Society Today   Second Edition

The cover photograph represents the primary subject
matter of sociology: the patterns of organization and
the processes of interaction among groups of people.

CRM BOOKS
Del Mar, California

SOCIETY TODAY
Second Edition

CONTRIBUTORS

Rodney Stark
University of Washington
General Advisor

Ronald L. Akers
Florida State University

Helen C. Arbini
California State University, San Diego

Richard Dewey
University of New Hampshire

Bruce K. Eckland
University of North Carolina

Glenn A. Goodwin
Pitzer College

Richard Greenbaum
*John Jay College of Criminal Justice
of the City University of New York*

Jeffrey K. Hadden
University of Virginia

Michael Hechter
University of Washington

Bernard Karsh
University of Illinois

Lewis M. Killian
University of Massachusetts

William Kornblum
University of Washington

James C. McCann
University of Washington

Marianne Rice
University of Washington

Peter I. Rose
Smith College; University of Massachusetts

John Finley Scott
University of California, Davis

W. Richard Scott
Stanford University

Neil J. Smelser
University of California, Berkeley

Mark Solomon
University of Oregon

Jeffrey W. Stone
Pomona College

Martin Trow
University of California, Berkeley

Pierre van den Berghe
University of Washington

Howard M. Vollmer
American University

Rita R. Weisbrod
University of Washington

Brief biographies of the contributers and attributions of their work in this text appear on pages 512-514.

2 3 4 5 6 7 8 9 10

Preface to the Second Edition

Society Today, Second Edition, is essentially a new book—it retains only about one-tenth of the text and art of the first edition. The second edition was created out of the experiences gained in doing the first, and it seems appropriate to preface the revision with a brief discussion of why and how we decided to produce a virtually new sociology text.   ¶ This edition has two primary goals: to coherently summarize the current state of knowledge in the areas of sociology normally covered in the introductory course and to communicate that knowledge effectively. We have learned that to meet the first goal it is necessary to coordinate the knowledge of a number of experts. The broad scope and rapid proliferation of knowledge in contemporary sociology make it very unlikely that one or two authors alone can produce a book that is comprehensive, equally authoritative across all topics, and current. ¶ To achieve the second goal of effective communication requires both clear writing and graphics that open up ideas. A good text must seize and hold student interest: unread books teach no one. Well-conceived and well-executed graphics can clarify concepts, demonstrate ideas, and personalize material. We have tried to meet these criteria in order to offer an attractive and authentic invitation to the study of sociology.   ¶ Many conversations with instructors and thousands of feedback questionnaires from students told us what was good about the first edition of *Society Today* and what needed to be changed. We believe the revision will continue to gain and hold student interest and that the content requirements of the introductory course will be well satisfied. The second edition is shorter, and the topical coverage and organization are entirely new. It still relates the substance of sociology to social concerns but pays more attention to the basic tools used by sociologists for *analyzing* these problems. The text still tries to teach what sociologists know, but it also indicates some of what they do not know and what some of the current debates are. ¶ The class testing of many new chapters showed us that students could learn a good deal more about sociology than we had anticipated—if the material presented is in the right form. For example, students ordinarily are both bored and made anxious by discussions of research methods. But we discovered that the average freshman can quickly and willingly understand much methodology if it is presented in the context of real research. Science writers have long used the detective-story model, and we found it extremely effective as a form for teaching research methods. (Eighty-three percent of class-tested students correctly read and interpreted a set of contingency tables after one reading of Chapter 2.) Similarly, we learned that students could readily learn to identify the basic components of a functionalist theory if the material is presented with the clarity achieved in Chapter 4. As another example, we found

that the theories and dynamics of social movements in Chapter 28 are clearly understood when the Women's Liberation Movement is used as a case study.
¶ Considerable efforts were taken to assure that the book is a complete and coherent introduction to sociology and not a collection of essays. The writing and editing followed a detailed and integrated blueprint. Editors worked closely with the contributors, with critical reviewers, and with a general advisor who guided the project from beginning to end.   ¶ Our commitment in revising the text has been to reveal sociology as it really is, not as any brand or school of sociology thinks it ought to be. This does not mean bland eclecticism, however. It means reflecting sociology as an ongoing activity and revealing the fundamental issues involved in the major current disputes. We believe that this is the most interesting way to display sociology. It is also an honest introduction to the field.

Roger G. Emblen
Publisher, Social Sciences
CRM Books

Note to Students

Besides the changes in substance between the first and second editions of *Society Today*, we have made several changes aimed at making it easy for you to use the book. These devices should help you integrate your reading and follow up on sociological questions and problems that particularly interest you.   ¶ *First*, an extensive system of cross references among chapters has been added so that you can compare theories and see the relationship between concepts as they are used in different areas of the discipline.   ¶ *Second*, all studies from which data have been drawn or whose conclusions are cited are referenced, and the full list of references appears at the back of the book. The date in parentheses following an author's name (or name and date following the data or conclusion) refers to the date of publication of the particular study. The studies are alphabetized by author, and all chapters that cite a particular study are listed in its bibliographic entry. Thus, if you found, in reading Chapter 13, for example, that you wanted to know more about the role of intelligence in social mobility, you could look up Bruce Eckland's study and see—besides the full information you need to find that study at the library—that Chapter 5 also contains some discussion of the relation of intelligence to social mobility and other factors. ¶ *Third*, each chapter is concluded by a selected list of further readings, chosen by the expert who wrote the chapter. You can thus quickly find material that will help you follow up on aspects of the chapter that interest you.   ¶ *Fourth*, studies whose data were used as the basis of charts and graphs are listed in the Credits and Acknowledgments section at the back of the book. They are listed by chapter and page number. If you wish to follow up on the results or methodology of the study whose data are displayed, the full citation in the Credits section will enable you to find the book or article at your library.   ¶ *Fifth*, the glossary has been expanded and completely rewritten. You may find it helpful in pinning down concepts and terms. ¶ The thorough documentation is designed not only to offer academic substantiation of the statements in the text but also to help you follow paths of learning in sociology that this introductory text can only point toward. We hope that the clear writing and vivid graphics in *Society Today*, Second Edition, will make you want to learn more— and that the reference systems will make it easy for you to do so.

Contents

Society Today   Second Edition

This textbook has two primary aims. The first is to introduce you to the subject matter of sociology. The second is to introduce you to sociology as an activity. Briefly, the subject matter of sociology is human *social* behavior. Consequently, sociology is itself an example of its subject matter. Like any academic discipline, sociology is not simply a huge collection of books and articles. Fundamentally, sociology is an ongoing, relatively organized human undertaking. Therefore, it cannot be understood

UNIT I
adequately simply by reading and learning what sociologists say about the social world. It is equally necessary to observe sociologists

SOCIOLOGY: A SUBJECT
in the act of studying social life. Only then can you judge the

AND AN ACTIVITY
worth of what sociologists say and understand the nature of their problems. ¶ Throughout this book we introduce you not only to sociology as a subject but to sociologists and their activities. Chapter 1 defines the subject matter of sociology and describes the difficulties that sociologists have in studying human beings. Chapter 2 lets you look over the shoulders of sociologists at work. It consists of three informal accounts of important sociological investigations that used different methods of research.

Chapter 1 What Is Sociology and How Is It Possible?

The social sciences ... are in fact a single science. They share the same subject matter—the behavior of men. And they employ, without always admitting it, the same body of general explanatory principles. This last truth is so obvious that it is still highly controversial.

GEORGE C. HOMANS (1967)

IF THE CLAIM OF UNITY among the social sciences is controversial, that is because the claim is both accurate and misleading. It is accurate to say that all social sciences attempt to understand human behavior. Yet the fact remains that an introductory course in sociology is very different from an introductory course in psychology, economics, anthropology, or political science. The difference exists because these various social sciences have concentrated their efforts on different aspects of human behavior.

As a crude analogy, let us suppose that each social science is a player on a football team. It would be accurate to say that each is playing the same game, according to the same rules, and that the success of the team depends on the joint efforts of all players. However, the social sciences would make a terrible football team. They have no coach or playbook. Each player carries out his own assignments as he sees fit. Nevertheless, each at least tries to be aware of his position on the team and usually lines up at more or less the right spot and does what he thinks ought to be done for the success of the team.

Although the dividing lines among the social sciences are fuzzy and their activities are poorly coordinated and often overlap, their characteristic specializations make it possible to tell them apart. To help you distinguish among them, we offer first a thumbnail sketch of each, and then we briefly point out how a particular problem might be divided among the social sciences.

THE SOCIAL SCIENCES

Psychology is mainly concerned with the bases of individual human behavior. Major areas of study include human development, behavior disorders, and learning; perception, sensation, and the biochemistry of the brain and nervous system; and individual emotions, motivation, personality, creativity, and the like. *Social psychologists* study the processes of social interaction, the ways in which individuals behave toward one another.

Anthropology is partly a biological, partly a social science; its method of studying human beings is usually comparative. *Physical* anthropology deals with the biological origins of the human species and biological variations within it, including racial differences. Major attention is on finding and classifying human fossils and artifacts. *Cultural* anthropology is devoted to observing or reconstructing the ways of life of simple, preliterate societies and to studying human social relationships in general.

Economics is primarily concerned with the production, consumption, and distribution of wealth within societies. In studying, for example, the gross national product, the unemployment rate, or the price of steel, economists are not simply studying statistics—these statistics reflect the behavior of individuals and the relationships among groups.

Political science specializes in the study of governments, the political processes by which social decisions are made, political parties and leadership, and individual and group political behavior.

Sociology emphasizes human relationships within groups and interconnections among social institutions. Its primary subject matter is human societies—their patterns and arrangements, their processes of development and change, and the interplay between these patterns and processes and the behavior of individuals and groups. If this definition seems very general, it is because the activities of persons calling themselves sociologists are spread over a wide range of topics. The work of individual sociologists often is concentrated on a particular problem, but the field itself is very broad. (In fact, many sociologists regard sociology as responsible for coordinating and synthesizing the work of the various social sciences.) Nevertheless, sociologists as a group can be recognized from among other groups of social scientists: Sociologists give much less attention to the individual and much more to groups than do psychologists. They are much more concerned with modern industrial societies and less concerned with simpler or preliterate societies than are anthropologists. Although many sociologists study economic matters, they tend to give more attention to the relationship between the economy and other aspects of society than economists usually do. Similarly, although sociologists are very active in the study of politics, they are more inclined than political scientists to connect political behavior and institutions to nonpolitical areas of life.

To make these differences among the social sciences more concrete, consider how each might approach the question of how best to reform the present welfare system in the United States. *Psychologists* might examine how welfare programs influence the mental health of recipients; the extent to which different programs would increase the individual's sense of personal worth and competence; or how best to retrain the unemployed. *Economists* might examine the impact of various welfare programs on taxation, on the unemployment rate, on consumer buying, or on inflation. *Anthropologists* might explore the patterns of self-help in isolated, impoverished communities or report on how simple societies deal with welfare problems. *Political scientists* might study the legislative processes through which welfare policies are made and the operations of government agencies administering welfare programs. *Sociologists* might examine the effects of welfare programs on family structure, public opinion, the birth rate, race relations, education, the formation of slums, or the distribution of power within society. They might also examine how each of these factors influences welfare programs or creates the need for such programs.

SOCIOLOGY AND COMMON SENSE

No student in an introductory sociology class is coming into contact with his subject for the first time. Students often see their first algebraic equation, their first molecule, or their first frog's heart in a classroom. But the subject of sociology is people, and all students know quite a bit about people. For example, here are some findings from sociological research that might confirm the common-sense notions you already have about the social world:

Wife slapping and marital violence occur most commonly among the poor, the uneducated, and blacks (Chapter 14).

Children from low-income homes are more likely to be delinquents than are children from upper-income homes (Chapter 14).

Revolutions are more likely to occur when living conditions continue to be very bad than when conditions are rapidly improving (Chapter 14).

The more religious a person is, the more likely he is to give time and money to general charitable activities (Chapter 20).

New birth control methods have reduced the birth rate in the United States (Chapter 24).

If these statements all seemed like simple common sense to you, then you can understand the surprise of many sociologists when research showed that each of the statements is false! A major problem for sociologists and all social scientists is that common sense so often misleads them.

Because sociologists study societies, social institutions, and the patterns of human interaction, much of what they study is a part of everyday experience. It is familiar, if not fully understood. The basic premises of sociology—that social life is patterned, that beliefs, values, and attitudes are learned, that we are as others see us—are premises that most people know intuitively. Yet things we know intuitively are sometimes true and sometimes not. In fact, many of the beliefs and preferences people hold are not based on fact but on conventional assumptions and other kinds of group-based prejudices. The majority of Americans would probably assume that most of the statements on the preceding list were true and rather obvious. As you read this book, you will find why each is not true and how sociologists find out whether such statements are true or false.

THE SCIENCE OF SOCIOLOGY

How can sociologists be sure that what they say about social life is any more accurate than what other people say—why should you believe sociologists? *The statements made by sociologists are more accurate than simple common sense to the*

Figure 1.1   These photographs suggest the objects of study of psychology (*top left*), economics (*bottom left*), anthropology (*top right*), and political science (*bottom right*).

extent that they are based on scientific observations and procedures. The basic attitude of science is vigilant skepticism. Nothing is to be taken for granted; everything is to be tested carefully against systematically selected and appropriate evidence. The scientific quest calls for the progressive refinement of theories on the basis of objectively and carefully collected observations.

But can sociology or any social science really qualify as a science? This question has caused considerable controversy for some time. The answer partly depends upon what one means by *science.* If science means testing theories against appropriate evidence, then most of the controversy has died down. Virtually all sociologists agree that they must use that standard to test their work, even if they battle mightily over what constitutes appropriate procedures for gathering evidence or what it is that sociologists ought to be studying. If, however, one takes a more restrictive view of science and means by it the formulation of powerful theories expressed mathematically and evidence based on extremely precise measurements, then one would judge little of social science to be scientific. It seems fair to point out, however, that few of today's most advanced sciences would have passed such a test at earlier stages in history.

This text uses the less restrictive definition of science. Sociologists are scientific to the extent that they scrupulously test what they suspect or believe against appropriate observations. That is the common denominator of all sciences. However, every science has distinctive techniques for making observations—techniques made necessary by the sorts of phenomena one needs to observe. Thus physicists need cyclotrons, biochemists need microscopes, and astronomers need telescopes in order to "see" what they are doing. Sociologists, too, have had to develop techniques and instruments to give them reliable, systematic observations of people and groups. They use laboratories filled with recorders and equipped with one-way mirrors. They conduct interviews with large, randomly selected samples of the population. In libraries they search out data, including documents, historical accounts, and facts

and figures. They often carefully observe people in natural settings to see what they do in their everyday lives. You will be able to judge for yourself the effectiveness of sociological research methods when you read the next chapter. There you are invited along on three sociological fact-finding expeditions.

Simply to say that the social sciences can be conducted scientifically is not to say that they are just like the physical or natural sciences. As we have pointed out, the social sciences use different methods of observation—a cyclotron would be useless to a sociologist, and a public opinion poll useless to a physicist. Furthermore, an extremely critical difference between the physical and social sciences arises from differences in subject matter. The social sciences face some unique difficulties because people are not simply aggregates of particles following physical laws.

THE PROBLEMS OF STUDYING PEOPLE

People are self-aware. Unlike gases subjected to heat or chemicals mixed in a vat, a person can to some extent choose his course of action. Freedom of choice raises three major problems: (1) because people are self-aware, the mere fact of observing them may change their behavior; (2) the fact of human choice makes it hard to predict what people will do—unlike chemicals, which can be counted on to explode when they are supposed to; (3) because people may change their behavior on the basis of social-science discoveries, they may make these discoveries outmoded—social-science knowledge has the capacity to self-destruct. Upon examination, these problems are not simply barriers to doing social science but are also among the chief virtues of doing social science.

That observation may change the behavior of persons being observed obviously makes it more difficult to do sociological research. For example, sociologists have ridden with policemen to see what they do during a normal day (Reiss, 1968). But on a *normal* day policemen are not being observed by sociologists; the presence of observers may change the behavior to be observed. But this problem is hardly unique to the social

Figure 1.2　Photographs are not reality, but they can capture many of its important features. Photographers trying to get people to "act naturally" have some of the same problems faced by social scientists: people can become self-conscious under scrutiny, and the representations of their behavior made by the camera or by social-scientific research no longer are close to the "natural."

sciences: Subatomic particles may not become self-conscious when physicists look at them, but observation is known to change their movements because the beams of light necessary to see or photograph such particles deflect their paths. Throughout this book you will discover many subtle means used by sociologists to look at people without disturbing them and means for compensating for whatever disturbances are caused by observation. Consider just one example: a group of researchers tested the idea that persons with conservative religious views were less trustful of their fellow men than were persons with liberal religious views (Forbes *et. al.*, 1971). They did this by counting the proportion of cars with locked doors in church parking lots during Sunday-morning services. The churches were all located in similar neighborhoods. When the researchers compared liberal and conservative churches, they found more locked doors in conservative parking lots. (A recent social-science book has been devoted to "unobtrusive measures"—ways of making undetected observations (Webb *et al.*, 1969).

Aside from posing problems for the researcher, the fact that human behavior can be influenced by observation means that human nature is not intractable—*we can be changed*. Thus we are not eternally condemned to being bigoted, greedy, violent, and ignorant. We can become better than we are. And that makes social science worth doing. A major goal of social science is to tell us what we are and how we can be changed.

It is true that people make conscious choices and that unlike atoms we are not ruled by blind nature. But it is not true that therefore it is impossible to explain or predict our behavior. It simply means that human consciousness—and choice making—must become an object of study. Frequently, it is not enough to look only at the external forces affecting humans; we must also understand how people perceive, respond to, and define their situations. Rather than making social science impossible, this search is one of the most fascinating activities of social science.

It is incorrect to think that only to the extent that people are irrational and ruled by unrecog-

Figure 1.3   The camera's eye sights an older woman in the crowd. A sociologist, while not ignoring her entirely, would be more likely to study the characteristics of the young crowd around her, of which she is not a typical member.

nized forces can social science explain their behavior. Indeed, if people were wholly rational, it would be much easier to predict their behavior. We would only have to determine where their best interests lay and we could be sure that they would act accordingly. But in reality people and nations frequently have imperfect knowledge of their best interests or are restricted in their choices by nonrational considerations such as traditions, fears, or friendships. Such considerations make it harder, not easier, to explain or predict people's behavior.

Finally, the capacity for self-destruction of social-science knowledge is one of the major justifications for engaging in social-science research. Usually social scientists study such problems as racism, poverty, crime, or mental illness not simply because they are interested in these topics but because they hope to use what they learn in order to *change* present social ills and inequities. If they could not use knowledge about human societies to change how societies operate, people would perhaps be better off not knowing what goes on.

The simple fact that men change their behavior in light of social-science knowledge in no way falsifies that knowledge. *All theories*, whether in physics or in sociology, *are applicable only under specified sets of conditions*. If these conditions are altered, perhaps on the basis of the theory, the theory no longer applies—but it does remain applicable to the original conditions. For example, an economic theory may state that when certain financial circumstances develop, a business recession will occur. The theory does not become false simply because people use it to avoid these circumstances and prevent recessions.

Similarly, a false theory does not become true simply because men alter their behavior in ways that seem to make the theory accurate. Robert K. Merton (1957) has greatly increased our understanding of the ways in which "self-fulfilling prophecies" operate in social life. For example, imagine that a completely inaccurate economic theory predicts a stock-market crash and that investors who know this theory try to get their money out before they lose it—their action results in a stock-market crash. Even though the predicted crash occurred, the theory does not account for the crash. We would need another theory to explain why this false theory caused the stock-market crash.

THE SOCIOLOGICAL EMPHASIS

The special problems created for social science by people's self-awareness are not the only problems there are. Many arguments against the possibility of sociological knowledge point to the *individuality* of human beings, saying that sociological propositions fail to deal with individual personalities. It is true that sociology does not explore the uniqueness of individuals. Instead, it seeks *generalizations about groups of people*. It produces such propositions as the following. Regardless of their income, Catholics are more likely than are Protestants to vote for the Democratic Party. Partners in second marriages are more likely to say they are happy than are partners in first marriages. Such propositions do ignore the unique features of individual Catholics and Protestants and of individual marriage partners. These statements are about groups of individuals, not about Ms. Jones or Mr. McCann. Sociologists do consider Ms. Jones and Mr. McCann but only insofar as they contribute to the groups in which they are observed, described, and classified. It is clear that sociology is possible only if unique individuals can be treated collectively.

Obviously no two people are identical. Each of us has had different experiences and possesses different knowledge. The question is, are we so different that our behavior cannot be studied in terms of the various groups that we belong to—groups of Americans, students, farmers, women, and so on? This question is an empirical one—subject to proof or disproof. Either sociologists can make relatively accurate generalizations about groups, ignoring many of the idiosyncratic features of the individuals who make up these groups, or they cannot.

The fact that sociologists have indeed produced accurate generalizations indicates that it is often possible to ignore individual differences. It turns out that much of what is unique about people is trivial for the purposes of sociological generalization. Such factors as shared religion, nationality, age, sex, marital status, and education have proved to be important determinants of what people believe, feel, and do.

People could be so unique that no important generalizations could be made about them. But that does not seem to be the case. Instead, humans behave more as Sherlock Holmes described them in Arthur Conan-Doyle's *The Sign of Four:*

. . . while the individual man is an insoluble puzzle, in the aggregate he becomes a mathematical certainty. You can, for example, never foretell what any one man will do, but you can say with precision what an average number will be up to. Individuals vary, but percentages remain constant.

AN INVITATION

It is the task of sociology to find out what the "average number" are "up to." And it is the purpose of *Society Today* to describe what sociologists are up to.

One thing they are most certainly up to is arguing with each other. Many introductory texts choose to ignore this fact. Instead, they present sociological knowledge as if it were carved in stone tablets—as if all the fundamental arguments had long been settled and harmony reigned throughout the field. In so doing they greatly distort reality. They present as truths statements about which sociologists are in heated disagreement. Worse yet, they take all the life and blood out of sociology.

Society Today has taken the opposite stance. It tries to present sociology as it really is. The excitement of sociology is that it is not all cut and dried. Rather, it is an intense, ongoing quest to understand ourselves and our social relations. Much is known; much more is in dispute. And very much more remains completely mysterious. The chapters that follow try to report honestly what sociologists know, what they argue about, and what they still need to understand. *Society Today* is not simply intended to teach sociology. It is also an invitation to become a sociologist.

Chapter 2   Doing Sociology

CHAPTER 1 ARGUED that sociology was possible. Despite the many special problems of studying people, sociologists have found ways to do it. One purpose of this chapter is to let you see for yourself how sociology is done. It offers a behind-the-scenes view of sociologists going about their business of attempting to learn the answers to some important questions about people and society.

Although the aim of the chapter is to give you some understanding of basic research procedures, it is not a manual of statistical techniques. It really consists of three detective stories describing how four sociologists solved some intriguing problems and discovered facts that increase our understanding of why we behave the way we do. Such understanding can lead to change.

A second aim of the chapter is to show you that sociologists are not inhabitants of another planet. Like the rest of us, they often blunder, have streaks of laziness, fall in and out of love, and have good and bad luck. Like anyone else, they have professional and personal biases, and as scientists, they have to be particularly careful to guard against these. This chapter will show you some of the measures that sociologists can take when they suspect biases in their own hunches or beliefs.

JOHN LOFLAND: PARTICIPANT OBSERVATION

In the fall of 1960 John Lofland arrived at the University of California, Berkeley, to study for a Ph.D. in sociology. He was determined to conduct close-up, face-to-face studies of social movements. Although there had long been active sociological study of such social movements as radical religious and political groups, these studies were mainly of two kinds: studies of the social and economic conditions during which such movements flourish and studies of their ideology. These findings taught sociologists little about how such groups operate on a day-to-day basis, how they recruit and keep their members, how they retain their commitment to their "unusual" beliefs in the face of a doubting world, or how they deal with failure to speedily transform society or to convert a large number of persons.

These were the processes Lofland wanted to understand. In order to pursue them, he first had to find a suitable group to study. It was not easy to find such a group. At the time there were not a great many radical religious or political groups developing. Furthermore, the group had to be located in the San Francisco Bay area—Lofland had neither the freedom nor the funds to go elsewhere. Finally, he had to find a group that would be willing to let him study it. Such groups are notoriously secretive, which is one reason why little in the way of close sociological study of them had been done.

Finding a Radical Group

For about two years Lofland poked around the occult religious enclaves in the Bay Area, looking for a serious-minded radical social movement. Most of the groups he found were interested in unusual or occult ideas and ideologies, but the members were more like audiences than social movements: they listened to varieties of doctrines but did virtually nothing about what they heard. Then, in February of 1962, he found the group he was looking for (fictitious names are used).

At a convention of the Flying Saucer Clubs—a loose audience of people who believe that contact has been made with creatures from outer space and speakers who claim to have traveled on flying saucers—a woman approached Lofland and told him that she represented a group that had had "a wonderful message from Korea." Further conversation revealed that this message involved a messiah—a returned Christ—and a doctrine that predicted the world would soon end. Lofland honestly described himself as a sociologist interested in studying new religious movements. The woman, who was later to be a major figure in his study, suggested that her group—the Divine Precepts—was one he must be sure to study. So Lofland accepted an invitation to the group's communal living quarters to hear more about their message. Upon arrival he was placed alone in a room to listen to a two-and-a-half-hour tape-recorded version of the message. It bored Lofland nearly witless. Afterward he was introduced to Miss Lee, who had been a college teacher in

Figure 2.1   John Lofland is the author of *Doomsday Cult* (1966), which reported his study of the religious movement he referred to as the "Divine Precepts" movement, as well as of several other books. In 1972 he founded the journal *Urban Life and Culture*, devoted to close-hand observational studies of urban life. At present he is an associate professor of sociology at the University of California, Davis.

Korea and who was the messiah's missionary to America.

He exchanged a few pleasantries with Miss Lee and with the woman who had invited him to the group. Then he made his escape. At the time he thought there were only the two of them, and perhaps one or two others, in the whole movement. That would have been much too small a group to study.

A week later Lofland and a colleague decided to drop in on one of the weekly meetings of the Divine Precepts group. They were already in the neighborhood, having just been turned away from the door of another occult group meeting, where they had been mistaken for plainclothes policemen. When they arrived at the Divine Precepts meeting, Lofland was shocked to discover a room filled with people and to learn that there were at least a dozen core members all living together and giving their full time and energy to seeking converts. He realized now that he had gained access to the kind of group he wanted to study—one with a radical faith and at an early stage of development.

A few years earlier a Korean engineer, Mr. Soon Chang, had announced that he was the returned Christ and that he would gather about him a group of the redeemed who would rule in heaven following judgment day, which was only a few years hence. He had gathered perhaps 10,000 followers in Korea, among them Miss Lee. In 1959 Miss Lee was dispatched to America to gather converts. She settled first in a college town in the Pacific Northwest, and she eventually gathered a small group of followers—all young people. Because some members had experienced conflict with neighbors and with members of their families, the group moved to San Francisco; several of them left husbands, wives, or children behind.

When Lofland found them, they had been in the city for nearly a year. They were beginning to look for new members again, after having spent most of their first year acquiring a large apartment house and a printing press, learning to operate the press, and printing an English translation of their holy book.

From the first encounter, Miss Lee and the group knew that Lofland was a Ph.D. candidate in sociology and that his own interest in the group was professional. (Lofland found out later that the group really thought that God had sent him to be a convert but that he was slow to recognize his mission.) The group accepted Lofland, and he immediately began to spend all his available time with them, questioning people closely about their past, their attachment to the group, and their everyday activities. Whenever he had the opportunity, he slipped away to write notes about what he was seeing and hearing. He also purchased a tape recorder and often sat in his car to record his observations after group meetings. Lofland's short handbook on conducting field research (1971) records in detail the techniques he began developing during this study. In order to check the validity of his observations and interpretations, he asked other sociologists to attend Divine Precepts meetings from time to time and make independent observations.

Theory I: Why People Convert

As time passed, Lofland began to fashion a theory about certain factors that caused people to convert to the Divine Precepts. Initially he based his theory (which is displayed in Figure 2.2) on reconstructions of the life histories of those who had become proselytes. He searched out the common patterns that seemed to explain why these young Americans gave up their conventional life goals to become full-time missionaries for a Korean-based Christ.

After he had constructed his theory, Lofland began the long process of testing and revising it. Any theory built upon a set of data cannot be tested by the same data. It could have been mere coincidence, for example, that all the converts he had interviewed shared certain features; because these shared features were the source of his theory, the data and theory would automatically agree. Lofland could gain confidence that he had isolated the real causes of conversion only if he could predict successfully who would convert in

Figure 2.2   Lofland's description of the steps
leading to conversion to a radical faith, based on his
study of the Divine Precepts cult. The first four
steps occur before the individual has any contact with
the cult, whereas the final three steps occur as a
result of continued and increasingly intense interaction
with the members of the cult.

A PERSON

PREDISPOSITIONAL FACTORS
Characteristics of persons that they bring
to the conversion process

1 The individual must experience an enduring, acutely felt tension or strain (for example, job failure or marital discord).

2 The person must hold a religiously oriented problem-solving perspective. He may well have rejected conventional faith, but he must still view the world in religious terms—see problems as having religious, as opposed to political or psychiatric, solutions.

3 On the basis of the first two characteristics, he must define himself as a religious seeker, a person who is open to new religious outlooks.

4 When he encounters the Divine Precepts group he must be at, or very shortly coming to, a turning point in his life. To convert, a person must be at a point in his life when old lines of action and commitments are completed or have failed or been disrupted (or are about to be) and when the opportunity (or necessity) of doing something different with his life arises. (For example, he or she may have just lost a job, been divorced, graduated from school, or recovered from a long illness.)

SITUATIONAL FACTORS
Characteristics of the interaction between
individuals and the group

5 The potential convert must form or already possess a close affective tie with one or more Divine Precepts members. Many converts already had such ties—they were married to, closely related to, or long-time friends with a Divine Precepts member. Others failed to convert until they had formed such a tie. In a sense, conversion meant coming to accept the beliefs of one's spouse, sibling, or friends.

6 Ties with persons outside the Divine Precepts group must be nonexistent or neutralized. Some probable converts were held back from conversion by the unwillingness of spouses to convert or by the counter persuasion and pressure of friends and families. Converts typically lacked any ties that could restrain them, and, if they had ties, they were neutralized by absence.

7 To become an active Divine Precepts member, to move from verbal agreement to actually giving one's life to the movement, required intensive, day-to-day interaction with group members. Some verbal converts whose physical circumstances prevented such interaction never became full converts. Others did so only when their circumstances changed so that such interaction occurred.

A CONVERT

	PARTICIPANT OBSERVATION	EXPERIMENT	SURVEY RESEARCH
Typical Cost	Inexpensive	Depends on equipment used	Depends on sample size and whether questionnaire or interview is used
Size of sample or group or number of subjects	Usually small	Limited by funds and time—usually small	Depends on size of population, funds, and time—can be very large
Type of interaction with subjects of study	Face to face—formal or informal	Face to face—formal	If questionnaire used, indirect (by mail). If interview used, face to face but formal.
Type of problem	Theory and variables generated in process of research—not controlled by researcher	Theory and variables known in advance and controlled in the lab	Theory and variables known in advance but not controlled by researcher
Can the independent variable be manipulated by the researcher? (Can events be timed?)	No	Yes	No
How are the variables controlled?	Through testing and revision of the theory	By random assignment to experiment and control groups	Through statistical analysis
Can the results be generalized to a larger universe (population)?	Yes (only if groups have been selected randomly)	No (sample not used)	Yes (by random selection of cases)
Must the theory be predictive?	Yes	Yes	Yes
Is it possible or likely that the act of doing the research will influence the results?	Yes: The researcher is a participant in the interaction to be studied	No	If questionnaire is used: No If interview is used: Yes
Can it be used to find out the distribution of a variable (for example, age) in a population	No	No	Yes
Where does the research take place?	In the field: In limited area	In the lab	In the field: In extended area or several areas
Criteria for selection of groups, subjects, or cases	Nature of the study, availability	Convenience	Random selection from the population

Figure 2.3 (*Left*) The uses and limitations of the three types of sociological research strategies discussed in the text: participant observation, experiment, and survey research. No single method is adequate by itself to answer all sociological questions. You may find it helpful to refer back to this table as you read about various studies in subsequent chapters.

Figure 2.4 These dancers are members of the International Society for Krishna Consciousness, a religious group that as a social phenomenon shares many of the features that characterize the Divine Precepts group studied by John Lofland.

the future. *Prediction* is the critical test of all scientific propositions.

Lofland had to wait until the group secured a significant number of new converts who would also exhibit the particular features that he had isolated in his theory. For example, each person prior to conversion should have bonds of close friendship or family ties with someone who was already a member. If a new convert lacked one of the features or elements in his theory, then Lofland would have to reconsider and change at least that part.

It was not enough just to keep track of new converts: Lofland also had to carefully study people who attended group meetings but failed to join the group. If the theory was valid, people who failed to become converts should *lack* at least one of the essential features. If anyone met all of the requirements of the theory but still failed to convert, then something important had to be missing from the theory.

For many months Lofland investigated every-

one who turned up at Divine Precepts activities. He moved in with the group for a few months to observe everyone closely, and he traveled to interview the former spouses of several early members, and he talked with other people who were aware of the group's early activities. Lofland compiled and typed hundreds of pages of field notes. At the same time he assisted the group by copyediting a new edition of the holy book—again printed on the group's own press.

As Lofland watched the group add more members and open two new headquarters, he became convinced that his theory of conversion was adequate: No one who met all its requirements failed to convert; no one converted who lacked any of the requirements. Colleagues who independently checked his observations and field notes agreed with his findings. In 1965 he published a paper, "On Becoming A World Saver: A Theory of Conversion to a Deviant Perspective," which he incorporated in his book *Doomsday Cult* the following year. Several years later Lofland was able to

Figure 2.5 (*Top*) A chart of the three-phase cycle of activities of the Divine Precepts movement. (*Bottom*) A picture of Jesus People during the missionary phase of the cycle, which Lofland has hypothesized to be descriptive of small social movements in general.

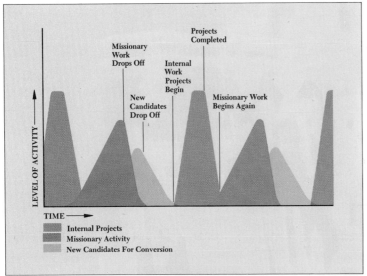

revise and generalize his theory to make it apply more broadly to socialization into any kind of deviant role (*Deviance and Identity*, 1969).

Theory II: The Cycle of Group Activities

From the beginning, Lofland was interested in more than the process and elements of conversion. He had begun with many other questions. For example, what kept the Divine Precepts group going when they failed to win converts quickly? Lofland became convinced that the ac-

tivities of the group had a cyclic pattern and that this repeating pattern gave group members a way to overcome their disappointments over failing to convert more people in a short time. The cycle of activities helped rejuvenate their hope.

Lofland noticed that people in the Divine Precepts group alternated between extremely energetic missionary activity and extremely vigorous internal projects. For example, when they suspended missionary projects, they would buy and completely refurbish a set of flats. Or they would print a new edition of their book on their basement press. Lofland became convinced that they followed a three-phase cycle. First, they would be very active outside the group, looking for potential converts. When they had succeeded in getting a number of new people (often about a dozen) to come to meetings, they would then slow down such external activity and concentrate all their energy on converting the new people they had gathered.

After a few months, usually all of these new people would drop out of group activities; the group would suddenly find itself with nothing going on, with (usually) no new converts to show for their effort, and with their high hopes of several months before dashed by failure. Instead of going back into the streets to gather a new group, at these times they would invariably launch one of their projects. This would deeply engross them for several months, and they would gain new energy and confidence with the success of the projects—a handsomely remodeled flat, a newly printed book. After finishing a successful project, the group had enough motivation to renew missionary work.

How could Lofland be sure that this cycle was more than coincidence? First, he was able to check back on earlier group activity to see what had gone on before he began his observations. With the group's guest book—in which all visiting potential converts recorded their names and the date of entry—he was able to reconstruct the patterns of past missionary activity. Lofland found periods in which virtually no new persons were signed up interspersed with periods of very heavy sign-ups. He was also able to date various group projects. All of the projects occurred a few months

Figure 2.6   One of the problems faced by participant observation is that the social scientist's presence affects to an unknown degree the social process he is studying. Would the Ghanaians shown at top with Michael Lowy interact as naturally in his presence as they would without him? The participant observer usually tries to become fully immersed in the interactions of the group he is studying. Fitting into the situation under study solves some problems of participant observation but it raises some important questions, especially those involving invasion of privacy and other questions of ethics.

after a heavy sign-in period, and during a period when virtually no new people signed up. Past patterns of group activity seemed to offer quite convincing support for his theory.

Lofland's theory of cyclic activity and its consequences, however, had yet to pass the test of prediction. He committed himself to predicting that at certain future times a group project would suddenly be proposed and carried out. And in fact he was able to tell in advance approximately when such projects would occur—well before any of the group members had thought of the project. As these predictions came true, Lofland gained considerable confidence that he had isolated a process or mechanism by which small social movements can maintain their hope in the face of discouraging circumstances.

Method: Overview

The method that Lofland used to collect his data is often called *participant observation*. Because the sociologist has face-to-face interaction with those he is studying, he is able to directly observe group processes as they unfold. For the kinds of questions Lofland was concerned with, participant observation is undoubtedly the best method of research. You will notice that what Lofland did differs sharply from everyday association with other people—for example, what you do when you are with your friends or in class. First, Lofland

systematically recorded his observations. He had formulated specific questions, and he made efforts to locate and record specific kinds of information. For example, data about the background of everyone who attended group meetings was obviously critical for answering questions about the process of conversion.

Lofland took many precautions not to delude himself, not to see only what he expected or hoped to see. His objectivity and his precautions against bias helped him understand the Divine Precepts movement better than did its members or leaders. Remember that he brought in outside observers several times during his study to judge independently the accuracy of his findings. Several of these colleagues periodically checked his methods of observation and his data during the entire course of the study in order to evaluate long-term as well as specific or isolated observations. It is precisely this painstaking attention that sociologists give to factual accuracy and to testing their theories against facts that qualifies sociology as a science and makes it different from a person's common-sense understanding of social life.

KAREN DION: EXPERIMENT

We know we *ought* to value people for their inner rather than for their outer selves; surely it is unfair and undemocratic if the accident of how one looks

Figure 2.7   Karen Dion is presently an assistant professor of psychology at the University of Toronto. She has continued her studies of the social effects of physical appearance begun while she was earning her doctorate at Minnesota and is the author of a number of scholarly articles on the effects of appearance.

greatly affects how one fares in life. Until several years ago even social scientists steadfastly ignored a person's physical appearance as a significant factor in his or her social life. This reluctance to consider physical appearance stemmed partly from convictions that science should not be concerned with such "superficial" traits and partly from an aversion that social scientists often express for genetic or biological accounts of behavior; they prefer environmental ones. (Chapter 5 discusses the "nature or nurture" controversy in detail.)

It is now clear that the extent to which we judge people by the way they look compels serious study. Although we know we ought not to judge people by their looks, we all know that to some extent we do. As George Herbert Mead and others have pointed out (see Chapter 7), we see ourselves as others see us—our identities are socially constructed. It seems likely that how we are seen is influenced to some extent by what is there to be seen. *What we are* may be shaped by *how we look*.

Two bold young women took up the study of the social significance of physical appearance in the mid-1960s. Ellen Berscheid, a social psychologist, and Elaine Walster, a sociologist, began with a study of dating choices among college students. They discovered that appearance was by far the most powerful consideration. Appearance took priority over other possible choice considerations, including the other person's values, interests, and activities (Walster, Aronson, Abrahams, and Rottmann, 1966; Berscheid, Dion, Walster, and Walster, 1971). Their pioneering work made the study of physical appearance suddenly respectable.

Several years later, in 1967, Karen Dion arrived at the University of Minnesota to study for a Ph.D. There she was soon exposed to the research findings of Walster and Berscheid, who had conducted their studies at Minnesota. Dion found their work exciting and decided to attempt to pursue the effects of physical appearance in situations other than ones of romantic attraction. The line of experiments that she conducted over the next several years dramatically revealed what we all secretly suspect but hope is not true: Physical appearance has a profound effect on the way people

respond to and evaluate one another—the effect even extends to how young women respond to the misbehavior of children.

Testing the Theory by Experiment

Dion began with a hunch that a person's interpretation of a child's misbehavior as harmless, serious, or even pernicious might be influenced considerably by the child's physical appearance. She thought it likely that people would see pretty children as "little angels" and would find excuses for their misbehavior; similarly, they would see homely little children as "little monsters" and would judge them harshly for committing exactly the same misbehavior.

Dion's next step was to devise a way to find out whether her suspicions were true. How could she determine whether beauty does in fact affect judgments this way? Her solution was to use an experiment. When it is possible to do so, social scientists always prefer to use experiments to test their theories because an experimental situation not only permits the manipulation of the factor believed to be the cause but also allows the experimenter to isolate this factor from other factors that may also be operating.

The success of an experiment rests upon successful prediction of outcomes in precisely the same way as did Lofland's test of his theory of conversion. However, while Lofland had to wait for events to happen in their own time, an experiment permits control over the timing of events. An experimenter hires or recruits *subjects*—persons on whom the experiment is conducted—and controls what happens to them and when.

Many kinds of human events, of course, cannot be taken into the laboratory. Lofland could hardly hire people and create in them the conditions outlined by his theory as leading to conversion. Given what he wanted to study, he had no choice but to work in a natural setting. But Dion's study could be done in a lab, and, in fact, it could be done much better in a lab. If she had tried to observe people in natural settings to see whether they seemed to treat children differently on the basis of appearance, she would have had to struggle with many other complications. No two children

Figure 2.8   (*Left*) A hypothetical account of misbehavior used by Karen Dion in her research on reactions to physical attractiveness and photographs of children similar to those used in the research. (*Right*) An incident of misbehavior.

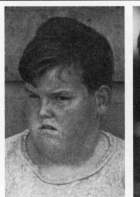

At one corner of the playground a dog was sleeping. Peter stood a short distance from the dog, picked up some sharp stones from the ground and threw them at the animal. Two of the stones struck the dog and cut its leg. The animal jumped up yelping and limped away. Peter continued to throw rocks at the dog as it tried to move away from him.
(From Karen Dion, 1972)

would ever have committed exactly the same act of misbehavior in exactly the same way. Thus, it would not have been clear whether reactions to them were based on differences in appearance or on actual behavior differences. Furthermore, since most children, like most adults, are of average appearance, it would have been hard to say whether one was more attractive than another. But in the laboratory these confusions can be sorted out effectively.

The Experimental Design

Dion chose a simple and effective experimental design. In order to rule out variations in the misbehavior of children, she created several written descriptions of misbehavior allegedly committed by a seven-year-old on the school playground (see Figure 2.8). In this way, Dion could attribute the *same* action to a pretty or to a homely child simply by attaching different photographs to the written account. But how could she objectively determine who is good looking when people's perceptions of beauty and ugliness are basically subjective?

By using a group of judges to rate a number of photographs as very attractive or very unattractive, she was able to choose photographs on which there was very high agreement among the judges; this procedure overcame idiosyncrasies of individual taste. The selected pictures ruled out variations in hair and eye color. The children in the unattractive category had no physical defects, and none of the children wore glasses—they were simply very pretty and very homely little children. Half were girls, half boys. The pictures and written accounts were the basic materials Dion used in the experiment.

For subjects, Dion recruited 243 female undergraduate students. Each met with the experimenter and was presented with a series of accounts of misbehavior and a picture of the child who had allegedly committed the act. After reading a given account, each young woman had to rate the seriousness of the child's offense, the severity of punishment the child should receive, and the likelihood that the child would commit such an act again; the women were also asked to rate the child on a number of traits, including "good" or "bad," "kind" or "cruel," and others. Ideally, Dion would have liked each woman to rate the same incident for both an attractive and an unattractive child to see whether she made a more positive judgment of the pretty one's behavior. But this procedure would have made it obvious that the pictures were not those of the actual child who had committed the act. Instead, the experimenter showed half of the subjects a picture of a very pretty child and the other half a picture of a very homely child for each given act of misbehavior. To determine whether appearance influenced judgments, Dion then compared the ratings given to attractive children and those given to unattractive children who had been guilty of the same behavior.

The results of this comparison confirmed Dion's expectations that the influence of appearance was very strong (Dion, 1972). When the offenders were very pretty children, most of the women found excuses for their misbehavior; they said that the acts were untypical and not a cause for serious concern. But when the same action was attributed to a homely child, the women's judgments were more often severe, and they de-

scribed the child more often as a chronic offender.

One young woman made this comment after reading about an attractive little girl who had supposedly thrown rocks at a sleeping dog:

She appears to be a perfectly charming little girl, well-mannered, basically unselfish. It seems that she can adapt well among children her age and make a good impression. . . . She plays well with everyone, but like anyone else, a bad day can occur. Her cruelty . . . need not be taken seriously.

All this woman had to go on was a description of cruelty to an animal and a pretty picture! When a picture of a homely little girl accompanied the same account of cruelty to a dog, another young woman concluded:

I think the child could be quite bratty and would be a problem to teachers. . . . She would be a brat at home. . . . All in all, she would be a real problem.

Clearly, beauty is not merely in the eye but also influences the judgment of the beholder.

With this general understanding of what Dion found and how she went about it, we can examine her experiment in greater detail. In it are all the critical elements of a proper experimental design. Figure 2.9 displays the elements, and the following discussion explains each of them.

The Independent Variable   All experiments include at least one independent variable over which the experimenter has control. It is called *independent* because it is the factor that is thought to be a cause of or to effect changes in something. *Variable* means that this factor takes more than one value. If the independent variable were electrical current, for example, it would be necessary at least to be able to switch it on and off. The accounts of children's misbehavior in Dion's experiment did not vary; they were identical regardless of the picture attached to them and therefore were *not* the independent variable.

The independent variable was the attractiveness of the child that the young women saw, and it took two values: very attractive and very unattractive. The independent variable in an experi-

Figure 2.9   A chart of Karen Dion's experimental design. The experimental method in sociology has the advantage of allowing the sociologist to manipulate the independent variable according to the purposes of the research and to control, through random assignment, sources of error.

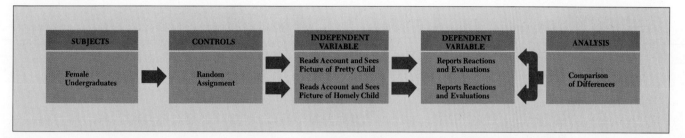

ment is *manipulated;* that is, Dion could decide which subjects saw pretty or homely children when they read a given account of misbehavior.

The Dependent Variable The dependent variable is the factor that you expect the independent variable to affect—this factor is *dependent* upon the independent variable. In Dion's experiment the degree of negative evaluation of children's actions is the dependent variable. Dion found that it depended on the attractiveness of the child. The homely children were more likely than the pretty children to receive negative evaluations for the same misbehavior. The independent variable, then, produced the changes that occurred in the dependent variable.

Controls In an experiment, to control means to exclude the possibility that some factor—other than simple chance—could be causing the changes in the dependent variable—in this experiment, the women's evaluations. Dion used *randomization* of the subjects to ensure against the operation of such other factors. Whether the subjects saw a picture of a pretty or a homely child with a given description of misbehavior was determined randomly. (A very simple way to randomize would have been to flip a coin to determine who sees what.) Had Dion not used randomization, she might have chosen subjects—accidentally or through her own unconscious bias—who were more than normally sympathetic toward all children when she distributed the pictures of pretty children. Less than normally sympathetic subjects might have received pictures of homely children. Differences in the subjects' sympathies for children—not differences in the children's appearance—could then have

caused the differences that Dion found in the evaluations made by the two groups of subjects. She might also have selected more educated subjects for one of the groups or subjects who had less experience with children. Using randomization, Dion had only to worry about simple chance differences that might occur.

Statistical Analysis How is it possible to compute the odds against the results' of an experiment being due only to chance? The experimenter knows that the laws of probability account for the extent to which randomization makes all possible differences (such as greater or less than normal sympathy toward children) equal between the two groups (except, of course, for differences resulting from manipulation of the independent variable). There is a computable probability, for example, of tossing seven heads in a row. The odds against chance-produced findings in an experiment depend on the number of subjects used and on the size of the difference found between the two groups on the dependent variable (in Table 2.1, the difference between 13.12 and 10.70).

The usual way to compute these odds is to use a *test of statistical significance.* As a rule of thumb, experimenters usually require that the odds be at least 20 to 1 against chance findings before they

Table 2.1   Perceived Likelihood of Future Transgressions*

Attractiveness of Child	Mean Rating	
Unattractive	13.12	$p < .001$
Attractive	10.70	

* Ratings range from 0 (very unlikely) to 17 (very likely).
Source: Adapted from Karen Dion, "Physical Attractiveness and Evaluations of Children's Transgressions," *Journal of Personality and Social Psychology* (1972).

Figure 2.10.1   Rodney Stark is coauthor with Charles Y. Glock of five books on aspects of religious behavior. His most recent book, *Police Riots*, was published in 1972. In addition to writing scholarly articles, Stark has written for a number of magazines, including *Harper's* and *Psychology Today*. Since 1971 he has been a professor of sociology at the University of Washington.

Figure 2.10.2   Charles Y. Glock has been a leader in survey research and in the revival of social-science studies of religion. He served as Director of the Bureau for Applied Social Research at Columbia until 1958, when he left to found the Survey Research Center at Berkeley. Much of the empirical research done on religion in the past decade has been done by Glock, his colleagues, and his students. He is the author of many books and articles and is presently a professor of sociology at the University of California, Berkeley.

call the results statistically significant or put any trust in their results. As shown in Table 2.1, the odds against Dion's main finding being the result of simple chance are at least 1,000 to 1. If she conducted this experiment 1,000 times and if physical appearance actually *does not* influence judgments about the likelihood that a child will commit future transgressions, then she would get differences this great on the dependent variable only once. This probability is what is indicated by $p < .001$ in the table—the probability (p) that these findings are the result of chance is less than ($<$) one chance in 1000 (.001). Clearly, Dion is betting on nearly a sure thing when she claims that appearance influenced the subjects' evaluations of children's misbehavior.

Applications

Was all Dion's effort worth it? As we pointed out in Chapter 1, human behavior is not forever fixed. On the contrary, it can be changed. But it does not change as long as we remain unaware of why we think and behave the way we do. Knowing the results of this study and of others built upon its findings, we can see that many children are probably being dealt with unfairly on the basis of how they look. If we think such discrimination is objectionable and contrary to our ideals, we should find ways of alerting people to their unconscious biases. For example, it would seem reasonable to put student teachers through such an experiment in order to demonstrate to them that they are influenced by outward appearances. Thus sensitized, they may guard against such biases when they enter the classroom. Considering such implications of Dion's experiment, we can see the virtue in the capacity of social-science findings to

self-destruct. If people do unfairly treat one another on the basis of physical appearance, we would hope that knowledge that they do so would lead to behavioral changes—that one day because of work such as Dion's, these findings would no longer apply to human behavior.

CHARLES Y. GLOCK AND RODNEY STARK: SURVEY RESEARCH

On Christmas Eve, 1959, a gang of German youths desecrated a Jewish synagogue in Cologne. The swastikas they crudely smeared on the walls showed that anti-Semitism had not died with the Third Reich. Worse yet, within days the Cologne incident was repeated in many other German cities. But this was only the beginning. The wave rapidly spread beyond Germany and then beyond Europe to the United States. By March, 1960, barely two months after the first German incident, at least 643 similar incidents had occurred in America (Caplovitz and Rogers, 1960). The incidents were a sensation in the news media for a while, but then the storm of incidents subsided as mysteriously as it had begun. Soon most people forgot about it. But one group did not.

The Anti-Defamation League (ADL) of B'nai B'rith, founded in 1912 to fight anti-Semitism in the United States, had faced an overwhelming task for many years. But times changed, and by the late 1950s, ADL leaders had come to believe that militant anti-Semitism had virtually died out in America. They had then turned most of their attention to subtle problems of institutional discrimination and to the black freedom movement. The outbreak of vandalism against Jewish property, accompanied by occasional violence against Jews, shocked them deeply. They decided that their most pressing need was for basic research on a broad range of questions concerning the sources, persistence, and potentialities of American anti-Semitism and of prejudice in general.

ADL leaders decided to seek the help of scholars at the University of California at Berkeley. Their choice was governed partly by history, for in the 1940s social scientists at Berkeley had conducted a series of studies of prejudice, including a classic work called *The Authoritarian Personal-*

ity (Adorno *et al.*, 1950). They also knew of the presence of an interdisciplinary group of sociologists, psychologists, and political scientists at Berkeley who were interested in tackling the problem once again.

The Uses of Survey Research

This group of social scientists quickly assembled itself under the auspices of the Survey Research Center and divided up the potential work into independent but related studies; the ADL initially supplied $500,000 to fund the operation. Unlike the kind of participant observation done by John Lofland, large scale *survey research*, the method generally employed by these scholars, is expensive. Lofland's expenses, other than supporting himself, consisted of a tape recorder, filing cabinets, and a lot of paper and typewriter ribbons. But to conduct personal interviews with several thousand people randomly selected from the adult population in selected regions across the nation costs a lot of money in salaries and travel expenses. To code these interviews for computer processing also requires a great deal of money and labor. One good survey analyst can easily use up several thousand dollars each month in computer time, and he may have to keep up this pace for a year or two. Survey research therefore requires extremely comprehensive and detailed preplanning. If you ask the wrong questions or fail to ask a significant one, you may have wasted the time and money allotted to you.

In spite of the pressures involved, survey research is the only reliable procedure to follow to acquire certain kinds of information. If you want to know the distribution of some trait in a *population*—for example, anti-Semitism or political preference—no other method suffices. If a cheaper method existed for accurately forecasting elections, nobody would pay the Gallup or Harris organizations tens of thousands of dollars to conduct a survey.

The study of anti-Semitism required survey research, not an experiment. People already are or are not anti-Semitic. One could not morally or practically find people who do not have attitudes about Jews and try to create positive or negative

Figure 2.11   Anti-Semitism is not just an attitude; it has also been manifested in behavior, of which this swastika painted on the wall of a Jewish synagogue represents only a minor example.

attitudes in them. Nor could the independent variables in which these social scientists were interested (such as level of education and religious preference) be manipulated in a laboratory: you cannot take people into a laboratory and create some of them as college graduates and some as high school dropouts. Nor could one raise some of them as religious conservatives and others as non-believers in a laboratory. The study on anti-Semitism had to take people as they were and try to determine why they were that way. Similarly, had Dion wanted to know what proportion of the population is very pretty or very homely, she could not have determined that in her laboratory. Nor could she have determined what proportion of the population discriminates against unattractive people. Either of these questions would have required a survey.

Charles Y. Glock, director of the center, and Rodney Stark, a second-year graduate student in sociology at Berkeley, were scholars planning one of the projects to study anti-Semitism. With considerable difficulty they managed to convince the other social scientists in the group that an in-

Figure 2.12 A path-analysis diagram of Glock and
Stark's research. The arrows linking the concepts
show the direction of the relationships studied. For
example, orthodoxy is seen to lead to religious
hostility, which in turn leads to secular anti-Semitism.
The thickness of the arrows represents the
strength of these relationships. Thus, the strongest
relationship was between orthodoxy and particularism,
whereas there was no relationship between
particularism and seeing historical Jews as "crucifiers."
(From R. Stark et al., 1971.)

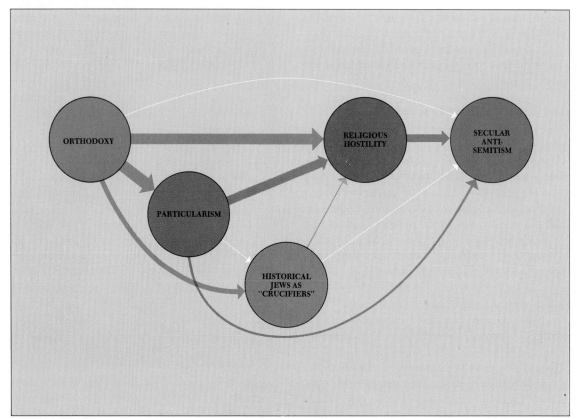

dependent study of the role of religion in generating and sustaining American anti-Semitism ought
to be done. Some members of the group felt that
this study took low priority because the relationship between Christian teachings and anti-Semitism was so obviously false. Others thought it obviously true. Glock and Stark thought such disagreement established the need for their research.

For the first eighteen months Glock and Stark
planned and prepared their questions and their
research methods. They studied the history of
Christian-Jewish relations, theological traditions,
and contemporary church literature. Out of this
planning came a general theoretical scheme.

The Theory and Model

It was clear from history that the major source of
anti-Semitism was religious conflict—religion was
the only important way in which Jews had differed from their neighbors. Ethnic differences
among Christians had never resulted in the sus-

tained conflict found between Christians and
Jews. Furthermore, the development of laws curtailing Jewish freedoms and rights—for example,
laws establishing ghettos within which Jews were
forced to live—had been encouraged by various
churches' decrees. The last legally enforced ghet-
toization of Jews in Europe before the rise of Nazi-
ism was in the Vatican State and was discontinued
only in 1870.

Viewing this history, Glock and Stark developed a theory about the way in which commitment to traditional Christian doctrines and teachings about the religious status of Jews and their
role in the Crucifixion would continue to shape
contemporary beliefs about Jews. This theory was
a series of abstract concepts linked by propositions—statements about how these factors influenced one another in cause-and-effect relationships. Figure 2.12 shows the conceptual scheme
of these factors in the diagram of a path analysis,
and it displays such concepts as *orthodoxy:* belief

in the traditional teachings of Christianity; *partic-ularism:* belief that Christianity is the only true religion and that salvation is only open to Christians; *negative religious images of the historic Jew:* belief that the ancient Jews are fallen from Grace and responsible for the Crucifixion; and *negative religious images of the modern Jew:* belief that the Jews are still unforgiven for the Crucifixion and therefore damned. Glock and Stark postulated a developing causal order, starting with orthodoxy and ending with a negative religious image of the modern Jew. They further postulated that these religious grounds for hostility would spill over into secular situations and make people especially susceptible to *secular anti-Semitism*—that is, stereotyping Jews, mistrusting and resenting them, and discriminating against them.

Testing the Theory by Survey

In order to test their model, Glock and Stark first had to develop methods to actually measure the elements in their theory. Specifically, they had to construct questions that would classify people's attitudes on each of these factors. For example, what set of questions would validly assess the extent to which people hold orthodox Christian beliefs? The process of developing suitable questions took a good deal of research. They consulted theologians, wrote drafts, and made trial runs. A group of volunteers from local churches gathered and filled out a draft of a questionnaire, with Glock and Stark present to discuss ambiguous items or ones that failed to give the volunteers suitable means for expressing their views. They sent a later draft to several hundred persons randomly selected from the rolls of local churches. They then analyzed the results to see whether they were promising. The results were good, so Glock and Stark continued their research.

Survey research can be done either by interviewing people or by having them complete a self-administered questionnaire. The questionnaire method is considerably cheaper because postage is cheaper than interviewers' wages. But the questionnaire method often has a poor return rate. The validity of results based on a random sample of a population depends on getting data

from most of the people selected for the sample. If, for example, researchers gather the presidential preferences of only half of the sample selected, it may be that the other half have very different preferences, and the researchers may be badly misled in predicting an election. With interviewing, however, the nonresponse rate is apt to be very small.

Glock and Stark had settled on the questionnaire method because their funds did not permit interviews of the length and numbers they wished to have. Furthermore, they knew that they would be able to insert their key measures in a study planned by Gertrude Selznick and Stephen Steinberg that would use nationwide interviews with a random sample of 2,000 adults. They decided to study the relationships between religion and prejudice in depth first and then to attempt to *replicate* their findings on nationwide data. To replicate a study means to repeat it—with another sample population in this case. Replication is the best way to guard against possible errors produced by oddities or chance factors in the original sample; replicating a study on a different population sample makes it possible to be sure that findings for one population apply to another. Glock and Stark had decided to limit their first study to church members in a single metropolitan area, but replication would permit them to tell later whether their findings could be generalized to the entire country. Their first problem was to pick an area for their study. With that choice made, they would proceed by first drawing a sample of Protestant and Catholic congregations and parishes. From these they would randomly select persons from the membership lists. But acquiring the lists, of course, required cooperation of the churches. And that was a problem.

After months of negotiations with church leaders in many parts of the country, they found cooperation easiest to obtain in their own area; thus, four counties on the west side of the San Francisco Bay made up the sample: urban San Francisco, wilderness Marin, wealthy San Mateo, and sprawling Santa Clara—a fair microcosm of the state of California. Glock and Stark randomly selected 21 Catholic parishes from a total of 137; they selected

Figure 2.13   Sample questions from the questionnaire distributed by Glock and Stark in their survey research on the causes of anti-Semitism. The questions are selected from the section dealing with relations between Christians and Jews.
(From C. Y. Glock and R. Stark, 1963.)

We turn now to relations between Christians and Jews. There is a great deal of disagreement about what Jews are like. Here are some things people have said at one time or another about Jews. For each statement, we would ask you to do two things:

First read the statement and decide whether you tend to think Jews are like this or not, and put your answer in Column A.

Then, whether or not you think Jews are like this or not, we would ask you to suppose that the statement actually were true. If the statement were true, how would it tend to make you feel toward Jews? Would you tend to feel friendly or unfriendly toward them because of this? Put your answer in Column B.

| COLUMN A | | | | COLUMN B | | |
| Do you feel Jews tend to be like this? | | | | If Jews were like this would it tend to make you feel: | | |
Yes	Somewhat	No		Friendly	Unfriendly	Neither Way
☐	☐	☐	Jews are particularly generous and give a great deal of money to charity	☐	☐	☐
☐	☐	☐	On the average, Jews are wealthier than Christians	☐	☐	☐
☐	☐	☐	Jews are more likely than Christians to cheat in business	☐	☐	☐
☐	☐	☐	Jewish children tend to get better grades in school than Christian children do	☐	☐	☐
☐	☐	☐	Jews are less likely than Christians to oppose Communism	☐	☐	☐
☐	☐	☐	The movie and television industries are pretty much run by Jews	☐	☐	☐
☐	☐	☐	On the average, Jews tend to drink less than non-Jews	☐	☐	☐
☐	☐	☐	Because Jews are not bound by Christian ethics, they do things to get ahead that Christians generally will not do	☐	☐	☐
☐	☐	☐	While many Jews attend synagogues and worship God, most Jews are not very religious	☐	☐	☐

97 Protestant congregations representing all major denominations. It was not easy to win cooperation from every parish and congregation. Some small churches drawn in the sample (located through the Yellow Pages and other means) had already failed and closed—one had actually been torn down. Furthermore, permission required many personal appearances by Stark before church boards. Finally, everything was set, and in April of 1963 the questionnaires were mailed to the respondents. Follow-up letters and other efforts were made to stimulate a high rate of return. But the big job was correcting the sample for faulty inclusions; church membership lists turned out to be filled with deadwood—many of those listed as members had moved from the area some

years before, and others had died, one as far back as 1929!

Finally, about 70 percent of the church members had responded to the study. While this is a fairly high rate of response, it is sufficiently far from perfect to permit bias in the findings. For example, the three out of ten who did not answer might have been less educated, older, poorer, or less religious than the seven out of ten who did answer. Glock and Stark used several techniques to guard against the possibility that their findings were biased because of differences between those who did and those who did not cooperate.

First, they chose a sample of persons who had not returned their questionnaires. They telephoned these persons and briefly interviewed them to determine their age, sex, occupation, church attendance, education, and so forth. They then compared the nonrespondents with the respondents on each of these factors. Finding only very small differences, they gained confidence that their findings would not be badly biased. They also knew that when they obtained interview data from the national sample—where there would be no appreciable response bias—they could check their findings against it.

Statistical Analysis

What does it mean to say that religion and prejudice are or are not related? Now that the researchers had data on the beliefs, activities, and attitudes of more than 3,000 persons, how could they proceed? What they did is at the heart of virtually all science: statistical analysis of the quantitative data, or evidence that has been transformed into numbers.

In the preceding section we discussed the most simple form of statistical analysis. The logic in all scientific analysis is the same although the analysis can take more or less complex forms. First, Glock and Stark had to give each person a score on each of the concepts in their theory. This is quite similar to one of the ways in which college teachers score objective quizzes—the number of correct answers assigns each student a grade.

Glock and Stark added up each person's answers to a set of questions designed to measure a particular concept or element in the theory. Unlike test scoring, these scores did not imply better or worse performances but simply different patterns of beliefs or attitudes. For example, orthodoxy was measured by a person's responses to questions about whether he believed in a personal God, in the divinity of Jesus, and in the existence of heaven and the devil. People who claimed firm belief in all four were given a score of four; those who rejected one belief were scored three, and so on down to a score of zero for people who rejected all four beliefs. In this way five groups were created for the concepts of orthodoxy, ranging from very orthodox down to very unorthodox believers. Other concepts were similarly measured and scored.

To see whether one set of scores is related to another set requires a simple comparison. The following example, taken from Glock and Stark's study, is based on two sets of scores. The first is a measure of what they called *religious dogmatism*—the independent variable. It combined the first three religious concepts in their theory into a single measure. The second is *anti-Semitic beliefs*—the dependent variable. To find out if religious dogmatism is in fact related to anti-Semitic beliefs, they first had to separate people into groups according to their scores on religious dogmatism. Glock and Stark condensed the original numerical scores into three groups; the result was as in Example A.

Example A		
Religious Dogmatism*		
High	*Medium*	*Low*
522 people	421 people	310 people

* Protestants only.

The next step was to see how each of these three groups was distributed on the measure of anti-Semitic beliefs. The results were as in Example B.

Example B			
Anti-Semitic Beliefs	Religious Dogmatism		
	High	*Medium*	*Low*
High	271	143	62
Medium	204	202	164
Low	47	76	84
Total	522	421	310

Glock and Stark then compared persons with high scores on religious dogmatism with those scoring lower to see in which group anti-Semitism is most common. Looking at the raw numbers above it would be very hard to make such a judgment. It is true that those scoring high on religious dogmatism have the greatest number (271) of high scores on anti-Semitic beliefs. But it is also true that they are the largest group.

When groups contain different numbers of people, they are hard to compare. The solution to this problem is to convert the simple numbers into percentages, which take account of size differences and make direct comparisons easy. You divide 271 by 522 to get the percentage of persons scoring high on religious dogmatism who also scored high on anti-Semitic beliefs: 52 percent. Similarly, you divide 62 by 310 to determine that only 20 percent of those scoring low on religious dogmatism scored high on anti-Semitic beliefs. When all of this division is completed (which is usually done by a computer in a tiny fraction of a second), the results are as in Example C.

Example C			
Anti-Semitic Beliefs	Religious Dogmatism		
	High	*Medium*	*Low*
High	52%	34%	20%
Medium	39	48	53
Low	9	18	27
Total	100%	100%	100%

Reading across this table, you will see that the percentage scoring high on anti-Semitic beliefs falls as one reads from those high on religious dogmatism to those medium and low on this measure: 52—34—20. Or reading across the third row of the table, you can see that the percentage scoring low on anti-Semitic beliefs rises as religious dogmatism declines: 9—18—27. Thus, more than half of the persons in the high-dogmatism group are high on anti-Semitism, but only one person in five among those in the low-dogmatism group is high on anti-Semitism. This clearly shows a relationship between dogmatism and anti-Semitism, confirming Glock and Stark's theory that religion plays a role in contemporary American anti-Semitism.

Although such findings confirmed Glock and Stark's expectations, they still had much work to do. Recall that in Dion's experimental design the people participating in the experiment were randomly assigned to treatment conditions. Randomization allowed Dion to control all other possible causes of differences—besides chance differences—between those seeing a pretty child and those seeing a homely child. It established (within known probabilities) that both groups would be equal in terms of background, age, attitudes, and the like; the only thing permitted to vary was the appearance of the children. In such experiments, the analysis of findings is complete when the initial comparison has been made. The investigator then uses a simple statistical method to determine whether the size of the relationship found—for example, the size of the difference in degree of anti-Semitism shown between people who scored high and people who scored low on dogmatism—is great enough to make it extremely unlikely that simple chance caused it. If the difference is statistically significant, the experimenter then publishes his findings with confidence.

When survey research is the method, however, one is not able to rule out other differences by random assignment of respondents. How people came to hold beliefs classifying them as high or low on dogmatism is not within the control of the investigator. Hence, because people who scored high or low on dogmatism differ in other ways, there is always the possibility that some factor other than dogmatism is responsible for the findings.

This problem, which Glock and Stark had to grapple with, is called *spuriousness*. When we can demonstrate that something other than dogmatism produced the findings, then we can say that the original relationship between dogmatism and anti-Semitism was spurious, not causal. Consider a silly, but apt, example of spuriousness: The more fire trucks present at a fire, the greater the fire damage will be. We can easily see that although these two phenomena will occur together, their connection is spurious, not one of cause and effect: fire trucks are not causing the damage. Instead we know that both the number of trucks present and the extent of the damage are produced by the size or seriousness of the fire.

Similarly, some other factor could be making it appear that religious dogmatism is the cause of anti-Semitic beliefs. Many sociologists would have

Figure 2.14 A hypothetical chart presenting a *spurious* (false) relationship between religious dogmatism and anti-Semitic beliefs. If Glock and Stark had been wrong in their assumption that religious dogmatism and anti-Semitism are causally related—if, for example, another factor, such as income level, were really responsible for both dogmatism and anti-Semitism—then the correlation between dogmatism and anti-Semitism would disappear, as it does below, when the researchers controlled for income level. However, in fact the survey researchers *did* control for income, and the causal relation between dogmatism and anti-Semitism *did not* disappear.

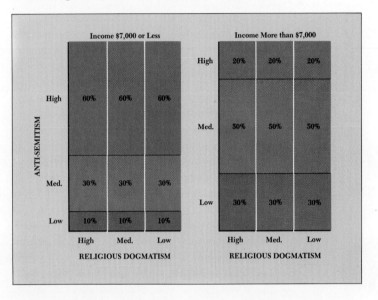

a hunch that social class might be producing high scores on both measures (see Chapter 14). They would argue that poor people are both more religiously dogmatic *and* more anti-Semitic than are well-to-do people. They would therefore say that those who scored high on religious dogmatism typically are poor people and for this reason scored high on anti-Semitism; those who scored low on dogmatism typically are well-to-do people, and therefore they scored low on anti-Semitism.

Sociologists use statistical controls to guard against spuriousness. They try to remove the effects of factors that might produce spurious findings. The principle involved is quite simple. In the Glock and Stark study they would examine the relationship between dogmatism and anti-Semitism separately for poor people and for the well-to-do. For the sake of simplicity, let us suppose that it would be sufficient to divide people into two income groups: those earning $7,000 a year or less and those earning more. Classifying people by income would be used to create two tables. One would contain only those earning $7,000 or less; the other, those earning more.

Figure 2.14 is a *hypothetical* illustration showing that income was the cause of a spurious relationship between dogmatism and anti-Semitism.

Although a researcher would need to study many more levels of income, assume for the moment that by separating people into these two income groups, we have assured that everyone in each group has the same income. Say that within each of the two income tables, income no longer varies; we have controlled for income differences. If it was variation in income that produced the original connection between dogmatism and anti-Semitism, then when income is controlled for, the original relationship ought to *disappear*. Notice that it has disappeared in the hypothetical table. For the group earning $7,000 or less, each level of dogmatism contains the same percentage of people who scored high on anti-Semitic beliefs; across the top row we read: 60—60—60. Similarly, for the group earning more than $7,000, the percentage of people who scored high on anti-Semitism is the same regardless of their score on

dogmatism: 20—20—20. We can also see that regardless of the degree of dogmatism, people earning more than $7,000 are much less likely to be high on anti-Semitism than are those earning $7,000 or less: 60 percent versus 20 percent. We use such a control procedure to find out whether a relationship is spurious; we know that it is when the outcome is like the one in Figure 2.14.

However, this is *not* what happened when Glock and Stark controlled for income. They found that the original relationship between dogmatism and anti-Semitism *reappeared* in each of the income tables: Regardless of a person's income, his religious views influenced his judgments of Jews. Finding out that income was not a possible source of spuriousness increased Glock and Stark's confidence in their original findings. Using similar procedures, they were also able to eliminate age, sex, education, denomination, political affiliation, rural or urban origins, and a number of other potential sources of spuriousness. Such controls greatly increased the probability that religious dogmatism does in fact cause anti-Semitism.

Glock and Stark first confirmed their theories on data collected from Northern California church members; then, when data from the national interview sample became available, they repeated their previous analysis and found virtually identical results. Confirmation further increased the probability that they were correct, but that was not a sufficient stopping place.

Applications of the Study

Recall why Glock and Stark had undertaken their study: to try to understand the causes of American anti-Semitism. Glock and Stark projected that perhaps as many as 17.5 million Americans at that time harbored ill-will toward Jews on the basis of their religious convictions.

The findings called for action. Glock and Stark were not content simply to publish their results. They believed that they were obligated to help find ways to change these pernicious patterns. Is this a violation of scientific neutrality? A proper scientist, whether sociologist or chemist, must be scrupulously impartial and careful in gathering and evaluating his evidence. But once he has done so, he is under no obligation to treat his findings neutrally or to do nothing about them. A chemist warns us that rising mercury levels in lakes and rivers endanger life. Glock and Stark had a moral abhorrence of prejudice, and they believed that churches have an absolute obligation to undo what they have done, that is, to find ways to stop fostering prejudice.

They first acted on their findings when they supplied a preliminary report to the Vatican Council II, a worldwide meeting of Roman Catholic prelates that led to many changes in the church. Through the Dutch Documentation Center they distributed copies of their report to all of the assembled bishops. The council did issue a historic statement condemning the notion that the Jews bore the guilt of the Crucifixion, and ADL leaders stated that Glock and Stark's report had been critical in prompting this action.

Shortly thereafter Glock and Stark published their findings in *Christian Beliefs and Anti-Semitism* (1966). The book received considerable press attention; it was praised and damned, believed and denied. Both authors received a great deal of mail. Some people wrote that the book had inspired them to work harder as ministers or at be-

ing good Christians. Some wrote abusive, threatening, or obscene letters. Glock and Stark were satisfied that they were provoking action. A number of Protestant churches made affirmations similar to the one made by the Vatican Council II (other churches had made such affirmations earlier). More important, church leaders generally agreed that positive action was necessary, that Sunday-school books and church literature needed considerable revision, and that educational campaigns at all levels were needed. For more than two years Glock and Stark toured the nation, meeting in seminars with church leaders, curriculum directors, and religious publishers, and they found that people listened to their results despite their misgivings. They had to listen because Glock and Stark had facts, not opinion. One of Stark's most effective lines in these sessions was: "Forget about our theory. For whatever reason, the fact remains that most of your members —your most active members—still blame the Jews for killing Christ and believe all Jews are damned to hell. Many also believe Jews cheat and steal and lie. If that's not what you want them to believe, you've got a serious problem whether or not they learned these beliefs in church." He was able to show statistics based on large random samples to back up his charges.

In 1971 these same authors, joined by two colleagues, published an additional replication of their study. This time the respondents in the survey were not church members or the general American public; they were Protestant ministers (Stark, Foster, Glock, and Quinley, 1971). The results were virtually identical to the earlier findings based on surveys with laymen and the general public as respondents. As a result, most church leaders agreed that they had a big job to do.

MORE THAN METHODS

Conducting sociological research requires more than common sense, general nosiness, or an understanding of statistics and computers. A body of knowledge guides sociologists in their quest to understand man in society.

First, they are guided by the *concepts* and *theories* of sociology. Concepts are ways of cutting up the world and naming the parts. For example, in the study by Glock and Stark, orthodoxy and anti-Semitism are working concepts. Theories are ways of ordering the conceptualized parts; they say how and why various parts are connected. For example, Lofland's theory of conversion tells how and why people join the Divine Precepts, and it can be generalized to other radical religious movements. The sociological body of knowledge is also made up of *empirical findings and generalizations*—all that social science has learned about people in society through countless efforts to observe and record social life.

Unit II provides an introduction to the principles of sociology: the main concepts and theoretical perspectives. The remainder of the book is devoted to combining these principles with the fruits of sociological thought and research in specific areas of interest. The three sociological studies in this chapter offer specific, detailed examples and references for the procedures, problems, and principles that you will be learning in Unit II and in later chapters.

SUGGESTED READINGS

Kaplan, Abraham. *The Conduct of Inquiry: Methodology for Behavioral Science.* Scranton, Pa.: Chandler, 1964.

Lofland, John. *Analyzing Social Settings.* Belmont, Calif.: Wadsworth, 1971.

Selltiz, Claire, *et al. Research Methods in Social Relations.* Rev. ed. New York: Holt, Rinehart and Winston, 1959.

Zeisel, Hans. *Say It With Figures.* 5th rev. ed. New York: Harper & Row, 1968.

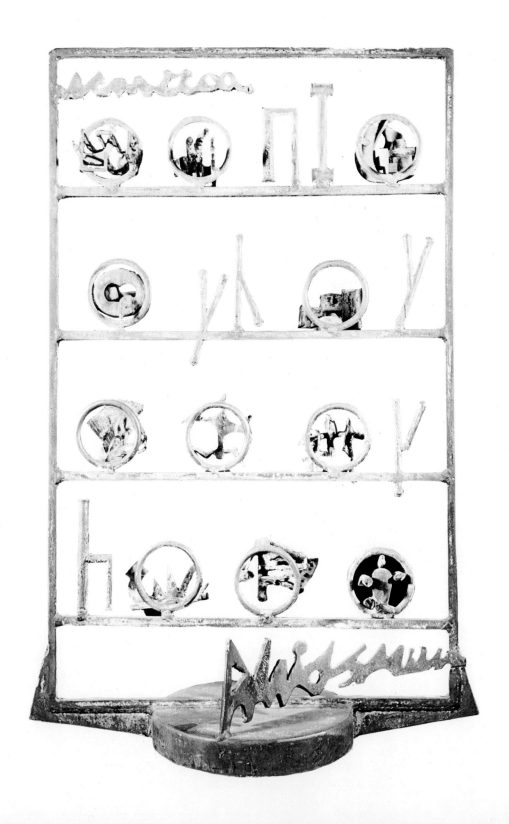

The major activities in all of science are *naming* and *explaining*. Both are necessary, but the difference between them is extremely important. Giving things names enables us to separate the world into identifiable units. The names that scientists use are called *concepts*. Concepts are used for *analysis*—which Webster defines as "separating or breaking up any whole into its parts." But once science has broken up phenomena into parts and named them, the job remains to put things back together. Statements that connect some set of concepts into an explanation are called *theories*. Concepts are therefore the necessary building blocks of theories. Theories unite

UNIT II
THE PRINCIPLES
OF SOCIOLOGY

two or more concepts and say how they are related to each other. For example, the more committed people are to beliefs about the religious inferiority of Jews, the more likely they are to be anti-Semitic; that is, *religious hostility* causes *anti-Semitism* (Glock and Stark, see Chapter 2). Two concepts, religious hostility and

anti-Semitism, are causally linked in this theory. The vital point to remember is that to name something is *not* to explain it. Naming some set of beliefs, feelings, and actions as anti-Semitism lets us know what we are talking about, but it says nothing about what causes (or explains) anti-Semitism. Only theories propose explanations.
¶ Chapter 3 explains how sociologists have disassembled and named major parts of social life. It offers you the vocabulary of sociology and identifies the major sociological concerns. Chapter 4 introduces you to the major theoretical perspectives that sociologists use to reassemble their concepts into explanations of social life. The concepts and theories of sociology together constitute the fundamental principles of the field.

Chapter 3 Basic Concepts

MARTHA MOSHER AND HER FAMILY are Americans. In some ways they are like all Americans and all other human beings. But in other ways they are more like some Americans and less like others. Some of these similarities and differences arouse the interest of sociologists, and some do not. All of the members of the Mosher family have brown hair. But that does not seem to have much influence on how they act, what they believe in, or how they conceive of themselves and others. Some of the Moshers are males and some are females; some are children, and some are adults. These characteristics do seem important. Furthermore, the Moshers are white, and that greatly affects their lives. That they are Jews also makes a great deal of difference in how the Moshers regard themselves and are regarded by others.

Sociologists are not greatly interested in Martha Mosher or any other individual. They are more interested in her family, her circle of friends, her classmates, and all the other groups in which Martha participates. Sociologists want to understand groups—what makes them tick? What goes on between groups? How are our individual lives shaped by groups?

To answer, or even to ask such questions, sociologists find it necessary to disassemble social life into components. We do not experience life this way, any more than we experience a watch as a pile of parts. But only by taking life apart can we comprehend it. We shall therefore look at bits of Martha Mosher's biography throughout this chapter as we explore the basic ways in which sociologists disassemble society.

When sociologists take apart the world they give names to the parts. These names are concepts. All sciences develop their own terminology to define and delineate the parts of the world with which they are concerned, and sociology is no different. To understand the ways in which sociologists divide up and study the "sociological world" you have to understand sociological language.

Frequently, scientists and investigators use words from common speech but use them slightly differently or in restricted ways. The accuracy of such words increases if they have few and pre-

cisely specifiable meanings. Such terms may denote important concepts for a discipline and are therefore both tools of investigation and building blocks of theories. The two most basic concepts in sociology are those of *society* and *culture*. The immediate task is therefore to define and discuss what sociologists mean by the terms society and culture and, following that, to introduce you to other basic concepts and terms.

SOCIETY

Society is a technical term in sociology, and it is used to refer to fewer things than it can refer to in everyday speech. For instance, Martha and her family do not belong to "high society"—their names never appear in the society pages of the *New York Times*—yet they are members of society. It is worthwhile to understand from the beginning what the term society does *not* mean for sociologists. Obviously, this term does not refer to what you read about in the society pages of the newspaper, nor does it refer to clubs or associations. Whether or not Martha ever joined the Girl Scouts, a book club, or a union would certainly be of interest to some sociologists, but nonetheless, when sociologists speak about society, such groups are not what they are referring to.

Sociologists have defined the term society in various ways, but all the definitions have essential similarities. The definition offered by Bernard Berelson and Gary A. Steiner (1964) is a good example. They define society as "an aggregate of people that is self-sustaining, that has a definite location and a long duration, and that shares a way of life." Another way of saying basically the same thing is to define society as *a group of people whose relationships are organized and structured by a culture.* This definition introduces the sociological concept of *culture.*

CULTURE

When sociologists use the term *culture,* they mean more than the way Martha uses her knife and fork or the number of paintings she owns. Simply put, the concept of culture refers to the entire complex of things acquired by Martha and anyone else through their collective experiences in society. The classic definition of culture offered in 1871 by the anthropologist Edward B. Tylor, which appears to include everything but the kitchen sink, is still adhered to by sociologists. Tylor (1958) defines culture as "that complex whole which includes knowledge, belief, art, morals, law, custom, and any other capabilities and habits acquired by man as a member of society."

If we adopt Tylor's definition of culture, we are taking culture to be *learned* (through collective experiences) and to be possessed by humans. Anything acquired outside of society (by heredity, for example) does *not* qualify as culture, according to this definition. Recalling the definition of society as a group of people whose relationships are organized and structured by a culture, we can now state that culture is the *principle of organization* in a society. In other words, without a culture there would be no human society as we know it. The relationships between people are studied in sociology by way of other important basic concepts that are introduced a little later on in the chapter.

If you have concluded that it is next to impossible to study society without also studying culture, you are right. The distinction between society and culture is made for the sake of convenience; it is primarily analytic—it is a useful way to take social phenomena apart. As contemporary sociologist Ely Chinoy (1968) put it: "Although we can distinguish between them analytically, human society *cannot* exist without culture, and culture exists *only* within society." Before moving on to a discussion of the concepts sociologists use to study society and culture, it is necessary to elaborate a bit on the concept of culture. This can be accomplished rather painlessly by examining some of the characteristics of culture.

SOME CHARACTERISTICS AND FORMS OF CULTURE

Culture, as was noted earlier, is a social *phenomenon*—it is learned through collective experiences of people in society.

Culture as Problem Solving

Culture can be thought of as the ways in which groups deal with the basic and recurring facts of their existence. People living in groups—that is, in societies—always have to develop ways to handle their lives. As social beings, they face problems and situations, many of which are universal and recur from generation to generation, for example: regulating the relationships between individuals; regulating those between the sexes; maintaining health; and accounting for the nonhuman universe and its workings. Another fact of social existence is that people must transmit culture itself from generation to generation. Culture, in Tylor's words, is that "complex whole" that handles all these problems.

Relationships between men and women, which form a subset of the relations between people in general, may serve as an example of how culture structures people's activity. How Martha and a man behave toward one another when they are interested in getting to know one another, how they might act, think, and feel if their relationship were to become intimate, how they would handle a long-term relationship, all this and more is regulated by various social rules (Tylor's "morals," "law," and "custom"). Some of these rules are manifested through the institutions of marriage and the family and are further revealed in courtship patterns.

The maintenance of health and sanitation is attempted through many practices, the most familiar ones having to do with taboos and requirements surrounding the handling and preparation of food and certain types of behavior required at times of birth and death. In our own society, health and sanitation practices also include such institutionalized means as professional medicine, hospitals, and community health programs. What the Moshers will or will not eat, whether or not they cook what they accept as food, the methods they have for avoiding contamination, their trips to the dentist and the doctor, their vaccinations and showers, their responses and behavior when birth is imminent or death occurs are some of the practices of interest.

The facts of the universe have historically been

Figure 3.1   Culture is reflected in the constructs or views of the world that different societies adopt at different points in time. (*Top*) A map drawn to depict the world view of a flat earth, which uses a mythological construct to account for the unknown. The cultures of modern industrial societies, by contrast, are characterized by the scientific view of the world (and unknown worlds) that they have adopted. (*Below*) A photograph of Earth taken from space.

explained or accounted for by mythology and religion. It can be argued that in our own society science has taken over part of this function and provides a world view that has some of the features of a religion. Martha accepts without question the scientific view that the universe is composed of an enormous or infinite number of stars and planets similar to the solar system in which she lives. Yet, although she is not "religious," her Jewish background does affect her feelings about death and the universe. These attitudes, in turn, condition her other attitudes and her behavior.

Culture is transmitted from generation to generation by education. Education covers a spectrum that includes what children learn as they interact with other children and with adults; more formalized routines, such as the telling of stories and tales around the fire; systems of apprenticeship; and the complex system of primary and secondary schools, colleges, universities, and professional programs of societies such as ours. Martha has learned and learns many things from her parents and friends, but she has also spent most of her life in school, from nursery school to postgraduate work at the university, and she would be shocked at the idea of never sending her children to some kind of educational institution.

Culture Is a Unity

It is for the convenience of study that we discuss Martha's life by breaking it down into segments that she shares with other Americans. But, of course, in real life all these aspects of culture, these attitudes and behavior patterns governing how life is conducted, fit together and affect one another. That is, a characteristic of culture is that it tends to form a unity—an integrated, coherent whole—whose parts are intricately related. If one aspect of a culture is significantly altered or changed it may have widespread effects. For example, the American civil-rights movement to organize and mobilize black people around the demand for full equality of participation in American culture had great effects on American life. Many changes have been experienced by Martha and her family and virtually all Americans in their traditional attitudes, beliefs, and behavior

Figure 3.2   Subcultures are groups whose
norms set them apart from the rest of society. Subcultures differ from one another in their orientation
toward the larger society. Street gangs (*top*) are an
example of a type of subculture in open conflict
with the norms of the larger society. A quite different
orientation is exemplified by the Amish of
Pennsylvania (*bottom*), who have actively isolated
themselves from American society.

Figure 3.3   William Graham Sumner (1840–1910) was one of America's first sociologists and was on the faculty of Yale University. He was greatly influenced by the work of Herbert Spencer and sought to apply to social life the principles Darwin discovered about biological species. His major work, *Folkways* (1906), is available in a popular paperback edition and has been read by generations of sociology students. Sumner argued that principles of natural selection operate in such a way that success goes to the most talented (see Chapter 15).

toward blacks as a result of this movement. Some of these changes are reflected in new state and federal laws and procedures that were passed in the 1960s and 1970s—as well as in the political rhetoric of the times. Indeed, many observers have noted that the current push for social changes in the status of subgroups in general may be traceable to the impetus that was initially supplied by the civil-rights movement.

Basic Culture Is Abstract

Such important changes in culture are felt not only in material life but in the ideas and opinions of the social participants. This brings us to note another characteristic of culture: *Basic culture is abstract.* It is made up of such things as ideas and values. These abstract or nontangible entities, however, are reflected in what is called *material culture:* architecture, industrial machines, washing machines and other products of technology, clothing, Barbie dolls, and the accouterments of the American way of life.

Subcultures

Earlier we pointed out that a culture tends to form a coherent and unified whole. But when we look at many large societies, it is obvious that groups with quite marked cultural differences may exist side by side within the same society. Sometimes these cultural dissimilarities stem from long-standing, historic differences, such as those between English- and French-speaking Canadians. Sometimes differences develop as a result of changes in the society, for example, when a generation gap occurs. Groups with distinctive cultures within the same society are often referred to as *subcultures.* Martha and her family are Jewish and part of the Eastern-European Jewish subculture in America; Martha is also in her late twenties and to a large extent considers herself part of the "youth culture" or "counterculture" and actively rejects many of the qualities of American life that her parents accept.

A *subculture* is a culture within a culture—a group that has developed its own set of beliefs, morals, customs, and practices that its members share but that are contrary to those prevailing in the larger society or in other major groups in the society. J. Milton Yinger (1960) defines subculture as "norms that set a group apart from, not those that integrate a group with, the total society." There are numerous examples of subcultures; ethnic minority groups, street gangs, communes, and the drug subculture are only a few.

The study of human beings, as we have seen, requires the study of culture and society. How do sociologists *conceptualize* the ways in which culture organizes and structures relationships among people in society? The following sections explore some of the basic concepts that sociologists use.

SOME OTHER BASIC CONCEPTS

It is common in sociology to speak of *social organization* and *social structure* synonymously with *society.* In fact, it is helpful to view society as the organization or the structure formed by culture. In getting at society through culture, sociologists have developed the concept of *norm.*

Norms

Norms are rules—they define what is required or acceptable behavior in certain groups or situations. They imply that the individual *should, ought,* or *must* follow certain behavioral patterns. Because norms embody the standards for *evaluating* the behavior of individuals or groups they are excellent reflectors of culture. Like all rules, norms generally carry sanctions for their violation and thus can be viewed as controls. In other words, it is through norms that society regulates relationships between its members. Norms run deep in all of us—they influence the phenomena of conscience, guilt feelings, motivation, elation, and depression—they are internalized rules and standards. Sociologists identify a number of types of norms; together these types constitute what is called the *normative order* or the *normative system.* Two types of norms that are essential constructs in sociology are *folkways* and *mores.*

Folkways   The term *folkways* was coined early in the 1900s by the American sociologist William Graham Sumner (1840–1910) in his classic book

Folkways (1959). Folkways are ways of doing things that are regarded as right and natural and that are not questioned, such as eating three meals a day and brushing your teeth. Folkways carry little or no sanction (punishment) for their violation. As Sumner wrote: "The folkways are the 'right' ways to satisfy all interests, because they are traditional. . . . In the folkways, whatever is, is right." Two types of folkways frequently identified in sociology are customs and fashions.

Customs are folkways that seem relatively permanent. They are practices that have gradually become accepted as appropriate modes of behavior and are maintained by group opinion. Observing particular religious holidays, participating in certain rituals (such as the marriage ceremony), and deferring to your professor in the classroom are all examples of customs. Customs resist change, which is how they differ from fashions.

Fashions are practices that are expected to undergo fairly rapid change; fashions very noticeably start and end. Rapidly changing fashions in clothing styles and slang vocabulary are accepted features of American life. Five years ago Martha and her friends wore miniskirts and said that things were groovy; now they are just as likely to wear "midis" and to say that things are "all *right.*"

Mores The term *more* (it rhymes with *foray*) was also coined by Sumner. Mores are a special group of norms about which the members of society are extremely conscious and that they regard as absolutely essential for the well-being of the group. There is an air of inviolability about the mores; they carry a *must* connotation and are accompanied by heavy negative sanctions for their violation. What a society defines as *moral* is revealed in its more structure; thus, the mores are the core of the normative order. In our society, clear examples of mores are provided by the ten commandments. There are different kinds of mores, and two important kinds are conventions and laws.

Conventions are relatively rigid rules governing certain social interactions. The major difference between conventions and *laws* is that violations of laws are punished by *legal sanction,* and violations of conventions by the negative re-

sponses of the group. As the pioneering German sociologist Max Weber (1864–1920) put it: "A violation of convention . . . often meets with the most effective and serious retribution in the form of social ostracism, which may be even more effective than legal sanction" (1964). The "professional ethics" of medicine and psychiatry are recognized codes of conventional behavior that govern how doctors and psychiatrists interact with their patients in certain recurrent situations. If Martha were to visit a doctor or psychiatrist who subsequently revealed details of her case, she might accuse him of violating his ethical code and could appeal to one of his professional organizations. When such conventional codes as professional ethics are violated, the offenders may be met with group sanctions that may be formal (say, expulsion from the county medical society or a fine) and informal (the disapproval of one's fellow professionals, a bad reputation in the field).

Laws are rules that are made by those who hold political power and that are enforced through the machinery of the state. Generally (although not necessarily) laws are viewed as *codified mores.* An example are the laws against murder and assault in American society. If Martha could prove, according to rules set up by the state, that her doctor willfully did her some injury, he might be convicted of violating a law and be punished by the state and by social censure as well. Many laws, however, do not carry the widespread moral conviction associated with the mores. If Martha's doctor had been caught milking the welfare system or cheating on his income-tax returns, for example, he might be punished by the government but escape professional and social censure.

We have seen that folkways and mores are types of norms and that norms are the *cultural* rules regulating relationships between people. When there is widespread *consensus,* or agreement, about norms, there generally is *conformity* to them. Behavior that does not comply to normative standards, which violates the rules, is termed *deviance.* The study of deviant behavior constitutes a subfield of sociology and includes such areas of investigation as the causes of crime and criminal behavior (criminology), mental illness,

Figure 3.4   Examples of norms (*top middle*),
values (*top right*), beliefs (*bottom left*), and attitudes
(*bottom middle and right*). Inherent in most
social interaction is a combination of these
four orientations.

juvenile delinquency, alcoholism, and drug addiction. (For an extended discussion of how deviance
is defined and controlled see Chapter 11.)

Two other sociological constructs that also
have to do with culture are *values* and *attitudes.*

Values

Values are views about what is desirable. Values
differ from norms in that norms are fairly precise
rules of behavior, whereas values are *general
standards* that are somewhat independent of specific situations. An example may help clarify the
difference: Martha's opinion that democracy is a
desirable form of government is a *value;* the *rules*
under which a democratic society actually functions (folkways, mores, laws, and so on) are *norms.*
Other examples of values in American society are
that the free-enterprise system is good and that
achievement and success are important goals. Val-

ues are preferences about the way things *should
be,* but they are generally derived from *beliefs,*
which are convictions about the ways things *are.*
Martha holds that some form of government is
probably necessary; that is a belief. Her view
about what kind of government is most desirable
is a value. The rules that actually regulate relationships between people under any form of government are *norms.* Now, let us muddy the water
a bit and introduce the concept of *attitude.*

Attitudes

The word attitude has been used inconsistently by
sociologists. Frequently it is used as a synonym for
opinions or sentiments. But the most widely used
definition classifies attitudes as the subjective and
individualized counterparts of values. Thus, attitudes involve *evaluations*—positive and negative
judgments. But attitudes also imply a *predisposi-*

Figure 3.5   Culture influences and determines not only large-scale institutions but also individuals' everyday tastes and preferences, including the kinds of foods they like and the way they like them prepared. (*Below*) A woman of the Libinza tribe in the Ngiri River area of the Congo prepares grubs for cooking.

tion to act; that is, persons holding a certain attitude will act differently in specific situations than will persons who do not hold that attitude or who hold a contrary attitude. Neither beliefs nor values necessarily imply any tendency to act. You can believe that government is necessary and support democratic values but still take no part in American politics. But if you hold strong attitudes about the virtues of the Democratic party you are quite likely to vote or otherwise act on its behalf.

SOCIETAL CONCEPTS

So far we have discussed some of the basic concepts sociologists use to study how culture structures and organizes people's relationships in society—norms and types of norms, and values, beliefs, and attitudes. Now it is time to take a further look at how sociologists conceptualize society. Perhaps the most significant *societal* concept in sociology is that of *social institution.*

Social Institutions

When sociologists talk about society, social organization, or social structure they are generally referring to *groups of social institutions.* Indeed, one of the most efficient and comprehensive ways to understand a total society is to understand its major institutions and the relationships that exist between them.

An *institution* can be defined as *an abstract set of norms, values, and beliefs that center on and define some segment of human life.* If you find it difficult to remember that definition you can take refuge in Sumner's simpler one: "An institution is a concept . . . and a structure" (1959). The "concept" part of Sumner's definition corresponds to the "abstract" part or intangibles of our definition, to institutional norms, values, and beliefs. The "structure" part of his definition refers both to the *organization of persons* (or functionaries) who bring into fact and action those norms and so on and to the *set of material instrumentalities used* to translate them into actuality. The military in American society is a social institution; it has its norms (folkways, mores, conventions, laws, and so on), values, and beliefs; it has its functionaries (ranging from the commander in chief down to the privates); and it has its set of material instrumentalities (ranging from side arms and missiles to binoculars and computers). A similar kind of analysis can be made of any other institution, such as the family, religion, and the educational institution.

Thanks again to Sumner, sociologists make a distinction between two types of institutions: crescive and enacted. *Crescive institutions* are those that emerge slowly out of the folkways and mores, such as the institution of the family. *Enacted institutions* are those that are consciously created, usually by people occupying positions of power and authority. They are often created (or enacted) by law. An example of an enacted institution is the particular form of government under which we live in American society.

The concept of *social institution* exemplifies the profound relationship between society and culture. As indicated earlier, culture affects or structures the way individuals feel about things. In human society even such phenomena as basic biological drives are controlled by culture, and culture effects this control through institutions. For example, the biological sex drive in humans can result in the build-up of tension—what is called covert or inner tension. The *overt*—the external or the acting out—aspect of the drive relieves this tension. There are often negative feelings associated with the overt aspect (guilt, shame, anxiety, and so on) when the drive is not satisfied through normative institutional channels (such as in the institution of marriage). In other words, it is through institutions that societies positively and negatively sanction the expression of the sex drive; and it is through institutions that differences in sexual practices between cultures are maintained. The processes by which the culturally appropriate attitudes, values, beliefs, and responses are instilled in individuals are collectively known as *socialization,* another concept that sociologists find essential to the study of society.

Socialization

Newborn infants have no norms, no attitudes, and no values. Martha's new baby, like all babies everywhere, has no culture. *Socialization* is the set of processes by which the baby will learn the norms, values, attitudes, and beliefs of her society. It is the never-ending process that transforms the individual from an organism into a *person.* Martha's baby will develop a self or personality and learn the rules of social life through her group (and institutional) exposures. Through these exposures the human being learns the various conceptions of statuses he or she occupies (or will occupy) and roles he or she must (or will) perform.

What kinds of groups do individuals find themselves part of or join in most societies? This is a question that is basic to sociology, and the next immediate task is to discuss some kinds of groups and intergroup social processes that interest the sociologist. Then, two of the most fundamental of all societal concepts—those of *status* and *role* —will be defined and discussed.

Groups

Sociologists make a fundamental division of groups into primary and secondary groups. The American sociologist Charles Horton Cooley (1864–1929) coined the term *primary group* to refer to any group that is very important— primary—to an individual. A primary group is relatively small, and its members maintain intimate, cooperative, and usually face-to-face relationships with one another. Primary groups are characterized by strong loyalty, and the relationships between the members (primary relationships) are considered *ends in themselves* rather than means to other ends. In other words, the members of a primary group interact with each other on a *holistic* (as opposed to a *segmented*) basis. The classic example of a primary group is the family, but the concept extends to any group dominated by primary relationships, such as some street gangs or friendship groups. Martha's family constitutes a primary group for her, but so do her women friends, with whom she is very close.

Secondary groups stand opposed to primary groups. The members of secondary groups maintain relatively limited, formal, and impersonal relationships with one another. These secondary relationships are *instrumental* toward achieving some special interest or need. Sociologists Kimball Young and Raymond Mack (1965) note: "Secondary groups are characterized by much more deliberate and conscious formation than primary groups. Almost always they represent partial and specialized interests or needs." The people in the class Martha is taking on silk-screening techniques constitute a secondary group, and so did her school classes, which came together for the instrumental purpose of pursuing a degree. The basic difference between primary and secondary groups is that the former are invaluable for giving us meaning in life, whereas the latter are necessary for accomplishing particular goals that are defined by the society.

Three other types of groups that are of central interest to sociology are *peer groups, reference groups,* and *ethnic groups. Peer groups* are composed of individuals who are social equals. The concept is generally, although not necessarily, used to refer to people of the same age. Children in a class at school are usually considered peers and are usually very close in age, but the peer

Figure 3.6   Throughout a person's life he or she belongs to many groups of different types, and often to several groups simultaneously. These photographs suggest some of Richard Nixon's groups: his family constitutes a primary group; the U.S. cabinet, a secondary group; and heads of state, a peer group.

group referred to in the phrase "a jury of one's peers" has more to do with equality of social position than with age. Peer groups often take on the qualities of primary groups (such as with street gangs), but secondary groups (such as a group of college classmates) can also be peer groups.

A *reference group* is any group whose standards an individual regards as important in evaluating aspects of his own life. That is, a reference group is any group whose values an individual takes into consideration when making a particular decision. Thus, a reference group could be a primary group (Martha's family), a secondary group (Martha's class), a peer group (Martha's fellow artists), or another kind of group.

The term *ethnic group* has been used in various ways by sociologists. Traditionally it has designated any group characterized by a unity of both race and culture, and it has also been used to refer to only cultural groups (such as religious groups) or to only racial groups. The term ethnic group is most frequently used in contemporary sociology to mean any group that is perceived *by others* as distinct because its members adhere to a certain

religion, have a particular national origin or language, or are racially different from the majority. Thus, a good synonym for ethnic group as it is used today is *minority group*. As the sociologists Tamotsu Shibutani and Kian M. Kwan (1965) tell us, an ethnic group "consists of those who conceive of themselves as being alike . . . and who are so regarded by others." Martha is a member of the Jewish ethnic group—and if she ever forgets it, there are many ways in which mainstream America will remind her of that fact. Two other examples of ethnic groups—minority groups—in contemporary American society are blacks and chicanos, or Mexican-Americans.

In view of relatively recent developments in American society, such as the urban uprisings of the late 1960s in Detroit, Watts, Newark, and other major urban areas, the importance of contemporary ethnic-group study in American sociology cannot be overemphasized. The findings of ethnic-group study can possibly be used to help alleviate tensions between particular minority groups in America or between such groups and the majority. Contemporary ethnic-group study

also reveals the essence of sociology, namely, the study of *group* characteristics and interrelationships. These relationships are studied within the context of certain *social processes,* some of which are revealed by the following basic concepts.

Conflict, Competition, and Cooperation

The concepts of conflict, competition, and cooperation, the "three *C*s of sociology," underlie virtually all substantive sociological inquiry. Sociologists see *conflict* as a social process that results when two or more groups consciously seek either to block one another in reaching a goal or to injure, defeat, or even annihilate one another. The first thing that strikes the sociologist about conflict is that some degree of conflict is always present in society. Indeed, this observation has led many sociologists to conclude with Lewis Coser (1956) that "a certain degree of conflict is an essential element in group formation and the persistence of group life." The most fundamental basis of conflict is the tendency to use one's own way of life as a standard for judging others. Following Sumner, sociologists call this tendency *ethnocentrism.*

Said another way, ethnocentrism is a dislike for people whose culture and ultimate goals differ from one's own. It often is associated with the belief that one's own race, culture, or society is superior to all others. Most people and most groups are ethnocentric to some degree. For example, the Moshers, like most Jews, value education highly and tend to be somewhat incredulous or contemptuous to discover that others do not. Like most Americans, they hold an individualistic bias and do not understand, and possibly do not respect, cultures in which subordination to the social group is valued more than individualism.

Conflict between groups may be inevitable, but there are various social mechanisms that operate in society to reduce conflict. Humor, for example, functions to remove tensions that might result in violence. In addition, groups that may potentially conflict with one another often set up patterns of behavior that minimize contact between them and thus greatly reduce the probabilities of immediate conflict. Martha grew up in a Jewish neighborhood that bounded on an Irish one, but the kids from each did not go very often into the other's neighborhood—unless they were looking for a fight.

Competition is another dynamic characteristic of life in groups. *Competition* is the *normatively regulated* process in which two or more groups strive toward a goal that can be fully achieved by only one of the groups. (In other words, competition is a rule-regulated process of outdoing others in achieving a mutually desired goal.) It differs from conflict in that competition is governed by a system of norms that precludes overt violence. When the competitors break the rules, conflict occurs. For instance, in New York, members of Martha's ethnic group struggled to "better" themselves socially by taking on positions of importance or prestige. Many of them became teachers and school administrators. In the 1960s many blacks in New York, who also were struggling to rise in the social system, noticed that because so many Jews were teachers, there were fewer places for blacks in the school system. The fight to achieve some measure of control over schools in black neighborhoods caused a great deal of conflict in New York in the late 1960s.

Competition can also be a dynamic social force: It stimulates achievement by lifting people's level of aspiration, it threatens failure (as well as success), and it adds an element of rivalry. *Cooperation,* in contrast to both conflict and competition, is the process of two or more groups working together to achieve a commonly desired goal.

The "three *C*s" are not the only social processes of importance in the study of group behavior. At least on a par with them are accommodation and assimilation, the "two *A*s" of sociology.

Accommodation and Assimilation

Conflicting social groups frequently cease conflict—by way of a truce, compromise, or willingness to subject themselves to arbitration—and try to work out a more harmonious situation or relationship. The cessation of conflict can lead to the process of *accommodation,* which William Fielding Ogburn and Meyer Nimkoff (1964) have characterized as "the actual working together of individuals or groups in spite of differences or latent hostility." When Grandpa and Grandma Mosher settled in New York's Lower East Side around the turn of the century, they and others like them learned to cooperate to some degree with the poor Irish immigrants who had preceded them and whose neighborhoods were so close to theirs. Both groups, through the process of accommodation, even began to share some aspects of their cultures in their new land.

One possible end point of the accommodative process is assimilation. *Assimilation* is the process by which culturally divergent groups become more and more alike. The concept was used most often in the studies of American immigrants undertaken early in this century at the University of Chicago. Although there is, theoretically, a "cultural give and take" in the process of assimilation, the term was most commonly used to denote the disappearance of the group characteristics that most strongly differentiated immigrants as they adopted the culture of American society. Martha's father, for example, cut off the long ear locks commonly worn by the Jewish men in Eastern Europe where he was raised. He also ceased observing many of the customs and conventions of his parents. This usage of the term is exemplified by Shibutani and Kwan's statement (1965) that "an immigrant becomes *assimilated* to the extent that he sees himself from the standpoint of Americans in general."

In summary, the "two *A*s" of sociology can be used to describe the various stages of acceptance of ethnic groups into society. In American society, the process of assimilation is underway for some *cultural* groups, as is evidenced by, for example, the partial fusion of Italians, Poles, and the Irish (to mention only three) into American society. This is clearly not the case with *racial* groups in America. Various voluntary organizations within the black group have different notions about which of the "*A*s" apply to blacks in American society. The Black Panthers possibly would describe the position of blacks in America as being only at the *accommodation* stage and would probably even articulate a *resistance* to assimilation. On the other hand, more middle-class, main-

Figure 3.7   Assimilation into white America is not a goal shared by all the members of the black community in the United States. Those who argue that equality for black people can be gained only by full assimilation have attacked norms and institutions that exclude blacks from full participation. Martin Luther King, Jr. (*left*), led sit-ins and other civil-rights demonstrations during the 1960s. Others within the black community, such as Malcolm X (*right*), have maintained that the assimilation of blacks into mainstream America would result in the loss of black identity and culture. Rather than favoring assimilation, these people call for accommodation, for liberation of black people from oppression, and for blacks and whites to retain distinct cultures.

stream black organizations such as the NAACP might describe the position of black people in America as approaching the stage of *assimilation* and would perhaps encourage it. What is clear with respect to blacks in America is that there is still a significant cultural resistance on the part of the dominant culture (white America) to assimilate blacks. In fact, much of white America even resists moving toward the accommodation of blacks in American society. Relationships between minority and majority groups in America thus remain a sociological powder keg, capable of exploding into open conflict at almost any time.

It should be amply clear by now that the study of groups and their interrelationships is fundamental to sociology. The emphasis on the study of groups, however, should not obscure the fact that we must inevitably link individuals to groups—to society and culture. We do this in sociology through the concepts of *status* and *role*.

THE CONCEPTS OF STATUS AND ROLE

In addition to providing the link between the individual and his or her groups—between Martha and her family, her other primary groups, her fellow artists, her society at large, and so on—the concepts of status and role are invaluable in demonstrating the relationships between society and culture.

Status

A *status* is a place or position in the system of social relationships. The system can be either hierarchical or nonhierarchical. In a *hierarchical* system of social relationships, statuses are ranked in terms of high or low positions (based on different degrees of esteem or disesteem). For example, Martha's aunt, who is managing editor in a corporation that publishes textbooks, can be considered as occupying a higher status than all the editors who work under her. In a *nonhierarchical* system of social relationships, statuses are defined as being merely different, one from the other. In her college, for example, Martha's status as an art major simply differs from that of her fellow student who majors in education. But the discussion on the concept of status is meaningless without bringing in the concept of role because status and role are always intimately related.

Figure 3.8   Because many roles are associated
with particular kinds of clothing or costumes, clothing
is an important element in the identification of
other people's roles—and one's own.

Role

When discussing a person's status, a sociologist inevitably thinks of the person's role, for a *role* is a set of expectations applied to an occupant of a particular status and is characterized by certain obligations (or duties) and privileges (or rights). In her interaction with her father, for example, Martha is expected to play the role of daughter. This means that she is expected to fulfill some duties or obligations (such as showing respect to her father); simultaneously, she expects to enjoy some rights or privileges from her father (such as receiving affection and, while she is dependent on her family, economic support).

Aside from the role of daughter, Martha plays many other roles—artist, wife, college student, and politically active feminist. This fact reveals an important characteristic of status or role, namely that *the same individual* can occupy each one of the statuses or play each one of the roles indicated. The artist can be a wife, a college student, and a feminist. On most occasions, a person plays one role at a time, but not too infrequently he or she may play different roles simultaneously.

The rights and duties inherent in a role are largely determined by one's society and culture. Martha's parents, being Americans, would play the role of parent differently than would their counterparts, say, in India. Underlying this difference in behavior are different ways in which the two societies and cultures define what the role of parent is supposed to be. People who live within the same society and culture, however, have by and large been socialized to understand in a similar way the sets of expectations attached to various roles. It is through such mutual expectations of the role players that reasonably smooth interaction between them is possible.

Types of Statuses and Roles

The discussion of status and role is not complete until we understand that sociologists distinguish various types of statuses and roles. You should be aware of the differences among *ascribed status*, *achieved status*, and *assumed*, or *voluntary, status* and of the differences among *prescribed role*, *subjective role*, and *enacted role*.

Ascribed Status An *ascribed status* is one that, with its attendant duties, obligations, rights, and so on, is imposed by the society on the individual on the basis of some characteristic of his, usually a biological one. An ascribed status derives from attributes an individual has no control over, such as age, sex, or skin color, or from membership in a group to which he is assigned by others, such as family, religion, or nationality. In regard to age statuses, it is interesting to note that all societies divide the life cycle into at least three stages—childhood, adulthood, and old age—all of which carry various behavioral expectations (roles) with them. Likewise, all societies have different expectations about role behavior for males and females. To identify someone in American society as a "Kennedy" or "Rockefeller" is to describe him on the basis of an ascribed status, and to describe someone as a six-year-old Negro boy is to describe him on the basis of three of them.

Achieved Status An *achieved status*, on the other hand, is one that a person can move into after meeting particular requirements. If Daniel Mosher meets the requirements for promotion at his place of work, he can move from salesman to buyer; if Linda Mosher passes her college courses, she could graduate with a degree in sociology and could eventually achieve the status of sociologist.

Status and Social Mobility The process by which an individual changes status is called *social mobility*. Mobility can be upward, downward, or horizontal. *Upward mobility* would be exemplified by Daniel Mosher's move from salesman to buyer; *downward mobility* would be a reverse move from buyer to floor salesman; and *horizontal mobility* would be exemplified by Daniel's staying a salesman but moving to a different store where the job content is the same.

The concept of social mobility is used occasionally in sociology to classify types of societies or social systems. Accordingly, societies in which social mobility is possible are sometimes called *class* or *open systems*, and societies in which such mobility is largely prevented (because of strict adherence to ascribed characteristics) are sometimes called *caste* or closed systems. The United States is often used as an example of an open or class system and India of a caste or closed system.

Assumed Status In *assumed,* or *voluntary,* status the individual (theoretically, at least) exercises a choice in taking on the status. Assumed status is similar to achieved status, but there is a fundamental difference between the two. You will recall that achieved status is based upon meeting particular requirements, most often having to do with skills that are associated with the position. An example of a person's moving into an assumed or voluntary status, however, is Louie Mosher's taking over his father's golf-equipment business and being appointed president of the corporation that runs the business. The only requirement Louie had to meet was to be related to the owner of the business—who was also the former president of the corporation. Louie, by the way, moved into another assumed, or voluntary, status when he got married last summer.

Prescribed Role A *prescribed role* is a set of expectations regarding one's behavior as prescribed by the social norms of society. Society imposes on all individuals generally uniform definitions of which rights and duties should constitute the set of expectations for any given role. A prescribed role is therefore sometimes called an *objective role.* All people who are playing the same prescribed role (say, of student) are expected to carry out the same role prescriptions. Thus, you and your fellow students should carry out the same obligation of learning as much as you can from your professor. At the same time you and your fellow students are similarly expected to demand as your privilege that your professor impart as much knowledge to you as possible.

Subjective Role Despite the imposition of a uniform role prescription on all students, there remains some variation among different students in carrying out the prescription, largely because of the function of *subjective role.* A subjective role refers to the specific expectations one holds concerning one's own and others' behavior. Given

the same prescribed role of student, various students are likely to subjectively define what the role means. For Tom, the prescribed obligation of "learning as much as you can" may mean studying *ten* hours a week; for Martha, it may mean studying *forty* hours a week.

Enacted Role Finally, the *enacted role* refers more to specific overt behavior than to the mere expectations that, as we have already seen, characterize the prescribed and the subjective roles. The term enacted role is often used interchangeably by sociologists with *role performance* or *role behavior.* The actual performance or enactment of a role is simply the observable implementation of both the prescribed and the subjective roles. For example, given the same prescribed role of student, a majority of students exhibit similar types of behavior if they subjectively interpret the student role similarly. On the other hand, a minority of students, given the same prescribed role of student, are likely to enact this role differently than the average students because they differ in their subjective roles.

A REVIEW OF FUNDAMENTAL CONCEPTS

Our excursion through the basics of sociology began with a discussion of the most fundamental concepts of all—society and culture. After making a distinction between the two, which included various characteristics of culture as well as a brief discussion of the concept *subculture,* we determined that society and culture were interrelated. We then proceeded, accordingly, to present some of the basic concepts with which we study society and culture. After introducing *norms* as essentially cultural in nature, the discussion moved to a presentation of two types of norms: *folkways* and *mores.* Having indicated that *customs* and *fashions* were types of folkways and that *conventions* and *laws* were types of mores, we introduced the concepts *values, beliefs,* and *attitudes,* which, though not considered norms, were also essentially cultural in definition.

   Drawing upon the discussion of norms, values, attitudes, and beliefs, we introduced what is probably the most fundamental societal concept in sociology, that of *social institution.* After identifying *types* of institutions and defining the concept of *socialization,* we then proceeded to distinguish between various kinds of groups that interest the sociologist. The discussion of *primary groups, secondary groups, peer groups, reference groups,* and *ethnic groups* concluded by leading us into a presentation of various social processes that are studied by sociologists, namely, the "three *C*s" of sociology, *conflict, competition,* and *cooperation,* and the "two *A*s" of sociology, *accommodation,* and *assimilation.*

The closing sections of the chapter were concerned with the concepts *status* and *role,* which we indicated were used to (theoretically) link the individual to society and culture. In addition to distinguishing different types of statuses, the closing pages of the chapter introduced the concepts of *social mobility, class,* and *caste.*

SUGGESTED READINGS

Berger, Peter L. *Invitation to Sociology: A Humanistic Perspective.* Garden City, New York: (Anchor Books) Doubleday, 1963.

Davis, Kingsley. *Human Society.* New York: Macmillan, 1949.

Williams, Robin M., Jr. *American Society.* 2nd ed. New York: Knopf, 1960.

Chapter 4 Theoretical Perspectives

THE PREVIOUS CHAPTER INTRODUCED some of the basic concepts used by sociologists to identify important aspects of social life. Although it is essential to give names to the objects one wants to study or discuss, naming is only the first step toward understanding. In the same way that a vocabulary list is not a language, a set of concepts is not an explanation. To constitute a language, a vocabulary list must be transformed into sentences according to some set of grammatical rules. Similarly, scientific explanations require that concepts be linked together in particular kinds of statements according to logical rules. Such statements are called *theories*.

Theories are the most general kinds of explanations that tell us why and when to expect certain things to happen. Scientists use *concepts* (names) to organize and identify the phenomena in which they are interested. Theories unify some set concepts into an explanation that expresses how the concepts are logically interrelated. For example, an adequate theory of revolutions might combine such concepts as social class, intergroup conflict, and others into a statement telling us when (and why) to expect revolutions to occur. However, not every sociological statement is a sociological theory, even though it may use sociological concepts and may seem to explain some sociological problem. Furthermore, the test of whether a statement is part of a theory does *not* depend on whether it is true. What is important is whether the statement, if considered in the appropriate context, *could* be true or false, or whether other statements, which themselves could be true or false, can be deduced from it. In other words, to qualify as part of a theory a statement must either be subject to disproof or give rise to some other statement that is subject to disproof.

Theories are risky statements; they entail predictions that may or may not come true. For example, any statement that predicts that a revolution will occur when the lot of deprived persons is rapidly improving *could* turn out to be false—if such conditions failed to result in revolutions, we would know the theory is false. Any assertion that could not *possibly* turn out to be false is not by

itself a theory. The statement that a revolution will occur when the people rise up with sufficient vigor against their oppressors is undoubtedly true. But it predicts nothing and most certainly is not a theory. Such a statement gives us no insight into when or why to expect a revolution. Such *tautological* statements, which are discussed later in the chapter, are equivalent to saying it will rain tomorrow if the weather is right. We are left not knowing whether to plan a picnic.

This chapter examines the current adequacy and role of theory in sociology. It outlines the major premises of some of the most influential theoretical positions in contemporary sociology. The purpose of the chapter is to give you an adequate background in some of the major theoretical issues being debated by sociologists, so that you will be able to recognize the different approaches sociologists take to specific questions discussed in subsequent chapters.

SOCIOLOGICAL THEORY: THE PRESENT STATE OF THE ART

As you will certainly discover in subsequent chapters, sociological theories—and the theories current in social science generally—often are relatively crude. In fact, much that has been called theory in social science is not theory at all, but only preliminary work toward constructing theories. The current state of social-science theory has been depicted by B. F. Skinner in his most recent book, *Beyond Freedom and Dignity* (1971):

Twenty-five hundred years ago it might have been said that man understood himself as well as any other part of his world. Today he is the thing he understands least.... Greek physics and biology are now of historical interest only (no modern physicist or biologist would turn to Aristotle for help), but the dialogues of Plato are still assigned to students and cited as if they threw light on human behavior. Aristotle could not have understood a page of modern physics or biology, but Socrates and his friends would have little trouble in following most current discussions of human affairs.

Current sociological theories are rather primitive compared to current theories in the natural and physical sciences. The major reason for this discrepancy is that the *scientific* study of society has begun only recently in comparison with the scientific study of the physical world: there were astronomical observatories in ancient Egypt; the Greeks did experiments in physics and chemistry; and grave robbers began to supply physiologists with corpses to dissect centuries ago. But while the physical and natural sciences developed, there were no social-science laboratories and no systematic fact gathering on the questions that social science might raise. The understanding of human behavior and of human societies was pursued mainly by speculation or deduced from theological and philosophical premises.

It was not until 1879 that Wilhelm Wundt founded the first psychological laboratory. The next year Karl Marx made one of the earliest attempts at survey research by distributing 25,000 questionnaires to workers. Sociology as a scientific enterprise was first proposed by the French philosopher August Comte in the 1830s. But sociology has only been in operation for about the last seventy-five years, and only for the last generation have there been substantial numbers of practicing sociologists and large-scale research programs.

The Relation Between Theory and Research

Philosophers of science and scientists in various fields with unquestioned reputations as "theorists" disagree quite vigorously among themselves about what scientific theory is, and especially about how scientific theory is to be distinguished from scientific research or evidence. In very general terms *a scientific theory can be regarded as a logically interconnected set of propositions that describe certain relations among those objects, events, or processes with which a particular field of science is concerned.* Often the parts of a theory are *axioms*—no axiom can be deduced by logical operations from any combination of the remaining axioms—and *hypotheses* or *derivations*, which can be so deduced.

An essential characteristic of the theories of any *empirical* science—as distinguished from such purely formal sciences as logic or mathemat

ics—is that the acceptability of the theory as "true" or "false," "confirmed" or "confuted," or "sterile" or "fruitful" is contingent in some way upon what scientists call *evidence*, or *empirical data.* A scientific theory is always involved in an interaction with evidence. Often we are told that the evidence comes first: if the theory does not fit the evidence, so much the worse for the theory. In practice it is not that simple. Often a conflict between a theory and evidence is resolved by collecting more evidence. Then, too, even when the evidence seems to refute one part of a theory, that part may still be regarded as "correct" or "true" if it has a tight logical connection with other parts of the theory that do fit the evidence. In such cases a theory is more likely to be modified or extended than rejected—a special axiom may be added to the theory to take care of the particular problem.

In practice, the elegance of a theory's logic has a great deal to do with whether scientists judge it to be acceptable or unacceptable. Closely related to the acceptability of a theory is the scientific ideal of *parsimony:* a scientific theory is parsimonious when it "explains the most with the least." A highly parsimonious theory that has only a few axioms and that explains 80 percent of the relationships in a given field may be preferred to a complicated theory that has many axioms and that explains 90 percent of the relationships. The "power" of a theory is not simply a matter of how much it explains but of how much theorizing it takes to perform that explanation.

The history of science shows that in practice neither theory nor research comes first. A theory that is true or false without any relation of any kind to evidence is not a scientific theory; similarly, a description that is not related to any kind of theory is not scientific research. What happens is that theory and research mutually guide and limit each other. Just as there is, in principle, no end to the number or kinds of theories that might be constructed, there is no end to the amount of evidence that might be collected. One important function of theory in science generally, and especially in sociology, is that it guides the collection of evidence. A theory tells us what data to collect —namely, those data that are relevant to the con

Figure 4.1 The relationship between theories and research hypotheses bridges the gap between the abstract and the concrete. Theories express causal relationships by indicating which concept represents the independent variable and which concept(s) the dependent variable(s). But a concept is an abstraction—we cannot see or touch it. We can only examine particular real instances covered by it. A theory saying that social class (independent variable) is positively related to political conservatism (dependent variable) can be tested only on the basis of concrete measures of each concept. Education, income, and occupational status can be selected as measures of social class. Expressed attitudes about social welfare, regulation of business, and support for Republicans may be selected to measure conservatism. We deduce from the theory that the higher an individual stands on the measures of social class, the more likely he will be to take conservative positions on the measures of conservatism. Predictions thus derived from a theory are called hypotheses. If a hypothesis is not borne out by empirical research, we then conclude either that the theory is false (or at least needs revision) or that we have not devised adequate concrete measures of the concepts.

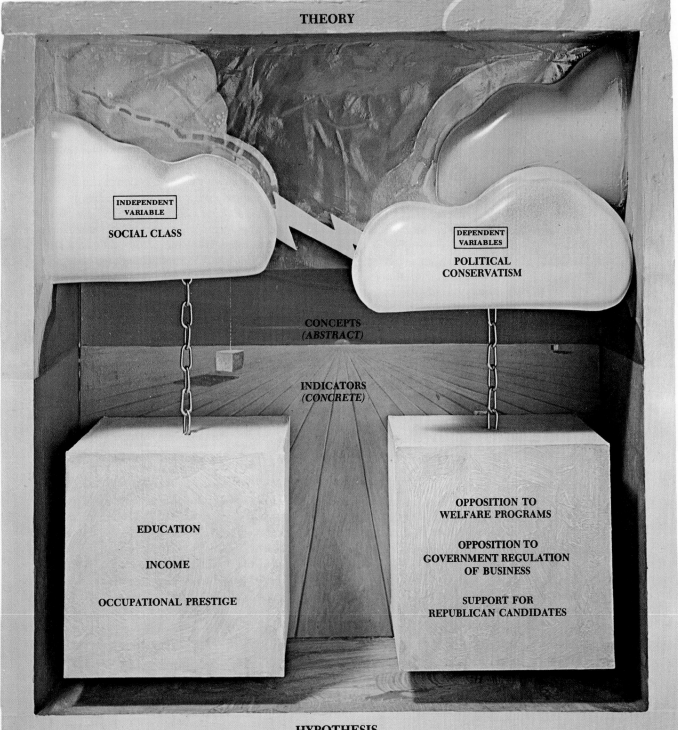

THEORY

INDEPENDENT
VARIABLE

SOCIAL CLASS

DEPENDENT
VARIABLES

POLITICAL
CONSERVATISM

CONCEPTS
(ABSTRACT)

INDICATORS
(CONCRETE)

EDUCATION

INCOME

OCCUPATIONAL PRESTIGE

OPPOSITION TO
WELFARE PROGRAMS

OPPOSITION TO
GOVERNMENT REGULATION
OF BUSINESS

SUPPORT FOR
REPUBLICAN CANDIDATES

HYPOTHESIS

firmation or refutation of the theory. Otherwise we might go around studying and measuring everything, ending up with great mountains of data but with no way of sorting them out or making sense out of what we have collected. Such nontheoretical sociology has often been called "outhouse counting," after the habit of some sociological researchers to collect great masses of information (usually from the United States Census) on plumbing facilities in American households, without ever interpreting the meaning of their research.

By the same token, one important function of research is to tell us how to build theories. Plausible and highly logical interpretations of social life have existed at least since the time of Plato, but without the check of scientific evidence, these interpretations could, and did, go off in every direction. As the sociological theorist Kingsley Davis observes, "Fantastic schemes of reasoning have existed for centuries and have finally died through lack of interest rather than through disproof" (1949).

The Language of Sociological Theory

Because of the relatively primitive character of sociological theories, it has not often proved very profitable to analyze them in the strict logical and mathematical way that works so well in the more developed sciences. Sociological theory is almost always presented as a verbal narrative, written in the ordinary language of the community in which the sociologist lives and works. It therefore has all the richness and subtlety of ordinary language. But it also retains the ambiguity and imprecision of that language. Unlike the specialized vocabulary of the natural sciences (which were forced to coin names for phenomena that had previously gone unnoticed), sociological terms often must struggle to retain their assigned definitions in the face of the less restrictive definitions of these same words in the natural language. We all can define such terms as age, sex, race, unemployed, poor, or radical. But our definitions may give meanings to these terms that are quite different from the ones that a particular sociological theory intends. Such inconsistency leads to a great deal of confusion.

Furthermore, use of everyday language in theories makes it hard to grasp that sociological concepts, like all scientific concepts, are *abstractions*. (An abstraction is more general than, and not fully represented by, any concrete instance of the class of objects or phenomena included in it.)

Because of all these problems, sociologists have become increasingly inclined to invent their own conceptual language. But when they do this—when they invent their own names for things that already have names in the common language—they frequently are ridiculed for the use of jargon and abominable prose. There is no happy solution. Until sociologists develop enough powerful theories they will probably have to make do with terms taken from the natural language and risk ambiguity and misunderstanding. Therefore, as the sociological theorist Philip Selznick once told a class of students in introductory sociology: "If you are planning to go on in sociology and can't tolerate a certain amount of vagueness and confusion in the concepts you use ... well, let's face it; you're in the wrong field."

All this is not to say that sociological theory has no virtues. One very redeeming feature is that it deals with questions that prove to be of persistent social and intellectual interest to people, sociologists and nonsociologists alike.

NONEMPIRICAL ASPECTS OF THEORIES

The elements of a sociological theory that can be accepted or rejected are its *empirical components,* or *testable propositions;* when these propositions are highly specific and refer to readily available data, they are usually called *hypotheses.* Some of these elements reappear so often that we can easily identify them. But we also need to be able to recognize the nonempirical, or nontestable, parts of a theory, so that we will not waste time or money trying to accept or reject them by amassing research results. The nonempirical elements of theories that we shall consider are: *tautologies*—statements that are true by definition of their constituent terms; the *classification scheme*—the system of "pigeonholes" used for organizing concepts and events; and the qualification *"other things being equal,"* a statement that is often attached to testable propositions but that severely restricts the kind of evidence that can be used to test them.

Tautologies

We have pointed out that concepts are simply the names scientists give the objects they study. Obviously, it would be silly to ask whether such names are true or false. A rose by any other name is still a rose. It is only necessary that we agree on what group of objects is defined by the word rose. By the same token, tautologies and, as we shall see, classification schemes do not raise the question of truth or falsity.

Tautologies are statements that are always true by virtue of the definitions of their terms and the logical relations among them. In fact, definitions are prime examples of tautologies. When we assert that the concept of upward mobility means that persons end up higher in the stratification system than did their parents, we are not asserting something that could possibly be false. Instead we are saying what the term "upward mobility" means. There is complete identity of meaning between a term and its definition; they are the same thing. To say boys will be boys is certainly true (if vague) because the subject and the object are the same word. To say that boys will act like juvenile human males is simply to put it another way. Trouble arises, however, when statements that appear to be theories, or are advanced as theories, turn out to be tautological.

The anthropologist Clyde Kluckhohn, in his classic work *Mirror For Man* (1949), claimed it was easy to explain why the Chinese dislike milk. He wrote that the Chinese do not like milk because of their culture. But as George Homans (1967) saw, this is not an explanation at all; Kluckhohn had merely asserted a tautology. For the fact is that Kluckhohn defined culture as the "total way of life of a people . . . [their] design for living." Part of the way of life of the Chinese is a dislike of milk. Thus, to say that they dislike milk *because* of their culture is simply to say their culture is caused by their culture. It says nothing of the major point in question, which is why their culture is this way

instead of some other way. Kluckhohn might as well have said the Chinese do as they do because they are Chinese. That is necessarily true. But it is not very interesting, and it certainly is not an explanation of anything. Had Kluckhohn merely used the case of the Chinese dislike of milk as an example of culture, all would have been fine.

Tautologies are vital to science—we must have definitions. But when they are mistaken for theories, they merely lead us to think we have gained understanding when we have not.

Classification Schemes

Classification schemes are merely complex definitions. Frequently they are created by cross-classifying several concepts. Thus we may use the concepts of employment and sex to create a scheme into which all Americans can be placed —employed males, employed females, unemployed males, unemployed females. We can multiply these four types into eight by distinguishing between persons in the South and those not in the South. By further subdividing on the basis of those over and under thirty years old we can create sixteen types.

Frequently in science it is very useful to construct elaborate classification schemes. For example, biology would be hopelessly confused without the Linnaean system, which classifies all living organisms into kingdoms, orders, phyla, genera, species, and so on. Sociologists, too, find classificatory schemes very useful. One of the better known classification schemes was created by Robert K. Merton (1957); it uses conformity to and deviance from social norms. Merton first stated that people can be divided into those who accept the goals of their society (for example, to get ahead in life) and those who do not. Second, those who utilize institutionalized (or legitimate) means for attaining goals can be distinguished from those who do not. Cross-classifying these two concepts yields four possible types.

Merton named each of these types of people. (He later added a fifth type, but that need not concern us.) The *conformist* accepts society's goals and uses institutionalized means to achieve them. The *ritualist* has given up on the goals

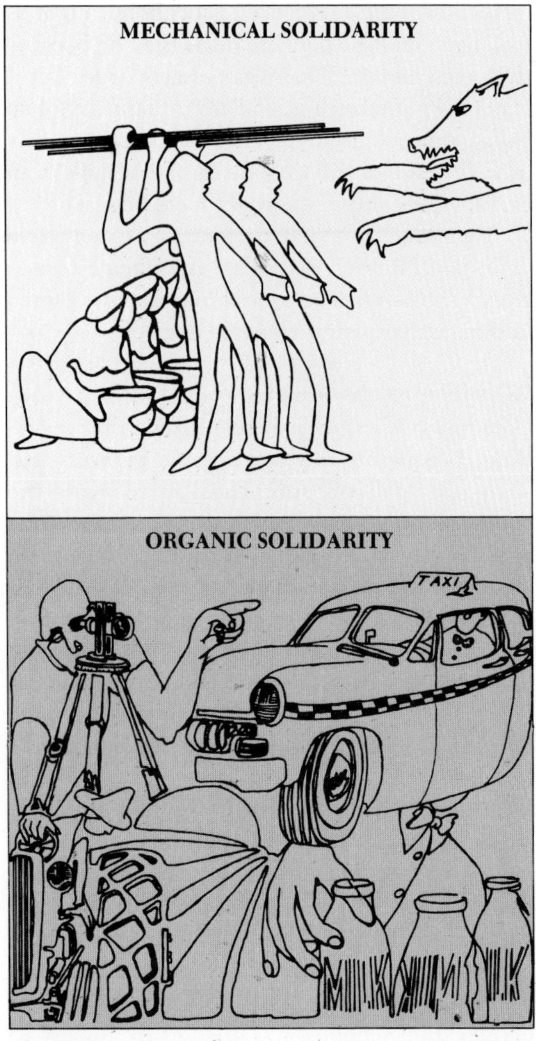

Figure 4.2   One of the earliest classification schemes in sociology was proposed by Emile Durkheim. Durkheim conceptualized societies in terms of the complexity of their division of labor and the type of solidarity they exhibit. Traditional societies rely on *mechanical solidarity* (*top*). In these societies the division of work roles and life styles is based on age and gender.

Individual variation is minimal, and people are tied together by shared norms, beliefs, and values (collective conscience). *Organic solidarity* (*bottom*) typifies societies with a higher degree of division of labor. It is based on the interdependence of diverse social parts and emerges when specialists share economic interdependence but tolerate and accept different life styles.

MECHANICAL SOLIDARITY

ORGANIC SOLIDARITY

tion an innovator, and the scheme will tell us nothing about who will become innovators until they have already done so. After the fact, a scheme such as Merton's can classify anyone—that is what it is supposed to do. But ahead of time it can predict nothing—and prediction is precisely what a theory *must* accomplish.

"Other Things Being Equal . . ."

Sociologists increasingly use the qualification "other things being equal" (sometimes indicated in Latin as *ceteris paribus*) in their explanations, and they have a very good reason for doing so. When a physicist declares in his theoretical statement that "X varies with Y, other things being equal," he does not stop in simply stating the theory—he goes on to test it. Because of the vast knowledge and technique acquired in 400 years of research, the physicist is able to test the theory in an experiment in which other things are literally *made* equal. As we show in Karen Dion's study in Chapter 2, the relation of X to Y is studied by causing X to vary while controlling the effect of all known extraneous variables, or reducing them to "zero effect" by holding them constant during the experiment, and then measuring the concomitant variation in Y.

Unfortunately, a great deal of sociological theory is concerned with events of such a character that little of the theory can be tested in rigorously controlled experiments. Sociologists test their theories principally by observation rather than by experimentation. Although observation can be subjected to some statistical controls, these controls are generally less effective than the direct control of variables used in the physical and biological sciences and to some extent in psychology. The sociologist must stress the "other-things-being-equal" qualification in his theories partly because he cannot manipulate the other variables that need to be made equal for the purposes of his research.

One can imagine a sociological theory that is so comprehensive that no "other-things-being-equal" clause is necessary because the variation produced by the "other things" is all accounted

but still goes through the motions of using the institutionalized means. The *retreatist* has rejected both goals and means. The *innovator* accepts the goals, but he adopts noninstitutionalized means to achieve them.

Sociologists frequently have used Merton's classificatory scheme as the basis for statements such as: A person became an innovator *because* he accepted the goals of our culture (to be wealthy, for example) but rejected the means (for example, hard work as opposed to racketeering). This seems a powerful explanation. In fact it is no explanation at all—it is a tautology. Such a person is by defini-

for by the propositions of the theory. Such theories have been attempted from time to time, but in practice they all have one fatal defect: the harder they try to explain everything in general, the less adequately they explain anything in particular. Consider, for example, the following very comprehensive theory: "Social behavior is a function of heredity and environment." As we shall see in the next unit, there are excellent reasons to believe that this statement is true. However, it tells us very little that we need to know and seems to have little practical application. What we need are more specific hypotheses on particular components of heredity and environment. In fact, the theory as posed comes very near to being a tautology—nearly every conceivable factor that can be imagined to have any effect on social behavior would seem to fall under the headings of heredity or environment anyway. The statement ultimately means: "Social behavior is a function of everything that can have any imaginable effect on social behavior." The theory could only be false if social behavior proved not to be affected by anything at all!

The limited usefulness of such very general theories—at least in the current stage of sociology's development—causes sociologists to pay more attention to more specific theories. The specificity of a theory—which means that it does not take account of every conceivable relevant factor—is what imposes the need for an "other-things-being-equal" clause on the theoretical side; the unavailability to sociologists of rigorously controlled experiments is what imposes the clause on the research side. Let us consider an example.

For many years, texts used in courses on marriage and the family asserted that premarital sexual experience led to unhappiness later in marriage (usually in the form of divorce). The statistical evidence seemed clear: if you studied a large number of married persons and established two groups—those who had engaged in intercourse before marriage and those who had not—you found the first group had a higher rate of reported unhappiness and divorce than the second group. Based on these data, textbook writers advanced tentative theories pointing to premarital experience as an effective cause of later unhappiness—through exciting jealousy, enhancing an interest in sexual variety, producing guilt feelings and anxiety, and so forth.

Are such theories correct? One thing is clear: it would be a practical impossibility to test the theory by an experiment. Using the general method of experimentation in the social sciences, you would first randomly assign unmarried individuals to "experimental" and "control" groups. Then you would require the "experimental group" to engage in premarital intercourse and prohibit the "control" group from doing so. After your subjects were married, you would measure rates of unhappiness. But of course you would never get that far because sociologists lack the authority to tell people when and when not to have sexual intercourse. Lacking experimental controls, the sociologist would be unable to determine whether premarital intercourse is always associated with marital unhappiness or whether the association is really the result of the fundamental link of premarital intercourse and marital unhappiness with some third, fourth, or any number of additional factors. The sociologist, in short, does not know whether premarital intercourse leads to marital unhappiness *when other things are equal.*

As it turns out, there is a third factor—a person's social class—that explains most of the observed relationship. It has been found that individuals in the lower or poorer social classes are more likely both to engage in premarital intercourse *and* to be unhappy in marriage (for example, the lower classes have a divorce rate several times that of the upper classes). The statistical control that is used in such a case to approximate the condition of "other things being equal" is the examination of the relationship between premarital intercourse and marital unhappiness *within each class group.* When this is done, it can be seen that the lower classes have a high rate of marital unhappiness and divorce and that the upper classes have low rates. However, within each class group it makes little difference for marital happiness whether one has had premarital intercourse or not—possibly because most premarital intercourse occurs between two people who subsequently marry each other (see Chapter 18).

From the experience of dealing with countless such cases of *spuriousness,* which is discussed in Chapter 2, sociologists are coming increasingly to understand that the qualification "other things being equal" is an implicit requirement of any theoretical statement. Whether a particular statement about a sociological relation is true is not a matter of comparing it to uncontrolled statistics or to common sense but of taking into account, as best one can, the "other things" that, if not made equal, are likely to affect the relation.

THEORETICAL PERSPECTIVES IN SOCIOLOGY

Thus far we have concentrated on the logical structure of theories. We now turn to the substance of sociological theories. Theories attempt to explain something definite, and most influential theories in sociology are addressed to a fairly specific facet of social life. They explain such social processes as prejudice, social inequality, or population growth. This chapter will not discuss such specific theories—you will find them in later chapters that cover specific subjects. Instead, we will cover broad theoretical perspectives that have a strong influence on the formation of more specific theories.

These major perspectives have been shaped by traditions of thought in social, political, and scientific philosophy; by the history of sciences and of societies; and even by the general intellectual development of the Western world. These perspectives rest on sets of basic premises about how men and societies operate. By understanding the fundamental assumptions of each major perspective, you will find it much easier to understand specific theoretical disputes.

Theoretical perspectives can be separated into two different levels of analysis. The first level is small in scale and tries to understand social behavior at the small-group or face-to-face level of human interaction. Theories at this level are called *micro* theories. The second level is large in scale and tries to understand the links among large social units—the impact of economic institutions upon political and religious institutions, for example. Theories at this level are *macro* theories.

John Lofland's study of the Divine Precepts movement (Chapter 2) is an example of a micro-level study. Norman Cohn's study (1961) of the effects of economic conditions on the creation of religious movements is an example of a macro-level study. Both studies are concerned with the same general subject matter but on a different scale. Both levels of study are necessary in order to provide a full account of such events as religious movements. Cohn tried to tell us when we can expect such movements to occur and why; Lofland tried to tell us, given that such movements occur, how they operate and why. A full sociological explanation requires a blending of both micro and macro theories. For this reason the distinction between micro and macro is somewhat artificial, and some sociologists work with theories combining both levels. In fact, George Homans (1964) of Harvard has long argued that *all* adequate sociological theories must begin with micro-level premises (which he sees as psychological) and only later should add statements concerning macro questions; however, many sociologists disagree.

The distinction between micro and macro remains useful because most sociologists concentrate their work at one level or the other. Additionally, micro and macro theories derive from different intellectual traditions and relate to different fields outside sociology. Microsociology has its closest links with psychology, and macrosociology is connected with such fields as history, economics, anthropology, and political science—which all deal with fairly large-scale aspects of the societies they study.

MICRO THEORETICAL PERSPECTIVES

Two major micro-level perspectives are currently prominent in sociology. At first glance they seem very different. One of them, *symbolic interaction,* is usually associated with observation of face-to-

Figure 4.3   Micro theories in sociology, including
symbolic interactionism and behaviorism, attempt to
explain interaction and behavior in small groups.
Micro theorists therefore focus on patterns of behavior
in small groups. Micro-level analysis represents a
choice of perspective on the subject matter to
be studied, not necessarily a particular area of study.

Figure 4.4 Macro theories attempt to explain
relationships among large social units, such as institutions or whole societies. Macro theories provide a
large-scale perspective on events and often serve to
explain the larger social context in which micro
processes occur.

Figure 4.5 Herbert Blumer has long been the major spokesman for the symbolic-interactionist position in sociology. He was an All-American football player at the University of Missouri, and he played with the Chicago Cardinals during the 1920s while he was a graduate student and teacher at the University of Chicago. He was a student of George Herbert Mead's, and upon Mead's death in 1931 he took over his course in social psychology. For many years Blumer was the editor of the *American Journal of Sociology*. In the mid-1950s Blumer left Chicago and became chairman of the sociology department at Berkeley, where he played a major role in raising that department to its present preeminent position.

face social situations, which gives the work of symbolic interactionists an appealing character; it is often full of human-interest detail. *Social learning*, on the other hand, developed out of carefully controlled laboratory studies of animal and human behavior and in some ways seems an affront to human self-conceptions. Yet in the judgment of many sociologists, these two perspectives are not completely incompatible. Some have been busy trying to synthesize the two into a single, more powerful, micro theory of social behavior (Akers, 1973; Scott, 1971). In later chapters specific applications of these perspectives are explained further when symbolic-interactionist and social-learning theories of socialization, roles, group dynamics, deviance, and other matters are treated in detail.

Symbolic Interaction

The fundamental insights of the symbolic-interaction perspective are expressed in the name itself. First, social life requires communication, and human communication is highly *symbolic*—we communicate through symbols such as words and gestures and even through the symbols of music, painting, sculpture, and billboards. Second, social life depends upon *interaction*—the process in which the activity of one person affects the response of another person, which in turn, through various feedback mechanisms, affects the continuing activity of the first person.

The Meaning of Symbols Symbolic interactionists stress that what is distinctive about human social behavior—what sets it off from the intensive social behavior of lower animals such as baboons, ants, and many species of birds and fish—is the extent to which human interaction is *mediated* by symbols. Symbols almost always intervene between one person's action and another person's response to that action. The symbolic interactionists therefore argue that we must get at the *meaning* that symbols convey.

For most symbolic interactionists, the meaning of symbols is not considered to be any objective part of the relationship between symbols and the activities or events to which they refer. For them, meaning is subjective—a matter of the intentions and interpretations that go on in the minds of actors. As the most influential living spokesman of symbolic interaction, Herbert Blumer, said, "Each individual aligns his actions to the actions of others by ascertaining what they are doing or what they intend to do—by getting the meaning of their acts" (Blumer, 1962). Many symbolic interactionists (including Blumer) go beyond this; the meaning of symbols and the interpretation of action are not only subjective but are at least in part indeterminate. Human response to and interpretation of action is held to involve a creative element; so no scientific theory—including the sociological—can ever perfectly predict what human beings are going to do.

From reading Chapter 3, you are already familiar with some of the central concepts of symbolic interaction. First, the concept of culture identifies the means by which people give meaning to acts. It is through such aspects of culture as language that we communicate our meanings, and through such aspects as norms and customs that we relate our meanings to actions. Socialization enables us to acquire culture. The socialization process is therefore a primary focus of symbolic interaction—it is mainly through symbolic interaction that humans are socialized.

The Social Self As will be considered in detail in Chapters 6 and 7, the central concept in symbolic-interaction theories of socialization is the *social self*. This concept was developed by the principal founder of the symbolic-interaction perspective, George Herbert Mead (1863–1931), who was Herbert Blumer's teacher at the University of Chicago. Until Mead's time, it was widely thought that such human traits as *minds* and *selves* existed prior to any social process (such as socialization) in which people became engaged. Mead turned this conception around and argued that the social processes come first: from social interaction arise the traits of mind and selfhood. Because of their highly developed ability to use and manipulate symbols, humans have minds and selves, and lower animals, for all practical purposes, do not. In human communication, symbols come to be recognized as objects in themselves, independent, at least to a high degree, of the events and objects to which they refer.

For Mead, *mind* is a social process in which *significant symbols* call out in the person who presents them the same response that they call out in the person to whom they are presented. The *self* for Mead is likewise a social process; it is our learning or internalization of the general content of others' responses to our conduct. Through his self-conception the individual can do two things: he can see himself as others see him, and he can take on the role of others; in so doing, he learns to identify with the way that other persons think of themselves and interpret social life. It is this ability to take on the role of the other that makes it possible for persons to comprehend the meaning of their own and others' acts and for meaningful social interaction to occur.

Through taking the role of others, the individual learns how to behave appropriately in situations; he learns the norms of groups; he understands the meanings attached by others to the physical and social environment; and he learns to shape his own actions and meanings to those of others. This process will be given more specific application in Chapters 6, 7, and 8.

The major thrust of symbolic-interactionist research has been to try to understand how persons engaged in social interaction perceive their situations and how they define one another's actions.

Most symbolic interactionists regard the *subjective meanings* attached to behavior as essential components for a satisfactory understanding of human social behavior.

Social Learning

The micro-theoretical perspective called *social learning* is quite new in sociology. Its most basic premises come from learning psychology, most recently from the learning theory of B. F. Skinner.

The Consequences of Behavior The starting point of Skinner's theory is that *behavior is shaped and maintained by its consequences*. Behavior that operates on the environment (both social and physical) in such ways as to produce consequences is called *operant behavior*. Most of what an organism—human or lower animal—does has effects on its environment, and often these effects feed back upon the organism in the form of stimuli. An activity's consequences that tend to increase the rate at which the activity is subsequently performed are *positive* and *negative reinforcers;* those that decrease the rate, *punishments*.

Skinner has offered simple illustrations of the way that reinforcers operate: "A slave driver induces a slave to work by whipping him when he stops; by resuming work the slave escapes from the whipping (and incidentally reinforces the slave driver's behavior in using the whip). A parent nags a child until the child performs a task; by performing the task the child escapes nagging (and reinforces the parent's behavior)" (Skinner, 1971).

Over many years of work with animals and humans, Skinner and his colleagues have learned much about the effects of reinforcers in shaping behavior. Sociologists were slow to recognize that conditioning pigeons to peck at levers for the reward of food was relevant to understanding human social behavior. But as early as 1941, psychologists Neal Miller and John Dollard in their book *Social Learning and Imitation* pointed out the essential mutual implications of sociology and learning theory. Social-learning theory provides a very simple and powerful explanation of how

Figure 4.6   George C. Homans was the first sociologist to make substantial efforts to apply the principles of learning theory to sociological questions and has been a leading developer of the social-learning perspective. He received his bachelor's degree from Harvard University in 1933 and through creative scholarship became a member of the Harvard faculty and rose to the rank of professor without having earned a doctorate. During World War II he served as captain of convoy escort ships in the North Atlantic. His research has ranged widely over studies of medieval society, bureaucracy, small-group research, and cross-cultural studies of marriage rules. His best-known book is *Social Behavior: Its Elementary Forms* (1961).

learning occurs, but many versions offer no theory of reinforcement as such. It is left to sociology to explain the organization of reinforcement and punishments. Or as Scott (1971) put it, "It is within the subject matter of sociology that the important reinforcers of human behavior are to be found." Let us see how and why this is so.

The first major sociologist to utilize learning principles in sociological theories was George C. Homans (1961). Homans took his premise from Skinner—*the more rewarding people find the results of an action (or the more rewarding they believe them to be), the more likely they are to take this action.*

Interaction   What Homans saw was that most of the reinforcements or rewards of social animals such as humans come from other animals of the same species. Here sociology enters, and the social-learning perspective comes to share many features of symbolic interaction. Both perspectives focus on *interaction.* Both view interaction as activity in which the actions of one person influence the actions of another, which in turn produces reactions in the first. Symbolic interactionists argue that people in interaction align their actions to the actions of others on the basis of the subjective meanings of these actions; social-learning theorists do not stress subjective meanings but concentrate instead on showing how interacting humans reciprocally reinforce one another's behavior in ways that produce an alignment of action.

Both symbolic interactionists and social-learning theorists agree that humans must learn to be human through interaction. Social-learning theorists have a powerful theory of how this learning occurs. Of the wide variety of acts that humans can perform, some are reinforced by the physical and social environment and therefore tend to be repeated; others are not reinforced and therefore tend not to be repeated. Symbolic interactionists offer detailed accounts of what will be reinforced and how. They tell us how certain norms arise in human groups and define certain actions as desirable (to be positively reinforced) or undesirable (to be ignored or punished).

Subjectivity and Determinism   The major conflict between the two perspectives has to do with the importance of subjective states of mind and the extent to which human behavior is conceived to be determined and scientifically predictable. Symbolic interactionists believe that it is essential to understand subjective states in order to comprehend human action, and they point out that the creative aspects of human action make it difficult to rigorously predict future acts. Social-learning theorists, on the other hand, are *behaviorists*—they believe that science has access only to public activities—that is, activities that, in principle at least, more than one person can observe. Whether the activity is intimate or private makes no difference to behaviorists as long as it can be observed. What the behaviorists are opposed to, however, is the study of individual private states of consciousness, such as feelings of anger or joy.

Let us take a simple observation—Tom is stamping his foot—and see how the two perspectives would deal with it. Someone might infer from his act that "Tom is angry." That inference may be incorrect. Perhaps his right foot is cold; perhaps he is squashing a bug. But, behaviorists say, if we study Tom's foot stamping under various carefully controlled conditions, we will eventually be able to predict and specify the conditions under which different strengths and frequencies of foot stamping will occur. Once we can do that, we have identified the "causes" of the behavior, and inferences about angry feelings are unnecessary.

Symbolic interactionists might respond to this line of reasoning by arguing that while it would indeed be a serious mistake to assume that feelings have always intervened, it is just as wrong to disregard any feeling that has in fact intervened. We need, in the interactionists's view, to take account of what the *person* (Tom) regards as important in his action. This point was well put by W. I. Thomas, one of the founders of the symbolic interactionist school: "If men define situations as real, they are real in their consequences." Thus, if Tom perceives his reaction as one of anger, that perception will have real consequences. If social scientists want to understand Tom's actions, they must also study Tom's perceptions.

The social-learning theorists follow the dictum of the psychologist Edward Chace Tolman(1886–1959): "Another organism's private mind, if he have any, can never be got at." Thus all we can know of another person's subjective states is what he tells us about them. His verbal statement, as a perfectly public aspect of his behavior, can be studied as such. But it is unwise to use it as a basis for inferring what is in his "private mind, if he have any." Indeed, social-learning theory renders verbal reports of internal states suspect because it argues that persons are less likely to give a scrupulous report of their internal states than they are to say what they believe will draw the greatest reward in a particular social situation. As for inherently creative or indeterminate aspects of human action, social-learning theorists are suspicious as to whether they exist. They argue that much human behavior *seems* to be "free" or indeterminate simply because science has neither the resources nor the interest to analyze and catalog all the factors that may in fact determine it completely. The social-learning theorist George Homans has put the matter quite briefly: "I be-

lieve that human behavior is utterly determined, right down to the last sneer."

Although symbolic-interaction and social-learning theories very definitely disagree on certain points, they both emphasize the role of social interaction in shaping human lives. Mead and his followers have concentrated on the social sources of reinforcement through which the self arises, and social-learning theorists have provided an understanding of the learning process by which these reinforcers shape the behavior that we acknowledge as human and reflective of the possession of a self. These matters will receive greater attention in the context of concrete sociological problems in subsequent chapters.

MACRO THEORETICAL PERSPECTIVES

Sociology has long been dominated by two powerful macro theoretical perspectives; conflicts between the two have been extremely bitter. The conflict has reflected the differing political commitments of sociologists more than any unreconcilable differences between the two theoretical perspectives themselves. For, as we shall see, the two perspectives have a great deal in common although they have a fundamental difference in emphasis. It is important to understand the basic similarities of and differences between these two perspectives because they underlie much of what sociologists argue about. These matters are discussed frequently in later chapters, especially those in Units V and VI.

Knowing that the founding father of one of these perspectives—*conflict theory*—was Karl Marx makes the political basis of dispute obvious. The other perspective—*functionalism*—in some ways reflects liberal opposition to Marxist analysis. The differences between liberal reformers and radicals in the political arena are often bitter indeed, but it does not necessarily follow that their theories of society are wholly different—even though it is often "good politics" for both sides to exaggerate and emphasize the differences. In any event, the disputes between functionalism and conflict theory are not nearly as intense as they once were. As is demonstrated in Chapter 15 and elsewhere, contemporary sociologists are attempting to build more powerful theories in a number of topic areas, by combining elements of both functionalism and conflict theory.

Functionalism

Functional theories are not unique to sociology. In fact, the logical form of functional theory in the social sciences is borrowed from biology, where it originated. Also, some aspects of the functionalist mode are better developed in economics than in sociology, and most sociological applications of this kind of theory were adapted from anthropology.

The distinctive feature of most forms of functional theory is that, like forms of learning theory, they *explain phenomena on the basis of their consequences.* The fundamental premise is that particular things happen or particular structures arise and are maintained because of the consequences they have. Physiologists, for example, explain the liver by referring to its consequences (functions)—it maintains a stable level of sugar in the blood. Such a stabilizing mechanism is necessary because our digestive intake of sugar is highly variable and blood coming from the digestive system sometimes has an extremely high sugar content and sometimes a very low content. Our body needs a much more stable level of blood sugar than the digestive system provides, and the function of the liver is to stabilize the sugar level.

Components of Functional Theories According to one recent commentator, functionalist explanations or theories have three key components (Stinchcombe, 1968):

1. A *structure or activity* whose existence is to be explained and that has as a consequence the maintenance of
2. some *variable within tolerable limits,* which would not be so maintained in the absence of (1) because of
3. some source of *tension or disruption.*

This scheme only sounds complicated. Returning to our physiological example, we can recognize that (1) the liver has the consequence of (2) keeping a stable level of blood sugar, which is threatened by (3) the wide variability in the amount of sugar coming from the digestive system. The liver, then, exists because it is functional; if digestive activity were constant, we would not expect the process of natural selection to produce animals with livers. In this type of functional explanation, the evolutionary process of "natural selection" provides the mechanism by which the consequences of an activity "feed back" so as to affect its subsequent development or rate of occurrence. Many (though not all) functional theories in sociology are evolutionary in this sense, especially those that explain the growth and persistence of the oldest and most stable components of social organization such as the family (as a group) or the economic division of labor (as a social process).

Let us consider a classic example of a functional explanation of a social process. During World War I Bronislaw Malinowski studied tribal life in the Trobriand Islands. He observed that the islanders had rich magical traditions. But he also saw that magic was especially linked to certain kinds of activities. For example, the islanders used little magic in preparation for fishing within the calm lagoon of the island, but they utilized a great deal of magic before launching dangerous fishing expeditions out onto the high seas. The islanders' selective use of magic led Malinowski to propose a functional explanation of magic in primitive societies. Magic is practiced because of its consequences; although it does not of course provide any real control, it reduces anxiety by giving persons a *sense* of control over the outcome of their activities. Magical rituals therefore will focus on controlling those activities over which people have the least control (Malinowski, 1948).

In Malinowski's example, the structure or activity to be explained (1) is magic; its consequence (2) is a sense of control over activities such as fishing on the high seas, where the sense of control is threatened by (3) the lack of effective means (such as advanced nautical technology) for insuring safe sea voyages. Like the liver, magic exists because it serves a function; if deep-sea fishing were safe, we would not expect to find magic practiced in connection with fishing expeditions.

Systems Functional theories make certain assumptions about the nature of the phenomena they attempt to explain. Chief among these is the assumption that the phenomena are part of a *system*—they are related to one another in such a way that a change in one part produces changes in the other parts. The assumption that human societies are systems leads to a search for functions. For if societies are systems, then particular structures have effects elsewhere in the system; the task of sociological explanation, then, is to determine what is influencing what, and how this process occurs. A second major assumption about societies follows from the first: for societies to operate as systems—for societies to hold together—some *balance* or *equilibrium* must be maintained among the various parts. The organization of societies cannot vary in too many ways.

Functional analysis in sociology thus concentrates on determining the effects that one part of a social system has on the other parts. Often a particular social arrangement (such as the family) is held to be vital to the balance of society as a whole (by providing essential functions of reproduction and socialization, for example). This line of explanation can be readily used in advancing conservative political positions. Defenders of the political status quo—for example, an absolute monarchy—can be encouraged by functionalist reasoning to argue that monarchy is necessary for the continuing operation of society, for it prevents destructive social disorder and the "war of all against all." As Arthur Stinchcombe (1968) has put it, "This conservative cast of functional theory is not logically necessary, but it is an inherent rhetorical opportunity in the theory."

Nothing in the general strategy of functional explanation, however, implies that there is only one way to fulfill necessary social functions. For example, in a few societies, the conventional human family gives way to various schemes of collective child rearing. Similarly, absolute monarchy clearly is not the only way (and among industrial societies, probably not a very efficient way) to prevent destructive social disorder. Further, functionalism does not assume that any particular society *ought* to be held together, nor that all societies *will* in fact be held together. To the extent that functional analysis provides conservatives with arguments for the *status quo*, it also provides radicals with strategies for making changes. Similarly, functional analysis often attempts to indicate which kinds of societies are likely to prosper and endure and which kinds are likely to break apart and be absorbed or dominated by other societies.

In providing a framework for theories about the relationship among various parts of a society, functionalism does not imply that such relationships are "good" or "bad," or that a society is "good" or "bad." Some functionalists have even found it necessary to distinguish between *functional* and *dysfunctional* social arrangements because they have identified relationships in social life that work to the detriment (dysfunction) of society as a whole.

Manifest and Latent Functions One contribution of functionalism that is especially useful to students is the distinction between *manifest* and *latent* functions. Manifest functions are the recognized and intended consequences of some structure or activity. Latent functions are unrecognized and unintended and may be either functional or dysfunctional. When President Hoover severely limited federal spending during the Great Depression, he did so to ease the tax burden on the nation. The unintended or latent consequence was to depress the economy further by making less money available. Economists made a major contribution in discovering this latent function and in pointing out that during depressions and recessions federal spending should be massively increased through deficit spending, which has the effect of boosting activity throughout the economy.

As another example, critics of present plans to create a wholly volunteer army fear that a latent consequence of this attempt to remove the unpopular threat of being drafted will be to make the army less responsive to civilian control. Their argument is that historically the draft has served the latent function of preventing conflict between the military and civilians by keeping a high proportion of civilian-oriented, nonprofessional soldiers in the army. They look at societies without civilian soldiers and notice that the armies in such nations tend to be more militaristic and to seek their own goals in opposition to those of civilian society—often taking over the government by military dictatorship. The critics conclude that civilian soldiers have kept the American Army relatively less militaristic and less inclined to usurp civilian power. Removal of civilians, who serve to keep militarism within tolerable limits, would thus be like removing an individual's liver. In fact, it can be argued that the function of civilian soldiers in demilitarizing the army was originally a manifest function. The Founding Fathers depended on civilian soldiers to protect civil rule from military despots. Over time we have largely forgotten this original manifest intention—and what was once a manifest function has become a latent function.

Seeking out such relationships among social arrangements is the most universal feature of functionalist analysis. If you want to know why some social process works the way it does, look to see how it influences and is influenced by other aspects of society.

Conflict Theory

Most functional theorists would argue that some minimum degree of integration is necessary for a society to persist. Other functionalists would argue that a high degree of agreement or *consensus* among members on the society's major norms and institutions is economical because the cost of *social control* (maintenance of the normative order) is less than it would be if the members disagreed. For example, societies such as Ireland with two competing religions have more internal conflict than such societies as Spain where one religion dominates—religion is a powerful agent in shaping norms and values.

However, most functionalists would not argue that a society *must have* a high degree of consensus on norms and institutions, for such an argument flies in the face of the facts: many societies around the world clearly exhibit a high level of *conflict*. Members of these societies disagree on norms and institutions, and groups and classes do not work together for any common interest so much as they compete for scarce resources.

The Emphasis on Conflict Contemporary conflict theorists use many of the premises of modern functionalism, but they differ on one major point. They hold that functionalists fail to take sufficient account of conflict in their theories of social organization and especially in theories of social change (van den Berghe, 1963).

Modern conflict theory derives largely from the work of the great nineteenth-century sociologist and social philosopher, Karl Marx. Conflict received careful attention from Marx in his concept of *class struggle*, but it is interesting to note that in other respects Marx was an early and special kind of functionalist (Stinchcombe, 1968). Marx clearly assumed that societies are systems and that change in one aspect of society affects many other aspects. Similarly, Marx explained the origins and persistence of particular social structures and activities on the basis of their consequences. Furthermore, Marx was a perceptive detector of manifest and latent functions and particularly of latent dysfunctions (see his argument in Chapter 14 about the latent dysfunctions that he believed would destroy capitalism).

Class Interest and Power The main difference between Marxists and ordinary functionalists lies in their answers to the question: *functional for whom?* Most functionalists would answer "functional for the society as a whole." They stress the links among all parts of a society and use the social system as a whole as their basis for assessing costs and benefits. Most Marxists would answer "functional for the ruling class." They stress the way in which particular social arrangements—especially the economic arrangements—serve *particular groups within societies at the expense of other groups*. Marxists use class interest rather than the whole society as the basis for assessing costs and

Figure 4.7   Karl Marx (1818–1883) remains the most influential of the early social scientists. He was born and educated in Germany, and his major work was done while he lived in England. He viewed history and life in society primarily in terms of inevitable conflicts between social classes. The major focus of his work was on the process by

which capitalism and social rule by the bourgeoisie would be superseded by socialism and proletarian rule (see Chapter 14). His best-known works include *The Communist Manifesto* (1848, written with Friedrich Engels), *The Class Struggles in France (1848–1850)* (1850), *Critique of Political Economy* (1859), and *Capital* (1867–1879).

is important to recognize here is that Marx believed that changes in power in societies cause changes in major social arrangements. As Stinchcombe stated over a hundred years later (1968), *"the greater the power of a class, the more effective that class is as a cause of social structures."*

Differential power, then, is the major focus of conflict theory. To understand why some structure or activity persists, conflict theorists recommend that we try to determine how it serves the interests of those groups that have the most power to shape social policies.

Theory and Ideology

It is often claimed that conflict theory is better able to account for changes in societies and that functionalism is better able to account for societies' persistent features. Most sociologists now believe that this is too simple a distinction. As will be taken up in Unit VIII, there are two major sources of change in societies. One source is external pressures, such as wars or natural disasters; the second is internal imbalances (or dysfunctions) that result in conflicts and a need to establish a new balance. Both theories can accommodate both sources of change, although conflict theory may provide a clearer explanation of internal change. It is probably a safe generalization that conflict theorists give greater emphasis to dysfunctions and social change because they are personally more likely to desire radical social change. Functionalists give more attention to functions and to social stability because they personally are less likely to desire radical change and more likely to prefer reform of present arrangements. Thus the ideological thrust of their theories reflects a desire on the one hand to know how to pull societies apart and on the other hand to know how to prevent societies from being pulled apart.

benefits, sometimes arguing that it is meaningless to speak of the interest of society as a whole in any sense that transcends the interests of particular classes. It is this emphasis on conflicts of group interest that gives rise to the label of conflict theory. Whereas functionalists stress the interdependence of all members of a society and the interests they have in common, conflict theorists emphasize exploitation of some members of society by others and interests they have separately.

The starting point of Marx's analysis of social history stated that over the course of time social arrangements change, so that arrangements that were good for one group tend to be replaced by arrangements that benefit another group. Marx charted the rise and fall of powerful or ruling groups in the history of societies. A fundamental thesis of conflict theory is that social arrangements are designed to give advantage to the most powerful groups in society. As Marx wrote in *The Communist Manifesto* in 1848: "The ruling ideas of any age are the ideas of its ruling class."

Details of Marx's argument about the dynamic behind the rise and fall of classes throughout history are presented in Chapters 14 and 15. What

In subsequent chapters you will find conflict and functionalist interpretations competing to explain many important social phenomena. Usually, the interpretations will be clearly identified. Nevertheless, it may help you to have some simple cues for recognizing each. When you read statements that emphasize the role of some social arrangement in serving the needs of *society as a system,* mention the needs of all the members of society, and refer to shared values or a consensus over goals, you are most likely reading a functionalist interpretation. When you read statements that stress *inequalities of power within societies* and mention class conflict, special interests, coercion, or exploitation, you are most likely reading a conflict-theory interpretation.

This chapter has attempted to present enough of the logical structure of contemporary sociological theories to enable you to distinguish theories from research results and to understand enough of the major assumptions of the various perspectives so that you may recognize their applications in later chapters. The truth is that no scientist can say anything about the world without making use of some kind of perspective as a device for interpretation, and he can do next to no worthwhile research without a theory to guide his efforts.

SUGGESTED READINGS

Blumer, Herbert. *Symbolic Interactionism: Perspective and Method.* Englewood Cliffs, N.J.: Prentice-Hall, 1969.

Homans, George C. *The Nature of Social Sciences.* New York: Harcourt, Brace & World, 1967.

Mead, George Herbert. *Mind, Self, and Society.* Chicago: University of Chicago Press, 1936.

Stinchcombe, Arthur L. *Constructing Social Theories.* New York: Harcourt Brace Jovanovich, 1968.

We have examined the way sociologists think about society and how they go about studying it. Now it is time to examine what they have found out (and also what they have not found out). The plan of the rest of the book is to begin at the micro level of study—with the most simple components of social life—and add complexity

UNIT III
until we have literally moved from the fertilized human ovum to functioning social systems. ¶ In the last chapter, we examined

THE INTERPLAY OF
the statement "social behavior is a function of heredity and environment."

HEREDITY AND ENVIRONMENT
We concluded that the

statement is very probably true but that it is also too vague to be meaningful. This unit discusses this basic premise of sociology and examines factors of heredity and environment that sociologists have found significant. We try to unravel some major ideas and arguments in what is often called the nature-nurture debate. How much of what people are stems from their heredity (nature) and how much from their environment (nurture)? Chapter 5 examines the extent to which hereditary factors limit and facilitate what human beings are and can be. Chapter 6 considers the influence of the environment—human culture and society—in making people human.

Chapter 5 The Biological Basis of Society

DURING THE LATTER PART of the nineteenth century, *biological determinism* dominated our views of human and social behavior. The monumental achievement of Charles Darwin's theory of evolution and natural selection led to enthusiastic but simple-minded applications of Darwinism to sociological and psychological questions. People attributed virtually all individual and group differences in human behavior to inheritance. For example, they explained differences between social classes and especially between societies as the result of biological differences produced by breeding and evolution. It was a time of great intellectual enthusiasm: all the difficult questions about human nature and human society seemed on the brink of solution. It was also a racist and bigoted time. People justified exploitation of the poor by the rich and of less technically advanced societies by Europeans on the grounds of innate biological superiority of the dominant groups. They argued that ruling elites and advanced societies were the result of superior bloodlines, that elites were thoroughbreds destined by nature to outperform the so-called atavistic or primitive varieties of the human species.

Consequently, many early psychologists spent considerable time trying to catalogue the set of *instincts*—or genetically determined behavior such as a spider's ability to spin webs—that produced the whole range of human behavior. Some early social scientists worried about the corruption of the best bloodlines (upper-class white Europeans) that might occur if social reforms either allowed interbreeding with outgroups or prevented competitive forces from eliminating the weak. Biological doctrines in part prompted strict immigration laws, segregation, opposition to unions, and eventually the doctrine of Aryan supremacy, which resulted in the massacre of Jews and other so-called inferior strains by the Nazis.

Modern sociology rose in opposition to the simplistic application of biological determinism; modern sociologists argued that much variation in human behavior and capacity is the product of environment, not of genetic inheritance, and that many behaviors are learned rather than governed by instincts. This controversy, which will be taken up again in Chapter 6, has been called the *nature-nurture* debate: Is man primarily a product of his hereditary nature or of the nurturing he receives after he is born?

Karl Marx challenged the notions that privilege is based on genetic superiority. Instead, he argued that economic advantages and disadvantages account for human variability. If the children of the poor and the children of the rich were raised in the same environment, they would end up equally talented and successful. Similarly, the French sociologist Emile Durkheim argued for the dominance of social and cultural factors over biological ones. In his famous study of suicide (1897), he analyzed empirical data based on official rates to disprove many biological and geographical theories of suicide; he demonstrated instead that suicide was related to cultural factors such as religion and to social factors such as close-knit family life.

ENVIRONMENTAL DETERMINISM

The ideological triumph in the social sciences of those arguing for environmental factors against heredity was soon virtually total (Benedict, 1959; Childe, 1951). During most of the twentieth century there has been little room for biological factors in the social sciences. Recall the main theoretical traditions of sociology presented in Chapter 4. Clearly, these are environmental, or nurture, theories.

Unfortunately, environmentalism was carried to as great an extreme as biological determinism had been. Sociologists lost all sight of man as a biological creature and gave all their attention to cultural and social factors. While racism and elitism were thus severed from their crude intellectual justifications in biological determinism, a new kind of bigotry resulted called *homocentrism* —human-centeredness, or a false pride in our own uniqueness as a species. The line between man and animal, so slight during the days of biological determinism, became an insuperable barrier. It was believed that man alone had culture and that culture was everything; whatever man shared with animals was of no importance.

Figure 5.1   Assumptions underlying homocentrism are being challenged. For example, the dolphin in the photograph (*top*), named Peter, and the woman, Margaret Howe, are taking part in an experiment in which the dolphin is learning to approximate human speech and communicate with human beings. (*Bottom*) Sound-wave patterns (sonic spectrograms) of Margaret saying "ball"

and Peter's subsequent vocalization of "ball." The upper traces are taken with a narrow-band filter (45 cycles per second), the lower traces with a wide-band filter (300 cycles). The vocalizations strongly resemble each other. However, the dolphin's pitch is somewhat higher than Margaret's, and he tends to raise the pitch at the end of the word, whereas she tends to lower it.

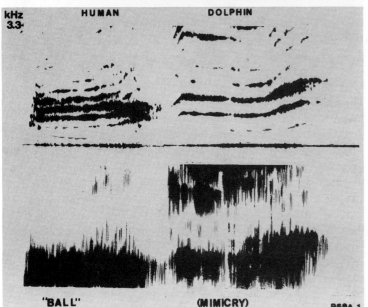

Much of the victory of nurture over nature was simply propaganda. It was no more based on solid research than were the racist doctrines of biological determinism. As a result, sociologists have recently had to begin reconsidering their position because the evidence shows that biological features do enter into the human equation in important ways (Eckland, 1967).

Decades of painstaking research in behavior genetics and in the study of the behavior of non-

human species have produced facts that have undercut our homocentrism: First, culture is not exclusively human. Many species learn ways of behaving, and the adults of some species even pass on crude technologies to infants; in fact, some nonhuman species—the chimpanzee, for example—have been observed not only using but making simple tools (Mazur and Robertson, 1972).

Second, such obviously inherited characteristics as body build and physical stature have been shown to be of extraordinary importance in individual and group behavior. Physical attractiveness, for example, appears to be as important as either intelligence or social-class background in its contribution to the mobility of women through marriage (Elder, 1969). Karen Dion's experiment, which is discussed in Chapter 2, shows that physical attractiveness also influences judgments about a person's character.

Third, geneticists have demonstrated that it is highly probable that inherited traits and capacities play a significant role in setting limits on human performance and in shaping human personality (Thiessen, 1972).

There has been a rebirth of communication between biology and sociology, and consequently, no adequate introduction to sociology is now possible without consideration of biological factors.

This chapter considers three main ways in which biology informs sociology. First, through the study of animal behavior—called *ethology*—we have recently gained vital insights into human behavior. Second, attention to human physiology is necessary in order to understand how human biological characteristics limit and shape what people are and can be. Finally, it is vital to determine the role of genetic inheritance in human behavior in order to understand the role of the social environment.

ANIMALS AND HUMAN BEINGS

The study of social behavior in animals has provided sociologists and other behavioral scientists with many useful insights into human nature. Studies of animals, from insects to apes, not only have contributed new ideas about the habits of

Figure 5.2 *(Left to right)* The first evolutionary steps toward human beings' eventual mastery of the environment were taken in the tropical forest in which our quadrupedal primate ancestor lived more than 20 million years ago. During Miocene times new environments were produced when mountains arose. One of these new environments, a transition zone between forest and grassland, has been used by three groups of primates. One group, the chimpanzees, has only recently entered this woodland savanna. Both the newly bipedal hominids and some ground-living quadrupedal monkeys, however, moved beyond the transition zone into open grassland. The quadrupeds, such as the baboons, remained there. The forces of natural selection in the new grasslands setting favored the bipedal hominid hunters' adaptation of the striding gait—typical only of humans. Once this adaptation developed, humans moved into most of the earth's environments. *(Adapted from John Napier, 1967.)*

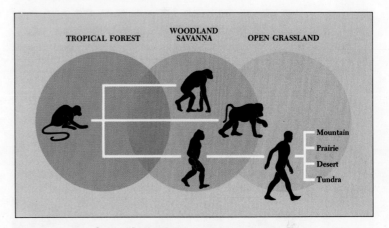

human beings but also have provided a convenient yardstick against which to measure and evaluate the characteristics that we consider uniquely human. Studies of other species, however, have shown that people probably do not possess any single trait that cannot be found in the physiology or habits of some other animal. What is uniquely human is therefore probably some combination of traits.

Comparative Ethology

Empirical observation of other animals has revealed important clues about human nature. To observe is not to reason by analogy or to assume, for example, that because something is true of white rats or greylag geese it must therefore be true of human beings (Scott, 1963). From comparative physiology and ethology we have learned which differences are critical between humans and other species. For example, man is one of the few animals, but not the only one, equipped with grasping hands that can manipulate objects. Numerous other primates—and some carnivores such as the raccoon—have good digital dexterity, but only humans couple this ability with fully erect posture, which frees their hands as they move about.

Other human advantages include stereoscopic vision, which enables us to judge distance and depth far better than most other mammals; year-around sexuality, which allows us to breed irrespective of the season and its particular food supply; and an oversize brain relative to body size (LaBarre, 1955). Various animals share each of these features with human beings, but in no animal other than man do all of these attributes appear together.

Instinct and Learning

Long before the development of modern genetics and ethology, the terms *instinct* and *innate* were used to refer to any inherited pattern of behavior. People thought that instinct or some other biological force ruled much of the observed behavior of animals and even of men, in some cases. These terms eventually took on so many different meanings that most social scientists abandoned them entirely (Lorenz, 1965; Klopfer and Hailman, 1967). But the question posed about human instincts persists: What human behavior patterns, if any, are automatic responses to environmental stimuli and do not have to be learned?

In animal experiments, the standard method of determining whether a behavior pattern is instinctive is to rear the animal in isolation so that it cannot learn behavior from other members of its species. If the young animal develops the behavior pattern characteristic of the species without ever having seen the act performed, we say that the response is instinctive.

Findings from biology and psychology show that learning, not instinct, in many cases is the means by which animals adapt to their environment. The importance of learning has long been understood for human beings, as we shall see in Chapter 6, but it now appears equally significant for many other species. Moreover, it seems that all animals have some capacity to learn; even the flatworm, with its highly restricted repertory of behaviors, can learn to traverse a maze.

If ethology has revealed that many animals besides man must learn, it has also revealed suggestions that man has certain inborn traits or instinctive bases of behavior. As is pointed out in the next chapter, normal human babies appear to possess an innate nuzzling and sucking response. They also seem to babble instinctively, whether or not they hear human speech.

Figure 5.3 Ethological studies attempt to determine which behavior patterns are innate in a species and which are learned. The sucking response is one that is innate in humans as well as in animals. Learning, however, appears to be as important to other animals as it is to humans in the development of many behavior patterns. The chimpanzee shown in the bottom series of drawings is displaying insight learning. The chimp in this experiment had had experience with the boxes; they had been left in its environment for some time before the bananas were hung out of its reach. The chimp suddenly piled the boxes as shown and ate the bananas. The next time it was presented with this situation, the chimp would show no hesitation. It had learned how to use the tools in its environment.

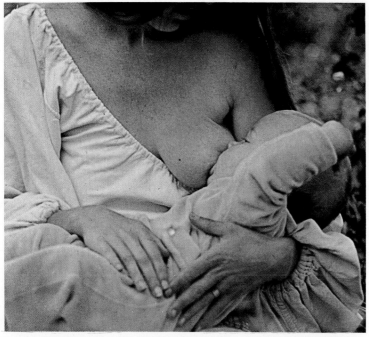

Undoubtedly the most controversial attribution of an innate characteristic to humans is Konrad Lorenz's recent claim that humans are born with an aggressive tendency. Lorenz believes that through socialization innate aggressiveness can be channeled in a number of ways, but he does not believe that aggressiveness can be eliminated (Lorenz, 1966). Whether or not aggressiveness is innate, it is certainly of value in competing for food, shelter, sustenance, and mates. However, for social animals such as man, aggression must be somehow redirected away from other group members; otherwise there would be constant war of all against all, and social life would be impossible. Ethologists find that social animals have developed a number of patterns for redirecting aggressiveness away from group members. A major pattern is the *appeasement ceremony*, which is characteristic of primates and is based on mutual grooming behavior. Mated pairs of baboons (Kummer, 1971) and chimpanzee groups (von Lawick-Goodall, 1969) will only groom one another. This grooming behavior—which involves the removal of parasites and the cleaning of fur and skin—is a central activity that promotes intimate, in-

Figure 5.4   Observers can often figure out the ranking of the individual hens in a dominance hierarchy by noting which hens take precedence over which others in obtaining food and water. As a rule, older animals dominate younger ones, and larger ones dominate smaller ones. In what ways does the dominance hierarchy in chickens resemble the social hierarchies of humans discussed in Unit V? (Adapted from W. C. Allee, 1938.)

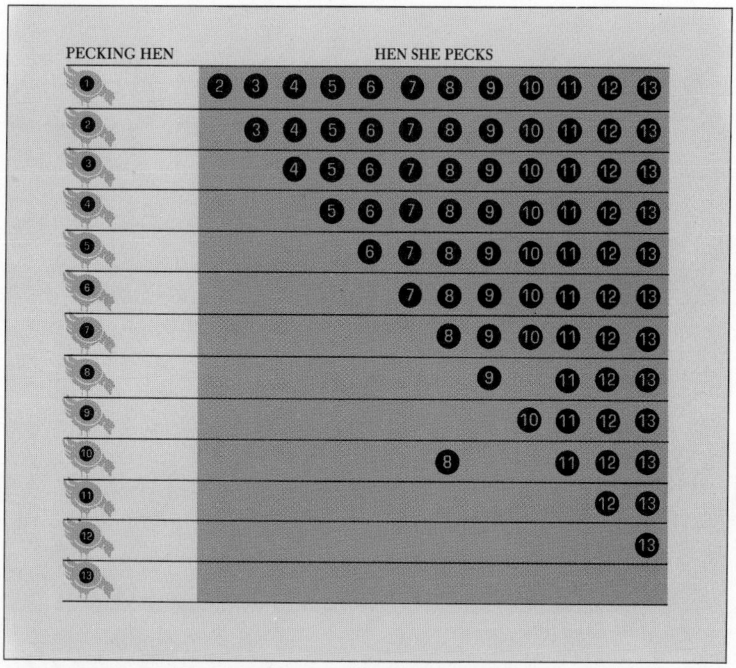

dividual social relationships. Wolfgang Wickler (1972) suggests that similar patterns help to channel human aggression; however, a great deal more must be studied before we can begin to settle fully questions about which behavior is learned and which is instinctual.

Animal Societies and Culture

Whether by trial and error, imitation, or some other device, animals, like men, do learn. Some animals that live in large communities evolve rules for governing the behavior of each individual; a division of labor with specialized roles; and territorial boundaries to keep the group intact. These groups are not just random assortments of individuals but, like human societies, are social organizations with a kind of cultural inheritance that is independent of the particular individuals who happen to be in the group and play its roles at any given time (Dimond, 1970).

When old members die, new ones assume the positions of the old, giving the society a continuity of character. In its most elementary form, social organization is simply the ordering of behavior among individuals into regular and predictable patterns. This organization is exactly what happens, for example, in the pecking order of chickens (see Figure 5.4).

An important question is the extent to which the network of social relationships in animal societies is learned or is tied to fixed biological mechanisms. To a large extent, *role differentiation* —the specialization of tasks critical to the maintenance of human and animal societies—has biological bases; as Chapter 17 points out, sex and age constitute the most common criteria. Role differentiation in insect societies is almost totally based on sex and size differences.

There is evidence, however, that many of the patterns of social behavior among primates and many other vertebrates are learned. The learning generally occurs in close dependency relationships, such as that between a female and her offspring, rather than in isolation or in a strictly trial-and-error manner. Jackdaws apparently learn their fears from their elders; sheep learn to follow each other and use old migration routes; and cats

learn from each other to kill mice, despite folk wisdom to the contrary.

Human beings, then, are not the only animals with the ability to develop culture by passing on acquired learning. However, animal culture, if we can call it that, is relatively uncomplicated. The behavior patterns in animal societies, although transmitted intergenerationally, seem to be learned quickly and directly by imitation.

Communication and Human Behavior

If the characteristics of learning and intergenerational continuity are shared by both animal and human societies, in what respect are humans unique in the animal kingdom? Some students of human behavior have attributed our uniqueness to our possession of language.

All organized groups of animals communicate among themselves. In some cases, animals communicate through physical contact, but they usually use some sort of auditory signal or sign language. Birds convey information to other birds with a limited number of sounds, most of which have been interpreted by human observers as denoting danger, hunger, the presence of food, or the assertion of territorial rights. Heredity deter-

Figure 5.5 Primates other than humans seem incapable of voluntary vocalization. Washoe, a chimpanzee, has been taught a form of communication that is considered a language, although it does not involve vocalization. She is shown here at about five years of age using the American Sign Language to say "hat" (*top*), "sweet" (*middle*), and "fruit" (*bottom*).

mines some of these signals but not all of them. For example, English sparrows raised with canaries will learn to sing like canaries.

The communication system of human beings is far more complex than that of any other animal. In its variability, grammar, and particularistic meanings, it is wholly independent of heredity. Yet, as some linguists have argued, the structure of the human brain may be largely responsible for the acquisition of language competence (Chomsky, 1965). Nearly all children, with minimal environmental stimulation, easily learn the structure of language within a very short period of time, and the research available suggests that this capacity does not vary by culture, social class, or race. Language universals probably are the result of humans' innate mental endowment.

Furthermore, humans possess highly specialized physical capacities for making vocal sounds. Attempts to teach monkeys and apes to speak have floundered because these animals are incapable of *voluntary vocalization.* Dogs do not decide to bark; rather, when they are in certain physical states of arousal, they do bark. The same is true for primates. Only aquatic mammals—such as whales and dolphins—share man's capacity to emit voluntary vocalizations; for this reason Elaine Morgan (1972) argues that humans passed through an aquatic period. Recent efforts to teach primates speech have thus turned to the sign language of the deaf and dumb or to plastic word tokens, for, in their natural state, primates communicate mainly by gestures.

It is possession of language that makes possible the rapid accumulation and dissemination of the knowledge necessary for the development of large and complex societies. A complex culture, if it is to survive and develop over time, requires a vehicle of this kind. Human beings cannot afford to grow up repeating by trial and error all the mistakes of the thousand preceding generations. At the most basic analytical level, verbal language, perhaps more than anything else, sets humans apart from all other animals.

SOME BIOLOGICAL FACTS OF SOCIAL LIFE

It is obvious that humans are of flesh and blood and that particular physiological processes have much to do with human capacities. Physiology not only sets humans apart from other species but also sets off some humans from others. In Chapter 13 evidence will be reviewed to show that physical differences such as beauty, height, and strength greatly influence a person's chances for success. To use obvious examples, although we may learn the appropriate rudimentary skills required, most of us are too small to play professional football or basketball, too insensitive to tone and rhythm to be great musicians, and too graceless to dance in the ballet.

Two of the most obvious and influential physiological facts of life are sex and age. Chapter 17 discusses the impact of age and sex differences on

Figure 5.6   Charles Darwin (1809–1882) formulated the theory of evolution that revolutionized modern biology. He observed that although the rate of reproduction of all species ought to lead to extremely rapid increases in their numbers, the actual population of a given species remains relatively constant over time. Darwin postulated that a natural selective mechanism must be at work—"survival of the fittest"—by which organisms survive in proportion to their natural advantages. This principle permits explanation of changes in species over time: The fittest organisms survive to breeding age and reproduce; by such selective breeding, species evolve; and characteristics with the greatest survival value tend to be perpetuated and others to die out. Darwin first laid out his theory in detail in *On the Origin of Species* (1859) and expanded it in *The Descent of Man* (1871). His evolutionary views contradicted Christian doctrines of creation and led to great furor. Darwin is today regarded as one of the giants of scientific discovery. However, early efforts to apply Darwinian principles directly to social life proved to be of dubious value.

social roles and explains sex and age as continuing bases for social inequalities. In this chapter we consider some major social implications of sex and age, not as roles, but as physiological phenomena.

Sex and Society

Human reproduction has considerable impact on what humans are and how human societies operate. Unlike the majority of animals, anthropoids, including man, do not have a breeding season. Rather than being sexually accessible only during a seasonal time of fertility, human females are fertile each month, and sexual excitation is psychologically rather than wholly physiologically produced. As a result human infants are not born during a short season but throughout the year. Thus, humans do not make up nearly so distinct age cohorts as do many animals. Furthermore, because human sexuality is constant rather than seasonal, stable relationships between males and females are encouraged. The males and females of many other species associate only during the breeding season. The stability of human relationships is further encouraged by the comparatively long term of human pregnancy and the degree to which the female is incapacitated in late pregnancy and by delivery. The long dependency of the human infant, too, encourages the formation of families, as is discussed later in this chapter and in Chapter 17.

These facts of human sexuality not only undergird the formation of families but also threaten the maintenance of families, thereby necessitating the development of customs and taboos to control the disruptive features of sex.

All known societies have developed rules and regulations governing sexual behavior, some of which prescribe courtship and marriage patterns. In no society are people allowed to mate at random. An incest taboo of some sort is, in fact, one of the few cross-cultural universals. In all societies sexual intercourse between a child and a parent is categorically prohibited. In many societies, however, marriage with one's first cousin, on either the mother's or father's side, is not only permitted but may be mandatory. Marital patterns are exceedingly varied, and the rules appear to be most complicated in some of the least "advanced" societies (Murdock, 1949).

The origins of the incest taboo apparently have very little to do with any instinctive aversion toward incestuous relationships or with concern for the dysgenic consequences that may follow from long inbreeding within a confined population. The taboo probably owes its origin to the nature of human family organization (LaBarre, 1955). The taboo against sexual relations between mother and son, for example, eliminates overt conflict between the father and the son for access to the mother. Only if the society forbids the male child to have sexual intercourse with his mother does it seem reasonable to expect the father to refrain from killing his male offspring, as stallions will often kill their colts. Furthermore, the taboo widens the sphere of communal relations by forcing alliances between unrelated groups. Bonds of marriage link families together because if children are to find mates, they must find them outside the family. If there were any groups that did not observe the incest taboo, they have neither survived nor left any accounts of their experience, although in the royal families of ancient Egypt and of Peru under the Incas, where the rulers were considered gods, incest between brother and sister was obligatory.

All societies must devise ways to control sexual behavior. In all societies, the rules go well beyond those prohibiting incest. Sexual intercourse outside marriage, irrespective of whether the partners are related, is usually limited by morality and sometimes by law as well.

Age as a Social Fact

Another problem for the social organization of human societies is the development of some system for the care of the very young and the very old. Again, the roots of the problem are biological. No infant in the animal kingdom is quite so helpless and so dependent for so long a period as the human child. Maturation proceeds very slowly, and for a substantial part of the time, the child must depend upon adults or older children for survival. Under unfavorable conditions, where average life expectancy might be no more than

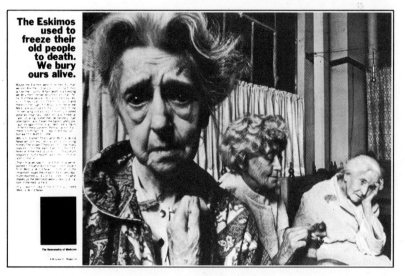

Figure 5.7   Every society must deal with the phenomenon of old age. In some societies, such as Japan, the aged are treated with respect and are considered a source of wisdom. In the United States, in contrast, old people generally are pushed aside as useless. Advertisements like the one reproduced here call attention to the fact that the elderly are left to sit idle and eventually die in old-age homes and retirement communities, which are often referred to as ghettos for the aged.

thirty years, the period of dependency might occupy almost half the total life span of many of the group's members.

It is not necessary, however, that the child be directly dependent upon his biological parents to fulfill his needs; sociologically speaking, any adults may fulfill the parental roles. In practice, child rearing is organized in many different ways, ranging from the small, isolated conjugal family in the United States to the collective child-rearing practiced on the Israeli *kibbutz.*

Societies assign individuals to different roles according to their ages. Childhood is a period of dependency that lasts until children are both biologically and socially mature enough to assume independent responsibility. In many societies the transition from childhood to adult status is marked by formal ceremonies—sometimes puberty rites, sometimes other kinds—all of them collectively known as *rites of passage* (Williams, 1972). In modern societies the passage from childhood to adulthood is usually less well-defined, but it generally occurs upon entry either into marriage or into the work force. However, such ceremonies as the Jewish boy's Bar Mitzvah or the Catholic child's first communion symbolize the earlier kinds of rites. In recent generations the age of puberty in the United States has declined slightly, probably because of improved nutrition; however, as a result of the ever-increasing extension of the length

of formal education, adolescence has been prolonged well into what previously would have been considered adult years. Although biologically an adult, the adolescent is socially still a child, and the period of adolescence fosters both adolescent discontent and generational conflict.

At the other end of the life span are the aged and the aging. All societies must somehow deal with their care and management, even if that means, as it does for some migratory groups, leaving them behind to die when they can no longer be useful to the tribe or care for themselves. Most societies develop some kind of provision for the aged, sometimes honoring them as guardians of the traditions and the sacred rites of the culture, sometimes casting them aside as useless. In the United States, and increasingly in other industrial societies, change proceeds so rapidly that the experience of one generation may have limited relevance for the next. It is the young, not their grandparents or even their parents, who are the transmitters of modern culture. Old people today discover that they have little to contribute to the primary functions of society. As a result, social and psychological problems attend old age in the United States.

How our society will handle these problems in the future is an open question because we are now in a period of transition. A system in which the responsibility for the care of the aged rested with the family has now changed to one in which the responsibility rests either with the state or with the individual himself, who may plan for his own retirement. In the meantime, the present generation of aged persons and the generation about to retire are caught between the expectations they held in their own youth and the expectations of their children and grandchildren.

Evolution and Race

People are social animals and do not live alone. Human beings, as far as we know, have always lived in organized groups, from small roving bands to large, territorially based societies. In the process of adapting to particular geographies and ecological niches, humans have developed varied forms of civilization. In fact, the differences

Figure 5.8 These children are taking part in Project SEED (Special Elementary Education for the Disadvantaged), a program designed to teach high-level mathematics to disadvantaged elementary-school students. Its goal is to raise the children's intellectual performance and their self-concepts. Another aim is to counter psychologist Arthur Jensen's contention that compensatory education cannot help such students develop conceptual reasoning on a par with that shown by middle-class whites. Evaluation studies show that black SEED students do as well as white children on the Raven Progressive Matrices Test, a test Jensen has used to support his claim that blacks show poorer conceptual reasoning.

among human social arrangements often are as large as the individual differences among members of the same group. So different are the manners, the morals, and the behaviors of various cultures that few genuine universals of human culture have ever been found.

Different forms of human behavior can largely be ascribed to cultural rather than to hereditary differences. The impact of culture is shown in cultural *diffusion*—the selective borrowing of behavior patterns or material artifacts of one culture by another—and in *acculturation*—immigrants' assimilation of the patterns of a new culture. The very great number of different cultures is itself one of the strongest arguments for the influence of culture on behavior (Firth, 1958).

Any relatively stable group is also a breeding population, which means that mating occurs more often among members of the group than between group members and outsiders. Eventually, such inbreeding causes members of the group to resemble each other more and more closely because they come to share more and more of the same genes. Moreover, as a result of such evolutionary mechanisms as natural selection and mutation, differences in gene frequencies arise between populations. This is the central biological meaning of race (Osborne, 1971): Various human groups have developed distinct genetic patterns that exhibit themselves in differences in skin

color, eye color, hair color and texture, and genetically based diseases such as sickle cell anemia.

One of the issues still facing modern social science is the extent to which observed *behavioral* differences among races can be attributed to differences among their gene pools. Most environmentalists have long argued that differences—excluding obvious physical and morphological ones—in behavior among groups can be largely if not entirely accounted for by longstanding environmental and cultural factors. At present this seems by far the most likely explanation.

THE DISPUTE OVER HEREDITY AND ENVIRONMENT

We come now to the most polemical and profound interplay between biology and sociology. As has been pointed out, sociology is concerned with *variations* in human social behavior. Some people are aggressive, some passive; some are successful, some unsuccessful; some are strong, some weak. What accounts for these differences? To what extent are they produced by differences in the physical and social environment—for example, by differences in family life, wealth, and education—and to what extent are they produced by differences in genetic inheritance?

We are just beginning to understand some of the basic outlines of the interplay between envi-

Figure 5.9   Biologists classify twins according to whether they arose from one fertilized egg (zygote) or two. Monozygotic twins (*right*), who are genetically identical, develop from the splitting of a single zygote and share the same chorion and placenta. Dizygotic twins develop when two egg cells are released from the ovaries at the same time and are fertilized by different sperm. Dizygotic twins (*left*) may be less like each other, physically and temperamentally, than they are like others of their siblings. As the drawing shows, before birth each has its own placenta and chorion. Whether there are one or two placentas in the afterbirth permits the two types of twins to be differentiated. (Adapted from L. B. Arey, 1954.)

ronment and heredity. Unfortunately, what has actually been determined or at least seems probable has also been greatly exaggerated and misinterpreted. Sociologists have been guilty of extreme and unfounded claims that environment determines everything. Biologists have been equally guilty of extreme reliance on genetic explanations.

Recently, misunderstanding has increased in the polemical dispute over genetic versus environmental explanations of interracial IQ differences. Following the suggestions of psychologist Arthur Jensen that blacks may be genetically endowed with slightly less intelligence than are whites, extreme charges of genetic inferiority of blacks have been made. Conversely, exaggerated denunciations of IQ tests have been made in reaction to Jensen—claims that the environments in which the children of blacks, chicanos, and anglos are reared are so different that their intelligence cannot be measured by the same tests. At present it can be said that there is no practical or reliable way for Jensen or anyone else to compare intelligence across racial boundaries or to confirm the presence or absence of genetic differences underlying interracial differences in measured intelligence. Furthermore, as is pointed out in Chapter 13, it seems plausible that the IQ differences that concerned Jensen may be produced by nutritional differences, so that nothing may be left for genetic factors to explain.

Twin Studies

Racial questions aside, biologists have amassed quite compelling evidence that *within* populations (both black and white) some quite basic characteristics are substantially inherited. They have done this by patiently searching out sets of identical twins for study, especially identical twins who have been reared apart.

Human twins are of two kinds. Dizygotic (DZ) twins occur in about two-thirds of all twin births. They result from two ova being fertilized at the same time. DZ twins are sometimes called fraternal twins because they are no more genetically similar than are ordinary siblings—on the average they are about fifty-percent genetically similar;

they may be of the same or different sexes. Identical twins—monozygotic (MZ) twins—are produced when a single fertilized ovum splits. They are therefore genetically identical—they look alike, are of the same sex, and have the same eye color and blood type; only MZ twins can give one another successful skin transplants. The genetic inheritance of identical twins is the same, and if such twins can be found who have been reared in quite different environments, it becomes possible to compare the role of environment with that of heredity.

Differences between MZ twins should reflect environmental differences alone. Studies of MZ twins reared together have found their IQ scores to be very highly correlated (+.87). If environment played no role, the correlation should be as close to perfect as the reliability of the tests would permit (or about +.95); if heredity played no role, the correlation should be only as high as the effects of being reared in the same environment would predict, which is about +.23 for unrelated children reared together. When identical MZ twins are reared in quite different environments (having been split up for adoption or placement with relatives) the correlation between their IQ scores remains extremely high (+.75). That the correlation is lower than it is when MZ twins are raised together suggests that environment does influence IQ. But that it remains so high suggests that heredity plays a very powerful role—heredity is estimated to explain at least half of the variance between individual scores (Eckland, 1967). Similarly, siblings should display considerable correlation of IQ scores (+.50) if only genetic factors were operating and mating patterns were random, and only then if the tests were perfectly reliable. Studies find their IQ scores correlated at slightly more than the expected level under a random mating model (+.55), indicating a small effect due either to shared family environment or to parents themselves sharing some of the same genes (assortative mating for intelligence leads to higher genetic parent-child and sibling correlations, as we shall see later in the chapter). In any case, there is a very large effect because of common parentage. Table 5.1 summarizes available

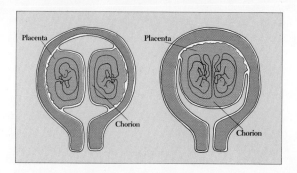

Table 5.1 Correlations for Intellectual Ability: Obtained and Theoretical Values

Correlations Between	Number of Studies	Obtained Median	Theoretical Value[*]
Unrelated persons			
Children reared apart	4	−.01	.00
Foster parent and child	3	+.20	.00
Children reared together	5	+.24	.00
Collaterals			
Second cousins	1	+.16	+ .14
First cousins	3	+.26	+ .18
Uncle (or aunt) and nephew (or niece)	1	+.34	+ .31
Siblings, reared apart	3	+.47	+ .52
Siblings, reared together	36	+.55	+ .52
Dizygotic twins, different sex	9	+.49	+ .50
Dizygotic twins, same sex	11	+.56	+ .54
Monozygotic twins, reared apart	4	+.75	+1.00
Monozygotic twins, reared together	14	+.87	+1.00
Direct Line			
Grandparent and grandchild	3	+.27	+ .31
Parent (as adult) and child	13	+.50	+ .49
Parent (as child) and child	1	+.56	+ .49

[*] Value one would expect if genetic factors alone were operating.

Source: A. R. Jensen, "How Much Can We Boost IQ and Scholastic Achievement?" *Harvard Educational Review* (Winter, 1969).

findings on IQ correlations according to various degrees of relatedness and under different environmental conditions. The obtained values come quite close to the genetically expected values and therefore indicate that intelligence—or whatever it is that IQ tests measure—is considerably determined by genetic factors.

Table 5.2 summarizes studies on a variety of other psychological traits comparing MZ and DZ twins. Some are reported in terms of *concordance rates.* A concordance rate shows the percentage of pairs having the trait in common. Thus, for 86 percent of the MZ twins, if one was judged schizophrenic, so was the other. Among DZ twins this match-up occurred only 15 percent of the time. These studies show that in all comparisons MZ twins, who have identical genetic make-ups, are much more similar to each other than are DZ twins, who have only about a fifty-percent genetic similarity.

Another source of evidence on the role of genetics is to compare the similarities between adoptive parents and adopted children and the similarities between the actual parents and

adopted children. One such study (Skodak and Skeels, 1949) found that there was only a very low correlation between the IQ of adoptive mothers and adopted children but that the correlation between the IQ of the real mother—who had not influenced the child's environment—and the adopted child was approximately the same as that normally found between mothers and children.

These studies suggest that for some human traits, especially intelligence, genetic factors play a potent role. This poses an extremely odd situation. The more uniform the environment—that is, the more we are able to give all children an equal chance in life—the greater will be the role of genetics in their intellectual development and, presumably, in their success in life. For if we ever could make environmental conditions uniform, only genetic factors would be left to cause individual variations. On the other hand, the harsher and more unequal the environment, the smaller the role of genetic factors. Richard Herrnstein (1971) has suggested that we are in the process of moving from a society in which inequality is fixed by the environmental advantages of birth to one

Table 5.2   Behavioral Traits of Monozygotic (MZ) and Dizygotic (DZ) Twins

Trait	Investigator[*]	Intrapair Concordance Rate		Intrapair Correlation Coefficient	
		MZ	DZ	MZ	DZ
Schizophrenia	Kallman (1953)	86%	15%	—	—
Manic-depressive psychosis	Kallman (1953)	93	24	—	—
Psychopathic personality	Slater (1953)	25	14	—	—
Alcoholism	Kaij (1960)	65	30	—	—
Male homosexuality	Kallman (1953)	98	12	—	—
Hysteria	Stumpfl (1936)	33	0	—	—
Suicide	Kallman (1953)	6	0	—	—
Intelligence	Newman et al. (1937)	—	—	.88	.63
Motor skill	McNemar (1933)	—	—	.79	.43
Vocational interests	Carter (1932)	—	—	.50	.28
Extraversion-introversion	Gottesman (1963)	—	—	.55	.08
Depression	Gottesman (1963)	—	—	.47	.07
Neuroticism	Eysenck & Prell (1951)	—	—	.85	.22

[*] See bibliography for full references.

in which inequality is fixed by the genetic advantages of birth. These matters are considered more fully in Unit V.

Having established evidence for the role of heredity in human affairs, we must now introduce some important qualifications. We have suggested above that the heritability of a trait such as IQ is always specific to the population under investigation. The degree to which heredity accounts for IQ depends upon how greatly the environment hinders or permits inheritance to be fulfilled.

Genes alone do not directly produce anything, at least not anything observable. Genes merely operate upon the physiological and biochemical processes that, along with the environment, determine behavior. Thus, heredity modifies the growth and continued development of the living organism and so limits what it can do. It only fixes what the organism can do in the sense that it determines a *norm of reaction*, or sets limits for each individual. The *phenotype* (the observed characteristic or behavior) is always the product of the *genotype* (the population gene pool for that particular trait) and environment, working together.

This bare assertion does not, perhaps, move us very far toward an understanding of how particular genetic factors interact with particular environmental ones to produce the results in terms of traits or behavior that we can and do observe. It may be more precise to say that sociologists are primarily interested in *polygenic* inheritance, that is, the heritability of traits such as intelligence that involve not a single gene but many genes in combination. These genes determine the potentialities of an organism, but the environment determines how much of these potentialities will be realized during development. Environment is thus a *threshold variable* that up to some critical point may suppress the development of genetically based potentialities and that, past that point, may have little influence on precisely how and how far those genetic potentialities will develop (Lerner, 1968). Genetics, environment, and culture all impose limits on the development of human potentialities and therefore on the development of society itself. At this time we do not know precisely where or what these limits are or how the limits imposed by one factor interact with and either reinforce or mitigate the limits that are imposed by other factors.

The Effects of Assortative Mating

Although no child is a perfect copy of another, like does tend to beget like. This fact of life has both negative and positive consequences. A child obtains precisely half of his genes from each parent, and even though there is a *regression toward the mean* of the adult population, the child is more likely to resemble its biological parents than to resemble some adult selected at random. Moreover, the more either inbreeding or *assortative mating*—the tendency of like to marry like—occurs, the more closely the child will resemble his parents.

These points can be illustrated by looking at the manner in which intelligence is distributed in the general population. No matter how it might be defined or measured, intelligence is a polygenic trait; many genes are involved in its determination. Bright parents may have some children who are brighter than they are, some who are equally bright, and some who are well below the population mean. Children born to bright parents, however, will tend to fall somewhere between the parents' level and the population mean; in other words, they will generally be brighter than the average but not quite as bright as their parents. Just how closely they will actually resemble their parents depends upon how closely the parents resemble each other.

Under conditions of *random mating*, on the other hand, the imperfect fit between the distribution of intelligence in a given generation of young people and the distribution in their parents' generation can be a dynamic social force. Despite the aspirations of bright middle-class parents for their children, some of the latter will be downwardly mobile because they cannot meet the society's standards of achievement. Conversely, some of the children of less intelligent lower-class parents will be exceptionally bright and, if given the opportunity, will advance well above their parents' social status (Waller, 1971).

The regression toward the mean operates in two directions: parents with below-average intelligence may have more intelligent, even brilliant, children, and above-average parents may have below-average children. In both cases, difficult problems in transgenerational communication and in the allocation of status may arise.

The long-range consequences of assortative mating for intelligence and rising genetic parent-child correlations are not well understood either by geneticists or sociologists. Some students of the problem argue, however, that societies that have both institutionalized mass testing programs and a highly stratified educational system—one that sorts and selects students on the basis of performance—are thereby encouraging the development of a genetically based class structure.

The purpose of this chapter has been to demonstrate that human beings are not the product of environment alone. Because sociology is concerned primarily with the effects of the social and cultural environment, it seems to be vital to gain some overview of the way in which biology sets certain limits and potentials for the environment. We turn now to how society and culture develop and shape this human biological potential.

SUGGESTED READINGS

Dimond, Stuart J. *The Social Behavior of Animals.* New York: Harper & Row, 1970.

Eckland, Bruce K. "Genetics and Sociology: A Reconsideration," *American Sociological Review,* 32 (1967), 173–194.

Lerner, I. Michael. *Heredity, Evolution and Society.* San Francisco: Freeman, 1968.

Mazur, Allan, and Leon S. Robertson. *Biology and Social Behavior.* New York: Free Press, 1972.

Chapter 6 The Cultural Basis of Society: Childhood Socialization

FROM TIME TO TIME the media report tragic cases of children who are found after years of having been locked in attics, basements, or closets, or who have been in some other way imprisoned in solitary confinement by deranged parents or guardians. These *feral* children—the word literally means untamed—are of special importance to social science: They provide a basis for judging the role of learning in becoming human. Deprived of all but the most trivial and fleeting human contact, these extremely neglected children have only their genetic resources to draw upon in order to become human. When found, they bear only superficial signs of humanity. Frequently they are mistaken for mental defectives. Although some are in their late teens when they are found, they can merely grunt, are indifferent to their surroundings, make no effort to control bowel and bladder functions, and frequently spend their time rocking rhythmically back and forth on their heels. Attempts to treat these children have been just sufficiently successful to demonstrate that they are not mentally defective and that their condition is the result of isolation. Not one of these children has ever become normal, but those who lived long enough did show considerable ability to learn (Davis, 1940*a*; 1947; 1949).

SOCIALIZATION

What these tragic children show us is that *humans must learn to be human.* Biological and physiological factors set important limits and provide certain initial capacities. But to become a human being requires a social and cultural process of intensive interaction between the developing child and other people—a process filled with emotional, physical, and cognitive stimulation.

The process through which an infant learns to be human is called *socialization.* When an individual has become adequately human, we say he has been properly *socialized*—he has been made *social.* As was pointed out in Chapters 3 and 4, humanness is essentially a social product. The self arises only through interaction with others. We learn who and what we are, we become what we are, through interaction with others. Children

locked away in attics do not become human—they remain, at most, potentially human.

Yet it would be incorrect to restrict the idea of socialization to human development. We now know that many animals do not become competent adults of their species simply through maturation. To be an adequate lion, ape, or wolf requires more than instincts. To some extent, all infant animals have to learn; they develop their behavioral potentials according to the environmental circumstances they meet in life. To become a lion, ape, or wolf involves more than having the body of a lion, ape, or wolf. Each animal must also learn how to behave like one.

The investigation of socialization is a major concern in various sciences: here sociology overlaps with psychology and anthropology, and all these fields intersect with biology and the health sciences. A major task for the investigator of socialization is to separate the influences of *nature* from those of *nurture*—to distinguish between what is innate and what is learned. Another task is to explore and understand the interplay between nature and nurture in the development of children. For sociologists, perhaps the most important task is to determine which social factors influence child development and how and why these social factors are influential.

THE EFFECTS OF DEPRIVATION ON DEVELOPMENT

The major part of this chapter will report on what sociologists know or suspect about the social factors that influence childhood socialization. But before taking up this material, we will first review research on deprivation of social contact in order to demonstrate some differences between nature and nurture that have been found.

Isolation and Deprivation

Over the past several decades some of the most exciting and important work on deprivation has been done by Harry Harlow in his laboratory experiments with rhesus monkeys at the University of Wisconsin. In one classic study, Harlow separated the satisfaction of hunger provided by nurs-

Figure 6.1   These monkeys were raised apart from their mothers. When a strange object, a large toy bear, was placed in the cage, the monkeys having terry-cloth-covered surrogate mothers ran to them for comfort (*right*) but later became curious enough to venture out and explore the bear. Monkeys with only a wire mother surrogate to cling to (*left*) remained fearful of the bear. The "contact comfort" provided by terry-cloth mother surrogates evidently was important to the monkeys' development.

ing from the physical comfort and cuddling that a mother's attentive presence provides infants. Ordinarily, of course, both comfort and satisfaction of hunger occur simultaneously. Harlow began his experiments with a number of infant monkeys that he raised in isolation. These little monkeys were provided a surrogate mother made of wire mesh and equipped with a milk-providing nipple. Some of these infant monkeys were also given a second surrogate mother constructed of soft terry cloth, but without a nipple. When frightened by the experimenters, the little monkeys with both kinds of mothers ran to sit on the lap of the terry-cloth mother, not to the feeding but uncuddly wire mother. Furthermore, little monkeys who had terry-cloth mothers were better able to adjust when they were later brought into contact with other monkeys than were the monkeys raised only with wire mothers. Although none of these young monkeys made normal adjustments to others, those who had received at least minimal cuddling from sitting in the lap of a terry-cloth mother showed better adjustment (Harlow, 1962).

Later, Harlow (1965) raised three groups of infant monkeys in three different environments: some wholly in isolation; some isolated with their mothers (real, not dummies); and some isolated with several other infant monkeys. The wholly isolated monkeys grew up to be very abnormal and adjusted very poorly to later social contact. But those raised in isolation with their mothers

were also very abnormal. Those raised as a group without mothers adjusted most normally of all. Of course, infant monkeys do not need to depend upon mothers for food or protection in a laboratory, whereas motherless monkeys would die in the wild. Furthermore, laboratory monkeys did not need to be taught many of the behaviors required to survive jungle life. Probably the most important point of Harlow's studies is that the effects of social isolation—from mother or from peers—are irreversible. Normal behavior and personality never developed even after long periods of renewed social contact.

Deprivation and Child Development

A major reason for the profound effects of social isolation is that it results in greatly reduced levels of stimulation. Research shows that normal infant development requires a variety of auditory, visual, and tactile stimulation and that a high level of such stimulation in infancy speeds learning. For example, the development of visual perception is greatly influenced by deprivation. Philip Salapatek and William Kessen (1966) found that the rate of development of perception depends on the amount of visual stimulation the child receives and the extent of the child's interaction with these stimuli. Thus, a high level of stimulation in and of itself seems not to be enough. The infant's attention must be engaged, usually by the mother, who, as a source of continuing rewards (reinforcements), is best able to guide the infant's involve-

Figure 6.2   In an effort to compensate
for the deprivations that poor children suffer,
preschool programs have been initiated in the United
States that are concerned with children's social and
emotional development as well as with the
development of cognitive skills necessary for their
academic success. Such programs supply language
instruction and cultural experiences and attempt to
provide a supportive atmosphere in which
children can develop optimally. Head Start is an
example of such a program.

ment in stimuli (Palmer, 1969). It has also been found that infants learn early language skills best if mothers talk to them while facing them and holding or patting them (Kagan, 1967). Note that there is no reason why it must be the mother rather than the father (or any other person, for that matter) who interacts with the infant in this manner; ordinarily, however, it is the mother who acts as the source of reinforcement (see Chapters 17 and 18).

In any event, these findings suggest that differences between the ways parents provide stimulation to their infants and the amounts they provide may account for some of the differences in the rate of intellectual development of young children. Lower levels of cognitive development characterize children of the lower class and those from families with many children (Clausen, 1966). It may be that these children receive less stimulation; that is, their parents may direct their attention to stimuli less frequently than do parents of children in the middle or upper classes or parents who have only a small number of children with whom to interact.

Studies by Wayne Dennis show that IQ scores of children are proportional to the length of time they spend in foundling homes awaiting adoption. He studied orphaned and abandoned children in the Middle East and found that the longer children stayed in foundling homes (and were thus deprived of normal levels of stimulation), the lower their IQ scores. During their stay in the institution, children developed, on the average, at only *half* the normal rate—thus falling a year behind what should have been their normal mental age for each two years in the institution. Upon adoption they began to develop at the average rate—one year of mental age for each year of chronological age. Thus, the effects of deprivation seem cumulative—the longer the deprivation, the greater the loss, and the greater the deprivation, the greater the loss. The losses also seem to be permanent. They are at least very difficult to make up (Dennis, 1938; 1960).

Attempts at compensatory socialization and education thus often come too late. By the time children get to school, they may have suffered a

lag in development that is difficult to overcome. To counter early deprivation, efforts such as Head Start have aimed at reaching preschool children.

THEORIES OF SOCIALIZATION

Because socialization is the process of learning to be human, it is not surprising that the major micro theoretical traditions in socialization are all forms of learning theories (see Chapter 4). Yet there are many differences among these socialization theories in terms of emphasis and scope. Much current work is rooted in behaviorism—theories primarily focused on the mechanisms of learning. Other work follows the symbolic-interactionist tradition and focuses on the role aspects of learning—how, through interaction with others, people learn relatively complex chains of behavior, namely, general roles such as son, daughter, male, playmate, and the like. A third tradition has been concerned with developmental stages in socialization. The Swiss psychologist Jean Piaget and his followers have been concerned with mapping and

Figure 6.3 Burrhus Frederic Skinner is a psychologist of learning and a contemporary spokesman for behaviorism and for behavioral engineering in the design of societies. He has developed a strong position on the behavior of organisms, including human beings, in which he emphasizes the role of learning (especially reinforcement) and rejects hypotheses about the inner dynamics of personality development. He is the father of the teaching machine and programmed learning. He bases his work on the principle of operant conditioning, which he illustrated at one point in his career by teaching pigeons to play table tennis through reinforcing their correct responses with grains of corn. His pigeons have also played the piano and operated systems for guiding submarines and bombs. Animal researchers observe and measure behavior with his Operant Conditioning Apparatus, widely known as the "Skinner box." He has written a novel describing his vision of a behavioral utopia—*Walden Two* (1948)—as well as such scientific works as *Science and Human Behavior* (1953), *Verbal Behavior* (1957), *Contingencies of Reinforcement: A Theoretical Analysis* (1969), and *Beyond Freedom and Dignity* (1971). Skinner is Edgar Pierce Professor of Psychology at Harvard University.

understanding cognitive stages of development. Freud was concerned with stages of emotional development; his work formed the basis for a fourth tradition of study, continued by his followers. Before actually discussing specific research in childhood socialization, one must gain a basic understanding of these theoretical positions.

Behavioral Learning Theories and Socialization

As was pointed out in Chapter 5, humans do appear to be born with some innate (inherited) traits. For example, all normal babies begin to babble at about four months, even the children of deaf persons who communicate only by sign language (Lenneberg, 1969). Normal babies also seem naturally to nuzzle in search of the nipple (Gunther, 1961). But nuzzling is not nursing, and most babies take several days of aided trial and error to learn to nurse. Nor is babbling speaking; the children of the deaf do not learn to speak and, in fact, cease to babble if they are not exposed to persons who speak. Whatever innate behaviors humans possess must be modified and developed by learning.

Behavioral learning theories, as was pointed out in Chapter 4, are based upon principles of conditioning and reinforcement. People learn what they are *reinforced* (or rewarded) for doing. Behavior that is reinforced tends to be repeated; behavior that is not reinforced tends not to be repeated. A little boy, upon seeing his first dog, may run to his mother, who then comforts and pats him to soothe his fears. This treatment increases the likelihood that he will run to his mother the next time he sees a dog because the comfort he received the first time reinforced this behavior. Another child who, upon seeing his first dog, approaches it and gets his hand licked is likely to approach other dogs in the future because getting his hand licked reinforced the approaching behavior.

Learning theorists such as B. F. Skinner believe that everything a person does is behavior learned through the process of reinforcement. Because parents often are unaware of reinforcement principles, they may foster in children the very behavior they wish to discourage. Therefore, learning theorists counsel very careful examination of child-rearing techniques to determine which actions reinforce which behaviors.

Rewards Versus Punishments Behavioral learning studies have proved that humans and animals learn efficiently and rapidly more as a result of rewards than of punishments (Ferster and Skinner, 1957). This phenomenon of learning seems critical to the possibility of instituting more effective child-rearing practices. It has been found that when a punishment is removed, frequently an unwanted behavior reappears. Thus, to remain effective, punishment—and a punisher—must be continually at hand. But behavior based on rewards does not require constant reward in order for it to continue to occur. That the behavior is *sometimes* rewarded turns out to be sufficient. In fact, it has been determined that an *intermittent reinforcement schedule*—rewarding the behavior only some of the time—produces higher levels of performance than does constant rewarding. Therefore, a person who gives rewards need not always be present to maintain a desired behavior. It is effective to reward desired behavior but not to reward it each time it occurs (Skinner, 1971).

Some studies seem to indicate that the preferred administration of rewards and punishments depends upon the learning context and type of behavior that one wants to elicit. In studying the learning of morals and ethics, Martin L. Hoffman and Herbert D. Saltzstein (1967) found that occasional punishment was beneficial. Their study showed that moral development is most advanced in children whose parents reserve the *right* to punish them, although they *rarely* do so.

Forgetting An important connection between learning theory and socialization involves *unlearning*—forgetting or extinguishing—responses. The experience of forgetting is one with which we are all familiar. But an important rule to remember is that people are less likely to forget what happened *first* in a chain of events. Thus, it is important that children get off on the right foot in new situations because what happens first is

Figure 6.4   (*Top*) Positive reinforcement. Permitting a child to spend a period of time watching television, an activity he enjoys, as a consequence of his having performed a desired behavior—say, picking up his toys—serves to reinforce the behavior of picking up toys. (*Middle*) Punishment. By stopping the child from watching his favorite program (a pleasurable activity) as a consequence of his having performed an undesirable behavior—say, hitting his sister—the mother hopes to discourage future performance of the undesirable behavior. (*Bottom*) Negative reinforcement. If the mother tells the child that an unpleasant condition (lack of television) will be lifted upon performance of a desired behavior—say, drawing a picture for his sister as a kind of apology for having hit her—and the boy performs the behavior, the removal of the unpleasant condition may serve to reinforce the desired behavior of apologizing.

very likely to be remembered. The child who was licked by his first dog will put up with a number of unsuccessful encounters in search of another friendly dog. The child who ran and was comforted will probably remain fearful even through supervised encounters with friendly dogs.

Often, when a particular response goes unrewarded for a very long time, the individual ceases to make that response. The response is thus *extinguished.* However, the extinction of responses cannot always be accomplished by removal of the reinforcement (or reward) for the response. An important finding is that if a person is emotionally involved in a learning situation, it is hard to extinguish his learned behavior (Bandura, 1969). Because emotion is so frequently involved in early childhood learning, early learning tends to be very resistant to later change.

Imitation   A second critical form of learning is modeling, or imitation. Imitation is characteristic of the socialization of humans and of many animals—the young act the way they see (or have seen) another person or animal act in a similar situation. Imitation is especially critical for language learning. Children repeat words and phrases back to the person they are copying until finally they are able to approximate the behavior of their model ("Say Daddy"—"Da"; "Daddy"—"Dahda").

Reinforcement often plays a critical role in imitative learning. Albert Bandura and Richard Walters (1963) have shown that children are likely to imitate behavior that they have seen a model being rewarded for or to imitate a model who is performing an act for which they themselves have previously been rewarded (see Figure 6.5). Mothers frequently taste the food children are resisting and express huge, lip-smacking pleasure over the taste in order to convince children that eating the food will actually be rewarding.

One of the classic studies of the role of imitation in socialization (Sears, Maccoby, and Levin, 1957) found that parents' nonaggressive responses to their children's aggressive behavior tended to diminish aggressive behavior among children, whereas parents' aggressive responses increased

Figure 6.5   The role of reinforcement in imitative learning is exemplified in the photos below. This young boy has just seen a film in which a model had been praised for exhibiting aggressive behavior toward the Bobo doll. When given the opportunity to interact with a similar doll, the boy imitated the complex set of behaviors he had seen with obvious vigor. According to Albert Bandura, the boy was behaving as if he himself had earlier experienced the reinforcement of praise.

children's aggressive behavior. Punishing aggression can itself be an act of aggression (for example, spanking) and provides a model for aggression. Because parents are much more powerful than are children, their aggression against children gets results (in the short run) but demonstrates to children that aggressive behavior works (because it is rewarded).

It seems that children will imitate even if they are not immediately reinforced for doing so. This is especially common in role play, a major concern of symbolic interactionists.

Symbolic Interactionism and Socialization

Children's dramatic play—when they pretend to be mother or father or store clerk—illustrates that children can perform long sequences of behavior that they have observed others perform. But there is more to this behavior than simple imitation. This kind of role playing is a critical part of successful socialization. Through such play children begin not only to prepare themselves for playing such roles in their adult lives but also to discover a great deal about themselves and the nature of social relationships. To some extent, by playing mother or father, a child comes to better understand her or his parents, as well as the nature of the parent-child role relationship.

Looking-Glass Self   Role play and role learning are major topics of Unit IV. But a few points that bear most directly on childhood socialization can be pointed out now. A critical feature of role learning is putting oneself in another's shoes so that one may look at oneself from the other's point of view. Charles Horton Cooley spoke of this feature of role learning as developing a *looking-glass self*. Thus, humans learn to develop a sense of rightness or wrongness about their behavior on the basis of their social relationships: they learn to regard themselves from the perspective of what George Herbert Mead called the *generalized other* (see Chapter 4 and Chapter 8 for an extended discussion of these concepts). What the symbolic interactionists assert is that conscience arises only in connection with our perceptions of what others expect of us. Such perceptions are

Figure 6.6 Jean Piaget. For almost half a century Jean Piaget has studied the intellectual development of children. On the basis of his painstaking observations of children performing various cognitive tasks, he has constructed a theory of the nature of intelligence and the stages of intellectual growth.

greatly enhanced by considerable role play. Symbolic interactionists emphasize that people behave as they do to a large extent because of the particular role they occupy at a given moment. A person will respond differently to the same situation, depending on whether he regards it from the role of father, husband, employee, or policeman.

Because of their emphasis on role behavior, symbolic interactionists pay considerable attention to how children develop role-playing abilities; they also attend to the effects that certain kinds of role playing have on child development. To this extent, their concerns coincide with those of the learning theorists, who also view imitation as an important feature of childhood socialization. From both these perspectives, it appears critical that children have appropriate behavioral models for important roles they eventually will play. Those who are serving as models for children bear an important responsibility. If they are poor models of such roles as parent, friend, or teacher, children who learn about these roles by imitating them may themselves become poor parents, friends, or teachers.

Sex Roles Presently, a major concern about role models is concentrated on sex roles. Efforts to raise the status of women by altering their characteristic roles through modeling are frustrated because of the shortage of high-occupational-status role models of women. Because there remains a superabundance of traditionally feminine role models (see Chapters 17 and 28), little girls continue mainly to imitate the role of housewife (that of mother and cook) and such traditional occupational roles as nurse and schoolteacher. Similarly, little boys during play treat little girls as subordinates because the models of women most available to them remain the subordinate, passive, traditionally feminine ones. Thus, children are still modeling themselves on the basis of traditional relations between the sexes. Little girls leave the imitation of such roles as doctor, astronaut, or fireman to little boys because these are not observable female roles.

At the same time there is a growing concern regarding the lack of male role models for little boys. It is only recently that most males have begun to grow up almost wholly in the company of adult women. In the past, little boys at an early age began to follow their fathers around the shop or the farm and to imitate adult male roles. But today, especially in the suburbs, little boys regularly see few men—all of them are away working. Some social scientists have begun to wonder what kinds of males will result from little boys who grow up without much contact with adult-male role models. As yet there is little information to go on, but because role play is critical to socialization of the young, it is generally expected that we will soon see some important consequences.

Piaget's Cognitive Stages

So far, little attention has been given to maturation—simple, age-linked physical development—in the socialization process. Neither behavioral learning theorists nor symbolic interactionists place major emphasis on maturation. Yet it is clear that maturation does, to some extent, determine when certain types of learning can occur. The work of Arnold Gesell and his associates on motor development shows that some kinds of skills are beyond children of certain ages; even practice will not permit children to master these skills earlier than other children of the same age who receive no practice (Gesell and Ilg, 1943). Certain kinds of coordination and conceptual abilities simply take time to develop.

Maturational factors limit the kind and speed of socialization. If social scientists can learn in detail about the maturational processes affecting human socialization, people can more intelligently judge how best to socialize children. Jean Piaget has devoted a long and illustrious career to this learning. He began with intensive observation of his own children, and from his tentative conclusions about their development he began to build a theory about the maturational stages in human cognitive development. Since then, many others have taken up his ideas, and considerable research has been done to test his constructs. In contrast to most behavioral learning theorists, who tend to treat learning as a steadily cumulative bit-by-bit process, Piaget postulates a series of cognitive

Figure 6.7   Piaget's four stages of cognitive development. The child in the sensorimotor stage (*top*) manipulates objects without understanding their function or the basis for his actions. He experiences the toy airplane in terms of the actions he performs with it, such as pushing and sucking; he does not know that "airplanes fly." The preoperational child (*second from top*) develops mental representations of people, objects, and events and begins to learn language. He now understands that an airplane flies. The concrete-operational child (*bottom left*) can categorize objects and events and mentally manipulate the categories. He can coordinate his thinking about concrete characteristics of objects and can therefore assemble the parts of a model airplane into a whole. The formal-operational person (*bottom right*) can think hypothetically and consider alternative hypotheses for a given event. Adult thought is formal-operational. The person shown here is using his understanding of the functioning of an airplane to design a new type.

stages that organize and determine learning. He also postulates sudden leaps from one stage to the next when the child is old enough and confronts a genuinely new stimulus. According to Piaget, human cognitive development passes through four stages: the *sensorimotor stage;* the *preoperational stage;* the *concrete-operational stage;* and the *formal-operational stage.*

The Sensorimotor Stage   This stage exists prior to children's acquisition of symbolic language. During this period, which lasts about the first eighteen months of life, children practice perfecting their contact with the objects that surround them. They adapt their basic reflex mechanisms so that they can interact with these objects. Thus, the intelligence of infants is displayed in their actions. When a one-year-old wants a toy that is out of reach resting on his blanket, he pulls the blanket toward him to get the object. This is a *scheme of action,* a general response used to solve a variety of problems. The infant acts out many of these schemes: for example, bouncing in his crib in order to make a toy attached to his crib move.

Two basic principles of Piaget's theory are *assimilation* (the incorporation of a new object into an existing scheme) and *accommodation* (the alteration of old strategies and schemes or the making of new ones in order to include new objects or experiences and to solve unfamiliar problems). Flexibility of thought is thus the key to Piaget's view of intelligence.

The Preoperational Stage   The child in the preoperational stage (eighteen months to about seven years) encounters reality on a new level, the representational level. During this period, the action schemes the child developed as an infant become internalized and consequently are available as the vehicle for representational thought. The child also demonstrates *egocentrism* early in this period; that is, he does not make an adequate distinction between his own perceptions, thoughts, and feelings and those of others. He does not realize there are points of view different from his own, so he cannot take other people's points of view into consideration. In one classic study, Jean

Piaget and Edith Meyer-Taylor (1962) presented children with a clay model of a mountain range. The children were asked to describe what it looked like from their own position and then to describe what it would look like to someone taking various other positions around the clay model. Strikingly, children at the early preoperational stage of development recognized no difference between the positions; they described all the viewpoints of the mountain range in exactly the same way—as they themselves saw it.

Two features of children's activities during the preoperational period reflect the shift from action to representation. The children begin to imitate the actions of others (and even the actions of objects around them), and they begin to use language (first symbols, then concepts). Although a three-year-old uses symbols, his or her thought is not usually organized into concepts and rules. This process is completed during the stage of *concrete operations*, which we shall now discuss.

Stage of Concrete Operations Children from about the age of seven to twelve years are distinguished from those at the preoperational stage because of several operations they can perform that the younger ones cannot. Children at this stage are able to *mentally represent a series of actions*. They also have an understanding of the operation of *conservation;* that is, they recognize that liquids and solids can be transformed in shape without changing their volume or mass. Piaget's most famous clinical experiment demonstrates that the typical five-year-old does not believe a quantity of water remains constant (is conserved) despite changes in the form of the container that encloses it. A seven-year-old will insist that both containers hold the same amount of water, saying, "They are the same because you can put the water back in the other glass, and then the height will be the same." The child is aware of the reverse operation that will restore the original situation.

The concrete-operational child has also mastered the operation of *class inclusion*. If a five-year-old (preoperational) child is shown eight yellow candies and four brown candies and is asked, "Are there more yellow candies or more can-

dies?" he or she is likely to reply, "More yellow candies." Piaget says that the preoperational child cannot reason about a part of the whole and the whole itself simultaneously, whereas the concrete-operational child can.

A fourth characteristic that distinguishes preoperational children from those at the stage of concrete operations involves *serialization*—the ability to arrange objects in order according to some quantified dimension such as weight or size. This ability is critical for understanding the relation of numbers to one another and therefore necessary to the learning of arithmetic.

Stage of Formal Operations At about age twelve, a child's thinking moves into the stage of formal operations. Characteristic of this stage is the preoccupation with *thought*. During this period, children no longer deal with the raw reality of data but with assertions or statements—propositions—that contain these data. In this stage, the child is capable of considering all the possible ways a particular problem might be solved and the possible forms a particular solution might assume. Thinking becomes self-consciously deductive. Also, operations are organized into higher-order operations—ways of using abstract rules to solve whole classes of problems.

Piaget identifies two substages in the period of development of formal operations. In the first (age twelve to age thirteen or fourteen), adolescents learn how to define the relevant variables in a problem and to formulate a general hypothesis, but they cannot set up an exhaustive method of proof. In the final substage (age fourteen or fifteen onward), they can set up an exhaustive method of proof by laying out all the possible variables and then varying a single factor at a time while excluding the other variables or holding them constant (Inhelder and Piaget, 1958).

It is in the periods of concrete and formal thought that Piaget accords a special place to the role of maturational factors. Piaget insists that children cannot be taught formal logic or formal cognitive techniques until they have acquired the necessary mental structures. Although the exact ages at which a child traverses these stages varies

Figure 6.8 Freud's psychosexual stages. According to Freud, an individual's development optimally passes through these stages rather smoothly, and the adult personality incorporates features from all stages. Neuroses can develop as a result of fixation at any of the pregenital stages; for example, an obsessive-compulsive neurosis results from fixation at the anal stage. Freud's account of development is clearer with respect to males than to females.

AGE	STAGE	ASPECTS OF DEVELOPMENT
Birth to about one year	Oral stage	Pleasure centers around the mouth—eating, sucking, spitting, biting, chewing. Adults who fixate at this level may displace their oral impulses by being gullible, possessive, sarcastic, or argumentative.
One year to three years	Anal stage	Pleasure centers around the retention and expulsion of feces; type of toilet training can affect the child's personality—depending on whether the training is too strict or too permissive, the child may become (as an adult) obstinate and stingy, or destructive and messy, or creative and productive.
Three years to six years	Phallic stage	The child discovers and derives pleasure from his genitals; the Oedipal conflict and castration anxiety occur.
Six years to about eleven years	Latency period	To relieve the anxiety stemming from the Oedipal conflict, the child represses his desire for his opposite-sexed parent and identifies with his like-sexed parent, repressing all erotic impulses toward the opposite sex.
Adolescence	Genital stage	Egocentric and incestuous love is replaced by heterosexual love and sexuality; the adolescent prepares for adulthood by channeling his drives into group activities and preparation for work and marriage.

from child to child and from culture to culture, Piaget insists that this sequence of stages is universal and invariant in children.

Freudian Theory

Sigmund Freud also insisted upon stages in child development. But for Freud and his followers these stages mark the development of emotional life, of personality, and of a sense of self in relation to other persons.

Stages of Development Freud was the first psychological theorist to emphasize the developmental aspects of personality and, in particular, to stress the decisive role of infancy and childhood in determining a person's basic personality struc-

ture. Freud believed that a child goes through a series of qualitatively different stages during the first five years of life. The three early stages, collectively called the *pregenital stage*, are the *oral*, the *anal*, and the *phallic*. Each of these stages is organized around a different zone of gratification in the body. Personality development involves the release of sexual energy progressively through the oral, anal, and phallic zones. However, *fixation* may block this progression and hamper normal development. Fixation can occur when either excess pleasure or frustration is associated with a particular zone.

The first source of an infant's gratification is derived from the mouth by eating—more specifically, by sucking. When teeth develop, the mouth is used for biting and chewing. These two modes

Figure 6.9   Sigmund Freud (1856–1939) formulated a theory of the inner dynamics of personality development and socialization. This psychoanalytic theory was among the first to postulate psychological causes for psychological disorders. Freud's theory, perhaps psychology's most complex and extensive theoretical undertaking, has influenced most current conceptions of human behavior and development. The impact of Freud's theory owes much to his great writing abilities; among his many books are *Interpretation of Dreams* (1900), *Totem and Taboo* (1912), *The Ego and the Id* (1923), *Civilization and Its Discontents* (1930), *General Introduction to Psychoanalysis* (1935), and *Moses and Monotheism* (1939).

of oral activity, ingestion of food and biting, are prototypes for character traits that develop later.

When toilet training begins (usually during the second year), children have their first experience with the external regulation of an instinctual impulse. Freud speculated that the particular method of toilet training used by parents and their feelings concerning elimination have far-reaching effects upon a child's development. If parents are very strict and repressive in their methods, children may hold back their feces in defiance of them and become constipated. Freud believed that if this mode generalizes to other forms of behavior, children may develop *retentive* characters; they will become obstinate and stingy. Or, in reaction to repressive toilet-training measures, children may vent their rage by expelling their feces at inappropriate times.

During the phallic stage of development, which lasts from about age three to age six, sexual and aggressive feelings associated with the functioning of the genital organs come into focus. The pleasures of masturbation and the fantasy life of the child that accompanies autoerotic activity set the stage for the appearance of the *Oedipus* (or *Electra*) *complex*. (The complex takes its name from the Greek king in Sophocles' tragedy who killed his father and married his mother. Electra was Oedipus' daughter.) Briefly, this complex consists of sexual attraction to the parent of the opposite sex and hostility for the parent of the same sex.

A period of latency follows (roughly from age eight until adolescence), during which the dynamics of the personality become more or less stabilized. Then, with the advent of adolescence, a new stage of development, the *genital stage*, upsets this stability; as the normal adolescent moves into adulthood, the stability returns.

Although Freud differentiated these stages of personality development and saw them as qualitatively distinct, he did not assume that there were any sharp breaks or abrupt transitions in passing from one stage to another. He believed that the final organization of personality represents contributions from all the stages. For many years Freud's stage theory was very influential in psychology and psychiatry. But it has never attracted much interest among sociologists, who have criticized it as both too vague and too narrow in its cultural base.

Identification   For sociologists, one central and influential aspect of Freudian theory is its emphasis on the importance of *identification* in childhood learning and thus in socialization (McCandless, 1967). Generally, identification takes place when a child chooses an adult or adults as behavioral models and attempts to imitate their behavior; these are adults whose lives the child wishes and dreams himself to be living. In Freudian theory, full identification with the parent of the same sex takes place when the *Oedipus* (or *Electra*) *conflict* has been resolved, that is, when a child's incestuous wishes toward the parent of the opposite sex are repressed and the child, in fantasy, identifies with the parent of the same sex, thus vicariously enjoying this parent's relationship with the parent of the opposite sex.

According to Freud, one comes to identify with the parent one initially fears and mistrusts most. In another hypothesis, based on social-learning theory, children are said to identify with the parent they see as the most rewarding figure. A third hypothesis, formulated by the sociologist Talcott Parsons, argues that the child identifies with the parent whom he or she sees as the most powerful figure (Parsons, 1955).

A study of these three alternative hypotheses of identification (the most feared parent, the most rewarding parent, the most powerful parent) has found that the power hypothesis best describes identification in boys and girls in the United States (Mussen and Distler, 1959; Mussen and Rutherford, 1963). In a similar vein, John W. M. Whiting, in examining cross-cultural data, proposed that a child identifies with his most successful rival for resources that he or she wants but cannot control (the *status-envy hypothesis*). He classified a number of cultures according to the likelihood that in those cultures a father will be nurtured by the mother, thus denying the son and arousing his envy of his father. Father identification should be greatest where the father is most favored and nurtured within the family. Whiting found, as he had predicted, that in *nuclear families* (a father, one wife, and children living together) father identification among sons is highest; in *extended* households where grandparents and other adults live with the nuclear group it is next highest; in *polygynous* families in which several wives and their children live under the same roof with the father it was next highest. The least father identification occurs in polygynous families where each wife lives with her children in a separate house and the father only visits (Whiting, 1959).

This review of socialization theories has necessarily been abbreviated; only key concepts and very major points have been presented. Furthermore, as pointed out at the beginning of this section, these are micro-level theories. Micro theories cannot provide a complete explanation of any phenomenon. Each micro theory must be embedded in a macro-level theory. Macro theories drawn from *functionalism* and from *conflict theory* have much to say about why children are socialized in various ways and about the consequences of each mode of socialization for individuals and for societies as a whole. Elements of such theories arise in the next section. However, a complete explication of major macro theories bearing on socialization would be too awkward for this chapter because these theories focus on such other complex social factors in identification as the family, the stratification system, education, population, politics, and religion. These aspects of socialization are treated in the context of macro theories in subsequent chapters. It is enough here to point out that functionalists tend to examine socialization in order to see the ways it serves (or impedes) the effective functioning of societies as systems, whereas conflict theorists try to see what class interests are being served by various patterns of socialization.

THE SOCIOLOGICAL STUDY OF SOCIALIZATION

Early in this chapter it was pointed out that the study of socialization intersects a number of fields. This fact is clearly reflected in the research on socialization, which has been conducted by soci-

ologists, psychologists, anthropologists, educators, pediatricians, nutritionists, and many other professionals. In consequence, the research lacks an organizing theory or even a systematic confrontation of opposing theories. Similarly, the topics chosen for study have been scattered, and many obvious questions have not been pursued.

Socialization, however, is one of the few areas of social science where frequent attempts have been made to conduct systematic cross-cultural studies, and several major reviews have tried to collect these findings and summarize the diverse research (Goslin, 1969; Zigler and Child, 1969; Stevenson *et al.*, 1963). Rather than summarize the summaries, it will be best to concentrate on several important topics and several recent and influential research studies. This material will give you better insight into the area. Seven studies will be reported. They fit into the four general kinds of studies usually done on socialization, as shown in Figure 6.10. Two studies of each of the three types AB, BC, and AC and one type of ABC follow.

Study I   A——▶B

Kohn (1969): *Social-Class Differences in Parental Values (A) and Child-Rearing Methods (B).* Do parents of different social classes (see Unit V) hold different values about what kind of child they would like theirs to be? If so, do these different preferences influence how they behave toward their children? These were the issues assessed by Melvin Kohn in a study based on intensive interviews with 200 white-collar and 200 blue-collar families with fifth-grade children, randomly selected in Washington, D.C.

From prior research, Kohn had developed a list of seventeen characteristics desirable in children of age ten to eleven (Kohn, 1969). He asked his sample of parents to choose the three they felt most desirable in their boy or girl. Although parents from each class agreed on many things, white-collar parents gave a higher priority to values that reflect individual expression and good interpersonal relations: happiness, curiosity, consideration, self-control. Blue-collar parents gave higher priority to behavioral conformity: obedience and neatness. Leonard Pearlin then con-

Figure 6.10   Chart of the seven studies of socialization that conclude this chapter.

		A **GENERAL SOCIAL FACTORS** *(such as social class, family size, stage of economic development)*	B **CHARACTERISTICS OF THE INDIVIDUAL PARENT** *(such as the behavior of mother or father, the child-rearing methods used)*	C **THE CHILD'S BEHAVIOR OR PERSONALITY**
A→B STUDIES	1	Social class influences	on parental values and child-rearing methods *(Kohn, 1969)*	
	2	The effects of family size	on child-rearing methods *(Elder and Bowerman, 1963)*	
B→C STUDIES	3		The effects of child-rearing methods	on need achievement in boys *(Rosen and D'Andrade, 1959)*
	4		The effects of mother-child communication	on the child's acquisition of language *(Brown and Bellugi, 1964)*
A→C STUDIES	5	The effects of birth order and sex		on the development of children's power techniques (how they get their own way) *(Sutton-Smith and Rosenberg, 1970)*
	6	The effects of an absent father		on deferred gratification *(Mischel, 1961)*
A→B→C STUDY	7	The influence of cultural factors	on mothers' behavior	toward aggressive behavior among children *(Minturn and Lambert, 1964)*

ducted a comparable study in Turin, Italy. The similarity between the findings was very great. In both countries white-collar families valued characteristics in children that involve self-expression and self-direction, whereas blue-collar families valued conformity to external standards. These relationships held when racial, religious, regional, and ethnic backgrounds were controlled.

But do these preferences influence how parents raise their children? Yes. Kohn asked parents how they would respond to eight situations involving children's misbehavior. His findings agree with those of Urie Bronfenbrenner (1958). Blue-collar families are more likely to use physical punishment; white-collar families are more inclined

to use isolation, reasoning, appeals to guilt, and threats of withdrawal of love. Blue-collar parents respond to misbehavior in terms of its immediate consequences; white-collar parents, in terms of its intent.

According to Kohn, the differences in what parents value in the behavior of their children reflect class differences in the requirements of work. White-collar jobs emphasize self-direction and the ability to work cooperatively with others. Industrial blue-collar occupations generally impose subordination and conformity to other people's standards. Kohn argues that the values stressed in the father's occupational setting are passed on by parents to their children. Blue-collar

Figure 6.11   Child-rearing methods have been
shown to correlate with the need for achievement,
or achievement motivation, in children. The parents
of boys with high achievement motivation are
those who encourage attempts at increasingly difficult
tasks, provide warmth and emotional support,
and tolerate failure more than do the parents of boys
with low achievement motivation.

and white-collar families are preparing their children to deal successfully with the world as they
have found it to be.

Study II   A——▸B

Elder and Bowerman (1963): *The Effects of
Family Size (A) on Child-Rearing Methods (B).*
Experiments on the behavior of small groups have
shown that the size of the group influences the
development of complementary leadership roles
—those of the task-oriented leader and the leader
devoted to emotional support of group members.
(See Chapter 8.) The larger the group, the more
likely these roles are to be differentiated and to
be held by different persons (Hare *et al.*, 1962).

Based on this research, Glenn Elder and
Charles Bowerman hypothesized that the larger
the size of the family, the more likely it would be
that fathers dominate and mothers offer emotional support. They predicted that as the number
of children rose, the father would be more likely
to be the disciplinarian and also that he would rely
more on external methods of control—physical
punishment and verbal abuse—than on persuasion or praise and approval as methods of control.

To test these notions, Elder and Bowerman
asked questions of a sample of teen-agers in
grades seven through twelve in schools in Ohio

and North Carolina. Their findings mainly supported their hypothesis. In all family types mothers were more likely than fathers to make and
enforce the rules governing their children's
behavior and were more likely to use persuasion
and such symbolic rewards as praise and approval.
But this behavior by the mother decreased as
family size increased. Correspondingly, the father's involvement in child rearing increased as
the size of the family increased. Furthermore, fathers' reliance on punishment and verbal abuse
also increased with family size. However, these
findings were modified by the sex composition of
the family and by social class. Blue-collar fathers
were more likely to be disciplinarians when their
large families included girls.

Study III   B——▸C

Rosen and D'Andrade (1959): *The Effects of
Child-Rearing Methods (B) on Need Achievement
in Boys (C).* We are all familiar with persons with
a strong need to succeed. In a series of studies
David McClelland (1961) has called such a need
achievement motivation—a strong psychological
desire to excel. For a long time social scientists
have speculated on the origins of such needs—
how is it that some people have a lot of achievement motivation and others have very little?

Bernard Rosen and Roy D'Andrade decided to
observe the interaction patterns between parents
and children to try to identify how achievement
motivation is fostered or suppressed. They selected a group of white boys between the ages of
nine and eleven from schools in Connecticut. The
boys were selected according to the degree of
their achievement motivation as shown on a need-
achievement test, which was administered in
their schools. Half of those chosen had been measured as high in need achievement, half as low.
Social class of the families was controlled.

The investigators then went to the home of
each boy and, in the presence of both parents, had
the boy perform a number of tasks. For example,
each boy stacked blocks blindfolded, tossed rings
at a peg, and the like. Parents were permitted to
talk to their son while he performed tasks but not
do them for him. In several of the tasks the par-

ents were permitted to make success harder or easier. For example, they could make the ring toss easier or harder by setting the distance the boy had to throw. Similarly, they could choose to have the child make easier or more difficult patterns with blocks. As expected, boys with high achievement motivation did much better at all tasks than did those with low achievement motivation. They also asked for less parent aid and were more likely to reject aid from their parents.

Their parents also behaved quite differently than did the parents of low-achievement-motivation boys. Fathers of highly motivated boys gave higher estimates of what their sons would be able to accomplish and chose more difficult task levels for sons to perform. But they were also much warmer toward their sons, gave them much less advice, shrugged off failures, and were generally much more at ease than were the fathers of boys with low achievement motivation. The mothers of high-achievement-motivation sons differed from mothers of low-achievement-motivation sons in much the same way. They too were warmer and chose more difficult task levels. However, unlike fathers, mothers of high-achievement-motivation sons were much more likely than the other mothers to be rejecting of failure, to push the boys to succeed, and to give specific advice.

Rosen and D'Andrade concluded that the fathers of high-motivation sons gave them an excellent model of high expectations combined with warmth and a "hands-off" policy. They were confident and relaxed. Mothers supplied the emotional impetus needed to instill strong needs to achieve—mothers offered both warmth and rejection. Whereas fathers of high-motivation sons were constant in their rewards, mothers differentially reinforced achievement—praise for success, disappointment for failure. This combination seems vital. Parents of low-achievement-motivation sons failed to ask much of their children and did not combine warmth with rejection.

Study IV   B——C

Brown and Bellugi (1964): *Mother-Child Communication (B) and the Child's Acquisition of*

Language (C). In October, 1962, Roger Brown and Ursula Bellugi began a longitudinal study of the development of language in two children, whom they called Adam and Eve. Every second week, they visited these children in their homes and made notes and tape recordings as these children and their mothers went about their normal routines. Everything said by the child and by the mother was recorded and later analyzed. Adam was studied from twenty-seven months of age until thirty-six months; Eve, from eighteen months to thirty-six months. These children were selected from thirty interviewed because they talked a lot and their speech was understandable to the observers. The point of the study was to systematically keep track of the development of children's speech. The findings have been of considerable importance.

First of all, Brown and Bellugi found that even when repeating a phrase or sentence an adult has just uttered, young children omit all but the most critical and meaningful words. Children are very likely to retain nouns and verbs (and less often adjectives); they are less likely to use or repeat auxiliary verbs, articles, prepositions, and conjunctions. (These terms are called *functors* by linguists because their grammatical functions are more important than their meaning content.) Children's early sentences tend to be restricted to high-meaning words; additional elements of syntax are omitted (see Table 6.1). In this sense children's early sentences are *telegraphic;* telegrams also often omit all but necessary words—"Arriving Sunday" instead of "I will arrive on Sunday."

Table 6.1   Some Imitations Produced by Adam and Eve

Model Utterance	Child's Imitation
Tank car.	Tank car.
Wait a minute.	Wait a minute.
Daddy's brief case.	Daddy brief case.
Fraser will be unhappy.	Fraser unhappy.
He's going out.	He go out.
That's an old-time train.	Old-time train.
It's not the same dog as Pepper.	Dog Pepper.
No, you can't write on Mr. Cromer's shoe.	Write Cromer shoe.

Figure 6.12   Does this girl, shown in a photograph taken at a child-care center, have a brother? If she does, is he older or younger than she? According to a study by Sutton-Smith and Rosenberg, girls are not likely to use physical force to get their way outside the home unless they have older brothers whose behavior may be imitated.

Table 6.2   Expansions of Child's Speech Produced by Mother

Child's Utterance	Mother's Expansion
Baby highchair.	Baby is in the highchair.
Mommy eggnog.	Mommy had her eggnog.
Eve lunch.	Eve is having lunch.
Mommy sandwich.	Mommy'll have a sandwich.
Set wall.	He sat on the wall.
Throw Daddy.	Throw it to Daddy.
Pick glove.	Pick the glove up.

Brown and Bellugi also found that when young children attempt to repeat an adult sentence, no matter what the length, they reduce it to between two and four morphemes. A morpheme is a meaningful linguistic unit that is either a word (as *talk, cat, child*) or part of a word (as the *ed* in *talked*, the *s* in *cats*, or the *hood* in *childhood*) and that contains no smaller meaningful parts. They suggest that this four-morpheme limit is a real limit to the length of a sentence that a child beginning to speak can utter or plan.

A second major finding was not only that children imitate parents, but that parents imitate children. Mothers were frequently recorded repeating a child's sentence, only in expanded form. The child would say, "There go one," and the mother would respond, "Yes, there goes one." In fact, the data showed that mothers more often imitated children than children imitated mothers. About a third of the time Adam's and Eve's mothers responded to their speech with an expanded imitation (see Table 6.2). Thus, the mother-child interaction tends to be built upon childish reductions of adult sentences and adult expansions of childish sentences. This interaction is probably vital to the development of children's language abilities.

Table 6.3   Child's Utterances Not Likely To Be Imitations

My Cromer suitcase.	You naughty are.
Two foot.	Why it can't turn off?
A bags.	Put on it.
A scissor.	Cowboy did fighting me.
A this truck.	Put a gas in.

Brown and Bellugi discovered an even more interesting phenomenon. Children's speech revealed many instances of what appear to be trial-and-error attempts to discover the grammatical structure of language—especially the appropriate use of functors (see examples in Table 6.3). The children spoke many sentences containing meaningful errors that were not likely to be imitations of anyone's speech, for example, "Cowboy did fighting me." Brown and Bellugi reason that this practice reveals an unconscious, bit-by-bit discovery of the rules of grammar, of what words are allowed in what positions in sentences. This process of discovery is not fully understood yet, either linguistically or psychologically. But it does suggest that childish speakers are more than passive imitators of adult speech who slowly, by reinforced imitations, come to master adult speech. It suggests that children slowly and experimentally build more complex mental structures as their speech becomes more complex and more correct.

Study V   A——C

Sutton-Smith and Rosenberg (1970): *The Effects of*

Birth Order and Sex (A) on the Development of Children's Power Techniques (C). A series of studies has shown that among siblings, the first-born use quite different power techniques—devices for getting their own way—than do second- or later-born children. Retrospective reports by college students consistently revealed that first-borns were more bossy, reprimanding, and inclined to use physical force toward the second- or later-born than were the second- or later-born, who relied more on pleading, whining, sulking, begging, and appeals to parents to deal with the first-born. These differences are not surprising because age differences in children imply strength differences. Little brother is unlikely to rely on strength to get what he wants from big brother. But these same studies produced a much more fascinating hypothesis: *outside* the home, things were virtually the reverse; first-borns seemed to be *less* bossy and reliant on physical power in their relationships with their friends than were second-borns. This finding suggests that second-borns model their use of power techniques with their peers after examples set by an older sibling at home.

Brian Sutton-Smith and B. G. Rosenberg decided to pursue these suggestions from earlier studies; to do so, they collected data from children involved in older-younger child relationships, and they did not depend on the recollections of persons at college age. They selected ninety-five fifth- and sixth-graders from a school in Ohio. Thirty-three of them were first-born, and sixty-two were later-born—only those with a sibling within four years of their own age were included in the study. The children were also separated into sex combinations. This separation resulted in eight combinations according to birth order, sex of the child, and sex of the older or younger sibling. Each child answered a battery of questions about strategies that he used to get his way and ways his sibling used. They were also asked to describe their means for getting their way with their best friends in school. There was close agreement between older and younger children on their respective behavior. Both older and younger siblings agreed that older children were bossier and that younger

children were more likely to cry, pout, sulk, or appeal to parents for help.

However, there were marked exceptions to this pattern according to the sex combination of the siblings. Younger brothers with older sisters tended to rely on direct rather than subordinate power techniques. They used blackmail, held possessions for ransom, and used physical force. Both the younger brothers and the older sisters agreed on this. They also agreed that the older sisters of younger brothers used relatively parental techniques, such as reasoning, explaining, taking turns, or claiming special status as a female—"You must do this for me because I am a girl." Older males used direct power techniques regardless of the sex of their sibling. Older females used direct power techniques *only* when their sibling was female.

The modeling hypothesis (that second-born children model their use of power techniques with their peers after the example set by their older sibling at home) was only weakly supported by the data. However, the data repeated the patterns found with college students: The older siblings were more cooperative, according to their friends, whereas the later-born were more bossy. Regardless of birth order, males were more inclined to use physical force; females, to seek help or ask for sympathy.

Thus, as with most animal groups, dominance within families tends to be decided by size. That the younger brothers of girls tend to use force rather than manipulation probably reflects both the fact that they may not be physically weaker than their sisters and the fact that cultural norms inhibit female use of physical force. In dealing with younger sisters, girls are reported to scratch, pinch, and tickle. This behavior probably would not be an effective physical deterrent to younger brothers, who are reported to wrestle, chase, hit, and break things. Chapter 17 will consider at length the possibility that inequality of sex status stemmed from differences in strength between men and women. In contemporary adult society such differences seem of little importance—few tasks any longer require considerable strength.

But in the relatively more primitive setting of childhood, especially within the family, sheer brute strength continues to play an appreciable role in dominance.

To some extent, then, female submissiveness continues to be developed in childhood because sex-based strength differences remain relevant. Efforts to change traditional sex roles will, in part, be frustrated until there is some way to overcome these dominance patterns among children. One possibility may lie in the fact that younger sisters of older brothers seem quite physically aggressive in dealing with children from outside their families. It would be interesting to know if women who had older brothers have found it easier to overcome or step out of the traditional feminine role of submissiveness. If so, one application of this knowledge might be to have more male elementary-school teachers, as they could suffice as a surrogate for older brothers and promote greater aggressiveness on the part of young girls.

Study VI A——▶C

Mischel (1961): *Absent Father (A) and Deferred Gratification (C)*. Recently, with the rise in the divorce rate (see Chapter 18), social scientists have become concerned about the effects on children of not having a father in the home. What difference does it make if children are raised in a household headed by a mother instead of in a normal two-parent family? Earlier in this chapter it was suggested that a lack of male role models may produce rather different adult males when the present generation of children matures. But we are only beginning to understand some of the ways in which they may be different.

In this study Walter Mischel explored the impact of the absence of a father from the home on the ability of children—both boys and girls—to *defer gratification*. This term refers to the inclination to reject a smaller immediate reward in order to obtain a larger reward at some future time. In Chapter 13 we point out that the ability to defer gratification plays a vital role in occupational success. For example, in order to become a surgeon, a person must struggle through twelve years of training beyond high school, part of it without

income and part with a very low income. Dropping out of school to take a job would result in a considerable immediate increase in income. But remaining in school will eventually produce a much higher income.

Mischel suspected that children who grow up without fathers develop less capacity to defer gratification. Such a capacity depends upon the development of trust that the promise of a greater later reward will be kept. In order to acquire this capacity, a child must have experience with fulfilled promises. Mischel reasoned that in nuclear households the absence of fathers, who are at work, sets up a condition for giving children experience with deferred gratification. Mothers frequently tell children that if they refrain from some action or desire, their father will provide even greater fulfillment when he gets home. "Can I have a cookie?" "Not now, dear, but when your father gets home we will drive over and get an ice-cream cone." When there is no father in the home, Mischel suspected, the opportunity for experience with deferred gratification is less. If this is so, then children growing up without fathers should display less ability to defer gratification than should children growing up with fathers.

To test his hypothesis Mischel worked with eight- to nine-year-old children on Trinidad and Grenada in the West Indies. Each child was interviewed individually at school and, along with other questions, was asked to answer "yes" or "no" to the following two statements.

1. I would rather get ten dollars right now than have to wait a whole month and get thirty dollars then.
2. I would rather wait to get a much larger gift much later than get a smaller one now.

After completing the interviews, the experimenter said he wanted to thank the group for their cooperation. He held up two candy bars (one a ten-cent size, the other a twenty-five-cent size) and said, "I would like to give each of you a piece of candy, but I don't have enough of these [showing the twenty-five-cent size] with me today. So you can either get this one [showing the small bar] right now, today, or, if you want to, you can wait for this one [showing the large bar], which I will bring back next Friday [one week later]." Each student wrote T (today) or F (Friday) on a piece of paper, and each received what he asked for.

Mischel's findings (see Table 6.4) show the effects he had anticipated. Children with fathers were much more likely than children without fathers to choose delayed rewards. We still do not know whether the reason they did so is the reason suggested by Mischel. But his explanation is the one presently most plausible. If it is indeed the explanation, then mothers who are raising children without fathers ought to be able to compensate for this particular consequence by providing many occasions for their children to experience deferred-gratification situations.

Study VII   A——▶B——▶C

Minturn and Lambert (1964): *A Cross-Cultural Study (A) of the Influence of Mothers' Behavior (B) on Aggressive Behavior Among Children (C).* A critical problem in social-science research is the extent to which study results are relevant only to those cultures in which they were found. The majority of social scientists are Americans or Europeans. Thus, most studies have been limited to the United States or Europe. Consequently, many things we believe to be universal features of human social behavior may, in fact, be merely universal to Western societies. It is therefore vital that social scientists test their theories in non-Western societies. This study of mothers and children in six cultures is extremely important to social science because it is based on comparable observations in both Western and non-Western societies: a village caste group in northern India, an American community in New England, an Indian village in Mexico, a Gusii village in Kenya, a barrio in northern Luzon, Philippine Islands, and a village on Okinawa. Because there was interest in comparing child rearing in each society, the communities were selected so that families within them were quite homogeneous in economic characteristics and cultural heritage.

A team of trained observers went to each community and selected two dozen children in the community for intensive observation. The moth-

Table 6.4   Presence of Father in Home and Deferment of Gratification

Presence or Absence of Father	Number Preferring	
	Immediate, Smaller Reward	Delayed, Larger Reward
Grenada Children		
Father Present	9	42
Father Absent	8	10
Trinidad Children		
Father Present	19	26
Father Absent	17	6
Total	53	84

Source: Adapted from Walter Mischel, "Father Absence and Delay of Gratification: Cross-Cultural Comparisons," *Journal of Abnormal and Social Psychology,* 63 (1961), 116–124.

ers of chosen children were interviewed in considerable detail on how they and the fathers dealt with the children. Eventually the researchers attempted to explore the relationships between how the parents dealt with the children and how the children behaved. Special attention was given to how parents dealt with their children's aggressive behavior toward other children.

The first important result of the study was the discovery that there was more variation in child rearing methods *within* any given culture than there was *between* cultures. Although the various cultures showed considerable differences in their average methods of child-rearing, each culture contained many people who were not even close to the average in the way they raised their children. In each community there were mothers whose methods were more like those predominant in another culture than like the methods predominant in their own culture.

A major interest of the study was in how mothers dealt with the aggressive behavior of their children toward other children. Mothers in the Indian village in Mexico were the group *most* likely to punish such behavior. The American mothers in the New England community were those *least* likely to punish aggressive behavior. In comparing the six cultures, Leigh Minturn and William Lambert found that in cases where rela-

Figure 6.13   According to a cross-cultural study by Minturn and Lambert, aggressive behavior in childhood is shaped by a combination of early child-rearing practices and peer-group interaction. A lively child, imitating aggressiveness in adults, may be aggressive in his peer group. If aggressive behavior is reinforced in his peer group, it is likely to be repeated.

tives lived nearby (sharing a central courtyard, for example), rules against children's fighting were strictest. Looking within any culture, they found that the more children there were in a family, the more likely parents were to punish fighting. These findings are congruent. Apparently fighting within families (even when the family is extended and includes relatives) is more disruptive than fighting among unrelated children.

Perhaps the most interesting question raised in this study was whether the techniques used by a mother to control aggressive behavior—did she punish or ignore such behavior?—have any influence on how children acted. Surprisingly, the answer seems to be no. Children who were punished for aggressiveness against other children were no more or less likely to be aggressive in the future than were children whose aggressive behavior was ignored by their mothers. Similarly, whether or not a mother punished aggressive behavior di-

rected at her by the child had no effect on the aggressive behavior of the child. Can it be that Konrad Lorenz (1966) is correct—that aggressiveness is an innate or physiologically based characteristic of individuals? Possibly so. (See Chapter 5.)

However, from the standpoint of sociology the most important result of the study was the link it demonstrated between the level of a child's activity and the degree to which he or she adheres to the socially approved level of aggressiveness. In Mexico, where the mothers tend to punish aggressiveness, the most lively children—those who display the highest levels of interaction with others—appear to be less physically aggressive with their friends than do the less lively children. The reverse is the case for New England children, whose mothers tend to ignore their aggressiveness. Thus, the most lively children seem to reflect the average family values about aggressiveness, even though particular children do not reflect their own mother's attempts to influence their aggressive behavior.

How does this happen? Minturn and Lambert suggest the following process. First, parental care and especially maternal care of babies provides the basis—probably in the form of self-confidence—that makes a child lively (a high social interactor). Second, through observation of adult behavior, children learn what behaviors are valued, and they model or imitate that behavior in their interaction with one another. Thus, it is the positive or negative response of other children to a child's aggressive behavior that plays the determining role in shaping individual behavior. The lively children receive more feedback, or reinforcement, because they do much more interacting. Thus, the livelier the child, the faster his or her behavior is shaped to meet the standards of the group. Here, as in Harlow's work on monkeys, discussed earlier, the critical importance of the peer group in the effective socialization of the young is evident.

This chapter has attempted to orient you to some of the basic issues and principles involved in the study of socialization although this area of study is much too massive to more than sketch in a single chapter. If this is an area you find of special interest, you might enroll in a course on socialization in your sociology department and a course on human development in your psychology department. This is not the end of the topic in this text. It is taken up again in many following chapters. For one thing, socialization does not end with childhood. People continue to be socialized all their lives. They continue to learn to play new roles and conduct themselves in new ways. Chapter 10 is devoted to the topic of adult socialization.

SUGGESTED READINGS

CRM Books. *Developmental Psychology Today.* Del Mar Calif.: CRM Books, 1971.

Goslin, David A. (ed.). *Handbook of Socialization Theory and Research.* Chicago: Rand McNally, 1969.

Minturn, Leigh, and William W. Lambert. *Mothers in Six Cultures.* New York: Wiley, 1964.

Sutton-Smith, Brian, and B. G. Rosenberg. *The Sibling.* New York: Holt, Rinehart and Winston, 1970.

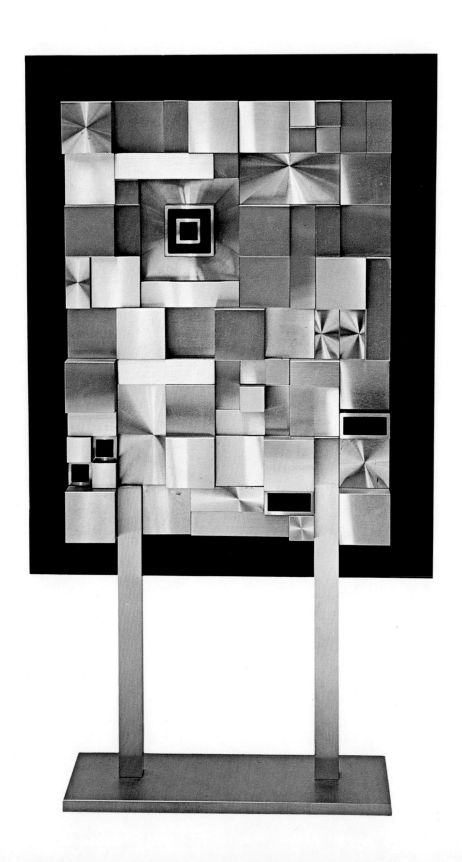

The self arises out of social interaction. It is shaped by the multiplicity of *roles* each human must perform—socially defined ways of relating to others in particular circumstances. Sociologists usually care much less about who is in a particular role than about characteristics of the role itself.   ¶ By definition, roles exist only in relation to *groups*. In fact, groups can be regarded as collections of roles. Some groups, like cocktail-party guests, are very informal and very loosely organized, but other groups, such as university faculties, are very formal and organized. The latter are called *organizations*. Furthermore, organizations are not merely collections of roles but are usually also collections of groups.   ¶ The first three chapters in this unit sketch the essential features of these three components of social organization. The final two chapters utilize them to explore some major problems faced by all forms of social organization.   ¶ *Socialization*, examined in Chapter 6, turns out to be a continuing process. Throughout our lives in groups and organizations we are required to learn new roles—and even unlearn old ones. Furthermore, many persons are cast into roles that they cannot perform or that are inappropriate. Serious lapses from appropriate role performances are labelled *deviant*. Some deviance is considered careless, foolish, or funny. Some is considered criminal. Efforts to exact proper role performances are called *social control*, which is the system of sanctions (rewards and punishments) that groups and organizations employ to gain conformity. When failures in role performance are judged sufficiently serious, extreme sanctions are employed to *resocialize* persons. Such sanctions range from strong group disapproval to confinement or imprisonment.

UNIT IV

PRIMARY COMPONENTS OF SOCIAL ORGANIZATION

Chapter 7 Social Roles and Interaction

BEFORE YOU READ THIS CHAPTER, please take a piece of paper, number it from one to twenty, and write twenty different words or phrases to answer the question: "Who am I?" Answer as if you were giving the answers to yourself, not to someone else, and write your answers in the order that they occur to you. Do not worry about logic or importance. Give yourself ten minutes to do the test.

This test is called the Twenty Statements Test (TST). It is a simple test developed by Manford H. Kuhn and Thomas S. McPartland (1954) and is used by sociologists to determine a person's self-image—how a person views himself or herself.

If you review your answers to the TST and compare your responses with those of your classmates and friends, you may notice that several interesting patterns emerge. First, you will notice that your set of answers is not exactly like that of anyone else. Some of your answers, for example, may have been "eighteen years old," "a student," "female," "religious," "a sister," "liberal," and "blond." One of your friends may have described himself as, among other things, "caucasian," "male," "a student," "a philosophy major," "a son," "a good chess player," and "a human being." It is highly unlikely that any two TSTs will be exactly alike. People differ in important ways, and these differences are reflected in their self-images.

You may also notice that, even though your list of self-images is not the same as anyone else's, some of the ways you see yourself are similar to some of the ways other people see themselves. For example, both you and many of your friends see themselves as students. It is unlikely that any image that you have of yourself will be unique; someone else probably has that image of himself or herself, too. Even though each individual may be seen as unique, there are important ways in which people are related. These social bonds are reflected in people's shared self-images.

A third factor that the TST brings to light is that self-identity is social identity. People cannot go far in describing themselves without giving clues about how they are linked up with other people in an ongoing set of social relationships within society. It would be meaningless, for exam-

ple, for someone to think of himself as a college student if there were not other students, professors, deans, departmental chairmen, and trustees of the college. Could you be yourself if there were not other people who were being themselves in relation to you? It is impossible to have a self-conception in isolation; what one is and how one views oneself is bound up with how one stands in relation to other people.

It was pointed out in Chapter 6 that people raised in isolation cannot rightly be called human, only potentially human. We must learn to be human beings; that is, we must learn to be social beings. By learning how we are related to other people, we learn who we are.

EMERGENCE OF THE SELF

If you were to ask a month-old infant girl to answer the question "Who am I?" you could expect a gurgle in response, perhaps a smile. It would, indeed, be amazing if the answer to your question bore any relation whatever to the question that you posed. For all intents and purposes, the human infant is a bundle of drives and impulses seeking satisfaction. When she is hungry or tired or cranky, she cries out. She does not know why she cries out, but if the people around her respond in appropriate ways (for example, by giving her milk, holding her, or putting her to bed), she stops crying. The infant does not yet have a self in the social sense. She develops a self as she grows up and takes her place within an ongoing set of social relationships.

How does the infant begin to acquire conceptions of himself and others? It is interesting to note that although the infant's impulses are "selfish," his first awareness is of others, not of himself. A study of small infants by Read Bain (1936) indicated that the other is known in experience before the self is. Bain studied the acquisition of self-related and other-related words of children from the time they were twenty-one days old until the time they had mastered self-words and other-related words. He found that the child knows the other before he is aware of his own self. The devel-

Figure 7.1   (*Top*) The Twenty Statements Test
(TST). Can you detect any patterns? How are your
own replies similar to or different from these
hypothetical answers? (*Bottom*) Drawings, like verbal
responses on the TST, may be used to express a
person's self-identity.

1. Paul Ramirez	11. 150 lbs.	1. woman	11. first-time voter
2. Mexican-American	12. strong	2. 20 years old	12. part-time salesgirl
3. 27 years old	13. good looking	3. blonde	13. roommate
4. working man	14. Catholic	4. sexy	14. Protestant
5. union member	15. Democrat	5. girl friend	15. religious
6. underpaid	16. Vietnam vet	6. student	16. intelligent
7. divorced	17. smart	7. sociology major	17. sensitive
8. boyfriend	18. humorous	8. junior	18. independent
9. brother	19. lucky	9. 3.5. G.P.A.	19. witty
10. 5'9" tall	20. voter	10. Young Democrat	20. tall

Age 27. "I am a housewife."

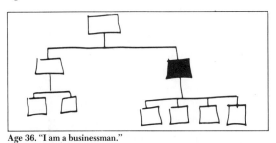

Age 36. "I am a businessman."

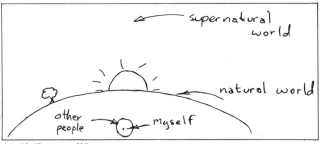

Age 18. "I am myself."

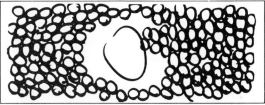

Age 45. "I am independent."

Age 15. "I am the best quarterback."

Figure 7.2   Charles Horton Cooley (1864–1929; *left*) and George Herbert Mead (1863–1931; *right*) are regarded as cofounders of the symbolic-interactionist perspective in sociology. A major focus of Cooley's interest was childhood socialization. Like Piaget, he worked largely from observations of his own children. In *Human Nature and the Social Order* (1902), Cooley set forth his theory of the social nature of the self. In *Social Organization* (1909), he developed the concept of the *primary group* and stressed its role in socialization. Mead graduated from Oberlin College

opment of a child's knowledge of self depends on the reactions of others toward his responses.

Let us examine the processes by which the social self emerges. In order to do this we will first look at the work of Charles Horton Cooley and George Herbert Mead, pioneer sociologists who laid the foundations for study of the social self.

Cooley: The Looking-Glass Self

Charles Horton Cooley (1922) conceived of the social self as a *looking-glass self.* We see ourselves, according to Cooley, as if through the eyes of other people.

> Each to each a looking-glass
> Reflects the other that doth pass.

The looking-glass self is composed of three main elements: our imagination of how we appear to others; our imagination of others' judgments of that appearance; and some sort of self-feeling, such as pride or mortification. How we view ourselves is influenced greatly by how we think others see us. It is as if one could stand in front of a magic mirror and ask, "Mirror, mirror on the wall, who is the fairest of them all?" and have the mirror talk back to us.

In a sense, according to the concept of the looking-glass self, we all stand in front of a magic mirror when we relate to each other. We all make judgments of other people and imagine what their judgments of us are. How we feel about ourselves and how we view ourselves depends on our relationships to other people. It is to Cooley that we owe the important insight that the self-identity is formed through relationships with other people. Cooley, however, did not actually explain how the social self emerges through the process of social interaction, how a person comes to de-

in 1883; in 1887 he studied with William James and Josiah Royce at Harvard University but did not pursue a doctoral degree. In 1894, at the invitation of James, he joined the faculty of the University of Chicago, where he remained until his death. Mead wrote little but was an influential teacher. His innovative ideas about the social origins of the self were compiled into three books by his students and colleagues after his death; much of the material is based on notes taken during his lectures. Of these volumes, the most influential is *Mind, Self and Society* (1934).

velop a social self. It was George Herbert Mead who took Cooley's initial insight and developed a theory explaining how the self comes into being.

Mead: Emergence of the Social Self

Mead (1934) discusses the emergence of the social self as a three-stage process: the preparatory stage, the play stage, and the game stage. During each of these three stages, people gain an increasing ability to view themselves objectively, as if from the standpoint of others.

During the *preparatory stage* children imitate the people around them. For example, a small boy may sit on his father's lap in a car and pretend to be driving. This imitation does not involve an understanding of the meaning of the actions in which the child engages. If the child gets tired of "driving," he can stop without serious consequences and go on to more exciting activities. The only limitations on the child's activity are his imagination and his physical capacity. Other people are not taken into consideration.

During the *play stage* the actual playing of roles occurs. The child may play mother, postman, truck driver, or cowboy. At this stage the child begins to learn that certain roles have meaning and that this meaning is in relation to other roles. The child learns to act back toward herself or himself. For example, the child may want to mail a letter. He learns during the play stage that there are certain people who are in charge of letters; these people are called postmen. The child can hand a letter over to an imaginary postman, then turn around and be the postman, take the letter from himself, and pretend to take it to the post office. It is during this stage that the child first begins to have a social self and is first able to direct activity back toward this self. This process of acting toward yourself as others act toward you is called *taking-the-role-of-the-other.* It is the essential feature in the development of the social self.

Children begin to learn to get outside of themselves at the play stage but, as yet, have no fully developed selves. A child's reference points for viewing herself or himself are particular other persons. One minute the child may be a postman; the next moment, a doctor or a fireman. Separate

Figure 7.3　Our self-identities are greatly determined by our relationships with other people. This young woman, confronting a mirror image of herself, inevitably judges her physical appearance on the basis of how she believes others, including her family and friends, see her.

identities are taken to suit the child's mood of the moment. The child also passes randomly from one role to another and takes roles one at a time. At this point the child has no organized and unitary view of the self. For a fully developed self to emerge, the child must enter the game stage.

In the *game stage* the child must be able not only to take a series of single roles of particular other persons but also to take several roles simultaneously. Mead uses the example of the baseball game. It is important for the person not only to know what his role is in the game but also to know the roles of each of the other players. If there is a man on first base and one out, the second baseman must be ready (in case of a ground ball to short) to receive a throw from the shortstop and then relay a throw to first for a double play. Similarly, the child who has arrived at the game stage must know not only his role but also the roles of the other people involved in the game. It is during this final stage in the development of the self that the individual comes to have an organized self.

At this point a person must do more than take the roles of particular other people; she or he must take the role of what Mead calls the *generalized other*—an objective, organized, and durable perspective on the self. By taking the role of the generalized other, a person develops a consistent standpoint from which to view himself or herself. What was during the play stage an inconsistent self that switched from moment to moment becomes in the game stage an organized self. This self reflects the individual's location in the ongoing social structure of which he or she is an integral part.

It is important to be able to view oneself from the perspective of the generalized other and to have a consistent self-image, for only a person with a fully developed self is able to maintain relationships over time. She or he can be expected to act in consistent ways and can expect that others will do the same. It is this consistent and durable feature of the social self that is the basis of social organization. People with organized selves can come to play organized roles. A discussion of roles and the relationships between the self and roles will be presented later in the chapter.

Research on the Self

The main assumption underlying the work of Cooley and Mead (and the work of other theorists of the self) is that the way we come to see ourselves is dependent, in large part, on the way others see us. If the attitudes of others change, the way in which we view ourselves will probably also change. That we tend to shift our self-images on the basis of others' attitudes is especially true in regard to our self-conceptions, which entail judgments and evaluations.

For example, research by Richard Videbeck has shown that an individual's self-conception changes according to others' evaluations of that individual. Videbeck used as subjects thirty introductory speech students who had been rated superior in speaking ability by their professors. He told the subjects that expert judges would rate their performance on a speech. Half of the students were told by these judges that their performance on the speech was inadequate; the other half were praised. Before and after the rating of their performances, subjects rated themselves on their own speaking abilities. Those subjects who were rated favorably by the judges later

Figure 7.4   According to Mead, a child's social self emerges in three stages as he gains an increasing ability to view himself from the perspective of others. During the *preparatory* stage (*top*), the child imitates the behavior of others without understanding the social meaning of the act. In the *play* stage (*middle*), the child can engage in meaningful activity and can take the role of the other toward himself, but the various roles he acts out are as yet random and unorganized. It is not until the child reaches the *game* stage (*bottom*) that he learns to view himself from several different perspectives simultaneously and to organize these views into a coherent whole—a social self. The unfolding of the social self is not completed even at this point; a person's self continually develops and changes throughout his life.

improved their own self-ratings. Those who were subjected to disapproval changed their self-conceptions and rated themselves as poorer speakers than they had on their first self-ratings. The results of this study support the hypothesis that a self-conception is learned in interaction with others and that changes in the reactions of others toward the individual can change his self-conception (Videbeck, 1960). Through interaction with others, those speech students who were rated inadequate in the experiment lowered their self-conceptions—even though they were initially judged by their professors to be superior speakers.

The Videbeck study was replicated by Martin L. Maehr, Josef Mensing, and Samuel Nafzger. These researchers studied a high-school physical-education class composed of thirty-one boys who were put through the same rating process. They found similar results. The boys' self-evaluations changed either positively or negatively according to how others' evaluations of them were experimentally manipulated (Maehr *et al.*, 1962).

A person's self-conception is influenced by other people's reactions to him, but it is also influenced by his subjective version of how others rate him. John J. Sherwood (1965) studied subjects in a public-relations training group. He had individuals rate themselves on various dimensions of self-conception. He then had other people rate the subjects; these subjects were then informed of how they were being rated. On their second self-rating, the subjects changed their self-evaluations to comply with others' evaluations.

We have seen that a person's self-conceptions can be changed through other people's reactions to his behavior. It is also true that self-conceptions can lead to particular types of behavior. A positive self-concept has been shown to be an insulator against deviant behavior. Walter C. Reckless, Simon Dinitz, and Ellen Murray (1956) showed that a positive self-concept can insulate a boy against becoming a juvenile delinquent. The researchers studied 125 sixth-grade boys in a high-delinquency area of Columbus, Ohio. These boys had been chosen by their teachers as good prospects for not becoming delinquent. The researchers checked into the boys' records and gave them self-conception tests, social-responsibility tests, and delinquency-vulnerability tests. The results of these tests indicated that the boys saw themselves as law-abiding and obedient. They conformed to the expectations of their parents, teachers, and other adults, and they evaluated themselves as "good" boys. Reckless and his colleagues viewed this positive self-concept as an effective deterrent to delinquency.

Studies of self-conception are concerned with the evaluative nature of the self. Studies of self-identity, on the other hand, emphasize where a person locates himself in society. Ronald G. Corwin (1961) studied nurses to find out to what extent a nurse's conception of the nursing role affected her career aspirations. Corwin found that a nurse's identification of herself as *professional* was frustrated in the hospital setting by the requirements of a bureaucratic role. These nurses maintained a self-identity as professionals but sought careers that would lead them outside the hospital setting, particularly into teaching.

Like the nurses in Corwin's study, most of us are frustrated when our self-identities are contradicted rather than confirmed by the people and situations we encounter every day. When people experience this kind of incongruence, they are likely to respond by changing their attitudes, behavior, or both. William R. Rosengren (1961) argues that the behavior of persons and their self-identities remain relatively stable and predictable as long as they experience a meaningful convergence of views: how they see themselves, how they see others, and how they think others see them. Rosengren implies that if people see that others are changing their attitudes toward them or find that attitudes of different others have become important, they will likely change their self-identities over an extended period of time. This altered self-identity will result in changes in their overt behavior. Rosengren's explanation seems to apply very well to the change in self-identity—and behavior—experienced by many college students who leave home with congruent attitudes about self and others but, finding the different attitudes of new others on campus to be important, change their attitudes over time. For

many students, a comparison of freshman TSTs with ones taken five years later will show interesting attitudinal changes.

Study of the Self in Literature
Literature can be a very fruitful area for the investigation of the emergence of the self. Using *The Red and the Black*, a novel by Stendhal, Francis E. Merrill (1961) showed how Julien Sorel, the main character, came to see himself as an object. Sorel came to define himself and evaluate himself in terms of how he perceived that others described and evaluated him. Julien saw himself through the eyes of *direct others, intermediate others,* and *ideological others.*

Julien's direct others were those persons with whom he came into direct contact, persons who had an immediate impact upon his self-conception and self-identity. Sociologists very often refer to direct others—important people in one's life—as *significant others.* Parents, friends, and teachers are examples of significant others. Intermediate others were those with whom Julien did not come into direct contact but who nevertheless had an effect on the way he saw himself—for example, the general population of his village, Vérrieres. Ideological others were, for Julien, the whole spirit of France in the early nineteenth century: the ". . . grandeur of Napoleon, the heroism of his revolutionary armies, the political adroitness of Talleyrand, and the seductiveness of Don Juan" (Merrill, 1961).

The important point made by Merrill was that Julien Sorel's self-conception and self-identity were finally formed by the conceptions that others had of him. Although Merrill's study does not represent a controlled experiment, it does show how the area of literature can provide useful insights into the study of the social self.

We have seen how the self develops: In the process of relating to other people, individuals learn to step outside themselves and view themselves objectively. Although this view may undergo some changes, a person with a fully developed self is able to expect things of himself or herself and can expect things of other people as well. The person with such a fully developed self is able to play roles in an organized, ongoing manner. We will now turn to a discussion of roles.

SOCIAL ROLES

Stated briefly, a *social role* is a set of *expectations* applied to an occupant of a particular *position* or status. (This terminology is also discussed in Chapter 3.) In order to understand the concept of role, one must first understand what is meant by *social positions* and *social expectations*. (Much of the following discussion on social roles is based on the work of Neal Gross and his colleagues in *Explorations in Role Analysis: Studies of the School Superintendency Role*, which offers excellent explanations of these points.)

Positions

A position is the location of a person or class of people in a system of social relationships. You, for example, occupy the position or status of student in the system of relationships that is called the college or university. As a student you are related to other people in that system who also occupy positions. In fact, without these other positions your own position would not exist. Within the classroom, for example, there are two positions, that of student (occupied by several people) and that of professor (occupied by a single individual). A characteristic of positions is that they exist only in relation to other positions and receive their meaning in relation to these other positions (Gross *et al.*, 1958).

Focal Positions and Counter Positions In order to fully understand a particular status, it is necessary to specify the other related statuses. If we call your status of student a *focal position* (the position on which we shall focus), the statuses related to it become *counter positions*. Let us return to the example of the classroom: you occupy the focal position of student along with all of your fellow students; together you and your fellow students stand in direct relation to the counter position of professor.

If we take the analysis out of the limited context of the classroom, we find that a particular focal position is related to many counter positions. As a student, you are related not only to other students and to a particular professor but also to the general faculty of your college or university—deans, university librarians, teaching assistants, and general staff. Each of these statuses stands in a particular relation to your status of student.

Your student status is not merely confined to the college or university campus. In the larger society it is important that you occupy this position. For example, if you go to a movie theater, your student position may get you a discount on admission. Or your student status may determine just what kind of off-campus housing you can find. Positions in one system have implications not only in that system but in other systems in which a person is likely to participate (Gross *et al.*, 1958).

Positional Sectors A *positional sector* is that portion of a position that is related to a particular counter position. One sector of your position of student puts you into relation to your professor; another sector, into relation to fellow students, and so on, until your entire student position is described. In other words, your position is completely represented when all of your relationships within a particular system or in the larger society are described in relation to your position within that system or society (Gross *et al.*, 1958).

Anticipations and Expectations

An *anticipation* is a prediction concerning how an occupant of a particular status will act in a given situation. If a professor gains a reputation for being a hard grader and giving difficult examinations, his students may come to anticipate that the exam they will take on the following Friday will be difficult.

An anticipation refers to a prediction about what a person occupying a certain status *will* do in a given situation. An *expectation* is an evaluative standard applied to an incumbent (occupant) of a position. An expectation concerns what a person occupying a status *should* do in a given situation. For example, take the case of a professor who habitually shows up five minutes late for his lectures. Students anticipate that he *will* be late yet

Figure 7.5   The position of student (*bottom center*) is linked to the counterpositions of dean, faculty, staff, and librarian. Each of these links establishes a position relationship. All the relationships within an institution, taken as a whole, constitute a position system. But the person who plays a role and therefore occupies a position in one institution may play many roles within a variety of institutions (*top*). From the point of view of an individual, his or her role set consists of all of the role expectations associated with a particular position he or she holds. Thus, a person may have several role sets: in his educational institution he is a student; in his family, a son; in his job, a worker; and in the political sphere, a citizen (a voter, taxpayer, and so on).

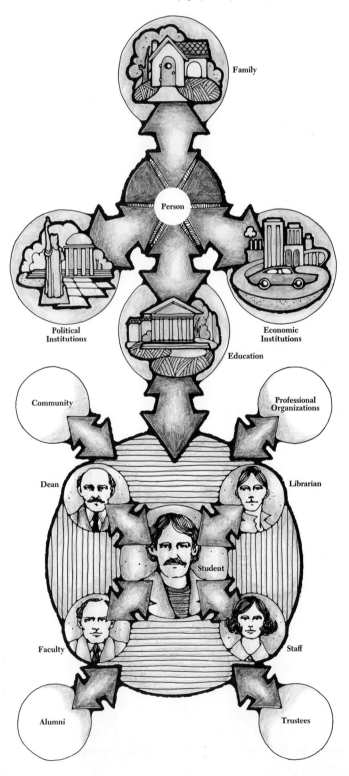

they still expect him to be on time; that is, the professor *should* be punctual.

When we discussed the emergence of the self, we saw that a person acquires a fully developed self when that person gains the ability to take the role of the generalized other, to expect things from himself and others, and to anticipate what he and others will do in given situations. A person with a fully developed self is capable of occupying positions in an ongoing social system. Such a person is also able to be the object of social anticipations and expectations.

Roles

A *role* is a *set of expectations* applied to an incumbent of a particular position. As we have noted, students are, by virtue of their position, in relation to those who occupy several counter positions in the social system—professors, librarians, and so on, each of whom has a set of expectations about the student. Other people in counter positions have expectations about the person in the focal position—and the set of these expectations is the person's role (Gross *et al.*, 1958). The student's role is the whole set of expectations that all people in counter positions have for him. The student, however, reciprocates with his own expectations of others. In order to fully understand what roles are, it is advisable to distinguish between *role relationships* and *role sets*.

Role Relationships   A role relationship is a term that sociologists use to describe the expectations that people who occupy a pair of positions in a social system have for each other. Students expect professors to come to class and give lectures, examinations, and grades and to know a lot about the subject matter they teach. Professors expect students to listen to their lectures, take notes, pass examinations, and be respectful. Role relationships, then, refer to expectations that members of a focal position have for a single counter position and the expectations that the occupants of the counter position have for the focal position (Gross *et al.*, 1958).

Role Sets   A role set, on the other hand, refers to the complex set of role expectations associated with a particular status. The role set of a student includes not only the expectations that professors have of the student but also the expectations of everyone else with whom the student stands in relation.

The importance of the concept of role set is that the person who occupies a particular status is subject to many expectations simultaneously. In order to be able to take the roles created by so many different expectations from others, a person must have a fully developed social self. A person who has only reached the play stage (in Mead's terms) is capable of being in role relationships, but he or she is not able to have an organized role set. A role set requires organization of a person's role relationships (Gross *et al.*, 1958).

Sanctions

All incumbents of positions hold expectations concerning each other's behavior. This does not guarantee, however, that people will actually live up to these expectations. Librarians expect students to return books on time (although they may anticipate the opposite). This expectation alone is not sufficient to ensure that the student will bring the book back within a specified time period. Librarians therefore may use sanctions (in this case, library fines) in order to gain a student's compliance to their expectation. A *sanction* is a reward or punishment applied to a person occupying a particular position by a person occupying a particular counter position. A reward is a *positive sanction;* a punishment is a *negative sanction.*

A professor, for example, expects students to gain an adequate knowledge of the subject matter. This expectation alone is insufficient to ensure that the students will actually become subject competent. The professor must also offer rewards (good grades) and punishments (poor grades) on examinations in order to maximize the chances that students will live up to the expectation.

To summarize, people are located within a social system through their occupancy of positions.

They are related to other people in that system by the ways in which their statuses are related to the statuses of these other people. Each of the positions within the system carries with it a set of expectations and anticipations concerning the behavior of those people who occupy those positions. These sets of expectations are called social roles. A role set includes all of the expectations applying to the occupant of a particular position within the system. The reciprocal set of expectations that ties the members of any two positions together is called a role relationship. People attempt to ensure that others to whom they are tied in a system of relationships will live up to the expectations that they have of these others by applying rewards (positive sanctions) and punishments (negative sanctions) to these others. Having outlined the necessary distinctions, we shall now turn to an examination of the relationship between a person's social self and social roles.

THE SELF AND SOCIAL ROLES

If you go back and look over your TST you can see that you occupy many positions and play many roles in various social systems. Each of the positions that you occupy carries with it many expectations that you are urged to perform. In your college or university, you occupy the position of student, and you may be expected to attend classes, take examinations, go through registration, fill out forms, and spend time studying. You are also a member of a family and have certain obligations to your parents and perhaps to your brothers and sisters. You may be expected, for example, to attend birthday parties, go home for vacations, and write letters to your relatives. For each of the positions that you occupy, people expect you to do certain things.

When you consider all the positions that you occupy—and consequently all the expectations that others have of you—you may find it overwhelming. You may wonder how it is possible to meet all of these expectations. In truth, it is not possible to meet all of the expectations of others with whom you have relationships. There are times, however, when it is necessary to choose to meet one expectation rather than another. Sociologists call such situations *role conflicts*.

Role Conflict

Role conflict is a kind of dilemma. When a person has two or more expectations at the same time and cannot fulfill all of them, he or she has to choose one and exclude the others.

Role conflict may arise because of incompatible expectations within a particular role. Take the obvious case of the unfortunate student who has signed up for two classes that meet at the same time. He cannot, of course, attend both classes, yet he is expected to attend each. Role conflict may also occur when an expectation applying to one of a person's positions conflicts with an expectation applying to another of his positions. It is possible, for example, to be a student and a political activist at the same time. If you have an important examination on Monday for which you are not prepared, it may be necessary to spend the whole Sunday before studying for it. This brings about a situation of role conflict if your friends want you to go to a political meeting with them Sunday morning. One way or another, cases of role conflict must be resolved.

Role Conflict Resolution

There are several techniques that can be used in order to resolve role conflict. One of these techniques is the establishment of priorities. For example, the student who is faced with the two classes that meet at the same time may decide that one of the classes is essential and the other not so important. The student may then drop the less important class in order to resolve the role conflict.

A person may also seek a compromise solution. He or she may, for example, choose to go to the political meeting but return home right afterwards in order to study for the examination.

A third possibility is to combine the various roles that are the sources of the conflict. If a person is invited to a movie by a friend but has a sociology class that same night, she might invite the class to go to the movie and argue that the

movie is relevant to the study of sociology. See whether you can think of some other ways of resolving role conflict.

The study of role conflict brings up the problem that people do not always do what is expected of them. In a situation of role conflict, for example, some expectations must go unfulfilled. Thus, role expectations and role behavior differ.

Role Behavior and Expectations

Role expectations point out what an incumbent of a particular status *should* do. *Role behavior,* on the other hand, is what a person in a particular status *actually* does. Two people who occupy the same position may play the role associated with that position in quite different ways. One student might attend classes regularly, take careful notes, and study hard for examinations; another student in the same class might come to class once in a while, fall asleep half the time, and never crack a book. Even though the expectations for these two students are the same, their behavior differs considerably. Similarly, a given individual may play one of her or his roles as expected and other roles with less interest or facility. A student who takes compulsory physical education and physics may be a good mathematician but a lousy athlete.

It is also possible that different roles will call for different degrees of involvement from the people who play them. One way of conceiving of these different degrees of involvement has been suggested by Theodore R. Sarbin (1966). He proposes the *organismic* dimension in role behavior: that is, the intensity with which a person plays specific roles. If all roles were performed with equal intensity and involvement, people would soon drop from exhaustion. In any society, roles have to be distinguished on the basis of the degree of organismic involvement that they require from the self.

Sarbin distinguishes seven levels of roles on the basis of how much organismic involvement a particular role requires. At the low end of the scale, the role and the self are highly differentiated; minimal involvement and little effort is required. An example of a role played at this level is that of the casual shopper. It is possible to per-

Figure 7.6 Not all roles require the same degree of self-involvement. College students who work part-time in a mailroom may be minimally involved in this role; they may sort mail while simultaneously thinking about performing more interesting roles (*top left*). Students in a gym class (*right*) exemplify a more moderate amount of self-involvement. During more extreme involvement in role playing, the self and the role become virtually indistinguishable; such a degree of organismic involvement may occur when a person is deeply immersed in meditation (*bottom left*).

form this role while daydreaming about many other roles.

The second level distinguished by Sarbin is the dramatic role that involves mechanical acting. The employee who "puts up a good front" to impress the boss is behaving on this level of involvement. He is slightly more involved than the casual shopper, but his self and his role are still highly differentiated.

On the third level, dramatic acting still occurs but is considerably more heated or intense; the actor behaves as if he were the character whom he portrays. At this level the person may put himself or herself into the role but can still distinguish between the self and the role.

A moderate degree of organismic involvement is exemplified by the fourth-level role that a hypnotic subject plays. Whatever the hypnotic suggestions call for, the person behaves as if he or she were in that state. While hypnotized, a subject can get full by eating an imaginary meal.

Level five is exemplified by the hysteric, the person who behaves as if he or she were afflicted with an organic dysfunction. At this level the self and the role are not differentiated and the person is highly involved in the performance of the role.

The sixth level of organismic involvement comprises those roles in which ecstatic states are reached. A person undergoing sexual climax, a mystical experience, or rites of passage is performing roles that involve a maximum of involvement. But in these roles the experience is transitory; a point of ecstasy is reached, then it subsides, and the person returns to a state of equilibrium.

The final level of organismic involvement may be irreversible. It involves the total involvement of the self with the role. A person who is the object of sorcery or witchcraft may be seen to be in a role in which his or her self is totally involved. Another example is a moribund person. The person's self-control is totally lost in the performance of this type of role (Sarbin, 1966).

On the one hand, different roles require different degrees of involvement from those who perform them. On the other hand, even when a given role, such as student, requires the same degree of involvement by everyone who performs it, different people playing the role may be more or less involved in the associated role behavior.

So far we have discussed situations in which people relate to roles in a positive way by meeting, with more or less enthusiasm, the expectations of the roles that they play. It is also possible, however, for a person to purposely avoid playing a particular role and fulfilling the expectations attached to that role. Sociologists refer to this phenomenon as *role distance.*

Role Distance

People who at least partly identify the self with a particular role and attempt to fulfill expectations associated with that role as well as possible are said to *embrace the role* (Goffman, 1961). Erving Goffman uses an example of a merry-go-round to show how people differentially embrace roles. To a three- or four-year-old child, riding a merry-go-round is a challenge. The child is seen to embrace the role of merry-go-round rider at this age and to put all that he or she has into performing the immediate role.

Role distance, on the other hand, is the expression of separateness between the individual and the role that individual is performing. The twelve-year-old would not be caught dead taking the role of merry-go-round rider seriously. While riding around, the twelve-year-old will show a great deal

of detachment from the role. She or he will goof around, kick the horse to get it to go faster, look bored, or do anything to show that he or she is above it all.

Role distance, of course, is not limited to the roles that children play. The student who breezes through an examination without any effort and the basketball player who makes it look easy on the court are exhibiting role distance.

Transitory and Permanent Positions

The extent to which a person gets involved in performing a particular role may depend, at least in part, on the permanence of the position associated with the role. A role may last a few minutes or extend over the entire lifetime of an individual. Contrast the role of the merry-go-round rider with that of male, for example. Throughout our lives we are continually moving into and out of various statuses or positions. Some of the roles that we play and some of the positions that we occupy hold little interest for us. Other roles are essential to our self-identity and extend into all of our relationships and cover our whole lives.

A *transitory position* is one that a person occupies for a limited time. Examples of transitory roles are four-year-old, customer, and college freshman. We are moving into and through these roles and associated positions all of the time. A *permanent position*, on the other hand, is one that a person occupies throughout his or her life. Although transitory positions may have importance for our self-identity, permanent positions are generally far more important in shaping who we are. Sex and race are statuses that people occupy permanently. From a very early age a girl learns that she is a girl, and expectations associated with this position are likely to shape the course of her life. Although the roles associated with her permanent status are changing, she remains a woman throughout her life. Permanent positions are discussed further in Unit V as ascribed statuses.

Career

The sequence of positions that an individual enters and leaves during his or her lifetime constitutes his or her *career*. The person moves through a series of related transitory positions and performs associated transitory roles. The student may be seen to have a career as he or she moves through the positions of freshman, sophomore, junior, and senior and finally graduates, thus ending a college or university career. Upon graduation an individual may begin another career, perhaps as a teacher, and may move from this position to the position of department chairman, principal, or school-board member. Or perhaps this person will go to graduate school and become a sociologist.

Each position that a person occupies helps shape his or her self-image. In each of these positions the individual is related to other people in a system of relationships. Each of these other people has expectations for the individual and each helps define who the person is. We are all moving through society, and society is moving through us. Who we are influences what we do, and what we do shapes who we are.

Expectations are the foundation upon which roles are built. Just as social roles are made up of expectations, groups are made up of social roles. In the next chapter we will examine the structure and nature of groups.

SUGGESTED READINGS

Goffman, Erving. *Encounters: Two Studies in the Sociology of Interaction.* Indianapolis, Indiana: Bobbs-Merrill, 1961.

Gross, Neal, Ward S. Mason and Alexander W. McEachern. *Explorations in Role Analysis: Studies of the School Superintendency Role.* New York: Wiley, 1958.

Manis, Jerome G., and Bernard N. Meltzer (eds.). *Symbolic Interaction: A Reader in Social Psychology.* Boston: Allyn and Bacon, 1967.

Mead, George Herbert. *Mind, Self and Society.* Chicago: University of Chicago Press, 1934.

Biddle, Bruce J., and Edwin J. Thomas (eds.). *Role Theory: Concepts and Research.* New York: Wiley, 1966.

Chapter 8 The Nature and Variety of Groups

ON A SUNDAY MORNING in June a stream of family automobiles unloaded a horde of little boys and their baggage at Camp Roaring River. The boys were from many different places, and nearly all of them were strangers to each other. During the course of the day they were assigned to lodges for a two-week stay. Each lodge housed fifteen boys under the supervision of an adult counselor. Residents of each lodge were given a collective name—the bears, the wolves, the cobras. Each group had its own schedule of activities and formed its own sports teams for competition with the other lodges. Within hours of being dumped together, some boys in each lodge had established their popularity, thereby earning some degree of authority; others were considered less popular, and one or two in each lodge were judged unpopular. Within several days the boys within each lodge had forged strong common bonds and had accepted responsibilities on behalf of the common needs of their group. They were proud to be bears, wolves, or cobras. But at the same time they were forming negative feelings and stereotypes about other lodges—"Bears are cheats," "Wolves are sissies," "Cobras are punks." Furthermore, it became apparent that no lodge group was simply a collectivity of fifteen boys. Internal cliques and coalitions developed within each group, and some of them reflected the boys' memberships in various groups outside the camp. Black and white boys tended to form separate cliques, as did Protestant and Catholic boys. Sometimes these factions led to internal conflicts, but these usually subsided the moment the group faced an external challenge from another lodge.

THE STUDY OF GROUPS

In this fictitious account of goings on at camp we can see essential features of social groups develop out of chance assortments of boys thrown together to enjoy two weeks of outdoor fun. This description was informed by the detailed study of group formation and conflict at summer camps by Muzafer and Carolyn W. Sherif (1953).

When sociologists talk about groups, they do not mean any bunch of people who happen to be

at the same place at the same time. In everyday speech, we sometimes refer to a crowd of people waiting to cross a street, passengers on an airplane, or persons in a theater as a group; sociologists call such gatherings *aggregates* or *collectivities*. We also often use the word group when we speak of persons sharing some characteristic—for example, males, college students, or salesmen; sociologists call these *categories* of people.

Sociologists reserve the word group to describe a *collection of people who are involved in some organized and recurrent pattern of interaction.* A group consists of some recognized set of roles and norms. Furthermore, groups are oriented toward some set of goals (whether the goals involve starting a revolution or simply enjoying friendship and play). Because of shared goals and recurrent interaction among members, groups give rise to a sense of belonging or solidarity among participants. Thus, groups have at least a vague notion of the boundary that distinguishes members from nonmembers. For a collection of persons to constitute a group in the sociological sense, members must perceive that they share a collective existence and common aims.

Why Are Groups Important?

People spend most of their everyday lives in groups—at work, at school, at play, at home. Groups are the most elementary units of social life: They are *social* because they involve more than one individual and *elementary* because they are more simply structured and depend more on face-to-face interaction than do larger units, such as organizations. In order to understand the inner workings of larger social units, it is necessary to understand the structures and functions of groups.

As has been pointed out in previous chapters, groups are essential not only for human survival but even for the possibility of being human. In Chapter 7 we pointed out that people's identities are shaped by the roles they perform. Outside of groups, roles are meaningless—the role of father, for example, is meaningless outside the context of the family. Indeed, such other critical interests of sociology as norms, customs, or culture are empty

Figure 8.1   Social aggregates, social categories, and social groups differ with respect to what their members have in common and to how recurrent and organized their interaction is. Members of *social aggregates,* such as these subway passengers in the left-hand photo, are together in a crowded space but probably have little else in common. The interaction of these particular individuals is not organized or recurrent. People who are part of a social category do share some socially meaningful characteristic; for example, the men in the middle photo constitute the *social category* of industrial workers. But even if the particular men pictured here all worked on the same assembly line, they would not constitute a social group: People in *social groups* have recurrent interactions that are organized according to a set of goals and norms. The members of the fraternal social club in the photo at right (or the industrial workers if they happen to belong to the same union) share common aims and feel a sense of belonging to their group that sets them collectively apart from nonmembers.

terms except as they apply to characteristics of groups. Therefore, sociologists have no choice but to study groups.

How Groups Are Studied

The sociological study of groups has followed two distinct paths. One is influenced by anthropology, the other by experimental psychology. One method sociologists use is *observing* groups in their natural setting, much as anthropologists systematically observe the life of villages and tribes. John Lofland, whose research was discussed in Chapter 2, used this method to study the small group that dedicated itself to spreading the doctrines of the Divine Precepts. This method has the advantage of dealing with natural behavior where it occurs. It has the disadvantage, however, of not being able to manipulate or control the variables being observed. Lofland could not manipulate the kinds of persons who came in contact with the Divine Precepts' message, nor could he require the group to adopt different missionary tactics. Because observation is extremely time-consuming and because it limits the number of persons who can be observed, sociologists frequently use survey research as a substitute for direct observation of groups. In survey research, group members are asked to be their own observers. For example, members are asked whom they like, whom they interact with, what person is dominant in the

group, and so on. Unfortunately, sociologists want to know much about group processes that members quite frequently are unable or unwilling to report accurately.

Unlike organizations or whole societies, groups may be small enough to bring into or create in the laboratory. A good deal of activity in sociology and social psychology is devoted to doing such laboratory studies, often called *small-group research.* Subjects are recruited and given tasks to perform collectively within a controlled laboratory setting. Often elaborate equipment, one-way mirrors, and the like are used to provide a careful record of what occurs. In these studies the experimenter may manipulate the nature of the tasks, the situation, or the group's composition in order to study how relationships among participants are developed and changed, how behavior is influenced, or how tasks are accomplished. The question arises, however, whether sociologists can apply knowledge about groups in laboratory situations to group behavior in real life.

Some researchers have blended elements of participant observation and laboratory experimentation into what is called the *field experiment.* Natural groups in natural situations are manipulated in certain ways, and the results are observed and recorded. The work of the Sherifs mentioned previously is based on field experiments. They used real summer camps and worked with whatever boys came to camp. Once the boys were in camp, the Sherifs saw to it that they were randomly assigned to lodge groups. They systematically varied the activities and treatment of various lodge groups in order to see how the boys reacted.

Unfortunately, this approach to the study of groups has limited applicability. Many natural groups cannot ethically or practically be manipulated for the sake of sociology. John Lofland, for example, could hardly have randomly assigned persons to undergo intensive interaction with Divine Precept missionaries. It is usually necessary to take either an experimental or observational approach, not both.

We have defined and have outlined why and how groups are studied. Now we need to get down to the business of what sociologists know about groups. First of all, they know that some fundamental types of groups can be identified in ways that simplify the task of understanding the role of groups in social organization. The first part of the chapter examines these types. Sociologists also know a good deal about how groups operate: how they are formed, how they are held together, how they influence individual behavior. The second part of the chapter will summarize what has been learned by sociologists about the structure and processes of groups.

TYPES OF GROUPS

Sociologists conceive of groups in a variety of ways. The purpose of any given conception is to isolate a few important features of groups. This section will deal with those conceptual types that have been found most generally useful.

Primary and Secondary Groups

The concept of *primary group* was first used early in this century by the American sociologist Charles Horton Cooley in response to the fact that although all relationships among humans are both intimate *and* impersonal, some relationships are more intimate than others. Groups characterized by a high degree of intimacy in the relationships among members Cooley classified as *primary*

groups. In his classic definition (1909), he said that such groups "are primary in several senses, but chiefly in that they are fundamental in forming the social nature and ideals of the individual." As a result, members strongly identify with the group. As Cooley put it, when persons find it natural to describe a group as "we" they are probably describing a primary group.

Cooley stressed the role of face-to-face interaction in defining and maintaining primary groups. Although it is true that face-to-face interaction among members is a frequent characteristic of primary groups, it is neither a necessary feature nor one that suffices to distinguish primary from secondary groups. As Kingsley Davis pointed out, some relationships may be very intimate but involve indirect contacts (as among members of a family that is geographically dispersed), and some involve face-to-face contacts but are very impersonal (as between prostitutes and their customers). Davis suggested three physical conditions conducive to primary groups: physical proximity, small size, and durability. In addition, a depth of emotional tone must be present in the relationships among primary group members (Davis, 1949). Examples of groups that tend to be primary are families, street gangs, play groups, some social clubs, and villages. It is obvious that such groups have considerable impact on our lives. They are the primary location for socialization, the scene of our "private lives," and a major source of identity.

If primary groups are basic to our identities, it is also the case that much of our lives are lived in groups not characterized by close bonds of intimacy. Groups within which relationships tend towards the impersonal are called *secondary* groups. Secondary groups are characterized by the involvement of only a limited part of a person's loyalties and feelings. Relationships tend to be based more on calculation, stereotyping, and utility. We tend to take part in such groups because of what they *do* for us, not for what they *mean* to us. Typical examples are work groups that never meet outside the office or shop, civic organizations, and college classes.

Sometimes, for brief periods, secondary groups can be transformed into primary groups.

Figure 8.2   Isaac Asimov's account of an occurrence in his own life illustrates how people, thrown together by circumstance, may become a close-knit, primary group but subsequently may drift apart when circumstances change.

I suppose we can all think of examples in which we participated in the formation of groups under unusual circumstances. Back in the middle 1940s, I spent some time in the army as a private. I hated it. I was not badly treated; I did not see combat; I was never in danger of any kind; but I just hated it. I hated the things we were required to do, the conditions under which we were required to live, the people with whom I was forced to associate.

Then the time came when we had to travel from Virginia to Hawaii. It was a ten-day trip by train and ship. Only a relatively small number of soldiers were going, and most were eighteen-year-olds with limited background and education. Seven of us, including myself, were older men with college degrees. We seven clung together. There was nowhere to go and no one with whom to interact except ourselves. There was nothing much to do, but we played bridge, talked, reminisced, told jokes. I never played bridge very much before that trip or since. I never even liked it very much; but it seemed the most remarkable and fascinating game in the world for those ten days. I couldn't have enough. And those six other guys—the nicest, sweetest, best guys in the world. We loved each other. We were like brothers. Everything was so warm and comfortable that I was actually happy. In fact, I don't know off-hand when in my whole life I was so continuously happy over so long a stretch of time. And in the army!

Occasionally, I remember, we would discuss the possibility of trying out for officer-training school. As officers, life would be easier, but we would undoubtedly have to stay in the army longer. We all thought we would remain privates and push for discharge. Of the seven of us, I was far and away the most vehement in supporting the private-and-discharge alternative.

Then one time the other six came to me, all together, and told me they had decided to opt for officer training. The advantages were simply too attractive. Wouldn't I join them? I was astonished. How could they be so foolish? So weak? I refused. I tried to dissuade them. They put the pressure on, argued, pleaded, listed the advantages. To the end I resisted and finally in black despair I cried out, "Go ahead, leave me. Desert me. To hell with all of you."

Then they broke down laughing and explained it was a put-up job. They just wanted to see if I could resist group pressure, and there were bets on as to whether I would or not. I tried to laugh, too, and boasted that I was immovable in my convictions. But I wasn't. I have never forgotten the despair of those moments and how near I came to agreeing to be an officer rather than have them leave me.

Eventually, we reached Hawaii and separated. It may have seemed to me on the wonderful trip that we were soul mates who would remain together forever, but the fact is that since I left the army—so long ago—I have never been in contact with one of them.

                                                                    I. A.

Isaac Asimov, introduction to Chapter 24, "The Individual and His Groups," in CRM Books, *Psychology Today: An Introduction*, 2nd ed. (Del Mar, Calif.: CRM Books, 1972), p. 471.

For example, during a strike, a work group may become a primary group. During the blackout in New York City many secondary groups, and even aggregates of people who were stalled in elevators, briefly resembled primary groups. Or, as in the account by Isaac Asimov in Figure 8.2, persons thrown into close contact by circumstance can become a primary group. But unless the initial conditions continue, these groups usually cannot retain their primary features, and so they drift back into the secondary-group category.

It is important to recognize that *primariness* and *secondariness* are matters of degree and emphasis. All groups have some degree of intimacy. And all have some degree of impersonality—spouses do not tell each other everything, nor do they discard all forms of etiquette. Particular groups must be compared and classified as relatively more primary or more secondary.

Gemeinschaft and Gesellschaft   Well before Cooley developed the concept of the primary group, European sociologists had been considering the same distinction. Their interest was in characterizing the long-term historical shift from small, rural, intimate, and traditional society to large, urban, impersonal, and modern society— the shift from intimate village life to impersonal urban life. In the mid-1880s, Ferdinand Tönnies introduced the concepts of *Gemeinschaft* (community) and *Gesellschaft* (society or association) to characterize old and new forms of social life. As will be discussed in Chapter 24, the shift from rural to urban life is extremely recent. (As recently as 1930 nearly half of the American population still lived in small towns or on farms.) The massive shift to urbanism was thus just beginning at the time Tönnies wrote. It was already clear at that time that this shift was the wave of the future and that it would transform the most fundamental features of social life.

In order to make sense of these transformations, it was necessary to isolate the critical differences between the past and the future. Tönnies saw *Gemeinschaft* as approximated by the old, rural, peasant village or community, a cohesive social unit organized on the basis of shared values

Figure 8.3   The Ainu of northern Japan (*left*) live in a *Gemeinschaft* ("community"). Social relations among them are predominantly primary and are organized on the basis of the values, norms, beliefs, and attitudes they hold in common. Contrasted to this form of social organization is the *Gesellschaft* ("society"), in which members pursue individual goals and have diverse values, beliefs, and attitudes (*right*). The concepts of *Gemeinschaft* and *Gesellschaft*, respectively, correspond roughly to Durkheim's concepts of mechanical and organic solidarity. See also Figure 4.2 in Chapter 4.

and norms that commanded strong allegiance from its members. They referred to themselves as "we." Individuals do not join a *Gemeinschaft;* they are born into it. Social bonds are formed by circumstance, not chosen.

In the *Gesellschaft*, individual self-interests dominate. There is little consensus on norms or values, and commitment to the group is low, or at least greatly limited. Change is continual. Traditions are called into question on the basis of more rational and efficient ways of doing things. In Tönnies view, the *Gesellschaft* is a mass society of loosely connected individuals, each of whom pursues his or her own interests as best and as efficiently as possible. According to Tönnies, *Gesellschaft*, with its complexity of secondary relationships, was gradually replacing *Gemeinschaft* as the dominant form of social organization—and Tönnies made it clear that he both regretted and feared the change.

From our perspective nearly a hundred years later, we see that the changes Tönnies predicted have occurred but that their results have not been quite as disastrous as he feared. He had underestimated the ability of humans to fashion primary groups and relationships within mass society, and he had idealized the warmth of relationships in the *Gemeinschaft*. As countless novels (such as *Main Street*, by Sinclair Lewis) have revealed, small intimate communities can be cruel and repressive as well as warm. For all our present concern that cities have become violent jungles, we would do well to remember that historical studies have shown that life in the *Gemeinschaft* was perhaps even more violent (Graham and Gurr, 1969).

The Sacred and the Secular   A third effort to classify these differences among groups was made by Howard P. Becker (1950). He distinguished between *sacred* and *secular* societies. Although Becker's sacred societies do greatly resemble Tönnies' notion of *Gemeinschaft*, Becker was primarily interested in the commitment of these societies to tradition and to mystical or superempirical beliefs. Similarly, in Becker's terms, *Gesellschafts* were usually, but not always, *secular* socie-

ties. Nazi Germany was, according to Becker's classification, both a *Gesellschaft* and a sacred society—it was a modern industrial society with an intense commitment to a near mystical ideology concerning the racial destiny of Germans.

For Tönnies, the transformation from *Gemeinschaft* to *Gesellschaft* was irreversible. For Becker, the historical trend was from sacred to secular societies, from religion to science, but the trend was not irreversible. Indeed, something to be feared in the modern world was the sacred *Gesellschaft* that combined the parochial sense of special virtue characteristic of *Gemeinschafts* with the vast industrial might of the *Gesellschaft*.

Both Tönnies and Becker utilized the fundamental ideas expressed in the concepts of primary and secondary groups as macro concepts to analyze large-scale historical trends. As we shall see in later chapters, especially in Unit VIII, these concepts have considerable utility in the study of social change. For instance, they are particularly useful in understanding the transformations from preindustrial to industrial societies. These concepts may also alert us to the kinds of disruptions that such transformations are likely to produce in the character of interpersonal relationships.

Reference Groups

The concept of *reference group* has become extremely important in sociological analysis. This concept has much in common with the notion of the primary group, but it is also importantly different. Many primary groups are also reference

Figure 8.4   (*Right*) A housing unit similar to
those in the student-housing complex where Festinger,
Schachter, and Back investigated the effects of proximity on friendship formation. (*Left*) Data from their
study that indicate the close relationship between
someone's physical proximity to you and your choosing
that person as a friend.
(From L. Festinger, S. Schachter, and K. Back, 1950.)

groups, but not all are; secondary groups also can serve as reference groups.

Quite simply, reference groups are those groups to which people refer in order to make comparative self-judgments. Individuals evaluate themselves according to the standards and values of their reference groups, and they orient their behavior, either positively or negatively, toward these groups. Thus, people take from their reference groups a set of values, standards of behavior, and even, in some cases, a certain self-image (Shibutani, 1955).

Often, people do not orient their behavior to the norms or expectations of the group in which they happen to be participating at the moment. They may violate the expectations of one group in order to fulfill the expectations of some other group. In fact, one may use some group as a reference group without actually being a member of it. A person may model himself on the basis of some group he hopes one day to belong to; for example, the young executive may model his behavior after that of top management. In a study of college professors, Alvin Gouldner (1957) found that some faculty members were attentive to their relationships with local colleagues. Others seemed to care little for the approval of their fellow faculty members, attending instead to their reputations among scholars in their field around the world. Gouldner used the terms *locals* and *cosmopolitans* to distinguish between these two types of professors and found that much of their behavior could be easily understood once one identified their reference group.

Sometimes people have negative as well as positive reference groups. Various activities may be disdained because they are thought to be associated with a group that the individual holds in contempt. Young people, for example, may avoid participating in certain activities because their parents engage in them.

GROUP STRUCTURES AND PROCESSES

Thus far some special types of groups have been discussed. But how do such groups actually operate? Let us now turn to this topic. The remainder of this chapter examines how groups are formed,

how they become cohesive, and how they induce members to conform to group norms. Questions about ranking within groups will also be explored. How does leadership arise, how is it maintained, and what is the relationship between various styles of leadership and various kinds of groups? Finally, the chapter will consider patterns of communication within groups.

Much of what we know about groups is the result of experiments conducted with small groups of persons assembled in laboratories. As mentioned earlier, one of the difficulties that plagues sociology is the extent to which findings based on laboratory experiments apply to situations in real life, outside the laboratory. When there is supporting evidence from nonexperimental studies, we are more confident that experimental findings do apply outside the lab. But on some of the matters discussed later, such evidence has not been collected. When corroboration from outside the laboratory situation is lacking, you should regard the findings as tentative.

The Formation of Groups

The obvious basis of most group formation is *goal achievement*. This is simply to say that most groups are formed for some specific purpose, that people join their efforts to achieve some goal they value. Couples marry and form families in pursuit of stable affectional relations, in order to rear children, and to gain economic security; people form social clubs to have fun; they form work groups to earn a living. As we shall see later, the purpose for which a group is formed often has consequences for its internal organization and for the nature of its leadership. For now, it is enough to recognize that goals give rise to groups and that existing groups often seek new goals.

Proximity   Groups, by definition, require considerable interaction among members; it seems equally obvious that groups would form among persons who happen to be close to one another. The point may be obvious, but the great extent to which sheer physical proximity shapes our lives comes as a shock to most people unfamiliar with the results of a number of studies.

SOCIOMETRIC CHOICE AND PHYSICAL DISTANCE			
Units of Distance	Number of Choices Given	Possible Number of Choices	Percentage Choosing
1	112	8×34	41.2
2	46	6×34	22.5
3	22	4×34	16.2
4	7	2×34	10.3

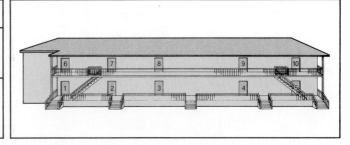

Consider the choice of a spouse. Obviously we choose the person we marry on a number of grounds, such as appearance, interests, or personality. Nevertheless, it has been demonstrated that in urban areas, geographic proximity is such an important factor in choice of marriage partners that the probability of marriage falls off in a regular gradient as the distance that separates potential partners increases. It is true that we tend to marry the boy or the girl next door.

Perhaps the most extensive examination of the effects of physical proximity on friendship-group formation was carried out by Leon Festinger, Stanley Schachter, and Kurt Back (1950), who studied the development of social interaction in married-student housing units at the Massachusetts Institute of Technology just after World War II. The availability of housing was extremely limited, and the students were assigned, almost at random, to housing units as they became available. Almost none of the students in any of the housing units had known each other prior to moving in. Figure 8.4 is a schematic diagram of the typical housing-unit pattern. It contains apartments on two floors, with stairs at each end. We can measure, very crudely, how far it is from any given apartment to any other apartment: for example, we can call the distance between two adjacent apartments "one unit" of physical distance, the distance between two apartments "two units," and so on; we can add a unit's worth of distance for having to go up or down stairs.

Each member of this housing complex, which actually consisted of many apartment units like the one schematized in Figure 8.4, was asked to list his best friends in the project. A basic question was: what is the probability that a person will choose his close friends on the basis of the number of units of physical distance that separate him from people? That is, what proportion of people listed as one of their close friends the person who lived next door to them, what proportion listed the person who lived two doors away, and so on? Partial results are shown in Figure 8.4.

As can be seen, even within these very narrow limits, the closer one lives to another person, the more likely one is to list him as a close friend.

People who live next door to a person are more likely to be listed as his close friends than are people who live two doors away. These people, in turn, are more likely to be listed than people who live three or four doors away. It is reasonable to assume that large physical distances make a difference in who our friends are—after all, we all know that when a formerly close friend moves to a town some distance away, the friendship tends to diminish. But should it make a difference whether a person lives six feet away instead of fifteen feet? The result of such small differences does indeed seem surprising, but it has been established many times in research.

In Festinger, Schachter, and Back's study, the result was consistent not only within apartment houses but between apartment houses. People were more likely to have friends in apartment houses adjacent to theirs, much less likely to have friends in apartment houses two units away, and still less likely to have friends in apartment houses three, four, or five units away. It appears that over a wide range of distances, the actual physical distance between your home and the home of another person is very important in determining whether you will list him as a friend. The difference between his living only 6 feet away and 15 feet away is important, but so is the difference between living 60 feet or 6,000 feet away. Before we leave this study, we should note one small anomaly: There were certain subjects who tended to be chosen somewhat more frequently than would be expected by chance. These were the people who lived in the apartment adjacent to the foot of the stairs. The garbage can was behind the stairs, and it appears that perhaps more people passed by their door (and therefore saw them) than passed by the doors of people living in other apartments.

Similarity Proximity is not the only factor that brings people together into groups. Obviously, we tend to prefer others who resemble us—those who share our interests, values, beliefs, and ideals. When people have free choice in forming or joining groups, they gravitate toward those whose members are similar to them in educational achievement, age, class, ethnicity, religion, and politics. Furthermore, the more people interact under conditions of equality, the more they come to share values and interests and to like one another (Berelson and Steiner, 1964). Groups tend to form among those who are already similar, and group membership tends to make people more similar than they were before.

Group Cohesiveness

The cohesiveness of groups—literally, how tightly they stick together—has been the object of considerable research. A common technique for assessing group cohesiveness is the *sociometric method*. Persons are asked to name their best friends. The extent to which persons in a group choose other group members rather than persons outside the group is used as an index of cohesiveness. As shown in Table 8.1, Rodney Stark and Charles Y. Glock (1968) found that Christian denominations in America differ greatly in their cohesiveness. Members of the more theologically liberal Protestant denominations, such as the Methodists, tend to have their best friends outside their church congregations. Members of more conservative denominations, such as the Southern Baptists, tend to select their best friends from

within their church congregation. Stark and Glock therefore characterized liberal Protestant congregations as "audiences," or secondary groups, and conservative denominations as "communities," or primary groups.

A major factor influencing group cohesiveness is *size*. The larger the group, the more difficult it is for members to interact with each other. Similarly, physical proximity influences group cohesiveness. In a classic study, Sherif and his associates (1953) showed that if a group of boys is divided and physically separated into two smaller groups—so that the pairs of boys who have begun to like each other are separated—the interaction within each of the new groups results in new attachments of liking within each group. When the two groups are then put in a competitive situation, dislikes in each group become focused on the other group, even though it contains former friends. When the two groups are then put in a situation calling for cooperation and interaction, the dislikes tend to dissolve and be replaced by liking. Similarly, Stark and Glock (1968) found that conservative Protestant denominations differed from liberal denominations in that the average size of conservative congregations was much smaller and that conservative church members

Table 8.1   Friendship Patterns Within Church Congregations

Religious Affiliation		"Of your five best friends, how many belong to your congregation?"				
		3–5	2	1	0	No Answer
Congregational	(n* = 151)	18%	11%	22%	49%	0%
Methodist	(n = 415)	24	17	16	43	0
Episcopalian	(n = 416)	20	19	21	39	1
Disciples of Christ	(n = 50)	42	10	12	36	0
Presbyterian	(n = 495)	23	19	18	39	1
American Lutheran	(n = 208)	20	14	15	50	1
American Baptist	(n = 141)	40	13	12	31	4
Missouri Lutheran	(n = 776)	25	15	19	40	1
Southern Baptist	(n = 79)	49	11	14	23	3
Sects	(n = 255)	67	13	7	9	4
Total Protestant	(n = 2,326)	29%	16%	16%	36%	3%
Roman Catholic	(n = 545)	36%	14%	14%	34%	2%

* n = number of people who were asked.
Source: Adapted from Rodney Stark and Charles Y. Glock, *American Piety: The Nature of Religious Commitment* (Berkeley: University of California Press, 1968).

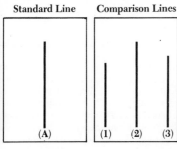

Standard Line   **Comparison Lines**

(A)   (1) (2) (3)

Figure 8.5   Solomon Asch (*far left*), a social psychologist, conducted a brilliant series of experiments on conformity to group judgments that has enhanced our knowledge of the factors associated with conformity and resistance to group pressure. (*Left*) These two cards, or similar ones, are shown to a subject during one trial in the Asch experiment. The actual discrimination involved is easy; control subjects (those not subjected to group pressure) chose line 2 as the correct match in over 99 percent of the trials.

interacted more frequently with one another. These are probably major reasons for their greater cohesiveness.

Another major factor influencing cohesiveness is *turnover*. Bernard Berelson and Gary A. Steiner (1964) report that "the larger the proportion of new members joining an established group within a given time (short of actually taking it over), the greater will be the resistence of the group to their assimilation." Although a few new members can usually expect to be welcomed into a group, too many new members at one time threaten the existing pattern of relationships within a group. Because they are not yet related to older members by bonds of friendship, these new members reduce the overall cohesiveness of the group. It follows that, as Berelson and Steiner report, the less turnover in membership, the higher the cohesiveness and morale of a group.

Conformity to Group Norms

Throughout this book we have asserted that groups greatly shape individual behavior—that groups maintain a set of norms governing behavior and that they impose sanctions on members in order to gain compliance to norms. A great many studies have been conducted on the nature and extent of the power of groups to obtain conformity to norms. Let us now consider some of the major results.

Perhaps the most famous study of conformity to group pressure was designed and conducted more than twenty years ago by the social psychologist Solomon Asch (1952). Since then, his study has been repeated many times.

The following is what you would experience if you were a subject in one of Asch's experiments. You and seven other students report to a classroom for an experiment on visual judgment. The experimenter says that you will be asked to judge the length of lines on a series of comparisons. He displays two large white cards like the ones shown in Figure 8.5. On one card is a single vertical line—the standard whose length is to be matched. On the other are three vertical lines of different lengths, and you are to choose the one that is the same length as the standard. One of the three is

actually of the same length; the other two are substantially different. The experiment opens uneventfully. The subjects give their answers in the order in which they are seated in the room; you happen to be seventh, and one person follows you. On the first comparison every person chooses the same matching line. The second set of cards is displayed, and once again the group is unanimous. The discriminations seem very easy, and you settle in for what you expect will be a rather boring experiment.

On the third trial there is an unexpected disturbance. You are quite certain that line 3 is the one that matches the standard, but the first person in the group announces confidently that line 1 is the correct match. The second person follows suit and declares that the answer is line 1. So do the third, fourth, fifth, and sixth subjects. Now it is your turn. What you thought was going to be an uncomplicated task has turned into a disturbing problem. You are faced with two totally contradictory pieces of information; the evidence of your own senses tells you that one answer is clearly correct, but the unanimous and confident judgments of the six preceding subjects tell you that another answer is correct. What do you do? Do you stick to your initial judgment, or do you go along with the others?

Your dilemma persists through eighteen trials. On twelve of the trials the other group members unanimously give an answer that differs from what you clearly perceive to be correct. It is only at the end of the experimental session that you learn how you have been duped: the seven other subjects were all confederates of Dr. Asch, who had instructed them to respond the way they did.

How do most people react in this situation? Asch put fifty subjects through this procedure and found that almost a third of the subjects conformed at least half of the time. What accounts for this high degree of conformity, and what factors explain why some people conform and others do not? Asch carefully observed the subjects' behavior during the course of the experiment and conducted intensive interviews with them afterward to ascertain both the psychological mechanisms underlying the behavior of the "independents"

Figure 8.6   Asch's classic experiment on conformity to group pressure is depicted in these photographs. Subject 6, sitting at the upper-right corner of the table, is the only real subject; the others are confederates of the experimenter. The subject listens to the others express identical judgments that differ from his own. He is in a dilemma: does he express his own judgment and risk being different from the group or does he conform to the group's judgment? Asch found substantial conformity

to the group on the part of his subjects. The amount of conformity depended on the size of the opposition. If only one other person was opposed, there was very little yielding; when the majority expressed contrary judgments, conformity became quite pronounced. Some subjects conformed to the group judgment even when they believed strongly that their own choice was correct and the group's was incorrect. What do you think you would have done if you had been a subject in Asch's experiment?

and the "yielders" and the conditions that promote conformity. Some of the independent subjects stuck to their guns very confidently, announcing their judgments loudly and spontaneously. Others were more withdrawn or tense but still managed to resist the pressure to conform to the group judgment. Among the yielders, very few reported that they actually *perceived* the majority's choice as correct. Most yielders said that they believed their own perception to be correct but that they yielded to the group pressure so as not to appear different from or inferior to the others. These subjects felt that if they did not follow the group's lead, they would be revealing some basic weakness in themselves that they preferred to hide.

Asch's illustrative descriptions of an independent subject and a yielder appear as Figure 8.7. Other studies, that by David Marlowe and Kenneth J. Gergen (1968), for example, have found that people with low self-esteem (that is, a generalized lack of self-confidence) are more likely to yield to group pressure than are people with high self-esteem. Clearly, it is the person who has confidence in his or her own abilities and basic worth who can afford to be less concerned with the opinions and approval of others.

Asch obtained a very interesting finding about conformity in the course of several variations of

this basic experiment: the *size* of the majority is not nearly so important as its *unanimity.* Just as much conformity was found when there were three or four confederates as when there were seven, nine, or even fifteen. But when just one of the confederates was instructed to give the right answers rather than go along with the majority, the amount of conformity declined dramatically: from 32 percent to 5 percent (Asch, 1952).

In 1961, Stanley Milgram repeated the Asch experiment with Norwegian and French students. He found that Norwegian students were considerably more likely than French students to yield to the group's judgments. He had predicted such differences on the basis of his informal observations of both societies. He judged that Norwegians would be more likely to conform because he believed Norway had a much more cohesive society than did France.

The degree of cohesiveness has a major effect on conformity to group norms. In the study of married-student housing discussed earlier in this chapter, Festinger and his colleagues found that the more cohesive a housing unit, the greater the degree to which residents conformed. The higher the proportion of friendships within a unit, the smaller was the proportion of residents who deviated from group standards (Festinger *et al.*, 1950).

One reason why cohesiveness influences conformity is that individuals are inclined to perceive a group's opinion as closer to their own than it actually is (Kelley and Thibaut, 1954). However, the more frequent the interaction among group members, the more correct are their judgments about group opinion (Berelson and Steiner, 1964). Interaction is more frequent in more cohesive groups. A second reason also follows from higher rates of interaction in cohesive groups. The more people interact, the more they are inclined to like each other; and the more they like each other, the more they stand to lose by offending group standards. It is relatively easy to shrug off disapproval by strangers, but the good opinion of our friends is valuable and we do not risk it lightly.

From the perspective of social-learning theories, the group is the major source of rewards and

Figure 8.7   Asch's descriptions of an "independent" subject and a "yielding" subject in his experiment on group pressure and conformity.
(From S. E. Asch, 1951.)

Independent	*Yielder*
After a few trials he appeared puzzled, hesitant. He announced all disagreeing answers in the form of "Three, sir; two, sir." At Trial 4 he answered immediately after the first member of the group, shook his head, blinked, and whispered to his neighbor, "Can't help it, that's one." His later answers came in a whispered voice, accompanied by a deprecating smile. At one point he grinned embarrassedly and whispered explosively to his neighbor: "I always disagree—darn it!" Immediately after the experiment the majority engaged this subject in a brief discussion. When they pressed him to say whether the entire group was wrong and he alone right, he turned upon them defiantly, exclaiming: "You're probably right, but you may be wrong!" During the experimenter's later questioning, this subject's constant refrain was: "I called them as I saw them, sir."	*This subject went along with the majority in eleven out of twelve trials. He appeared nervous and somewhat confused, but he did not attempt to evade discussion at the close of the experiment. He opened the discussion with the statement: "If I'd been first I probably would have responded differently." This was his way of saying that he had adopted the majority estimates. The primary factor in his case was loss of confidence. He perceived the majority as a decided group, acting without hesitation: "If they had been doubtful I probably would have changed, but they answered with such confidence." When the real purpose of the experiment was explained, the subject volunteered: "I suspected about the middle—but tried to push it out of my mind." It is of interest that his suspicions did not restore his confidence or diminish the power of the majority.*

punishments for the individual. A group therefore reinforces behavior that it wants members to perform. As George C. Homans (1961) put it:

Men give social approval, as a generalized reinforcer, to others that have given them activity they value, and so make it more likely that others will go on giving the activity. One of the kinds of activity some men find valuable is that their own behavior and that of others they are associated with in a group should be similar in conforming to a norm. . . . People that find conformity valuable reward conformers with social approval, but they withhold approval from those that will not conform, or even express positive dislike for nonconformists as having denied them a reward they had a right to expect.

Individual autonomy is thus restricted by the expectations of our friends and associates. Indeed, the simple fact of *social* life means that individuals cannot be wholly free to pursue their own impulses and interests; their freedom inevitably impinges on someone else's freedom. The child who takes all the toys deprives all the other children of playthings. Furthermore, what we want to do— our impulses and goals—are learned from the group.

Nevertheless, as is discussed in Chapters 10 and 11, some groups require more conformity than do others, and some individuals conform more fully than do others. In his influential book *The Lonely Crowd* (1950), David Riesman and his associates argued that, initially, traditional societies *(Gemeinschafts)* require greater member conformity but that, as a result, persons brought up in such societies become less susceptible to group pressures. The values and standards inculcated by traditional societies become permanent features of individual character, according to Riesman, and function as a kind of inner gyroscope. Later in life this gyroscope will permit the individual to stick to his principles and resist group pressures to act in different ways. Riesman called such persons *inner-directed.* In contemporary societies *(Gesellschafts),* according to Riesman, people learn how to orient their behavior to the expectations of those around them. They are *other-directed.* If the inner-directed person has a gyroscope, the other-directed person has social radar. He is sensitive to the shifting expectations that accompany membership in a great many groups. Riesman thus argued that the typical American character type had been shifting over time from inner- to other-directed. However, later research based on forgotten questionnaire studies of school children dating back to the late nineteenth century suggests that Americans have not changed very much—Americans have always been fairly other-directed (Greenstein, 1964). Furthermore, it may be that other-directedness is not nearly as culturally determined as Riesman and many other sociologists think it is. Recent studies of our closest primate cousins, the apes, reveal that they may be even more hungry for group approval than are humans. A great deal of ape activity is designed to attract approving attention, and dominance among apes is determined according to how good a show an ape can put on for the others (Morgan, 1972). For an account of one such show see Figure 8.8.

Ranking Within Groups

Groups are never made up of a set of equals. Inevitably, in the words of George Orwell, "some are more equal than others." In all groups there is some degree of ranking of members in terms of their dominance over other members. It turns out that no matter how group members are asked to rank one another, the structure of ranks in the group turns out to be the structure of leadership. Whether members are asked to choose the most popular, admirable, talented, or powerful persons in the group, the same general ranking of the same individuals tends to be produced. Thus, to study ranking within groups is to study the nature of group *leadership*.

The more complex the group and its tasks, the more leadership tends to be widely delegated and specialized. However, even in very simple laboratory groups, two distinctive leadership functions can be observed.

Expressive and Instrumental Leadership Leadership in groups must fulfill two necessary but somewhat contradictory needs of the group—the need to pursue the goals of the group *(instrumental leadership)* and the need to create harmony and affection among group members *(expressive leadership)*. Usually these two functions of leadership—to guide the group toward its goals and to sustain interpersonal liking and affection—are not fulfilled by one person. Although leaders usually begin in both roles (that they are well-liked helps them dominate task-directed activities), they

Figure 8.8 Other-directedness may not be determined totally by culture. The human need for group approval is a quality shared by our closest primate relatives, the apes, who go to great lengths to attract attention and win approval.
Elaine Morgan, *The Descent of Woman* (New York: Stein and Day, 1972), pp. 187–188.

First the dominant gorilla starts by hooting. He gives anything up to forty hoots at an increasing tempo. He picks a leaf and puts it in his mouth. He stands up on his hind legs, grabbing a handful of vegetation and throwing it into the air. Then he beats his chest up to twenty times with his hands, using them alternately, and slightly cupped. Sometimes for good measure he kicks one leg into the air while he is doing it. Immediately after the chest-beating he starts a curious sideways run, first a few steps bipedally and then charging sideways like a gigantic crab, sweeping one arm through the vegetation, slapping at the undergrowth, shaking branches, breaking off or tearing up whole trees. Finally he thumps the gound, usually with one palm but sometimes with two, as who should say "Follow that, buster!" Of course no one can, though even infant gorillas of six months old have been known to rise shakily onto their hind legs and slap at their puny chests, watched by their mothers as fondly as if they were aspiring Hollywood tots at their first audition.

rarely hold both very long. In more than half the groups taking part in a series of small-group experiments, the same group member was rated in first place on both "liking" and "ideas" after the first session. After the second session, however, only 12 percent of the groups ranked the same individual first on both instrumental (ideas) and expressive (liking) leadership. This proportion of groups dropped to 8 percent by the fourth session (Slater, 1955).

Those who direct group activities—who dominate the group—tend to lose some of their popularity. To be the most popular member, a person must devote himself to keeping members happy (expressive leadership). When faced with a choice, most group leaders will give up the instrumental-leadership role in favor of gaining popularity. In a series of experiments by Robert Freed Bales (1953), nine persons who started out as both best liked and as having the best ideas dropped the best-ideas role in favor of being best

Figure 8.9 Regardless of gender or social class, popular children tend to have higher IQ scores than unpopular children.
(From M. Roff and S. B. Sells, 1965.)

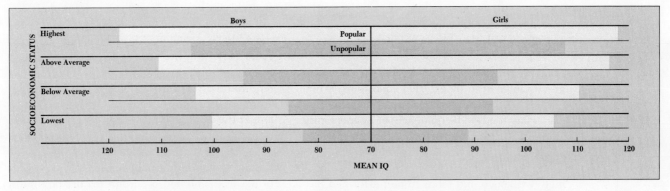

liked. Not a single person dropped the best-liked role in favor of the best-ideas role.

Who Leads? The individual characteristics that are associated with leadership are fairly obvious to all of us. They are traits that give the individual competitive advantages in gaining the admiration of others and in serving the needs of the group. Physical size—height and weight—are of major importance in leadership within children's groups. The strongest are better able to get their way and to excel in games (Berelson and Steiner, 1964). But, as reported in Chapters 13 and 17, size is also associated with leadership among adults. The same is true of beauty. Leaders are judged to be better looking than followers. Similarly, leaders are found to have higher IQ scores than do their followers. However, they must not be too much more intelligent. As Cecil Gibb (1954) found, IQ differences of about thirty points seem to be the limit; beyond that relations between leaders and followers seem to break down. Leaders have also been found to be more sociable, more determined, more energetic, and more self-confident than followers (Berelson and Steiner, 1964). They have also been found to be more liberal, even when they are leaders of conservative groups (Stouffer, 1955).

How Do They Lead? When groups have established norms, it is very difficult for leaders, no matter how talented, to change the groups' procedures or goals very much. If a leader tries too hard, he will lose his leadership position. Nor-

mally, it is easier for leaders to influence means and tactics than to influence goals. Indeed, leaders conform to group expectations because persons tend to become leaders who already closely conform to the standards of the group (Berelson and Steiner, 1964).

In one influential experiment, groups of children were formed and allowed to interact for sufficient time so that they developed traditions concerning their activities. Then a leader was introduced into each group. Each leader was a somewhat older child selected because he or she had previously demonstrated leadership skills. As it turned out, the newcomer was forced by the group to engage in the activities it had developed prior to the newcomer's arrival. Attempts by a leader to initiate new activities were mainly unsuccessful. "In the overwhelming majority of our cases the leader was forced to accept the group's traditions—that is, he proved weaker than the group but still managed to play the role of the leader" (Merei, 1958). Thus does laboratory research confirm the famous remark by a French socialist, "My followers are on the barricades; I must go and lead them."

Nevertheless, leaders do have some independent effect on group behavior. For one thing, leaders will tend to direct the group toward activities in which the leaders are proficient and away from activities in which they are less competent (Berelson and Steiner, 1964). Furthermore, leaders will be followed more faithfully if they make it possible for members to achieve private goals as well as group goals. For example, when we say the President is calling in his political I.O.U.s in order to pass a particular program, we mean that in the past he has helped congressmen achieve private goals for which they are now indebted.

Styles of Leadership Leadership in groups is greatly influenced by external conditions. When groups are free to determine their own activities, leadership tends to be quite active. Leaders initiate, persuade, and even coerce members. However, when the activities of the group are imposed from outside the group, leadership is correspondingly weakened and tends to be performed passively. Passive leaders operate as mediators and as behavior models (Berelson and Steiner, 1964).

In a famous study, groups of boys were formed and three styles of leaders were introduced into the various groups: autocratic leaders, democratic leaders, and laissez-faire, or permissive, leaders. It was found that democratic leaders were most effective in holding groups together and in accomplishing the work of the group. Groups led by autocratic, or domineering, leaders bogged down in internal dissention. Groups led by laissez-faire leaders tended to get little work done (White and Lippitt, 1960). It must be pointed out, however, that in this experiment the subjects were American boys who were perhaps already socialized to respond negatively to autocratic leaders. Furthermore, in such situations autocratic leaders had limited means for coercion. In the real world, autocratic leaders often have been able to use terror to control groups quite effectively.

In his best seller, *Up The Organization* (1970), Robert Townsend has argued that organizations should have a change of leaders about every five years. He claims that leadership becomes ineffective over time because past decisions and conflicts tend to restrict future options. Townsend's views are supported by small-group research. The longer the duration of leadership, the less open is the communication within the group and the less efficient the group tends to become in solving new problems (Berelson and Steiner, 1964). This brings us to another important feature of groups, the patterning and processes of internal communication or interaction.

Communication in Groups

It has been pointed out earlier that group cohesiveness is not only a result of the amount of interaction among members but also leads to interaction among group members. According to circumstances, however, there is considerable variation in the amount of communication or interaction in the same group. Internal disagreements or dissension may cause considerable increases or decreases in interaction, depending on the cohesiveness of the group. In groups that are very cohesive, dissension causes a sharp reduction in interaction until the dissension is resolved. People try to protect their emotional stake in the group by avoiding open disagreement. But in groups with little cohesiveness, interaction tends

Table 8.2   Acts Toward Others in a Small Group

Initiator of Act	Target of Act						Total Individual-Directed Acts	Group-Directed Acts	Total of Acts Initiated
	1	2	3	4	5	6			
1		1238	961	545	445	317	3506	5661	9167
2	1748		443	310	175	102	2278	1211	3989
3	1371	415		305	125	69	2285	742	3027
4	952	310	282		83	49	1676	676	2352
5	662	224	144	83		28	1141	443	1585
6	470	126	114	65	44		819	373	1192
Total of Acts Received	5203	2313	1944	1308	872	565	12208	9106	21311

Source: Adapted from Robert F. Bales, Fred L. Strodtbeck, Theodore M. Mills, and Mary E. Roseborough, "Channels of Communication in Small Groups," *American Sociological Review*, 16 (1951), p. 463.

sharply to increase as members recognize they disagree on an important matter (Berelson and Steiner, 1964).

Furthermore, when there is dissension, interaction will be directed primarily toward members perceived as holding the minority view (the deviants)—so long as the majority believe there is some chance to convert them to the majority view. Once the majority believe that those holding the minority viewpoint are unpersuadable, interaction with the deviants is greatly curtailed. Such minority members are, in effect, expelled from the group (Festinger and Thibaut, 1951).

It is clear that interaction within groups is neither randomly patterned nor equally distributed among members. In fact, a careful compilation of who addresses whom in a group reveals the dominance ranking of group members. Bales has conducted many studies of communications in small groups. Table 8.2 shows the distribution of all interaction in eighteen sessions of six-man groups. These findings show that if group members are ranked according to the total number of interactions they initiate, they are similarly ranked: (1) by the number of interactions they receive; (2) by the number of interactions they address to other specific persons; and (3) by the number of interactions they address to the group as a whole. It is quite easy to see that person 1 is the leader of the group and that person 6 is an extremely marginal member—no one talks to him much and he talks little to anyone (Bales *et al.*, 1951).

Communication within a group tends to be directed from equal to equal and from higher-ranking persons to lower-ranking persons. Henry Riecken and George C. Homans (1954) found that this pattern was influenced by the nature of the group activity. Communication is primarily between high- and low-ranking members in task situations and between equals in social or leisure situations. Similarly, there is more communication with instrumental leaders during task situations and more communication with expressive leaders during social situations.

All of these tendencies in groups are heightened as groups grow in size. The larger the group, the more the leadership dominates communications, the more the group tolerates direction by the leader, and the more formalized the group's procedures become (Bales and Borgatta, 1955). The critical size seems to be from five to seven members. Smaller groups tend to be informal with less differentiated leadership; however, beyond that size the domination by leadership increases rather rapidly. Apparently, unless groups are very small, all members in a group cannot pay equal attention to all others. If everyone tries to talk there is chaos. Recall from Chapter 6 that parents were much more autocratic in large than in small families. This behavior reflects the general pattern of group functioning and also tells us something about why relationships are more impersonal and more governed by formal rules in *Gesellschafts* than they are in *Gemeinschafts*. Participatory democracy as practiced in the New England town meetings requires that everyone can fit into the town hall. Mass societies tend towards impersonality simply because they are large.

This chapter has discussed the basic structure and operations of groups, emphasizing small, face-to-face groups. Building on this base, we now turn to a special kind of group—the formal organization. Indeed, one way of looking at formal organizations is as a cluster of small groups united in a common enterprise.

SUGGESTED READINGS

Berelson, Bernard, and Gary A. Steiner. *Human Behavior: An Inventory of Scientific Findings.* New York: Harcourt, Brace & World, 1964, Chapter 8.

Festinger, Leon, Stanley Schachter, and Kurt Back. *Social Pressures in Informal Groups.* New York: Harper & Row, 1950.

Hare, A. Paul, Robert F. Bales, and Edgar F. Borgatta (eds.). *Small Groups: Studies in Social Interaction.* Rev. ed. New York: Knopf, 1965.

Homans, George C. *The Human Group.* New York: Harcourt, Brace, 1950.

Chapter 9 Formal Organizations

CHAPTER 8 MAINLY WAS CONCERNED with small, informal groups in which members engage in considerable face-to-face interaction. Many groups, however, are large, formal, and impersonal. *Formal organizations*—groups that are bureaucratic, have officially defined positions and roles, and are structured and guided by rules and regulations —are perhaps the most distinctive feature of modern, industrialized society. The transformation from *Gemeinschaft* to *Gesellschaft*, as characterized by Tönnies, whose views were discussed in Chapter 8, has been a shift from informal community life to life within formal organizations. A useful way to understand what formal organizations are is to examine why and how they came into existence.

Consider the medieval shoemaker. He was a self-employed craftsman who personally performed all of the operations of his trade. He purchased leather from the tanner, made the shoes, and sold them. Ordinarily he worked alone or with his son, and his family lived in the back of his shop. For hundreds of years this is the way shoes were made.

But one day something happened. A village began to grow rapidly, and the local shoemaker found he had many more customers than he could take care of. How could he increase production to provide shoes for everyone? Our hypothetical shoemaker decided to hire some helpers. The helpers were not trained shoemakers, but the shoemaker found that he could teach each of them to perform a few of the operations required to make shoes. He trained one to buy leather from the tanner, another to cut out soles, and another to sew. And he made an unemployed innkeeper his salesman. Thus was a small shoe factory born.

The shoemaker soon discovered that by having a number of helpers specializing in one repetitive step in the shoe-making operation he could not only make more shoes but could make them faster and cheaper—his factory was *efficient*. Efficiency is a consequence of the organizational principle our shoemaker had discovered: the *division of labor*. As used in social science, the concept of the division of labor means what it says: the division of members of a work group into spe-

cialized roles. Instead of each person performing the same series of tasks independently, members perform different aspects of an operation that contribute to the completion of the final product: in this case, shoes.

Thus far our shoemaker had invented the *horizontal* division of labor: persons specializing in particular parts of the shoe-making operation. But as time went on he faced a new problem. Someone had to take charge of coordinating the activity of his workers. There were endless disputes and problems to be solved, and the shoemaker could hardly get any of his own work done. Then he realized that his own work no longer entailed shoe-making; rather, his work was running a shoe factory. His job had become that of manager. As he hired more and more workers, he found he could not manage things by himself; so he hired his wife's brother to help him manage. Pretty soon the two of them could not keep up with things either. They began to streamline their tasks by promoting some workers to be foremen and by hiring an unemployed poet to keep their accounts. Thus was *vertical* division of labor introduced into shoe making. People not only specialized in tasks but specialized in their use of authority and power as well.

The conversion of a one-man shoe-making shop into an assembly line illustrates more than the difference between preindustrial and industrial forms of production. This example also illustrates the primary features—the concern for efficiency and specialization with respect to both tasks and authority—of nearly all organizations in modern societies. Even organizations not devoted to production—for example, hospitals or political parties—are characterized by both horizontal and vertical divisions of labor.

There is much more to know about formal organizations than simply that they are based on the division of labor. Let us go on to consider some other perspectives on organizations.

TWO PERSPECTIVES ON ORGANIZATIONS
Sociologists have developed two approaches to the study of formal organizations that are both somewhat conflicting and somewhat complemen-

tary (Gouldner, 1959). One is the *rational-system* approach, which views the formal organization as a distinctive type of social group having many unique features. The other is the *natural-system* approach, which focuses on those features that the formal organization shares with many other types of social groups.

For the rational-system analyst, organizations are rational instruments for attaining some specified goal or goals. Organizations are rational in the sense that they are set up to achieve predetermined goals with a maximum of efficiency and a minimum of waste. Karl Mannheim (1950) referred to such rationality as *technical* or *functional* rationality. In economic terms, such rationality attempts to maximize output per unit of input. Investigators who employ the rational-system approach (in addition to Max Weber, whose views will be described subsequently) include Frederick Taylor, the founder of the school of scientific management, and Henri Fayol, a leading advocate of the administrative-management approach.

The natural-system analyst sees organizations as having many features in common with other social groups. For example, it has been postulated that all groups (ranging from such primary groups as the family and friendship groups to such secondary groups as the formal organizations we study here) face the same set of problems: keeping the group's members working together, attaining group goals, maintaining lines of communication, checking hostility and dissension, and so on. Other elements are also shared by all groups: for example, power, leadership, roles, role differentiation, and norms.

The natural-system analyst, then, is more interested in the generic social processes underlying *all* types of groups, and he sometimes looks at formal organizations because they are abundant and readily visible, often much more so than more informal types of groups. Leading advocates of the natural-system view of organizations include Robert Michels, a German sociologist who wrote a now-classic monograph on the operation of the Social Democratic Party at the turn of the century; Elton Mayo, one of the founders of the

human-relations approach to organizations; and Philip Selznick, a contemporary student of formal organizations.

Throughout this chapter, we will follow mostly the first line of analysis because our purpose is to discuss the distinctive aspects of formal organizations. The student, however, may wish to think about what we present here in the context of the previous chapter on groups in order to gain more insight into the second line of analysis.

Goals and the Rational-System Approach

The point of departure for the rational-system analyst is the recognition that most behavior in formal organizations is goal-directed. What sets off formal organizations from other types of social groups is the specificity and explicitness of their goals; that is, their goals are usually clearly defined. Members of an organization must choose among many courses of action in order to implement its goals (March and Simon, 1958). The more precisely goals may be defined, the easier it will be for organizational members to design a structure that will attain these goals in as rational a way as possible. Thus, decisions concerning goal implementation—how tasks are to be performed, what employees are needed, how resources, including personnel, are to be allocated, who should exercise power over whom, and how incentives should be distributed—may be most rationally made when the goals are clear, as they often are for industrial-production organizations or as they were for our hypothetical shoemaker.

But many organizations are faced with goals that are not so clear-cut. The goals of a university, for example, are less clearly defined (and their attainment less easy to measure) than those of a business firm. A rational-system analyst would predict that because the university cannot arrive at a clear definition of its goals (what, for example, constitutes a good education and how can it be measured?) the university suffers much difficulty in attempting to rationalize its internal structures so as to promote the attainment of good education. Decisions concerning student admissions, graduation requirements, and the distribution of scarce resources among various departments are

Figure 9.1   The rational-system approach to the study of formal organizations concentrates on the specific goal-directedness of such organizations. A professional basketball team, for instance, is a formal organization that has specific and clear-cut goals—to win games and make money. But the members of this formal organization may also have their own individual goals— possibly to maximize their economic advantages, set

scoring records, or play long enough to receive a pension. As natural-system analysts note, individuals' goals conflict at times with organizational goals, and thus members' actual behavior is often incompatible with the professed goals of their organization. In the natural-system view, therefore, organizations are not necessarily characterized by a high degree of goal specificity.

constantly being made and remade while the very philosophy underlying institutions of higher education continues to be debated by administrators, faculty, and students. The business firm's effectiveness, on the other hand, can be more easily evaluated by using such criteria as the profit-and-loss statement or the balance sheet.

Goals and the Natural-System Approach

Sociologists who take the natural-system view of organizations are by no means convinced that organizations are necessarily characterized by a high degree of goal specificity, even in the case of business firms. These analysts argue that, in fact, few organizations actually pursue highly specific goals. Rather, organizations typically have multiple, complex, and often conflicting aims (such as the university has) many of which go unrecognized even by organizational decision makers themselves. Natural-system analysts note that in many organizations the true purposes are obscured from the participants and that the officially professed goals do not correspond to the operant objectives (Perrow, 1961). These professed goals even seem to be incompatible with the actual behavior of those who command the organization's resources. Indeed, if we look at the members of an organization instead of at its charter or bylaws, we see that they typically pursue their own individual goals, which may or may not overlap with those officially professed by the organization. Detailed studies of organizations have shown that this is one of the prime causes of inefficiency: considerable organizational time is spent by members pursuing their own interests (Michels, 1949; Dalton, 1959). Thus, the actual behavior of organizational members is often incompatible with professed goals.

Perhaps the most important point made by sociologists of the natural-system school is their insistence that all formal organizations, like all other social groups, share one overriding objective—to survive. When their survival is at stake, organizations will abandon their officially stated goals in order to save themselves (Selznick, 1949; Sills, 1957). Philip Selznick's study of the Tennessee Valley Authority (TVA) showed that this government agency, over a period of time, abandoned many of its original objectives and modified other objectives in order to assume a more conservative stance. This organization attempted to adapt to—and thereby survive—a political environment that had been rather hostile prior to this shift (Selznick, 1949).

It has also been noted that the successful attainment of an organization's professed goal is followed by a frantic search for some new goal that will justify its continued existence. An instructive example is the March of Dimes organization. Following the introduction of the Salk and Sabin polio vaccines, the organization attained its goal of conquering polio, and it began to concentrate on stamping out birth defects (Sills, 1957). Should this organization be as successful in this new campaign, it will undoubtedly justify its continued existence by finding some new malady to wipe out.

The natural-system view concludes that much organizational behavior is incomprehensible unless we see it as directed to self-maintenance and unless we realize that members' goals are at least as important as official ones (especially as members are the actors and goal implementers within the organization).

FORMALIZATION

As pointed out at the end of Chapter 7, any social group may be viewed as a network of social roles. A role was there defined as a set of expectations applied to the occupant of a particular position. In informal groups (for example, groups of friends), roles depend on the unique personalities of the particular individuals as well as on the positions they fill. Role behavior may stabilize (that is, become more organized and patterned) in such informal groups; for example, a leader may gradually emerge by contributing to group goal attainment in a manner that is acceptable to other group members.

Although stable social roles do emerge from informal interactions, they can also be created by decisions that predate the interactions themselves. A set of relationships may be called *formal* to the extent that social positions and accompanying roles are defined independently of the particular individuals who will fill them. An organizational designer may create the position of supervisor, for example, specify its activities and its relationship to other positions such as workers and managers, and then find a person who will fill this position and play its associated role. The formal definition of the position serves to structure in advance the expectations and some of the attitudes that will be directed toward the occupant of the position, whoever he or she may be and whatever his or her personality traits are..

Formalization and the Rational-System Approach

Formalization is an attempt to make behavior more predictable by standardizing and regulating it. From the viewpoint of the rational-system analyst, formalization greatly contributes to the rationality of the organization because it objectifies (makes visible and explicit) the relations among all the participants. Thus, we can speak of a formal organizational structure. This formal structure—for example, a government office or an industrial firm—can be mapped by a diagram, and the relationships among the positions can be designed and redesigned. Those responsible for the shape of the organization can attempt to determine which relationships among positions and which behaviors on the part of each position will most efficiently implement the organization's goals.

Formal structures are thus artificial rather than natural social units and, at least in theory, render organizations independent of the feelings and idiosyncrasies of particular members. As Robert K. Merton notes, "Formality facilitates the interaction of the occupants of offices despite their (possibly hostile) private attitudes toward one another" (1957). In fact, many organizations discourage the development of friendships among members for fear that such emotional ties will undermine performance or interfere with rational operation. According to Talcott Parsons (1951), organizational behavior should be governed by universalistic, not personal, norms.

In such formal structures it is not even essential to recruit superior people to leadership positions because the behavior of the incumbent is expected to be governed by the position or the office rather than by his or her personal characteristics. Robert MacIver (1947), writing in reference to political structures, has noted that: "The man who commands may be no wiser, no abler, may be in some sense no better than the average of his fellows; sometimes, by any intrinsic standard, he is inferior to them. Here is the magic of government."

More generally, here is the magic of formalization. Not only are formalized structures less dependent on finding and holding superior individuals than are other types of social groups, but such structures are not even dependent on the participation of any particular persons. Individuals may come and go, and the structure of relationships will remain intact. The *process of succession*—the movement of individuals into and out of positions—can be routinized so that one appropriately trained person can replace another with minimal

Figure 9.2 Peter M. Blau is a professor of sociology at Columbia University. He has been active in many areas of research but is best known for his studies of bureaucracy and formal organizations. In 1955 he published *The Dynamics of Bureaucracy*, a work based on intensive observation of the bureaucratic process in both a public and a private organization. In 1956 he published *Bureaucracy in Modern Society*. In 1962, with W. Richard Scott, he published *Formal Organizations*, a major theoretical work.

disturbance to the organization's smooth functioning. It is in this sense that formal organizations have the capacity to be immortal, although, in fact, most of them do cease to exist or merge into other organizations.

Informal Structures: A Natural-System Perspective

Although natural-system analysts do not deny the existence of such formal structures, they do question their impact on the behavior of the organization's members. It is easy enough to draw diagrams of the organization's structure and to talk officially about how the organization should function, but it is quite another matter to persuade participants to perform according to the diagrams and the official pronouncements. F. J. Roethlisberger and William J. Dickson (1939) were among the first investigators to systematically examine these departures from the formal structure; they noted that an *informal structure* existed parallel to the formal one. In their decade-long investigation of the Western Electric Company, these investigators documented the existence of stable norms, expectations, and patterns of behavior diverging from those prescribed by the formal rules and job definitions. The importance of informal structure was established by these researchers, and its ubiquitous presence has been confirmed by hundreds of later investigations (for example, Blau, 1955; Dalton, 1959; and Roy, 1954).

This informal structure, which does not appear on any organizational chart, is composed of cliques, friendship groups, and crosscutting personal loyalties that may either strengthen the effectiveness of the formal structure, undermine it, or transform it. Thus, Peter M. Blau's study (1955) of a group of federal investigators demonstrates how the informal consultation patterns that developed among officials contributed positively to the quality of decision making even though such discussions were prohibited by official policies. By contrast, Donald Roy's study (1954) of the work practices of operators in a machine shop describes the elaborate techniques these workers used to

restrict their production to a level that they regarded appropriate.

In some cases, the informal structure merely supplements and fills out the formal network of relationships. In fact, it is often this informal structure that allows the work of the organization to get done at all—work that, were it all to be handled as the formal tables prescribe, would become hopelessly entangled in organizational red tape and bureaucratic formalism. Attempts on the part of the organization's leaders to limit the role of informal structures and to break up friendship groups, often undertaken in order to ensure their own control, frequently impair both the organization's effectiveness vis-à-vis its external environment and its ability to provide satisfaction to its own members.

In addition to noting the importance of informal structure, the natural-system analysts point out that formalization also places an extremely heavy burden on the designers of formal structures. No planners are so far-seeing that they can anticipate all the possible contingencies that may confront the occupants of particular positions as they attempt to carry out their assignments. Given that the designers' knowledge is incomplete, that there are inherent limitations in dealing with complex information, and that circumstances are constantly changing, attempts to program in advance an organization's behavior or that of its personnel will often be foolhardy and dysfunctional. In a highly formalized structure, participants are not expected to exercise personal judgment but only to carry out their assigned duties in the specified manner. Such programming can easily become maladaptive and lead to behaviors both ineffective and inefficient, the *trained incapacity* that Thorstein Veblen (1918) described more than half a century ago and for which some organizations are notorious.

As with the specificity of goals, the degree of formalization of an organization must also be regarded as variable. Some organizational structures exhibit a high degree of formalization; others exhibit lesser degrees. In contrast to other types of social groups, however, formal organiza-

Figure 9.3   The irrationality of rationality.
Bureaucracy, often considered the most rational form
of social organization, may sometimes function
according to an irrational plan.

Mail Plan Requires 2,309 Miles For 20-Mile Delivery of Parcel

WASHINGTON, Sept. 26 (UPI)—A package mailed from Modena, Utah to Panaca, Nev., a distance of 20 miles, will have to cover a 2,309-mile route before delivery under the United States Postal Service's new bulk mail system, Representative Robert N. C. Nix charged today.

The extreme example was one of 52 instances the Pennsylvania Democrat cited to show added travel for parcels that will result in some sections of the nation when the new system becomes operational in 1976.

Mr. Nix, chairman of the House Postal Facilities and Mail Subcommittee, made the charges in prepared remarks as his panel renewed hearings on the Postal Service's construction program.

The system calls for construction of 21 large sorting centers and 12 auxiliary centers around the country where all parcels will be shipped for sorting by machine before being sent out for delivery.

The Postal Service contends that machine sorting will greatly speed the handling of parcels and result in quicker delivery. Mr. Nix conceded that it would probably "benefit mass mailers."

Cites Standard for Agency

"We are not interested, however, in what, if any service can be obtained by big business mailing houses," Mr. Nix said. "The standard for the Postal Service as a Government agency is what, if anything, such an agency will accomplish directly for the American mail patron."

A Postal Service spokesman acknowledged that some long-distance routes would result but added, "We don't think it's fair to pick out 50 isolated cases when the mass bulk mail system will be greatly improved."

In the Modena example, a truck now delivers such a package the 20 miles to Panaca. Under the new bulk system, Mr. Nix said, the package would go from Modena to Salt Lake City, then to Denver, then to Los Angeles, then to Las Vegas and finally to Panaca, a distance of 2,309 miles.

Aides to Mr. Nix said the Modena - to - Panaca example would occur because Modena was on one side of the boundary line for a postal area that had Los Angeles as the controlling center and Panaca was on the other side, meaning the parcel would have to go to Los Angeles and back.

Other examples listed by Mr. Nix included, the following?

¶From Joplin, Mo., to Tulsa, Okla., a distance of 77 miles, would go from Joplin to St. Luis, to Dallas, to Oklahoma City and then to Tulsa, a total of 1,129 miles.

¶From Duluth, Minn., to Superior, Wis., a distance of four miles, would go from Duluth to Minneapolis and then to Superior, a total of 288 miles.

¶From Niles, Mich., to Cassopolis, Mich., a distance of eight miles, would go from Niles to Kalamazoo, to Detroit, back to Kalamazoo and then to Cassopolis, a total of 500 miles.

Similarly, a package mailed from Chapel Hill, N. C., to Carrboro, N.C., a distance of one mile, will "under the new postal organization, with its businesslike methods, travel 160 miles to arrive at the same destination a mile away," Mr. Nix said.

tions usually have a relatively formalized set of positions and a structure that can be depicted by an organizational table.

BUREAUCRACY

The term *bureaucracy* is sometimes used as a synonym for all formal organizations. The term may also be used as an epithet for any rigid, rule-bound, inefficient, and labyrinthine organizational form. The Kafkaesque features of bureaucratic life, such as red tape and "officialese"—the language of bureaucrats—cannot be totally denied, and Kafka's novel *The Trial* depicts them nicely. But let us consider the concept of bureaucracy in a more limited and analytical fashion.

For our purposes, a bureaucracy may be conceived of as a specialized administrative staff responsible for maintaining an organization as a going concern and for devising, overseeing, and coordinating the activities of this organization's other participants (Blau and Scott, 1962). *Bureaucratization* refers to the development over time of this specialized administrative apparatus. Reinhard Bendix (1956) points out:

Seen historically, bureaucratization may be interpreted as the increasing subdivision of the functions which the owner-managers of the early enterprises had performed personally in the course of their daily routine.

The size of this administrative component has increased rapidly over the last half-century and reflects the increasing complexity of modern organizations. Examining only industrial firms and using the number of salaried employees as a crude index of the degree of bureaucratization, Bendix found that in five industrialized Western nations the percentage of salaried administrative officials expressed as a proportion of production workers, or of hourly-wage workers, increased from approximately 7 percent in 1900 to approximately 20 percent in 1950 (Bendix, 1956).

In the case of most types of organizations, bureaucracies are only components of total organizational systems, whether these are industrial, commercial, or service organizations. However, in other instances, best exemplified by governmental agencies, the bureaucracy is coterminous with the entire organization because such units function as administrative segments of a larger system: the state. However, the degree of bureaucratization as a defining variable of organizations will not be used in this chapter. Although the reservations of the natural-system analysts must be kept in mind, the working definition of organizations proposed here is still those social groups that exhibit relatively high degrees of goal specificity and formalization of structure.

THE EMERGENCE OF FORMAL ORGANIZATIONS

The existence of social units whose members allow themselves to be "organized" in the pursuit of limited, specific purposes is a relatively recent social development. Many sociological analysts have concerned themselves with examining the social conditions under which such specialized forms arise.

Basing his conclusions on the work of many predecessors—including Ernest Barker (1944), Otto Hintze (1908), Thomas F. Tout (1916), and Max Weber (Gerth and Mills, 1946)—the Israeli sociologist S. N. Eisenstadt has suggested that there are certain social conditions that are prerequisite to the emergence of formal organizations. A high degree of differentiation among roles is one condition. Another is the allocation of critical roles according to *universalistic* rules (applied uniformly to a class of eligible people such as trained accountants or mechanics or lawyers) rather than to *particularistic* criteria (that is, choosing people not according to their ability but on the basis of their personal relationship to the selector). Also among these prerequisite conditions are: the extension of the community boundaries beyond those of any single group; an increase in the complexity of social life; and attempts by groups to develop and pursue political, economic, and social-service goals that extend beyond the boundaries of any particular group. Finally, another prerequisite for the emergence of a formal organization is the development of differences

among various groups regarding the priority of goals and the consequent competition among them for scarce resources (Eisenstadt, 1959).

Such conditions are themselves the product of more basic changes in the structural foundations of a society. These changes result from the gradual release of human and material resources from their moorings in such *ascriptive units* as kinship and ethnic groups. (See Unit V for an extended discussion of ascription.) Resources then become free-floating in the sense that they are available for harnessing in the service of specific and limited purposes. Of course, these resources are subject to the competing claims of special-purpose groups that emerge.

Most of the documentation for these extremely broad assertions comes from a variety of historical studies that focused on the emergence of a specific organization in a particular context. One of the best and most readable historical-analytical descriptions of this process is provided by Hans Rosenberg (1958), who carefully describes the slow and painful emergence of the Prussian bureaucracy from its origins in a decentralized group of competing patrimonial princedoms. However, additional evidence comes from Stanley Udy's comparative study of the characteristics of thirty-four production organizations in thirty-four different nonindustrialized societies. Udy's data reveal that the greater the degree of an organization's insulation or separation from the ascribed ethnic and kinship structures characterizing a society, the greater the rational characteristics exhibited by this organization. Such rational characteristics included a concentration on limited objectives, an emphasis on performance, formalization in the sense of specific job assignments and specialization, and centralized management (Udy, 1962).

An important prerequisite for technical rationality, then, is the organization's power to determine its own sphere of operations (that is, its own objectives, the personnel it will hire, how it will divide and coordinate their work, and how it will compensate them). Only in relatively recent times have the preconditions outlined by Eisenstadt been realized; organizations have been suffi-

Figure 9.4   In analyzing formal organizations, rational-system analysts concentrate on the formal relationships between members, as exemplified by the formal channels of communication in the chart. The actual pattern of relationships existing within a particular organization, however, may not conform to the formal structure. For example, note the discrepancies between the formal and informal channels of communication in the same corporation. Natural-system analysts believe informal structure is at least as important as formal structure in determining what goes on in formal organizations.

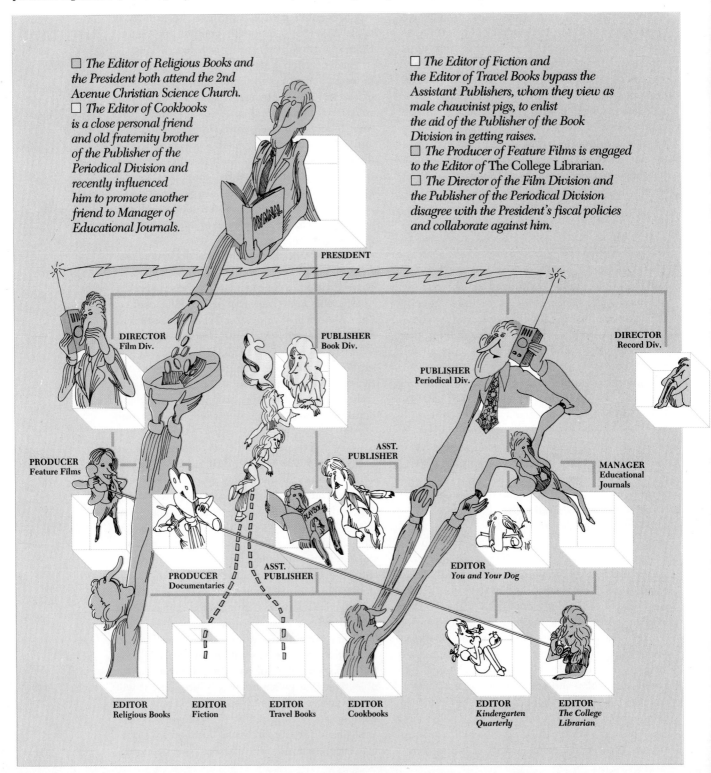

Figure 9.5   Max Weber (1864–1920) greatly influenced contemporary sociology, especially the development of macro sociological theories. He grew up in Berlin, where his father was a member of the parliament, and, for a brief period at the end of World War I, Weber was himself in politics—he was a consultant to the German Armistice Commission at Versailles and helped draft the constitution of the Weimar Republic. Weber worked in law, history, and economics in

addition to sociology and merged all these concerns in his monumental four-volume *Economy and Society*, published in 1922, after his death. Unfortunately, this work did not appear in English until the mid-1960s. Meanwhile, his brief monograph, *The Protestant Ethic and the Spirit of Capitalism*, published in German in 1904–1905, was published in English in 1930 and has been the main basis of his fame—although many now judge it to be one of his poorer works.

ciently freed from surrounding social pressures to be capable of determining their mode of operation. In industrialized societies, special-purpose organizations such as political parties, publishing companies, and universities are ubiquitous. That such organizations perform important functions in these societies has been emphasized by Parsons (1960):

The development of organizations is the principal mechanism by which, in a highly differentiated society, it is possible to "get things done," to achieve goals beyond the reach of the individual.

THE STRUCTURE OF ORGANIZATIONS: WEBER'S MODEL

Merely to say that an organization is characterized by a formal structure indicates nothing about the precise nature of that structure. Formalization permits design and redesign, but what pattern is to be followed? One model that has received much attention is that created by the great German sociologist Max Weber. Weber attempted to specify a set of structural characteristics that he believed would collectively promote rationality in administrative activity. He enumerated many specific structural characteristics but among the most important were the following:

1. The organization is guided by a set of explicit and specific purposes from which a system of rules and regulations is derived that governs the behavior of officials.
2. There is a distribution of activity among offices so that each incumbent has a specified sphere of competence.
3. The offices are arranged in a hierarchical pattern so that each official exercises authority over those subordinate to him and is subject to the authority of his superiors, but only in his capacity as an officeholder and within the limits established by organizational rules.
4. Officials are personally free, bound to their offices only by a contractual relationship that involves services in return for compensation, normally a salary. Officials do not own their offices, nor are they allowed to appropriate to themselves the means of administration.
5. Candidates for positions are selected on the basis of technical competence, and they are

promoted on the basis of seniority, performance, or both. Officials are appointed rather than elected.
6. Officials must carry out their functions in a disciplined and impersonal manner.
7. The organization maintains detailed written records, the contents of which are often treated as "official secrets."
8. The individual's commitment to his office is his primary work commitment.

Weber (1947) contended that actual structures approximating this model were capable of achieving the highest level of efficiency and were therefore the "most rational known means of carrying out imperative control over human beings."

Through this model, Weber hoped to isolate those characteristics of organizational structure that differentiated contemporary organizational forms from those of an earlier age, in particular, patrimonial and feudalistic forms. In such earlier forms, offices were frequently owned by their incumbents; indeed, offices were sometimes sold to the highest bidder. Incumbents were usually selected because of their family background, wealth, or personal influence. Authority relations were apt to be diffuse (encompassing the whole of a person's existence) rather than specific to the job, and the job itself was often a secondary concern of its occupant (Eisenstadt, 1963).

Weber's Structural Rationality

Weber insisted that rationality resides in the structure of an organization and not in the individual participants. In Weber's scheme, rationality is embodied in rules that are calculated to implement goals and in authority relations that ensure attention to duty and the proper coordination of activities. Weber believed rationality is also embodied in reward systems that motivate participants to carry out their prescribed duties and in technical criteria according to which the organization's participants are selected and promoted. According to this view, such organizations are fundamental to the maximization of formal rationality in human life, a rationality that must not be confused with personal rationality in the psychological sense. As a latter-day proponent of the rational system, Herbert Simon (1957), concludes:

The behavior patterns which we call organizations are fundamental, then, to the achievement of human rationality in any broad sense. The rational individual is, and must be, an organized and institutionalized individual.

Weber's Critics

Critics of Weber have pointed out that he overlooked the existence and importance of informal structure; that some of the characteristics of his model conflict with others or are dysfunctional for the attainment of goals; and that he appeared to confuse authority based on possession of office with that based on the personal competence of the officeholder (Blau, 1956; Blau and Scott, 1962; Gouldner, 1954; Parsons, 1947).

The shortcoming of Weber's analysis most consistently pointed out by later sociologists is his failure to recognize that there is no single type of rational organizational structure. Rather, structural forms can and must vary according to the nature of the goals pursued and the state of technical knowledge applied in the pursuit. Given different sets of goals and different states of technology, the same structural pattern may be rational in one case and irrational in another.

Nevertheless, Weber's work remains seminal in the history of sociology. It opened up a new area of inquiry and has provided the model from which literally all other work in the field has started. If a theory or model is to be judged not by its absolute truth but by its ability to stimulate further thought and inquiry, then Weber's work on the structure of formal organizations must rank as one of the monumental achievements in the history of sociology. In any case, the criticisms we have cited do not discredit Weber's basic thesis concerning the historical transition of organizations from earlier feudal forms to more rationalized forms of authority and administration.

GOALS, TECHNOLOGY, AND STRUCTURE

Consider two types of goals and technologies. In the first case, goals are precise, scientific knowledge is well developed, and the degree of organizational formalization is high. Thus, foolproof technology can be constructed. It is possible in this first case to specify and organize in advance the types of activities to be carried out; in James March and Herbert Simon's terms (1958), "performance programs" can be devised. Decisions concerning appropriate task activities can be centralized and specific sequences of standard activities assigned to particular participants. The tasks involved lend themselves to subdivision, and the efficiencies associated with specialization are ushered in: short training periods, replaceability of participants, easy evaluation and control of the work process, and so on. Note that extreme specialization does exact costs: fatigue and boredom caused by repetitive activities, lack of motivation, lowered worker satisfaction, and, in the absence of a union, job insecurity—all symbolized by the single word *alienation,* a topic that will be discussed later in this chapter.

Under such advanced technological circumstances, a large administrative staff will be required to design the performance programs; to recruit, train, and supervise the work force; to handle unusual problems, including those of flagging motivation; to direct the flow of materials; and to coordinate the contributions of various participants. But given specific goals and a technology of proven efficacy, a bureaucratic structure on the Weberian model is likely to present itself as the most rational arrangement (Litwak, 1961; Perrow, 1967).

In the second hypothetical case, organizational goals are diffuse and ill-defined, and the degree of organizational formalization is low. Work cannot be routinized or minutely subdivided, and the success of the enterprise may depend on the judgment, ingenuity, and expertise of the individual members of the organization. Because individuals are required to exercise more discretion in handling tasks, it becomes less feasible to subdivide and routinize work tasks. Under these circumstances, an individual must carry out an entire meaningful sequence of activities, making adjustments at later stages according to the results of earlier phases.

Professionalization

Greater discretion in handling tasks is usually predicated on greater individual competence, the development of which requires long and costly training. In cases where individual discretion increases, a smaller administrative staff usually results because less planning, supervision, and coordination are required (Litwak, 1961; Thompson and Bates, 1957). An arrangement in which individuals are granted such broad discretion in managing their work and in attaining their goals is characteristic of the work of professionals. Research by Richard H. Hall (1967) reveals that when the work force is more professionalized (when workers have high individual competence), less reliance is placed on a hierarchy of authority to effect control; there is less division of labor among workers; and there are fewer rules and procedural specifications. In such circumstances the formation of coalitions among professional practitioners is likely to ensue. Professionals form such coalitions in order to establish and maintain standards of performance and to prevent undue interference with their work on the part of outsiders, all those not possessing similar training and skills (Goode, 1957). *Professionalization* is likely to develop wherever substantial numbers of highly trained people participate in an organization; professionalization is characteristic of hospitals, clinics, law firms, universities, and scientific research organizations.

Incompatible Structures

Organizational structures that are devised do not always turn out to be compatible with the goals to be pursued or with the state of existing technology. When a bureaucratic structure is devised to pursue diffuse objectives or utilize imperfect technologies, the result is often ineffectiveness. Because the standard, prescribed routines of a bureaucracy do not permit enough flexibility to cope with complex and often only partially understood problems, a high proportion of errors and failures results. Such a situation is exemplified, at least to a considerable degree, by the operation of public welfare agencies in this country. Over the protests

of the professional social-work community, a profession not yet strong enough to dictate the conditions under which its members will work, an incredibly diverse client group is "processed" by the performance of standardized sets of activities that are often irrelevant to the actual needs of the clients. The costs associated with the operation of these agencies is unfortunately borne by the clients themselves and also, indirectly, by the general public (Wilensky and Lebeaux, 1958).

A different kind of cost is involved when professional structures are used to carry out routine tasks. In this case, the cost is an inefficient and economically irrational allocation of a scarce and valuable resource, that is, competence. It is inefficient to use highly trained persons to perform tasks that can be done as well by those with lesser skills and training. Such inefficient allocation of resources occurs, to a degree, in medical clinics where physicians are often forced to treat routine conditions that could as easily and perhaps more effectively be handled by medical assistants.

POWER AND AUTHORITY STRUCTURES

One of the crucial factors to keep in mind when examining any organization is that it is a power structure (Etzioni, 1962) whether or not the dimension of power is explicitly recognized by the participants. Power may be defined as the ability and willingness of one person to sanction another by manipulating rewards and punishments that are important to the other. As Peter Blau (1964), George C. Homans (1961), and others have argued, power differences quickly emerge in informal groups as a consequence of differences in such personal attributes as wealth, intelligence, physical strength, or sexual attractiveness.

Personal attributes that render individuals differentially useful or attractive also enter into the structure of power relationships within formal organizations, but the formal structure, as opposed to the informal, is rarely determined by such personal differences. Rather, formal organizations establish a formal *hierarchy* of positions. Built into the definition of each position (and into the specification of relations among positions) is differential access to the rewards and penalties that are controlled by the organization. These rewards and penalties can be used to influence the behavior of participants.

Power, however, is not authority, and no organization can be content to rely solely on power to control its members (Weber, 1947). Authority may be defined as normatively regulated power. Authority exists to the extent that a set of generally accepted social norms operates to legitimate power relations by defining them as correct or appropriate. These norms, however, work two ways: On the one hand, they specify that subordinates in a power relationship must comply with directives from their superiors; on the other hand, they specify the limits within which power may be exercised by superiors. The person who wields power is both upheld and constrained by the social norms that legitimate his or her power.

Two types of authority structures may be distinguished: endorsed power and authorized power. The difference depends on the location of the group upholding the norms that constrain the power holder. *Endorsed power* exists when the social norms are enforced by the group of persons subject to the exercise of power. It frequently happens that a group of persons, all of whom are subject to a single individual's exercise of power, collectively develop norms that both support and circumscribe the individual's exercise of that power (Blau and Scott, 1962). The relationship that grows between a leader and the members of his street gang may serve as an example of endorsed power.

Authorized power, on the other hand, exists when the norms that circumscribe the power wielder are enforced by a person or group of persons not themselves subject to the exercise of that power (Scott, Dornbusch, Bushing, and Laing, 1967). This kind of authority structure is more characteristic of formal organizations and, in fact, is implicit in the meaning of a *hierarchy of offices*. In short, power may be regulated from above as well as from below.

Power relations become authority relations by endorsement, by authorization, or through both methods. A prison guard who exercises power under norms prescribed by his superiors has authority by authorization, regardless of whether the exercise of his power is or is not endorsed by the inmates of his cellblock. An informal inmate leader who exercises power under norms established by his fellow prisoners has authority by endorsement, regardless of whether his position and his actions are or are not recognized by prison officials. However, the person whose exercise of power is both authorized by his superiors and endorsed by his subordinates may be said to enjoy greater legitimacy than one whose power is only authorized or only endorsed. The practical effect of this greater legitimacy is that the exercise of power under such a condition is likely to be more effective in attaining goals and more stable than an exercise of power commanding only one source of normative support (Scott, 1970).

ORGANIZATIONS AND INDIVIDUALS

The organizational structures that are designed to be most effective in attaining the organization's objectives are not necessarily those that maximize the satisfactions of individual participants or that provide them with the optimal conditions for the development of their personal potentialities.

Alienation

Among the earliest and most trenchant critics of organizations was Karl Marx, who believed that workers' lack of control over their work situation results in their alienation from the work process and its products. Marx thought that workers' alienation, epitomized by their social position as *wage slaves* and their psychological degradation to a mere "appendage of the machine," would produce their estrangement from the factory system and, ultimately, from the capitalist system itself. Weber attempted to extend Marx's analysis beyond the industrial sphere. Hans Gerth and C. Wright Mills (1946) note that Marx's emphasis upon the workers' alienation from the means of production becomes, in Weber's perspective, only one aspect of a pervasive modern trend: the separation of individuals from control over the conditions of their own lives. Thus, the modern soldier

Figure 9.6   In performing their jobs, people may get caught up in ritualism, a form of goal displacement. Conformity to procedural rules then becomes a goal in itself rather than a means to accomplishing the actual goals of the organization. This gas-station attendant may be losing sight of his organization's goal, which is to make a profit, as well as his own personal goal, which is to earn a living. Instead he is totally absorbed in the ritual performance of the means, "serving the customer."

is equally separated from control of the means of violence, the scientist from control of the means of inquiry, and the civil servant from control of the means of administration.

The theme of individual alienation continues to attract the attention of sociologists, psychologists, and psychoanalysts. Empirical studies have revealed that job satisfaction increases with the individual's occupational position (higher officials are more satisfied with their work than are those in relatively subordinate positions) but that no group evinces a high level of job dissatisfaction (Blauner, 1964). In part, this lack of high levels of dissatisfaction can be explained by the tendency of those who do monotonous and menial jobs to assign less importance to their work in the formation of their self-image: they are less likely than executives and professionals to consider their work their "central life interest" (Chinoy, 1955; Dubin, 1958; Morse and Weiss, 1955).

Humanizing the Organization

Most attacks on formal organizations point out that individual needs for independence, autonomy, creativity, and self-realization are seldom met by highly specific and circumscribed jobs and that many organizational positions encourage infantilism and dependency rather than maturity and independence (Argyris, 1958). Those subjected to such positions often respond by engaging in covert sabotage, restriction of output, and emotional withdrawal—attitudes that simultaneously enable them to reject the organization emotionally and allow them to make the minimal contribution necessary to retain their positions within the organization. Chris Argyris and others argue that only a fundamental restructuring of the work environment of millions of people can change this situation. Jobs must be enlarged and rendered challenging; hierarchical dependency must be reduced; and workers must be allowed to participate in making those fundamental organizational decisions that affect their fate as members of the organization. The consequence might well be more satisfied and more humanized workers and executives, and organizations at once more effective and more efficient.

Although they do not disagree with the goal of humanizing organizations, other analysts question the extent to which individuals actually desire challenging work and an opportunity for self-realization. Further, it is suggested that Argyris and his colleagues underestimated the costs associated with the radical transformation of organizational structures. Also, the advantages of such a transformation for organizations may have been overrepresented. Humanized structures may not necessarily be the most effective and efficient structures. This qualification does not mean that efforts should not be made to improve organizations as environments within which people must live and work. Rather, humanization must be defended and propounded as an important end in itself, not simply as a means toward greater productive efficiency (Strauss, 1963).

Ritualism in Formal Organizations

Robert K. Merton (1957) has suggested that a structural pattern that produces effectiveness in some circumstances may prove ineffective in others. Merton argues that the formal definition of positions, the proliferation of rules and regulations, and the reward systems of formal organiza-

Figure 9.7   People who hold bureaucratic positions over an extended period may come to lose sight of the problems of working men and women. In order to combat the tendency toward a "bureaucratic mentality," in China bureaucrats spend a short period of time each year working in factories and on communal farms. Chen Yung-Kuei (*in front*), Vice-Chairman of the Shansi Provincial Revolutionary Committee and Secretary of the party branch of the Tachai brigade, is shown here joining commune members in building terraced fields as part of a current mass campaign to develop water-control and irrigation facilities.

tions all encourage timidity, conservatism, and a narrow technical approach among organization members; in short, these elements of formal organizations encourage *ritualism.*

Ritualism may be thought of as a special instance of a more general social phenomenon—that of *goal displacement*—in which conformity to rules becomes an end in itself rather than a means toward accomplishing the organization's or one's own objectives. Ritualism, of course, is not unique to organizations; indeed, society thrives on goal displacement. Means are forever becoming ends: eating becomes dining; shelter and clothing become socially valued ends in themselves rather than means of protection from the elements.

Such transformations are also the primary bases of much occupational specialization. Good health is only a means by which people can live their lives fully, but the maintenance of health becomes the primary objective of the physician and of other medical specialists. Science is a means for understanding and, ultimately, for gaining control over the environment, but for scientists its advancement becomes the ultimate aim of their lives. In short, the bureaucrat who transforms his job from a means into an activity performed and valued for its own sake enjoys good company.

This transforming behavior can be tolerated so long as those who indulge in it do not lose complete sight of the fact that their jobs exist in order to serve the organization's clients and, finally, the interests of the larger society. All too often, however, these larger interests become obscured, and the organization's business comes to be conducted primarily for the benefit of its permanent bureaucratic staff. It is a commonplace among sociologists who have studied hospitals, for example, to find that many rules and regulations justified as being essential to proper patient care really exist to simplify and make more convenient the work of the staff (Goffman, 1961).

Individual and Organizational Goals

Obviously, individual motives and organizational goals do not necessarily coincide. Nor will the discrepancy between individual and organizational goals necessarily be bridged by recruiting people whose motives as individuals are congruent with the goals of the organization. Physicians genuinely devoted to helping people are not necessarily better physicians than those who wish to make money or improve their social status. People participate in organizations for a variety of personal motives, including desire for money, desire for status, and more altruistic objectives, such as public service. Indeed, a recent study of volunteer political groups by James Q. Wilson (1962) emphasizes the multitude of problems that occur when organizations must mesh their purposes with individual motives. For example, political groups whose adherents are motivated by a desire to see a particular candidate in office must deal with the troublesome problem that every group member's desired candidate cannot run and everyone's candidate cannot win. Because personal and organizational goals do conflict, it is important that individual goals and personal motivations do not overwhelm and exclude the goals of the organization as a whole. To some extent, the processes of recruitment into the organization can control this problem, but it is primarily the critical task of the organization's leadership to deal with conflicts between individual and organizational goals as they come up.

ORGANIZATIONS AND SOCIETY

A host of problems are raised for the larger society by the existence and the functioning of a multiplicity of formal organizations (Ellul, 1964; Faunce, 1968). One of these problems has to do with the question of whether the federal bureaucracy—the administrative structures primarily associated with the executive branch of the government—is, or should be, master or servant of the people. In a democracy, the vast and ever proliferating administrative apparatus of the state is typically expected to be politically neutral. The development of a civil service in which people have tenured careers is one mechanism specifically designed to insure this neutrality as well as to insure continuity of administration and appropriate levels of competence. The problem arises because the very continuity of tenure and the technical expertise of the career civil servants give them distinct advantages over elected political officials whose specific qualifications for their jobs may be few and whose tenure of office is usually limited.

On the one hand, government bureaucrats are often criticized for not being sufficiently responsive to the elected political leadership; for example, Seymour Martin Lipset (1950) reports that conservative civil servants acted to undermine the political programs sponsored by the socialist government in Saskatchewan. On the other hand, bureaucrats are sometimes criticized for being overly responsive to the demands of political regimes. The American civil servant, for example, is often criticized on the former ground, but German civil servants were criticized on the latter ground by Herbert Jacob (1963) and others for their "spineless quality" in responding too readily and too efficiently to the will of the Nazi political overlords during the 1930s and 1940s.

Another problem raised by the function of organizations in modern society relates to the rationality of organizations. Throughout this chapter, the argument has been presented that formal organizations are capable of achieving a high-level rationality, that is, rationality of an entirely technical sort. In practice, therefore, organizations may be rational in their goal-implementing activities, but organizations may be irrational, from a logical or substantive point of view, in their goal-selection process. This phenomenon may be called the problem of *bounded rationality*. The factors that organizations take into account in the selection of their goals may be unduly restricted or dictated by severely limited perceptions, perspectives, and interests. What results is an effective, efficient instrument that is aimed in the wrong direction.

From the society's standpoint, more frequent results are organizations created with overlapping objectives that needlessly duplicate services, organizations working at cross-purposes to each other, and organizations failing to meet vital social needs. One of the most important problems of our time is to make the selection of organizational objectives more responsive to the needs of those that the organizations have been established to serve. Bendix (1952) points out that as with society itself, organizations, too, are the creation of people, and people may still, through the political process, determine how and for what ends those organizations will be used.

SUGGESTED READINGS

Blau, Peter M., and W. Richard Scott. *Formal Organizations.* San Francisco: Chandler, 1962.

Etzioni, Amitai. *A Comparative Analysis of Complex Organizations.* New York: The Free Press of Glencoe, 1961.

March, James G. (ed.). *Handbook of Organizations.* Chicago: Rand McNally, 1965.

March, James G., and Herbert A. Simon. *Organizations.* New York: Wiley, 1958.

Chapter 10 Adult Socialization and Resocialization

AS CHAPTER 6 MADE CLEAR, humans must learn to be human. This learning process is called socialization. What people learn through the process of socialization is their culture—the beliefs, customs, habits, information, and technology of their society. The amount and quality of culture that human beings slowly have accumulated and passed on most distinguishes them from other animals. Variations in the nature and extent of their cultures set societies apart from one another. For example, human beings in some societies depend upon nomadic hunting and gathering for their livelihood; people in other societies manufacture moon rockets, hula hoops, and nuclear warheads.

Socialization does not end with infancy or graduation from school. Within all societies humans undergo a lifelong process of acquiring culture. The more complex the society, the more intensive is this continuing socialization process; however, the socialization process continues in all societies, regardless of their complexity. The content and effectiveness of socialization account for many variations in the behavior and outlook of adult members of particular societies. For example, males who serve in the army become somewhat different from males who do not. Some occupational groups, such as the clergy or the police, sustain distinctive outlooks; persons entering these occupations tend to have their views changed accordingly (Stark, 1972b). Similarly, people who live in cities come to be noticeably different from people who live on farms (Berelson and Steiner, 1964).

In addition to providing new training, adult socialization is required to maintain the effects of early socialization. When adults are isolated they tend to regress even from childhood training. For example, some niceties of toilet training tend to disappear among firewatchers who work in solitude (Scott, 1971). Similarly, prisoners kept in solitary confinement tend to become extremely ill-adjusted over time (Schein, 1956).

Often, it appears that the socialization process has failed badly. People seem unable to perform their roles in a socially acceptable manner. Terms like *deviant, criminal,* or *psychotic* are applied to such persons. Frequently, the judgment is made that these persons need such extensive changing that it makes more sense to speak of *resocializing* them than of socializing them. Resocialization measures may range from private psychotherapy sessions to incarceration of persons in prisons and mental hospitals.

This chapter deals with adult socialization and resocialization and examines the lifelong process of social learning that characterizes the human condition. Special attention will be given to the ways in which roles, groups, and organizations shape and reshape behavior and self-images.

SOCIALIZATION AND ROLE CHANGES

One reason socialization is continuous is because all societies are *age-graded.* As people mature, they are expected to perform new roles. Chapter 17 discusses at length the ways in which age differences are related to inequalities in all societies. What concerns us now is how the maturation process makes it necessary for people to be socialized into new roles.

The physical maturation of humans is a relatively slow process. A colt can run within an hour or two after birth, but a human cannot walk until more than a year after he or she is born. Most mammals are sexually mature within months, but human puberty does not occur until adolescence. Building upon these simple physical facts, human societies have elaborated a virtually universal set of roles in the life cycle—infant, child, juvenile, young adult, spouse, parent, grandparent, elder. As Chapter 7 points out, each of these roles carries a different set of expectations that people must learn to fulfill adequately.

Humans begin to be prepared for these roles long before they are physically or socially qualified to fulfill them. From an early age, many children are oriented toward marriage and raising a family. Through such activities as playing mother and father, they begin to learn how to be mothers and fathers. Similarly, children frequently begin to learn about sex and reproduction well before the time they are physically mature enough to

Figure 10.1   Rapid change is characteristic of life in modern industrial societies. For example, technological innovations in medical diagnostic methods are constantly being made. The machine shown here is a radioisotope scanning device, used in diagnosing brain conditions. Isotopes are injected into a patient's bloodstream. Organs are delineated on the black screen in the upper-left panel of the machine by the scanning

of the machine, which is sensitive to radiation. The physician then studies the images for "hot" or "cold" spots. A hot spot is an area of increased blood flow, which indicates the presence of a tumor. A cold spot is indicative of an abcess in which there is fluid or pus but little blood. In order to become aware of and use such innovative technology, doctors must continue their education throughout their professional lives.

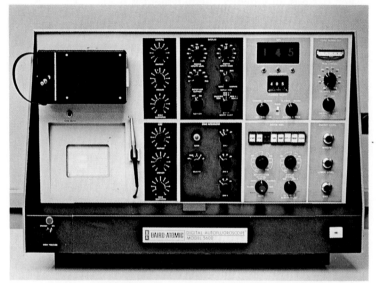

engage in such activity. Children also begin to fashion some notion of what they are going to be when they grow up, say, a fireman or teacher.

This early training, however, is far from sufficient for actually performing adult roles. Upon marriage, young couples require considerable adjustment to settle successfully into their roles as spouses. In fact, many do not succeed and require special tutoring by marriage counselors in order to learn their new roles. The same learning and adjusting process is also true of sex. Humans must learn how to interact sexually. (They are not alone in this: Harry Harlow's monkeys raised in isolation failed to learn how to engage in sex even after long exposure to members of the opposite sex. See Chapter 6.) It is equally obvious that people must learn how to perform occupational roles; sometimes years of training both in school and on the job are required to develop specific occupational abilities.

Adult socialization is a continuing process because cultures and societies themselves change during an individual's lifetime. Social change is especially characteristic of our complex, contemporary societies. Rapid social change makes new demands upon people for which neither their childhood nor previous adult socialization has prepared them. The troubles the elderly have with

"newfangled gadgets" is a common source of humor, but such jokes are unfair to the elderly. We all face learning to deal with "newfangled" things all the time. Such professions as medicine and engineering expend great effort on continuing educational programs in order to help their members keep up with the rapid pace of innovations. In fact, social change is often so rapid these days that a number of occupations have become obsolete long before those trained in such work have retired. Such has been the fate of many harness makers, cowboys, radio actors, and battleship admirals, to name a few.

Today, women's roles are rapidly shifting. Women were traditionally cast in roles of dependence, submissiveness, and domesticity, but they are now gaining self-reliance and equality in relation to men (see Chapter 28). Their childhood socialization and much of their prior adult experience did not prepare most women for these emerging feminine roles; nor have most men been prepared for the shifts in male roles necessitated by new conceptions of female roles. The disorienting impact of social change can be seen in the anger and anxiety with which many people react to women's demands to establish new types of sex-role relationships, especially in the family and in work (see Chapters 18 and 22). Extensive reorientations of major roles produce periods of considerable confusion. Perhaps reorientation to social change can never fully occur until people can be socialized for these changes from early childhood.

There has been concern that rapid social change is itself becoming a chronic social problem. In his best seller, *Future Shock* (1970), Alvin Toffler suggests that rapid technological change and the resulting strain on people produced by the need for constant relearning and reorientation may cause society to remain in a chronic state of moderate instability. As will be discussed in Chapter 19, at the very least, rapid social and cultural change has transformed educational goals from the learning of specific information and skills to an emphasis on learning to learn. Rapid social change has also led formal organizations to de-

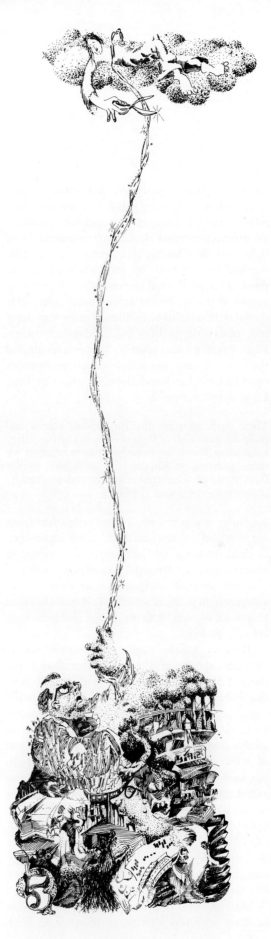

Figure 10.2   The "generation gap" may be an inevitable consequence of the differences in childhood and adult socialization in our society. Whereas children are encouraged to be idealistic—to have ideals that "soar to the sky"—adults are supposed to be practical and rooted to the experiences of their daily lives—to be "down to earth."

velop elaborate training and retraining programs to help keep individuals abreast of changing role requirements in their society.

DIFFERENCES IN ADULT AND CHILDHOOD SOCIALIZATION

Although both childhood and adult socialization involve the learning of culture, the two differ considerably in the *content* of what is learned and the *sources* from which it is learned. For example, learning a new language is quite different from learning to talk. Most young children learn from their parents; most adults do not.

Content Differences

There is a larger proportion of new material in the content of childhood learning than in that of adult learning (Brim and Wheeler, 1966). There is some truth to the saying that everything is new to the young but the old have seen everything before. Much adult socialization involves a synthesis of old and new learning—a recombination of already-acquired skills and knowledge. Adults learn new languages on the basis of the vocabulary and grammatical command of languages already learned and build new job skills upon those they already possess.

Furthermore, childhood learning is more *hypothetical* and therefore *idealistic*, and adult learning is more *concrete* and therefore more *realistic*. Inevitably, a considerable discrepancy exists between ideals and realities. By definition, an ideal is a hypothetical standard against which we gauge the value of concrete instances. However, children are typically socialized by being taught idealized notions that neglect concrete circumstances. Parents encourage children to have ideals that "soar to the sky," according to Kingsley Davis, "because they have so little social experience —experience being largely kept from them" (1940b).

Similarly, Max Weber's arguments have been utilized by Seymour Martin Lipset to shed light on the inevitability of a *generation gap* that results because of differences in childhood and adult socialization. Weber observed that young people tend to follow "a pure ethic of absolute ends" rather than an "ethic of responsibility"—that is, an ethic concerned with the consequences of their actions. Clearly, the young are not constrained by responsibility for what happens. Indeed, they are denied responsibility. Lipset suggested that the young often make impossible demands that ideals be fulfilled because they have not yet experienced the contradictions between what should be and what is, between ideals and the practical limits of concrete situations: "experience has not hardened them to imperfection." Lipset further argued:

Their contract with the [professed] moral and political standards of their society is abstract; they encounter them as principles promulgated by older persons, as imposed by authority, rather than as maxims incorporated into and blurred by their own experience (1965).

Similarly, engineers, physicians, or lawyers fresh out of school require considerable job experience in order to adapt all their academic training to concrete circumstances. Classes in civics and government are not adequate preparation for involvement in political activity. Textbooks tell how things ideally ought to work but not how they actually do work.

Because much adult socialization occurs through experience with real rather than hypothetical situations, it less often leads to a disjuncture between what is learned and what is actually done. Unfortunately, this characteristic of adult socialization may produce short-sightedness in adults; they may too readily accept, in the name of practicality, not only less than ideal solutions but very bad solutions. Snell Putney (1972) has called this tendency "crackpot realism." He cites people who defend pollution as a necessary consequence of preserving the productive level of business. Such a "realistic" defense ignores the fact that the long-term results of ecological damage may destroy all future possibilities for conducting business at all.

Most parents intentionally seek to instill ideals in their children that they themselves have

greatly modified through experience. Even though many parents may recognize that moral training is eroded by experience, they believe that some ideals—such as those implementing sexual prohibitions—are appropriate to the needs of the young, even if these ideals will be modified by later experience. Furthermore, to some extent, most parents, like most adults, mourn the loss of their own innocence. They still hope for a better world and know that to seek it idealism is needed.

Socializing Agents

The agents of socialization for children and adults are very different. The family clearly is the group most responsible for teaching children basic social roles, values, attitudes, and motivation. The emotional intensity that characterizes family relationships helps to insure that children learn the basic elements of their culture and specific social group.

The family becomes more peripheral in adult socialization. As a person grows older, more and more of his or her socialization occurs in the context of *secondary* relationships—relationships that are often less intense and more impersonal than family and other primary and peer relationships. (See Chapter 8 for definitions of primary and secondary groups.) Socialization after childhood is closely bound to the large-scale, bureaucratic organizations that dominate so much of life in contemporary society. To an increasing extent, as people mature, the agents of their socialization shift from their families and friends to people-processing organizations: schools, colleges, corporations, training and rehabilitation centers, mental hospitals, jails, prisons, and others (Brim, 1966). These organizations have been explicitly designed to provide contexts in which new learning or relearning can take place.

THE ORGANIZATIONAL CONTEXT OF ADULT SOCIALIZATION

The process of adult socialization occurs in two ways: either as *developmental* socialization or as resocialization. In developmental socialization, efforts are made to build upon the individual's prior socialization, to blend new skills and understand-

Figure 10.3   Resocialization may be voluntary;
for example, the men in the left-hand photograph are
voluntarily participating in a rehabilitation
program for drug addicts. But resocialization can also
be involuntary; involuntary resocialization is
suggested by the prison scene at right. Whether or
not resocialization is involuntary depends on the nature
of the social institution undertaking the resocialization and on the goals of the resocialization procedures.

ing with the old. A person's developmental socialization seems to that person a normal extension of
his or her past. Resocialization efforts are designed
to massively reshape the person and to replace old
self-images and modes of behavior with new ones.
The line between developmental socialization
and resocialization is often difficult to draw, but
we shall try to make a few distinctions in the following examples.

Developmental Socialization

The ways in which organizations engage in developmental socialization of adults are both numerous and obvious. The United States has become a
nation of students. Several thousand colleges and
universities, as well as thousands of technical and
vocational schools and training programs, are engaged in the developmental socialization of this
nation of students. Training programs have
become a major budget item for the modern corporation and the governmental agency. As Chapter 19 clarifies, we have much to learn about making educational processes effective and efficient.

Still, attempts at developmental socialization
have been more successful than have attempts at
resocialization in this society.

Resocialization

The goal of resocialization is to create a new person or to restore a damaged one. Resocialization
is an effort to compensate for grave deficiencies
in prior socialization (at least as judged by those
conducting the resocialization) or to replace prior
socialization that has been lost or forgotten.
Consequently, resocialization is a disjunctive and
often traumatic process. Whereas developmental
socialization may be experienced as routine, resocialization marks a significant break in people's
lives, especially for those who must involuntarily
submit to resocialization (for example, those incarcerated in a prison or a mental hospital). Furthermore, resocialization often is stigmatizing—ex-
convicts and former mental patients often have
trouble getting jobs or resuming old friendships.
Developmental socialization is meant to increase
the competence of persons within the social

Figure 10.4 People undergoing involuntary re-socialization often feel little or no commitment to the resocialization programs. Many inmates of prisons, for example, have come to feel that the very authority and purpose of the prison system are illegitimate. An important contributor to recent prison unrest and riots is institutional racism, discriminatory practices based on race that are built into the very structure of a social institution. In 1971 these black inmates of Attica State Prison in New York rebelled to protest unfair treatment and conditions at that time; they presented a list of demands, several of which appear below. Institutional racism within the prison is only the last instance in a long string of such instances that led to the almost solid mass of black faces in this photograph. Discrimination in many institutions that are involved in socialization and resocialization—in schools, in employment practices, in law enforcement, and in the legal system—contributes to the disproportionate numbers of black men in prison today.

During the prison rebellion at the Attica State Correctional Facility in 1971, prisoners formulated demands that included:

"... 'complete amnesty' and freedom from 'physical, mental and legal reprisals,'

'speedy and safe transportation out of confinement to a nonimperialistic country,'

a Federal takeover of the prison,

'true' religious freedom,

an end to censorship of reading materials,

the right to communicate with anyone at their own expense,

the 'reconstruction' of the prison 'by inmates or under inmate supervision,'

more recreation and less cell-time,

'competent' doctors,

coverage by state minimum wage laws and freedom to be active politically."

In addition, the prisoners also called for improvements in their diets, specifically the inclusion of fresh fruit.

framework; resocialization is intended to return to that framework those whom society regards as deviant. (See Chapter 11 for a sociological definition of deviance.)

Contingencies Inside the Organization

Nowhere can the differences between developmental socialization and resocialization be so clearly seen as in the context of the organization. Depending on whether people are being resocialized or developmentally socialized by an organization, people's *level of initial commitment* to the socializing process and to the organization will vary. In addition, the *degree of individual choice and decision making* that members of an organization enjoy, the *typical patterns of interaction* in which they engage, and the *amount of organizational control* that is employed over them differ greatly. Stanton Wheeler (1966) has proposed these four dimensions to evaluate and contrast developmental socialization and resocialization.

Level of Initial Commitment People involved in the process of developmental socialization usually are well-disposed toward it. Often they greatly desire the training they are receiving; for example, commitment is typically high in students who are enrolled in professional schools such as medicine and law. In fact, they may have made considerable sacrifice to gain admission to such programs. Typically, the reverse is true in resocialization. Most resocialization is, to some degree, involuntary; people usually resist and resent it, especially inmates of prisons and of most mental hospitals.

Initial commitment makes a great deal of difference. When commitment is high and participation is voluntary, the process of socialization can proceed and the chances for success are high. When commitment is low and participation involuntary, efforts must first be made to instill commitment; otherwise, socialization must be attempted without it. However, coercion frequently gains only superficial compliance; so attempts at resocialization are frequently unsuccessful.

Perhaps half of those sentenced to prison are

one day returned to prison; obviously, their resocialization has been ineffective. In fact, even many people who do not commit subsequent offenses cannot be considered successfully resocialized. They were originally sentenced for offenses they were unlikely to repeat and therefore were not in need of resocialization. For example, someone convicted of manslaughter as a result of a traffic accident is unlikely to repeat his offense, whether or not he initially served time in jail.

Low commitment, negative attitudes, and resistance to organizational demands are typical of people undergoing involuntary resocialization. These people often come to feel that the authority and purpose of the resocializing organization are illegitimate, and therefore their commitment to resocialization programs is nil.

Individual Choice and Decision Making   An individual undergoing resocialization typically is permitted little individual choice, either in initiating resocialization or in giving it direction. In developmental socialization, however, the individual usually has considerable choice and may participate in making decisions that concern him or her. The extremes may be represented by an experimental college and a prison. The college students control many choices about what courses to take, what major to pursue, where to live, and how to distribute their time; prisoners, however, have virtually all their decisions made for them. Students supposedly want to be in college. Few convicts probably want to be in prison.

Patterns of Interaction   A third organizational contingency of adult socialization and resocialization involves two perspectives on patterns of interaction: First, one has to look at interaction between people undergoing socialization and those doing the socialization (usually the staff of the socializing organization); second, at patterns of interaction among people who are themselves being socialized or resocialized.

As a starting point, assume that people in an organization really feel the impact of that organization through the *amount* of interaction they have with the organization's staff. Socializing organizations frequently make this assumption; for example, schools use student-teacher ratios as an index of educational quality (that is, the effectiveness of socialization), presumably because that ratio reflects the likelihood of meaningful interaction between the two groups. The fewer students in a class, the more time a teacher may spend with each. Prisons, mental hospitals, and other resocializing organizations use staff-inmate ratios in a similar fashion. These ratios, of course, do not reveal the *actual* extent of interaction between the two groups. It is possible, for example, that the larger the staff, the more they talk to one another and avoid inmates.

In most socialization settings, interaction among those being socialized is perhaps as significant as member-staff interaction. Whenever people find themselves in similar situations, they begin to form social relationships and a *subculture* of their own. The particular form that a subculture takes can have an important effect on the impact of the socializing organization.

Subcultures form in two different ways. People who enter an organization all at one time may form a group or groups that help them adapt to their new environment, as when entering freshmen form groups. However, in some organizations, such as prisons or unwed mothers' homes, entering members usually encounter a preexisting subculture.

One study of students in medical school done by Howard S. Becker and his colleagues showed how the students adapted to their new environment by developing collective responses to it. Faced with the overwhelming detail and variety of the curriculum and the heavy faculty demands, students had to decide what was important to learn, memorize, and work on and what was not. The social relationships among the students enabled them to make tacit agreements to scale down their work loads in similar ways and in terms of their own needs rather than the faculty's. The resulting subculture also aided the development of new role identities among students through their collective interpretation of what it means to be a doctor, what a doctor's responsibilities and priorities are, and how the professional role of doctor should be incorporated into one's own personality—all matters not directly approached or covered by the medical curriculum. Learning how to be a doctor, then, entails more than simply learning how to heal, and the existence of a subculture among students serves to facilitate learning about the more informal side of being a doctor as well as to help students adapt to the medical-school environment (Becker *et al.*, 1961).

Interestingly enough, student subcultures typically do not play a very important role in success in graduate and professional school. Research by Carin Weiss (1972) based on a nationwide sample of students in American graduate and professional schools reveals that involvement in the student subculture had little or no influence on success in school or on the development of a self-conception as a scholar, scientist, or professional. On the other hand, her research showed that the amount and quality of contact between students and professors had a very powerful influence both on success and self-conceptions.

The other type of subcultural formation occurs as new members of an institution or organization become socialized into the subculture that exists among those who are already there. This socialization occurs most strikingly when people enter an organization alone or in small groups and learn the ropes from veterans of the institution, for instance, in prisons, jails, and mental hospitals. Erving Goffman's *Asylums* (1961) provides some interesting descriptions of socialization into subcultures in the mental hospital he studied. There he found a rich and complex *underlife* among inmates, into which new inmates were socialized. Even though inmates' personal freedom was limited and the staff imposed considerable regimentation on them, they were still able to carry on social relationships and develop collective responses to, and definitions of, their situation. They even succeeded in hoodwinking the staff once in a while.

Individuals enter the organization either in large groups, small groups, or singly. In any of these cases, two levels of socialization occur. One level is socialization into the informal subculture among members of the organization; the second level is the socialization or resocialization dictated by the purpose of the organization. The two levels are not necessarily compatible or consistent. For example, part of learning the ropes is learning how to get around or combat organizational demands. The studies by Becker and Goffman both illustrate the ways in which collective subcultural formations function to reduce the effectiveness of the staff (and thus their socializing or resocializing impact). This does not mean that socializing agencies should or even could eliminate relationships among members, for to attempt to do so might invoke considerable alienation and even further resistance to organizational demands. And it is well known that such subcultural relationships occur even in very highly regulated and regimented organizations such as prisons (Sykes, 1958).

On the other hand, in cases where the relationships and culture among members support organizational goals, as in some professional schools, subcultural formations can be a powerful aid in achieving those goals. Subcultures may facilitate quick adaptation to a new and strange environment and reinforce staff values. For example, the barracks subcultures that arise among Marine recruits are especially devoted to the aims of the corps—to transform recruits into Marines.

Whether or not a cohesive, viable culture develops among members of a socializing organization depends on several factors. One factor is the turnover of members. When turnover is high—as is the case when adults return to school for short refresher courses or stay at a temporary detention center while in route to prison—we expect little interaction among members. When students spend years in college or inmates spend half their lives in prisons or mental hospitals, we expect a great deal of member interaction. Another factor that influences the successful development of a subculture in an organization is the extent to which people can congregate; when they can, there is more chance for a subculture to develop. Troublesome inmates in a prison or mental hospital are isolated precisely in order to reduce their influence on others.

Organizational Control Underlying the three factors that we have discussed—commitment, choice, and interaction—is the amount of organizational control that the organization maintains over members' lives. All socializing organizations maintain some control over their members; otherwise they could have little if any impact. But there are wide variations in the amounts and kinds of control exercised. Schools, for example, always have control over at least students' academic and classroom behavior. But boarding schools and residential colleges become twenty-four-hour living establishments, and the extent of the schools' control widens to include activities and behavior outside the classroom.

A socializing organization, however, may also gradually diminish its control. When a convicted man who has done time moves from prisoner to probationary status, the law enforcement and court systems relinquish control over certain parts of his life.

Extensive control over members' lives is typical of agencies of resocialization: presence is involuntary, commitment is low, and attitudes are negative. Organizations maintain control by physically separating people from the outside environment. Prisons and mental hospitals may isolate inmates inside walls and barbed wire; they may use electronic surveillance, guards, and geographical remoteness. The more an agency must force socialization on an individual, the more it will be likely to use these methods to obtain extensive control. Agencies of developmental socialization rarely use force and coercion because extensive control is not crucial or even instrumental to their successful functioning.

Methods for maintaining extensive control over members are considered necessary in certain kinds of resocialization. In order to bring about radical changes in role behavior and values, resocializing organizations must put the individual in a situation where supports for previous identity, behavior, and values are absent and where supports for the desired changes can reinforce new identities and values. Resocializing agencies that perform this function have been called *total institutions* by Goffman (1961). These institutions become, in effect, an around-the-clock environment that marks a sharp break with the individual's previous way of life.

Resocialization and Total Institutions

As we have already suggested, resocialization is a traumatic, intense process that few individuals find pleasant and that involves extensive organizational controls. Radical changes in adult social behavior, values, and identities are extremely difficult to accomplish. By adulthood, behavior patterns are deeply ingrained and have had lifetime reinforcement. Resocialization programs must suppress this prior learning in order to supplant it with new patterns.

Goffman investigated how the organizational structure in a mental hospital can effect such changes. He found that the mental hospital functioned as a total institution. How do total institutions supplant lifelong identities? They cut off patients from the situations, people, and props that had maintained their past identities and self-images. They not only physically remove the patients from familiar surroundings but also subject them to regimented and standardized practices that reduce their individuality. By stripping a patient of much of his or her previous self, the staff in Goffman's hospital could begin to replace this self with a more conventional identity—with a self resocialized to social demands—through individual and group therapy (Goffman, 1961). What has been called brainwashing is simply this stripping process that has been carried to an extreme (Schein, 1956).

Few people are ever subjected to brainwashing, although many are subjected to milder forms of resocialization that they may not recognize as "stripping" attempts. Military boot camp and basic training are examples. New recruits are socialized into military culture by first being isolated from civilian influences. Then they are subjected to standardized treatment, and their individual identities are suppressed through uniform clothing, haircuts, and barracks life. Little privacy or indulgence is allowed while the recruits are being

Figure 10.5

"There are 60 million homes in the United States and over 95 percent of them are equipped with a television set. (More than 25 percent have two or more sets.) In the average home the television is turned on some five hours forty-five minutes a day. The average male viewer, between his second and sixty-fifth year, will watch television for over 3000 entire days—roughly nine full years of his life. During the average weekday winter evening nearly half of the American people are to be found silently seated with fixed gaze upon a phosphorescent screen."

Nicholas Johnson, *How To Talk Back To Your Television Set* (New York: Little, Brown and Company, 1970).

Figure 10.6   Resocialization into military life is literally a "stripping" process. New recruits are removed from the familiar people, situations, and props with which they have built and maintained their self-images. Suppression of their individual identities proceeds further as the men are subjected to regimented and standardized practices. For example, as they enter military life they are given identical haircuts and lined up in towels to wait until uniforms are issued to them. Note that in the photograph they are set apart from and are situated lower than the authority figure—a commanding officer—looming in the foreground.

taught how to become soldiers. During this process, civilian norms and values are ridiculed as sloppy and undisciplined; at the same time, drill sergeants praise the glory of military discipline.

NONORGANIZATIONAL CONTEXTS OF SOCIALIZATION AND RESOCIALIZATION

Socialization or resocialization occurs not only in the context of formal organizations but between individuals or in informal groups. The impersonal system of communications characteristic of technologically advanced societies also plays a part in the socialization process; books, newspapers, magazines, movies, and television greatly influence our lives. Nonorganizational socialization has already been touched on in the discussion of how informal subcultures operate within organizations. We will now take up other forms of nonorganizational socialization.

Psychotherapy

Each year a great many persons who believe they have difficulty coping with their lives seek the aid of psychiatrists, psychologists, marriage counselors, and other professionals engaged in what Goffman (1961) has called the "tinkering trades." Although some therapy occurs in such organizational settings as prisons or mental hospitals, much psychotherapy involves interaction between an individual and a therapist outside a formal organizational setting. The goal of all such therapy is the construction or reconstruction of a more adequate and satisfied self. Traditional therapies, such as those practiced by the followers of Freud, Rogers, Sullivan, and others have aimed at changing underlying components of the individual psyche. The patient is helped to bring to the surface repressed knowledge and feelings and to thereby reorient his whole personality in the light of what he has discovered about himself. The assumption is that if one first changes essential character traits, changes in behavior will follow as a natural consequence.

Recently, a new form of therapy called *behavior modification*, based on the work of learning psychologists such as B. F. Skinner, has broken with traditional views. Behavioral therapists concentrate on changing what a person does; they argue that changes in self-conceptions follow from changes in behavior. To illustrate the basic difference between Skinner's position and traditional therapies, we can consider the case of an extremely shy person. Traditional psychotherapists would seek the psychological causes of the person's shyness and try to reconstruct the patient's self-image so that he or she could become less shy. The therapeutic process could take years. Behavioral therapists would try to change the patient's behavior with reinforcements and punishments: Less shy behavior would, of course, be rewarded; shy behavior, punished or not reinforced. By changing the person's behavior they would expect the person's self-image to rapidly change—if you stop acting shy, you will stop feeling shy. Behaviorists claim that their methods take less time and that new symptoms of disorder do not crop up in place of the "extinguished" behavior. (See Chapter 4.)

Status Socialization

How do people learn to fulfill the expectations attached to statuses or positions that are so general that they do not necessarily imply specific roles? This kind of learning, too, is socialization. General statuses in society do imply distinctive cultural patterns—particular life styles, outlooks, and modes of interaction (for example, appropriate manners). Sociological literature is filled with descriptions of the particular cultural patterns associated with various social statuses—for example, the upper classes, tenant farmers, factory workers, suburbanites, blacks, immigrants, and the like. Each of these statuses is associated with distinctive cultural patterns that new members of each group must learn.

William Whyte's study of the *Organization Man* (1956) reveals that working for a corporation involves much more than simply performing a job successfully five days a week during business hours. Working in the upper echelons of a corporation sooner or later means that a man requires an "organization wife"; a house in the right suburb; proper conversational habits; and appropriate tastes in food, drink, and clothing. Having to acquire the accouterments of one's status may not be enforced so much by the organization itself as by the people in it on whom one depends for promotion, for approval, or for friends.

Elliot Liebow's study (1967) of a ghetto neighborhood in Washington, D.C., shows that life among lower-income, underprivileged groups has its own bases of conformity too. Such is the case among *streetcorner men*—unemployed men who hang around on the streets and have developed intricate interaction patterns. To take one last example, Howard S. Becker's study of marijuana smokers and his study of jazz musicians (1963) illustrate that each group has a distinctive life style and set of values, norms, and habits. New members must learn what it means to be a marijuana smoker or jazz musician by learning each group's way of life, just as organization men do in the suburbs and streetcorner men do in the urban ghettos.

The point is that people all come to live in a specific and distinctive place within the broader culture of their society. The place a person inhabits invariably has its own peculiarities—others around him or her expect certain things that are not expected in other social settings. The learning of these peculiarities is an important part of adult socialization, especially in contemporary societies where people experience considerable social mobility and often live in social settings much different from those in which they were raised as children. This type of adult socialization is more subtle and less obvious than that which occurs in the context of people-processing organizations and total institutions, but it is important nonetheless and rests on many of the same interpersonal processes that childhood socialization rests on.

Media Socialization

Marshall McLuhan (1965) has argued that television has rapidly transformed our sprawling and impersonal mass societies into a global village. Through electronic images we now see and hear what is going on everywhere in the world, within moments of its occurrence. There is much truth in McLuhan's assertion. Fads, styles, and even popular songs once took months or even years to spread across the United States, but they are now transmitted rapidly. Vietnam is the first war that people have watched in their homes.

In addition to television, we are exposed to a host of other mass media—radio, movies, magazines, newspapers, and books. Obviously, these media play a significant role in both childhood and adult socialization. And social scientists are increasingly concerned about the nature and extent of the socializing effects of the mass media.

One important aspect of the mass media's effect is the part the media play in status or life-style socialization. Cultural patterns of major status positions are frequently depicted by the media. Through news coverage, documentaries, dramas and comedies, and advertisements, the media let us glimpse how others live—the rich, the middle classes, the poor, and various ethnic groups. Whether these glimpses are accurate, they shape many people's beliefs and ideas about others.

Advertisements particularly exploit life-style differences in order to glamorize products. Famous athletes use a particular men's cologne. Beautiful and happy young women use a specific brand of hair rinse or drink a liquid breakfast. Successful executives prefer a particular car. Whether or not these advertising claims are true, they are usually presented in a context that implies to the public something about the life these persons lead. A consequence of such advertising is that it reinforces people's attachment to particular cultural values and conceptions of beauty, youth, and success.

A second aspect of media socialization is that it brings rapid reports of challenges to, or shifts in, prevailing roles, values, or norms. For example, when the student protest movement arose at the University of California at Berkeley in 1964, students around the world rapidly learned through media coverage of student grievances at Berkeley and of their efforts to establish new roles for students, faculty, and campus administrators. To the extent that these students believed they shared the grievances of the Berkeley students, they began to try to redefine the roles and positions on their own campuses. Soon similar student demonstrations spread across the nation and around the world. Had it not been for the message from the media, it may have taken a long time for events at Berkeley to be noticed elsewhere. Similarly, it is from the media that many people learn most of what they know about social movements (such as those aimed at the liberation of women or Third World communities) which challenge prevailing norms and roles. No longer must social movements depend wholly on word of mouth or on sending organizers from town to town. If people can get their views covered by the mass media, they can reach nearly everyone at once.

This use of the mass media has led to the nonevent or the media happening. In order to get news coverage on television there must be something to show—something worth filming. Rarely is a message enough; it must be an acted-out message. Thus, many activities (staged by people in social movements, by politicians, and by anyone else seeking to get his position publicly known) are designed to give television a picture. For ex-

ample, welfare mothers may picket city hall to protest the inefficiency and patriarchal nature of the welfare system. Their action against city hall will be effective primarily because they can communicate their protest through the television networks—their picket line provides action film. Likewise, a political candidate tours slums in order to get his plans for urban renewal (and thus the platform upon which he is waging his political campaign) aired on television.

The discussion of socialization and resocialization in this chapter assumes that society judges some persons as having been missocialized, that is, socialized in ways that society finds abnormal or even dangerous. Such persons violate social norms. The more norms they violate, the more likely it is that action will be taken to resocialize them (and also, often, to punish them for their violations). Such persons are referred to as deviants by sociologists.

It is vital to recognize that people are not born deviants; they learn to be deviant, just as others learn to conform to norms. We are not born knowing how to be drug addicts, criminals, or prostitutes, just as we are not born knowing how to speak English, play the piano, or become sociologists. Such roles are learned, whether the content of the learning is labeled disreputable and deviant or conventional and respectable.

The next chapter is devoted to deviance and social control. It will discuss what behavior is considered deviant and why; how people become deviants; and how society attempts to limit and contain deviant behavior.

SUGGESTED READINGS

Brim, Orville G., Jr., and Stanton Wheeler. *Socialization After Childhood.* New York: Wiley, 1966.

Goffman, Erving. *Asylums.* Garden City, N.Y.: (Anchor) Doubleday, 1961.

Scott, John Finley. *Internalization of Norms: A Sociological Theory of Moral Commitment.* Englewood Cliffs, N.J.: Prentice-Hall, 1971.

Whyte, William H., Jr. *The Organization Man.* New York: Simon and Schuster, 1956.

Chapter 11 Deviance and Conformity

TWO YOUNG WOMEN SAT at a table in a modern-day ice-cream parlor arguing with a man and a woman at another table. One of the young women at the first table took out a flute and began playing it loudly enough so that the waiters were unable to hear and take orders from those sitting at nearby tables. One of the customers and a waiter asked the woman to stop playing; she reduced the volume for a few seconds and then began playing loudly again. As they were leaving, her companion turned to the man with whom she had been arguing and said, "You're just a no-good ——er." Those at nearby tables heard but did nothing. The man turned to reading a book and then deliberately and loudly broke wind. That act earned him a few scornful looks from some people in the place; others tried to hide snickers; and still others ignored it or pretended not to hear it.

WHAT IS DEVIANT BEHAVIOR?

Deviant behavior is any disapproved act that violates the social norms within a social system. These norms may be the expectations of right and proper behavior shared by people in a particular setting, or they may be more general expectations, which prevail across many different situations. Deviant behaviors may be minor acts that few people take seriously, or they may be taken very seriously by, and evoke strong reactions in, a great many people, in which case they are said to be of major social concern.

Although there are some acts that seem never to be encouraged, what is considered deviant is generally relative to time and place. The same behavior that is considered unacceptable in one group or society may be defined as proper in another. Within the same social system, what is considered evil at one time in history may become permissible or even honorable later on. Behavior thought to be appropriate for some roles and statuses is inappropriate for others. The major forms of deviant behavior in society today may reflect the norms of the powerful groups in society, or the standards agreed upon by the majority, or both.

The kinds of behavior that are included within the general definition of deviance but are usually not considered of major importance are illustrated by the actual case described at the beginning of the chapter. The unsolicited and disruptive flute playing, the obscenity, and the flatulence were all deviant in this particular context. Most people present for this incident and most of those reading the description of it would agree that the actions of the woman and the man violated the norms governing manners at this kind of public place. However, the reactions to these violations were unorganized, informal, and mild. Such instances of norm violations occur often but do not offend people deeply or affect great numbers of people, and the behavior is not upsetting enough to those in a position of power that they feel called upon to take strong action to control such behavior. In the case cited, the manager of the ice-cream parlor could have taken action if he felt provoked enough by the behavior in question. Lying to a friend, cheating at cards, being rude and discourteous, wearing the wrong styles of clothing, and improperly dressing for a party begin a list of deviances that anyone could expand upon at length. (It is also possible for a person to be considered deviant without doing anything. One may be deviant simply by failing to conform to the prevailing standards of normal appearance and anatomy—being obese, terribly ugly, deformed, or handicapped.) Other types of nonconformity may violate the rules of organizations and groups and be reacted to in stronger, perhaps formal, ways; for instance, cheating in school, booing the preacher in church, violating rules in the factory, or elbowing a player in a basketball game are behaviors that can usually be counted on to invoke strong and swift reactions.

Although sociologists do designate behaviors like these as deviant, they have focused their efforts on describing and explaining such behaviors as crime, delinquency, mental illness, alcoholism, prostitution, and suicide because they deviate "in a disapproved direction, and of sufficient degree to exceed the tolerance limit of the community" (Clinard, 1968). That is, the criteria sociologists use in deciding what deviant behaviors to study are: (1) they must be of major importance to a great number of people in the society, as evi-

Figure 11.1   Some acts, such as prostitution (*top*),
are currently considered serious enough to require
official legal sanctions. Other types of behavior—such as
the eccentric style of dress this man has adopted
(*bottom*)—may disturb or offend the sensibilities of
some people, but such behaviors are not considered so
threatening to the community that they require formal
social control. Sociologists of deviant behavior have
focused primarily on the former type of deviance—
illegal behavior.

denced by (2) the existence of effective, formal
social-control mechanisms that are specifically
aimed at restraining the deviance.

WHAT IS SOCIAL CONTROL?

Social control is any social mechanism for encouraging conformity and curtailing deviance.
The very norms that evaluate behavior as good or
bad are themselves mechanisms of social control.
As pointed out in Chapters 6 and 10, through
childhood and adult socialization, people learn to
regulate their own behavior with regard to the
roles they play and the statuses they occupy in
society. Social sanctions are applied to our behavior both to teach us proper conduct and to keep
us in line with the norms at any given time. Other
people attempt to reward us with positive sanctions when we do what is right (in their eyes) and
to punish us with negative sanctions when we do
wrong (from their point of view). The informal
show of approval and acceptance by those close
to us, whether through word or gesture, is the
most common and effective positive sanction. But
more formal and public sanctions, such as monetary rewards and symbolic awards, are also positive gestures that encourage conformity. Minor
deviations are apt to be met with the withdrawal
of affection, a frown, or words of rebuke.

Most of us conform most of the time because,
as a result of being socialized, we have developed
self-control. The informal sanctioning that occurs
in primary groups and the more indirect restraints exerted by secondary and reference
groups are forces of social control that teach people to exercise self-control and to conform rather
than to commit deviant behaviors.

However, the principal social-control response
to behaviors defined as deviant by the majority or
by powerful groups in modern society today is to
enact laws against these behaviors. Formal organizations are set up to administer the treatment
stipulated by these laws and, in some cases, to
apply penalties to those who commit deviant
behaviors. Indeed, in complex societies the formal
control system is nearly synonymous with the legal control system. Therefore, sociologists' concentration on the major forms of deviance means

that the sociological study of deviance is, for the most part, the study of illegal behavior. And the form of social control most often studied by sociologists is control through law.

The list of actions covered by criminal law are well-known: murder, assault, rape, burglary, robbery, fraud, embezzlement, arson, vandalism, prostitution, certain kinds of gambling, public disorderly conduct, and so on. In addition, there are the violations of laws and regulations not a part of traditional criminal law, for example, restraint of trade, adulteration of food and drugs, and environmental pollution. Alcoholism is not illegal but public drunkenness and driving while drunk are. Drug addiction is not illegal but possession of certain drugs is. The law defines as delinquency not only those acts by youth that would be crimes if committed by an adult but also some kinds of behavior, such as drinking, incorrigibility, and running away from home that are considered deviant only when committed by minors.

The government also sets up public (and helps finance private) formal organizations to control some forms of deviance by treating deviants. Deviants are sometimes forced by the state to undergo treatment involuntarily. It is not a criminal offense to be mentally ill, but the law provides for the official designation of some people as mentally ill and for their involuntary incarceration. In some states, drug addicts may be committed by law to treatment centers for a specific period of time, and they must remain until the period ends even if they want to leave. Even in situations where treatment is not legally coerced, as in some suicide-prevention and crisis clinics, community mental-health agencies, and drug rehabilitation centers, the organizations that run the clinics and agencies may be supported and regulated by the state as part of an overall public policy to control the deviant behavior.

EXTENT AND VARIATIONS OF DEVIANT BEHAVIOR

Although sociologists are very interested in how it is that certain actions come to be considered deviant and how society attempts to control these actions, the question that has most preoccupied

them is one of causation: How and why does deviance occur? In order to propose answers to this question, one must have some answers to questions about the extent and variations of deviant behavior: How much is there and who is doing it?

How Data Are Obtained

How does a sociologist obtain data on deviance? Any of the social-research methods—observation, experimentation, and surveys—are available for, and have been used in, the study of deviance. The fact that crime, some types of sexual behavior, drug use, and the other forms of deviant behavior are especially sensitive subjects, however, makes direct study difficult. Gaining entry into and rapport with deviant groups or experimenting with deviant acts requires that the sociologist overcome more difficult practical and ethical problems than are likely to be present in the study of nondeviant groups or behavior.

Official Records Probably because of these special difficulties, studies of deviance have been heavily dependent upon the formal agencies of control for information and access to subjects. Therefore, what is known about the extent and variations of deviance is filtered through the police, courts, coroners, narcotics agencies, prisons, mental hospitals, and the other organizations set up to control deviant behavior. Who gets caught as a deviant is not just a matter of who commits deviant acts; it is also a matter of how offenders come to official attention and what decisions are made about them. It may be that the "facts" about deviance from official records are based on an unrepresentative sample—that the selection process through which some deviant acts are officially recorded and others are not reflects factors other than the behaviors themselves. These factors may include not only the social characteristics of the deviants but also the beliefs, biases, and characteristics of the control agents. Thus, one must be cautious in generalizing from the official statistics.

Self-reports Fortunately, sociologists' knowledge of the extent and variation of deviant behavior is not wholly dependent upon these official

Figure 11.2   The percentage change in crime
·rate and in major index crimes compared to the
population increase in the United States from 1960
to 1970. (Major index crimes include murder,
forcible rape, robbery, aggravated assault, burglary,
larceny for amounts of over $50, and automobile
theft. The crime rate indicates the number of
offenses per 100,000 population.)
(Adapted from Federal Bureau of Investigation, 1971.)

Figure 11.3   Trends in court cases trying
juvenile offenses compared to the juvenile population
from 1940 to 1968.
(From the Office of Juvenile Delinquency and
Youth Development, 1970.)

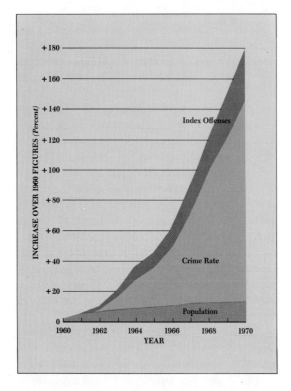

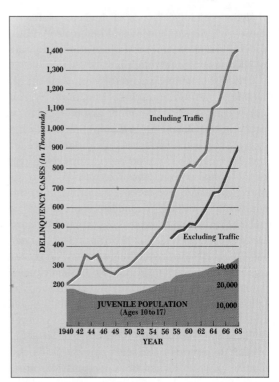

sources. A number of studies have been conducted that by-pass the official agencies by surveying representative samples of the general population with *unofficial* measures of deviant behavior.
Deviant behavior may be unofficially measured
by administering anonymous questionnaires or by
conducting confidential interviews in which people *self-report* their own deviant behavior or report the deviance known to them. In recent years
other measuring techniques have been developed, such as *victimization* surveys, in which respondents report the times they have been victims of crime, for example, have had their cars
stolen or houses burglarized, have been assaulted
or robbed, and so on.

Participant Observation   A frequent technique
for studying deviance is face-to-face observation
of deviants or deviant groups. Recall that Chapter
2 showed how John Lofland used this technique
to study the Divine Precepts, who, whatever else
they were, were a deviant group in that their
behavior violated important religious norms of

American society. (Many who came once to hear
their message became quite agitated when they
discovered that the Divine Precepts were "not
Christians.") Sociologists have done many participant observational studies of deviant groups, of
embezzlers (Lemert, 1972), hold-up men (Irwin,
1970), mental patients (Goffman, 1961), homosexuals (Humphreys, 1970) and street gangs (Whyte,
1943), to name only a few examples.

Extent of Crime and Delinquency: Official Measures

To what extent do crime and delinquency occur
in the United States? Table 11.1 shows the total
number and the rate (per 100,000 population) of
officially reported major crimes in 1970. It is clear
from this table that crime in the United States is
mainly property crime; the rate of reported property offenses is about six times the rate of violent
offenses. The difference would be even more
striking if robbery, which is counted as a violent
offense in the table, were counted as a property

crime. However, the actual amount of crime (all kinds) is much higher than the amount that is officially recorded. A recent national survey of households found that the crime rate calculated on the basis of unofficially reported victims of crime is about twice as high as the official rate (Ennis, 1967).

Table 11.2 shows that crime is predominantly an activity of the young (at least as indicated by the number of young people who are arrested for and charged with criminal offenses). Juveniles (young people under eighteen years of age) account for a sizable portion of these arrests. Although persons aged ten to seventeen account for only 16 percent of the general population, one-fourth of all arrests and almost half of the arrests for major crimes are of persons under eighteen. The overrepresentation of juveniles is most evident for property crimes; half of those arrested for property offenses are under eighteen, and more than two-thirds are under twenty-one. Arrests on charges of violent crimes are more likely for those over eighteen, especially in the age group including those eighteen to twenty-four; this group makes up less than 15 percent of the population but represents more than a third of arrests for violent offenses.

The arrest figures indicate that adolescents account for more than their share of criminal arrests (and presumably more than their share of crimes). However, another way of measuring the extent of delinquency is to look at the proportion of the general adolescent population that gets included in the police and court statistics. As it turns out, this proportion is quite small. In 1970, less than 6 percent of the juvenile population (ages ten to seventeen) was arrested by the police (FBI, 1971), and only 2.5 percent of the juvenile population actually appears before the juvenile courts in a year (Office of Juvenile Delinquency and Youth Development, 1970).

Are Crime and Delinquency Increasing?

Figures 11.2 and 11.3 leave little doubt that the official rates of crime and delinquency had been steadily increasing until 1970. The increase in

Table 11.1 Major Crimes* Officially Reported in the United States, 1970

Type of Crime	Actual Number	Number per 100,000 Population
All Major Crimes	5,568,200	2,740.6
Major Violent Crimes		
Murder	15,810	7.8
Forcible Rape	37,270	18.3
Aggravated Assault	329,940	162.4
Robbery	348,380	171.5
Total	731,400	360.0
Major Property Crimes		
Burglary	2,169,300	1,067.7
Larceny (over $50)	1,746,100	859.4
Auto Theft	921,400	453.5
Total	4,836,800	2,380.6

* Major crimes are those reported to the police and acknowledged by them to have occurred whether or not they know who has committed them. The Federal Bureau of Investigation collects data from police reports on twenty-seven categories of crime and two juvenile-status offenses. But the seven crimes shown here are set aside as "major index" crimes and are the only ones for which the number reported is compiled. On the other offenses only arrest data are reported.

Source: Adapted from Federal Bureau of Investigation, *Crime in the United States, Uniform Crime Reports—1970* (Washington, D.C.: Government Printing Office, 1971), p. 6.

property offenses (up 146 percent from 1960 to 1970) was greater than the increase in violent offenses (up 126 percent). In fact, the homicide rate had been decreasing during the first half of the decade; it started upward in 1965 (FBI, 1971). The increase suggested by these statistics does not mean that the streets became less safe. In most cases of interpersonal violence the offender and victim are relatives, neighbors, or acquaintances. For example, a relatively small proportion of homicides result from the commission of a planned crime such as armed robbery; rather, four out of five murders result from arguments and fights between lovers, between friends or acquaintances, or within the family unit; indeed, 16 percent of all murder victims are killed by their spouses (FBI, 1970).

During the 1950s and early 1960s less than 2 percent of the juvenile population was officially handled by the juvenile courts in any given year

Table 11.2   Arrests by Age, 1970

Age	Percentage of Arrests			
	All Arrests	Major Crimes	Major Violent Crimes	Major Property Crimes
Under 18	25.3	46.1	22.6	51.7
Under 21	39.1	63.2	40.2	68.6
18 to 24	27.1	30.0	36.0	28.3
25 and older	47.6	23.9	41.4	20.0

Source: Adapted from Federal Bureau of Investigation, *Crime in the United States, Uniform Crime Reports—1970* (Washington, D.C.: Government Printing Office, 1971), pp. 126–128.

(Teeters and Matza, 1959; Perlman, 1964). But, as shown in Figure 11.3, there was a definite upward trend in juvenile arrests and in juvenile court cases, although this increase was uneven. The rate of juvenile court referrals dropped in 1959, came up in 1960, dipped again in 1961, rose once more in 1962, and persistently increased in the following years (Office of Juvenile Delinquency and Youth Development, 1970).

Who Is Committing Crime and Delinquency?

In order to attempt solution of the riddle of what causes criminal and delinquent deviance, the sociologist must know not only the extent of crime and delinquency but also who is committing crimes and delinquency. A person's age and sex, the region and community in which he or she lives, and the race and class of which he or she is a member are all factors that have been found to be decisive variations in determining whether or not this person will commit criminal or delinquent acts.

Age and Sex Statistics in the preceding paragraphs showed that adolescents and young adults predominate among the officially apprehended population. Statistics also show that crime and delinquency are male-dominated activities. In 1970 and 1971, about six males were arrested for each female arrested, and there were four boys for each girl who came to the attention of juvenile courts. These ratios represent less difference than in prior years. In 1960, the ratio of male to female arrests was eight to one, and the ratio of boys to

girls in juvenile court cases was about five to one (FBI, 1971; Office of Juvenile Delinquency and Youth Development, 1970). There has been some speculation that these changed ratios reflect a decline in traditional sex-role differences.

Region and Community Most crime is concentrated in the urban areas of the United States, where the rate is about two-and-a-half times that of suburban areas and more than five times that of rural areas (see Table 11.3). The region with the highest overall crime rate is the West; the lowest rates are in the South and the North Central states. The South, however, has the highest rate of violent crimes (except robbery).

Race and Class Not only is crime primarily an urban phenomenon, but in the big cities the official statistics show crime to be concentrated in the lower-class central districts and among the nonwhite minority populations. In all areas, persons with minimum education, low income, and lower-class occupations are arrested and incarcerated way out of proportion to their numbers in the population (Voss and Peterson, 1971; Sutherland and Cressey, 1970). For example, black people comprise about 11 percent of the general population, but 27 percent of all arrested offenders are black, and 36 percent of those arrested for major crimes are black (FBI, 1971).

Official Statistics: Pro and Con

Some sociologists maintain that changes in official crime and delinquency rates are entirely the result of variations in enforcement and reporting policies. Thus, if there is a reported increase in official crime rates, they say it reflects better detection and reporting of crimes. If the official rates show a disproportionate number of males, blacks, lower-class youth, and those from urban communities, it is said to be simply because official agencies are more likely to move against people with these characteristics—not because people with these characteristics are actually more involved in crime and delinquency (Chambliss and Nagasawa, 1969; Kitsuse and Cicourel, 1963). Although official statistics are a relatively crude index of actual deviant behavior, perhaps only some changes and differences in official statistics can be attributed to variations in official policy.

Unofficial Measures of Crime and Delinquency

The studies using such unofficial measures as anonymous self-reports in surveys of deviance indicate that the amount of undetected delinquency is several times greater than the amount indicated by official statistics (although the discrepancy is much less for very serious offenses). Further, many factors related to official delinquency are only slightly related or are totally unrelated to unofficial delinquency. For instance, the factor of race shows little significance in the overall amount of self-reported delinquency; that is, the unofficial rates do not show blacks to be disproportionately represented. The factor of sex, while still significant, shows the ratio of male to female offenders to be closer to two or three to one instead of the official ratio of four to one. Perhaps the relationship that has been most strongly called into question by the unofficial studies is that

between social class and delinquency. A number of studies have found no significant relationship between the total number of self-reported delinquencies and social class (Nye *et al.*, 1958; Akers, 1964; Voss, 1966; Hirschi, 1969). This finding is considered in detail in Chapter 14.

Extent and Variation of Other Deviant Behaviors

In order to attempt to answer the question of what causes deviance, the sociologist must also be informed about the extent and variations of deviant behaviors other than crime and delinquency —such behaviors as drug use, alcoholism, suicide, and mental illness.

Drug Use The number of opiate addicts (most of whom are heroin addicts) is probably something less than 200,000, although some recent estimates reach as high as half a million. Even the highest estimates would place the proportion of the general population who are addicts at a fraction of 1 percent. If nonaddicted users and former users and addicts are added to this percentage, there may be as much as 4 percent of the general population who have had some experience with opiates (Blum, 1967). Addicts tend to be young, male, and concentrated in the large cities among nonwhite and among lower-class groups (Chein *et al.*, 1964; O'Donnell and Ball, 1966; Blum, 1967). Some evidence, however, shows an increase of addicts among middle- and upper-class groups and soldiers in Vietnam (*Newsweek*, July 5, 1971).

At one time this description of opiate addicts also fit users of marijuana. But use of marijuana, LSD, and other *hallucinogenic* drugs, as well as

Table 11.3   Major Crime Rates (Number of Major Crimes per 100,000 population) and Community Size, 1970

Community	Total Rate of Major Crimes	Rate for Major Violent Crimes	Rate for Major Property Crimes
Large cities*	5,335.1	980.4	4,354.7
Suburban communities	2,137.0	176.7	1,960.3
Rural areas	927.4	120.0	807.4

* Over 250,000 in population.

Source: Adapted from Federal Bureau of Investigation, *Crime in the United States, Uniform Crime Reports—1970* (Washington, D.C.: Government Printing Office, 1971), p. 6.

Figure 11.4   Young heroin addicts take part in a "confrontation session" at Odyssey House, a privately supported rehabilitation center in New York City. The boy and girl (*bottom*) are, respectively, eleven and fifteen years old.

6 to 10 percent are alcoholics—problem drinkers. The alcoholic is most likely to be a lower-class Catholic man in his mid-forties living in a large city in the northeastern or western part of the country (Cahalan, 1970).

Suicide   Each year in the United States about 20,000 persons (about .001 percent of the population) take their own lives, and about eight times that many attempt suicide. This rate has remained fairly constant in the twentieth century, except for a period of higher rates in the Depression of the 1930s and a period of lower rates in the 1950s. The vast majority of suicides (about seven out of ten) are men, but most suicide attempts are made by women. Suicides are most likely to occur in a large city on the west coast and among older people (mid-sixties and older), whites, unmarried persons, Protestants, and upper and lower classes. Suicide rates are not consistently related to climate or season (Labovitz, 1968; Maris, 1969).

Mental Illness   The best estimates indicate that less than 1 percent of the population at any given time is under "treatment" for diagnosed mental illness; this figure represents persons who are patients of public and private hospitals and clinics (Dunham, 1965). However, some surveys of samples from the general population in large cities have judged as much as 23 percent to be *mentally impaired* (Srole *et al.*, 1962). Overall rates of mental hospitalization tend to increase with age, and there is some evidence that these rates are higher for whites and for men. As is taken up in detail in Chapter 14, lower-class persons are disproportionately represented in public mental-hospital populations; middle- and upper-status persons predominate among private patients (Faris and Dunham, 1939; Hollingshead and Redlich, 1958; Weinberg, 1967).

SOCIOLOGICAL THEORIES OF DEVIANT BEHAVIOR

The sociological theories of deviant behavior can be viewed as tentative answers to two interrelated questions: Why do certain groups and seg-

use of amphetamines, increased among young middle-class, whites during the 1960s (Goode, 1970). The increase was especially evident among college students but was also noticeable in the general population. The 1971 Gallup Poll found that 42 percent of the college students who were asked admitted to use of marijuana; the 1972 Gallup Poll revealed that 11 percent of the adult population had used marijuana at least once (compared to 4 percent in 1969).

Alcoholism   About two-thirds of the adult population (and in some communities the majority of the teen-age population) drink alcohol, but only

Figure 11.5   Although the number of heroin addicts is estimated to be a fraction of 1 percent of the general population of the United States, some portions of the general population are much more exposed than others to the possibility of addiction from a harrowingly young age onward. Heroin is easily available to children and adolescents, especially nonwhites of the lower classes who live in the inner cities. The quotation below is from a composition written under a fictitious name by a Puerto Rican child living on the Lower East Side of New York City.

> *Sometimes I feel like giving up, it is no use to fight problems. Last year when I was in the 5th grade I tried to take the needle from some older kids who were shooting it in the school yard. I really felt that anything, even dying, was better than being here in this life. Death has to be better than this.*   CARMEN
>
> *Can't You Hear Me Talking to You?*
> Bantam Books Inc.

ments of society have higher rates of deviant behavior? And what is the process by which individuals come to commit deviant acts and play deviant roles? There are differences in the answers propounded by various sociologists, but all the theories emphasize that the social environment—the larger social structure surrounding an individual and the more immediate social situations and groups to which he or she belongs—plays a major part in the causation of deviant behavior. Each theory is consistent with or derived from one or more of the general sociological theories presented in Chapter 4.

Social Disorganization, or Anomie

The social disorganization theory views deviant behavior as an adaptation to basic conditions of social disruption, lack of consensus on norms, and social malintegration. These conditions are collectively called social disorganization, or *anomie*, and whenever they prevail, higher rates of deviant behavior are expected. For instance, the explanation offered by this theory for the high rates of officially reported crime, delinquency, addiction, prostitution, and mental illness in the lower-class areas of the city is that these neighborhoods are socially disorganized (Faris, 1955). Another major version of this theory is that although all people (especially males) are socialized to aspire to success and achievement in American society, there is unequal access to legitimate means or opportunities to achieve success. This discrepancy between means and ends is a form of anomie that produces strain in the system by exerting particular pressure on lower-class and minority groups (who are most likely to be denied legitimate opportunities). Thus, people in these groups are more likely than people in other groups to turn

to illegitimate, or deviant, means to attain their ends (Merton, 1938).

Albert Cohen (1955) argues that the development of delinquent subcultures results from the reactions of lower-class male adolescents to their inability to live up to the conventional (largely middle-class) criteria of status and achievement. The delinquent subculture provides a set of anti-conventional, deviant criteria of status and achievement that the adolescents are able to meet. Richard Cloward and Lloyd Ohlin (1961) agree that a delinquent subculture arises in response to the denial of opportunities to pursue legitimate ways of achieving success and status. They add, however, that the particular form that the subculture takes reflects differences in the availability of illegitimate opportunities in neighborhoods where lower-class male adolescents reside. In the most disorganized areas there is a relative deprivation of even criminal opportunities; there are few successful deviant models to emulate and few structured criminal activities into which the adolescents can become integrated. In these areas the delinquent subculture is most likely to be focused on nonutilitarian gang fighting. In other neighborhoods, where criminal adults can be found and illegitimate opportunities are available, a more utilitarian theft subculture evolves. A *retreatist* subculture revolving around drugs is resorted to by those who fail in both the gang-fighting and theft subcultures.

Although anomie theory has been applied primarily to crime and subcultural delinquency, it has also been used to explain other forms of deviance. For example, alcoholism is often viewed as a response to the anxiety-producing conditions of anomie. The more disorganized the social groups and culture, the higher the rate of alcoholism (Ullman, 1958; Snyder, 1964). Similarly, suicide rates have been accounted for by lack of integration or disruption in status, group, or society (Durkheim, 1951; Gibbs and Martin, 1964; Maris, 1969).

Conflict Theory

Conflict theorists do not agree with anomie theorists that all people are socialized into the same

Figure 11.6   Edwin H. Sutherland (1883–1950), a highly influential criminologist, entered the field of criminology in 1924 with the publication of his textbook *Criminology,* which offered a comprehensive criticism of conventional criminological theory. This textbook and its revisions, all entitled *Principles of Criminology* (1934, 1939, 1947, and a revision done by Donald R. Cressey in 1960), have been re-garded as most authoritative. Sutherland's theory of crime causation—the theory of differential association —conceives of criminality as participation in a specific cultural tradition through association with representatives of that culture rather than as the consequence of some physical or psychological abnormality. Sutherland's other books include *The Professional Thief* (1937) and *White Collar Crime* (1949).

cultural values or that deviance is a response to disorganization. Rather, they contend that society is composed of conflicting groups that hold different sets of values and interests; society, therefore, has no genuine consensus on values. Instead, the more powerful groups have their values embodied in the law, and their values thus become predominant in society. When those in the less powerful groups conform to some of their own norms, they may violate the norms of the dominant groups, and their actions are branded as deviant (Vold, 1958; Quinney, 1970).

Ethnic and racial minorities, immigrants, and others may do things deemed deviant simply because they are adhering to a set of norms at variance with those of the dominant groups (Sellin, 1938). Some conflict theorists view the delinquent behavior of lower-class youths as an effort to achieve status by realizing the values of their separate lower-class subculture rather than as a reaction to their inability to attain to middle-class standards (Miller, 1958). Also, these theorists point out, murder, violence, property damage, and other crimes are committed on *both* sides of the conflict when protest and revolutionary groups attempt to challenge the established order. Witness the history of union formation, radical protest, and urban riots in this country. Both unions and management commit crimes, and both protestors and police commit them too.

Labeling Theory and Deviant Identity

The labeling perspective shares with the conflict approach an emphasis on the less powerful being branded as deviant by the more powerful. But to this emphasis is added the symbolic interactionist's notion that the individual constructs a self-identity on the basis of how others behave toward him and what he thinks they think of him; this self-identity then leads him to behave in certain ways. Therefore, the actions taken to label a person as deviant (and to control him) may result in a *self-fulfilling prophecy,* in which an originally nondeviant person becomes so, and a slightly deviant person becomes more committed to a deviant way of life. Official apprehension and public labeling of an individual as a deviant, rather than deterring him from norm violations, may induce others to treat him differently, to cut him off from nondeviant alternatives, to push him into participation in deviant groups and roles, and to facilitate the development of a committed deviant identity (Becker, 1963, 1964; Lemert, 1972).

Thus, the minor offender may become a serious delinquent. Rejection of the homosexual by straight society pushes him further into exclusive association with other homosexuals and strengthens his self-image as a homosexual. The branded addict finds it difficult to think of himself as a nonaddict; consequently, he will have trouble convincing others to think of him as a nonaddict and to support his efforts to keep away from drugs. Another implication of the labeling perspective is that the passage of laws forbidding the possession or consumption of some goods or services (drugs, gambling, prostitution) often drives the distribution and supply system underground into the hands of organized criminal syndicates. The public policy designed to control one deviance therefore may foster the conditions necessary for the continuation of other deviances.

Erving Goffman (1963) and John Lofland (1969) should be included in a discussion of labeling theorists because they, like symbolic interactionists, give central importance to the development of a self-identity in a deviant career. Although most labeling theorists focus on the role of formal control agencies in affixing a deviant label on persons, Goffman gives more attention to the response of informal, face-to-face audiences to individual deviance. Also, whereas most labeling theorists are concerned with unlawful deviance, Goffman has broader concerns. He asks how individuals manage any kind of stigmatization in social interaction; he studies the ways in which people deal with being crippled and deformed as well as how they deal with being alcoholics, homosexuals, or criminals.

Lofland attends to the entire process of becoming deviant, including the commission of the deviant act, the impact of labeling, and the assumption of a deviant identity. His analysis is based on a major expansion of his theory of conversion, outlined in Chapter 2. He has laid out the step-by-step process by which people are recruited and socialized into such deviant roles as prostitute or professional check-forger.

However, most illegal and most deviant behavior is not the product of stable deviant roles. Most deviant behavior is committed by "normal" persons; for example, most murders are not committed by "criminals" but by friends or relatives of the victim . Role analysis, thus, is not relevant to a great deal of deviance.

Control Theory

When social control is adequate, deviance is prevented; when internal or external controls are weak or broken, deviance occurs. This central proposition in control theory indicates that this theory is not as concerned with finding motivation for deviating from norms as are the theories reviewed thus far. Rather, it is concerned with locating at what point social control breaks down so that people are set free to deviate. Other theories question why people deviate; control theory asks under what conditions people conform.

For Walter Reckless and his colleagues (1956; 1967), the fact that many people are deviant in some parts of society means that external control—*outer containment*—is not strong enough to counter the impetus to deviance. The boy who remains conforming even in lower-class, high-delinquency areas of a city does so because he has been socialized into a "good" self-concept that insulates him from the delinquency-producing influences of a bad environment. His peers, who lack this *inner containment,* succumb to the same environment. (Refer to Chapter 7 for an account of Reckless' research.) In Travis Hirschi's view (1969), deviance results when the bonds to conventional society's groups, institutions, and beliefs are broken or weakened. The more strongly adolescents are attached to parents, conventional adults, and peers, the more they are involved in school and other conventional activities, and the more they are committed to conventional beliefs, the less likely they are to be delinquent. The

weaker these ties, the greater is the likelihood that they will become delinquent.

Differential Association and Social Learning

Edwin H. Sutherland's differential association theory contends that a person undergoes the same basic socializing process whether learning conforming acts or deviant acts. Through symbolic interaction with others, principally in primary groups, a person learns the techniques that make him able to deviate and violate the law. He also learns the attitudes and *definitions* (meanings given to behavior that make it seem right or wrong, justified or unjustified) that make him willing to violate the law. Given that an individual is exposed to both law-breaking and law-abiding patterns in his associations, whether or not he will commit criminal or delinquent acts depends upon the balance of favorable and unfavorable definitions to which he is exposed in regard to breaking the law. If a person is exposed to criminal definitions while relatively isolated from conforming definitions—if he is exposed to criminal definitions first, more frequently, for a longer time, and with a greater intensity than to anticriminal definitions—then he will violate the law (Sutherland, 1947; Sutherland and Cressey, 1970).

Robert L. Burgess and Ronald L. Akers (1966) agree that the same basic socializing process is involved in learning deviant and conforming behavior and that only the content differs. However, they believe that Sutherland's theory inadequately specifies the mechanisms of learning involved. Therefore, Burgess and Akers reformulated differential association theory, using the behavioral learning principles of operant conditioning (reinforcement theory). The reformulated theory is essentially a social-learning approach that retains Sutherland's emphasis on learning in social interaction and learning of definitions favorable to criminal behavior. But the theory integrates these factors into the basic learning mechanisms of *reinforcement* (reward) and punishment. Thus, deviant behavior will be committed if, under similar circumstances in the

Figure 11.7   Although most people agree that there must be official efforts to control certain acts, such as murder and rape, debates rage over laws that attempt to regulate such behavior as drug use and sexuality. Some groups are fighting for the repeal of all laws that make crimes of activities that have no "victims."

Betty and Sue are married. To each other.

Betty and Sue live like any other young married couple.
Betty pursues a successful career in publishing. Sue prefers to do the chores at home. Both will tell you they wouldn't have it any other way . . . except for one thing. Sometimes they feel very alone.
This week Eyewitness News explores the predicament of Betty, Sue and many others like them in a candid documentary entitled "Lesbians."
Hear lesbians talk openly about their philosophy and way of life. Learn about the social pressures that have forced them into hiding.

Watch "Lesbians." With Fred Anderson and the Eyewitness News team. This Monday through Friday, November 16-20 at 4:30 and 11:00 p.m.
Call the Eyewitness News team anything you like. Except indifferent.

eyewitness news
kabc·tv/4:30 & 11:00pm
bonds/lawrence/nahan/sloane

past, it has been rewarded more frequently (and punished less frequently), in greater amounts, and with a higher probability than alternative conforming behavior. Definitions favorable to deviant behavior are themselves learned through reinforcement. These definitions then increase the probability of committing deviant acts by functioning as *discriminative* stimuli that signal or cue the actor as to what behavior is appropriate in a given situation.

Both Sutherland's differential association theory and the reinforcement revision of it were formulated to deal specifically with criminal and delinquent behavior. But differential association theory has been applied to many other forms of deviant behavior, and Burgess and Akers specifically claim that theirs is a general theory applicable to all deviance (Akers *et al.*, 1968; Akers, 1973).

The sociological theories of deviant behavior attempt to answer questions about the causation of deviance and are central to the sociologist's investigation of deviance. But sociologists are also very interested in how certain behaviors come to be considered deviant and in how society attempts to control these behaviors.

DEFINITIONS AND CONTROL OF DEVIANCE

Why is it that certain behaviors are defined as deviant and controlled? One type of sociological answer to this question is: Behavior that is treated as deviant by society, and is therefore termed illegal, reflects a widespread societal consensus on what is right and wrong. The older view of this consensus was that the law is a formal expression of a society's *folkways and mores* (Sumner, 1959). The more modern view is that disapproval of certain behavior and people is functional for the whole society as an ongoing and orderly system. Thus, such violent acts as murder and armed robbery are defined as deviant because if these acts were not controlled, they would be dysfunctional for society. Sexual promiscuity, homosexuality, and prostitution are disapproved because they are disruptive to a social order that relies for its continuity on enduring and interdependent heterosexual relationships organized around a stable family system (Davis, 1966). Kai Erickson (1966) argues that the singling out of some individuals and groups as deviant is itself functional for society, regardless of whether their disapproved behavior is dysfunctional, because this singling out allows other members of society to gauge the outer limits of socially acceptable behavior. Also, seeing negative sanctions applied to those persons who violate the norms helps people who remain conforming to reaffirm the validity of the norms.

Other sociologists explain the current definitions and control of deviance as an outcome of the compromises, defeats, and victories of group conflict. (See the preceding discussions of conflict and labeling theories.) The laws and public policy regulating deviance therefore result from the same process of conflict among political interests that produces any governmental decision, whether legislative, administrative, or even judicial. Both through direct political pressure and through influence as reference groups, the more powerful social classes, regions, groups, and population segments can see to it that their norms become dominant in the law and in the prevailing moral sentiments of society. The more powerful can impose the label of deviant on others and resist being called deviant for their own actions (Quinney, 1970; Chambliss and Seidman, 1971).

There is little doubt that certain kinds of actions would be very disruptive (even destructive) to society if not controlled. It is also the case that the various kinds of behavior defined as deviant by legal policy (and therefore to be controlled legally) also tend to be judged as serious deviances in public opinion polls (Simmons, 1965; Lofland, 1969). There is a core of acts defined in the criminal law (for example, murder, rape, fraud, theft, and destruction of property) whose undesirability few people would dispute. It is also difficult to find groups who support alcoholism and suicide as positive contributions to society.

Beyond this core of acts, however, many behaviors labeled deviant are being vehemently questioned by dissenting groups that object to one or another of the labels. Furthermore, controversy and conflicting opinion abound concerning the best policy for dealing with deviant behavior of all types. This fact is amply demonstrated by the long-standing conflict over capital punishment (Bedau, 1964) and the more recent dissension over the proper way to deal with civil disorders (National Advisory Commission, 1968; Walker, 1968). But perhaps the areas of legal control of deviance about which there is the greatest controversy today are: the public policies on drugs (Kaplan, 1971; National Commission on Marijuana and Drug Abuse, 1972), on pornography (Commission on Obscenity and Pornography, 1970), on gambling, on prostitution, and on homosexuality. These are all *crimes without victims*—actions by adults that, although legally prohibited, involve no injured, unwilling, or complaining victim (Schur, 1965). Crimes without victims involve either the individual doing something to himself or the willing exchange between partners or between supplier and customer. Although there is still some public consensus on keeping these acts under legal control (the 1972 Gallup Poll, for instance, found that 81 percent of the public think

marijuana should remain illegal), that consensus has been eroding in recent years, and the groups pushing for the decriminalization of such behavior are gaining in political strength.

The Criminal Justice System

In addition to studying the question of how much laws reflect social conflict or consensus, sociologists want to know how and with what success the formal structure set up to implement the law operates. The organizations and procedures that are provided to enforce the law (or to do something about behavior defined as a public problem) vary with the behavior in question. Mental illness, for example, is dealt with formally through a *mental health* or *lunacy commission*. This commission declares persons to be mentally incompetent and consigns them to various organizations for treatment or safekeeping, including state-run mental institutions. White-collar offenses, such as restraint of trade, false advertising, environmental pollution, commercial and consumer fraud, and fraudulent practice in professions are regulated by various state and federal boards and commissions. But the heart of the formal control mechanism is the *criminal justice system*. This administrative and judicial system consists of these major sectors: (1) the *police* (or more generally, *law enforcement* officers, including agents of the Federal Bureau of Investigation, the Treasury Department, and other agencies); (2) the *prosecutor;* (3) the *courts,* including (a) local *misdemeanant* courts for minor offenders, (b) *superior* or *district* courts for felony cases, and (c) *state* and *federal appellate* and *supreme courts* that hear appeals and decide questions of constitutionality; and (4) *correctional-treatment organizations and agencies,* including prisons, delinquency institutions, special treatment programs, and probation and parole offices.

The police serve as the principal gateway through which the suspected deviant is funneled into the control apparatus. That gateway leads to a system of adjudication and correction for adults charged with crime and a separate system for juveniles charged with delinquency (and for neglected children). Figure 11.8 maps the major

Figure 11.8   The criminal justice system processes millions of reported criminal offenses annually. The system is organized according to the type of offense, the seriousness of the offense, and the jurisdiction of the courts.

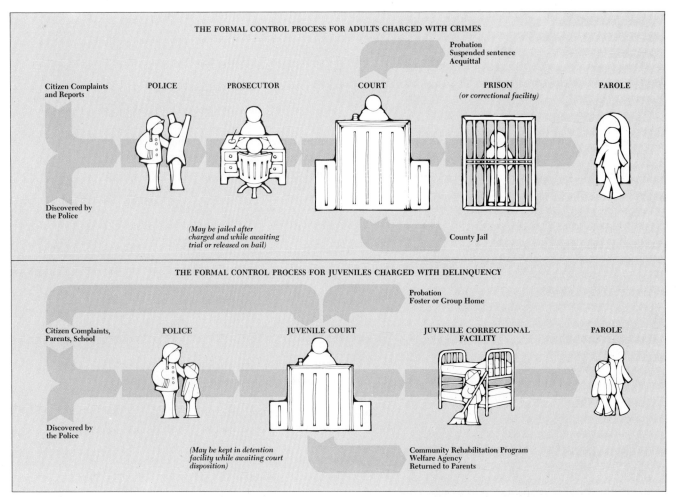

THE FORMAL CONTROL PROCESS FOR ADULTS CHARGED WITH CRIMES

Probation
Suspended sentence
Acquittal

Citizen Complaints and Reports   POLICE   PROSECUTOR   COURT   PRISON *(or correctional facility)*   PAROLE

Discovered by the Police

(May be jailed after charged and while awaiting trial or released on bail)

County Jail

THE FORMAL CONTROL PROCESS FOR JUVENILES CHARGED WITH DELINQUENCY

Probation
Foster or Group Home

Citizen Complaints, Parents, School   POLICE   JUVENILE COURT   JUVENILE CORRECTIONAL FACILITY   PAROLE

Discovered by the Police

(May be kept in detention facility while awaiting court disposition)

Community Rehabilitation Program
Welfare Agency
Returned to Parents

steps through which the adult and the juvenile are processed in the legal system.

Uses and Abuses of Discretion   At each stage of this processing system, *discretion* is exercised as to whether a person should be kept in the system and moved along to the next step or should be released. If everyone who violated legal norms were discovered, reported, arrested, charged, given a jury trial, found guilty, and incarcerated, the criminal justice system would self-destruct. As it is, the whole system is overloaded—even though the mesh in the law enforcement sieve is wide enough, and enough people are excluded, so that only a small fraction of the possible load is handled. Of all major criminal offenses known to

the police, less than 20 percent are cleared by arrest (this percentage is much higher for infrequent offenses such as murder), and of those persons arrested, less than 15 percent are actually imprisoned.

The exercise of discretion in acting against some and releasing other supposed deviants is necessary for the functioning of the system. But the exercise of discretion may have unintended consequences. Police discretion, for instance, sometimes leads in the direction of unnecessary violence (Westley, 1953), unstable overreaction to crowd control (Stark, 1972*b*), corruption, discrimination on the basis of race and class, and other acts counter to the rules of law and of due process (Chambliss and Seidman, 1971; Quinney, 1970;

Ferdinand and Luchterhand, 1970). Processes whereby these injustices come about are detailed in what follows.

The prosecutor decides which cases will be tried and the charges on which a conviction will be sought. He may engage in *plea-bargaining* negotiations with the defendant and his or her lawyer to work out an arrangement whereby the prosecutor agrees to reduce or dismiss certain charges in exchange for a plea of guilty by the defendant (Newman, 1956; President's Commission on Law Enforcement and Administration of Justice, 1967—popularly known as the Crime Commission). Many convictions are obtained in this way, and about eight out of ten felony convictions are on guilty pleas (negotiated and otherwise) before a judge, without a jury trial, presentation of evidence, or a prosecution-defense confrontation. The aim of this whole proceeding sometimes seems to be the attainment of bureaucratic efficiency in processing cases rather than the finding of truth and the assurance of justice. Further, there may be social and racial bias in the sentencing of those convicted (Bullock, 1961).

Thus, the practice of discretion may not only sacrifice legality for efficiency but may also provide opportunities for the abuse of authority. Persons entrusted with legal authority may allow their private prejudices and self-interest to influence how they use their discretionary powers. Indeed, a major complaint of American minority communities is that the police and the courts do not deal with them impartially. Recent government reports such as those compiled by the Kerner Commission, the Crime Commission, and the Violence Commission have agreed that abuse of discretionary powers by police and prosecutors is a serious problem (Stark, 1972*b*).

However, careful studies of the problem have revealed a somewhat complex picture. For example, the police are much more prone to be violent toward some kinds of crowds than toward others. What have been called "police riots" are mainly directed at crowds composed of kinds of persons whom the police regard as unconventional—blacks, Chicanos, students, political dissenters. But the police do not riot even when faced with

Figure 11.9 Police discretion may function to save the state time and money and alleviate crowded courtrooms. But in exercising their discretionary powers, police may also abuse their authority. For example, police often have been observed to overreact in riot situations, applying more force than is necessary to restore peace.

comparatively unruly crowds made up of what the police regard as conventional persons—delegates at fraternal conventions or celebrating sports fans (Stark, 1972*b*). However, mass confrontations are relatively unusual events. In the course of routine circumstances, studies have shown that the police do not frequently act on their prejudices. Thus, Albert J. Reiss, Jr. (1968) found in his observational studies of the police force that the bigotry freely and loudly expressed in the patrol car did not manifest itself in actual discriminatory behavior.

In practice the police seem to behave mainly in a routine fashion and so do the courts. Both, according to recent studies, seem to decide what action to take mainly on the basis of the seriousness of the offense with which a person is charged and his prior record. When seriousness of offense is controlled there no longer appear to be interracial differences in the length of sentences or the amount of fines imposed by the courts.

But, many wonder, how can this be the case when blacks are disproportionately arrested and sent to prison compared with whites? The answer is that the effects of racism in this society operate so that blacks have a higher rate of involvement in serious crimes. However, at the point where persons accused of crimes enter the criminal justice system, racism seems to play a minimal role. Blacks and whites suspected of similarly serious offenses ordinarily are treated similarly by the police, the prosecution, and the courts (Terry, 1967). Undeniably, political motives sometimes do influence the criminal justice system. Prosecutors of one political party do from time to time press flimsy cases against officeholders of the other political party. And periodically the courts have been used to harass political dissenters.

Correctional Organizations   After the court has judged an adult guilty of a crime or a juvenile to be a delinquent, he or she is legally sanctioned by sentencing to a specific type of *correctional* program. The judge may place the adult on probation; that is, he serves his sentence while remaining in the community under the supervision of a probation officer. If the offense is a misdemeanor, the sentence may be served in the county jail (or some substitute, such as a county farm or an alcoholic treatment center). If the offense is a felony, the person may be committed to a prison (or some substitute, such as a prison camp or *training center*). Once committed, few serve the maximum time of the sentence in prison. Most are released earlier and serve the remainder of their sentences on parole—that is, release back to the community under supervision of a parole officer. The conditions of probation and parole may require residence in a half way house or some type of re-

habilitation program in the community. The possibilities for the juvenile are much the same, except that there is a wider range of options before commitment to an institution and a wider range of correctional facilities available. (See Figure 11.8 for some alternatives.)

These correctional programs are supposed to protect society by restraining convicted people from additional law violations and by preventing them from repeating their deviant behaviors in the future. This protection of society is supposed to be accomplished through maintaining the convicted person in *custody* and *punishing* him for his transgressions or *rehabilitating* (resocializing) him (see Chapter 10). The philosophy of rehabilitation is a latter-day imposition on the older philosophy of punishment, and both philosophies exist today in an uneasy and contradictory mixture within the criminal justice system. Prisons, with their attendant custodial regimentation and deprivations, built to serve punishment aims, are now the site of such *treatment* programs as education, training, work-release, and counseling. Special treatment facilities erected to carry out the rehabilitation ideal are also charged with maintaining secure custody over their inmates. The juvenile court system and special institutions for delinquents were intended to be rehabilitative alternatives to the extant criminal court and prison system, but the juvenile courts and rehabilitation institutions have practiced treatment virtually indistinguishable from punishment (Platt, 1969).

Is the System Effective?   The question is: Through the deterrence of punishment or through rehabilitation, does the criminal justice system work to control deviance? The answer is: Not very well. Although it is probably true that there would be more deviance if no system at all existed, the current system seems to be doing less than an adequate job of deterring or rehabilitating. In both the older-style custodial prison and the newer treatment-oriented institutions there has evolved an adaptative inmate culture and social system that does little to further the goal of making the inmate less likely to commit crimes after release (Hazelrigg, 1969; Cressey, 1961).

(See Chapter 10 for a discussion of the formation of such subcultures.) The *rate of recidivism* (the rate at which those who have been imprisoned are reapprehended for violations after release) is close to 50 percent for many prison systems. Even the lowest recidivism rates—about 30 percent —recorded for some prison systems (Glaser, 1964) leaves one skeptical about the effectiveness of imprisonment in controlling deviance. The evidence is somewhat contradictory, but research has yet to establish clearly that either certainty or severity of imprisonment reduces the crime rate (Tittle, 1969; Chiricos and Waldo, 1970).

The success of special treatment and rehabilitation programs is not much more impressive. These programs have been based on a variety of theoretical and practical premises; they employ a spectrum of treatments ranging from individualized therapy to group counseling. They have operated within the confines of a closed institution and within residential and nonresidential facilities in the open community. Most of these programs are more humane and are infused with more dignity and respect for the inmate than is characteristic of the usual institutional regime. However, although some of these programs show tentative signs of success, at this time none has been shown to be clearly more effective in reducing recidivism than the traditional custodial programs (Kassebaum *et al.,* 1971; Empey and Lubeck, 1971;

Lerman, 1970). Likewise, programs for special types of deviants, such as drug addicts, have not shown a record of success (Glasscote *et al.,* 1972).

Community-based programs as *alternatives to incarceration,* both public and private, are proliferating. Many are residential and semiresidential programs in which ex-convicts live together in the attempt to help one another reintegrate into conventional society.

The federal government has spent millions of dollars in recent years to underwrite law enforcement and treatment programs to improve the criminal justice system. Most of these newer efforts have not yet been evaluated, and how successful they will be remains to be seen. But knowing the complexity of the problem and the history of such attempts, the sociologist is bound to predict that progress will be slow and painful.

SUGGESTED READINGS

Cressey, Donald R., and David A. Ward (eds.). *Delinquency, Crime, and Social Process.* New York: Harper & Row, 1969.

Gibbons, Don C. *Delinquent Behavior.* Englewood Cliffs, N. J.: Prentice-Hall, 1970.

Glaser, Daniel. *Social Deviance.* Chicago: Markham, 1971.

Rushing, William A. (ed.). *Deviant Behavior and Social Process.* Chicago: Rand-McNally, 1969.

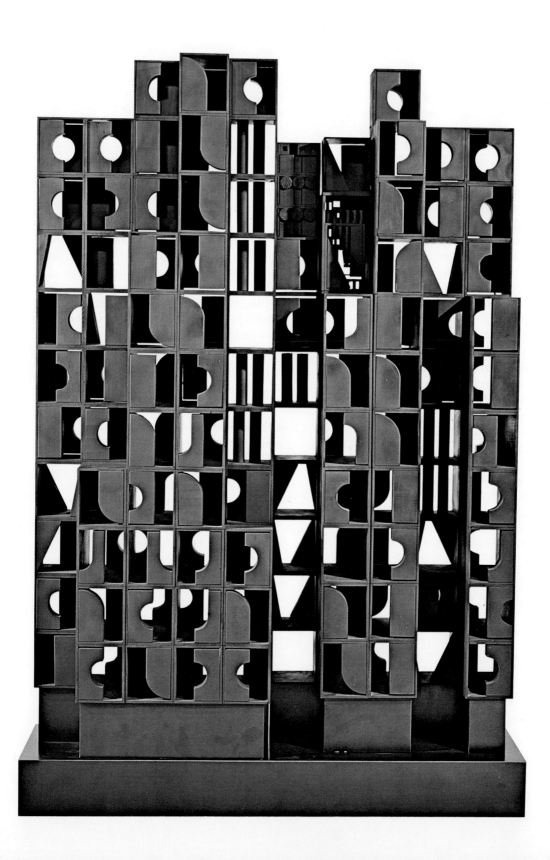

Inequality has always been a universal feature of human society. All known societies have been hierarchical, with some people on the bottom and some on top. For thousands of years people have wondered why this is so and whether it has to be that way. They still wonder. Those who wonder about such questions for a living are engaged in the study of *social stratification*, defined by Gerhard Lenski as the unequal distribution of scarce values in societies (1966). Social stratification is studied

UNIT V

by members of all the social sciences, but the majority of those who study it are sociologists. The study of stratification is one of the

STRUCTURES AND

major activities in sociology. ¶ The first chapter in this unit lays out the central

PROCESSES OF INEQUALITY

questions around which the study of social

stratification is organized. It also introduces the basic concepts used in stratification and describes the major historical and cross-cultural variations in stratification systems.   ¶ Chapter 13 examines the ways in which people and groups rise or fall in the stratification system. Chapter 14 looks at the consequences of stratification, both for the individual and for entire societies. Next, in Chapter 15, the most compelling question about stratification is asked: Is inequality necessary? The last two Chapters of the unit take up major sources of inequality: Chapter 16 examines inequalities based on race, religion and ethnicity; Chapter 17 considers inequalities based on sex and age differences.

Chapter 12 Stratification

By SOCIAL STRATIFICATION sociologists mean the unequal distribution of "scarce values" among members of any society. Stratified literally means layered. The term is used by geologists to describe layers on the earth's crust—topsoil, subsoil, clay, rock, and so on. As the phrase "upper crust" applied to high society makes clear, the term is also appropriate for describing the social strata of societies—groups of persons possessing progressively greater amounts of the good things in life, with the impoverished making up the bottom layer and the rich and powerful the top.

SOCIAL STRATIFICATION AND THE CONCEPT OF CLASS

Social thinkers have used this imagery of layers for centuries and often have referred to particular layers or strata of society as *classes*. Although all sociologists frequently use the concept of class, they have disagreed a great deal about what it ought to mean—what is the basic test for judging someone's class?

The Concept of Class: Karl Marx and Max Weber

The first modern attempt to fix the meaning of class was made by Karl Marx (1818–1883). Because Marx wrote a great deal over a long period of time and addressed so many complex matters, he tended to use the concept of class in a number of different ways. However, the definition he used most often, and for which he is famous, is that a class is a group of people who share a common relationship to the means of production: factories, machines, raw materials. In Marx's view, there were only two basic relationships to the means of production: either you owned the means of production or you had to sell your labor power to those who did own them. Thus, Marx saw essentially two classes in capitalist societies: owners and workers, or as he called them, the *bourgeoisie* and the *proletariat*. (As we have suggested, Marx actually considered other classes, but these are the ones he paid the most attention to.) Furthermore, Marx insisted that a group sharing a common relationship to the means of production could only be

considered a true class if its members possessed *class consciousness*, or a realization of their common position in the organization of production, their common interests, and their common antagonism toward the other major class. Today many sociologists make a distinction between a person's *objective class*, the actual rank he holds in society, and his *subjective class*, the rank he thinks he holds. Marx foresaw the possibility that a person's subjective-class awareness might not correspond to his objective position in society—workers, for example, might vote for monarchist parties. He called this *false consciousness*.

For Marx, the fundamental feature of class was economic; that is, a person's position in the economic order played the major role in fixing his place in society—his prestige, his political power, and even his family life.

Max Weber (1864–1920) elaborated on Marx's view, placing less emphasis on economic factors. Weber saw social stratification as based on three principal factors. He argued that these three factors varied somewhat independently and that their interplay had to be understood in order to comprehend social stratification fully. First, Weber distinguished the *economic order*, which he defined in a way fairly similar to Marx's concept of class. The economic order was based on a person's economic life chances or opportunities. The second factor that he saw in stratification was the *social order*, by which Weber meant the distribution of social honor, prestige, and deference in society. The third factor was the *political order*, by which Weber characterized the distribution of power in society.

Socioeconomic Status and the Modern View

Considerable research by modern sociologists has established grounds for Weber's distinctions. The three features of stratification—property, power, and prestige—do operate somewhat independently. Not all rich people have high prestige. Not all powerful people are rich. Therefore, it has often proved useful to keep these three stratification factors separate. On the other hand, it has also proved useful to think of stratification primarily

Figure 12.1   False consciousness occurs when
one's objective class (the status one actually occupies)
and one's subjective class (the status one thinks one
occupies) do not correspond. An industrial
working-class person, for example—such as the one
in the center of the cartoon below—may consider
himself a member of the "genteel poor."

as Marx did—as composed of classes that are conscious of their objective position and interests.

In practice, sociologists do both. But in the bulk of empirical research on stratification, the researcher employs a measure based on a combination of income, occupational prestige, and education. This combination is called *socioeconomic status* (SES). Although SES includes aspects of power and prestige, it is weighted toward economic factors.

Sociological theorists and researchers today rely more on the threefold conception of class that Weber made explicit than upon Marx's definition of class (although all three elements were implicit in much of Marx's work). This reliance is reflected in the title of the most influential collection of work on stratification over the past two decades: *Class, Status and Power* (Bendix and Lipset, 1953, 1966).

CONCEPTS: PROPERTY, POWER, AND PRESTIGE

Inequality means the uneven distribution of the good things in life. Contemporary sociologists

working from the legacy of Marx and Weber classify these "good things" under three main headings: *Property* refers to *rights* over goods and services of all kinds; *power* is the capacity to get your own way regardless of the opposition of others; *prestige* means enjoying social honor.

Each of these factors in social stratification is considered a *variable*—people vary in the degree to which they possess property, power, and prestige. In other words, we speak of the amount of one's property, the degree of one's power, the extent of one's prestige.

Admittedly, there are some good things in life that do not come under one of these three definitions—for example, health, knowledge, and pleasure. But it can be argued that these are less central to stratification. There is more truth in the saying that "money isn't everything, but it buys the rest" than in the sayings "you can't buy happiness" and "good health is priceless." Figures 12.2 and 12.3 substantiate this point. Furthermore, these other "good things" have much less impact on the patterning of social life than do the "three *P*s." For example, where there are laws or formal agreements about how the good things in life are to be distributed, these rules tend to be concerned mainly with property, power, and prestige.

Property

Sociologists refer to more than wealth and possessions when they use the term *property*. By property they indicate the fundamental *rights* over goods and services. Obviously, an individual has certain rights over his money or his real estate; subject to legal limits he can do with them as he pleases. But a person may also have property rights over things he certainly does not own. For example, a parent possesses certain rights and privileges over his child, even though the parent does not own the child. We still say that it is *my* child or *your* child.

When you view property as a set of rights, you can also see that such rights are limited by the competing claims of others. For example, the father's rights over his child are limited both by others' claims (the mother's rights) and by legal or moral restraints (parents may not kill their children). Furthermore, rights usually entail responsibilities: a parent loses rights over a child if he fails to fulfill minimal parental responsibilities. Similarly, land or money used illegally may be confiscated.

The nature of property is substantially defined by the culture of a society; indeed, even the concept of property itself varies considerably from one group to the next. In some cultures property is substantially represented in beads and artifacts, and land is not even regarded as property. In some cultures it is inconceivable to possess water; other cultures are intensely possessive of water. Nevertheless, all known human societies recognize property rights.

Sources We can make certain generalizations about the sources of property.

First, a person may acquire property *from simple membership in a group,* such as a family or a commune that holds some property in common. For example, a child comes to own his bicycle or to have property rights over the family food supply. Similarly, being an American brings the right

Figures 12.2 and 12.3   Does money buy health? (*Top*) The death rates for men and women with incomes over $10,000 are lower than the death rates for those with lower incomes. Does money buy happiness? (*Bottom*) Regardless of their sex, age, education, or income, most people sampled reported being "pretty happy." However, more higher-income people said they were "very happy," and more lower-income people reported being "not too happy."
(Adapted from E. M. Kitagawa and P. M. Hauser, 1969.)

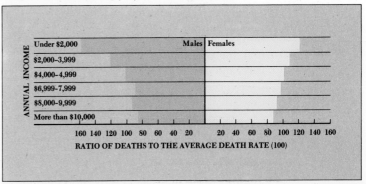

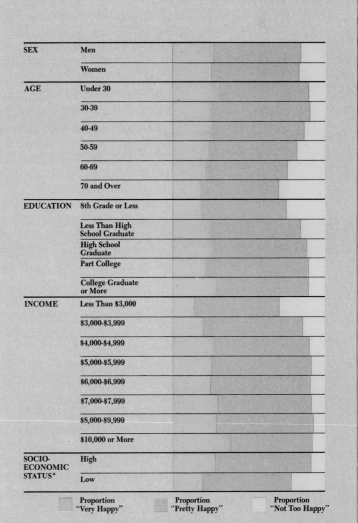

Respondents were divided into two social classes. "High" consists of people who have at least two of the following attributes: Family income of $5,000 or more, high school graduate or more, and white collar occupation. "Low" consists of those with none or only one of the above attributes.

(From N. Bradburn and D. Caplovitz, 1965.)

of citizenship; and belonging to a certain social category—being one of the elderly or a priest—brings rights to certain goods and services. In general, the elderly possess special rights to medical care, and priests are regarded as possessing rights over certain rites, which are a kind of property, as we shall see when we discuss role-use property.

Second, property rights are also won *in exchange for providing goods or services to others*. Exchange is the central feature of all economic relations. One receives certain property rights for granting such rights in return. For example, a worker exchanges his labor and skill for money; the boss obtains labor in return for his money.

Third, property is received *for organizing the production and distribution of goods and services*. In societies too complex for simple, direct exchanges of goods and services, such exchanges require large-scale organizing. The organizer or entrepreneur who puts together the capital, equipment, and manpower required to produce goods on a large scale or who creates the organizations for distributing these goods in exchange with others takes earnings from this process in return for his organization of the enterprise.

A fourth source of property comes *from capital investments*. Those who provide the property—including land, money, or equipment—that others use to earn property obtain rewards in the form of interest or dividends for their trouble and risk.

A fifth source is *gifts and inheritance*. Transferring property from parents to children is a nearly universal practice, as is the process of passing poverty from generation to generation.

Role-Use and Role-Reward Property   There is an important distinction between *role-use property* and *role-reward property*. Essentially this is the difference between property you get *to use* in order to perform some role—property that comes with the job, for example—and that which you get *to keep* as payment or reward for performing the role. The property that a corporation manager uses to get his job done is role-use property; that which he receives as salary and stock options is role-reward property. Whereas there are limits

and regulations governing all uses of property, role-use property is more closely regulated. The President of the United States has an incredible amount of role-use property, but he is held accountable for how he uses it. He may dispose of his annual salary much more freely. There is frequently a great disparity in people's possession of role-use and role-reward property. Many governmental leaders, corporation presidents, and generals lose a great deal of property when they retire. Indeed, the enormous gap between the amounts of money that bankers and company accountants utilize on the job and the amount they take home is a source of the chronic problem of embezzlement.

Power

Power is the capacity to get one's way even against opposition. The word capacity is used to indicate that power is a potential: it is not really something concrete to be possessed in the same way as property. Perhaps power can best be understood by examining its sources.

First, power may be based on *institutional position*. As with property, one must consider how power may be built into a role. For example, a president, general, bishop, or parent has role-use power. People in certain other roles, such as soldier or child, are expected to take orders on the basis of role relationships, which are discussed at length in Chapter 7. Power attached to roles usually is regarded as legitimate and normally is accepted by those who are subordinate to it. *Legitimate power* is often called *authority* in order to distinguish it from power based on other sources, such as force.

A second source of power is *force*. Here we meet the dictum "power grows out of the barrel of a gun." A person's power can be based on his capacity to overcome opposition by threatening or actually imposing physical harm or even death. In more primitive times such power was often a result of muscle power, as in fact it often is among animals. Force is also the source of power of the mugger and the hold-up man.

Legitimate power often rests on the potential use of force. Governments of modern nations at-

Figure 12.4   All societies have been stratified by caste, estate, or social class. There are four main classes in the United States. The top figure represents an upper-class elite. Moving down the pyramid, one sees the middle class, working class, and lower class. Some social thinkers, especially functionalists, believe that social stratification is necessary and inevitable. Conflict theorists, however, especially Marxists, argue that stratification by social class was created by human beings and therefore can be eliminated by human beings.

tempt to maintain a monopoly on the uses of force, such as police and the military power. People also use nonphysical force—for example, by threatening the withdrawal of love or by resorting to some other form of psychological blackmail.

Property is a third source of power. Power can be bought, and it exists wherever the ability to extend or withhold valuable goods and services exists. Employers have power based on the right to hire, fire, and grant raises and promotions. Workers have power based on the ability to withhold their labor. It is too simple to think that wealth equals power. Demonstrably, some wealthy people have little power, and some relatively poor people have a good deal of power. Nevertheless, there is a strong connection between the two.

A fourth source is *personal qualities*. Some individuals have the power to influence others to do their bidding through their charm, cleverness, attractiveness, force of personality, and other such characteristics. At the turn of the century Max Weber used the term *charisma* to describe the personal capacities of some religious and political leaders to persuade others to follow them. The word came into common usage when newspaper reporters (who had probably had an introductory sociology course) used it to describe how John F. Kennedy's personal qualities enabled him to influence public reactions.

Prestige

Prestige is defined as social honor—the respect one is given by others. Like power, it is best understood by considering some of its sources.

First, *institutional position* is a source of prestige as well as of power. That is to say, honor often goes with the job. We honor generals more than privates, physicians more than nurses, quarterbacks more than kicking specialists. Figure 12.5 displays ratings for many other positions. The amount of prestige attached to a particular role depends upon a number of factors about the role, including the income and power attached to it, the skill it requires, its importance to society or the institution, and the sacrifices required to attain or perform it. Prestige is not quite as role-

Figure 12.5　(*Top*) When asked to rate the relative prestige of a selected group of occupations, random samples of Americans repeatedly have ranked them as shown. You may find some of the comparisons surprising—would you rank an undertaker higher than a radio announcer? The average prestige score assigned by the public strongly reflects the average income and education of persons engaged in a given occupation. (*Bottom*) This table can be used to compare and contrast different categories of occupations. The three columns compare the ranges and relative positions of prestige ratings for high-level government officials, physical and social scientists, and various occupations associated with building and construction.

(From R. W. Hodge, P. M. Seigel, and P. H. Rossi, 1964.)

SCORE	OCCUPATION	SCORE	OCCUPATION
94	U.S. Supreme Court justice	72	Policeman
93	Physician	71	AVERAGE
92	Nuclear physicist	71	Reporter on a daily newspaper
92	Scientist	70	Bookkeeper
91	Government scientist	70	Radio announcer
91	State governor	69	Insurance agent
90	Cabinet member	69	Tenant farmer who owns livestock and machinery and manages the farm
90	College professor		
90	U.S. congressman	67	Local labor union official
89	Chemist	67	Manager of a small store in a city
89	U.S. Foreign Service diplomat	66	Mail carrier
89	Lawyer	66	Railroad conductor
88	Architect	66	Traveling salesman for a wholesale concern
88	County judge	65	Plumber
88	Dentist	63	Barber
87	Mayor of a large city	63	Machine operator in a factory
87	Board member of a large corporation	63	Owner-operator of a lunch stand
87	Minister	63	Playground director
87	Psychologist	62	U.S. Army corporal
86	Airline pilot	62	Garage mechanic
86	Civil engineer	59	Truck driver
86	State government department head	58	Fisherman who owns his own boat
86	Priest	56	Clerk in a store
85	Banker	56	Milk route man
85	Biologist	56	Streetcar motorman
83	Sociologist	55	Lumberjack
82	U.S. Army captain	55	Restaurant cook
81	Accountant for a large business	54	Nightclub singer
81	Public school teacher	51	Filling station attendant
80	Building contractor	50	Coal miner
80	Owner of a factory that employs about 100 people	50	Dock worker
78	Artist whose paintings are exhibited in galleries	50	Night watchman
78	Novelist	50	Railroad section head
78	Economist	49	Restaurant waiter
78	Symphony orchestra musician	49	Taxi driver
77	International labor union official	48	Bartender
76	County agricultural agent	48	Farmhand
76	Electrician	48	Janitor
76	Railroad engineer	45	Clothes presser in a laundry
75	Owner-operator of a printing shop	44	Soda fountain clerk
75	Trained machinist	42	Sharecropper who owns no livestock or equipment and does not manage farm
74	Farm owner and operator		
74	Undertaker	39	Garbage collector
74	City welfare worker	36	Street sweeper
73	Newspaper columnist	34	Shoe shiner

95	U.S. Supreme Court justice / Government scientist	Nuclear physicist	
90	Cabinet member　U.S. congressman	Chemist　Psychologist	Architect / Civil engineer
85	U.S. Foreign Service diplomat	Biologist　Sociologist	
80			Building contractor
75		Economist	Electrician
70			
65			Plumber

bound, however, as are property and power. Retired presidents, generals, and quarterbacks retain more of the social honor than of the power and property that went with their jobs.

Property is a second source of prestige. Merely possessing it often brings prestige, especially in those societies where there are great inequalities in wealth. Underlying this source of prestige may be certain assumptions about the merits of the effort required to acquire property, the style of life that property makes possible, or the power inherent in property. On the other hand, we know very well that property does not always translate into prestige—otherwise we would have no conception of the "vulgar" rich or the "genteel" poor. Indeed, many people have earned considerable prestige from the fact that they spurned personal property in order to better serve humanity.

Power, too, is a source of prestige, and it is obvious that people with great power are often accorded great prestige. However, prestige is often accorded partly for the restraint or responsibility that guides the use of power. The naked use of power often does not inspire prestige.

Personal qualities are an obvious source of prestige. In every society certain personal traits and qualities tend to be given more public honor than others. Among such traits are beauty—recall Dion's experiment in Chapter 2—physical strength, courage, integrity, intelligence, and holiness. These qualities may not be only those directly attached to an individual but may also be those of a group of individuals. In this way, prestige is often associated with such factors as age and sex (see Chapter 17), race, religion, or nationality (see Chapter 16). Individuals may receive prestige simply for being older, white male Christian Americans. Although these are individual traits, the source of these prestigious characteristics is group membership.

Fifth, prestige is accorded for *deeds and achievements*. Considerable honor is reserved in any society for those who accomplish outstanding deeds—who achieve the extraordinary. Such deeds and achievements include unusual bravery, uncommon accomplishments in warfare, athletic

triumphs, inventions and discoveries, artistry, holiness, or the capacity to perform magical or supernatural rites of one kind or another.

One important qualification must be made about prestige: It is necessary to distinguish between prestige in a local community or small group and prestige in the larger society. Calling someone "a big fish in a small pond" reflects this point. The president of a small manufacturing firm may have extremely high prestige in the town in which his firm is located but may be a virtual unknown and enjoy little prestige nationally—or even 100 miles up the road. Oddly enough, the reverse is not uncommon. Famous artists, musicians, writers, and scientists may be unknown in their home community.

STATUS

Having discussed the three main components of social status, we now examine several of their joint characteristics. What happens when some persons or groups enjoy high position on one dimension of stratification and a low position on others? What rules govern how people acquire status?

Status Inconsistency

We have seen that property, power, and prestige are interdependent but that they also may vary independently. A person shows *status inconsistency* if he ranks considerably higher on one dimension of stratification than on another; status consistency, if he ranks about evenly on each dimension.

Since the early 1950s, sociologists have empirically examined the effects of status inconsistency, the ways in which it may influence a person's attitudes and behavior. Gerhard Lenski (1954, 1956) argued that any combination of unequal rankings should influence social participation and lead to political liberalism. He postulated that a status-inconsistent person would present himself to others on the basis of his own highest status, while others would respond to him in terms of his lowest status. For example, a man with high income but low prestige would present his status on the basis of his wealth, but others would put him in his

POWER PRESTIGE PROPERTY

INSTITUTIONAL POSITION		You Have Been **ELECTED CHAIRMAN** OF THE BOARD **PAY EACH PLAYER $50**		INSTITUTIONAL POSITION
FORCE	**ADVANCE TO GO**		**COLLECT TWICE THE RENT ON NEW YORK AVE.**	FORCE
PROPERTY	TAKE A RIDE ON THE READING IF YOU PASS GO COLLECT $200	TITLE DEED **BOARDWALK**	READING RAILROAD	PROPERTY
PERSONAL QUALITIES	YOU HAVE WON **SECOND PRIZE** IN A **BEAUTY CONTEST** COLLECT $10			PERSONAL QUALITIES
POWER	**GET OUT OF JAIL, FREE**		**INCOME TAX REFUND COLLECT $20**	POWER
DEEDS AND ACHIEVEMENTS		**PAY HOSPITAL $100**		DEEDS AND ACHIEVEMENTS
IN EXCHANGE FOR GOODS AND SERVICES			**RECEIVE** FOR SERVICES **$25**	IN EXCHANGE FOR GOODS AND SERVICES
ORGANIZING ECONOMIC FUNCTIONS			Grand Opera Opening **COLLECT $50** FROM EVERY PLAYER	ORGANIZING ECONOMIC FUNCTIONS
CAPITAL INVESTMENTS			FROM SALE OF STOCK YOU GET **$45 ***	CAPITAL INVESTMENTS
GIFTS AND INHERITANCE			**YOU INHERIT $100**	GIFTS AND INHERITANCE

This card represents role use. The $45 received from stock is role reward property.

Figure 12.6 A person's social status is a combination of power, property, and prestige, each of which is derived from distinct sources, as the chart below indicates. For example, although the exchange of goods and services is a source of property, it is not generally thought to lead to power or prestige. An individual who ranks high on one aspect of status yet low on others shows *status inconsistency.*

place by responding to his low prestige. In this way, Lenski argued, all status-inconsistent persons would feel deprived of their "true worth" and be led to oppose the system by which status is distributed; that is, they would turn to politics of change.

Lenski's early studies seemed to support his views, but later studies have suggested that he is wrong (Blalock, 1966; Hyman, 1966). As Lenski (1966) himself later recognized, his early formulation may have been misapplied. When we examine Figure 12.7 we see many examples of people who have succeeded in some ways but not in others. On intuitive grounds it seems likely that this must make a difference to them. And perhaps it does, for all of the instances of inconsistent statuses in Figure 12.7 are of people who are members of social elites in some ways but not in others. Lenski's early work, however, was mainly concerned with status inconsistency among average people. His data were based on national samples of the adult population, and thus most people were of middle- or lower-class rank. Virtually all of the status inconsistency that he examined concerned status differences between middle ranks on some status measures and lower ranks on others. The data now suggest that such persons feel lucky about their higher status rather than deprived because of their lower ones. But it seems likely that elites are different and that Lenski's theory may well work when applied to elites. This will be considered in more detail in Chapter 13, where the circulation of elites is taken up.

Ascribed and Achieved Status

Simply put, *ascribed* status is based on who you are; *achieved* status, on what you do. Ascribed status is based on characteristics with which a person is born or into which he matures: for example, family background, race, age, sex, religion, and ethnicity. The most obvious case is inherited nobility—the eldest sons of kings and barons and dukes become kings and barons and dukes by simple succession to their fathers' positions. Achieved status is based on aspects of the individual over which he or she has at least some control: diligence, bravery, knowledge, and honesty; and on

Figure 12.7 Because the three sources of social status —power, property, and prestige—are independent, high rank on one factor does not guarantee high rank on the others. The chart below compares status-consistent people, those who rank equally on all three dimensions of status, with various types of status-inconsistent persons, those who rank high on one or more dimensions of status but low on others.

	HIGHER PRESTIGE		LOWER PRESTIGE	
	MORE POWER	LESS POWER	MORE POWER	LESS POWER
MORE PROPERTY	Corporation Presidents, Some Attorneys	Sports Stars, Actors	Mafia Leaders, Black Bankers	Successful Bank Robbers
LESS PROPERTY	Journalists, Some Scientists	Artists, Poets, Most Clergymen	Bureaucrats	Migrant Workers, Clerks

☐ Consistent Statuses   ◻ Inconsistent Statuses

individual qualities that are not *necessarily* inherited: intelligence, strength, beauty, and various talents.

All societies display both status by ascription and status by achievement. But some put more emphasis on one than the other. Societies with caste systems, for example, are extremely ascriptive in their status system. Industrial societies are quite achievement-oriented. Such cross-cultural variations will be discussed in the next section, and they are treated in Chapters 13, 16, and 17.

VARIETIES OF INEQUALITY IN DIFFERENT SOCIETIES

The extent and nature of inequalities differ from one society to another. These variations are closely connected to the way these societies make their living, to their technical capacities for producing the necessities of life. Anthropologists and sociologists have concentrated on five major types of societies (Goldschmidt, 1959; Lenski, 1966). Although there is considerable variation of detail among societies belonging to one type, their general similarities are great. But the contrasts among types are pronounced. These types progress from the primitive to the modern and can be thought of as stages in the historical development of

Figure 12.8   Gerhard Lenski is a professor of sociology at the University of North Carolina. He first gained international prominence with *The Religious Factor* (1961), which was one of the first survey studies of religious behavior. He then turned his attention to stratification and launched the study of status inconsistency. In 1966 he published *Power and Privilege,* a major theoretical attempt to synthesize functionalist and Marxist theories of social stratification.

societies—although many societies existing today have not made this evolutionary journey. To conclude this chapter, we will briefly sketch the characteristic systems of social stratification associated with each type of society. The discussion relies greatly on the work of Lenski (1966).

Hunting and Gathering Societies

Societies that earn their keep by hunting game and gathering wild edibles are the most primitive form of human societies. As recently as ten thousand years ago they were the only form of society ever known to man. Such societies still exist: the Aborigines of Australia, the Pygmies and Bushmen of Africa, a number of remote Indian tribes in the Amazon basin in South America, to name only a few. People of these societies depend upon materials taken directly from nature for their tools and clothes as well as for their food. With few exceptions, they must keep moving as they exhaust game and wild plants. They have no more than the rudimentary means for preserving food, and their life is one of feast and famine, mostly the latter. As to the former, adults have been reported to eat twenty-five to thirty pounds of meat in twenty-four hours when the hunt was successful (Holmberg, 1950). These societies are also very small; they average about fifty members and probably never exceed several hundred.

Hunting and gathering societies are the least stratified societies known to man, especially on the dimensions of property and power. The reasons for relative equality are fairly obvious. If one man in such a society took *all* the property the group possessed, he still would not have much except privacy (after the others die from starvation or run off to another group). There simply is very little property in such societies and virtually no surplus beyond the bare necessities of life. Similarly, these societies are comparatively egalitarian in terms of power. The headman's position is part-time, and he ordinarily engages in the same daily activities as other males. Usually his power is based on persuasion and consent. When a headman goes against the group, he often is replaced or simply ignored. As Alfred R. Radcliffe-Brown (1948) pointed out about the Andaman Is-

landers, the leading men have little or no authority, but they have a good deal of influence. Leadership is by consent; one tough man can perhaps force several to do his bidding, but he can hardly force half-a-dozen to do so. In these societies all normal adult males are fairly equally trained and equipped for fighting. The resources do not exist to allow a leader to buy supporters. In similar fashion, the shaman or medicine man holds a part-time position and possesses power only somewhat beyond that of other adult males.

Prestige differences, however, are more marked in these societies. As Lenski (1966) pointed out, prestige, unlike power and property, is not in short supply, and inequality on this dimension of stratification does not impair the group's effectiveness. Nevertheless, there are fewer prestige inequalities in hunting and gathering societies than in more advanced societies. People probably are just too familiar with one another in such small groups and the usual differences among them too small to support great inequalities in the distribution of honor. The main consequence of prestige is to create political influence (power). Its main source is personal accomplishments—in hunting, fighting, magic, and even in bearing many children. In fact, in these societies the major source of power and property also lies in personal characteristics. A man with more property typically gets it by being a better hunter and because his wife is more efficient at domestic skills. And a man typically has power because he gives what the group judges to be better advice.

The main criteria of inequality in these societies are age and sex. Men have higher rank than women; older persons, higher than younger persons (see Chapter 17). But the overall stratification system is simple and fairly equalitarian. Status is won mainly through achievement, and ascription is based only on age and sex.

Simple Horticultural Societies

For approximately 10,000 years some human societies have known how to raise their own food. At the first stage are societies that rely on small gardens for most of their food; these are distinguished from more advanced societies that can be said to farm. The latter societies are discussed in the next section. Simple horticultural societies rely on the digging stick rather than on the plow, do not understand fertilization, and are unable to work metal into farming tools.

A gardening economy is basic to many differences between horticultural and hunting and gathering societies. First of all, horticultural societies are larger. Lenski (1966) estimates their average size at about 200 members (four times the average of hunting and gathering societies). But instances of much larger horticultural societies are known—for example, the Iroquois Indians may have had a population of 16,000 members in a single society at one time (Murdock, 1934). Furthermore, whereas hunting and gathering societies are limited to a single community, horticultural societies frequently consist of several communities, although seldom more than ten (Lenski, 1966).

Horticultural societies are considerably more productive than are hunting and gathering societies. They typically produce surplus food, but some of this surplus is taken up by population growth. Although members of hunting and gathering societies have to spend most of their working hours seeking food, members of horticultural societies have leisure, which in turn permits the production of more elaborate property—large houses, fancy dress, and other goods. Furthermore, it is feasible for members to accumulate property because horticultural societies are not constantly on the move. They ordinarily stay in one place from two to a dozen years, depending on how rapidly they exhaust the fertility of the soil. In contrast, possessions in hunting and gathering societies are necessarily limited to what people can carry.

With relatively fixed locations come boundaries. And with boundaries, plus property worth capturing, comes warfare (a rarity among hunting and gathering societies). With surplus food, the production of more elaborate property, and warfare comes a more complex division of labor. In hunting and gathering societies, tasks are divided mainly on the basis of age and sex. In horticultural societies, "specialists" appear. Thus, the Kiwai

Papuans tend to leave such skilled production as making canoes, drums, harpoon shafts, and artwork to a few highly skilled, part-time specialists (Landtman, 1927). At a less developed level, the Iroquois left weapon and tool manufacturing to the elderly and sickly men incapable of fighting (Murdock, 1934). Indeed, various horticultural societies tend to specialize as communities in the production of certain goods and to engage in trade with other groups.

The division of labor also extends to leadership and religious roles. Among horticultural peoples, both tend to be full-time rather than part-time positions, to be based more on power than persuasion, and, in fact, to reflect the considerably greater stratification of people in horticultural societies as compared to hunters and gatherers.

In part, this is because horticultural societies have a greater *capacity* for inequality. In hunting and gathering societies the individual is hard-pressed to feed himself and his family. There is no surplus to support a leisure class. But in horticultural societies, chiefs often are furnished their food, as are shaman and medicine men. In fact, in many such societies the women feed the men who devote their time to war and ritual.

In horticultural societies there are marked differences in property, power, and prestige among members and especially among male members. Prestige is typically based on wealth—how many pigs, plumes, shell ornaments, and how big a house does a man have? The most important property inequality, however, is in wives. Horticultural societies typically are polygynous. Women are the basis of production because they do the gardening. And women are in limited supply. Because in any society male and female births are about equal and because women in primitive societies have a higher mortality rate (due to childbirth), it is obvious that when one man has several wives another man must have none. The more wives a man has, the wealthier he will be; the wealthier, the more wives he will be able to obtain; and the more wives he gets, the higher his prestige. Among the Kuma the ideal of men is to have ten wives. When studied, however, no one had ten, but in one clan, with eighty-seven men old enough to marry, one had four wives, five had three, twelve had two, fifty had one and nineteen had none (Reay, 1959). Men without wives were treated with contempt.

Prestige is not only a reflection of property in horticultural societies; often prestige is directly purchased. Frequently the well-to-do give away their goods to others in order to enhance their own reputations. As Lenski (1966) pointed out, in such societies most property has limited marginal utility, and property is not capital goods—that is, most property does not generate more property in the way investments, machines, and land do. Men have only a limited capacity to "consume" plumes, shell ornaments, vegetables, or pigs. When they acquire more than they can use, they frequently give the surplus away to persons who cannot repay, thus demonstrating their superiority and establishing a moral debt. However, because they do consider wives capital goods, they never give wives away. As Lenski noted, the result of such gift giving, which is very characteristic of horticultural societies, is to continually reduce inequalities of property and continually increase inequalities in prestige.

Power, too, is considerably more stratified in horticultural societies than in hunting and gathering societies. But power in horticultural societies is not a result of personal attributes. With specialization, power becomes somewhat attached to offices. Chiefs in horticultural societies often are able to exert power as a function of being chiefs. Their exercise of power is facilitated by having a sufficient surplus so that they can afford to support a group of retainers. At this stage of social evolution, then, it is possible to base power on force.

Whereas hunting and gathering societies are stratified mainly in terms of prestige, horticultural societies are more stratified on all three dimensions, especially more so in terms of power and property. In addition, status ascription based on factors other than age and sex occurs in horticultural societies; for example, the position of chief often is hereditary. However, this norm is frequently violated in favor of achievement criteria. Among the Kuma, for example, a study showed that in 36 percent of the cases in which succession

was supposed to pass from father to son, someone else had actually succeeded (Reay, 1959).

Advanced Horticultural Societies

Advanced horticultural societies represent a quantum leap in the development of human societies. They are much larger, much more specialized, much richer, and much more unequal than are simple horticultural societies.

The basis for this leap is technological. The most important technological achievement is metal working, especially making metal tools. The metal plow permits much more effective farming and greatly increases crop yields because the soil can be worked more finely and deeply than with a digging stick. Most advanced horticultural societies also irrigate, fertilize, and because they possess a much greater variety of cultivated plants, frequently rotate their crops. Consequently, the individual farmer is vastly more productive than he is in simple horticultural societies. A study has shown that the average Mayan farmer could raise enough food with forty-eight days of labor to supply his family for an entire year (Morley, 1946).

This great increase in a farmer's productivity has many consequences. First of all, it gives him considerable free time to devote to other activities (from pyramid building to warfare). Second, it permits much larger populations and much greater population density—as many as 100 persons per square mile are estimated for advanced horticultural societies (Lenski, 1966). Such advanced horticultural societies as the Inca and the Maya have had several million members (Steward and Faron, 1959; von Hagen, 1961). Third, surpluses permit the development of relatively large cities. Mayapán, the Mayan capital, had an estimated population of 20,000 (von Hagen, 1961).

The most important consequence of increased productivity is to facilitate the creation of complex governments and empires. Simple horticultural societies lack the resources to create permanent armies and elaborate governmental structures. There is not sufficient surplus to support a large group not engaged in production. By the same token the productivity of potential victims is too meager to make conquest profitable.

Figures 12.9 In hunting and gathering
societies, stratification is based almost
completely on age and gender. Women take care of
household duties, including child care and cooking, and
thé adult men hunt. In simple horticultural
societies women still engage in domestic labor but
men's work becomes more differentiated and stratified
as specialists develop. (*Left*) Men of Australian
aboriginal tribes are hunters and gatherers. (*Right*)
This man of the Solomon Islands is a specialist in
making ceremonial "red feather money."

Because they cannot support their oppressors, they limit warfare to raiding and plundering. But advanced horticultural societies can support armies and governments, and they are sufficiently productive to make it profitable to conquer their enemies. The consequence is empire building and the enlargement and elaboration of the state. Classes of professional soldiers and full-time officials appear. Government develops a number of levels—from the king through his retainers on down to a local village headman. Other occupational specialties also appear, including artists, entertainers, and a great variety of craftsmen.

Furthermore, power frequently becomes tyranny in these societies. Indeed, it is in these societies that slavery first appears to any substantial degree. Simple horticultural societies base much of their wealth on wives; with advances in production, however, it becomes profitable to own people in order to gain the surplus fruits of their labor. In advanced horticultural societies a slave is worth his keep, including the keep of soldiers to keep him enslaved.

In simple horticultural societies and hunting and gathering societies, it is hard to pass on wealth because so much depends upon the qualities of the individual. In advanced horticultural societies, however, there is a great increase in hereditary status because of three new factors: (1) the

development of formal notions of property rights; (2) the formalization of the idea of office; and (3) the tangibility, and therefore transferability, of assets (Lenski, 1966). With the greater geographic permanence of advanced horticultural societies, it becomes feasible to consider land as being someone's property. Similarly, slaves are more obviously property than are wives. With full-time specialization of officials, whose role gives them power over and above their native abilities (through wealth and coercion), it becomes easier for a son of modest talents to hold benefits wrested by a superior father. Finally, cattle, land, slaves, and even primitive money are tangibles that are readily possible to pass on from father to son. With inheritance, even greater accumulations of family wealth are possible, for each generation can add to the holdings. Consequently, these societies exhibit hereditary classes and very marked inequalities of power, property, and prestige. We see for the first time societies with inequalities as great as those between a distant king—endowed with almost godlike status—and a slave working under the overseer's whip.

Agrarian Societies

The stunning ruins of Mexico—monumental pyramids, temples, elaborate cities—were left by advanced horticultural societies that had neither the

Figure 12.10   Stratification systems in five
types of societies. In preindustrial societies—including
hunting and gathering, simple and advanced
horticultural, and agrarian societies—the development
of technology and an increasingly complex division
of labor are associated with increases in stratification.
Hunting and gathering societies are not highly
stratified, and what stratification does exist is based
on age and sex. Horticultural societies are more
highly stratified. Agrarian societies, based on a feudal
division of labor and more advanced technology, are
the most highly stratified societies. But as societies make
the transition from an agrarian base to an industrial
one, the trend toward increasing stratification reverses.
In industrial societies the gap between the very rich
and the very poor narrows as the middle classes expand.
The diagram below schematically represents the
stratification systems, in terms of power, property, and
prestige, of societies of different types. Technological
level, presence or absence and degree of
industrialization and urbanization, and size differ
among these societies as well.

HUNTING AND GATHERING
Crude Hunting Implements

SIMPLE HORTICULTURAL
Development of Simple Farming

ADVANCED HORTICULTURAL
*Development of Metal Working and
Plow for Easier Farming*

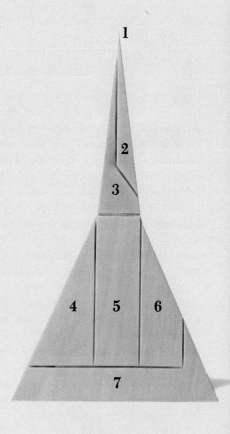

1   Men
2   Women and Children

1   Shaman and Chief (Full-time)
2   Warriors
3   Women and Children

1   King
2   Professional Soldiers
3   Full-time Officials
4   Artists
5   Entertainers
6   Craftsmen
7   Slaves

AGRARIAN

*Invention of Wheel and
Domestication of Horse*

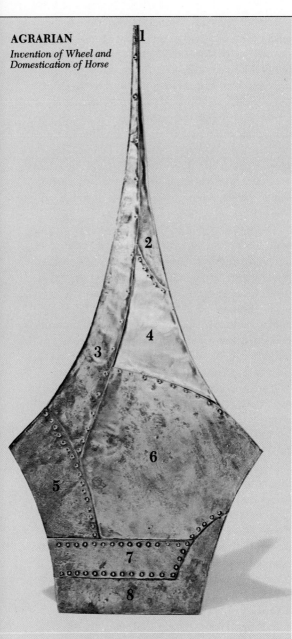

1   **The Ruler**
2   **Governing Class**
3   **Merchants**
4   **Retainers and Priests**
5   **Artisans**
6   **Peasants**
7   **The Unclean and Degraded**
8   **Expendables**

INDUSTRIAL

*Harnessing of Energy Other
Than Muscle Power and
Invention of Complex Machines.*

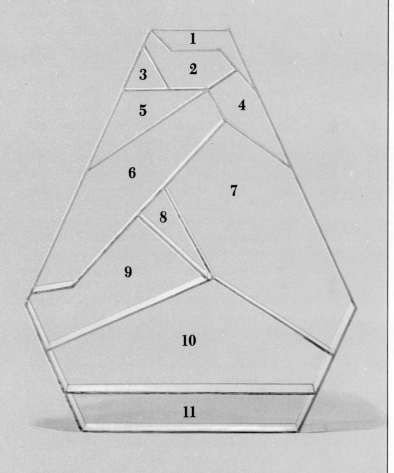

1   **Old Rich**
2   **The Nouveau Riche**
3   **Doctors**
4   **Professionals**
5   **Political Office Holders**
6   **White-collar Workers**
7   **Skilled Blue-collar Workers**
8   **Craftsmen**
9   **Semiskilled Workers**
10   **Unskilled Workers**
11   **Culture of Poverty**

horse nor the wheel. Without these, such societies could not reach the next major stage in human social evolution: agrarian societies. When societies such as Rome, Greece, medieval Europe, China, and the Moslem Empire domesticated and harnessed the horse and learned to utilize the wheel, people achieved two critical capacities: They were able greatly to increase their work strength and the speed, range, and payload of their communications.

It has been accurately pointed out that Rome did not become an empire as much because of its armies as because of its roads—because of the speed with which armies, officials, and booty could be transported. Furthermore, one man with a horse and plow could produce so much agricultural surplus that large armies could be fed; and with horse-drawn wagons food could be transported to distant armies or back from distant farms ruled by the empire. Large cities could also be fed, and it is only with the advent of agrarian societies that we find cities beginning to approach the size we now expect cities to be. There is considerable debate over how big these cities actually were (Davis, 1955), but some may have reached a half million. Perhaps twenty-five to thirty thousand is more typical of capital cities of agrarian societies; as late as the fourteenth century, London had fewer than 40,000 people (Russell, 1958). Nevertheless, these societies characteristically form around a sizable core city from which they are ruled—despite the fact that at least 90 percent of the population remains on farms and in rural farming hamlets (Sjoberg, 1960).

Furthermore, these societies are much larger in both area and population than are advanced horticultural societies. The Roman Empire at its peak controlled more than two million square miles, as did the Chinese. Spain during the eighteenth century controlled five million square miles; the Arab Umayyad Empire controlled more than three million. These are extremes, but they establish the point. Similarly, although advanced horticultural societies probably never have exceeded four million members, a few agrarian societies have reached a hundred million or more (Lenski, 1966).

It would be oversimplified to limit the technological gains of agrarian societies to the horse and the wheel. Many further technological refinements followed, especially in the area of metallurgy and simple machines. These were the societies, after all, that created the pyramids, the great buildings of Rome, the cathedrals of Europe. This technology stemmed from and gave rise to further specialization in the division of labor. The tax roles for Paris in 1313 listed 157 different crafts alone, not to mention other occupations such as official, priest, soldier, and farmer (Clough and Cole, 1941).

The empires of agrarian societies are not the result of simple growth or peaceful joining of neighboring groups. They all have been formed by *conquest*. As a result they are composed typically of varieties of ethnic, language, and even racial groups. Sometimes these differences quickly melt away following conquest; sometimes they persist and become the basis of castes and, for generations, of ascriptive inequality, as in India (see Chapter 16).

If advanced horticultural societies find warfare and conquest financially worthwhile, advanced agricultural societies find it profitable almost beyond belief—for the ruling classes at least. Sulla, the Roman dictator, is estimated to have plundered 480,000,000 sesterces from his campaign in Greece and Asia Minor (it is estimated that at that time a free Roman laborer and his family lived on 1,000 sesterces a year). Because of the profitability of conquest, agrarian societies live in a state of almost constant war—they are either trying for conquest or defending themselves against it. When not fighting others, they usually fight internally over who will hold the fabulous wealth of governing.

Lenski (1966) argues that because of their militarism, these societies almost always are governed by monarchs—powerful rule is more effective for societies at war. Furthermore, constant war creates a highly developed warrior class and restricts the means of warfare. No longer does the average male citizen possess access to adequate arms or have adequate training to serve as a warrior. Thus, the average man is subject to coercion.

Figure 12.11   In contrast to hunting and gathering societies (*top panel*) and simple horticultural societies, advanced horticultural societies have relatively permanent geographic locations. Staying in one place allows the members of advanced horticultural societies to amass surplus wealth, which can be passed on through inheritance procedures. Formal systems of property management develop (*second panel*); the idea of public office is formalized (*third panel*); and assets become tangible and therefore transferable (*bottom panel*). These three factors contribute to the increased importance of inheritance in determining status and come to serve as sources of the enormous differences in wealth that develop among social classes in agrarian societies.

In agrarian societies the wealth of the ruling classes is enormous even by modern standards, and the poverty of the masses is also extreme. The annual incomes of kings run to many millions. In the nineteenth century, the czars of Russia *owned* almost twenty-seven-and-a-half million people —serfs working the czars' lands whom they could dispose of as they wished. Recently, the premier of Thailand was reported to have accumulated an estate valued at $140 million over a ten-year period in a society with an annual per-capita income of less than $100 dollars (Lenski, 1966).

There are several reasons for the extreme stratification of agrarian societies. For one thing, they possess much greater wealth than do less developed societies. For another, they are tyrannically governed. But most important, the surplus wealth is very concentrated—the ruling classes are so small a portion of the total population that there is a great deal to go around. Rarely does the ruling class exceed 2 percent of the population, and often it is very much smaller than that. In France just before the revolution, it is estimated that only 0.6 percent of the population was made up of the nobility of all ranks and grades (Gottschalk, 1929). A tiny elite possesses the power, prestige, and property whereas the great bulk of the populace live in poverty. According to Marx, these extreme inequalities stem mainly from the institutions of government. Lenski (1966) accepted Marx's view and argued that it is through domination of the state and its coercive powers that a small group enriches itself at the expense of the rest. A second major base of inequality is control of religious institutions. Church and state are closely tied and between them exact most of the society's surplus into the hands of the few.

Agrarian societies also provide for the appearance of several new social categories. The first of these is *merchants*. The complexities of specialized production and trade provide an opening for some people to become specialists in the distribution of commodities. Sometimes merchant families have acquired sufficient wealth and power to enter the ruling class. But in the later stages of all agrarian societies merchants have existed at a higher level of wealth, status, and power than the average man. They constitute at least the beginnings of a middle class.

The second new social category Lenski (1966) calls the *expendables*. These are numbers of people who lack any legitimate claim to a living, those whom the society does not find it profitable to employ. The emergence of a ruling class, privileged beyond credibility, has as its obverse the creation of a class of the dispossessed: persons literally turned out to starve, steal, and beg. In London during the 1500s it is estimated that from 10 to 15 percent of the population were beggars (Lenski, 1966). Little wonder that citizens were fearful to appear on the streets after dark.

On all three dimensions of stratification, agrarian societies are the most unequal yet devised by man. Out of whimsy, rulers can and do have people and even large communities put to death. Masses of people become slaves or serfs. Large numbers starve in the streets, while the rich live in luxury. Prestige differences are also extreme, with the average man owing great deference to those above him. Moreover, agrarian societies show the most extreme reliance on ascriptive as opposed to achieved status. Although it is possible for some commoners to rise to elite status in such societies, the norm is status based on one's birth.

Industrial Societies

The most recent type of society is the one in which we live: the modern industrial state. It is obvious that industrial societies are profoundly different from any kind of society man has known previously. But we cannot yet fully characterize these differences because although there exist fully developed societies of the other types, we have not yet seen a fully mature example of an industrial society. Such societies are all still changing and developing rapidly.

We can distinguish among earlier and present stages of these societies and make at least educated guesses about future trends. Industrial societies developed from agrarian societies and have existed for about 200 years. In their earliest stages, they retained many characteristics of the stratification systems of agrarian societies. Kings continued to rule while impoverished factory workers replaced an impoverished peasantry as the basic source of economic surplus. This change-over proved unstable, and soon a surprising trend emerged. For the first time since human societies began evolving, the trend toward increasing inequality with increasing social complexity was *reversed*. Industrial societies soon became less stratified than agrarian societies, and this trend has continued. What happened in industrial societies to make this reversal possible?

First, the *power* of the ruling classes was curtailed. Kings were cast out or converted to harmless symbols. The claims of nobility to the rights (by birth) of military and political leadership were discredited. Universal suffrage greatly increased the political power of the average person. More important, individuals and groups gained the right to organize in order to defend and seek their interests through political parties, unions, and other organizations. Legal developments provided increasing protection of the weak from the powerful.

Second, *economic* inequality was greatly reduced as industrialization developed. For one thing, the total amount of wealth of nations increased by staggering amounts. Consequently, the absolute living conditions of those on the bottom of society greatly improved. The poorest resident of Harlem enjoys a standard of living beyond the dreams of the poor of Calcutta or the army of beggars in fifteenth-century London. Furthermore, the distribution of wealth has become more equal proportionately. Lenski (1966) estimates that in agrarian societies the top 1 or 2 percent of the population usually receives no less than *half of the total income of the nation*. He reports statistics from a number of modern industrial nations, showing that the top 2 percent now receive no more than 10 percent of the total wealth. Therefore, although industrial societies are still unequal in terms of property, they are very much less so than are agrarian societies.

Third, the distribution of *prestige* has also changed. "Commoners" no longer bow and scrape to their "betters." No one is executed for gazing upon the president or even upon the queen. The importance of ascriptive status has also greatly diminished, and the importance of achieved status has increased. Rather than feeling ashamed of humble origins, many successful people in industrial societies express pride in rising from poverty. Universal education systems have been created to facilitate success based on individual merit rather than on birth.

This is not to suggest that industrial nations are not stratified. Even the attempts such societies actually have made to reduce inequality have fallen far short of success. Poverty is still with us. Not everyone starts life with an equal opportunity for success. Huge inherited fortunes still remain. Some people have much more political power than others. Some persons are internationally admired; others are anonymous. But the trends have turned sharply toward greater equality.

Among the critical features of industrial societies that have influenced these trends are energy sources other than the muscle power of man and beast, machine technology, rapid and efficient communications, huge populations, urban living, and changes in the nature of warfare that have made it ruinously expensive instead of profitable.

Little needs to be said about the revolution in technology, energy, and communication. Muscle power provides less than 2 percent of the energy used for work in the United States today (Lenski, 1966). Your grandparents were the first generation to have automobiles. Your parents probably belong to the first generation to fly on commercial airliners. Your generation was the first to grow up with television.

Unit VII provides detailed examination of the massive shift from rural to urban living and of the rapid growth of populations in industrialized nations, especially in agrarian nations that have learned modern techniques of public health. It is perhaps enough to say here that nearly all members of agrarian societies live in rural areas and that the majority of people in industrialized nations live in cities. Recall that the largest population that any agrarian city reached was probably only about one-half million and that the average population for major cities stayed in the twenty-five-to-thirty-thousand range. Today we have cities of nine million.

Changes in the profitability of warfare will transform industrial societies, one way or the other. Agrarian societies have found warfare extremely profitable and have therefore engaged in it almost constantly. Although they were slow to recognize the fact, warfare for industrial societies is economically ruinous (Putney, 1972). France and England are still paying for the costs of World War I—a war that was fought partly in hope of economic gain. The United States is still paying debts incurred in World War II; rather than reap the spoils of our victory, we found it necessary to contribute to the relief of the vanquished. But even if we had carried off all the wealth of Germany, we still would have come out much behind. Even in a war with a small agrarian opponent in Vietnam we have run into prohibitive costs—staggering budget deficits, higher taxes, unemployment, inflation, and the curtailment of needed domestic programs. Furthermore, the armaments of modern war, even the nonnuclear varieties, devastate populations and property to a previously undreamt-of extent. Consequently, modern industrial nations find themselves in a position very similar to that of hunting and gathering societies—war is not worth the price. If such nations nevertheless engage in nuclear war, they may find themselves quite literally in the position of hunting and gathering societies.

Precisely why industrial societies have reversed the trend toward increasing inequality is not wholly understood. But a number of factors clearly played a part.

First of all, with industrialization the division of labor has become extremely complex, as have the jobs many subordinate persons perform. Consequently, those at the top of society can no longer understand the work performed by many below them, and workers have become far less interchangeable. This results in skill monopolies for many subordinate persons. Society cannot run without them, and they are in scarce supply (Galbraith, 1967; Drucker, 1969). This powerful bargaining position has been used to extract a greater proportion of scarce values and is reflected in the

great expansion of the middle classes in industrial societies. As Marx and others recognized, the great social revolution that gave rise to capitalism was a revolution of the middle classes against the feudal order of our agrarian past. Over time, the ranks of the unskilled have been shrinking, and the ranks of the skilled middle classes have been greatly expanding. (See Chapter 13.)

A second force toward equality in industrial societies has been the concentration of exploited groups into factories and firms and in cities. This trend led Marx to predict a revolution by the proletariat when workers, now gathered in proximity instead of spread across the rural landscape, developed class consciousness.

To a considerable extent, a shared consciousness of common grievances did develop just as Marx had predicted. But Marx failed to anticipate the survival potential of the capitalist system. Instead of fighting blindly to hold their privileges, as the nobility had done before them, the ruling classes accommodated their system to the demands of labor. Instead of revolution, the result was reform and the reduction of inequality. Indeed, to date, Marx's predicted revolutions have occurred only in late agrarian societies—for example, Russia, China, Cuba—not in industrial nations.

A third factor that helped reduce inequality in industrial societies was the incredible increase in productivity. Industrialization resulted in so much wealth that the upper classes could share it without having to reduce their own standards of luxury. Furthermore, gains in productivity in industrial societies, unlike earlier societies, have not outstripped population growth, so that gains have not immediately been eaten up. Although we have undergone a population explosion, the birth rate still has been considerably reduced in industrial nations, thereby facilitating a rising standard of living.

At this point something must be said about inequalities in the two basic political varieties of industrial nations—the capitalist and socialist systems. Socialist countries such as the Soviet Union have sustained a political ideology denouncing all social inequalities, whereas capitalist societies such as the United States have only committed themselves to an ideology of equal opportunity, not of equal attainment. It is the case that neither socialist nor capitalist countries offer full equality of opportunity and that both are stratified on all three dimensions of status. However, there are distinct differences. The Soviet Union displays considerable stratification of property. For example, the average wage is 800 to 900 rubles a month, but many Soviet executives earn salaries in the 7,500-ruble-a-month bracket (Lenski, 1966). Great as these wage inequalities are, they are smaller than those in the United States, where some executives earn more than $500,000 a year and Howard Hughes is estimated to earn $3 million a week. On the other hand, the Soviet Union is still more stratified in terms of power than is the United States, and socialist countries in general are more power-stratified than are capitalist countries. Consider merely the degree of individual freedom that citizens have to dissent or to control where they live and work. The average American can influence his government more than can the average Russian. He can also more easily move to another country if he wishes.

It is hard to say which system makes for greater prestige inequalities. Clearly, political leaders and officials enjoy greater relative prestige in socialist countries. On the other hand, there are probably fewer celebrities in socialist nations. In order to reward workers, socialist countries do attempt to use prestige as a substitute for property; they give medals to heroes of labor, for example, and they give much effort to honoring the work-

ing class. But it is hard to say that this reduces prestige differences between managers and workers or that American notions about the worth of the average man are any less pronounced than they are in the Soviet Union. In any event, socialist nations seem to be becoming more capitalistic and capitalistic nations more socialistic. Soon they may not be importantly different.

It is difficult to read the future, but it seems likely that modern industrial nations will continue the trend toward greater equality. This is not to predict that one day they will be wholly equalitarian. It may be possible that they can become equalitarian in terms of opportunity. But whether all men can ever be wholly equal in terms of their actual property, prestige, and power seems questionable. As Chapter 15 will demonstrate, this is an issue sociologists have debated violently for many years. The majority today doubt that total equality is possible, even in principle. Of course, they could be wrong.

SUGGESTED READINGS

Bendix, Reinhard, and Seymour Martin Lipset (eds.). *Class, Status and Power.* New York: Free Press, 1966.

Bottomore, T. B. *Classes in Modern Society.* New York: Pantheon Books, 1966.

Drucker, Peter F. *The Age of Discontinuity.* New York: Harper & Row, 1969.

Galbraith, John Kenneth. *The New Industrial State.* Boston: Houghton-Mifflin, 1967.

Lenski, Gerhard. *Power and Privilege: A Theory of Social Stratification.* New York: McGraw-Hill, 1966.

Chapter 13 Social Mobility

NO SYSTEM OF SOCIAL STRATIFICATION is entirely static. Even in the most caste-ridden agrarian societies, individuals and groups continually move up and down the ladder. Such changes are called *social mobility*. *Downward* mobility refers to losses; *upward* mobility, to gains.

Sociologists are particularly interested in *intergenerational* mobility—whether children end up with a higher or lower position than their parents attained. A banker's son who ends up a factory worker is downwardly mobile. A factory worker's son who becomes a banker is upwardly mobile.

What factors produce or inhibit social mobility? Why do differences in mobility occur? This chapter will identify sources and causes of mobility and discuss the amount of mobility in various types of societies, especially industrialized ones. In discussing the sources of mobility, we will treat separately features of the society in which mobility occurs and characteristics of individuals and groups that influence their mobility.

SYSTEMS OF SOCIAL MOBILITY

Two main factors determine the amount of upward and downward mobility in any society: The *capacity* of the system, which means the total amount of mobility it can support, and the *characteristics* of the system, or the conditions under which mobility is permitted.

Capacities

The capacity of a society to support mobility depends upon changes in the *amount* of property, power, and prestige available in the society and upon changes in the *distribution* of property, power, and prestige across the population. Put simply, the proportion of people who are upwardly or downwardly mobile in a society depends on whether the proportion of upper-status positions is expanding or contracting. Obviously, when "scarce values" are becoming scarcer or are being increasingly concentrated in fewer hands, downward mobility must be occurring. Some who have possessed greater amounts of property, prestige, or power—or whose parents did—must be

dispossessed and pushed down the social ladder. When scarce values are becoming less scarce and are being more generously distributed, some people must rise. Because the long-term trend in industrial societies has been toward expansion of the privileged classes, and correspondingly toward shrinkage of the most disadvantaged classes, these societies have shown relatively high rates of upward mobility.

In the last chapter we saw that the extent of stratification changes when societies change their chief means of making a living. A major aspect in the transformation from the exaggerated stratification of agrarian societies to the decreased stratification of industrial societies is an expansion of the upper classes and middle classes and a contraction of the lower classes. Consequently, a great many persons flow upward from humble origins to fill these vacancies in the system. Substantial upward mobility under such changing conditions is assured. This is dramatically illustrated in Figure 13.1, which shows changes in the overall stratification system of Mexico between 1895 and 1960—a period covering transformation from a highly stratified agrarian society to a less stratified early industrial society. During this period the lower class shrank from 90 percent of the population to approximately 40 percent; the upper, middle, and transitional classes expanded proportionately. Necessarily, during this sixty-five-year period a great many people—probably more than half of the population—experienced upward mobility merely as a result of changes in the stratification system. Mexico greatly increased its capacities to support upward mobility and a less stratified population.

This process is characteristic of all societies that have undergone the transformation from an agrarian to an industrial base. Furthermore, the greater upward mobility that results from expansion of the upper and middle positions has continued to operate in industrialized societies. In contrast, as Gerhard Lenski (1966) has pointed out, *downward* mobility predominates in agrarian societies as a result of high fertility and a static stratification system. Because the proportion of high-ranking positions remains relatively constant

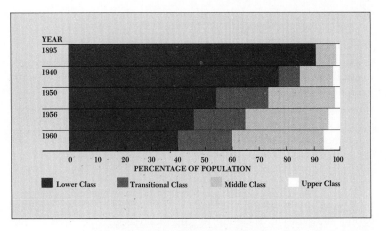

Figure 13.1   Changes occurred in the stratification system of Mexico during industrialization. In 1895, Mexico was highly stratified, but by 1960 many people had achieved upward mobility and the number of middle-class people had increased. (Adapted from H. F. Cline, 1963.)

in agrarian societies, and because the upper classes bear children in excess of the number needed for simple replacement, some upper-class children must experience downward mobility. There is simply no room for all of them at the top. In fact, much of the impulse for conquest exhibited by agrarian societies comes from younger sons who lack the right of succession to their father's wealth and position and who therefore go out to seek their fortunes at the expense of surrounding societies.

The pattern is sharply reversed in societies in which upward mobility predominates. Technology has had its greatest impact in eliminating the lowliest and least skilled occupations and in expanding the middle- and upper-status positions. Peter M. Blau and Otis Duncan (1967) report that farm workers in 1900 outnumbered professional and high-level technical workers in America by more than ten to one. Today professional and high-level technicians outnumber farm workers by nearly two to one. (See Chapter 22.) Similar changes have occurred in all industrialized nations. The elimination of low-status occupations and the expansion of high-status occupations has been a continual source of upward mobility in industrial societies.

The predominance of upward mobility in industrialized societies has, however, suffered periodic reversals. Economic depressions, wars, natural disasters, and civil wars have sometimes caused a shrinkage in upper-level positions and

have therefore forced large numbers of persons down the social ladder. For example, most industrialized nations, including the United States, experienced a severe economic depression in the 1930s. Many of those displaced during this period later regained their positions when conditions improved (but those whose downward mobility took the form of jumping out of their office windows did not). Similarly, the devastation caused by wars and civil wars has caused considerable downward mobility, as we will see in a later section. But these have been abnormal interludes, and the pattern of considerable upward mobility has been reestablished as soon as normal relations prevailed.

We will discuss how much mobility various industrialized nations exhibit, but first we should deal with the cultural rules according to which various societies permit mobility.

Characteristics

Industrialized societies have much more capacity for mobility than do less developed societies, such as the agrarian or horticultural types. But their greater capacity is not the only way in which they differ from less developed societies. An equally important difference lies in the rules governing stratification. Chapter 12 clarified the difference between status *ascription* and status *achievement:* rank can be attained on the basis of who you are (or who your father is) or on the basis of what you do. No one asks Queen Elizabeth II's son Charles what he is going to be when he grows up. As heir to the British monarch, he is going to be king. On the other hand, most people in Great Britain do have to worry about what they will be when they grow up because their future is open. To a considerable extent, what they will be depends upon what they will be able to do.

An open future is not typical of less developed societies, except hunting and gathering ones, but even hunters and gatherers have to operate within the severe limits of what *any* person in the society can hope for. In horticultural and agrarian societies, most people are in the position of England's Charles. They too know their future be-

Figure 13.2   Agrarian societies, such as the old American South, are based upon a feudal division of labor. *Ascription* serves as the primary basis of stratification in such a society. The sons of slaves were also slaves (*left*), regardless of their personal talents or effort. Industrialization, which shifted the emphasis from ascription to *achievement* as the basis of stratification, combined with the abolition of slavery, made it possible for a man like George Washington Carver, the grandson of a slave, to move up in the social hierarchy (*top right*). Status based on ascribed characteristics, however, has not entirely disappeared, even in the most advanced industrial societies. Race, for example, is still a great barrier to social mobility. The great-great-great-great-grandson of a slave can still expect to suffer discrimination because of his race (*bottom right*).

cause it is inherited. In these types of societies, ascribed status extends to such details of stratification as what specific occupation a person will perform. Sons of cobblers inherit their fathers' occupation. Peasants inherit peasantry. And the rich and powerful inherit riches and power.

It is not true that all status is ascriptive even in the most tradition-bound agrarian societies. Incompetents still lose their high positions, and the talented and bold still rise. Indeed, as often happened in India, a whole caste—that is, a group holding an ascribed status position—may slowly make gains in power, prestige, and property. Nevertheless, the trend toward increasing inequality as societies become more complex has been accompanied by increases in the degree to which inequalities can be based on ascription. Like the degree of inequality, however, the degree of ascribed status also reverses with the rise of industrialized societies.

Two factors have been chiefly responsible for this reversal: (1) the expansion of needed upper-status positions created shortages—and empty places that had to be filled—so that considerable upward mobility resulted in spite of ascriptive rules; (2) the complex nature of work in industrialized societies greatly increased the need for individual competence and talent, thereby making status by ascription unpractical and inefficient.

A glance back at Figure 13.1 makes it evident that Mexico could not have undergone such substantial changes in its overall stratification system unless great numbers of people had risen above their original ascribed statuses or those of their parents. The alternative would have been to prevent the development of industrialization. Massive upward mobility quickly makes ascriptive norms outmoded and replaces them with achievement norms. The trend toward achievement-based status is also required by the very complex nature of industrialized societies.

We have already mentioned the complex nature of work. In addition, as Weber pointed out, the chief characteristic of modern industrialized societies is an emphasis on rationality—they are increasingly organized to pursue goals in the most efficient, predictable, and effective ways. Concerns for maximizing performance run counter to norms of status by ascription. To pay attention to who a person is gets in the way of picking the person who can do the job best. The more complex the technology and the more demanding the occupation, the greater is this need to apply universalistic criteria to select who is to do what. The greatest pressure for achievement-based status is therefore at the *upper* levels—precisely where ascriptive rules are most stringent. Thus, ascriptive status rules were broken not for moral reasons of unfairness but because they were inadequate for the needs of industrialized societies.

This is not to suggest that family background plays no role in a person's success in industrialized societies. It does, as we shall see later in the chapter. But family background does not automatically lead to a high ascribed status. It is much harder in industrialized societies to directly inherit superior status without also legitimating it through

Figure 13.3 The diagram below depicts the changes that occur in the stratification systems of societies undergoing industrialization. From the perspective of the society as a whole, the number of upper-status and middle-status positions in the society increases, and lower-status people move up to fill the vacancies. From the point of view of an individual within the society, upward social mobility is attained through the completion of higher levels of education and the acquisition of job skills necessary in the specialized positions that are created in the increasingly complex division of labor.

Figure 13.4   Reinhard Bendix arrived in the United States in 1938 as a young refugee from fascist Germany and did undergraduate and graduate work at the University of Chicago, where he received his doctorate. He is a professor of sociology at the University of California, Berkeley. In collaboration with Seymour Martin Lipset he has produced some very influential work on stratification. He is also the sole author of a number of books, including *Work and Authority in Industry* (1956) and *Nation-building and Citizenship: Studies in Changing Social Order* (1964). Perhaps above all, Bendix is famous as an interpreter of the work of Max Weber. His *Max Weber: An Intellectual Portrait* (1960) provided a systematic overview of all of Weber's work and led to a reconsideration of Weber's contributions.

one's own achievements and capacities. Thus, as we shall see, superior family origins in the United States influence status primarily because they increase children's chances of obtaining a superior education, which in turn facilitates status achievement for such children.

Not all ascriptive criteria have been equally overcome by industrial societies. Race and ethnicity still block or facilitate status achievement in many such societies—for example, race still plays a sad part in American stratification; these matters occupy Chapter 16. As Chapter 17 will examine in detail, sex is also a continuing source of ascriptive status in industrialized societies. We should not minimize the seriousness of these forms of continuing ascription, but we must recognize that even here industrialized societies have greatly reduced inequality. With the exception of the Nazi aberration, religious and ethnic minorities are no longer slaughtered or legally barred from civic life in industrialized nations, but these are common patterns in agrarian and horticultural societies. Nor do industrialized societies any longer practice slavery, which is a common practice in less developed societies. Nor are women excluded from power, property, and prestige to the degree that they are in less developed societies. Although extremely serious problems of ascription remain in industrial societies, the inequalities that result from ascriptive status have decreased significantly.

Comparative Upward Mobility in Industrial Societies

The landmark empirical study of comparative mobility was published in 1958 by Seymour Martin Lipset and Reinhard Bendix. Prior to that time, sociologists had relied on impressions and speculations about the relative openness of opportunity in various industrial societies. Much theorizing had been devoted to explaining why America was a land of opportunity in comparison with other industrialized nations.

Lipset and Bendix poured cold water on this problem. Their data showed that not only did several industrial nations have higher rates of upward mobility than did the United States but that, overall, industrial societies also display quite similar patterns of mobility. (See Figure 13.5.) They were forced to the conclusion that generic features of industrial societies, not special features of the United States, are responsible for mobility. We briefly outlined these major features in the last section. Lipset and Bendix stimulated a great deal of subsequent study of mobility in industrialized societies; and, as should be the case, our understanding has progressed considerably beyond their original analysis.

As pioneers, Lipset and Bendix had to work with very imperfect data gathered from a great variety of sources. These data only permitted them to study mobility across a two-class system: manual and nonmanual occupations. Therefore, they could only measure upward mobility as movement from manual (or blue-collar) into nonmanual (or white-collar) occupations and downward mobility as movement in the reverse direction. It is essential to study the chances that people have to rise into a society's elites if we are to gain an adequate picture of opportunities. For example, if industrialization results in many sons of craftsmen becoming lowly paid clerks (as it does), such a movement is not a basis for talking of opportunities for upward mobility.

As it turned out, later research indicated that when more adequate data were examined there was some limited truth to the notion of America as a land of opportunities. Table 13.1 shows the proportion of the sons of manual workers who rise into elite occupations, that is, professions and high-level technical occupations. It also shows mobility into elite occupations by sons of middle-class fathers. Although mobility across the line dividing blue-collar and white-collar positions is very similar among industrialized nations, it is apparent in Table 13.1 that Americans born into low-status, manual families have a good relative advantage in rising to elite occupations. Nearly 10 percent of American sons of manual workers achieve elite status, with Japanese and Dutch sons a distant second in their chance of rising.

Figure 13.5   (*Top*) Chart of total intergenerational
mobility compared with upward and downward
mobility for several societies. Two patterns emerge:
The total intergenerational mobility for the United
States and Switzerland is about the same, but the two
societies differ considerably in the percentages of
people who are upwardly and downwardly mobile.

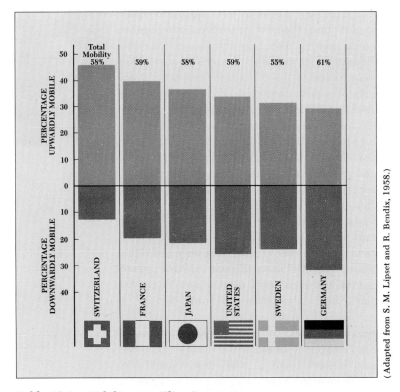

(Adapted from S. M. Lipset and R. Bendix, 1958.)

Table 13.1   Mobility into Elite Occupations

| Country | Manual Class into Elite | | Middle Class into Elite | |
	Percent	Mobility Ratio	Percent	Mobility Ratio
Denmark	1.07	.32	4.58	1.39
France	1.56	.25	10.48	1.71
Great Britain	2.23	.30	8.64	1.15
Italy	.35	.13	5.76	2.08
Japan	6.95	.59	15.12	1.29
Netherlands	6.61	.60	11.55	1.04
Sweden	3.50	.53	18.09	2.72
United States	9.91	.85	20.90	1.80
West Germany	1.46	.32	8.28	1.81

Source: Adapted from S.M. Miller (1960) as revised by Peter Blau and Otis Duncan,
The American Occupational Structure, New York: Wiley and Sons, 1967.

The second column in the table shows this
same comparison in terms of mobility ratios. A
mobility ratio of 1.0 would indicate the chance all
males in a society have of achieving elite status

(regardless of their origins). When the ratio is less
than 1.0 it means that people from that group are
somewhat handicapped in achieving elite status
in comparison with the population as a whole.
Ratios over 1.0 indicate an advantage. The table
shows that sons of American manual workers are
slightly disadvantaged in gaining elite status—
their chance is six-sevenths (.85) of that of the
population as a whole. Compared with the
chances in other industrialized nations shown in
the table, this is a very *high* chance to enter elite
occupations. The sons of Dutch manual laborers
have the next best chance, six-tenths of that of the
overall population, closely followed by sons of
Japanese workers. Manual sons in most industrialized European nations have much less chance of
entering elite occupations than do the sons of
American workers.

The fourth column in the table shows, however, that when it comes to the chances of middle-
class sons to enter elite occupations, the United
States is not outstanding. Therefore, it is in offering much greater opportunities for low-status sons
to enter the elite that the United States differs
most from other industrialized nations. As Blau
and Duncan (1967) put it:

There is a grain of truth in the Horatio Alger
myth. The high level of popular education in the
United States, perhaps reinforced by the lesser
emphasis on formal distinction of social status, has
provided the disadvantaged lower strata with outstanding opportunities for long-distance upward
mobility.

Still, most sons of manual laborers do not rise, and
there is no industrial society that is completely
free from ascriptive status.

SOURCES OF INDIVIDUAL MOBILITY

Industrial societies are characterized by relatively
high rates of social mobility. Obviously, however,
not everyone is mobile. Many stay in the same
social stratum into which they were born. In this
section we seek understanding of who is mobile
and why.

Figure 13.6   Otis Dudley Duncan is a professor of sociology at the University of Michigan and is one of the nation's best-known demographers. He is coauthor with Peter M. Blau of *American Occupational Structure* (1967). Duncan is a leader in the ecological analysis of urban communities and has made many important contributions to statistical methods.

Education

The most comprehensive study of occupational mobility in American society was published by Blau and Duncan in 1967. One of their major contributions was to recognize that it is occupational achievement, not mobility as such, that is the correct topic for explanation. If a sociologist focuses on mobility rather than occupational achievement, his findings are masked by one simple fact: the lower the level at which a person begins, the greater the probability that he will be mobile, because a greater number of possible occupations offer him upward mobility. Put another way, people at the bottom have nowhere to go but up unless they stay put; people at the top can only stay put or go down.

Blau and Duncan wanted to explain how people come to hold higher- or lower-status occupations, so they assigned a status score to each of a great number of occupations. The father's status was one of the factors they analyzed. They found that a person's social origins—that is, his father's occupation and education—exert considerable influence on occupational success but that his own educational achievement is much more important. In fact, they found that the main way in which a father's success affects his son's success is by affecting his son's educational achievement. The sons of successful fathers are more likely than sons of unsuccessful fathers to complete high levels of education and are therefore more likely to succeed. But poorly educated sons of successful fathers are not in a much better position than poorly educated sons of unsuccessful fathers. Similarly, educated sons of unsuccessful fathers are not much disadvantaged in competition for jobs with the educated sons of successful fathers. Some effects of social origins remain even when the sons' educational achievements are taken into account, but the effects are not very substantial.

The key to equality of opportunity, then, appears to be equality of educational opportunity. To the extent that mass education in industrial societies has been successful, considerable mobility has resulted. A major qualification of Blau and Duncan's work however, concerns racial minori-ties. As we point out later in this chapter and again in Chapter 16, educational achievement has much less impact on the occupational achievement of racial minorities than it does on the success of whites in America. Superior educational achievement so far has not brought nearly the proportionate occupational success to blacks, for example, that it has brought to whites.

Deferred Gratification

A major factor in upward mobility involves waiting for the two birds in the bush rather than settling for the bird in hand. Indeed, taking the bird in hand leads to downward mobility. An obvious instance is in educational achievement; it is better to stay in school and defer financial rewards than to drop out to take a job. People who drop out of college ordinarily enjoy a considerably higher immediate standard of living than do those who remain in school. But this is a short-term advantage: the college-educated enjoy considerably higher average incomes than do those leaving college. (Lassiter, 1966). Similarly, deferring marriage and children is associated with upward mobility, whereas early marriage and early childbearing is associated with downward mobility (Blau and Duncan, 1967; Lipset and Bendix, 1958).

Family

Not only is early childbearing associated with downward mobility, so is a large family. Upwardly mobile persons have fewer children than do those who are not mobile or who are downwardly mobile (Blau and Duncan, 1967). Late marriage accounts for part of the difference. Upwardly mobile people tend to delay marriage, and the older the couple is at marriage, the shorter their period of fertility. Not only does *producing* a large family influence occupational achievement but *coming from one* also greatly reduces chances of success. Chances of success are greatest for an only child or one with only one sibling (Blau and Duncan, 1967). In large families the eldest and youngest have the highest chances of success. All of these

Figure 13.7   At every level of educational achievement, blacks have lower median incomes than do whites. In fact, the higher the educational level, the greater the gap between median incomes of blacks and whites.
(From U.S. Bureau of the Census, 1971.)

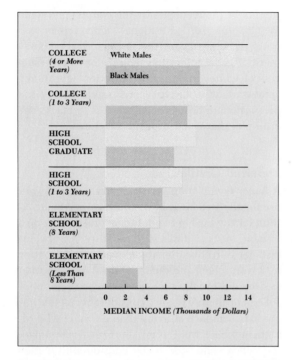

findings seem to stem from the division of family resources, particularly as they influence educational achievement. Other things being equal, the fewer the children, the larger their share of attention, supervision, and family finances. Parents seem to devote disproportionate resources to the education and training of their oldest child. The youngest child also gets a greater share of the family's resources because older children have become self-supporting. The major consequence of large families is to substantially reduce the educational achievements, and therefore the occupational success, of children (Blau and Duncan, 1967). Occupational success is also affected by broken families, apparently for the same reason—broken families have fewer financial and emotional resources than families that are intact.

Marriage

We have seen that early marriage is a barrier to mobility. However, marriage itself can be a source of upward or downward mobility, depending on the status of the spouse. The notion of marrying for money or social position is a cultural cliché that is usually applied to women. Men fairly often marry women of lower social standing or educational achievement than their own; women do so much less often. As a result, a substantial number of women improve their status through marriage, but men usually have to rely on their own efforts. In part, this is because family status greatly depends upon the status of the male; men can marry down without suffering any status loss, but most women who marry down lose status. As is pointed out in Chapter 17, this pattern may well be changing in industrialized societies, but at present it remains in force. A by-product of this pattern is a comparatively high proportion of upper-class women who never marry. Because women are less likely to marry "beneath themselves" than are men, for every upper-class male who marries down, there is an upper-class female left without an appropriate mate (Scott, 1969).

Intelligence

We have little direct evidence about the degree to which intelligence differentials affect mobility. Bruce Eckland (1967) has suggested that we cannot adequately assess the efficiency of systems of social mobility until we understand the link between mobility and intelligence.

As was pointed out in Chapter 5, there is substantial evidence that inheritance operates in determining a person's intelligence. If this is the case and if intelligence does matter a good deal in occupational success, then we must revise our basis for measuring the openness of stratification systems. At present, sociologists use as a standard of openness the assumption that in a wholly open society there would be no correlation between fathers' and sons' occupational achievements; that is, family background would play no part in individual success. No society has yet displayed this degree of openness. But if intelligence is partly hereditary and if it does affect success, then we would expect some correlation between fathers' and sons' successes, simply on the basis of the relationship between fathers' and sons' intelligence. Thus a society wholly open in terms of opportunities for success would still exhibit some apparent effects of family background. However, at the present time the degree to which intelligence does facilitate success has not been studied. We do know that there is a strong relationship between intelligence and educational attainment and performance (Hirschi, 1969; Coleman, 1966). It is possible that this is really the *only* way in which intelligence influences success, but it seems unlikely that intelligence plays so limited a role.

Motivation

Discussions of social mobility have given a great deal of attention to the effort a person makes, that is, to psychological variables such as *achievement motivation* (McClelland, 1961). It is fairly obvious that people must want to succeed if they are going to be very likely to succeed. But a critical question concerns the distribution of achievement motivation among society's members. If everyone equally desires success, then examination of factors influencing success gives some reading of the basis for achievement. Many sociologists take the position that achievement motivation is virtually universal (Barber, 1957; Luckman and Berger, 1964). Certainly, social-learning theories, outlined in Chapter 4, are based on the notion that reward seeking is a universal human trait; such theories would support the view that achievement motivation is universal if it is true that people universally regard high status as a reward. However, some sociologists challenge the assumption that all social strata are equally motivated toward achievement (Porter, 1968; Miller and Riessman, 1964). They argue that people born into lower-status families do not develop as strong desires for success as do people born into more advantaged families. Lacking motivation would, of course, compound the initial disadvantages of the poor, causing many not to even pursue success. Even if we assume that these studies are incorrect and that the poor have as strong an achievement motivation as the middle and upper classes, the poor would still be disadvantaged. As Suzanne Keller and Marisa Zavalloni (1964) point out, because lower-class young people have much farther to go, they may need more intense achievement moti-

vation than do middle-class young people in order to succeed. Keller and Zavalloni suggest that it may not be much of a sign of ambition for a middle-class youth to desire to go to college, but it might be a sign of great ambition among ghetto youth. Similarly, it may require considerably greater motivation for the children of unskilled laborers to become skilled blue-collar workers than for the children of middle-class fathers to become professionals. An understanding of relative differences in the distance to be traveled up the occupational ladder must shape our explorations of achievement motivation and success.

Race

It has been pointed out that education fails to produce the same payoffs in occupational success for blacks that it does for whites. Worse yet, the differential is greatest at the upper educational levels. The difference in average occupational status is *twice as great* between blacks and whites who have graduated from high school or attended college as it is between blacks and whites with no more than eight years of schooling. Thus, the careers of well-educated blacks lag further behind the careers of educated whites than do the careers of uneducated blacks behind the careers of uneducated whites. Blau and Duncan (1967) explored several causes of this lag. Part of the difference stems from the fact that blacks are disproportionately Southerners, and Southerners—white or black—are less successful than Northerners. Part of the difference also stems from differences in the quality of black and white education. Inner-city schools are inferior to suburban schools. Blacks also tend to be concentrated in lower-quality colleges and universities. All of these differences mean that blacks with the same amount of schooling as whites have probably received qualitatively less education. Furthermore, blacks start from more disadvantaged positions than do whites because their fathers have less education and lower incomes.

Taking all of these factors into account, Blau and Duncan nevertheless conclude that discrimination in the occupational system accounts for

Figure 13.8 A photographic essay on environmental factors that affect social mobility. (*Below*) Children from large, poor families, according to some sociologists, have less motivation to achieve and may become downwardly mobile. (*Opposite page*) People with environmental advantages, such as good educational facilities and housing, are more likely to be upwardly mobile. Community action programs against poverty help improve the social mobility of people whose environments put them at an unfair disadvantage.

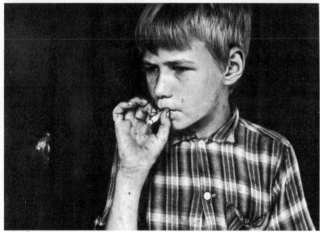

much of the black disadvantage. Although the mean education of blacks has risen strikingly over the past few years, it has so far not helped reduce occupational and income inequalities between blacks and whites. Education has simply not offered blacks the same road to upward mobility that it has to disadvantaged whites. *Even within the same occupations, blacks earn less than do whites* (Blau and Duncan, 1967).

These facts make a mockery of the widespread feelings among whites that blacks must earn equality in the same way as earlier disadvantaged white ethnic groups did (by "pulling themselves up by their own bootstraps") and that giving special advantages to blacks is unfair to whites. Even after paying his dues by sticking to the books and achieving a high-status occupation, a black, it

seems, cannot *earn* full economic equality under present conditions.

Nutrition

Poor nutrition greatly affects a child's general physical and mental development. Malnutrition has long been known to play a significant role in the poor learning performances of the children of poverty. These disadvantages conspire to keep poor families poor. Their children fail to develop the physical and mental liveliness to compete on an equal basis with well-fed, healthy children.

Scientists are now beginning to suspect that poor nutrition may hold an alternative solution to one of the most bitter debates of our time. It has long been known that the average measured intelligence of blacks trails slightly behind that of

whites in the United States. For a long time it was believed that these differences meant nothing more than that blacks had been the victims of cultural deprivations—poor education, poverty, unstimulating rural life, and the like. And, in fact, studies showed that such factors do account for some of the difference between the average IQ scores of blacks and whites. However, even when these cultural factors were controlled, some interracial IQ differences remained. This led the psychologist Arthur Jensen (1969) to suggest the existence of genetically based racial differences in intelligence. Jensen reasoned that there is solid evidence that genetic factors do influence intelligence, that whites and blacks are somewhat genetically different, and that possibly this genetic difference extends to the slight differences

in average IQ. (See Chapter 5.) Understandably, Jensen's suggestions aroused extremely bitter and polarized responses. His argument was based only on a chain of inferences, and many feel that it gave unwarranted support to racial bigotry and needlessly wounded the self-esteem of black people. Others leaped to embrace Jensen's inferences as established scientific justification for educational discrimination. In so doing they ignored the fact that the IQ differences in dispute are small differences between average scores and thus, even if Jensen were right, would not rationally lead to segregation. In any event, an alternative explanation to Jensen's, based on nutrition, is beginning to develop.

It has long been known that an infant's weight at birth is influenced by the mother's nutrition

Figure 13.9   Although there is some social mobility in every society, people from high-status families are more likely than those from lower-status families to attain high status themselves.

and that birth weight is related to the child's subsequent development. Small infants have a higher mortality rate, have a higher rate of birth defects, and tend to be of lower average intelligence (Watson and Lowrey, 1967). It is also well-known that the average birth weight of black infants is significantly lower than that of white infants in the United States (Watson and Lowrey, 1967). Black infants also have higher infant-mortality and birth-defect rates than do white infants —as would be expected on the basis of the birth-weight differences. However, recent research by David Rush (1972) has found that when birth weight is taken into account, the differences in infant mortality that have existed between white and black babies disappear. That is, when black and white babies of the same birth weight are compared, they display similar rates of mortality. It is true that adequate data do not yet exist to show that birth-weight controls would wipe out the interracial IQ differences, but it seems very plausible to expect they could. It also seems likely that birth-weight differences between black and white babies stem from the average black mother's having a poorer diet than has the average white mother. At present, research is under way both in the United States and abroad that should show what the linkage is between a pregnant woman's nutrition (and thus that of her fetus) and the infant's capacity for intellectual development. If the outcome is as is now suspected, we may find that present IQ differences between blacks and whites are neither genetic nor the result of test biases against blacks. Instead they may prove to be the result of another instance of the hardships imposed on blacks by social inequalities: an inferior diet.

Other Sources

There are a number of other factors that probably influence social mobility. Physical attractiveness probably enters into mobility, especially women's upward mobility through marriage. Studies have shown that height influences the occupational success of males—corporation executives are disproportionately tall in comparison with other males, and corporation personnel recruiters seem to prefer taller men for management training programs (Deck, 1971; Feldman, 1971).

Simple good luck probably also plays an important part in mobility. Although the role of luck has never been studied, it seems instructive that the Horatio Alger stories, often taken as the prototype of the American faith in success, turn almost entirely on good luck. The plucky, hard-working young hero never rises because of his hard work but only through lucky breaks. He finds a wallet and returns it. He marries the boss's daughter (Wohl, 1953). Good luck has certainly been a major factor in many individual fortunes based on oil discoveries. As yet, however, we know little about how commonly people just stumble on success.

SOURCES OF GROUP MOBILITY

Status is not wholly an individual or even a family matter. To some extent, even in industrial societies, status is ascribed on the basis of group membership. We have seen that merely by being black, an American may have limits imposed on his quest for success. Earlier in American history the same was true for Catholics and Jews (and, as we shall see, ascriptive status on religious grounds still persists at the elite level). Similarly, women as a group are denied status on ascriptive grounds. By the same token, membership in such groups, which are ascribed lower status, can lead to upward mobility—to the extent that the status of the entire group rises; for example, insofar as being black has become less of a status hindrance, the social position of the average black has risen. Similarly, as the position of women as a group improves, the position of the average woman rises. This is more than a truism: A great deal of social mobility in history has been the result of group mobility, both upward and downward.

Caste Mobility

E. Digby Baltzell (1964) pointed out that "history is a graveyard of classes which have preferred caste privileges to leadership." This has been especially true of agrarian societies. For example, the Roman senatorial aristocracy eventually lost their power to despots because they degenerated

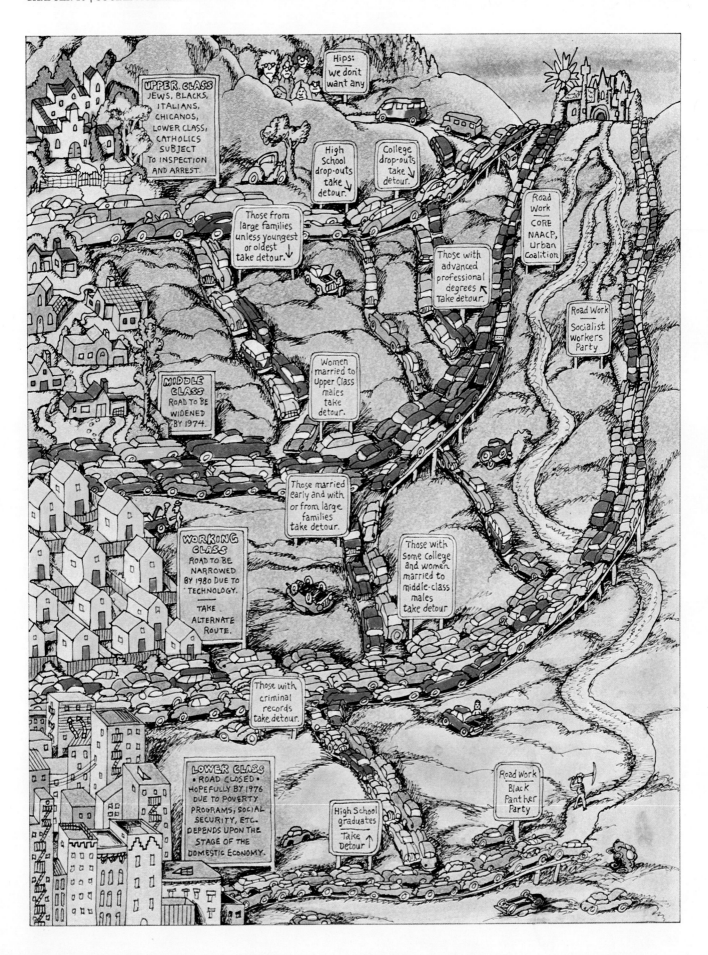

into a class unable to renew their ranks from the rising military and business classes. The nobilities of prerevolutionary France and Russia followed a similarly self-destructive course. Even in such an intensely ascriptive caste system as India's, a good deal of caste-based mobility has occurred historically and continues at present. A frequent pattern of upward caste mobility comes from taking control of a particular occupation such as money lending or mining that gains more social importance over time. Similarly, much downward caste mobility stems from the loss of importance of some role dominated by the caste. In modern India, for example, the historically exalted Brahmin caste is experiencing downward mobility. This priestly class has become more numerous than the contemporary Indian society can support at the level to which it is supposed to be entitled. Caste rules prohibit Brahmins from moving into more lucrative occupations (lest they lose their caste purity); many are therefore reduced to an impoverished level, and the prestige of the entire caste declines (Scott, 1972).

Circulation of Elites

In Chapter 12 it was suggested that Lenski's theory of status inconsistency may have been misapplied to the general population and that it may be applicable only at the elite levels of society. We now return to this matter to suggest that status inconsistency can help account for conflict within elites, especially conflicts that involve the denial of elite membership to upwardly mobile groups. Baltzell's (1964) theory of elite circulation—the turnover in membership of elites—suggests that ruling classes tend to become castes and thus resist claims to prestige made by new groups who are rising in property and power. He pointed out that the WASP (White Anglo-Saxon Protestant) establishment in America has excluded successful Jews and Catholics (especially Irish, Polish, and Italian Catholics) from "high society." Although Jews and Catholics have long been successful financially and have established considerable political power, they have been excluded from the most prestigious clubs, neighborhoods, and social circles.

Baltzell suggests that this reaction of the WASP establishment may, in fact, be at the expense of its power. As with previous ruling classes, they must now choose either to admit new members on the basis of achievement or to risk becoming a progressively feeble closed caste.

There are certainly strong connections between Baltzell's and Lenski's theories. In a later application of his theory, Lenski (1966) postulates that people who achieve wealth or property but who also are denied status because they are members of the "wrong" religion, race, ethnic group, or family background will try to alter the system under which they are denied status. The Democratic Party preferences of upper-class Catholics, blacks, and Jews offer support for Lenski's theory (see Chapter 14).

The combination of Baltzell's and Lenski's theories also offers a possible solution to a problem in Marx's theory of revolution. This solution was first proposed in 1916 by Vilfredo Pareto (1935), who pointed out that Marx was never able to explain adequately the source of leadership for a proletarian revolution, nor was his collaborator Friedrich Engels able to supply an answer. Marx and Engels were forced simply to assert that some members of the bourgeoisie would become disaffected and reject their class interests in order to provide needed sophisticated leadership to the proletarian revolution. They could not say *why* some bourgeoisie would become disaffected. The answer may lie in the fact that some claimants to elite status are denied full elite membership. Status inconsistency at the upper levels would lead to disaffection; some persons or groups who have elite rank on some criteria but are denied elite rank on others would then turn against the status quo. Indeed, the prominence of Jews (including Marx) in left-wing European politics seems to be a major example of this phenomenon (Cohn, 1958). Wealthy Jews were excluded not merely from high-prestige positions but even from conservative political parties. The word anti-Semitism was not coined by social scientists but by conservative European political parties who declared their opposition to the participation of Jews in civic life. Little wonder that educated and wealthy Jews did not find their interests served by the political right and that they turned instead to provide leadership to the proletarian left.

The mobility of castes and the circulation of elites are not simply the results of long-term social changes. In times of general social disorganization produced by civil unrest or natural disasters and in times of war, these processes greatly accelerate. For example, Wolfram Eberhard (1966) reports that high rates of upward and downward mobility occurred in China following the Mongol conquests and during periods of civil war and famine. Ho Ping-ti (1962) showed that there was much upward mobility during the early years of the Ming dynasty (1368–1644) when many persons moved up through banditry and rebellion and many established families were evicted from the elite. In fact, Ho Ping-ti's study showed that periods of considerable fluidity lasted for some years following the establishment of new dynasties in China. Obviously, this has been the case in the aftermath of many wars and virtually all revolutions: A change in who holds power is often the reason why wars and revolutions are conducted.

Youth Counterculture in American Society

To conclude this discussion of group mobility something must be said about the possible implications of American youth counter culture for upward and downward mobility in American society. Historically, we see that classes have lost their upper positions when they have become incompetent to defend their privileges. In the early 1800s, during the Regency Period in England, people of the old agrarian, landed aristocracy looked with disdain on the vulgar ambitions of the new industrial and business classes. Soon these "vulgar strivers" had taken away all their money,

land, and political power and had left the aristocrats only their empty titles and wistful remembrances of past glories (Scott, 1972). The affinity for an anti-materialistic counterculture shown by many children of privileged American families today may have similar results. As Peter and Brigitte Berger (1971) pointed out in their essay "The Blueing of America," for every middle- and upper-class young person who rejects the occupational structure, an opening is created for some poor or minority young person with ambition to move up.

Thus, the Bergers argue, "Marx may, in a paradoxical manner, be proven right in the end." The sons and daughters of the proletariat may well be coming into power as a result of a class struggle based on cultural styles. The most important positions in society seem to require the traditional virtues that the counterculture rejects—"discipline, achievement orientation, and also a measure of freedom from gnawing self-doubt." Thus, to the extent that middle- and upper-class young people lack these virtues, the powerful positions in society will go to ambitious lower-class young people who have not embraced the counterculture. If this happens it would hardly be the first time in history that engrossment in the beautiful things of life has marked the decline of a powerful class.

SUGGESTED READINGS

Baltzell, E. Digby. *The Protestant Establishment: Aristocracy and Caste in America*. New York: Random House, 1964.

Blau, Peter M., and Otis Dudley Duncan. *The American Occupational Structure*. New York: Wiley, 1967.

Lipset, Seymour Martin, and Reinhard Bendix. *Social Mobility in Industrial Society*. Berkeley: University of California Press, 1958.

Chapter 14 Consequences of Inequality

COMPETENT SURVEY-RESEARCH interviewers today always assess each respondent's social class—usually by asking about occupation, education, and income. A person's social class has been found to be crucial for understanding his behavior. The same is true at the macro level of analysis. Social inequalities are critical for understanding how societies change, hold together, or break down. Virtually everywhere sociologists have looked, they have found evidence of the potent, far-reaching consequences of social stratification. This chapter summarizes some of the more important consequences of social inequalities, both for the individual and for society as a whole.

INDIVIDUAL CONSEQUENCES

A person's position in the stratification system has been found to affect an extremely long list of individual beliefs, preferences, and behaviors. The following are among the most interesting and important findings.

Life Style

Obviously, the rich and the poor do not live alike. But what is not so obvious is that many of the ways in which they live differently cannot be attributed directly to income differences. Often enough the rich and the poor exhibit quite different preferences that do not seem to be based on money. It is not clear whether these preferences reflect real cultural differences or indirectly reflect income differences that operate to produce differences in education and diversity of experience. Whatever their initial source, the differences are no less real.

The editors of *Society Today* found a number of recurrent life-style differences between blue-collar and white-collar families by looking through the large accumulation of national survey studies conducted by such major organizations as Gallup, Harris, the National Opinion Research Center, and others, which are on public file in the International Data Library and Reference Service, Survey Research Center, University of California, Berkeley. Among these differences are that blue-collar families watch much more television and read many fewer books than do white-

collar families. They also subscribe to fewer magazines. They are much less likely to belong to any clubs or organizations and are poorer attenders when they do belong. Blue-collar men are more inclined to like baseball and to attend games but are less likely than white-collar men to enjoy or attend football games. They are more likely to drink beer, less likely to drink scotch or gin. They are more likely to smoke cigarettes, less likely to smoke marijuana. Blue-collar families entertain their friends less often and entertain their relatives more often. They are less likely to go to movies, plays, and concerts and are more likely to go bowling, fishing, or out for a ride. They more often play cards, except bridge, which is a predominantly upper-middle-class game. Ever since Kinsey, studies have shown that blue-collar couples have sexual relations less frequently and with less success. They have a higher divorce rate (see Chapter 18); they are less likely to feel that they are very happy (see Chapter 12). Not surprisingly, some of their unhappiness is related directly to their jobs (see Chapter 22).

Blue-collar and white-collar life-style differences do not exhaust the class contrasts to be found in the United States. As C. Wright Mills (1956) and others have pointed out, the upper classes are quite different from everyone else. It is not simply that they have a great deal more money and consequently have fine houses, servants, and expensive possessions; there are also very marked differences in manners, speech, and dress between the upper class and the rest of society—although often these differences are so subtle that they go unnoticed by everyone except the upper class. As is the case with the European upper classes, many of these subtle life-style traits of the American upper classes stem from the influence of exclusive schools and clubs. A characteristic difference can be found in language usage. Pronunciation differences are not as class-related in the United States as they are in England; the major difference in this country is in vocabulary choice. Surprising as it might be to most Americans, the upper class is more plain spoken than are the middle and lower-middle classes. They speak in a more straightforward, less pretentious way and use fewer euphemisms. As Clifton Fadiman (1956) and others have noted, upper-class useage prefers "begin" to "commence," "sweat" to "perspire," "died" to "passed away," "kin" to "relative." When an airline stewardess asks, "Would you like to purchase a cocktail?" she reflects middle-class standards of good usage. An upper-class person would say instead, "Would you like to buy a drink?" Upper-class people seem more casual in their dress. Often their clothing seems a bit old, but to the trained eye it is better cut—it is very quietly expensive. The rich are more likely to have fur linings in cloth coats than cloth linings in fur coats. The true upper-class person's name is also less likely to appear in the newspapers —especially in the society section—than is the name of the slightly less than upper-class person.

Crime and Delinquency

It was pointed out in Chapter 11 that the lower a person's social class, the more likely he is to commit a crime. A variety of reasons were considered. For a long time it also was assumed that juvenile crime—delinquency—was concentrated among the poor and the socially deprived. However, a series of empirical studies culminating in the recent research of Travis Hirschi (1969) found *no* association between the social status of the family and the delinquency of children. After pursuing the matter further, Hirschi discovered that in fact social inequalities do result in a greater propensity to commit delinquent acts; however, it is not the status of the family, but that of the child, that counts.

At first glance, it may seem odd to speak of teenagers as having a class position independent of that of their families. After all, their wealth is almost wholly dependent on their fathers' wealth. Nevertheless, by their early teens most people have already established a career line that is rapidly solidifying. By high school, students have established an academic record and a level of learning and experience that will greatly influence the extent of their further education and training and therefore the status level they can hope one day to occupy. Relative to their fellow students, they

have already established a status position that is highly related to the status that they will hold as adults. The teenager who is compiling a poor academic record, who is not gaining educational skills, and who has a relatively low status position among his fellow students has to a considerable extent established his adult status as low. This is true regardless of how high a position his father may hold—within extreme limits, of course, for even stupid and repulsive eldest sons of kings tend to become kings, although they also tend to have a harder time becoming king and staying king than they would if they were smart and attractive.

Recognizing the fact that low status in adolescence often means low adult status, Hirschi used a variety of measures of young people's own status positions and found them powerfully negatively related to becoming delinquents. Lower-status youth, whether from high- or low-status homes, are much more likely to commit delinquent acts than are higher-status youth. Hirschi argues that this occurs because lower-status youth are much less bound to observe the law by the various mechanisms of social control, which are discussed in Chapter 11—they have less affection and respect for their parents and their friends and therefore have less need to keep their respect. Furthermore, because their status is already low, they have less to lose through acts of delinquency.

Interpersonal Violence

If one single class-related difference would seem self-evident it is that the poor are more likely to resort to physical violence than are the well-to-do. This, however, is a good example of why the obvious and self-evident must be checked against the facts.

Rodney Stark and James McEvoy (1970) tested this view on data from a national sample of Americans by the Harris Poll for the President's Commission on the Causes and Consequences of Violence. They found it to be only a false impression. As Table 14.1 shows, lower-income persons are even slightly less likely than upper-income persons to have been in fights, to approve of slapping between husbands and wives, or to have ever

Table 14.1 Interpersonal Violence and Income in the United States*

Experience of or Attitude toward Violence	Income		
	$4,999 or less	$5,000– $9,999	$10,000 or more
Has been slapped or kicked	12%	16%	14%
Has slapped or kicked another	14	19	20
Has been punched or beaten	11	13	13
Has punched or beaten another	7	16	15
Could approve of a husband slapping his wife's face	14	22	23
Could approve of a wife slapping her husband's face	18	24	24
Has spanked a child	81	85	87
Has been threatened or cut with a knife	9	8	8
Has been threatened with a gun or shot at	6	7	7
Has defended himself with a knife or gun	5	5	8

* Childhood incidents and experiences in military combat have been eliminated.

Source: Adapted from Rodney Stark and James McEvoy III, "Middle-Class Violence," *Psychology Today*, Vol. 4, No. 6 (November, 1970), p. 54.

spanked a child. (Stark and McEvoy also found that racial differences had been exaggerated.)

It is true that official statistics on murder and serious assault indicate an over-representation of the very poor. But Howard Erlanger (1971) argues that these statistics have been misinterpreted to indict the poor for being violence-prone generally. Erlanger suggests that extreme violence represents a discontinuity both in violent behavior and in the class structure. He argues that acts of extreme violence are committed primarily by persons virtually outside normal society, somewhat akin to Gerhard Lenski's "expendables" (see Chapter 12). Thus it is inaccurate to see them as simply one step below the working poor on the status ladder—they are not really on the status ladder. Furthermore, Erlanger argues that it is equally incorrect to regard violence as shading from the very to the less serious: hitting your wife is not simply less serious than killing her, it is altogether different.

Stark and McEvoy argued that the stereotype of the poor as more violent is based on the relative invisibility of middle- and upper-class violence, which occurs in private homes rather than in thin-walled tenements and in clubs rather than in public taverns; it is dealt with by psychiatrists, mar-

riage counselors, divorce lawyers, and clergymen rather than by the police or social workers.

Prejudice

The lower a person's social class, the more likely he is to be intolerant of people of other races and religions. Social class is the single most powerful factor uncovered by studies of prejudice (Selznick and Steinberg, 1969). Class has this effect not only among members of racial and religious majorities but also among members of *minorities*. For example, Gary Marx (1967) found that anti-white attitudes among American blacks were most widespread among the poorest blacks. Stark (1964) found anti-Protestant attitudes most widespread among working-class Catholics.

The work of Gertrude Selznick and Stephen Steinberg greatly increased our understanding of the basis of working-class prejudice. They found that the principal factor is not income or occupational prestige but education. Table 14.2 shows the powerful effect of education on anti-Semitism and anti-black attitudes. Selznick and Steinberg argued that prejudice is largely based on a lack of exposure to cultural diversity—lower-class people are not only more intolerant of Jews, Catholics, and blacks, but of foreigners, people with beards,

Figure 14.1   Even though interpersonal violence is
fairly equally distributed among the social classes,
working-class violence tends to be more visible,
creating the idea that working-class people are more
violent than middle-class and upper-class people.
(*Below*) A scene of violence among middle-class
people from the film *Who's Afraid of Virginia Woolf?*

and political dissenters. Against previous theories
about working-class authoritarianism, Selznick
and Steinberg demonstrated that authoritarianism, which characterizes rigid, intolerant personalities, is probably a product of education
rather than of early childhood socialization. They
argued that intolerance of differences is the common cultural inheritance of most Americans and
that education functions to help us *unlearn* our
prejudices. The poorer people are, the less chance
they have to unlearn prejudice. They receive less
education, and they have much less exposure to
people who differ from them. Therefore, it is not
surprising that poorer people fail to develop a capacity to accept people who are different.

Politics

As Chapter 15 pointed out, in all industrialized
societies—and in many contemporary agrarian
ones as well—social inequalities are strongly
related to political behavior. The worse a person's
status or position is, the more likely he is to support political candidates, programs, and parties
that promise to reduce social inequalities—parties
to the left of center. On the other hand, the better
a person's position is, the more likely he is to support the status quo, to support conservative parties that want to maintain the stratification system
in its current form (Lipset, 1960). In nations with
a wide left-to-right political spectrum—in France,

Table 14.2   Prejudice and Education in
the United States

Prejudice	Educational Level Completed			
	Grade School	High School	Some College	College Graduate
Anti-Semitic	68%	43%	30%	17%
Antiblack	68%	49%	32%	23%

Source: Adapted from Gertrude J. Selznick and Stephen Steinberg, *The Tenacity of Prejudice* (New York: Harper & Row,
1969).

for example, where parties as far right as mon-
archists and as far left as communists compete
for support—politics are extremely class-based.
Where parties keep toward the middle of the
road, as do the Democrats and Republicans in the
United States, politics are less class-based (Lipset,
1960). Yet even in this country, poorer people are
very likely to be Democrats and wealthy people
to be Republicans—except wealthy members of
disadvantaged racial and ethnic groups, who vote
for Democrats (Campbell *et al.,* 1960). Religious
commitments may modify these tendencies, however. In both Europe and the United States, regardless of their social class, people with conservative religious views tend to vote for conservative
political candidates (Stark, 1964; Glock and Stark,
1965). Furthermore, as Samuel Stouffer (1955)
and Seymour Martin Lipset (1960) noted, the "liberalism" of working-class voters is limited to economic or bread-and-butter issues. On issues of
procedural liberalism—support for the freedoms
of the Bill of Rights, for example—the working
classes are less liberal than are the middle and
upper classes. This is reflected today by the many
union members who are demanding increasing
pay and benefits and at the same time demanding
that the government and police clamp down on
"unpatriotic" dissenters and students.

Class also affects political *participation.* Numerous survey studies have shown that blue-collar
adults are less likely to belong to political organizations, to vote, to be registered to vote, to write
letters to political officeholders, or to know who
is running for political office. Only a few months
before the 1964 election, according to the Gallup

Figure 14.2 Educational performance and social mobility are affected greatly by social-class background and home environment. During early socialization and throughout the school years, lower-class individuals, many of whom come from large families and may have to drop out of school to help support their families, may be deprived of a home environment conducive to study and of the cultural stimulation experienced by members of the middle and upper classes.

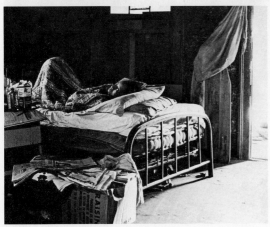

Poll, nearly half the American adult population could not correctly identify Barry Goldwater. Blue-collar voters are Democrats and are less likely to get to the polls. Thus big voter turnouts favor Democrats, and a major activity of Democratic Party workers is to get voters registered and to the polls on election day. Republicans, on the other hand, are often helped by bad weather, which holds down blue-collar voting.

Education

Chapter 13 discussed the major role of education in upward mobility, especially for white Americans. Unfortunately, the poor are handicapped by the fact that their children are much less likely to receive advanced or high-quality educations or to perform well during their school years. However, in comparison with other industrialized nations,

the children of poor Americans have extremely high educational opportunities. In many European nations now, for example, only from 5 to 10 percent of young people receive any college training. In this country about half do. In fact, a rural Southern black has a higher probability of going to college than does a white Englishman. It is such marked differences in educational opportunity that probably account for the much greater entry into elite occupations by the children of American manual workers.

Religious Commitment

Since well before the time of Christ, prophets, philosophers, and sages have claimed that the poor are especially religious because religion provides them with comforts and compensations for their worldly suffering. The Apostle Paul thought religion had little appeal for the high and the mighty and that only the "low things of this world" could enter in. Marx shared this view but spoke of religion as an "opium of the people," which perpetuated their exploitation and suppression by turning their attention from social inequalities to heavenly blessings. But there have been dissenting voices. Many have noticed that church congregations seem heavily overpopulated with the wealthy and successful and have wondered whether religion is not in fact a predominantly middle- and upper-class affair.

Recent research has confirmed both views: the poor are more religious than the rich in some ways, and the rich are more religious than the poor in other ways. Studies by Rodney Stark and Charles Glock (1968) have distinguished ways in which people typically express their religious commitment. The two main patterns are (1) religiousness that can function to provide compensations for earthly suffering and (2) religiousness that is in and of itself a form of social reward. The first variety comprises such aspects of religiousness as belief in God and the existence of rewards after death, acts of personal devotionalism such as praying, and ecstatic religious experiences. The second includes such factors as having formal church membership, holding positions of power and influence in religious organizations, and par-

Figure 14.3   Who are more religious, the rich or the poor? According to studies by Glock and Stark, the answer to this question depends on what one means by "religious." If one means belief in church dogma and principles, the poor are more religious than the rich. But if one means church membership and regular attendance, the rich are more religious. Churchgoers from an evangelical sect (*top left*) and Hasidic Jews (*bottom left*) stress commitment to religious beliefs. Both groups draw their membership primarily from the lower classes. The rich, in contrast, tend to emphasize church attendance and the maintenance of external symbols of commitment (*right*).

ticipating in worship services and in the various social and cultural activities of the churches. Stark (1972*a*) found that the poor are more religious than the rich when the first, or comforting, kind of religiousness is investigated. He also found that the rich are more religious than the poor when the second, or directly rewarding, aspects of religiousness are assessed. As in other aspects of social life, higher-status people tend to monopolize the rewards. But, perhaps having less need of them, they are not as inclined to seek the comforts of faith as are the needy poor.

Marriage and Fertility

In industrialized societies, social class is negatively related to divorce. The higher one's income, the less likely one is to become divorced. The same holds when education and occupational prestige are used as class measures. (The most notable ex-

ception is that among American blacks, the higher the education, the higher the divorce rate.) Generally, it is among the poor, not among the rich, that marriages are most unstable (Goode, 1962). In fact, the divorce rate is only one of many signs of less satisfactory family life among the poor. It was pointed out earlier that the poor have more sexual incompatibility. A blue-collar worker is also less likely than a white-collar worker to report warm or effective communications with his spouse (Komarovsky, 1964).

As is considered in greater detail in Chapter 23, the poor marry younger and have more children. However, class-based fertility differences have done considerable shifting over time. Beginning in the 1870s and 1880s, fertility began to drop sharply in Europe and the United States. The upper classes led this decline, and fertility differences between the classes increased rapidly. But

Figure 14.4   Poor people have greater nutritional deficiencies than do people in higher socioeconomic classes. Nutritional deficiencies and substandard living conditions among the poor not only contribute to higher rates of infant mortality and to a higher death rate than among upper-class people but also add to the psychological stress they suffer, possibly accounting for the higher incidences of mental illness among them.

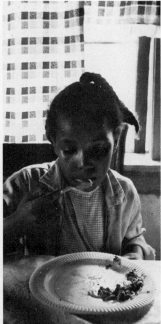

by around 1910, the fertility decline began to appear in the working classes as well, thus somewhat reducing the fertility differences between classes.

This pattern continued for the next three decades. After World War II, however, came the "baby boom." Fertility rose very rapidly among all social classes in Europe and the United States. This produced a slight decrease in class fertility differences (Wrong, 1958). Since the baby boom, the birth rate has been sharply declining again in industrialized nations. However, noticeable class differences in fertility have persisted.

Health and Mental Health

We reported in Chapter 12 that the poor have a higher death rate than do the rich. Chapter 13 pointed out that there are also differences in infant mortality between the rich and the poor. However, surprising as it may seem, social class no longer appears to be related to the incidence of ill health and disease in industrial societies.

Until recently a person's health was greatly affected by his social class. In fact, disease is still more prevalent among the lower classes of agrarian societies and societies that are in early stages of industrialization. This relationship no longer seems to hold in advanced industrialized societies such as the United States (Kadushin, 1964). In these countries, studies of the incidence of illness find only trivial and inconsistent relationships between disease and income, occupation, or education. The disappearance of social-class effects upon illness seems due to the upward movement of the whole economic level of industrialized nations. The poorest have been raised to standards of nutrition, sanitation, and housing that are sufficient to reduce disease, and public health immunization and disease prevention efforts seem to have reached all classes. For example, studies used to find that quality of housing was related to disease. They no longer find such a relationship in the United States (Kadushin, 1964). Similarly, a study conducted during the Depression in 1935 and 1936 found that the very poorest—those on relief or those earning less than $1500 a year—had higher rates of serious illness than did the rest of the population but that above this level there was no income effect. Today, no meaningful relationship between income and illness turns up in studies (Kadushin, 1964).

Although low social class does not seem to lead to illness, it does lead to a greater fear of illness and to much higher rates of taking sick leave from work. Charles Kadushin (1964) suggests that the greater fear of illness may stem from less understanding of disease and greater reluctance to go to the doctor. Absenteeism may stem from two factors: less job satisfaction and less responsibility on the job. In some instances illness and injuries may prohibit the performance of manual work but not interfere with white-collar tasks; for example, a broken leg would sideline a carpenter but not an architect.

If changes in industrialized societies have removed physical illness from the class-related list, the same has not occurred with mental illness. Varieties of studies have found that mental health increases with income, education, and occupational prestige (Srole *et al.,* 1962).

In the famous Midtown Manhattan Study, it was estimated that 12.5 percent of people in the upper-status level had symptoms of fairly marked psychological impairment but that 47.3 percent of those in the lowest status level had these serious symptoms. Similarly, 30 percent of the upper-status group were classified as wholly well psychologically, but only 4.6 percent of those at the lowest status level were judged wholly well. Upper-status persons were almost three times as apt to be wholly psychologically well as they were to be seriously impaired. Lower-status persons were ten times as likely to be seriously impaired as they were to be wholly well (Srole *et al.,* 1962).

It appears that industrialized societies have found the means to take much of the physical suffering out of inequalities, but they have not found the means to remove the mental anguish.

SOCIETAL CONSEQUENCES: CLASS CONFLICT

For Karl Marx, the key to history was class conflict. As technology and economic organization change, new classes are created, and their chal-

lenge to the established classes leads to progress: New classes rise, casting old classes into history and cleansing society of its old ways while establishing the new. Because Marx focused much of his analysis on technological change and increased productive capacity, his model of history fits reasonably well with the evolution or succession of types of societies discussed in Chapter 12; however, whether class struggle was the central feature of this evolutionary progress has been subject to dispute. As Chapter 4 pointed out, all modern social theorists agree with Marx that class conflict is a dynamic element in social life. But some, the functionalists, for example, give less primacy to conflict and instead stress the mutual interests that bind various classes together. Both views will be treated at length in Chapter 15.

In this section we will examine the changing role of class conflicts in industrialized societies in order to understand the consequences of inequalities for societies as a whole. First, we will review Marx's theory of the revolution of the proletariat in industrial nations and consider some reasons why such revolutions have not occurred. Then we will consider impediments to the development of strong class consciousness, and therefore of sharp class conflict, in industrialized nations. Finally, we will review some modern theories about the conditions under which marked class conflict and revolution may occur.

Marx and Perlman

In Marx's model of capitalist society, the property-owning upper class (the bourgeoisie) and the propertyless working class (the proletariat) are locked in an *inevitable* and *unceasing* struggle for power and the fruits of productivity. Their interests are wholly antithetical. In the beginning the bourgeoisie successfully exploit the proletariat, but ultimately the bourgeoisie will disappear because history is on the side of the proletariat.

At the time Marx wrote, the conflict between capitalists and labor was bitter, especially in Europe, and the degree of exploitation of the proletariat was great, perhaps increasingly so. Marx projected these trends into the future. He also predicted an unyielding selfishness on the part of the bourgeoisie and a wholly unregulated capitalist economy. From these assumptions a number of predictions seemed to follow: Unfettered capitalism would inevitably lead to overproduction and hence to high unemployment. This would sharpen class antagonism and class consciousness. Ultimately, capitalism would lead to the overthrow of the bourgeoisie by the proletariat, who would then take the means of production into their own hands and fashion a more equitable socialist state. It was this analysis—that the forces for revolution were inherent in capitalism—that led Marx to call revolution inevitable and to say that the capitalist system carried within itself the seeds of its own destruction.

Despite all the antagonism to Marxism in current political discourse, there are virtually no economists or political theorists who do not admire the lucidity and creative genius of Marx's theory. However, there is considerable dispute among these scholars about the adequacy of Marx's theory. The problem with Marx's theory is that revolutions did not occur when and where predicted; what has actually happened as capitalist societies have matured is different in some ways from what Marx anticipated. For example, class conflict and class consciousness have diminished, not increased, in industrial societies since Marx's day, and capitalist economies have become highly regulated to guard against wild swings in unemployment and against the unlimited exploitation of labor.

Writing in the 1920s, the economic historian Selig Perlman (1923) tried to explain why the revolutions Marx had predicted in industrial societies had not occurred. He concluded that Marx had failed to foresee the role of labor unions for making social reform rather than for making revolution. Perlman observed that although American workers organized into unions and sought to improve their wages, working conditions, and job security, they refused to back political radicalism. Perlman rejected Marx's assumption that ownership or nonownership of the means of production was the key to class struggle or the key for understanding the desires and actions of industrial workers. He argued that workers were concerned

Figure 14.5   With the development of labor unions, workers gained the legal right to organize and bargain collectively. Their exercise of this right contributed to the enactment of legislation concerning minimum wages, maximum hours, and decent working conditions—and to the abolition of the kinds of office rules shown below.

PROPRIETOR ZACHARY U. GEIGER
18   72

1. OFFICE EMPLOYEES will **DAILY** sweep the *floors*, dust the *furniture, shelves,* and *show cases.*

2. EACH DAY fill *lamps*, clean *chimneys*, and trim *wicks*. **WASH THE WINDOWS ONCE A WEEK.**

3. Each clerk will bring in a *bucket of water* and *scuttle of coal* for the day's business.

4. MAKE YOUR PENS CAREFULLY. You may whittle your nibs to your individual taste.

5. This office will open at 7 A.M. and close at 8 P.M. daily except on the **SABBATH**, on which day it will remain closed. Each employee is expected to spend the SABBATH by attending CHURCH and contributing liberally to the cause of the **LORD.**

6. MEN employees will be given an evening off each week for *courting purposes*, or two *evenings* a week if they go *regularly* to CHURCH.

7. After an employee has spent 13 hours of labor in the office, he should spend the time reading the **BIBLE** and other good books while *contemplating* the *glories* and building up of the **KINGDOM.**

8. EVERY EMPLOYEE should lay aside from each pay a *goodly sum* of his earnings for his benefit during his declining years, so that he will not become a *burden* upon the charity of his betters.

9. ANY EMPLOYEE who *smokes* Spanish cigars, uses *liquor* in any form, gets shaved at a *barber shop*, or frequents *pool* and *public halls*, will give me good reason to suspect his **WORTH, INTENTIONS, INTEGRITY,** and **HONESTY.**

10. The employee who has performed his labours FAITHFULLY and WITHOUT FAULT for a period of *five years* in my service and who has been THRIFTY and attentive to his RELIGIOUS DUTIES, is looked upon by his fellowmen as a SUBSTANTIAL and law abiding CITIZEN, will be given an increase of *five cents per day* in his pay, providing a just return in profits from the business permits it.

BE WORTHY OF YOUR HIRE

primarily with the conditions for marketing their labor and that they were motivated by the desire to maximize their personal gain from their labor; they could succeed in gaining more through effective unions. According to Perlman, as unions flourished they led not to greater class consciousness and an organized base for revolution but to concessions to labor and to a reduction in class conflict and class consciousness. Because unions monopolized the labor supply in industries they organized, they could extract better wages, hours, work rules, job security, and benefits, the costs for which were in turn passed on to customers, thus leading to considerable redistribution of wealth. As a result, the antagonism of labor would decrease, Perlman predicted, and the working class would tend more and more to concentrate on concrete economic issues, not on far-reaching social reorganization. The result would be greater equity in the operation of capitalist systems and would certainly not be the revolutionary changes foreseen by Marx. Furthermore, Perlman argued, the relatively high rate of social mobility in industrialized societies would cause workers to be unwilling to see themselves as *permanently* locked into the proletariat; the desire to be upwardly mobile would make them less class conscious. Thus, for Marx, class consciousness, class struggle, and ultimately the proletarian revolution were inevitable; for Perlman, they were highly unlikely.

However, there are some grounds, taken up again in Chapter 29, for thinking that Marx may have come closer to the truth than examination of industrialized societies alone would lead us to believe. Present-day Marxists argue that the reduction of inequalities and thus of class conflict in industrialized nations has been at the expense of the less industrialized and agrarian nations of the Third World. In this view, nations such as the United States have been replacing an *internal* proletariat with one that is *external*, and the contradictions inherent in capitalism have changed from a national to an international stage. Seen in this light, one would seek to understand the relationship between industrialized and nonindustrialized nations in terms of exploitation, repression, and international class conflict. It would follow, if

these arguments are true, that the revolutions predicted by Marx have not been thwarted but have been simply delayed.

Impediments to Class Consciousness and Conflict

We have seen that the major disagreement between Marx and Perlman is over whether or not workers in capitalist societies develop a strong sense of class consciousness and consequently strong class antagonisms. Generally speaking, Perlman seems to have been right. Modern industrialized capitalist societies seem best characterized as having relatively muted class conflicts and vague class consciousness. We will discuss a number of factors that seem responsible for this blunting of class consciousness and conflict.

Income Overlap and Diversity   In the spring of 1972, members of the steamfitters and other craft unions struck for higher wages at the University of California in Berkeley. At the time of the strike, journeyman members of these unions earned more money than the majority of faculty members—a faculty that has been rated as the finest in the country (Cartter, 1966). This is a striking example of a major barrier to class consciousness —in Marxist terms—in modern industrial nations. Many relatively low-prestige jobs that require manual labor pay better than do many higher-prestige white-collar jobs.

Today, white-collar and blue-collar salaries actually overlap to a considerable extent. In fact, many small capitalists—for example, owners of small plants, farms, and businesses—earn much less than do many who do not own the means of production but who only sell their labor. For example, many corporation executives earn huge salaries but own no part of their company. And many small grocery store owners earn less than do the truckdrivers who deliver their merchandise. These extreme pay overlaps in industrialized nations tend to obscure the line between owners and workers; the terms "owner" and "worker" are no longer synonymous with "rich" and "poor." Indeed, when one looks at unionized industries, it may be the case that managers earn more than workers, but it is also the case that they normally work far longer hours, under much greater pressure, with much less job security, and without protective work rules. Thus the proletariat contains considerable economic diversity, as does the bourgeoisie, and the two classes overlap considerably. This greatly modifies the economic base for developing class consciousness.

Large status and wage differentials within the working class make it difficult for workers to see themselves in a common situation and to band together behind a class-based ideology. Similarly, as the conflicts between small businessmen and large corporations demonstrate, it is difficult for the bourgeoisie to overcome their large internal status and income differentials to discover substantial mutual interests.

Geographic Political Representation Ordinarily, parliamentary and representative political systems are based on territorial rather than on occupational or strictly party representation. Therefore, elected officials usually are forced to represent the conflicting interests of several classes and a number of special interest groups; rarely does an official represent one group to the exclusion of all others because his district seldom is entirely controlled by a single group. To a greater or lesser degree, most elected representatives try to balance the claims of competing classes and interest groups and to appeal to all classes and groups. Parliamentary and representative systems therefore mute the degree to which naked class interests can surface for direct political confrontation. As the election of 1964 demonstrated, successful politics is coalition politics.

Cross Pressures Marxist writers have often treated economic facts as the real facts and all else as "superstructure." Perhaps. But it would have been hard to convince a wealthy American Catholic that his "real" interests lay with Richard Nixon in 1960 rather than with John F. Kennedy.

Industrial societies are characterized by considerable ethnic and religious diversity and by a wide range of other multiple group affiliations. Many of these crosscut social class and greatly

Figure 14.6 An Irish-American Catholic factory worker and war veteran does not know which candidate to vote for—Catholic Democrat Adams or Protestant Republican O'Brien. The voter is cross-pressured by his own conflicting ethnic, religious, political, and class affiliations. He agrees with O'Brien's positions on four of the issues and with Adams' positions on the remaining four. Voters whose group affiliations conflict typically find it hard to choose between candidates whose positions on issues mainly follow traditional party lines.

	Republican Candidate O'Brien (Protestant)	Democratic Candidate Adams (Catholic)
Aid to Parochial Schools	Against	For°
Legalized Abortion	Against°	For
Abolish Draft	Against°	For
Tax Corporations	Against	For°
School Busing	Against°	For
Raise Social Security Benefits	Against	For°
Raise Welfare Benefits	Against°	For
More Funds for Public Transportation	Against	For°

°The Voter's Issue Preferences

press against simple class-based decisions. Thus, a man may be a member of a militant union, which presses him toward class consciousness, but also be a Polish Catholic war veteran, all of which push him toward defining himself in terms of other commitments. The many roles—aside from the economic—that people typically hold in industrial societies work to militate against a simple class consciousness. Political decisions are seldom clearcut. Consider an Irish Catholic factory worker and war veteran faced with the candidates displayed in Figure 14.6.

On the issues the candidates are tied four to four. On ethnicity and religion they cancel out. Voters are often enough cross-pressured to this extent. Their decision then probably hinges on whether some of these issues are more important to them than others, or on traditional party loyalties, or on the personal charm of the candidates.

Perhaps the most serious cross-pressures in American society stem from racial and ethnic splits that crosscut class lines. Friedrich Engels, Marx's collaborator, looked at the American labor movement, as it developed after the Civil War, and noted that manual workers were split into a variety of different nationality groups literally speaking different languages. When workers cannot even understand one another it is difficult for

Figure 14.7   It is difficult for class consciousness to develop among working-class people in countries like the United States, where many workers make as much money as people with higher-status occupations—and sometimes considerably more.

them to develop any class solidarity. Engels recognized that it would be impossible at that time to unite the Irish Molly McGuires of eastern Pennsylvania, the black coal miners of southeastern Ohio, the German radicals of Chicago, and the Italian anarchists of New York and Boston. After a hundred years, these language divisions have largely vanished. But in their place are barriers of mutual antagonism between white and minority workers. Historically, the economic exploitation of blacks has been a source of conflict with white workers— blacks have been exploited as scabs and strikebreakers and have been used to hold manual wages down, especially in the South. Conversely, whites often have excluded blacks from their unions, especially from the more elite craft and construction unions. Consequently, blacks and other racial minorities have turned to bloc politics—politics based on group rather than class affiliation. Their demands for social justice impinge most directly on the white workers; it is their jobs, neighborhoods, and schools that blacks are entering. The support that white workers have given to George Wallace reflects not only their usual class antagonisms toward government but their antagonism toward blacks. As a result, the development of class consciousness among workers flounders on racial and ethnic conflicts within the working class itself.

Common Values and Allegiances   We have seen that the multiple roles that members of industrialized societies play often crosscut class lines. Individuals also play roles that are common to *all* members of a society and tend to hold values that all share. One of the most severe disappointments to socialist hopes came at the start of World War I. During the prewar years, the confederations of European socialist workers' parties and trade unions had denounced capitalist wars and had pledged to oppose sacrificing the blood of the proletariat for the gain of the bosses. It seemed obvious that the class interests of the proletariat were international. But when war came, it turned out that the overwhelming majority of workers had far stronger nationalistic than class ties. Workers saw themselves as German, or French, or English first and as workers only secondarily. So they marched. Similarly, during World War II, workers in the United States and Great Britain put the interests of the nation first and agreed not to strike. All members of industrial nations are citizens whatever else they are. And citizenship has proved to be a strong common allegiance that muffles class divisions.

A number of sociologists have also stressed the extent to which people in modern societies are committed to common sets of values such as democracy, due process, religion, and the like (Lipset, 1960; Bellah, 1968). Although the idea of *value consensus* undoubtedly has been carried too far by many sociologists, it nonetheless plays a significant role in reducing class conflicts. Approximately 95 percent of American people say they believe in God. Although there is considerable variation in the kind of God they believe in and in the strength of this belief (Glock and Stark, 1965), the general consensus provides a basis for appeals to unity in the name of religious values.

In similar fashion, regional and local commitments serve to unify people across class lines, as in the appeal to "my fellow Texans. . . ." Perhaps one of the most neglected sources of community solidarity across class lines is local sports teams.

When the home team is playing, one hears in public places a great deal of concerned conversation and communication across class and ethnic lines.

Common Consumerism   At the end of his life some twenty years ago H. L. Mencken derided life-style changes among printers: "They tell me they now play golf in checkered trousers. In my day printers spent their time in saloons, where they belonged." We noted earlier in the chapter the differences in upper- and lower-class life styles. Nevertheless, today the influence of the mass media and the rise in general affluence has resulted in consumption tastes that often crosscut class lines. This makes it harder for any one group to see itself as excluded from and subordinate to another. Class membership cannot readily be inferred from clothing, automobiles, or leisure-time activities. Especially in the Far West, it is difficult to tell factory owners from factory workers after work; they all wear casual sports clothing of about the same style.

The change in workers' clothing reflects some tendency toward conspicuous consumption on their part; meanwhile the rich have become circumspect underconsumers. Peter Blau and Otis Duncan (1967) say that working classes use consumer goods as a very visible status symbol and that it may be precisely in order to reject workers' claims to equal status that the rich have stopped driving Cadillacs and wearing fur coats. Whatever the case, it is hard to sustain militant class consciousness among working men who drive expensive cars, own a few shares of General Motors, and are planning where they will go for their annual hunting vacation.

Mobility   As was pointed out in Chapter 13, industrialized nations are characterized by relatively higher rates of social mobility, and status is determined much more by achievement than by ascription criteria. These factors work against class consciousness because they make class membership *impermanent*. A manual worker need not assume that his son will also be a manual worker because a great many sons of manual workers do rise into higher-status occupations.

Figure 14.8   Common values and allegiances often cut across class lines. This man considers himself an American first, a working man second.

Reinhard Bendix and S. M. Lipset (1958) say that the openness of their sons' futures also convinces workers that the reward system is fair—that people get the rewards they deserve and that *the individual, not the system,* is responsible for his fate. Class consciousness is never built on conceptions of individual merit—it requires instead an awareness of a common group situation and a belief that the system is responsible for the unequal circumstances in which the group finds itself. High rates of mobility therefore challenge the premises of class consciousness and emphasize the fairness of the system. We must grant that a pure meritocracy—a society in which status is given only on the basis of individual merit—remains stratified. The stratification, however, is not permanent intergenerationally; you can hope your children will be more talented than you are. Furthermore, it is hard to blame a merit system for your personal fate. Perhaps the clearest example of a meritocracy is sports. A five-foot eight-inch office worker may forever be saddened that Wilt Chamberlain, not he, is the center for the Los Angeles Lakers. But he must blame his failure to be a Laker not on an unfair stratification system but on the fact that the top of his head is seventeen-and-a-half inches too close to the floor.

Class Conflict and Revolution

How much inequality can societies sustain before they are torn apart by class conflict and revolution? Recalling agrarian societies, we are aware

Figure 14.9.1 Davies' J-Curve theory of revolutions applied to the French Revolution of 1789. Following continued economic growth from the beginning of the eighteenth century, a severe fiscal crisis in the 1780s helped create the conditions for revolution: the rising expectations of the French people could not be met by the faltering economy. The revolution broke out in July, 1789.

(From J. C. Davies, 1969.)

Figure 14.9.2 Davies' J-Curve theory of revolutions states that during periods of improved conditions, people's expectations about the future rise. Although there may be a slight gap between what people want and what they can get, they consider the disparity tolerable.

If there is a setback in the actual satisfaction of their needs without a corresponding reduction in their expectations, according to Davies, a revolution is likely to occur.

(From J. C. Davies, 1969.)

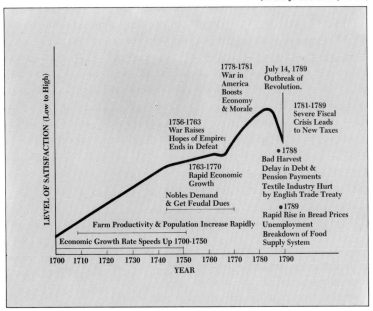

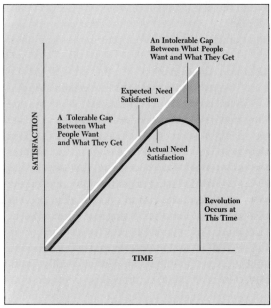

that societies can sustain enormous inequalities and remain entirely stable and tranquil.

It is not the absolute amount of inequality that produces class conflict. Instead it is *change*, especially rapid change, *in the amount of inequality* that produces internal strain on societies.

Relative Deprivation A critical concept for understanding how such changes in the degree of inequality produce strain is *relative deprivation.* This concept was developed by the sociologist Samuel Stouffer and his colleagues (1949) to account for the fact that soldiers in units where promotion was frequent and rapid tended to be more dissatisfied about promotion procedures and more impatient for their own promotions than were soldiers in units where promotion was slow and infrequent. Common sense would argue that the reverse should have been the case. As Stouffer pointed out, however, men awaiting promotion in units with rapid promotion felt more deprived relative to their comrades and relative to their own expectations for promotion than did soldiers whose comrades were not promoted frequently and who therefore had little expectation of being promoted anytime soon. Thus, it was not the *absolute* amount of deprivation but the *relative*

amount (the gap between expectations and actualities) that mattered.

Revolution of Rising Expectations The same process occurs in what is called the *revolution of rising expectations* in developing nations. When the situation of the lower classes begins to improve as agrarian economies enter the earliest phases of industrialization, it happens that their aspirations for a better life rise more rapidly than does the economy's capacity to satisfy them. Antagonism and dissatisfaction develop as the gap opens between what people hope for and what they have. In agrarian societies people expect little because they have no grounds to hope for much; therefore, they are not very dissatisfied. But when change gives people a reason for hope, their hopes for a better life soar more rapidly than do their prospects.

Davies' J-Curve Theory Modern sociological theories of revolution place major emphasis on relative deprivation and on the revolution of rising expectations. Much of the political unrest in developing nations is seen as a consequence not of simple deprivation but of the rapid improvement of the lot of the average man. The most potentially revolutionary situation occurs with economic setbacks.

James C. Davies (1969) has produced a formal theory of revolutions based on economic setbacks. He calls it the J-Curve theory. Davies' depiction of his model is shown in Figure 14.9.1. The line showing "Actual Need Satisfaction" takes the form of a "J" slanted face down: Davies predicts that revolutions are most likely to occur when "a prolonged period of rising expectations and rising gratifications is followed by a short period of sharp reversal, during which the gap between expectations and gratifications quickly widens and becomes intolerable." Davies argues, as did Marx, that revolutions depend in part on the state of mind of groups of people within societies—that groups must develop class consciousness. This happens, according to the J-Curve theory, when people fear not simply that things will no longer continue to get better but that they will actually get worse, that is, when they see the gap between what they want and what they get opening rapidly. Davies has analyzed a number of historic revolutions, including the French Revolution (see Figure 14.9.2) and the rise of the Nazis in Germany. Each case seems to fit the J-Curve. Revolution came when an upward trend in conditions suddenly reversed.

The J-Curve is not a complete theory of revolution, however. As Davies himself acknowledges, it does not predict when or why economic setbacks occur; it only says what will happen when they do occur. Furthermore, such setbacks may be necessary, but not sufficient, for revolutions to occur; that is, such economic setbacks do not always result in revolutions. The Depression led to the Nazi revolution in Germany but not to any revolution in Great Britain or the United States. It is true, however, that working-class consciousness and militancy did increase quite strikingly in all industrialized countries during the Depression. Even modest business recessions usually result in American workers' voting much more solidly for the Democratic Party than they do in times of prosperity.

Clearly, then, the amount of class conflict present in a society depends in part on the speed and direction of changes in the economic conditions of the average worker. When conditions are bad and unchanging there is little class conflict. When they are improving there is more class conflict. When they change for the worse after a period of improvement, class conflict is highest.

Other Factors Just how severe class conflict will become during such periods and whether revolution will result depends upon a great many factors that we do not yet fully understand. One critical factor during such periods is whether a sophisticated leadership offering a revolutionary program is present to galvanize and channel class conflict. In Chapter 13 the theory of status inconsistency was used to explain some elites' disaffection and willingness to cast their lot with that of workers. Revolutions are more likely to occur when the form of a society's elite is like a closed caste that resists entry by new groups. Castelike elites are most typical of societies in the very early stages of industrialization when they are still partly agrarian in their status arrangements. Historically, these societies have been prone to revolutions: Czarist Russia, China, Latin America.

Obviously sociologists learned much from Marx about the revolutionary potential of class conflict. It is equally obvious that they have learned much about these same matters since Marx lived and wrote. Despite the increase in our knowledge of when and why revolutions occur, it is evident we need to know a good deal more. Revolutions still occur when not expected and fail to take place when they are.

SUGGESTED READINGS

Berger, Peter L., and Brigitte Berger. "The Blueing of America," *New Republic*, 164 (April 3, 1971), 20–23.

Davies, James C. "The J-Curve of Rising and Declining Satisfactions as a Cause of Some Great Revolutions and a Contained Rebellion," in Hugh Davis Graham and Ted Robert Gurr (eds.), *Violence in America: Historical and Comparative Perspectives*. New York: Bantam, 1969, 690–730.

Mills, C. Wright. *The Power Elite*. New York: Oxford University Press, 1956.

Thielbar, Gerald W., and Saul D. Feldman (eds.). *Issues in Social Inequality*. Boston: Little, Brown, 1972.

Chapter 15 Is Inequality Necessary?

NO ONE HAS EVER managed to create an unstratified society. Even in the smallest utopian communities there have always existed differences in power and prestige and usually in property as well. Because of the universality of inequality in human societies, a number of theorists have suggested that some degree of stratification is inevitable, that stratification would not be universal unless it played some vital role in human social organization. From this it follows not only that there has never been an unstratified human society but that there can never be one.

Other theorists, distressed by the consequences of inequality, have argued that unstratified societies would be possible if sufficient effort were made to resocialize people into new character patterns—to replace individualism with a cooperative ethic. Whether all persons can be equal in terms of power, property, and prestige has been debated throughout history among intellectuals, and the hope for equality has given rise to countless wars, rebellions, riots, and revolutions.

In this chapter we will review the sociological theories that are rooted in this ancient controversy. The two most influential positions are the *functionalist* and the *conflict-theory* perspectives, which were outlined in Chapter 4. Recently a third position has emerged, which unites the key elements of both positions and seeks a resolution to the debate. All three positions on whether a society free from all inequalities is possible will be considered. In summarizing this debate, we have to gloss over considerable disagreement *within* each of these general viewpoints. In order to communicate the issues most effectively, sometimes the participants must be treated a bit unfairly. In particular, contemporary conflict theorists are somewhat misrepresented in what follows. Today most of them do not argue that an unstratified society is possible, although some continue to do so. In fact, Marx himself usually did not claim that an unstratified society was possible. However, to best understand the present position of conflict theorists, it is important first to see the position from which they have moved. Similarly, most functionalists now admit the importance of the

insights of conflict theory. But we are getting ahead of the story.

FUNCTIONALISTS: YES

Explanations of social stratification that today are called functionalist are at least partly derived from a conservative tradition of accounting for the distribution of scarce values: Who gets what? Why and how do they get it? What are the consequences? This line of analysis appears in very ancient religious writings. The common element is the judgment that stratification is in the very nature of things. In ancient times stratification was thought to be God-given—to be inherent in the way God created the world. Thus, men were created in different classes and with different destinies. Some were to lead, others to follow; some were to own, others to serve. Yet even in arguments holding that stratification is divinely ordained, it is clear that it is so ordained because stratification is good for societies as a whole. The argument is that each must play his assigned role in order for societies to survive or prosper.

The Influence of Darwinism

The rise of Social Darwinism in the latter part of the nineteenth century brought new justification to the old argument about the importance of social stratification. Darwin argued that natural selection based on survival of the fittest was the mechanism whereby life rose from the slime and man evolved from the apes. Stratification was thus seen both as a consequence of biology—classes and races were dominant because they were biologically superior—and as necessary to maintain the evolutionary process. Because the poor were the least biologically fit, it followed that to artificially increase their chances for survival and reproduction would sap the human race. Further evolution depended upon the fittest of each generation having a greater chance for survival.

One of the major sociological figures among Social Darwinists was William Graham Sumner

Figure 15.1 Social Darwinism, the application of Darwin's theory of evolution to social and economic structures, views laissez-faire economics and competition as natural processes. Survival of the fittest, accordingly, must apply to social change just as it applies to the evolution of biological species. Viewed from this perspective, Cornelius Vanderbilt's railroad monopoly, which overran smaller competitors, was seen as a natural expression of survival of the fittest.

(1840–1910). His book *Folkways* was extremely influential in the early development of American sociology; in it he viewed society as an arena in which men struggle for survival and advantage. Sumner argued that the class system measured the social worth of people—that to know a person's class was to know how talented he was. He admitted that once in a while luck could enter into who got what, but essentially he believed talent would out. The rags-to-riches stories of so many nineteenth-century American capitalists struck Sumner as proof of his views, and if the sons of successful men were disproportionately successful, that was mainly because they inherited their fathers' superior talents.

As was pointed out in Chapter 5, this application of Darwinism was extremely naive. Without cultural and social equality of opportunity, it was nonsense to speak of the most privileged as the fittest. The simple fact that the royal families of Europe had so many genetic defects, such as hemophilia, should have revealed the poverty of such arguments. (See Chapter 17.) Instead of justifying the status quo, Social Darwinism logically should have led to radical equalitarianism of opportunity and dog-eat-dog competition.

While Sumner and the Social Darwinists were active, an Italian social theorist named Gaetano Mosca (1858–1941) was developing yet another prefunctionalist argument that stratification was inevitable. In his study *The Ruling Class* Mosca laid out a devastating argument against then-current socialist arguments for the possibility of an unstratified society. Mosca's argument was based on three points: (1) Human societies cannot exist without political organization. (2) Political organization inevitably requires inequalities in power because there must be leaders. (3) Because of the self-seeking nature of man, power will always be exploited to obtain other privileges, such as economic advantages.

Mosca thus dismissed Marxists as naively utopian. Twenty years before the Russian Revolution, he predicted that if Communists ever came to power they would require political leaders—officials—and they would form a new ruling class.

The Functionalist Theory of Stratification: Davis and Moore

Following World War I a new view began to emerge in social science. It was called *functionalism* because of its basic insight: human societies have certain features because these features make positive contributions, or perform beneficial functions, for societies as systems. As pointed out in Chapter 4, functionalism sees societies as sets of interrelated parts; what goes on in one part influences other parts—for example, what happens in the family affects the economy. As functionalism developed, Talcott Parsons, a Harvard sociologist, came to play a major theoretical role. And it was one of his students, Kingsley Davis, who took the lead in formulating a functionalist theory of stratification. He argued that the need for inequality is inherent in the operational needs of societies (Davis, 1942, 1949, 1953; Davis and Moore, 1945).

Davis pointed out that efforts to explain the causes of something are not efforts to justify it. To explain why gravity causes unsuspended objects to fall to earth is not to be an apologist for gravity or an enemy of man's desire to soar off into the clouds. The discoverer of gravity may dash such hopes by his discovery without being glad about it. Davis wanted to free the debate of its historic ideological and moral commitments. He posed the question: Why is it that all known societies have been stratified?

He once summed up the answer in a sentence: "Social inequality is . . . an unconsciously evolved device by which societies insure that the most important positions are conscientiously filled by the most qualified persons" (Davis, 1949).

The first general statement of the functionalist theory of stratification was published by Davis and Wilbert E. Moore in 1945. They began with the obvious fact that societies are complex organizations made up of a great variety of roles or positions that must be filled. Any society must have some method for distributing its members among these positions. As people die, others must be put in their place and must be motivated to perform the duties of a particular position. If all positions in society were equally pleasant to fill, were

Figure 15.2.1   Kingsley Davis (*below, left*) is a native of Texas who received his doctorate from Harvard in 1936. Perhaps no contemporary sociologist has made significant contributions to so many areas of sociological concern. Besides proposing the leading functionalist theory of stratification, he has written classic papers on prostitution, feral children, and the population of ancient cities. His book *Human Society* (1949) was intended as an introductory text but has instead been studied as a major theoretical work. Above all, Davis has made major contributions to demographic transition theory (see Chapter 23) and to understanding fertility and urban growth. He is a professor at the University of California, Berkeley.

equally important for the effective functioning and survival of the society, and required the same amount of training or ability, there would probably be no real problem because it would not make much difference who went into which position. But, as Davis and Moore pointed out, in real life it makes a good deal of difference who gets into which position. The positions themselves are unequal. Davis and Moore note that some positions are naturally more enjoyable, some require special talents and skills, and some are functionally more important. It follows that positions serving important functions in the society must be filled by people who are both skilled and committed. According to Davis and Moore, a society must have rewards to use as inducements and a way to distribute these rewards according to position. "The rewards and their distribution become part of the social order, and thus give rise to stratification" (Davis and Moore, 1945). They then pointed out that prestige, power, and property are the primary rewards that nearly all societies can use as inducements.

The essential point is that many positions cannot be filled by just anyone. They require persons with special training and unusual talent. If society is to function effectively, arrangements must be made to ensure that such persons are attracted to these positions. In fact, in order to attract the best people to such positions, it is necessary to make people want them so much that they will compete for them. But how can this be accomplished? Many of society's most important positions are not intrinsically attractive. Typically, they entail unusually long periods of training, call for long and hard hours on the job, and impose considerable stress and responsibility. For example, surgeons must study for at least twelve years beyond high school in order to become competent. Their work is physically exhausting and stressful, and their hours are long and somewhat unpredictable. Furthermore, only a limited number of people possess the intelligence, the manual dexterity, and the psychological qualities required to be a good surgeon. How can we arrange that a sufficient number of persons with such characteristics want to be surgeons? Davis and Moore argued that so-

ciety can only accomplish this if the position of surgeon carries with it comparatively greater rewards than more attractive and less critical positions; the rewards have to be great enough so that people want to make the sacrifices necessary to be a surgeon.

Because positions differ in their importance and because they differ in the extent to which the ability to perform them is scarce, positions must also differ in the rewards they receive. If this is true, then it is obviously inevitable that rewards will be unequally distributed in any society—societies are stratified because that is the only way to make them work effectively. If societies were not stratified, everyone might be content to be a beachcomber, critical tasks might not be performed well, and the society might soon perish.

Davis and Moore's theory thus predicts that positions that are extremely important to the society and for which capable personnel are in *short supply* will be highly rewarded, and less important positions for which personnel are plentiful will be much less rewarded. This is certainly the case in modern industrialized societies. Those who perform unskilled tasks—tasks that anyone could do—receive little in the way of pay, power, or prestige. The most technically demanding occupations—those requiring much training or talent—receive considerable pay, power, and prestige. In fact, as occupations rise in relative importance and complexity, so do their relative rewards. In the nineteenth century, when medicine was relatively ineffectual, it was extremely easy to become a doctor, and the rewards were

Figure 15.2.2 Wilbert E. Moore (*opposite, right*) has written extensively on the topics of industrial development and social change. In 1951 he published *Industrial Relations and the Social Order* and *Industrialization and Labor*. In 1963 he published *Man, Time and Society* and *Social Change*. He is a former president of the American Sociological Association. After some years as a professor of sociology at Princeton, where he was associated with the Office of Population Research, he joined the staff of the Russell Sage Foundation.

low. As medicine became effective, it became difficult to become a doctor and the rewards became very high.

It follows from the functionalist argument that societies will be most effective (or function best) when social mobility is the result of individual merit and achievement. To the degree that ascriptive status rules are used to decide who gets which position, society is not making the most effective use of scarce talent. But many societies do utilize ascriptive rules of stratification, and this fact presented a problem for Davis and Moore's original theory: How can functionalism account for status by ascription? Davis subsequently recognized this problem and attempted to deal with it. He argued that his theory explained inequalities among *positions* in society, not among individuals.

Even though a high-caste person occupies his rank because of his parents, this fact does not explain the high evaluation of the caste's *position* in the community. The low-estate sweeper as compared with priestly classes cannot be explained by saying that the sons of sweepers become sweepers and the sons of Brahmins become Brahmins (Davis, 1949, 1953).

It is because of the positions they occupy, the roles they play in the life of societies, that different castes enjoy different levels in the stratification system, according to Davis. Admittedly, this may not guarantee that the most qualified persons play these roles. Davis would probably argue that ascriptive status rules are only possible when the complexities of even highly important positions are not great and when, with proper training (which caste membership provides), average people can fill them reasonably well. Furthermore, he could argue, it is precisely this tension between ascription and the need for scarce talent that made upward mobility possible even in highly ascriptive agrarian societies. A common route to the top was through the military, a role obviously vital to the survival of societies constantly at war. Indeed, Davis would probably argue that the great reduction in ascriptive status that has accompanied industrialization further strengthens his case: that rewards are a function of the impor-

tance of a position, and inefficient means of filling important positions will not persist because they are dysfunctional—either these means will be changed, or they will disappear because the societies that do not change them will perish.

The functionalist theory of stratification has the virtues of great simplicity and close congruence with the fact that all societies have been stratified. However, it is far from the whole story. Although it remains essentially unrefuted, there is a great deal about social inequalities that it cannot explain.

CONFLICT THEORISTS: NO

We have already suggested that many conflict theorists today no longer believe in the possibility of an unstratified society. But this is a relatively recent development. Although Marx frequently admitted that some stratification was inevitable in societies, his prophetic vision seemed to promise a new day when social inequalities would disappear. Thus, many Marxists (although not Marx) proclaimed that following the revolution of the proletariat and the creation of a true socialist state, men would literally be equal.

Marx's analysis was mainly directed at uncovering the nature of inequality in capitalist societies. His discussions of the coming unstratified socialist society were much less developed. Following Marx, however, other conflict theorists devoted considerable effort to explaining how such a society could be created (a recent attempt was made by Melvin Tumin in 1953). Their analysis rested on several basic assumptions about human abilities and motivation.

Environment, Ability, and Motivation

First, these conflict theorists adopted a wholly environmentalist explanation of human variation. They banished heredity from the human equation —in fact, they firmly embraced Lamarckian genetics, which held that acquired characteristics could be inherited (see Chapter 5). They therefore concluded that differences in human abilities were the result of environmental differences. With an equal environment, all men would be

Figure 15.3   In explaining social stratification, functionalists argue that *inherited* differences in intelligence and ability make such stratification necessary, whereas conflict theorists argue that *environmental* differences among social classes help maintain stratification. Educational institutions, they point out, are major agents of early socialization and of the transmission of values from generation to generation.

In a Chinese classroom, students are taught to "serve the people" and consequently to oppose class stratification. The debate between the functionalists and the conflict theorists hinges on the relative importance of heredity and environment. If the effects of environment are controlled, will the effects of heredity on stratification still hold? If so, support is given to the functionalist theory; if not, to conflict theory.

equal in ability, and talent would not be scarce. If their conclusion is true, it overcomes the central proposition in the Davis-Moore theory.

Second, they argued that all jobs in society are equally important (Tumin, 1953). If factories require engineers, they also require workmen. If armies require generals, they also require soldiers. It is not possible to argue that one position is more vital or necessary than another because all are necessary.

Third, they took the position that self-interest as the mainspring in human motivation is a cultural artifact. With proper socialization, people can be reared to act on altruistic grounds. The new socialist man would selflessly give his all for the betterment of all and would not seek his own best interests or be concerned about differences in the attractiveness of the tasks assigned to him as compared with tasks assigned to others; people sent to the coal mines would not be concerned that others had easier, safer, cleaner, and more interesting work. All would be content to make their contribution to humanity.

Finally, they simply discounted Mosca's analysis that societies will be stratified because they

require political organization and political organization necessitates inequalities in power. Although party chairmen and factory managers necessarily have more power than the rank and file, it was thought that they would use this power for the collective good, not for personal advantages. Besides, committees elected by the rank and file could keep tabs on them.

In general, these premises have not been borne out by research or experience. Modern genetics rules out the possibility that individual differences in such characteristics as intelligence are wholly or perhaps even mainly the product of the environment. Recall from Chapter 5 that the more environmental equality we achieve, the greater the role heredity will play: if there were no environmental effects—if we each realized our full potential—then variations in intelligence, physique, and the like would be wholly hereditary in origin. Thus, it is simply not the case that talent can be made abundant or that any person can be competent for any task.

Nor does the argument hold up that all jobs are equally important because all are necessary. For the most part, the importance of a job depends on how vital it is for the survival of society and how easily it can be effectively filled. Clearly, almost anyone can perform unskilled labor jobs, and at one time or another almost everyone has. Indeed, when little or no talent is required to fill a job, employers spend nothing on training and little or nothing on recruitment. But some jobs, obviously, are hard to fill. Unless it were required for the job, no one would train engineers, and no one would do the homework to become one. The functionalist argument rests on the relative scarcity of trained talent for some positions, not on the simple fact that all jobs must be performed.

Similarly, there has been little encouragement for the view that some new form of socialization can create humans who operate primarily on the basis of altruism. Learning theory suggests that reward-seeking is basic to the behavior of all organisms, including human beings (see Chapters 4 and 6). Rewards can come in forms other than property, power, or prestige; people can and do act for the good of others. Yet in no society have

Figure 15.4   The communal movement is one attempt to do away with stratification. Attempts have been made (although they have not always been successful) to eliminate inequalities through the equal sharing of tasks and by the rotation of jobs. One type of social stratification that is most resistant to change, even in communes, is stratification based on gender.

we ever seen men wholly or even primarily animated by altruistic motives—everywhere self-interest is a major determinant of behavior. No experimental utopian community has ever managed to overcome self-interest among its members. No experimental child-rearing programs, such as those attempted by child-care centers and schools in some socialist countries, have produced anything resembling selfless human beings. This is not to say that all people are wholly self-centered or to deny that people can be reared in ways that make them less self-centered. The

"Women's work" is still distinguished from "men's work" in many communes. In this area as in others, communes in China have an advantage in that they are integrated into the larger society and share its values and goals; American communes are isolated and receive little support—and frequently are met with outright hostility—from the larger society.

hope for a truly unstratified society, however, rests on nearly absolute selflessness, and although human beings do make sacrifices for their family, friends, group, or nation, or even for the whole of mankind, it seems unlikely that they can be led to make altruism their usual basis for action.

In all honesty, the question of whether stratification is inevitable is so hypothetical that it is probably unanswerable. An infinite series of hypothetical ifs can always be raised. There is no way anyone can prove finally that altruistic people cannot be created. We can only say that it has not been done, we do not have any idea of how to do it, and everything we know suggests that it cannot be done. But the possibility remains open.

Self-Interest

The majority of conflict theorists have abandoned the whole argument about absolute equality as futile and irrelevant. Instead, they have concentrated on a much more fruitful proposition: societies are much more stratified than they need to be. It may not be possible to make the janitor as powerful as the party chairman, or the nurse's aide as rich as the surgeon, but societies tend to become much more stratified than functionalist "necessities" require. It is here that conflict theorists have contributed powerful and critical insights into how and why societies operate the way they do.

As was pointed out in Chapter 4, conflict theorists take their name from the fact that they analyze societies in terms of the conflicts among individuals and groups for the possession of scarce values—property, power, and prestige. While functionalists stress the common interests shared by all members of society to promote the effective operation and survival of society, conflict theorists examine the selfish, private interests of dominant individuals and groups who exploit others for their own benefit. While functionalists emphasize consensus, conflict theorists emphasize coercion—the extent to which societies are run by force rather than by consent. In fact, when discussing how and why societies presently operate, conflict theorists give much more emphasis to self-interest than do functionalists, despite the fact that they reverse the emphasis when discussing hypothetical future societies. Conflict theorists essentially argue that people will seek to maximize their self-interests and that therefore, given any degree of inequality to start with, those with advantages will use them to gain even greater advantages. Conversely, people only give up as much as they must. Thus, society is a jungle. Worse yet, those with advantages will cynically defend their position, arguing that it is for the greater good of all, and thus try to spread false consciousness among the exploited. It is in this sense that conflict theorists call functionalist theories bourgeois and argue that functionalism attempts to hide the self-interest of the ruling classes behind a rhetoric about how inequalities serve the society as a whole.

THE EMERGING SYNTHESIS

To a considerable extent functionalists and conflict theorists talk past one another. Each theory seems able to account for factors that the other cannot explain. For example, conflict theory is unable to explain how to motivate highly talented people to spend the twelve years of study and hard work necessary to become surgeons. Functionalists can explain this. However, unlike functionalists, conflict theorists can successfully predict that surgeons will utilize their monopoly on their vital skills to obtain considerably greater rewards than would be needed to ensure an adequate supply of trained talent. For example, it seems extremely unlikely that the quality or quantity of corporation executives would noticeably decline if they were paid only $100,000 a year instead of $200,000.

When two competing theories display complementary interpretations, each succeeding where the other fails, there is an extremely high probability that a better theory could be constructed by combining the two.

Ossowski

This was precisely the point made by the Polish Marxist sociologist Stanislaw Ossowski in 1957.

Unlike previous participants in the debate between conflict and functionalist views, Ossowski did not ask which theory is correct. Instead, he tried to demonstrate that both views are fundamentally correct. This is possible, he argued, because human societies are far more complex than either functionalists or conflict theorists have recognized. Each theory emphasizes a different aspect of social reality.

Ossowski made explicit some intellectual trends that had been developing for years. Marxists had been aware for a long time that stratification had not disappeared in the Soviet Union and was not likely to do so. Indeed, Marxists had been victims of considerable misunderstanding when they spoke of creating a "classless" society. They had long since ceased to mean by this an unstratified society but meant instead merely one without classes in the Marxist sense. What they were talking about was a society with equality of opportunity in the sense that people rise or fall according to individual merit, not family position. In short, Marxists were describing a meritocracy indistinguishable from that described as the most functional—and therefore the most desirable—by functionalists. Functionalists had meanwhile become increasingly concerned about the persistence of poverty, of ascribed status arising from racism and sexism, and of inherited wealth, power, and prestige in modern industrialized societies. Their theory could not say why these dysfunctional arrangements persisted. Clearly, some sort of synthesis was called for.

Yet, despite various gestures of reconciliation exchanged between functionalists and conflict theorists, each camp has mainly continued to tend its own particular garden, and neither has done much work to produce a synthesis. To a considerable extent this noncooperation reflects the continuing effects of their different historical roots. Functionalists, from a "liberal" perspective, see the strengths of society and hope to make things better. Conflict theorists, from a "radical" perspective, see the weaknesses of society and hope to make something new that will be better. They are like the two men describing the same bottle

Figure 15.5 Lenski argues that although some
degree of stratification is inevitable in any society,
societies tend to be more stratified than is necessary.
In agrarian societies the wealth is concentrated
in very few hands, which creates huge differences
between the strata in power, property, and prestige.
This etching depicts the extreme stratification in
the Middle Ages. Serfs, at the lowest rung of feudal
society, must stand meekly aside as knights, the
armed might of the feudal lord, ride past.

as half full or half empty. Nevertheless, synthesis
of the two theories seems inevitable. In fact, the
effort has begun.

Lenski

The major effort so far to synthesize a more comprehensive theory of stratification from functionalism and conflict theory was made by Gerhard
Lenski, an American sociologist, in 1966. He began by blending functionalist and conflict-theory
premises in a way that makes some social stratification necessary but that also suggests societies
will tend to be more stratified than they need to
be. Then he examined a number of economic,
technological, environmental, and historical factors that also influence the nature of systems of
social stratification. The theory is lengthy and
complex, and we shall only outline some of its
major points.

Lenski's first premise is the obvious fact that
man is by nature a social being. Throughout this
book evidence has been presented that humanness lies in culture, which is socially created and

transmitted; indeed, the self arises only out of interaction with others. Radicals and conservatives
alike accept this premise.

His second postulate hardly glorifies the human species, but the weight of evidence seems to
justify it: *"When men are confronted with important decisions where they are obliged to choose
between their own or their group's interests and
the interests of others, they nearly always choose
the former—although often seeking to hide this
fact from themselves and others."* This is a statement combining the central conclusion of social-
learning theory—that the more rewarding men
find the results of an action, the more likely they
are to take this action—and the assertion that we
find it more rewarding to fulfill our own desires
than to fulfill those of other persons.

Lenski's third premise is that *most of the
things we value are scarce.* The supply of power,
prestige, and property is smaller than the demand; people would always take more if there
were more.

From these three premises it logically follows
that *"a struggle for rewards will be present in
every human society."* If all people were equally
able participants in this struggle, a standoff would
likely result, and everyone would end up with
relatively equal amounts of rewards. But, Lenski
pointed out, that is not the case. People *"are unequally endowed by nature with the attributes
necessary to carry on these struggles."* Thus, some
degree of inequality is inevitable. Furthermore,
Lenski posited that *people tend to be creatures of
habit and thus to be considerably bound by customs and traditions.* Thus, whatever patterns
become established in societies will tend to persist
longer than it would seem to make objective sense
to continue them.

Finally, Lenski argued that inevitably *all societies are to some degree imperfect as systems;* none
ever performs quite the way it is supposed to because inefficiency and error are unavoidable.
Many established patterns may actually work
against the effectiveness of society; some important goals are incompatible, and thus their full
achievement is impossible—for example, com-

plete external security tends to be incompatible with complete internal freedom; both internal co-operation and conflict are within certain limits normal for any possible society.

In Lenski's analysis the foregoing features of human beings and societies are relatively constant—they vary little from one time or place to another. These features thus define the basic *limits* within which any stratification system must operate: all societies will be somewhat stratified. But, Lenski pointed out, it is obvious that not all human societies have been equally unequal—some are more unequal than others. The remainder of his theory attempts to identify the critical factors that cause differences in the kind and extent of inequality observed in human societies.

Many of the factors Lenski thinks important were suggested in Chapter 12, in which we reviewed stratification in five basic types or stages of human societies. A major set of factors concerns *technology* and *productivity*. Hunting and gathering societies cannot be greatly stratified; with so little wealth available, no one can be very rich. The more productive a society, the more surplus wealth, and thus the greater the degree of possible stratification, as in agrarian societies. In industrial societies, however, technology changes the pattern: Technology is critical to increasing productivity, but it eventually works to limit inequality. As the division of labor becomes more complex, a greater proportion of people have skill monopolies that they can use to limit the extent to which they are exploited.

Lenski is concerned with many other factors besides technology and productivity. For example, he says that the degree of *external threat* also influences stratification because it influences the degree of constitutionalism in government. Extreme external threats produce tyrannical governments because these are most efficient for war making. Tyrannical governments will in turn produce greater inequalities in the stratification system because power will be highly concentrated, and wealth and prestige will tend to follow power. Similarly, the degree to which the common man plays a vital role in military affairs will influence inequalities. Where war making is restricted to a

small group of specialists, inequalities will be great; where the common man plays a major role in war making, there will be less inequality.

Lenski also argues that *ideology* plays an independent role in stratification. A society's beliefs will influence how it organizes itself. While it is true that what a society believes will be influenced by what it does, ideas can exert an independent influence. Here Lenski draws upon functionalist arguments that shared sets of values—religious, philosophical, political—function to unite societies and that these values impose limits on what any group, despite its power, can do and still continue to be regarded as legitimate. When Marx denounced false consciousness, he was saying the same thing, except he regarded it as "bad," while functionalists have regarded it as "good." Lenski argues that beliefs do affect stratification, that things simply happen this way, good or bad. For example, in a society powerfully committed to a doctrine of free will (that men choose their own fates), there will be less willingness to ameliorate social disadvantages—even on the part of the disadvantaged—than there will be in a society that believes men are shaped by their environment.

Unlike many sociologists, Lenski even makes provision in his theory of stratification for the role of *personal idiosyncrasies of leaders*. For centuries, history was told in terms of the desires and actions of great men. Then things went to the other extreme. Following Marx, many have argued that great men play virtually no independent role in history but that currents in economics and technology alone shape history. Both views are rash (Hook, 1943). Napoleon may have claimed that "God is on the side of the big battalions," but he himself frequently beat superior forces. Clearly, leaders are constrained by circumstances, but equally clearly, they retain some independent capacity for making the best or the worst of their possibilities. Lenski argues that leaders have some latitude within which to influence the distributive system of their society and increase or decrease inequality.

Perhaps Lenski's theory is most significant because it plausibly suggests that to understand how and why societies are stratified as they are—and how and to what extent they can be changed—we must examine a very wide range of factors. It will not suffice simply to examine the needs of the system for scarce talent, as orthodox functionalists do, or to point to the narrow self-interests of ruling classes, as orthodox conflict theorists do. We must understand a whole host of factors from genetics and individual psychology to the impact of technology, economic development, the environment, religion, politics, population changes, and leadership.

This is a huge task, and our ignorance is much greater than our knowledge. Lenski is not deceived about this. He does not argue that he has produced the final theory of stratification. Rather, to evaluate his own contribution, Lenski quotes Winston Churchill: "Now is not the end. It is not even the beginning of the end. But it is, perhaps, the end of the beginning." If social scientists have stopped hurling their convictions at one another and have begun to search for tested generalizations, then perhaps we can say that it is at least the end of the beginning.

SUGGESTED READINGS

Davis, Kingsley, and Wilbert Moore. "Some Principles of Stratification," *American Sociological Review*, 10 (1945), 242–249.

Feuer, Lewis (ed.). *Marx and Engels.* Garden City, N.Y.: (Anchor) Doubleday, 1959.

Ossowski, Stanislaw. *Class Structure in the Social Consciousness.* Sheila Patterson (tr.). New York: Free Press, 1963.

Tumin, Melvin M. "Some Principles of Stratification: A Critical Analysis," *American Sociological Review*, 18 (1953), 387–393.

Chapter 16 Race and Ethnicity

ARABS AND JEWS ARE engaged in yet another round of a war that is entering its third decade. Catholics and Ulstermen play out a too familiar drama of death in the streets of Londonderry and Belfast in Northern Ireland. East Indians and Africans, far from their native lands, struggle to gain and hold control of the South American country of Guyana. Pakistan and Bangaladesh continue to be fragmented by ethnic conflicts. In Uganda, Africans seek removal of the Asians in their midst. And here at home, in what Walt Whitman once warmly called "the nation of nations," racial discrimination and the growing opposition to it by black, brown, and red Americans are persistent features of national life.

The common theme in all of the situations mentioned here is *intergroup conflict.* Whoever is right or wrong and whatever the merits of any position in such conflicts, the collisions are between identifiable categories of people. These individuals do not only share in common certain religious, cultural, racial, or tribal characteristics; they often use these differences to justify claims of superiority and demands for territory or, in the case of those in subordinate positions, to demand freedom from oppression by the groups in power.

When we speak of intergroup conflict, we usually refer to relations between *dominant groups* and *subordinates.* Dominant groups may be thus defined as those who have the power to control the life chances of subordinate groups. Dominant groups—in South Africa, for example—may be relatively small but extremely powerful, powerful enough to keep larger, weaker bodies in check. Or they may consist of large, even vast, numbers of people suppressing the rights of those who are quite literally minorities. To avoid confusion, Richard A. Schermerhorn (1970) suggests that dominant groups may be considered to consist of either *elites* or *majorities;* subordinates, of either *mass subjects* or *minorities.*

RACE CONSCIOUSNESS AND CULTURE

The differences that exist between peoples—especially the kind that lead to and perpetuate intergroup conflict—are often passed down from one generation to another through the agents of socialization; for example, oppressed groups of people develop defenses to cope with the physical, psychological, and social barriers erected to "keep them in their place."

To say that differences are passed on socially is not to deny that certain attributes are genetically transmitted. Of course they are. When physical anthropologists speak of *race,* for example, they usually mean a group of persons who share some set of genetically transmissable physical characteristics.

Although pure races are difficult to find, it does not take a very skilled observer to recognize gross differences between the average person from China and one from Italy or from the Congo. The question is, "What do these differences mean?"

Recognizable racial differences frequently serve as a means for *labeling* or pigeonholing people according to how they look. Such labeling has been used throughout history by those who erroneously connect physiognomy with potentiality. Furthermore, this labeling has usually reflected invidious judgments about racial superiority and inferiority—and both majorities and minorities have engaged in these invidious judgments.

The use of invidious racial labeling by majorities is obvious. The doctrine of white supremacy has a long and sad history. In fact, as was pointed out in Chapter 5, until quite recently even social scientists correlated people's racial appearances with their proclivities. Because most social scientists were Europeans (or Americans of European origin), it is no surprise to find that they almost invariably determined that white Europeans were the most industrious, decent, and civilized of all varieties of human races and nationalities (Rose, 1968). For a long time, social scientists reinforced rather than combated the racism of their societies.

Minorities have also engaged in considerable labeling on the basis of recognizable racial differences. Just as do majorities, most minority persons who share certain physical traits tend to attribute to race alone what they should attribute to culture. Simply put, people often feel that those oth-

Figure 16.1 Persistent domination of one social group by another may lead to overt conflict. In Northern Ireland (*top*), the Catholic minority is at war with the Protestant majority over the issues of civil rights and British control. The new state of Bangladesh came into existence after a long, bitter struggle between the Bengalis of East Pakistan and the dominant Punjab majority of West Pakistan. The East Pakistani woman (*bottom*) fled after the invasion by West Pakistani government troops.

ers who happen to possess their looks also possess their outlooks.

There is a good explanation for this. Being persistently relegated to separate or inferior positions frequently has caused people to develop their defenses and their communities with one factor uppermost in mind: the fact that they are (or are seen to be) different. Not infrequently, racial discrimination has led directly to the formation of what seem like "racial cultures" and intense racial consciousness.

We must note the inclusion of the qualifying words *seem like,* for race *per se* has nothing whatsoever to do with culture or the potentialities for one way of life or another. As one young black put it recently: "It is not the fact that I am black but the meaning of being black that gives me my special character." Race and culture may be related, but they are separable phenomena and should not be confused.

Hard though it may be to believe, white and black Southerners in this country have more in common with one another than the white Southerners do with their (Caucasoid) English forebears or the black Southerners do with their (Negroid) African ones. Recognition of such facts of social life should not lead to the abandonment of the concept of race. It remains an important variable in the study of human relations.

Ethnic Groups

The trouble with the term *race* is that, as we have tried to suggest, it is often used to describe something other than physical differences. When speaking of race today, many social scientists, and laymen too, should tack on a qualifying adjective, for what they are usually describing is what Pierre van den Berghe has referred to as a *social race.* A social race is a group that "is socially defined but on the basis of physical criteria" (van den Berghe, 1967). Others, such as the Dutch sociologist Harry Hoetink, speak in terms of a "somatic norm image," again stressing social definitions of biological features (Hoetink, 1967). According to Marvin Harris (1968),

social races differ from other stratified groups (such as classes with low rates of out-mobility) in their methods of maintaining membership and group identity. Social races accomplish this by a special ideological device, the idea of descent.

What we have here defined as a *social race* comes very close to what others would label an *ethnic group,* save for one important fact: gross physical similarities are not necessary for membership or participation in an ethnic group. Most sociologists would agree that ethnic groups consist of "people who conceive of themselves as being alike by vir-

Figure 16.2 In South Africa black people are severely oppressed. Even though they are a numerical majority of the population they are relegated to an inferior position in their society. The advertisement depicted here reinforces the cultural notion that white is right. They must also conform to the restrictive rules and regulations imposed upon them by a white-supremacist government: they may sit only in specially designated areas (*top right*), and they must carry identity cards (*bottom right*).

The Extra Secret of
Success is

SKIN LIGHTENING CREAM

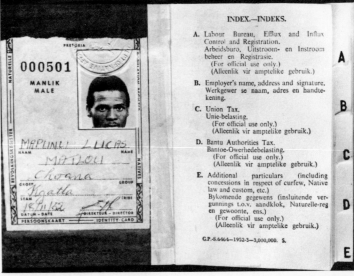

tue of common ancestry, real or fictitious, and are so regarded by others" (Shibutani and Kwan, 1965). Although the people of Southern Italy share certain "Mediterranean" features with Greeks and East European Jews (and although outsiders may be unable to make distinctions among them on the basis of looks alone), only the Southern Italians share the love of pasta, the Roman Catholic tradition, and the notion of *la misèria* (despite the fact that each of the other groups has its functional equivalents). And it is these distinctive cultural differences, not the physical appearance that these groups share, that make them separate ethnic groups.

Ethnic Stratification

The term *ethnicity* means the degree to which ethnic identity is held to be important by individuals, groups, or societies. An individual's ethnicity reflects the extent to which he feels (or is made to feel) part of some ethnic group. Individual ethnicity frequently reflects the extent to which others regard the individual in terms of his ethnicity. Acceptance by others outside the ethnic group often (but not always) loosens the degree of ethnicity or ethnic identification, and rejection by others outside tends to strengthen it. In many societies ethnicity is of considerable significance, and ethnic (and racial) criteria are used to place people within the stratification system. An individual's wealth, power, or social honor is

Figure 16.3   Gunnar Myrdal, a Swedish social economist, is the author of *An American Dilemma* (1944), the classic study of American racial relations that documents the sufferings of American blacks and the institutional arrangements of segregation and discrimination. The book was extremely influential in awakening American intellectuals to the problems of race relations, and it continues to be widely read. In 1968 Myrdal published an even more extensive work, *Asian Drama: An Inquiry into the Poverty of Nations,* a three-volume study of underdeveloped nations based on ten years of study. He has often headed United Nations committees and is the director of the Institute of International Economic Studies in Stockholm.

therefore likely to be based on his or her ethnic background. This is called *ethnic stratification,* and is defined by Donald Noel (1968) as "a system of stratification wherein some relatively fixed group membership (for example, race, religion or nationality) is utilized as a major criterion for acquiring social positions with their attendant differential rewards."

Ethnic stratification is found in almost every modern industrial society and, as Chapter 12 explains, in many others as well. Perhaps the most blatant example of ethnic stratification is the social structure of the Union of South Africa, where the descendents of the Boers have the favored positions along with the old English settlers (with whom *they* fought for many years). Then come the Jews (mostly from Eastern Europe), the Asians (from India), the Cape Coloreds, and at the bottom, the indigenous blacks. Each group is accorded a decreasing amount of social—and, for those nearer the bottom, physical—space in which to move.

South Africa is not the only place where ethnic and racial criteria are used for assigning status. One sees somewhat similar patterns in many Caribbean states, in Rhodesia, and in certain East African nations (though there the rank order of various groups has recently been altered: it used to be Englishmen on the top, then Asians, then Africans; it is now Africans on top, then Englishmen, with Asians on the bottom). Moreover, ethnic categorization remains a fixed feature of social life in the Soviet Union, in India, in Belgium, and even in Canada. Even the "homogeneous" Scandinavian countries relegate their Lapp populations to a position not unlike that of American Indians and, along with the "freedom-loving" Swiss, impose severe restrictions on workers from Southern European countries. By the same token, the United Kingdom is attempting to cope with its own intergroup problems, in part, by enacting such legislation as the Commonwealth Immigration Acts, which are decidedly "racialistic," to use their own phrase.

In the United States the castelike patterns of racial (and, in some areas, religious and ethnic) discrimination belie the widely touted notion that ours is a truly democratic society. Some writers, such as van den Berghe, suggest that the United States, like South Africa, is a "*herrenvolk* democracy"—free for the whites but not for the others (van den Berghe, 1967).

Implications of Pluralism

Restrictions placed on people because of their color or creed or national origins are anathema to those who truly believe that all should have equal access to life, liberty, and the pursuit of happiness. Gunnar Myrdal, a Swedish social scientist who did extensive research on relations between blacks and whites in this country some thirty years ago, contended that there was an obvious discrepancy between what people professed to stand for and their actual behavior. He went further and suggested that such inconsistencies gnawed at the heartstrings of most (white) Americans and would eventually cause them to do something to assuage their guilt (Myrdal, 1944).

Others have argued that few white Americans felt (or feel) either responsible or particularly guilty for the plight of Negroes but that many do feel quite anxious about the changes they see around them and even fearful of what increasing pressure for changes might portend. Myrdal's thesis was instrumental in bringing about civil-rights legislation, but it tended to play down the pluralism of American society.

Ours is not a society made up of whites and blacks, although as Nathan Glazer (1969) has suggested in a recent article, it may now be heading in that direction. For the present, as in the past, the United States is best characterized as a checkerboard of ethnic groups who remain structurally separate and, for all intents and purposes, separable, despite a decline in the kind of outward differences "that once made dialect humor a vaudevillian drawing card" (Rose, 1965). Whether we view differences as healthy or invidious, we cannot overlook the pluralistic character of the American social structure.

Ethnic Ties and Mobility   Upward mobility in the United States is in large measure related to the ability (and willingness) to accept the life styles

Figure 16.4   Bilingual signs and posters and the types of items in local food stores, restaurants, and newsstands often identify particular ethnic neighborhoods in the inner city and serve as reminders that residents of such neighborhoods share a culture that is different in some respects from that of the mainstream.

and values of the dominant group and, of course, to be accepted by its members. It appears to be the case that the lower one goes down the status ladder, the more one finds remnants of old-country culture and the retention of ethnic ties. Hundreds of thousands of people find solace and comfort in their old neighborhoods and jobs with people whose identity—and often whose kinship—they share. The "tribal ties" are often quite strong. Indeed, many of New York City's ethnic groups carved out their own niches in the social and economic structure and, rising within it, clung to the security they found in being able to control a piece of turf or a particular trade as did, for example, Irish politicians and policemen, Jewish garment workers and teachers, Italian builders and sanitation workers (Starr, 1969). Many other Americans, however, have foregone ethnic ties, left ghetto life behind, and sought to emulate the manners and mores of the dominant groups in their society.

Some people argue that in a complex society

some retention of ethnic differences is desirable and functional. Ethnic pluralism provides and even encourages *Gemeinschaft*-like or intimate relationships in what is otherwise a pretty impersonal social world. On the other hand, some argue that any sort of separatism (even voluntary) that is built on racial or ethnic lines can only serve to exacerbate differences and stifle opportunities for informal social interaction, which is so essential for getting to know people as individuals. They argue further that the few advantages of separatism for minorities are offset by the pain induced by discriminatory and differential treatment.

Accommodation and Assimilation Accommodation and assimilation are rather different phenomena. People may find ways to get along but remain different. Or people may have no trouble getting along because they have ceased to be different.

Accommodation is a word like "tolerance." It can have many meanings from "to get along with" to "to put up with." Among different races or ethnic groups it is usually achieved by mutual adjustment of the sources of conflict so that each group can enjoy reasonable freedom and security without surrendering all cultural differences. Accommodation may be informal; for example, two ethnic groups may share a park as common property, bloc vote for ethnically balanced local political tickets, and yet agree to stay out of each other's home neighborhoods. Or accommodation may be formalized and cast in laws regulating relations among groups, as in the case of the Walloons and Flemings in Belgium or the Chinese, Indians, and Malays in Singapore.

Assimilation is a more specific word. It means putting aside "foreign ways" (meaning one's ethnic culture) and becoming like the dominant group. Assimilation is generally a one-way process. Dominators rarely assimilate their culture to the culture of the dominated (although sometimes nomadic conquerors have been assimilated into cultures of agrarian societies they conquered).

In earlier times, assimilation in America was called "Anglo-Conformity." Today it is known (at least by most blacks and many young people of all groups) as absorption into the white bourgeoisie

mold. And, as is well known, it is increasingly rejected as a goal.

To many members of the black community —and of the Puerto Rican and Mexican-American communities, too—true assimilation is impossible to attain even under the best of circumstances. They recognize the extent to which traditional social patterns are matched by psychological resistances on the part of many (perhaps most) white Americans who do not want too close an association with them (Pinkney, 1969). They know, too, that attitudes and behavior are closely linked.

Patterns of Intergroup Hostility

We noted earlier that perceiving racial differences may result in labeling others and in mistaking cultural characteristics for biological ones. It is obvious that many of the tensions in this country and others arise partly because people make distinctions not on the basis of real information but in terms of what "we" think "they" are like.

Ethnocentrism Ethnocentrism is a term that William Graham Sumner used to describe people's sense of their own superiority to others and their use of their own cultural standards to judge others. Ethnocentrism is a critical element in group *prejudice*, the unfavorable beliefs and feelings people have about certain racial, religious, and ethnic groups.

Prejudice and Discrimination The distinctions made on the basis of race, color, religion, or national origin often show themselves in patterns of categorical denial, or what is commonly called *discrimination*. Discrimination is obviously related to prejudice, but it is not the same thing (Rose, 1973).

There are people who dislike others intensely and carry this hostility over into their behavior, sometimes going as far as to participate in organized campaigns of vilification and violence. At the other extreme there are those who have nothing but love in their hearts for their fellow-man and would never do anything harmful to anyone. They claim to judge people and act solely on the basis of individual criteria. (Needless to say, such saintly types are very few indeed.) Between the two poles are most Americans and, perhaps, most human beings. Collectively they have been called "the gentle people of prejudice," though, as sociologist Robert K. Merton (1949) once pointed out, even this broad group can be subdivided into *reluctant discriminators* and *timid bigots.*

Reluctant discriminators are those who are free (or relatively free) of prejudices against particular groups of people but who find it hard to challenge the norms of their social world. And so they go along with the crowd. If state, local, or neighborhood standards (sometimes written into law, more often part of a tradition) are discriminatory, then they, too, discriminate. Timid bigots are not much different. They are the sort of people who harbor all kinds of negative attitudes about particular groups but, again, because of what is considered appropriate and inappropriate, are often afraid to act out their hostile feelings—at least in those situations where the norms are clearly nondiscriminatory (Merton, 1949). It is not surprising that people suppress their true feelings in such situations; recall the studies of group conformity presented in Chapter 8.

Two lessons are to be learned from this typological treatment of prejudiced discriminators, nonprejudiced nondiscriminators, nonprejudiced discriminators, and prejudiced nondiscriminators. The first is obvious: The difference between the two key concepts of prejudice and discrimination is that the first is a set of attitudes and the second is the expression of those attitudes in behavior. Behavior includes any outward expression that affects others, including name calling. It is said that "sticks and stones may break my bones but names will never hurt me." That is a lie. Name calling hurts plenty and is discriminatory behavior.

The second lesson is less obvious, but it is no less important. Merton's typology, and its underlying assumptions, is important because it recognizes that it is necessary to know not only what people think and do but also the contexts in which they act—are they swimming with or against the social tide? What is absolutely central to any understanding of the dynamics of intergroup relations in this, or any, country is an understanding

of the *normative structure:* what is expected, what is required, and what is forbidden; the imputed sources of authority; and the ability to effectively enforce the rules.

Institutional Racism　In the United States *institutional racism* has pervaded the social order. Various segments of society—for example, schools, industry, and even churches—have systematically denied equal opportunity to certain specific groups in a way that, in one sense, makes everyone involved in discriminatory patterns. For many people, such involvement is inadvertent; many persons feel entrapped in a web of social relationships (the reluctant discriminators previously mentioned are a case in point). Many others do, in fact, harbor prejudices, having learned them as a part of a general socialization experience in a prejudiced society.

It is ironic but true that most people learn both their prejudices and the appropriate ways of acting toward others through contact with prejudiced others, not through interaction with the people of other ethnic groups who are the objects of their attitudes and discriminatory actions. We learn to be and do and act from those who set and enforce the standards—parents, peers, political leaders, and the like.

LAW, PERSUASION, AND CHANGE

We know that discriminatory behavior is psychologically injurious to individuals and damaging to the broader society, but how do we effect changes? This is a problem that has confronted community leaders, politicians (at least certain types of politicians), and social scientists for many years. Various techniques have been tried, including exhortation, education, contention, and negotiation (Watson, 1947).

Exhortation, the first mentioned, is one of the most widely used and least effective techniques. Preaching to followers to abide in the true spirit of Christ is not likely to work very well when the message is sounded in segregated churches.

Education is a bit better. However, if teaching is unsupported by changes in the normative structure, it is hard to sustain. (We speak here of specific intergroup teaching. We would be remiss not to point out the extensive evidence that the more highly educated a person is, the less apt he is to think stereotypically and the more amenable he is to changes of attitude and, under the right circumstances, behavior.)

Contention has become a favored technique of those who have recognized how ineffective the other methods have been in significantly changing entrenched patterns of discrimination; such disenchanted people have consequently taken their arguments to the streets. Contention serves several functions. It serves to rally people on both sides of any debate, and it enhances cohesion. It offers a locus for free-floating hostility and narrows the target for an attack upon the system. And, if skillfully executed, it scares to death people who are reluctant to get involved!

The past decade has seen the growth of contention in activities ranging from sit-ins at lunch counters to forays by whites and blacks into each other's communities to put on the pressure. "Black Power," "Red Power," "Chicano Power" —and, once again, "White Power"—are all expressions of this form of attempting to effect (or, for "White Power," to inhibit) social change.

Contention is usually accompanied by some form of *negotiation*. Although few militant civil-rights leaders will publicly admit that they will settle for anything less than total victory, the record clearly shows that the negotiated settlement has been the rule rather than the exception. To those most embittered, such bills as the Civil Rights Acts of 1960, 1964, 1965, and 1968—and similar acts at state and local levels—were token measures taken to keep the country cool and to assuage the guilt of white liberals. To others, these acts were classic examples of successful negotiations that could ultimately effect changes because they were essentially instruments of legislating morality, albeit a particular liberal-democratic one.

However one views them, the bills and similar acts suggest that with assiduous enforcement (something we have not yet seen in many places) old norms may be altered and people made to accept new standards of behavior. With federal and state legislation, the reluctant discriminators could become nondiscriminators without the censure of their peers, and the prejudiced discriminators would be forced to stop denying others what they themselves so often take for granted.

RESPONSES TO ETHNIC STRATIFICATION

Quite obviously, much of what was said in the preceding section could be construed as the voice of those who wish to lower the barriers, open the doors, and make integration a reality. However, there are many members of the dominant groups and many subordinates as well who feel quite differently about integration.

Some mass subjects and minority-group members, perhaps a substantial percentage, would like nothing better than to find their way into the mainstream of American society, to assimilate, to leave behind not only their ascribed status in one or another ethnic category but also the marks of their biological heritage, which they view as stigma. Some such people are deeply wounded and filled with self-hatred. Others are simply eager to get out of what they see as an impossible situation and to have a better life for themselves, especially for their children. There are others motivated by the belief that they (and their people) must merge in the great melting pot that (they think) America is or blend into another culture in another land. They often find, to their dismay, that the melting pot is more a dream than a reality.

There are those who opt for social integration and yet desire to retain the right to cultural pluralism. Others want to leave behind their old ways but retain the social patterns and traditions—for example, endogamous marriage (see Chapter 18) —that are so characteristic of racial and ethnic minorities in this country and elsewhere.

Increasingly of late, there has grown another response pattern, the response of those who reject the notion of integration in any form and prefer to live in and work for their own communities or, as in the proposed Republic of New Africa, in their own country. The widespread movement to develop black consciousness is a current example of the separatist philosophy. People often equate it with the separatism of the traditional segregationists, but in reality, the two movements have little in common.

Black separatism is, by and large, a reaction against the persistent failure of integration. It is an attempt by blacks to "get it together" and to "go it alone" because nobody else will do it for them. White segregationism is based on the desire to keep certain people (black people) "in their place." These movements should not be confused (Carmichael and Hamilton, 1967).

ETHNIC TRAITS AND INDIVIDUAL EXPRESSION

Caution must always be exercised in considering ethnic stratification, intergroup relations, or responses to discrimination. There is a tendency to deal with groups as if all members were entirely similar in outlook and behavior. There are, to be sure, many traits shared by those who have undergone common experiences and have been accorded similar treatment. Thus, one can speak of ethnic styles, particular patterns of communal organization, and, to some extent, differential values. White Southerners (a very definite ethnic group in our society) are indeed different from Boston Irish or New York Jews (Killian, 1970). And even within a single city like New York, gross ethnic differences play a significant role (Glazer and Moynihan, 1971).

Still, one must be careful not to overgeneralize about ethnic traits, just as one must be careful in using another useful but overworked concept, *national character*. It has been said that "we are like all other men; like some other men; like no other men." As human beings, people share certain needs and wants and fears. As members of various societies, cultures, and subcultures, people find—or rather, are given—alternative means to meet the functional requirements of survival. We have tried to suggest that for racial and ethnic group members survival means more than simply

Figure 16.5   Riots broke out in the summer of 1968 in the Watts area of Los Angeles, a black ghetto. Following the riots, black community leaders presented a list of proposals to city, state, and federal officials. These proposals were directed toward eliminating the underlying social and economic causes of unrest, conditions that exist in large cities throughout the country.

In the aftermath of the riots that took place in the black ghetto of Watts in Los Angeles, Black union leaders recommended the following proposals to be put into effect in the ghetto area:

The immediate starting of slum clearance and new housing projects with public and private resources.

The construction of a fully equipped hospital.

The cooperation of all levels of government in an intensive program of counseling for job and school placement.

The re-establishment of destroyed business and community services through the Small Business Administration and other agencies.

getting by. Finally, as individuals we differ markedly from one another no matter how similar our upbringing. This is true whether one is a Bushman living in a social world tightly circumscribed by tradition and limited in contacts with others or an Englishman living in the heart of London, whether one is a black preacher in Harlem or a Nisei farmer in the Imperial Valley of California.

Despite the interdependence of fate and the very strong fellow feeling of most members of ethnic groups, particularly subordinate ones, differences *within* groups still abound. Each and every group seems to have its saints and sinners, its shining lights and dullards, and even its old guard and young Turks! Some of these differences in temperament, in manner, and in commitment to the status quo or to change are often of great value to the group. Indeed, in most but not all cultures, it is rarely the average man, the modal type, who rises to positions of leadership. Rather it is the one

Figure 16.6 Gordon's concept of *ethclass* refers to a subsociety created by the "intersection" of social class and ethnicity. The concept of ethclass can be represented two-dimensionally as a grid with vertical and horizontal stratifications. In three-dimensional form, the concept can be represented as a cone. The higher the class level, the fewer the members and the greater the similarities of behavior across ethnic lines—except that in the upper class, minority-group members are excluded from class privileges.

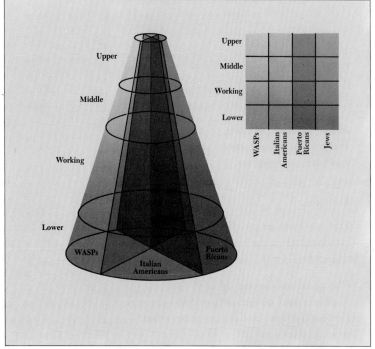

who stands out or, in certain cases, stands up and hollers.

Different sorts of people come to speak for different sorts of groups and for different segments of these groups. Ethnic groups, especially large ones, are often highly stratified. In Boston, for example, one knows the difference between people called "lace-curtain" Irish and those called "shanty" Irish (and one knows how resentful people are to have themselves labeled the latter). Moreover, when they are found in various parts of the country, regional variations may affect the success of intragroup communication or consensus. For example, the late Reverend Martin Luther King could arouse his people to great activity in Georgia, Alabama, and Tennessee, but he had difficulty rallying support in Watts and in Chicago's South Side. The social class and region of an ethnic group's members, then, strongly influence the group from within.

The Ethclass

Because of the importance of both ethnicity and social class for understanding society, Milton Gordon (1964) has introduced the concept of the *eth-*

class. In combining the words ethnic and class, Gordon is trying to combine vertical features of the stratification system (all ethnic groups are stratified, but some stand higher relative to others) with the horizontal distinctions of ethnicity (unassimilated ethnic groups are parallel within the class system).

Gordon argues that most cultural behavior is class-based; that is, poor people are more like one another regardless of ethnic affiliation than they are like people of higher socioeconomic status in their own group. Although this point is a debatable one, we would hypothesize that the higher one goes in all status hierarchies, the greater the similarities of behavior across ethnic lines. Social participation tends to be limited to one's ethclass: If one is a middle-class Jew, one tends to associate with other middle-class Jews.

And now we come full circle. Group identification, according to Gordon, is by and large racial or ethnic in character. One sees oneself *in regard to all others* according to his or her group label, that is, as a Puerto Rican or a Jew or a Pole or a black. And when the group is threatened, even those who have become quite assimilated find it difficult not to rally around the flag.

American politicians are well-aware of Gordon's theories even though they may have never read a word the sociologist wrote. They know the strength of ethnic identity and its pulling power in this structurally pluralistic society.

The Struggle for Power

Much of what we have discussed comes down to a question of *power*, the uses of which are discussed in Chapters 17 and 21. Depending on the balance of power, either *repression* or *conflict* often result. Racial and ethnic relations usually involve struggles over repression between those in control and those who seek greater freedom and equal access to opportunity (as do Catholics in Northern Ireland today) or independence (as do certain French Canadians). But sometimes, in situations of relative parity—in Guyana, for example—the conflicts center on *competition* for the right to rule, and political parties are almost entirely racial or ethnic in character.

In the United States both repression and competition patterns are in evidence. The civil-rights movement and its various offshoots speak for those people who are marked by repression and who are eager to have their burden lifted; some of them feel there is little hope of true integration, or even of freedom, and want to set up their own new society.

However, many other ethnic differences in America are the basis for competition. This is obvious in the ethnic composition of the two major political parties. The Republican party is quite disproportionately controlled, and supported, by WASPs (White Anglo-Saxon Protestants). Similarly, the Democratic Party is the party of Catholics and Eastern European ethnic groups (see Chapter 21). Although both parties use ticket balancing in order to appeal to as wide a number of groups as possible—"Elect O'Conner, Morelli, and Goldfarb!"—this strategy is more elaborately practiced by Democrats. Indeed, the "new politics" of party reforms that brought so many young people, women, and nonwhites to the 1972 Democratic Convention can be considered a logical extension of the balanced-ticket approach of the "old politics."

SUGGESTED READINGS

Allport, Gordon W. *The Nature of Prejudice.* Cambridge, Massachusetts: Addison-Wesley, 1954.

Gordon, Milton M. *Assimilation in American Life.* New York: Oxford University Press, 1964.

Greeley, Andrew. *Why Can't They Be Like Us?* New York: Dutton, 1971.

Killian, Lewis A. *The Impossible Revolution? Black Power and The American Dream.* New York: Random House, 1968.

Kurokawa, Minako (ed.). *Minority Responses.* New York: Random House, 1970.

Rose, Peter I. (ed.). *Nation of Nations: The Ethnic Experience and Racial Crisis.* New York: Random House, 1972.

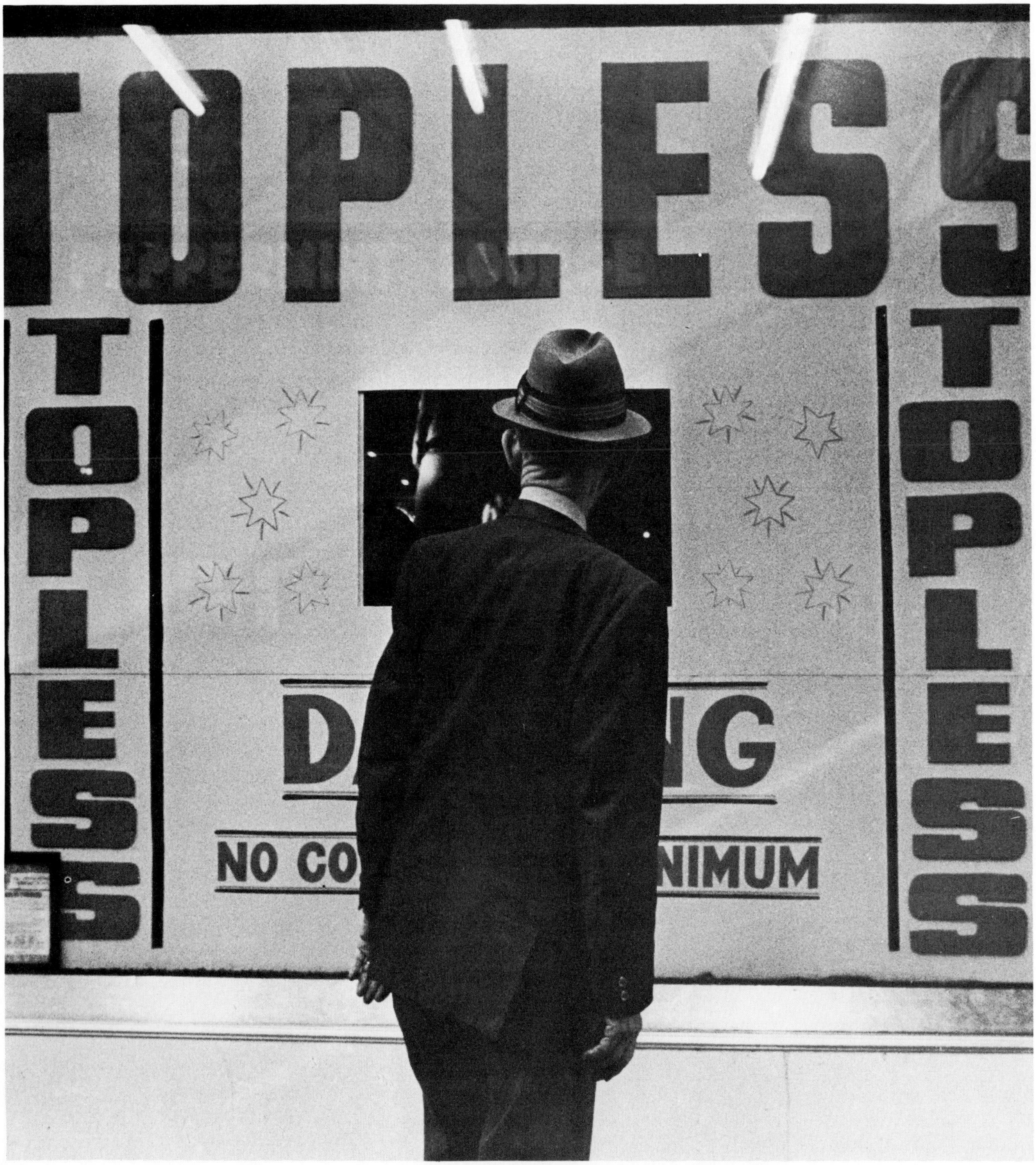
TOPLESS
TOPLESS
TOPLESS
NO CO NIMUM

Chapter 17 Sex and Age: The Tyranny of Older Men

AGE AND SEX ARE the most universal sources of social inequality. Our present understanding of sex and age stratification is quite imperfect, and it is important to consider what we do know and what we can only guess about. An effort to *explain* the causes of age- and sex-based inequalities must not be misunderstood as an effort to *justify* them. Rather, if we are going to make headway against such inequalities, it is vital to know the precise difficulties that we have to overcome.

Human beings did not have to invent age and sex inequalities; they were well established millions of years ago among ancestors who were not yet human. Although the degree and character of sex and age inequalities vary considerably from culture to culture, in all known human societies females have been subordinate to males; the young have been subordinate to adults. Mature males have always been the top dogs.

THE SOURCES OF SEX AND AGE STRATIFICATION

The universality of age and sex discrimination seems to be partly a function of human biology. While racial and ethnic differences, for example, are not always potential bases for invidious comparisons, sex and age differences always are. This is probably why they are the most intractable and universal sources of inequality.

The Evolution of Age and Sex Differences

Humans are not unique in having adult-male dominated societies. Many other mammals, including nearly all of our close cousins, the higher primates, live in societies dominated by adult males (Kummer, 1971). The gibbons and the chimpanzees are relatively egalitarian, but most other monkeys and apes, like human beings, show a good deal of adult-male dominance. An extremely important determinant of gender dominance in any given species of primates is the degree of secondary sexual differences between males and females. Secondary sexual characteristics are not directly related to the genital and reproductive organs; they include such characteristics as size, plumage, and hair growth. Perhaps the best single predictor of the degree of male dominance in a species is the ratio in size or weight of males to females. In the extremely male-dominated baboon species, for example, adult males weigh approximately twice as much as females; among the more sex-egalitarian chimpanzees, females usually weigh about 85 percent as much as males; *Homo sapiens* fall in between, but the weight ratio of females to males is closer to the one for chimpanzees.

It may not be very flattering to the male ego to realize that male supremacy probably lies in brute strength, but all the evidence for both people and primates points that way. Indeed, most other socially significant characteristics are either equally distributed by gender or give women a slight edge, as we shall see later.

Age inequalities also confirm the importance of sheer brute strength in male dominance. For people and primates alike, the adult female is generally dominant over infants and juveniles of either gender whom she outweighs. Similarly, the ranking order among males is in large part a function of their relative strength: fully grown males in their prime are generally the most dominant. In most groups of primates, then, a ranking of individuals by physical strength—measuring it by weight or size and taking age into account —would yield a fair approximation of the actual prevailing order of dominance.

As, in turn, physical strength and size are closely related to both age and sex, all primate societies are, in fact, differentiated by both age and sex. Indeed, the subhuman primates seem to be *principally* differentiated by age and sex; only man has invented numerous other bases for injurious comparisons. Because age in a given species bears a closer relationship to strength than does sex, age differences typically take precedence over sex differences. In simple terms, primate societies are even more thoroughly *adult*-dominated than they are *male*-dominated.

What Kind of Primate is Man? To understand age and sex differentiation in *Homo sapiens*, we have to do more than admit the obvious fact of our primate heritage; we have to take an unflinching look at what kind of primates we are.

Our ancestors emerged as hominids at least two or three million years ago, probably in the open plains of the tropical savannas. As the most hairless of primates, the human being is by nature a tropical animal, and only his technology has enabled him to survive elsewhere. Without weapons, a human being is also one of the most helpless primates. Completely terrestrial, he cannot escape predators by taking to the trees, as even the largely earthbound macaques and baboons do in search of safety. Furthermore, compared with these other terrestrial primates, humans lack prominent canine teeth and can easily be outrun by canine and feline predators. Only their technology enabled human beings to escape feeding the lions long before the Romans revived the practice as a spectator sport.

A Hunting Technology   For all but the last eight or ten thousand years of their evolution, hominids evolved as primates specialized in killing. Other primates, especially baboons and chimpanzees, occasionally kill and eat other animals, but man is by far the most efficient and aggressive killer of all and is indeed unique among mammals in the frequency with which he destroys members of his own and other species for the sheer fun of it.

Life as a predator and a scavenger—perhaps stealing kills from large felines—was made possible through tool and weapon making, itself a concomitant of brain development. Humans are not unique as tool makers, for chimpanzees have been observed making tools, but even the paleolithic hunter was much better at using weapons than any other primate was. It is important to note that hominids used weapons as defensive instruments of survival as much as they used them to get food and to kill competing humans. Another survival aid to the paleolithic hunter came with the domestication of the dog; as a fellow scavenger it was a natural choice as man's best friend. Besides helping track game, the dog was also the human being's earliest advanced warning system.

Social Organization   A predatory and scavenging existence also required a specialized social organization based on age and sex. Infants'

prolonged dependence on women and the incapacitation caused by pregnancy and lactation made for an obvious division of labor at the very start of hominid evolution: Adult males went hunting and scavenging, leaving women and children behind under some kind of protective shelter. In this respect, humans differ from the other terrestrial primates, like baboons and macaques, which are also highly social but which are mostly vegetarian—their females and young have to forage in the open under the protection of adult males. For humans, however, the surplus production made possible by an efficient hunting technology enabled females and young to remain at least semisedentary and resulted in a sharply drawn division of labor by age and sex (Gough, 1971; Washburn and De Vore, 1961).

The same division of labor still exists. George Murdock (1949) found in a sample of 175 contemporary societies that hunting is confined to males in 97 percent of the cases studied and is chiefly a male pursuit in the remaining 3 percent. Although it is true that there are very few hunting and gathering societies left today, it is equally true that humans were hunters for well over 99 percent of their social evolution. It is clearly unrealistic to believe that man's history of being a hunter is not in some way related to his present behavior.

Reproduction and infant nurturance required a sharp division of labor by age and sex among human hunters, and efficient hunting, especially of large game, also necessitated the banding together of several adult males. These additional requirements gave rise quite early in hominid evolution to the two characteristically, but not exclusively, human forms of social organization: the *family* and the *band*.

The family in its minimal form involves a stable sexual and economic relationship between at least two adults of opposite sex and their subadult offspring. In all human societies, such a relationship is socially recognized through marriage. *Polygyny* (a marriage of one man and more than one woman) is preferred in about three-fourths of contemporary societies; however, a large number of these societies are small tribes of hunters and gatherers or are in the horticultural stage. The

overwhelming majority of marriages are monogamous. As was pointed out in Chapter 12, even in
polygynous societies, the average man has only
one wife.

An additional feature of the human family is
the incest taboo, which results in the need for
several families to establish marital-exchange relationships with one another. Marriage not only
makes for stable ties between spouses and among
parents and children but also cements ties among
different families.

In all probability, the primordial type of social
organization for practically all of human evolution
was the hunting band made up of families linked
together through ties of marital exchange. More
complex societies evolved from this basic blueprint of the minimally viable human group. It is
interesting to note that some other terrestrial primates, notably the Hamadryas baboon (Kummer,
1971), have a very similar type of social organization; although they do not, of course, have marriage, they have stable polygynous families band-
ed together into foraging groups through cooperation among adult males.

Cross-cultural Comparisons: The Family

So much for the evolutionary origins of age and
sex differentiation in humans. We must now take
a closer look at the family in cross-cultural perspective: The family is the most universal and persistent of human groups and the one that is most
conspicuously stratified by age and sex.

There are two traditional sociological approaches to looking at the family. The first derives
from *functionalism,* which views the family as the
cornerstone of the social order. Functionalism is
discussed in greater detail in Chapter 15. The second view comes from *conflict theory* and sees the
family as equally important but also sees in it a
primary source of inequality; the family, in
Friedrich Engels' view, is a microtyranny dominated by adult males. Because our concern here
is with age and sex as sources of inequality, we
shall draw mostly from the second perspective.

A few interesting generalizations emerge from
a cross-cultural perusal of the family (Murdock,

1949; Goode, 1963; Stephens, 1963; Lévi-Strauss,
1968; D'Andrade, 1966).

Adult-Male Domination Families are micro
political systems in which adults are dominant
over children, and generally, men over women.
Some individual women may dominate individual
men, but in no known society is this the norm.

Marriage as Exchange In the great majority of
societies, marriage is considered to be an arrangement between two kin groups rather than a
mutual choice between two individuals. Typically, marriage is an exchange of ineligible kins-
women for eligible ones—men swap women of
their own kin group (whom they are forbidden by
exogamy rules to marry) for women from another
kin group. The exchange is either direct or indirect through the intervening step of a dowry.

Division of Social Life Most societies divide social life into the smaller, more private sphere of
the family and the public sphere of the larger
society. Men are invariably dominant in the public affairs of the society at large, including everything from the local community to the centralized
state. Women and children typically play a minimal role in the public sphere; their activities are
largely confined to the domestic sphere. Even
within the family, where women play an important role, they are generally subordinate to the
men, although they have some authority over
children of both sexes.

Seniority and Authority Seniority is the most
frequently invoked principle in the exercise and
transmission of authority within family groups.
Generation and birth order of siblings often determine the hierarchy of male kinsmen, but seniority
of husband and order of marriage frequently establish priority among married women. Senior
women sometimes exercise some authority over
junior men within their own kin group.

The Status of Women The degree to which
women are subordinate to men varies from
extreme to moderate, with sometimes near-

Figure 17.1   Most current human societies are
adult-male dominated. Women, as a rule, are forced
to take subordinate and stereotyped roles and
to perform labor for low or no wages. The subordination of women seems to approach a cross-cultural
universal. Domestic chores, classified as "women's
work," are much the same in Austria (*top left*),
Greece (*bottom right*), and the United States
(*bottom left, top right*).

egalitarian relations within the domestic sphere. Contrary to a widespread misconception in the West, there is no evidence that the status of women is any lower in polygynous than in monogamous societies. Rather, the greater independence that widows or unmarried women sometimes achieve indicates that marriage itself, irrespective of its particular form, contributes to the subordination of women. Polygyny typically results in a greater age difference between husband and wife than exists in monogamous societies, but far from depressing the status of women, it enables co-wives to coalesce against their husbands in some circumstances. *Polyandry* (a marriage of one woman and more than one man) is a rarity in any case and is more an indication of female infanticide (resulting in fewer women) than it is of a high status of women.

Patrilineal and Matrilineal Societies There are quite a few *matrilineal* societies, that is, societies in which descent is traced in the female line, but there is no evidence that any of them is now or indeed has ever been *matriarchal*. Many societies have a myth of matriarchal origins, but none has ever proven to be female-dominated. There is some evidence that women tend to be somewhat less subordinate and to inherit more property in matrilineal societies. However, in viewing the main difference between *patrilineal* and matrilineal societies, we do not ask which *sex* rules but rather which *males* hold power. In patrilineal societies, a woman is under the authority of her father, husband, or husband's father; in matrilineal societies, under that of her brother or mother's brother.

The cross-cultural evidence clearly suggests that in all societies the family is adult-male dominated, irrespective of its particular structure. Adults always have authority over children, and seniority is the most common principle used to establish the line of authority within kin groups. Marriage invariably results in an unequal relationship between the sexes. In patrilineal or bilateral societies, the husband—or his senior male relatives—directly dominates the wife. In matrilineal societies, the authority of the husband and father

over his wife and children is much more limited, but the women sent into marriage do remain under the authority of their brothers or mother's brothers. Marriage in this way remains largely an exchange game played between groups of male kinsmen. The basic insight of Marx and Engels (1964) that the family is the root cause of human inequality is validated by the ethnographic literature, although their earlier ideas that matriarchy was the original condition of mankind are not.

BIOLOGY AND CULTURE IN SEXUAL INEQUALITIES

The most fundamental difference between gender and age as bases of differentiation is that gender status is permanent and age status changes. Not surprisingly, people learn sex roles very differently from the way they learn age roles, and there is a great deal of cross-cultural regularity in this respect. As Chapter 6 points out, children in all societies learn sex roles primarily within the family and at a very early age. The learning that accompanies changes in age roles, on the other hand, is almost invariably entrusted, at least in part, to socializing agents outside the family; this learning receives wider social recognition through *rites of passage*, which we will discuss at length in a later section.

Gender Identification

Let us examine how people first acquire sex roles. Several striking facts about sex roles show great consistency across societies. First, a child's ability to correctly identify his or her sex occurs very early, around the middle of the second year in all societies. Gender identification is established in a relatively short time interval—a few weeks or months. Second, once established, gender identification is virtually irreversible; attempts to reverse it—for example, in the treatment of hermaphroditism—often cause serious emotional disorders. Third, all societies force practically all individuals into either a male or a female role although some societies tolerate a few instances of the assumption of the sex role opposite to one's own biological sex.

Figure 17.2   The acquisition of sex roles
starts early in life. Children acquire sex-typed behavior
after observing their parents, other significant adults, and
older children. Such behavior, which starts early
and affects almost every aspect of a person's self concept
and interactional patterns, is difficult to change
in later years.

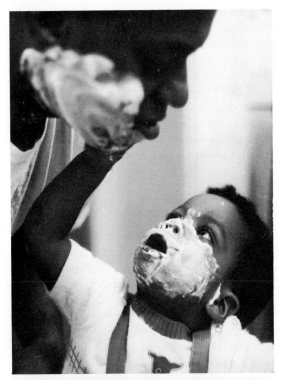

These astonishing regularities in the acquisition of gender roles suggest that the process is *not* purely cultural. It seems very similar to what students of animal behavior have called *imprinting,* a kind of learning process in which behavior is irreversibly established during a limited phase of the organism's maturation; the behavior is established as a consequence of biological predispositions being triggered by specific environmental stimuli. It is probably no accident that gender identification occurs simultaneously and inevitably in humans when they acquire speech. Gender identification, bipedal locomotion, and speech distinguish the infant from the child and mark the acquisition of genuinely human status—in the social sense. Just as a speechless human of normal intelligence is unthinkable, so is a genderless one.

Sex Roles

Beyond these cross-cultural uniformities in the process of gender identification, societies vary widely in the actual content of *sex roles.* Gender identification, it is worth noting, is achieved long before children are capable of assuming the roles culturally ascribed to either sex.

The Sexual Division of Labor   One of the most significant aspects of sex roles concerns the division of labor. With few and infrequent exceptions, men do all or nearly all of the warring, hunting, and grazing of livestock, while women do practically all of the fuel gathering, water carrying, food preservation, cooking, and infant care. In short, men engage in those occupations that involve both risk and spatial mobility, and women do more sedentary and routine tasks that do not interfere with pregnancy, lactation, and infant care (D'Andrade, 1966). There are exceptions to this generalization, of course. Sometimes in some societies women do heavier work than men do. But usually this is not the case.

Beyond these uniformities, however, societies differ enormously in the kinds of jobs they ascribe to men and women. Although pottery making and weaving are often women's tasks and metal work is frequently reserved for men, the exceptions are becoming more numerous. Ritual specialists, including priests, diviners, and medical practitioners, are among the first specialized occupations to arise even in minimally differentiated societies, and they are frequently held by men; however, most societies also reserve some ritual roles for women. Men typically have the lion's share of political offices, but a number of societies reserve some offices of secondary importance for women. Agriculture is engaged in by both sexes; the men usually do the most arduous labor, such as land clearing and harvesting, and the women do the more routine and less strenuous jobs, like weeding and seeding.

Sexual division of labor, then, has obviously been determined in part by biological constraints; it is equally obvious that cultures elaborate greatly beyond these constraints. In the majority of societies, most jobs are culturally defined as either men's or women's even when there is no apparent biological basis for the sexual division of labor. Some of the technologically simplest hunting and gathering societies and some of the most technologically advanced, especially the socialist ones, have a somewhat less rigid sexual division of labor than do the pastoralist and agricultural societies in the intermediate range of complexity.

In fact, the same relationship that generally holds between technology and inequality (see Chapter 12) also holds between the degree of technological complexity and the overall status of women relative to men. With a number of exceptions, the status of women is relatively lower in the agrarian societies than it is in either the simpler hunting and gathering societies or the more complex industrial societies. The complex agrarian societies tend to be the ones in which occupations are most rigidly ascribed not only on the basis of sex but also on the basis of caste or class. Complex agrarian societies constitute the high-water mark of inequality in social evolution. Chapter 12 discusses the differences among five general types of societies in detail.

Two salient conclusions can be drawn from a cross-cultural examination of the sexual division of labor: First, most occupations could be filled without regard to sex with no appreciable cost in efficiency, yet most societies come close to *maximiz-*

ing the sexual segregation of work. Second, the sexual division of labor is usually *invidious:* the males utilize their political power to reserve for themselves the jobs that they regard as more desirable in terms of honor, pay, interest, excitement, or other rewards. This second finding is confirmed by the fact that those societies that have the greatest degree of occupational segregation by sex also tend to be the ones in which the general status of women relative to men is lowest and in which ascribed inequalities on bases other than sex are most pronounced. The lot of women is relatively worse where other principles of inequality are also firmly entrenched.

Personality, Ability, and Intelligence Another important aspect of sex roles concerns the distribution of abilities and personality attributes (Maccoby, 1966). The debate on how much of the differences between males and females is ascribable to biology and how much to culture is still raging. By now, however, it is clear that either the environmentalist position—emphasizing the cultural determinants of behavior—or the biological reductionist position—emphasizing genetic determinants—is inadequate by itself. As we made clear in Chapters 5 and 6, all human behavior is determined by a complex interplay of heredity and environment, and we are now only beginning to be able to specify the balance of each in concrete aspects of behavior.

It is quite clear that physiology plays a role in gender differences in behavior, temperament, and ability. Although Western cultures overstress the extent of some of these differences, women clearly have less muscular strength than men. Women's records in sports are constantly somewhat lower than men's, but, of course, female athletes do considerably better than untrained men. For unexplained reasons, females have a Basal Metabolic Rate some 5 percent lower than that of men (when differences in body size are taken into account). Different hormonal balances undoubtedly affect temperament. For example, the sexual drive is affected by the secretion of androgen, which, being more salient in men, probably accounts for their lower threshold of sexual arousal.

Figure 17.3   Although there quite possibly are hormone-related differences in temperament between men and women, numerous psychologists have pointed out that differences in temperament *within* each sex are greater than the differences *between* them. And evidence for differences between the sexes in *ability* other than those involving sheer physical strength is virtually nonexistent. Women of ability have appeared in every age and in every society (*left side*); but cultural definitions based on gender (*right side*) have shaped women's behavior and placed them in roles that feature passivity, subordination, detachment, and even social parasitism.

In a number of respects, females have an advantage over males. They mature somewhat faster, which may well account for the consistently greater precocity of girls in the achievement of both motor and verbal skills. Little girls consistently learn to walk somewhat earlier than boys do, and they also talk earlier and more.

Females show much lower visible incidence of a number of deleterious genetic traits such as baldness, color blindness, and hemophilia. The reason is that the X chromosome contains many more genes than the Y one. A female has two X chromosomes, but in a male, the X chromosome pairs off with a Y chromosome. If a female carries a rare deleterious recessive gene on one of her X chromosomes, the probability is very high that its effect will be masked by a normal dominant gene on her other X chromosome. Among males, however, the corresponding Y chromosome lacks many of these genes, and one recessive gene on the X chromosome is sufficient to make the recessive trait appear, or become visible.

Chromosomal composition may also help explain the greater longevity and resistance to some diseases that females show. If one discounts the hazards of childbirth, which kills many women in preindustrial societies, females live longer than males. Women show somewhat greater resistance to diseases, with some exceptions like gonorrhea, than do men and therefore have lower mortality rates in all age brackets.

Notwithstanding the ethnographic *curiosa* reported by some anthropologists (Mead, 1935), there is abundant cross-cultural, and indeed cross-specific, evidence of gender differences in temperament. Males tend to be more dominant and aggressive and females more nurturant, not only in nearly all human societies but in most primate ones as well. Culture almost invariably elaborates on and reinforces these biological predispositions, but it very seldom succeeds in neutralizing or reversing them. Scarcely anyone would question the immense influence of culture in shaping the specific sex roles in a given society, but it would be equally foolish to deny sex-linked biological predispositions, which are probably regulated in good part through hormonal balances.

Much research has been conducted on the distribution of intelligence by sex because intelligence is one of the most socially significant human abilities (Maccoby, 1966). Apart from the slightly greater precocity of girls, most differences seem attributable more to environment than to heredity. Despite great individual differences in both sexes, males and females as groups seem to be endowed with the same biological quantity and quality of intelligence. Eleanor Maccoby (1966) reports some differences; the children who excel in intellectual tasks tend to be the more "feminine" boys and the more "masculine" girls, but these differences are so obviously related to cultural stereotypes in American society as to be almost certainly attributable to sex-role socialization. Unfortunately, we socially define intellectual boys as "sissies" and girl mathematicians or chess players as "unfeminine."

BIOLOGY AND CULTURE IN AGE INEQUALITIES

Having explored both the biological and the sociocultural bases of sex differentiation, let us now do the same for age differentiation. The physiology of maturation and aging is still very imperfectly understood, but its gross behavioral consequences are clear enough. Indeed, the biological limitations inherent in certain phases of the life cycle impose even more stringent limits on the performance of social roles than do sex differences. A twenty-five-year-old woman may not be quite as good as a twenty-five-year-old man at throwing spears at lions, but she throws them much better than does a two- or an eighty-year-old male. It takes a "male chauvinist pig" to deny a woman a pilot's job on a jet airliner, but to deny even a brilliant five-year-old access to the cockpit could hardly be construed as an act of adult chauvinism. Even if the controls could be reduced in scale to put them at the child's fingertips, we would justifiably raise questions about a child's attention span, need for sleep, and judgment in emergencies.

Not surprisingly, then, societies are even more differentiated and stratified by age than they are by sex, although the impermanence of age takes

Figure 17.4   As this pedigree chart shows, hemophilia
(a rare inherited blood disease that can be carried by
women but that is expressed only in men) was transmitted to most of the royal families of Europe through
the children of Queen Victoria.

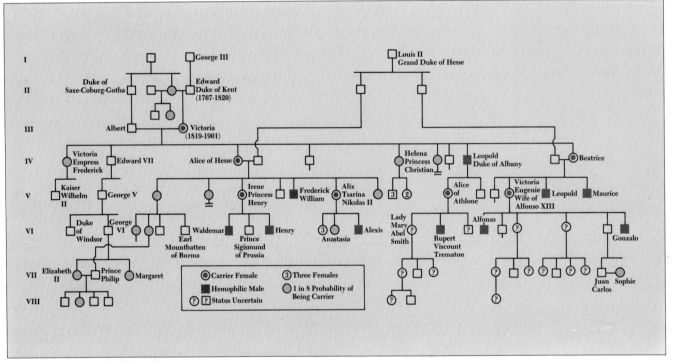

Maturation

much of the sting out of age differentiation. Indeed, as we shall see, some societies that are quite
rigidly stratified by age (and sex) come closest to
being democratic (for males) in other respects.

Maturation

The biological constraints of age in *Homo sapiens*
are obvious enough. Human infants are among
the slowest maturing and helpless of mammals. As
any parent knows, attempts to teach skills before
the child has achieved the necessary physical
maturation are doomed to failure. A puppy can be
housebroken in a few weeks, but the far more
intelligent human infant may take a few years to
control his bowels and bladder. Human infants
learn to focus on objects, sit up, control their
hands, crawl, walk, speak, and so on within rather
narrow time spans that are remarkably constant
from culture to culture; these activities are therefore probably biologically determined.

Those maturational constraints on our social
learning are most rigid in early infancy, but they
do not disappear thereafter. Adolescence, for example, seems to be an important learning thresh-

old. Around adolescence, our capacity to learn
certain skills, such as speaking a foreign language,
diminishes rapidly within a short time span.
Before puberty, nearly all persons of normal intelligence can learn to speak a foreign tongue like
a native, and after that only a gifted individual can
do so. The onset of old age marks another acceleration in the decline of a wide range of abilities,
from strength and sexual potency to intelligence.

Basically, maturation is marked by a slacken-
ing of our vital pace; it is a process of ever dimin-
ishing plasticity in our physiological responses to
our environment. In short, as organisms we gradually freeze and wind down, albeit not at a constant
rate. Death is merely a sudden acceleration of the
process, but even then we do not die all at once.
Our body temperature, basal metabolism, ther-
mal homeostasis (ability to maintain constancy of
body temperature), level of kinetic activity, capacity to learn and remember, sensory acuity, and
recuperative ability from injury decline from
childhood or adolescence. In early adulthood, intelligence, strength, and fertility begin their
downward skid at an accelerating pace with every

Figure 17.5   Some careers can allow for the fact that as a person's physical abilities are declining, his experience and knowledge are increasing. Bob Cousy started his career as a professional athlete, but when his playing ability declined with age, he took advantage of his experience to become a professional coach.

successive decade. We have used our brains to increase our longevity, but if we were left wholly to nature, most of us would be toothless by our middle thirties and most cases of appendicitis would be fatal. The biology of maturation and age-ing, then, is an extremely important part of our social abilities and disabilities, but the effect of learning in establishing age differentiation and hi-erarchy is equally important.

Learning and Experience

Age stratification is clearly a product of both bio-logical and sociocultural factors. We have seen that all societies are adult-male-dominated be-cause male adults have more brute strength than do children and females. But societies are also typically ruled by males in late middle age, that is, by persons who are well past their physical prime but not senile. It seems that in the vast majority of societies, the age span from forty to sixty years represents the optimum intersection between two curves: a declining curve of physio-logical abilities, which has not yet reached the downward tumble of senescence, and an ascend-ing curve of knowledge and experience, which has not yet leveled off at the point where learning ability declines.

If physical strength and abilities were all-important, most societies would be ruled by male athletes in their early twenties. Fortunately, none is. Even where physical abilities count the most—for example, in warfare and sports—it is young men in their prime who do the killing, dying, and running, but they are almost invariably *being run* by men at least a quarter of a century beyond the peak of their physical powers. Young men often resent domination by their seniors, but they typi-cally lack the knowledge and experience neces-sary to capture power.

Generational conflicts are much more com-monly characterized by a middle-aged group wanting to accelerate the retirement of a senes-cent one than by "young Turks" seeking to over-throw a middle-aged ruling class. Interestingly, even youth movements based on the premise that "you can't trust anybody over thirty" are inter-nally ruled by the most senior of the young, not,

as the logic of the ideology would imply, by the youngest. For example, the student-power move-ment of the late 1960s in the United States was dominated by graduate students, not by fresh-men, even though many of those leaders were suspiciously close to the disqualifying age limit of thirty years. Even among student radicals, experi-ence counts, and knowledge about "the establish-ment" comes in handy in attempts to overthrow the power structure.

Conversely, if knowledge, experience, and seniority accounted entirely for age stratification, then we would expect most societies to be geron-tocracies. In fact, real gerontocracies, or political systems ruled by the oldest, are quite exceptional either as total societies or as specialized organiza-tions. The Curia and the College of Cardinals of the Roman Catholic Church and the French Acad-emy are probably among the best examples of ger-ontocracies, whose secular power is quite limited.

In highly industrialized societies, where the pace of technological change has become so rapid that it more quickly makes skills and knowledge obsolescent, there has been a tendency toward earlier retirement and, consequently, a lowering of the average age of the ruling class. Even in the most rapidly changing industries, however, managerial experience counts. Young engineers fresh out of M.I.T. may think they would do a better job of running factories than their elders do, but few people are willing to give them a chance to put their managerial skills to the test.

Cross-cultural Differences and Similarities

The social organization of age—that is, the utilization of age as a principle of social differentiation—reveals a number of interesting cross-cultural similarities as well as differences.

Absolute and Relative Age   An important distinction is to be drawn between *absolute* and *relative* age. In Western societies, our compulsion to measure time precisely has led to a great but unusual concern for absolute age. We attribute an uncommon importance to the fact that we were born on, say, November 13, 1956, and a wide number of actions are contingent upon our ability to prove it through a birth certificate or "I.D." Without one of those exotic documents, we find it difficult to obtain a driver's license, register to vote, marry, qualify for a pension, get a passport to travel abroad, purchase or consume alcoholic beverages, and so on. Both our *identity* and our *identification* are closely tied to our absolute age, but our *relative* age has secondary significance. We frequently do not know precisely who among our associates is our junior or senior, nor do we attach much social significance to relative age unless age differences are great.

In the vast majority of the world's societies, however, relative age is of far greater consequence than absolute age, which, indeed, is frequently not known with any degree of precision. In many parts of Africa, for example, people traditionally did not know their birthdays, which were not socially important, but they knew precisely who, among hundreds or even thousands of persons around them, was their junior or senior.

Only recently were birth certificates introduced in most new African nations and with incongruous results. People now choose a birth date

at random within a plausible range and have it certified on official documents; then they are expected to stick by it. However, when it is in their interest to make themselves younger or older to qualify for a job or a pension, they frequently attempt to prove that they could not possibly have been born in, say, 1932, because their senior brother was born in 1933, the year when there was a catastrophic failure of the cocoa crop.

Seniority and Authority   In all societies, age is a paramount principle in the distribution of authority, both within and outside the family. The family is a grouping that quite naturally lends itself to division into generations. In its minimum *nuclear* form, the family normally has two generations living together, with the parents having authority over their children. In the far more common *extended* form, the family includes three or four generations of relatives and their spouses. The most common principle for the succession to authority within kin groups is seniority, the rules of which usually provide for exclusion of the mentally incompetent and retirement of the senile. For example, in a system of patrilineal descent, authority typically passes from the father to his eldest son, then through the line of brothers until the death of the last male in that generation, then through the eldest male in the next generation.

Seniority therefore applies not only between *generations* but also between *siblings*—many kinship systems use completely different kin terms for elder and younger brother. Even in the Western tradition of transmitting power and property, the principle of primogeniture—which defines the inheritance rights of the eldest son—was once much more widespread than it is now. In polygynous societies, seniority also plays an important role in establishing rights and privileges among co-wives. Order of marriage most often determines the rank of a wife in a polygynous household; older wives are rewarded in status for what they may lose in sexual attractiveness.

Status: Rites of Passage   In all societies, the significance of age transcends that of the family,

Figure 17.6   Rites of passage: A young woman emerges from the ritual seclusion that follows the onset of puberty among the Thonga people of southern Zambia.

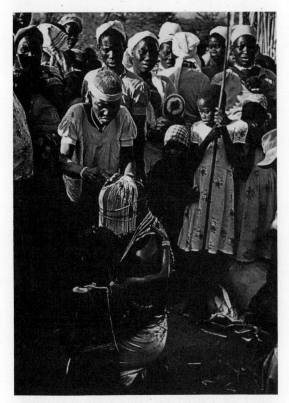

typically has less importance because women are not expected to play as important roles in public life as men are. Initiation is almost invariably a *public event* that transcends the confines of the family group; it is a collective ritual that is too important to be entrusted to individual kin groups. Even stateless societies, in which political power is not centralized or concentrated in a group of permanent office holders, run initiation ceremonies as a public, collective concern of the entire society. Furthermore, nearly all societies have some system of *public schooling* in preparation for initiation. In initiation schools the typical procedure is to isolate the initiates for a period of weeks or even months from the rest of society (including their families); elders usually give them instruction about adult roles, national history, religious traditions, sex, and so forth.

Education   The Western model of education obviously has many of the features of initiation schools. Indeed, in Western societies where age has taken second place to other more injurious bases of status differentiation like race and ethnicity, the one institution that is still rigidly stratified by age is the school system. The stratification is perfectly clear to everybody who is a freshman or a sophomore in high school, but the significance of these age classes diminishes in adulthood. Western schools, then, are extremely lengthy and elaborate initiation schools leading to the ritual of graduation or commencement; unfortunately, they also lead to dropout. The main difference between initiation schools in most other societies and in Western ones is that Western schools also try to convey a great deal of technical training and knowledge and that they produce a high attrition rate because of their social and intellectual selectivity. Schools in primitive societies rarely produce dropouts. Perhaps we would do better if, instead of endlessly discussing the pros and cons of democratic versus elitist education, we were clearly to separate two distinct functions of education: we would have common, democratic initiation schools wherein failure would be virtually impossible, and we would have a wide range of selective technical institutes where job skills

whether it is nuclear or extended, and in some societies age is the most significant criterion of stratification. Societies vary widely in the extent to which they have corporate, self-conscious, precisely defined age groups, but all societies at least distinguish among broad age categories, and all societies mark important events in the life cycle by means of *rites of passage*.

In Western societies, baptism, circumcision, confirmation, Bar Mitzvah, marriage, and funerals are religious rites of passage, but they also have a significance similar to many secularized occasions such as high-school or college graduation ceremonies and baby showers: they clearly mark passage from one age status to another.

There is also great cross-cultural uniformity in the way that formal socialization outside the family precedes rites of passage, particularly the all-important initiation that marks the shift from child to adult status. All societies formally initiate their male members into adulthood; a great many societies also initiate females, but female initiation

would be imparted. Instead of parochially dismissing non-Western societies as primitive and uneducated, perhaps we could learn much from them.

Age Conflicts   An interesting feature of age as a basis of stratification is that it is probably the least injurious or invidious and therefore the least ethically problematic. The young may find it galling to be under the authority of their elders, but they know that all they need to do for the tables to be reversed is to bide their time and survive: "Time is on our side." Generation conflicts are endemic in most societies, but they are very seldom revolutionary or even ideologized because "angry young men" have a way of quickly becoming not-so-angry not-so-young men, and eventually they may become "old guard." It is often critical to the historical reputations of revolutionaries to have died at a young age.

Any parent whose authority is challenged by his offspring—and this means practically every parent of normally intelligent children—has learned the pacifying nature of the argument: "wait until you grow up." Being told to wait probably makes children more impatient to grow up and makes the passage of time in childhood seem so agonizingly slow.

It is interesting to note that age conflicts are frequently ritualized. Halloween in American society, hazing in fraternities, the lampooning of teachers in school theatrical performances, and the like are rituals of rebellion that give vent to pent-up hostilities generated by power differentials. The rituals, however, do not represent any real challenge to the age hierarchy.

Age Stratification and Social Organization

Many of the world's most democratic societies—for males—have been rigidly stratified by age, and age stratification seems to be the least harmful way of integrating societies of up to hundreds of thousands of people. Examples can be found in many of the pastoralist societies of Eastern Africa, as we shall see when we view the Masai society.

Age-Set Societies   In broadest outline, societies that are stratified by *age-set* have made age the main principle of social organization beyond marriage and kinship. The system works roughly like an American college system stretched over an individual's entire lifetime and over the society's complete political and military organization. All the boys in such societies become lifelong members of a named age-set that retains its corporate identity until the death of the last of its members. As a given initiation period is closed and a new one opened, at intervals of approximately fifteen years, every age-set is automatically promoted to the next more senior *age-class;* in other words, if we call age-class the rungs in the hierarchy and age-sets the groups of people who move bodily through the system, we see that an individual remains in the same age-set for life but changes age-classes with the beginning of every new initiation cycle. The American collegiate equivalent would be that John Smith by entering Harvard in 1970 belongs for life to the age-set that we misleadingly call "the class of 1974," but he remains only one year in the freshman age-class.

The Masai Male   After initiation, the Masai boy enters the warrior age-class, which is internally subdivided into junior and senior subclasses. For the years that he remains in that age-class he may not marry, and he must perform what amounts to lengthy, compulsory, and universal military service. He will live with his age-mates in segregated warriors' villages, which are scattered throughout Masai land. The group of young men who inhabit a given village is in effect a military company fighting shoulder to shoulder. All warriors at any given time are and will remain for the rest of their lives members of the same age-set, subdivided into junior and senior warriors. When the next initiation cycle opens, the distinction between junior and senior warrior loses significance, and the whole age-set previously in the warrior class gets promoted to junior-elder status. Now allowed to marry, the junior elders devote their fifteen years in that status to raising a family and caring for their cattle herds. Junior eldership is primarily a time for private family concerns that is sandwiched between two periods of public service.

With the opening of the next initiation cycle,

the surviving junior elders, now typically in their forties, get promoted *en bloc* to senior eldership. For the next fifteen years, the age-set currently in senior-elder status will be concerned mostly with public affairs, especially with the running of the initiation system and the training of the young initiates. Many political decisions are made at large assemblies that include all initiated men, but senior elders come closest to being the Masai ruling class. Even so, their power is collective and quite diffuse. For initiated males—not females— Masai society is as democratic as any the world has ever seen. After fifteen years of senior eldership, the survivors of the age-set, now around sixty years old, go into respected but powerless retirement as "elder statesmen." A few members of up to three superannuated age-sets remain at any given time.

As can readily be seen, the Masai age-set system clearly stratifies all males, ascribes specialized tasks to the various age classes, integrates the various kin groups into a single, self-conscious, powerful military nation, and manages to maintain an uncentralized, democratic, yet highly cohesive political system in which every Masai man feels as good as any other. In fact, for a pastoralist society at a low level of technology, the age-set system is probably one of the best ways of welding widely scattered family groups into a cohesive nation organized for permanent raiding and conquest, as the military success of the Masai testifies. Unsettling as it may be, many of the world's most democratic nations have also been among the most bellicose nations.

CAN AGE AND SEX INEQUALITIES BE CHANGED?

In conclusion, let us review the history and take a tentative look at the future of age and sex inequality. Some two hundred years ago, the Founding Fathers of the American Republic—all adult white males of far-above-average wealth, education, and intelligence—declared that all men were created equal. It was a bold idea, but unfortunately, even they did not really believe in it. Viewing the political context of the time, it is clear that "men" meant literally adult males, not male and female humans; the concept of male equality, being restricted to the white male colonists, also excluded slaves and Native Americans, or Indians. Even among adult white males, however, it was obvious that some were "more equal" than others. The infant republic was in fact ruled through an uneasy alliance of convenience between Northern plutocrats and Southern slavocrats. Such are the shaky ideological foundations of the land of the free.

If a country allegedly committed to egalitarianism has been so notoriously unsuccessful in eliminating blatant inequalities based on such superficial criteria as skin pigmentation, what are the prospects for eliminating age and sex inequalities, which have some biological basis?

We may reasonably assume that age inequality is here to stay. A totally age-egalitarian society is practically unthinkable, and even the most radically egalitarian utopias have not come even close to applying their ideals on the age dimension.

The power of adults over children is the most fundamental form of human dominance, and it is no accident that its political blueprint, *paternalism*, has been extended to other forms of domination. A common way of keeping groups of adults subordinate is to identify them with children: this has been done to women, slaves, colonial peoples, every minority group, and even the rank and file during tyrannical regimes. The benignly smiling portraits of dictators project the image of a *father figure*. Irrespective of ideology, the model of paternalism is very pervasive—even where the groups kept under subjection show little of the dependency and helplessness that one associates with children. It therefore becomes extremely difficult to conceive of how this model would disappear in situations where the dependency and the disparity in size and strength are glaring.

Sex equality, on the other hand, seems much less utopian an achievement. To be sure, men are bigger and stronger than women. But whatever social significance this biological fact once had is now attenuated by our modern production technology, which makes muscular strength increasingly obsolete.

Figure 17.7   Women are often publicly treated as intellectual inferiors, and sexual inequalities that prevail in Western society are often reinforced or fostered by the mass-communications media.

The men who are going places always know how to get there. And when the place is Chicago, the 'how' is a United Club Commuter.

Club Commuters offer the business flyer a choice of airports there (O'Hare and Midway) and here (La Guardia, Newark, Kennedy).

Plus a choice of 23 departures every business day. And premium liquor service. (Cocktails on us in First Class, $1.50 in Coach.)

As the Travel Agent in the cartoon knows, we attract the successful businessman.

It's another case of success following success.

Fly the friendly skies of United.
The Club Commuter to Chicago.

"Since you're interested in meeting lots of charming, successful men, I suggest we begin your trip with a Club Commuter to Chicago."

Dear Sir:

Just tell me on the enclosed postpaid card how many office supervisors you have and I'll send each of them a FREE copy of the valuable Handbook "SUPERVISING WOMEN."

This is the Handbook that explores those areas in which supervising women presents specific problems that require an altogether different sort of handling!

Let's face it...supervising women properly is an acquired skill. It's not enough to be democratic, unprejudiced, or to have a "good heart." There are actual techniques involved, sensible things to do in tricky situations that are forever coming up. For example:

Women tend to be late to work and absent more often than men. Their home responsibilities account for it. How do you handle this problem?

	FOR HER	FOR HIM
RECORD PLAYER	This unit plays the record.	You have your choice of turntable with separate tonearm and cartridge of your choice, or an all-in-one record changer. The latter also changes the records automatically.
SPEAKER	The music you hear comes through the speakers. They must be kept sufficiently apart. You need two speakers for stereo.	Let your own ears determine your choice of speakers. From the variety made to component high fidelity standards, you can always find the one you like to listen to. Music can be piped into other areas of your home simply by adding speakers.

As Chapter 12 pointed out, very little work in modern industrial societies depends on muscle power. To the extent that muscle power was responsible for sexual inequalities, technology can be regarded as the great emancipator of women. However, unlike some primates, human females are not all that much weaker than males anyway. Muscle power, at any rate, is not the only factor that created sexual inequalities. Industrial technology may be a *necessary* (and available) condition for the liberation of women, but it probably is not a *sufficient* condition.

At least as important as the technology of *production* is the technology of *reproduction*—the ability to separate at will sexual and reproductive behavior in order to free women from the impediments of pregnancy, nursing, and child care. Contraceptive technology has made enormous progress in recent decades. Sex and reproduction can be fairly reliably separated. Similarly, technology has made it possible for humans to delegate the feeding of their infants to others by use of bottles and nursing formulas. Until very recently this was only possible for the rich, who could afford to use a wet-nurse. Now, by becoming parasitic on the females of such other mammals as cows, the price has been brought within the reach of nearly everyone. Although it is reported to be on the way (Rivers, 1972), we do not yet have a technology of extrauterine gestation, or pregnancy outside the female. But perhaps this is not necessary for the full liberation of women. Pregnancy is not usually very disabling, nor does it last very long. Few career lines could not readily allow for several maternity leaves.

Child care—thought by some to be the least difficult problem to solve—may present the most intractable difficulty. As John F. Scott (1972) noted, if one were to transfer the primary child-rearing functions of the family to employees, the cost would "soar out of sight." He cites the case of Israeli *kibbutzim* to show that when parental responsibilities are "industrialized," the cost cripples the organization rather than produces economies of scale.

Discussions of women's liberation often take up the case of the Soviet Union. It is clear that one of the factors behind much of the women's liberation in the Soviet Union was the high casualty rates of young males during World War II, which resulted in an increase of unmarried women; another factor, for married women, was the role of the grandmother as the child rearer. However, both factors seem to be one-generation phenomena: The present marriageable generation is not short of males, and the liberated Soviet women have no intention of retiring to grandmotherhood in their fifties. So their daughters must find a new form of child care. It is not clear how this problem will be solved in the Soviet Union or elsewhere.

Obviously, not all women must face the problem. But some women must have children, and many will want to, despite career aspirations. High-level businesswomen, professionals, and the wealthy can afford full-time child care. But who will do this child care? Less advantaged women?

Possibly the problem can be overcome by assigning the least productive, or lower-income, parent the job of early child rearing. But that creates a circular problem: Until women are freed from child care, they will not have an equal chance against men to be the most productive partner in a marriage; until they have an equal chance, they cannot be freed from child care. But perhaps the future trends for work in industrial societies provide a solution: a diminution of average working time through technology and corresponding increases in productivity. Consequently, it may be possible not only to support a family by working a few hours per week but also to divide those hours between spouses. Both spouses would then have considerable time for child rearing, and sex differentiation could be overcome.

We begin to see the outlines of the possible. Although age inequality will always be with us because children are naturally less competent than are adults, there no longer exists a natural basis for sexual inequality. That fact alone, however, will not produce sexual equality. As will be considered at length in Unit VIII, change does not automatically follow when old practices are no longer needed; it does not even follow from a definite need to discontinue them! Change must be won against the inertia of societies. It is only the squeaky wheel that gets grease. As ethnic, religious, and racial minorities have demonstrated, inequalities are only rectified when it becomes easier for society to do so than not to do so. And it is precisely this feature of change that necessitated and motivates the contemporary Women's Movement, which Chapter 28 treats.

SUGGESTED READINGS

Maccoby, Eleanor E. (ed.). *The Development of Sexual Differences.* Stanford: Stanford University Press, 1966.

Morgan, Elaine. *The Descent of Woman.* New York: Stein and Day, 1972.

Morris, Desmond. *The Naked Ape.* London: Jonathon Cape, 1967.

Tiger, Lionel, and Robin Fox. *Imperial Animal.* New York: Harcourt, Brace & World, 1971.

Cubi XXVII by David Smith (1965). The Solomon R. Guggenheim Museum Collection.

Thus far, we have seen that social life is made up of roles, groups, and organizations and that these are stratified. In this unit, we find that roles, groups, and organizations are not randomly distributed within societies. Instead, they tend to be clustered

UNIT VI
around certain vital needs or functions of societies. Such clusters are called *social institutions*. For example, all societies must deal

SOCIAL INSTITUTIONS
with matters of sexual relationships, child rearing, and kinship. The

cluster of roles, groups, and even organizations primarily devoted to these matters is called the institution of the family. Other major institutions are those dealing with education, religion, politics, and economics. Each of these institutions takes up a chapter of this unit. ¶ Sociologists use relatively broad definitions of these institutions and take the position that they are to be found in every society. In fact, sociologists argue that each major institution is fulfilling a vital social function and that a society could not exist if it lacked one of these institutions. A society without economic or political processes, for example, is unimaginable. By definition, a society consists of a set of basic social institutions. Therefore, upon completion of this unit, we will be able to discuss society as a whole.

Chapter 18 Family and Kinship

THERE IS CURRENTLY considerable speculation about the future of family life in our society. Quite a number of people maintain that families, as we have known them, are on the way out. Since families exist, in some form, in all known human societies and seem to have existed ever since anyone can remember, that is really rather a startling assertion. But even the rankest skeptics cannot afford simply to deny the assertion that the death of the family is imminent. The pace of change in our society in the twentieth century is such that it would be unintelligent to dismiss something as impossible just because it never happened before. After all, not very long ago, people laughed at the idea that we might one day fly, much less visit the moon. The unprecedented changes of the twentieth century have made the unthinkable often not just thinkable but real. So when President Nixon asserts that he vetoed the 1972 child-care bill because it threatened the existence of the American family, we can reflect that he is not alone in wondering about the future of that institution in American life.

In addition to the increasing amount of talk in advanced industrial societies, particularly in America, about the family's imminent demise, there are and have been some actual efforts in various quarters to actively do away with or radically change the institution. For example, attempts to change or eliminate existing family structures may accompany the attempt to build a socialist society after a social and political revolution, and, on a more modest scale, many young Americans are trying alternative living arrangements, such as communes.

For a real appraisal of the possibilities, however, armchair speculation will not suffice. Nor can fragmentary data, such as rising divorce rates, increasing numbers of people living together without a formal marriage contract, and greater sexual permissiveness, be taken as adequate evidence for the death of the family. If you have been thinking while you were reading, you may have noticed that we have been talking about "family" and "marriage" as if they were the same thing—which, of course, they are not. This should serve as a caution against making final judgments about

institutions without first looking at the larger picture. In fact, we have been talking about "the family" without even saying what that is.

How, then, are we to go about deciding the fate of the family? Obviously, we need to supply ourselves with a few definitions. And, after that, we should examine the various forms that the institution of the family has taken throughout history, in our culture and in others, and the various functions the family has served. We might then be in a position to make a critical appraisal of the changes in form and function that the family has undergone in modern industrial society. A comparative cross-cultural and historical perspective will help us to see American family organization as one possible ordering among many.

FAMILY ORGANIZATION

The first thing we must do is to define the concept of family, at least loosely, so that we know what we are talking about when we say that the family is one of the few universal facts of human society. We can begin by thinking of the family as a long-term association of adults, one of whose major concerns is the having and raising of children and the transmission of goods and culture from one generation to the next.

Anthropology, the study of different cultures, particularly less advanced ones, grew out of the interest aroused by early exploration and consequent contact between Europeans and radically different cultures. Central to the concerns of early anthropologists was the analysis of family patterns. The organization of the family, it was found, often provided the key to understanding the organization of the society; failure to discover the principles determining the structure of the kinship system often left the other aspects of a culture largely unintelligible. The study of families in other cultures provided Westerners with a new perspective for viewing their own.

In order for you to understand the various family structures that exist, you will need to equip yourself with a number of new concepts. As you read this section you may begin to get a sense of how much most of us take for granted about our particular family system.

Let us begin by making some fairly obvious yet important distinctions between the terms *marriage, family,* and *kinship systems.* The term *marriage* refers to a set of socially approved rules relating to the establishment of sexual unions. The term *family* designates a culturally defined social unit that at minimum usually consists of a married couple and their children. However, as we shall see, this is a limited conceptualization. *Kinship system* is a more inclusive term; it refers to the culturally prescribed means by which a society defines and organizes succession, inheritance, and socially prescribed attitudes and behavioral patterns among group members, called *kinfolk.* A society's kinship system, in short, defines who is related to whom and how they should behave toward one another.

It is very important to realize that these terms all designate relationships that are defined by a society. When a social scientist speaks about a family, for example, what he or she refers to is not a biological grouping but a cultural one. In our society, the socially defined family usually corresponds to the biological one: it ordinarily consists of a woman, a man, and the children they have had together. In many areas of the world that is not the case. In some societies, for example, the kinship system is such that a man has no rights over most of his biological children, and they do not claim descent or inheritance from him.

Types of Families
The most common type of family organization is the *nuclear family,* usually characterized by a married couple and their dependent children. This basic unit is also referred to as the *conjugal family.* (Sometimes distinctions are made between these two family types, but for our purposes we may regard them as synonymous.)

Most adults belong to two nuclear families: the one into which they were born and the one they enter by marriage. The family into which a person is born is called the *family of orientation,* and the family he or she establishes through marriage is called the family of *procreation.*

A second type of family organization is the *extended family.* In America we think of an ex-tended family as consisting of children and their parents, grandparents, and great-grandparents, if they are living. In other words, the extended family takes the form of three or four generations of nuclear families of lineal descendants. Looser conceptualization of what an extended family is embraces all relatives of an individual. Sociologists and anthropologists, however, generally use the term *extended family* in a more technical sense to refer to *more than one nuclear family living together or very near each other under the head-ship of one person whose position of leadership is defined by the rules of descent.*

At this point the study of the family and kinship becomes significantly more complex than we normally suppose by looking at our own culture. In our own society a young couple marry, traditionally with the woman adopting the man's last name, establish their own residence, and have and rear children, who, in turn, repeat the cycle. The relatives of the wife and of the husband are considered to be of equal importance, and variations in interaction are determined largely by proximity of residence, sentiment (how much you like or dislike them), and a sense of duty.

This pattern, the most common in industrial societies, seems relatively simple and logical. However, closer examination from a cross-cultural perspective proves it to be neither simple nor logical in many respects. Our family pattern and kinship system, like all kinship systems, involves a unique combination of *rules of descent* and *rules of residence,* one of a vast array of possible combinations. But before discussing descent and residence, let us examine a third type of family organization, the polygamous, which is now not legal in the United States, although Mormons formerly practiced it.

A *polygamous family* is composed of two or more nuclear families united by a common marriage partner. Polygamy, of course, can take one of two forms: *polygyny,* in which one man is married to two or more women, or *polyandry,* in which one woman is married to two or more men (although this form, as Chapter 17 notes, is quite rare). These patterns are illegal in our society, which is characterized by *monogamy.* Nevertheless, some observers contend that our society is increasingly characterized by *serial polygamy:* Instead of having more than one spouse at one time, many Americans have a number of spouses one at a time, through the process of divorce and remarriage.

This discussion of types of families clearly does not exhaust the topic. For example, *group marriage,* the culturally sanctioned union of two or more men with two or more women, although it is very rare, does occur, and the children of such a marriage do belong to a family.

In addition, in our own society there are borderline cases and deviant patterns that challenge the neat picture we have been painting. For example, in many marriages the adult partners do not have children, either by chance or design, yet they are still considered a family; in most cases a family is defined by a legal contract drawn up as a sign of marriage. Yet the law does recognize that some unions are *de facto* marriages, even though no "license" has been obtained. These unions are granted recognition (if they last long enough) as "common-law marriages," in which everyone concerned is considered to be participating in a lawful union and to have all marital and family rights, including descent and inheritance. Many long-term relationships, however, do not ever earn this social recognition: the relationship between a man and a woman (a "mistress") is usually not so recognized because the partners do not live together in what is called a household. Similarly, long-term relationships between two adults of the same sex (homosexual unions) may not gain social or legal recognition as marriages, even though the partners and their friends may definitely regard them as such.

You should be aware, also, that different societies considered to have the same *type* of family structure do vary greatly in their particular living arrangements, socially prescribed ways of choosing sexual and marriage partners, and so on. In some societies the unit that qualifies as a nuclear family may never live together or have much to do with one another either before or after the marriage ceremony. The Nayars of India, for example, as E. Kathleen Gough (1959) has reported,

Figure 18.1 Homosexual marriages are not legal in most of the United States. Although homosexual couples may find support for their relationships among their friends, they may suffer abuse or legal prosecution in the society at large.

formerly had an unusual arrangement: A young girl of the Nayar caste had to be married before puberty to a man of the appropriate subcaste. After the marriage, which might or might not be consummated, each partner returned to his or her family of orientation to live. The wife then took lovers from her own subcaste or higher ones or from the high landowning caste of Nambudiri Brahmans. If she became pregnant, one of her lovers had to acknowledge his biological paternity by paying the costs of delivery, but he then had no further responsibility toward or rights over the child. If no one made such acknowledgment, penalties for the Nayar mother and child were severe: expulsion, if not death. The point of such acknowledgment of biological fatherhood was evidently to ensure that the family was not "polluted" by contact with a lower caste. Children were expected to resemble their biological fathers. If the required gift was made, the child was accepted into the mother's lineage. The Nayar woman could have any number of lovers at once, and there was often some rivalry among the women to see who could collect the largest number, though the usual number in the eighteenth century was three to eight regular ones. All of a woman's children called all her current lovers by a word meaning "lord." In one area inhabited by the Nayars, the children called their mother's legal husband by a special kinship term. Among all the Nayars, the wife and all her children had to observe the death-pollution customs when the legal husband died.

This arrangement, which seems strange to us, is by no means the only one among the world's peoples that might violate our ideas of what a family is. In at least one society, that of the Nuer of Africa, marriage and the family are founded on the basis of cattle ownership. A woman who becomes wealthy enough in cattle to pay a bride price can buy herself a wife and become the husband and the legal father of her wife's children, who are then her (the "husband's") heirs (Evans-Pritchard, 1940).

It was asserted early in this chapter that the family was a universal of human societies, that a cultural unit that is recognizably a family is a functioning entity in every culture. It should now be clear that we can think of the family as universal only if we allow for wide cultural variation in how that institution is defined. *Historical* evidence, as Norman W. Bell and Ezra F. Vogel (1968) point out, is often contradictory about the forms and functions of families in early civilizations—and often subject to the biases of its interpreters.

Foundations of Family Organization

According to Friedrich Engels, in his *Origin of the Family, Private Property, and the State* (1964), the organization the family takes varies with the organization of the society as a whole. In primitive societies, he felt, group marriage predominated; in "barbaric" ones, what he called the "pairing family" prevailed; and in advanced societies, monogamy plus adultery and prostitution prevailed. Engels felt that monogamy marked the foundation of family form not on "natural" but on *economic* conditions—a victory of private property over a natural collectivism. Thus, for Engels, the two family functions of economic production and the regulation of the rights of inheritance (and therefore of descent) underlie the monogamous family. He goes on to note that "the first division

of labor is that of man and wife in breeding children" and that "the first class antagonism appearing in history coincides with the development of the antagonism of man and woman in monogamy, and the first class oppression with that of the female by the male sex." In Engels' point of view, then, the family both rests on and helps determine inequality of men and women in society and the patterns of individual inheritance. Consequently, he felt, the family as a long-term, functional unit would disappear if and when society owned all economic goods in common. In such a society, a man would not need to be sure he knew which children were his so that he could pass his goods on to them and only them. Advancement in such a society would be totally a matter of individual achievement rather than ascription by family background. Finally, women would not have to surrender personal rights in exchange for the economic security provided by a man, partly because the raising of children—their care, education, and socialization—would be a function performed by society as a whole, collectively.

Of course, Engels' views are far from being accepted by all social observers. Aside from the question whether the historical evidence he cites is adequate, there are two other questions: Can the functions Engels mentions ever be fully taken over by other social institutions? Would all the actual and potential functions of the family be exhausted even after such a shift? What do you think? (The general question of the functions of the family is explored in greater depth later in this chapter.)

Engels' critique of the family as socially enforced slavery for women and, more broadly, as a social institution tied to a particular economic organization led to the attempt in Soviet Russia, early in the postrevolutionary period, to take steps to hasten the disappearance of the family. For example, divorce and abortion were made readily obtainable, and the adoption of children was made illegal. Numerous arguments were made in favor of weakening the family. One of the central issues, of course, was to make women independent, as social beings and as economic consumers. Klara Zetkin (1929), a prominent leader

Figure 18.2   Primary, secondary, and tertiary
relatives of "ego." Double lines represent marriage bonds.

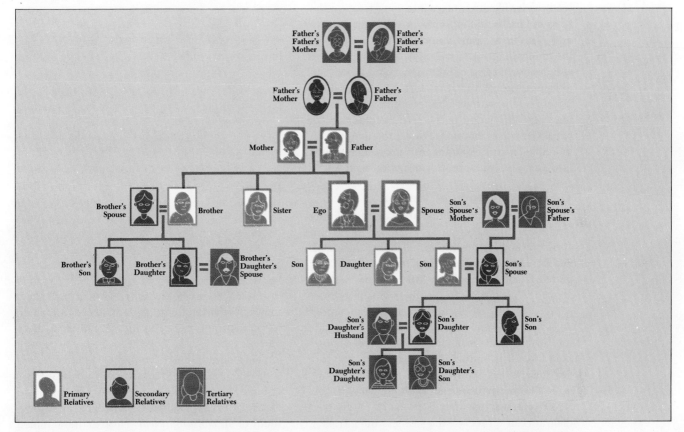

of the Communist movement, quoted Lenin as saying "The home life of a woman is a daily sacrifice to a thousand unimportant trivialities." Lenin then went on to point out that women's subsidiary position put them in a state of mind that causes them actually to hinder the move toward socialism: "The backwardness of women, their lack of understanding for the revolutionary ideals of the man, decrease his joy and determination in fighting." The key to women's freedom was seen as their integration into the work force because the result of such integration would be their economic and social independence.

The Soviet Union, however, as H. Kent Geiger (1968) points out, did not have the resources necessary to provide adequate care for homeless children or economic support for children of divorced mothers, to collectivize housework, to provide for enough public dining halls, and so on. The lack of new, supportive institutions left individu-

als floundering. Crime and delinquency also increased, and the birth rate dropped sharply. By the end of the 1930s the antifamily policies were completely reversed. The new, "Soviet socialist" family was instead extolled as a model of the new Soviet socialist society as a whole and as the best institution for instilling Soviet ideals in children and encouraging Soviet practice in adults. This model parallels the view of the family in most traditional societies and in many societies, such as Nazi Germany, seeking to reorder social values and priorities. Before we close this discussion, we should note, as Geiger does, that "the proposition that human society can do without the family was never seriously tested in Soviet Russia."

KINSHIP

So far we have concentrated on marriage and the family. But kinship system, as was noted earlier,

Figure 18.3   The bilateral descent system, by which American society organizes succession and inheritance. Circles with attached arrows represent males; circles with crosses represent females. Double lines represent marriage bonds. Single horizontal lines show generation, and single vertical lines, descent. Solid lines indicate ego's lineage. In a bilateral descent system, each person is a member of both the mother's and the father's group and inherits through both lineages.

is a broader idea that takes into consideration the issue of family relationships, or relatives, in general. Kinship systems determine the makeup of the family in terms of who may marry whom and also define patterns of inheritance and succession (that is, descent) and residence. Kinship also determines how various families are linked through marriage, a function that is far less important in our society than in ones in which the family is an individual's basic orienting institution. Let us turn now to an examination of rules of descent.

The Descent Aspect of Kinship

Every society assumes that its way of defining families and kinsmen not only makes sense but also is the only reasonable way of doing so. Indeed, family and kinship systems are so taken for granted that groups have little reason to think about them until some members violate the accepted patterns or the group comes into contact with another group that defines these systems differently. Most modern societies have experienced both violations and alternative systems, but earlier societies probably encountered other groups with different patterns only rarely or never.

Anyone who has ever examined a family-tree diagram can appreciate the vastness and intricacy of kinship links. To begin with, let us distinguish between *primary, secondary,* and *tertiary* relatives. Taking the point of reference of any individual—you—*primary relatives* consist of your parents and siblings (that is, your family of orientation) as well as of your spouse and children (your family of procreation). There are then seven types of primary relatives: mother, father, sister, brother, spouse, sons, and daughters. *Secondary relatives* are the primary relatives of your primary relatives, exclusive of your own; for example, your father's father, your spouse's sisters, and your son's wife are secondary relatives of yours. An elaboration of all these possible combinations produces thirty-three types. *Tertiary relatives* are the primary relatives of your secondary relatives, again exclusive of your own primary and secondary relatives. For example, your tertiary relatives include your mother's brother's wife and your son's daughter's husband. There are 151 possible types

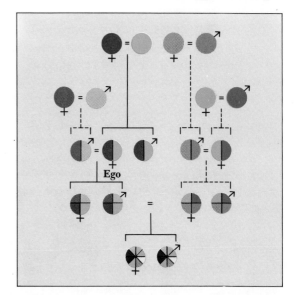

of tertiary relatives, and whereas your genealogy may not include them all, it is likely to include more than one person from a number of these various types.

This description of types of relatives gives some indication of the tremendously complicated task faced by all societies: who shall be recognized as a relative? Obviously, the formal acknowledgment of all *consanguineal relatives* (those linked by blood or common ancestry) and all *affinal relatives* (those related by one or more marital bonds) is theoretically possible but from a practical standpoint unmanageable. For instance, whom do you invite to the wedding?

In resolving this problem of too many relations, all societies evolve *rules of descent* that determine how names, property, power, and privilege—succession and inheritance—are passed from one generation to the next. These rules, obviously, serve to define not only inclusion in but also exclusion from a kinship group.

A rule of descent is either unilateral or bilateral. In *unilateral descent,* children inherit only through one side: descent is *patrilineal* if inheritance occurs through the father's side and *matrilineal* if it occurs only through the mother's side. In *bilateral descent,* inheritance occurs through both parents' lines. The bilateral descent pattern is firmly institutionalized in the United

States and throughout the Western world, although in some parts of it women's right to inherit and hold property in their own names is a very recent acquisition. It should also be noted that this descent pattern does present the problem of too many relatives. An informal but common solution consists of ascribing a sense of closeness to some pairs of relatives and not to others. Inheritance is by and large defined by formal law and social custom, but "closeness" of kinship tends toward informal determination, with sentiment and nearness of residence being important factors.

In a patrilineal system, descent and inheritance are defined totally through the father. Although blood ties exist, children remain excluded from their mother's family. Similarly, in a matrilineal system, descent and inheritance occur only through the mother's line, and no relationship to the father's family is recognized. Societies characterized by matrilineal descent are in the minority. Of the 565 distinct societies catalogued by anthropologists, matrilineal descent prevails in only 84, or fewer than one-seventh of them (Murdock, 1957).

Yet another pattern of defining relatives is known as *double descent*, a system that *selectively* identifies kinship on both sides of the family. For example, an individual may be considered a kinsman of the males of the father's lineage and the females of the mother's lineage, or vice versa.

Rules of Residence

The question of residence is important to the married couple because it determines to a great degree the quality of life that they will experience. Where one lives and with whom one lives makes a lot of difference. Obviously, it would be quite awkward if each member of a married couple remained in their own families of orientation. Rather, they usually live together. The *rules of residence* of a society are those determining where newly married couples will live. The most common pattern in simple societies is called *patrilocal*: the bride and groom establish residence with or near the groom's family of orientation. *Matrilocal residence*, another option, involves the groom's leaving his family to reside with or near

the bride's family. *Bilocal* residence in a society means the newly married couple may reside with the parents of either the bride or the groom. In this instance, the wealth and status of the two families of orientation usually determine which family receives the newly married couple, but in some cases the couple's preference may be an important consideration.

In our society we are accustomed to a pattern termed *neolocal*—literally, "new locale." This means that the newly married couple establishes an independent household. Sociologists and anthropologists have argued that this model, dominant in the industrialized world, is a functional necessity in urban societies. The great population shift from rural to urban areas and the concomitant shift from agricultural production to salaried employment (discussed more fully in Unit VII) are critical factors in the emergence of the neolocal residency pattern.

A fifth pattern of residence is termed *matri-patrilocal.* In this case the couple initially resides with or near the bride's parents and then later establishes permanent residence with or near the groom's parents. There are a variety of reasons for the development of this scheme. The temporary residence may give the bride an opportunity to make the transition in status from daughter to wife; the groom's labor for his in-laws may be considered part of a bride price; or, in some cases, the temporary residence may give the bride's parents a chance to be sure they are willing to have their daughter live permanently with the groom.

A sixth pattern of residence, one that occurs only rarely, is the *avunculocal:* the married couple establishes residence with or near a maternal uncle of the groom.

Some Consequences of Descent and Residence Patterns

Every social pattern, or socially determined way of doing things, has consequences for how life is experienced by people, and certainly descent and residence patterns are important in determining how life is lived. Every society's way of life is different from that of every other society's, but there are certain features and certain problems that are

Figure 18.4   Rules of residence vary among societies. Depending on the society they live in, a newly married couple may go to live with the groom's family (patrilocal residence), the bride's family (matrilocal residence), the groom's mother's brother's family (avunculocal residence), or by themselves (neolocal residence). Another possibility in some societies is for the couple to live with the bride's family for a while and then move in with the groom's family (matripatrilocal residence). Although the most common pattern is the patrilocal, the neolocal pattern is widespread in modern industrial societies such as ours.

likely to attend the presence of particular important institutions in a society.

The woman's eldest living brother in a matrilineal society usually wields the most effective power, although women as a group exercise more power than they do in patrilineal societies. In a society characterized by both matrilineal descent and matrilocal residency, the wife has an advantage over her husband: she is living among her own blood relatives, whereas her husband, who is a member of a different lineage, is a latecomer to his wife's home. Also, the wife in a matrilineal society usually controls much of the food supply, since the crop belongs to her lineage rather than his. Because the crucial social relationships in such a society are those between the mother and her children and the mother's brother and her children rather than between the children and their biological father, matrilineal systems work best when the husband is absent for long periods of time. Here we see a case where the social father is not the same as the biological one. Conflicts in matrilineal societies are far more likely to occur between the husband and his wife's eldest brother than between the husband and his mother-in-law.

It should be noted that whatever the operative principle of descent and residence and whatever the relative weight of blood relationship against affinal relationship, each descent and residence rule carries with it specific prescriptions for interpersonal behavior. And it should also be emphasized again that these patterns of descent and residence are socially established.

The reason why a culture has evolved one system rather than another may be unclear, but when it is possible for observers to trace the history of a culture, some logical (or, in sociological terms, functional) reason why certain patterns of descent and residence emerged generally becomes apparent.

At this point in the discussion you may be wondering what the preceding look at the wide variety of family organizations could possibly contribute to an understanding of the family in American society. The answer is that it allows us to see the contemporary and future American family in the context of a broad array of family patterns and consequently to think about it in terms other than those of disintegration and demise. American society is experiencing a period of change unprecedented in human history. Certainly then, it is not surprising that family structures should experience turmoil and disorganization and face an uncertain future. This is the plight of all institutions in our society. However, to understand the incredible variety of family forms through history and across cultures and to recognize the persistence of the institution is to gain a perspective that suggests that the family may not be disintegrating so much as it is struggling, like other institutions, to evolve a new shape and new functions viable in the emerging social order.

FUNCTIONS OF THE FAMILY

In the earlier discussion of Engels' critique of the family, it was noted that he believed that the family would become a superfluous or regressive institution if and when its functions were absorbed by other social institutions. Just what does the family do for the individual and society? In sociological language, what are the functions of the family? Are these functions changing? Are there universal functions of the family irreplaceable by other institutions and without which human societies could not survive? The answers to these questions are neither obvious nor simple.

As our society has moved in the direction of ever greater complexity and increasing diversification, other institutions have come to share, and in some cases virtually to assume, functions that were earlier considered the exclusive responsibility of the family. For example, the making of clothing and the production of food are no longer considered primarily a family responsibility. However, because we have no experience of a society without families to draw on, it remains impossible for us to definitely confirm or deny their functional necessity for human survival. Closer examination of the functions of the family should, nevertheless, provide some perspective for speculating on the future. We will examine six functions traditionally filled by families and common to all cultures. A review of each of these will make apparent that there is no necessary, inherent reason why any of these functions *must* be performed by a family. But two important questions should be kept in mind: (1) What is the efficiency and effectiveness of the family in performing these functions as opposed to the current or possible efficiency and effectiveness of other institutions in performing them? and (2) What would be the consequence for individuals and society if these functions were not performed at all?

Social Continuance

The first and most critical function of the family is to provide an institutional structure by which the *continuation of the group* can be assured. Even the most optimistic (or pessimistic) speculators about the future do not foresee immortality for human beings. Certainly, human societies must have institutional means for replacing membership in order to assure continuance.

Child Care

The continuation of the group means having babies. Having babies means having to cope with the long period of utter dependency that is characteristic of human infants. There is no logical necessity that the long-term care required by infants be provided by the biological parents; the family—whether or not its adult members are the child's biological progenitors—provides the social means for handling this critical function. In numerous societies, in fact, it is specifically not the responsibility of one or both of the biological parents to care for their infants, because membership in a family depends not on biological but on social relationships. In any case, *care of the physical needs of the young* until they are able to care for themselves constitutes a second important function of the family. As is pointed out in Chapter 17, there are strong economic reasons, as well as obvious emotional ones, why child care is usually consigned to the family.

Economic Support

Marriage also provides a convenient means for the *economic maintenance* of adults. Until the in-

dustrial revolution, the family was the basic unit of production. There seems to be at least some division of labor according to sex in virtually all cultures. In a study of 224 tribes scattered throughout the world, George Murdock (1949) found distinct patterns in work responsibilities between males and females. In more than three-quarters of these societies, men performed tasks requiring very strenuous physical exertion, such as lumbering, mining, and quarrying, and women performed tasks requiring somewhat less physical strength, such as grain grinding, cooking, gathering fuel and vegetables, and making and mending clothes.

It is interesting, however, that this division of labor according to physical capabilities is far from universal. Furthermore, it should be noted that the very idea of one sex being stronger than the other is culturally determined. For example, in some African tribes where women do the agricultural labor, women are considered to be obviously stronger (probably in the sense of having better endurance and stronger constitutions) than men (Albert, 1963). In another tribe, where women bear heavy burdens on their heads, informants told anthropologists that women were naturally suited for such work because their heads are harder. Perhaps a more relevant factor in determining who will do what is that women, because of the need to stay near the children at home, tend to be assigned chores that are primarily local, while those requiring greater physical mobility and absence from the tribe fall to men. With increasing social complexity the physical basis for the division of labor diminishes, but the family still remains the dominant institution for economic cooperation between the sexes.

Childhood Socialization

The preparation of members to become full-fledged participants in the ongoing social order is the family's fourth critical function. This process of *socialization* involves more than simply mastering the skills necessary for self-preservation. Rather, socialization (as we have seen in Chapters 6 and 10) is the process whereby the totality of a

Figure 18.5 We tend to think of strenuous physical activity as "men's work," but that is not true everywhere. These women carry heavy jars on their heads as a matter of daily routine.

culture is transmitted to each new generation. This involves not only learning how, what, and why but also internalizing the knowledge, customs, and values of the society.

As societies have become more complex many institutions outside the family have shared in the socializing function. Schools were created to educate people in formal intellectual skills and social behavior; religious organizations have been formed to instruct them in faith and values; groups have been developed around recreation and sports. Furthermore, the society as a whole has moved to ensure the individual's motiva-tion and participation by providing protection through police, economic support systems, and medical and health programs.

Even though the family has relinquished, at least in part, many of its traditional functions to other institutions, it continues to participate in the socialization of children and the transmission of culture. The family still remains the critical institution from which children learn most of their ideas of right and wrong. Through their families they also acquire their first view of what the world is all about. There is little doubt about the importance of early socialization in shaping the personality of adults. Although socialization is now regarded by social investigators as an ongoing process occurring for the duration of the individual's life, the family does provide the fundamental context in which personality is formed and a view of life acquired. In thousands of ways parents consciously and unconsciously participate in constructing realities that they transmit to their children.

Many may argue that families are generally failing to transmit values adequate and appropriate for a changing world, but it would be hard to argue that families transmit no values. All parents affect their children; even parents who endorse complete individualism and spontaneity are communicating a basic value orientation.

Regulation of Sexual Behavior

A fifth function the family performs is the *regulation of sexual behavior*. There is a great variety of accepted patterns of sexual behavior in human societies. And although deviation from recognized norms occurs in all societies, it is amazing how much of sexual behavior conforms to the established rules.

The Incest Taboo The most widely held and rigidly enforced restriction on sexual behavior is the *incest taboo* or incest prohibition, a rule forbidding sexual relations and marriage between close relatives. Societies vary as to which relatives are included under the incest rule, but the principle applies almost universally to the nuclear family:

brother and sister, mother and son, father and daughter.

Other Regulations When we examine the wide variety of restrictions other than incest placed on sexual behavior, it seems that the avoidance of sexual rivalry plays a central role in the emergence of sexual taboos. A large proportion of human societies permit *adultery*—sexual intercourse after marriage with someone other than one's marital partner—but the conditions, the time, and the persons involved are culturally regulated. In other words, complete sexual freedom is never condoned. The degree to which violation of established norms occurs varies from society to society, as does the severity of sanctions against those who get caught. During the seventeenth century, for example, adultery in Massachusetts carried the death penalty.

Western Society Western society, since about the time of Christian dominance, evolved very restrictive rules governing premarital and extramarital sex. Empirical evidence indicates that these historical prohibitions are now breaking down in American society. Yet, in spite of the large number of persons in our society who occasionally violate the cultural norm and have sexual intercourse outside of marriage, the great majority adhere to the norm most of the time. Even among the unmarried, the majority have sexual intercourse only with a partner they intend to marry (Luckey and Nass, 1969). Although empirical data on sexual behavior in this society date back only about twenty-five years, substantial evidence suggests that our values and behavior are in a period of transition, although probably not so great as advocates of sexual freedom seem to believe. The future will, in all probability, see even greater sexual freedom, especially among the unmarried.

To note transition in our society is not to suggest a present absence of norms. We seem, in fact, to be moving toward clearer definition of norms delineating, for example, when and under what circumstances extramarital sexual relations are permissible. The family as institution will indeed see changes occurring, but within some regulatory limits. Finally, the current confinement of most sexual activities within marriage presents a two-sided issue. One may choose to view this confinement negatively as an imposition placed on individuals to prevent social chaos. But in a more positive vein, marriage assures individuals of the right to a sexual partner for the release of their strong biological drives.

Ascribed Statuses

Another critical function of the family is the *confirmation of social status.* As you have seen, social status may be inherited *(ascribed)* or achieved. Ascribed status significantly affects an individual's chances for achievement. In order for a person born into an upper-class family to fall into a low social status he must fail miserably, whereas one who is born into a lower-class family must combine great individual effort with good fortune to raise his social standing substantially. The "breaks," whether in show business, politics, business, or another sphere, come disproportionately often to those whose families already have comparatively high social status.

Personal Intimacy

A final function is one that relates to the individual and that may be far from last in importance. In fact, it is possible that as various functions of the family are taken over by other institutions the establishment of a long-term *intimate personal and sexual relationship* between two adults that characterizes marital and family relationships may become the most important function of the family in advanced industrial society.

THE FAMILY IN INDUSTRIAL SOCIETY

Most investigators have, like Engels, seen the industrial and technological revolution as the principal cause of the emergence of the nuclear family. William J. Goode (1963), however, who has done a comprehensive study of the relationship between industrialization and family organization, sees a reciprocal and countervailing influence. He argues that "the ideology of the conjugal

Figure 18.6 William J. Goode is a professor of sociology at Columbia University. He is best known for his studies of the family. His *World Revolution and Family Patterns* (1963) received the MacIver Award from the American Sociological Association. His other writings include *After Divorce* (1956) and *Religion Among the Primitives* (1951) as well as many articles and essays.

(nuclear) family has generally entered a country before any substantial industrialization has taken place." The precise causal relationship between industrialization and the emergence of the nuclear family can never be known, but industrialization has clearly had profound consequences on the organization of the family. Goode has presented some of these effects. First, by elevating physical mobility to a pattern of life for many families, industrialization decreases both the amount and the closeness of contact between kin. Similarly, class mobility becomes more and more a characteristic of industrial society, and differences in life styles and incomes often serve to lessen rapport among relatives. A third factor helping to loosen kinship bonds is the development, concurrent with the sophisticated urban and industrial systems, of a multiplicity of agencies, organizations, and programs to handle needs for protection, support in time of need, and so on. People are thus no longer solely responsible for aiding their relatives in times of illness and need. Industrialization also alters value systems, which produces a fourth factor: the precedence of ability and achievement over birth in many instances. A person's kin can now ordinarily offer some opportunity for success, but not an assurance of it. A final, related point is that in the complex industrial state, with its thousands of jobs and vocations, it is far less likely that relatives can obtain jobs for one another.

Isolation of Individuals

Generally, the emergence of the nuclear family in industrial society has been viewed as a great step forward in the liberation of individuals from the rigid bonds of the extended kinship network. The emergence of the nuclear family has aided the development of individualism and sexual equality, but we have paid some heavy tolls for our "progress." Freed from restrictive kinship obligations, people in industrial societies can strike out on their own. But as Marx and many other observers have noted, millions have become captives of the competitive spirit that characterizes the industrial era. Competition and striving to achieve often become insatiable drives, depriving

individuals and families of the time and energy needed for mutual psychological and emotional support. Furthermore, parents often must leave their children alone or in poor and makeshift arrangements while they work. Although the nuclear family may facilitate the growth of intimacy between husband and wife, if rapport is not established, couples are left without the psychological assistance of the extended group.

There is also a clear tendency toward the isolation of children from a larger network of adults from whom they might learn and might gain emotional support. This loss has been mourned by Paul Goodman, Peter Marin, Ivan Illich, and most other proponents of new kinds of schools and a new view of schooling. Children in modern society have few and infrequent opportunities to develop close ties to adults other than their parents. Similarly, the substantial reduction in family size in industrial societies reduces the amount of interaction a child has with children of different ages. Further, if industrialization has encouraged an ideal of social equality of the sexes, its attendant nuclear family has served, as was noted earlier, to isolate women and tie them to an endless repetition of household chores and other service functions that in the extended family were shared. Because of the demands of family life, many of the burdens of which now fall solely on them, women often find themselves playing subordinate roles and missing out on many of the advantages theoretically open to them. Furthermore, many hangovers of patriarchal society seem to linger on in the definition of roles within the modern nuclear family, which puts strains on both the female and the male members.

Another serious negative accompaniment of the emergence of the nuclear family is the repeal of the authority of the aging and their estrangement from the mainstream of society. Historically, the elders of a family always received great respect as the bearers of wisdom and experience. In industrial society we treat the aged as obsolete. Except for a very small minority, elders are excluded from decision making, forced into retirement, given woefully inadequate pensions, and dismissed to "retirement communities"—either

Figure 18.7   In contemporary industrial societies the primary reason for divorce is emotional incompatibility, a cause that may be related to the strains placed upon people in the isolated nuclear family and to the social definition of their roles. (From U.S. Department of Health, Education, and Welfare.)

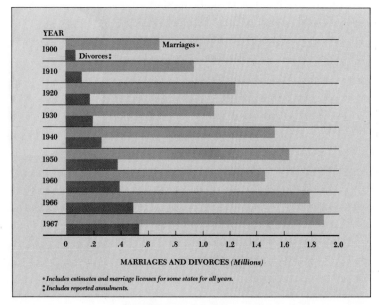

Divorce

Divorce is also considered to be a negative result of the industrial revolution. Divorce, of course, is not unique to modern societies: it exists in many nonliterate and peasant cultures, it is mentioned in the Bible, and it was well-known in Athens and Rome. But inadequate data make comparisons of cross-cultural and historical rates of divorce virtually impossible. Desertion, *de facto* bigamy, and psychological or emotional separation of couples who continue to occupy the same residence exist in many cultures; but we have no statistics on the frequency of adaptation to unsatisfactory marriage. We can speculate that in rural nineteenth-century America, most women found it an economic necessity to endure marriage, no matter how intolerable it may sometimes have seemed. Now, much of the increase in divorce in Western society is accounted for by the rising status of women and their increased economic power (Goode, 1962).

Popular journalists, as well as some social scientists, have tended to exaggerate the divorce rates

new plastic heavens in sunny suburbia or crumbling tenement havens in dingy central cities—where they can only watch other forgotten ones die while they await their turn.

and their negative consequences. For example, one in four marriages now ends in divorce. For those marrying the first time, the present rate of divorce is closer to one in six. Most marriages that end in divorce seem to begin to crumble in the first year of their existence, though the final breakup may not occur until several years later. About a third of all divorces do not involve children. And, with the exception of a few occupational categories, the divorce rate declines as one moves further up the social scale (Divorce Statistics Analysis, 1964).

Some research has shown that children are less likely to suffer emotional disturbance if their parents separate rather than remain together unhappily "for the sake of the children" (Nye, 1957). This contention does not negate the emotional trauma divorce brings for many adults and children. But divorce may offer a much healthier and wiser course, causing fewer lasting wounds than the alternative of remaining married despite incompatible interests and emotional needs.

Until recently, divorce was a serious social handicap that people sought to hide. Today, Johnny Carson, who exemplifies our cultural image of the all-American nice guy from a Nebraska farm, can joke about his divorce on national television. In the future our attitudes seem certain to become even more liberal. Similarly, courts are likely to continue to move in the direction of more lenient divorce procedures.

However, this does not mean divorce rates will continue to rise indefinitely. For many years the age at which people marry has been declining in the United States. People who marry when they are very young are more likely to get divorced. But assuming that our society's codes of courtship and premarital sexual behavior become even more permissive, young people will probably be less anxious to rush into marriage, and hence the average age at marriage will begin to rise. If this does happen, then we might expect people to do a better job of selecting mates on the basis of more permanent qualities of compatibility and thus effect a decline in the divorce rate. Another possibility is the establishment of more than one kind of marriage contract: for example, a temporary contract for those without children, easily dissoluble, and a more permanent contract for the rearing of children.

THE FUTURE OF THE FAMILY

The far-reaching changes we are experiencing in American society and the world make any predictions about the future of the family quite problematical. The isolation imposed by industrial societies has indeed put excessive strains and burdens on marital and parental roles, and in the future we can expect to see structural changes to ease them. But it is unclear precisely how they might be accomplished.

In looking for answers to the question of whether the family will survive, we have looked at evidence that the family is not restricted to an institution of the precise form it has taken in our culture; we have noted that families may perform any or all of numerous functions; and we have noted that the family seems to be universal—that is, there is an institution in every known society that can be identified as a family.

Perhaps the most certain thing about the family of the next quarter century or so is its potential for diversity. The trend toward fewer children will probably continue. It is also likely that modern societies will maintain the pattern of high physical mobility. It follows, therefore, that with the exception of a very small minority, few extended kinship ties will endure. We may, however, move toward creating surrogate families, perhaps themselves transient, fluid, and flexible, for fulfilling some of the functions earlier met by extended families.

It seems that the psychological functions of the family—intimacy, emotional support, a special sense of belonging—may survive the loss of all the larger social and material ones, such as economic support, transmission of cultural beliefs and values, and education. Israeli *kibbutzim*—communal agricultural communities—are often cited as examples of how societies may structure alternatives to the nuclear family. Yet, as Melford Spiro (1968)

has pointed out, there is still a strong *sense* of family on the kibbutz, even though children are not raised by and do not live with their parents and are not directly supported by them. Instead, these functions have been ceded to the kibbutz, which Spiro suggests may itself be regarded as a familylike group. It may also be important to point out that the kibbutzim function within the context of a Western-type society and thus by no means characterize Israeli social organization as a whole.

You may have noticed that many communes in the United States pattern themselves on the family as well, and, in fact, each commune usually refers to itself as a family. It is conceivable that if such groups continue they may provide one of the future patterns for family life in America. If Western society continues to grow more tolerant, and if governmental opposition abates, it is possible that a number of different family styles may come to exist simultaneously: those governed by temporary or trial marriage, limited contractual marriage, homosexual marriage, group marriage, communes, professional child rearing, and other forms. At the same time, the nuclear family pretty much as we know it today will not disappear. In spite of the limitations of the nuclear family, in many ways it suits modern society. The future may bring adaptation of the basic model rather than its abandonment.

SUGGESTED READINGS

Bell, Norman W., and Ezra F. Vogel. *The Family.* New York: Free Press, 1968.

Goode, William J. *World Revolution and Family Patterns.* New York: Free Press, 1963.

Murdock, George P. *Social Structure.* New York: Macmillan, 1949.

Parsons, Talcott, and Robert F. Bales. *Family, Socialization, and Interaction Process.* Glencoe, Ill.: Free Press, 1955.

Spiro, Melford E., with the assistance of Audrey G. Spiro. *Children of the Kibbutz.* 2nd ed. New York: Schocken Books, 1967.

STUDY THE PAST

Chapter 19 Education

IN ORDER TO SURVIVE, a society must transmit its values, attitudes, knowledge, and skills to each new generation. As we saw in the previous chapter, the process of primary socialization begins in the family, but as societies become increasingly complex, formal educational institutions develop to prepare new generations for participation in society. And in industrial societies, education not only helps transmit knowledge and skills but is the principle means of individual social mobility.

Education is the United States' largest industry: Nearly sixty million full-time students between the ages of three and thirty-four—well over a quarter of the American population—are enrolled in schools and colleges staffed by more than three million teachers and professors. Millions more study part-time in adult and extension courses or in schools and training programs operated by the armed forces or private industry. Millions of industrial and white-collar workers supply these students and teachers with buildings, books, blackboards, and other goods and services required in the actual work of education.

Formal education also embraces an increasing proportion of the individual's life span. For many occupations, the bachelor's degree from college provides only preliminary training. With graduate and postgraduate training becoming more important, an increasing number of people in our society spend a quarter to a third of their lives in formal education.

The United States was the first nation to achieve universal secondary education, the first nation to develop a system of mass higher education, and is now the first to aim at achieving universal higher education. As a result, over 80 percent of young Americans now finish high school, and over half of these obtain some form of higher education.

The pattern of universal secondary education and mass higher education is increasingly being emulated by underdeveloped societies. Social scientists, such as Aldo Solari (1967), have measured the "advancement" of underdeveloped or developing countries in Latin America by the extent to which each country has embraced universal or mass forms rather than traditional elitist forms of secondary education.

A FUNCTIONALIST ACCOUNT OF AMERICAN EDUCATION

Several theoretical perspectives have developed to account for the growth of formal educational institutions in mature industrial societies. This section considers the historic rise of education from a *functionalist* perspective. The next section presents arguments against the functionalist approach and offers an alternative interpretation based on *conflict theory*. The basic assumptions of both views are discussed in detail in Chapter 4.

Sociologists such as Martin Trow (1961), S. N. Eisenstadt (1956), and Burton Clark (1962) view secondary and higher education in industrial societies as resulting from extensive economic and professional specialization. Because the family alone cannot transmit all of the specialized technical knowledge that has been accumulated, schools have become the almost universal device for the transmission of this knowledge (Solari, 1967).

The functionalist perspective examines education in terms of the functions it fulfills for society. This perspective has been used to describe the development of mass secondary and higher education as a response to shifts in the occupational structure of the United States. Although the roots of our educational system lie partly in the early Puritan emphasis on being able to read God's word as revealed in the Bible, the real thrust toward the growth of American mass secondary education came with the shift from an agrarian to an industrial economy following the Civil War.

Education and Work in American History

According to many scholars and educators, successful operation of the emerging industrial economy required knowledge and mastery of new skills and techniques that only extensive education could provide. Life in the developing industrial towns and cities was changing accordingly: The division of labor multiplied occupations by the thousands, and new professions and semi-professions began to emerge. The link between

Figure 19.1   The members of this nineteenth-century
high-school graduating class probably came from
wealthy families, and the men most likely went on to
college and then into elite occupations and professions.
Most young people from less advantaged families
either did not complete high school or, if they did, got
jobs as soon after graduation as they could.

educational institutions and occupational structure becomes apparent as one traces the development of American secondary education.

In 1870 there were roughly 80,000 students
enrolled in secondary schools throughout the nation, the bulk of them in private academies. The
16,000 high-school graduates of 1870 made up
only about 2 percent of the seventeen-year-olds
in the country, but a very large proportion of this
number went on to college.

Prior to 1870, the secondary-school system offered a curriculum and enforced standards of
scholarship that were geared to the admission requirements of the colleges. American education
at this time could be characterized as elitist; the
small proportion of high-school and college-age
students were primarily upper- or upper-middle-
class youth who went on to fill the traditional
professions of law and the ministry. However,
after 1870, changes in the occupational structure
brought about the growth of the American high
school and college and a reorganization of the curricula of these institutions. Since the Civil War,
and especially since World War I, the economy

base has shifted to huge bureaucratized organizations characterized by central decision making,
mass production, and mass marketing. As small
organizations became large, written orders replaced verbal ones. Organizational growth demanded new occupations and skills for the re-
ception, recording, retrieval, evaluation, and
transmission of information. The phenomenal expansion of the secondary-school system after the
Civil War occurred largely as a response to the
economy's demand for a labor force of white-
collar employees with better credentials than the
bare literacy provided by elementary school.

After 1870 the number of public high schools
began to grow. By 1910 nearly 15 percent of the
fourteen- to seventeen-year-olds—a total of more
than 1,000,000—were enrolled in secondary
schools, and 90 percent of them were enrolled in
the more than 10,000 public high schools then in
operation. As the 1930s drew to a close, public and
private secondary schools included 65 percent of
the children from the ages fourteen to seventeen.
Between 1870 and the end of World War II, the
growing mass secondary system provided a useful

and increasingly vocational education for the new group of white-collar workers.

Occupational Structures and Mobility

Since World War II, changes in occupations in the United States have resulted in changes in secondary education and higher education. Between 1940 and 1950 the number of engineers in the country doubled, and the number of scientific research workers increased by 50 percent. Between 1950 and 1960 the total labor force increased by only 8 percent, but professional and technical positions grew by 68 percent. Largely because of the sustained economic prosperity following World War II and the subsequent demand for highly trained people, middle-class youth are now expected to go to college. College enrollment has increased also because college graduation has increasingly become a general expectation and requirement for entry into the white-collar job market, even though it may not be essential for the performance of most jobs.

As recently as 1940, college students represented only 15 percent of the eighteen- to twenty-one-year-old age group. By 1954, that proportion had risen to 30 percent and by 1960 to approximately 37.5 percent. In 1970, institutions of higher education enrolled a student body of nearly half of that entire age group—more than 7 million people. Since 1930, the rate of college enrollment has increased nearly eight times as fast as that of the total population, and since 1910, graduate enrollment has multiplied more than forty times as quickly as the growth rate of the total population of the United States.

College enrollment levels also have affected secondary-school curricula. The impetus to develop college preparatory courses in high schools was no doubt aided by the demands of parents who wished to assure their children a middle-class life style.

The rise of higher education reflects the growing expectation of acquiring a college degree and upward social mobility. Indeed, the American dream of the land of opportunity is inextricably linked with education. Many Americans in this century have used first the high-school diploma

Figure 19.2 Enrollment rates in secondary and higher education in the United States from 1870 to 1980 (projected). In Phase One, secondary and higher education was available only to an elite minority. Phase Two saw the growth of mass secondary education, but higher education was still the privilege of a small but growing minority. Only relatively recently has there been a rapid rise in higher-educational enrollment, as higher-status positions have increased in the society (Phase Three).

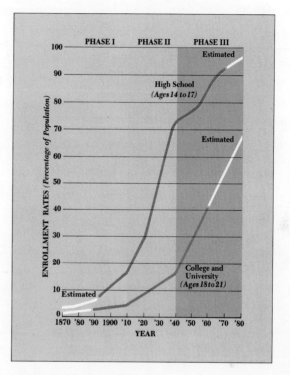

and then the college degree to improve their social status.

Although the functional analysis of education provides a plausible account of the development of educational institutions in the United States, it does not completely explain the peculiar history of American educational development, as compared with educational development in other industrial societies. Seymour Martin Lipset and Reinhard Bendix (1966) indicate on the basis of cross-cultural data that the long-term effect of industrialization has been the expansion of the middle classes. As industrialization advances in both the United States and abroad, the proportion of professional, official, managerial, and white-collar positions increases while that of manual positions declines. However, because the structure of the labor force has changed in societies with a variety of educational systems, it is difficult to prove that mass public education has played a necessary role preparing individuals for particular occupations. Moreover, the educational upgrading that is characteristic of American society may not have been caused by the increasing complexity of

Figure 19.3   According to functionalists, education in an industrial society provides formal training that enables people to fill specialized occupational roles and possibly to achieve high status solely on the basis of their own achievements. Conflict theorists, in contrast, point out that educational institutions serve as mechanisms for occupational placement of different status groups. Thus, as this picture suggests, one young man from a privileged background may emerge from the halls of higher learning and go on to become a corporation president or top university administrator; another young man, from a more modest working-class or lower-middle-class family, may go through a program of higher learning only to take a subordinate position in either of these specialized organizations. Is getting a college degree actually the key to upward social mobility for everyone in the educational system, or does a college degree groom for benefits only members of certain elite groups?

occupations. The jobs themselves may not require more education; in fact, jobs that require a year or two of college training in the United States are being staffed in Germany and Great Britain by high-school graduates (Lipset and Bendix, 1966).

EDUCATION AND STRATIFICATION

According to Randall Collins (1971), the functionalist theory of education is a special application of the more general functional approach. This general approach states that occupational positions require particular kinds of skilled performance and that positions must be filled by persons who have either the training or native ability to perform the occupational role.

The functionalist theory of education also states that the occupational structure creates demands for particular kinds of performance and that training is one way of filling these demands. In this way, the functional theory of education is tied to the functional theory of stratification developed by Kingley Davis and Wilbert E. Moore (see Chapter 15). The growth of education is seen primarily as a response to the demands of increasingly specialized occupations in industrial society. Those with enough talent and perseverance to endure extensive schooling will enter new occupations created by the emerging industrial order. Many individuals, irrespective of their social origins, will be able to enter high occupational positions because occupational attainment will be based upon achievement (on educational credentials or certificates), not on inherited wealth.

Arguments Against Functionalism

Collins questioned the validity of the functionalist theory of educational development on several grounds. First, educational requirements for jobs in industrial societies have not increased primarily because of an increase in jobs requiring a great deal of skill and a decrease in jobs requiring little skill. Collins estimates that only 15 percent of the increase in educational requirements imposed on the American labor force during this century can be attributed to a replacement of low-skill jobs by high-skill jobs. Most of the educational upgrading has gone on *within* job categories—the education required to obtain a particular job has been raised over time. For the most part, Collins argues, well-educated people are presently doing the same kind of work that less educated people used to do.

Second, the functionalist theory of education assumes that formal education provides training in actual job skills. However, most skilled manual workers acquire their skills on the job or as part of union apprenticeships. Also, vocational education for manual positions is virtually independent of occupational attainment. Graduates of vocational programs are not, in fact, more likely to be employed than high-school dropouts (Plunkett, 1960; Duncan, 1964).

The importance of formal schooling for nonmanual occupations is more difficult to specify.

Because the traditional professions of medicine and law have legal requirements that prohibit noncertified individuals from practicing the arts of the occupation, there are no noncertified practitioners to study for comparison. In 1950, however, 40 percent of engineers lacked college degrees, which indicates that even highly technical skills may be acquired by on-the-job training.

Third, formal education seems to be more of a status-achieving mechanism than a mechanism for imparting new knowledge. For example, the professional occupational associations of teaching, social work, and nursing have consistently tried to make educational qualifications a legal necessity for practice; this restriction of entrance to a select group of people helps improve the group's economic position on the labor market. As a result, numerous semiprofessional groups, such as beauticians and morticians, have sprung up in American society.

Last, beyond the stages of mass literacy, formal education does not necessarily contribute to economic development. Time-lag correlations between education and economic development show that mass secondary education has not preceded industrialization; in fact, industrialization and economic development occurred in Western Europe and the United States after only 30 to 50 percent of the seven- to fourteen-year-old age group was in school.

Collins' main argument is that education serves functions other than preparing people for the labor force. Indeed, there is a strong relationship between educational institutions and systems of stratification in all societies. In all industrial societies, mass public education has meant increasing reliance on achievement criteria, but not the end of status ascription. Achievement and ascription are discussed at length in Chapter 12.

The Conflict Model and Stratification

Collins provides what can be called a *conflict model* of education and stratification. According to this model, society is made up of status groups. Such groups consist of families and friends, but they may extend to religious, educational, or ethnic communities. In general, members of a status group share a common life style or culture that defines particular styles of dress and patterns of social behavior. Individuals in all societies derive their social identity through membership in these groups. Individuals may identify themselves in certain ways that reflect their status group. For example, an upper-class or even middle-class individual often identifies himself as having "breeding" or "respectability," and an individual with less income may identify himself as "just plain folks."

The social basis for these status groups is the system of stratification itself: Individuals have different life styles because they hold different economic positions, and they have affiliations with different ethnic, religious, educational, and cultural groups.

People struggle to obtain what is highly valued and scarce—in other words, property, power, and prestige. Most of the conflict concerning access to valuable goods is actually conflict between status groups. For example, in large governmental, military, or industrial organizations, status groups may hire individuals on the basis of their status-group affiliation, not merely on the basis of their native ability or acquired skills. The elite members of American business often select their successors on the basis of certain life-style traits they believe junior executives should exhibit. Elite status groups may also manipulate lower-level employees by indoctrinating them with the idea that the power of the controlling status group derives from its superiority. Educational requirements serve a dual purpose: they limit applicants for elite positions to those who share an elite culture, and they secure the respect of lower-level employees who do not have the requisite formal training.

Viewed from the perspective of conflict theory, the increase in secondary and higher education and in educational requirements for jobs in the United States results more from the desire of status groups to maintain their positions in the occupational hierarchy than from the need for more formal training. Educational institutions,

then, are seen as being the link between various status groups and occupational prestige.

Educational institutions provide students not only with educational skills but with certain values and patterns of behavior that will identify them with a certain status group and therefore make them eligible for certain positions. In this sense, formal education provides a life style. In the 1880s, for example, private secondary schools for children of the WASP (White Anglo-Saxon Protestant) upper class were founded when mass public secondary education no longer provided their children with a distinctive elite culture. However, even the American public high school was founded by WASP elites who wished to instill their values of propriety and industry in the growing number of immigrants from Catholic and non-Anglo-Saxon countries of eastern Europe.

The scope and functions of the public secondary school expanded to include preparation for social and civic responsibility, healthful living, and recreation. Functionalist scholars say that this diversification of high-school curricula has resulted from the growing need for occupational specialization. However, the emphasis on such subjects as etiquette, personal hygiene, and American government indicates that educators were as much concerned with "Americanizing" and "middle-classifying" high-school youth as with preparing them for future employment (Cremin, 1964).

The functionalist view of education fits the pattern of growth of formal educational institutions in all industrial and industrializing societies. The conflict model of education, however, emphasizes the way educational institutions work as a mechanism of occupational placement for different status groups. As we have seen, there is abundant evidence to suggest that the conflict-model view of the roles that schools and universities play is accurate. Indeed, the university, college, or even the high school that an individual attends is an important predictor of his future career pattern, irrespective of the skills he learns in these institutions. Employers in large corporations are dubious about how much actual skill is acquired in formal education, but they nevertheless require a college degree for higher levels of management because they think that individuals with college degrees have demonstrated sufficient "motivation" and "social experience" to enable them to assimilate managerial ideology (Gordon and Howell, 1959). Nationally organized corporations and large law firms in the United States consistently recruit from upper-class Ivy League schools and thereby perpetuate the employment of elite WASPs. The smaller manufacturing and retail trade occupations and the solo practices, such as the practice of law, draw people primarily from other ethnic minorities such as Jews, Italians, and blacks. Educational prestige also influences placement in government positions. Local government offices are dominated by many ethnic groups, but particular branches of the federal government such as the State and Treasury departments typically recruit members from WASP elite universities.

American Values and Occupational Structures

In conclusion, both functionalist and conflict-theory explanations are useful; perhaps only a combination of viewpoints fits all the facts in the American educational system. Shifts in the occupational structure in the United States offer an incomplete explanation of the extraordinary growth in secondary and higher education. Still, the growth of education and the increasing supply of educated persons has made education a requirement for many jobs. The growth of educational institutions has unquestionably raised the aspirations of the American population, and the schools have responded to popular demand. Americans, believing in a causal connection between education and both individual and national welfare, have at times seemed to see education as a sovereign remedy for all the ills of society.

Other countries such as Great Britain, however, have experienced comparable revolutions in their economic structure without comparable transformations in education. According to Joseph Ben-David (1963), the middle classes in Great Britain have alternate routes to social mobility

and therefore do not demand extensive higher education as do the American middle classes. In Great Britain, an individual can enter many professions such as law and medicine on the basis of apprenticeship or be technically trained on the job in engineering and business. In the United States certification by formal educational institutions has traditionally been the avenue of social mobility (Ben-David, 1963).

The general endorsement of equality of opportunity, the great power attributed to education throughout our history, and the role of education as a means of upward mobility have all contributed to the unique American commitment to mass secondary and higher education. The structural need for education (emphasized by functionalists) and American values combined with the demands of various status groups (emphasized by conflict theorists) have altogether produced a unique educational system in this country.

INEQUALITY IN EDUCATION

In the United States, as in other industrial societies, an individual's level of education determines to a large extent his position in society. However, as mentioned previously, despite the proliferation of American schools and colleges and the emergence of achievement criteria, or credentials, for most occupations, an individual's social origins are still a major determinant of his or her occupational success. Whether the educational system is a servant of the status quo or a vehicle of social mobility is a matter of constant public debate. As James S. Coleman (1972) notes, the problems of equal educational opportunity traditionally have been discussed in terms of the quality of textbooks, size of classrooms, age of school buildings, and extent of teacher training. However, sociologists recently have been looking at the influence of several other factors on an individual's opportunities for educational attainment.

Social Origins

Recent studies indicate that blacks and other minority groups actually constitute a small frac-

Figure 19.4   James S. Coleman is a professor of social relations at Johns Hopkins University. Coleman is a prominent figure in survey research, mathematical sociology, simulation games, and educational sociology. He is coauthor with Seymour Martin Lipset of *Union Democracy* (1956) and author of *The Adolescent Society* (1961) and *Introduction to Mathematical Sociology* (1964). He is perhaps most widely known as author of the "Coleman Report," which gave the results of an extensive study of the public schools undertaken for Congress. The report appeared as *Equality of Educational Opportunity* (1966). His findings that the educational achievement of teachers and the quality of school buildings and equipment had little or no influence on student performance touched off a controversy that still continues.

tion of those who are disadvantaged throughout life as the result of inequality of education—most persons so disadvantaged are white. The studies show that cumulative inequalities stem from social origins. Social class is therefore a better predictor of educational achievement than is race.

William Sewell (1971) has conducted one of the most comprehensive and thorough studies of the impact of social origins on educational attainment. He summarized the results of his study in his presidential address to the American Sociological Association in 1971. Sewell and his associates followed the career development of 9,000 randomly selected Wisconsin high-school seniors for fourteen years beginning in 1957. Dividing his sample into four Socioeconomic-Status (SES) groups, Sewell found that those in the highest quartile had a 2.5 times greater chance of continuing in some kind of higher education than those in the lowest quartile. The individuals in the highest SES groups were four times more likely to attend college, six times more likely to graduate, and nine times more likely to receive graduate or professional training. On the whole, the higher the SES group an individual belonged to, the more likely he was to achieve a higher level of education in his lifetime.

Sex

Sex was also found to be an important factor in determining achievement in higher education. Males were more likely to attain higher education than were females, but again, social origin was an important factor in determining probabilities. In the highest SES group, males were 28 percent more likely than were females to complete college, and they had a 29 percent better chance of going on to professional or graduate school. In the lowest SES group, the sex differences were much more marked: males had an 86 percent better chance than did females of graduating from college and a 25 percent greater chance of going on to professional or graduate school (Sewell, 1971).

Various women's liberation groups have conducted their own studies on inequalities of opportunity determined by sex. These studies indicate that children's books, advertising, and other image-making media inhibit feminine initiative and ambition. Sewell's study showed that women of higher SES backgrounds achieved a higher educational status than did women of lower status, but in all SES groups women attained less education than men did.

The Educational Environment and Segregation

Sewell's research also showed that family income is not the only variable to be considered in understanding a child's performance in school: Home environment also matters. The educational attainment of the parents significantly affects the child's educational attainment. Sewell found that each year of either parent's education was worth one-tenth of a year of higher education for their child—after taking into account the effects of the father's occupational status and family income. The children of parents with only grade-school education obtained on the average one and one-half years less education than did children of parents who were both college graduates—even if their fathers had similar jobs and their families had similar incomes.

The 1964 Civil Rights Act in part called for a survey to study unequal access to educational opportunities in the United States. The effect of the educational environment on a student's performance has been most extensively examined by the Coleman Report (1966). James S. Coleman and his associates tested and questioned nearly 600,000 students in first, third, sixth, ninth, and twelfth grades in 4,000 public schools across the nation. The Coleman team found that racial minorities scored significantly lower than did whites on achievement tests upon entering school and that these differences increased with each grade level. By the twelfth grade, blacks, Puerto Ricans, American Indians, and Mexican Americans were on the average three to five grade levels behind whites in reading comprehension and four to six grade levels behind in mathematics achievement.

The low level of school performance of these minorities is partly a result of the increasing "class segregation" of American students at the primary and secondary level. The suburbanization of the middle classes has had dire consequences for lower-class students, irrespective of their ethnic origins. In 1950 there were 98.3 million persons in our major metropolitan areas, but by 1960, the number in those areas had increased by 26.4 percent. However, the increase in central cities was only 10.7 percent, whereas suburban areas expanded 48.6 percent. This growth of suburban populations has been accompanied by the migration of relatively young, well-educated, and wealthy parents of school-age children. In contrast, the central cities increasingly are composed of rural and small-town migrants of a much lower socioeconomic status.

The significant consequence of these population shifts is poor education for the central-city child. Because school districts are supported by local taxes, the migration of upper-income groups out of the city has meant less tax expenditure on the segregated lower-class child.

Coleman's research demonstrates that a child's performance, especially a working-class child's performance, is greatly benefited by his going to school with children of stronger educational backgrounds. Moreover, as long as the school enrolls predominantly middle-class students—60 percent or more—the smaller group of lower-class students seems to have no detrimental effect on the performance of middle-class students. In these schools, there seems to emerge a pattern of *cultural dominance;* that is, middle-class norms prevail, and students and teachers alike strive to maintain the relatively high standards of performance characteristic of middle-class schools.

The work of Coleman and Sewell suggests that inequality of education is not a problem that can be eliminated by merely pouring more money into educational facilities. American cities remain residentially segregated by class as well as race. Students of lower social origins are usually segregated in schools where they interact only with students like themselves, who generally have not been encouraged by teachers and parents to achieve. The net effect is a total milieu that dis-

courages educational performance at every level.

Ideally, the establishment of a public system of education for all citizens should remove the environmental handicaps imposed by birth or poverty. As Chapter 5 points out, if environmental handicaps were removed, genetics alone would determine intelligence: the school system would function to give innately intelligent children from all social classes free and equal access to preparatory schools, colleges, and universities. However, sociological research indicates that the problem is much more complex. Because intelligence is determined not by heredity alone but also by culture and environment, there must be alternate ways of providing equal access to those environmental factors that develop intelligence —or whatever it is that intelligence tests measure.

Research findings have greatly influenced court decisions ordering racial integration and busing. However, there are obvious limitations on the effectiveness of such programs. For example, although blacks constitute a minority of only 11 percent in our society, the large majority live in urban areas where they represent much greater proportions of the population. The sheer logistics of busing enough students to achieve the desired balance is staggering, and perhaps busing on this scale is administratively impossible. In addition, the resistance of so many people to busing may make it politically improbable.

There are no easy solutions to the present inequality of opportunity. Marion Stearns' report (1971) on the preschool programs under Project Head Start and the Elementary Secondary Education Act specifies many of the difficulties of programs that aim to reduce the cultural disadvantages of children from low-income families by placing them in prekindergarten classes. Stearns points out that these programs, which reach about one-half million children every year, are initially successful in changing the intellectual and social behavior of children but that the effects of their preschool training gradually decrease. By the end of the first grade the nonpreschooled children begin to catch up. By the third grade there are no significant differences in either intelligence or

academic achievement of disadvantaged children who have or have not had preschool compensatory education—both groups have fallen behind their grade level. The short-term effects of these programs do not mean that they are worthless but that continuing programs are needed to help counterbalance the environment of poverty.

Status Inflation

The strong relationship between educational achievement and social and economic success will continue to be a pressing social issue. However, not all sociologists agree that improving educational opportunities will appreciably alter inequality. Murray Milner (1972) argues that the

value of an education actually decreases as the average level of education increases within the society. Although lower-class persons who receive a college education obtain a higher status than they would have if they had not attended college, the net consequence of spiraling education is the creation of *status inflation*. In other words, in all occupational categories, educational requirements will increase, but individuals who are better educated than their parents will not reap a significantly higher standard of living.

Inequality of education is prevalent not only at elementary and secondary levels but also at higher levels. The work of Martin Trow (1962) suggests that the massive expansion of American higher education has not removed inequality at the college level.

For example, between 1930 and 1961 the number of students enrolled in higher education rose from about 1.3 million to over 3.9 million. In 1939, college and university enrollment comprised about 14 percent of the eighteen- to twenty-one-year-old population; by 1961, about 38 percent of that population. Despite this increase, social-class origins still influence a child's future income because social origins affect not only the probabilities of a child's going on to college but help determine which college he or she will attend. The selective and often expensive private colleges and universities draw students from higher social strata than do large public universities, state colleges, and the junior colleges. The college a student attends affects his probable future income as well as his chances of going to a good graduate school and achieving distinction.

Systems and Policies

The California system of higher education provides one example of the trend of American higher education. In 1960 there were approximately 276,000 full-time students enrolled in California colleges and junior colleges; the number doubled by 1970. The California system of higher education includes three independent systems—junior colleges, state colleges, and the University of California—and each system provides a different form of higher education.

Each institution has academic admission policies that largely determine the SES composition of the student body. The junior colleges have an open-door policy: they are required to accept any individual with a high-school diploma. The state colleges are more selective in their admission policies: they recruit their students from the top half of the high-school graduates. The University of California has the most restrictive policy toward undergraduate admission and selects from the top 12 to 13 percent of the state's graduates.

The consequences of California's system are apparent when one takes into account the SES composition of the student body of each of the three systems. Although tuition to each of the colleges is minimal, social origins once again determine which college a youth will attend. The junior and state colleges are almost wholly nonresidential, but the University campuses draw their students from greater distances and most of them live in college dormitories or residential areas around the campus. It is unlikely that school fees bar many who are otherwise qualified from attending the California public system of higher education, but living costs are a significant factor.

A study carried out both in the Midwest and California indicated that the likelihood for working-class students to attend college is determined by the availability of local colleges to attend (Trow, 1962). The effect of the availability of public education on lower-class youth is very clearly seen: where the community offers a local public junior college, half of the boys from lower-class backgrounds go on to college, as compared with only 15 percent of boys from similar backgrounds living in communities with no local college. The presence of a four-year state college in the community raised the proportion of students going to college among these lower-class boys to nearly a third. Students from professional and other white-collar backgrounds are much more likely to go to college out of town. Therefore, the effect of local public institutions on the proportion who go to college is smaller, but still appreciable, among boys of middle-class origins and still smaller among those who have upper-middle-class origins.

The California system of higher education not only reflects the various social classes in the community but offers different opportunities for students. Burton Clark's case study (1960) of a junior college in California indicates that only approximately one-third of the junior-college students go on to a four-year program; the rest are channeled into vocational courses requiring only two years—which means that the student becomes, say, an engineering aide rather than an engineer. Similarly, the four-year degree offered by state-college system usually does not lead to scholarly research or the professions. Only the University of Cali-

Figure 19.6   Two types of classrooms in England. Debates have raged for centuries concerning the most appropriate form of schooling for children. The spectrum of schooling advocated by adults ranges from the "open classroom" (*top*), stressing creativity and self-direction, to the traditional, regimented schoolroom (*bottom*), in which students are all required to learn the same things at the same time.

in the quality and prestige of colleges and universities result in inequalities that affect the student's chances once he enters the job market.

THE QUALITY OF AMERICAN EDUCATION

The quality is no less important than the inequality of education; in fact, the two are related in many respects. The public debate over the quality of American education began with the first satellite launched by the Soviet Union in 1957. As a nation, we were concerned that anyone had been able to outpace us to such an astonishing degree in scientific and military achievements. The bulk of the criticism fell on our educational system. Educators, the critics contended, had become concerned with the psychological adjustment of the child rather than with his basic-subject competence, especially in mathematics and science.

This furor led to unprecedented government investment in education, primarily in higher education. The results are now history. By winning the race to the moon, Americans demonstrated that they were not inferior. But over the last fifteen years the turmoil over the quality of education has continued to intensify. Today almost everyone even remotely concerned with education has had a hand in casting a few stones. There is no area of education that has escaped controversy and chastisement. This public outcry against education is not without precedent. Consider the following editorial comment in the *New York Sun* in 1902:

When we were boys, boys had to do a little work in school. They were not coaxed; they were hammered. Spelling, writing, and arithmetic were not electives, you had to learn. In these more fortunate times elementary education has become in many places a vaudeville show. The child must be kept amused, and learns what he pleases. Many sage teachers scorn the old-fashioned rudiments, and it seems to be regarded as between a misfortune and a crime for a child to learn to read.

The debate over the form and content of education dates back much further than the turn of the

fornia system provides a center for academic research and professional training and affords the student greater opportunity to achieve an elite occupational status.

In conclusion, although the expansion of mass public education at all levels in the United States is unmatched by systems of education in other advanced nations, such expansion has not meant the decline of inequality in education. An individual's sex, social origins, family income, parents' education, school milieu, and the college he attends greatly influence his or her future educational level and occupational achievement. As the California system exemplifies, the vast differences

century. Plato, Aristotle, and even the presocratic philosophers argued about educational issues. The issues do not seem to change a great deal: What knowledge or skills should education impart? What are the goals of education? What are the best methods or techniques to accomplish these goals? How do you reform an educational system that falls short of its goals? Can we possibly achieve consensus on the goals of education?

The persistence of concern points to the importance of one function of education discussed earlier in the chapter—socializing youth to the wisdom, ways, and skills of their societies. To the extent a society permits its members to disagree, we should expect to find educational issues at the center of controversy. After all, whichever viewpoint wins and shapes the young minds of the present effectively molds the future.

Martin Trow (1966) has discerned two aspects of American education at the center of recent controversy over schools in the post World War II period: the education of the culturally deprived and the academic preparation of students going on to higher education.

Education for Students with Different Needs

Criticism of American public education was generated outside the school in the case of the urban slum child. The concern of black civil-rights organizations and their white supporters for equality in all aspects of American life naturally focused on public schools. Federal, state, and local agencies also have recognized that there is a growing number of poorly educated slum youth who are unemployable in our economy and who constitute future tax burdens on the rest of the population. Also, research documenting the low performance of black youth when compared with white students in schools in the same cities led to concern about *de facto* segregation of blacks and the quality of teachers in primarily black schools.

There is an intimate connection, then, between the quality of education and equality of education. All groups who criticize the quality of education do so in hopes of improving the child's

chances for upward mobility. But as Trow has pointed out, the criticism of education for deprived children and for youth preparing for college is based on two different conceptions of the nature of education.

The Liberal Conception In the demand for the reform and extension of college preparatory work is found a more traditional, *liberal* view of education, which applies not to deprived children but to higher SES youth. From the liberal perspective, the reform of education assumes that the provision of a higher quality of education will be sufficient to guarantee a student's success in later life. The demand for change is based upon the belief that innate intelligence can be transformed into learned skills and capacities only if the opportunities for education are made available. The child's motivation to succeed or his intelligence are not the center of debate; only the access to better curricula and teachers are in question.

The Radical Conception Pressures to reform education for the urban slum child often entail a *radical* view of the function and nature of education. The radical conception of education not only focuses upon increased expansion of educational opportunities for children but also assumes that schools must expand their jurisdiction over the child to include aspects of his home environment as well.

This perspective assumes that intelligence is not entirely hereditary but is partly achieved. The policy implications of this view are that the school should take active measures to help the family provide the opportunity for a child's intellectual growth through what might be called "compensatory socialization," or "compensatory education," a term coined in academic conferences in the early 1960s.

What the radical conception of education realizes, and what sociological research increasingly documents, is that motivation and intelligence, like wealth and power, are not distributed randomly throughout the population but are part and parcel of the stratification system itself. In order to overcome the problem of inadequate educa-

Figure 19.7   Can you pick out which school is
the lower-class one, which is the middle-class one, and
which is the upper-class one on the basis of the
equipment available in these different chemistry
laboratories—and the different degrees of interest
shown by the students and teachers? The difference
in amount and kind of facilities is only one mani-
festation of the unequal distribution of educational
resources in the United States.

tion one must also overcome barriers to learning
created by the family, teachers, and the overall
environment of the student.

The radical conception of public education is
gaining momentum in this country with various
governmental attempts to provide compensatory
education to an increasing number of culturally
deprived students. By the middle 1960s, many
compensatory programs sponsored by federal
grants went into effect in many of the urban
school systems throughout the country. Operation
Head Start, a program established by the Office
of Economic Opportunity, was much influenced
by the work of Martin Deutsch and others during
the late fifties and early sixties in applying the
fundamental idea of compensatory education in
the most direct possible fashion. Here, the idea
was to use extensive preschool training to compensate for deficient training in the family before
the child attends schools at which he would have
a distinct cultural disadvantage. Head Start was
more than a traditional nursery school in that it
stressed experiences assumed to be lacking in
lower-class homes. There was an emphasis on verbal experiences of many types—children listened
to stories read by the teacher, listened to their
voices on a tape recorder, and became familiar
with the shapes of letters of the alphabet. The
school became a center not only where the individual realized his talent but where his talent
was *created* by the institution.

If one applies the traditional liberal point of
view to deprived children, the child's performance is not considered a problem as long as there
exists a school for the child to attend. If a child
fails, it is because of his own lack of intelligence
or motivation to learn. The newer, radical conception of education has led both laymen and educators alike to question the school's role in the child's
failure or success. People with a radical conception of education are giving increasing attention
to the child's background and especially to the
types of teachers who teach slum children. As we
shall see, the teachers' conceptions and stereotyping of students in deprived areas can be very
harmful to such students.

Deprived Children and Their Teachers

The quality of education is determined in large part by the quality of teachers. Schools in urban slums are staffed for the most part by new teachers who lack tenure and job experience and therefore cannot get work in more attractive school districts. Teachers in all cities continue to "do their time" in ghetto schools and leave them as soon as possible. The teachers' view that ghetto schools are unattractive is reflected in their treatment of students. Teachers in deprived areas seem to view their students as inherently inferior and incapable of profiting from normal curricula (Trow, 1966). What is most important, however, is that these attitudes in turn affect the student's performance. A self-fulfilling prophecy seems to go into effect: where the student is perceived as incapable of learning, the student accepts this definition of himself and does not learn. Teachers also tend to have middle-class attitudes that lower-class youth do not share about the value of an education. Conflict results, and much of the daily educational routine is more disciplinary and custodial than academic; that is, teachers spend more time keeping classrooms quiet and under control than teaching (Silberman, 1970).

Teachers also respond negatively to students with low IQ scores. IQ tests have been criticized on two grounds: first, they test skills that lower-class youth have not acquired in their home environment; second, IQ tests label the lower-class student as incapable of great academic performance—teachers therefore do not expect or encourage learning among low scoring pupils.

The controversy surrounding the education of urban slum youth extends into every facet of the educational process. Teachers, home environments, school environments, and measures of skill and achievement all become targets for innovation and change.

Preparation for College

Criticism has been directed not only at educational failures with deprived children but also at the inadequacy of education for middle-class youth or youth aspiring to middle-class status. The great expansion of American higher education and the increasing educational requirements of jobs that confer middle-class life styles have made schools more oriented toward providing adequate college preparation. Educators have focused primarily on secondary-school courses but have also changed elementary-school curricula to include language, science, and mathematics.

Efforts to reform the secondary public school system derive from the liberal perspective that was discussed earlier. The demand for change focuses on academic deficiencies in schools, not on the student's motivation or intelligence. The emphasis in American high schools on basic reading, civics courses, and psychological adjustment of the child was sufficient prior to 1950 when the majority of youth ended their school careers upon high-school graduation. As higher education now expands in the 1970s to include 50 percent of the college-age youth, high schools have had to include courses that coincide with traditional college curricula—for example, foreign languages, higher mathematics, and science.

Again, the teacher in the public school becomes a target for discussion and debate. Teacher training has been somewhat upgraded by requiring teachers to have majors and minors in college so that teachers with credentials will be subject competent. Along these lines, the National Science Foundation has provided opportunities for older teachers to return to school to upgrade their knowledge in English, science, social science, foreign languages, and mathematics.

The impetus for reform, however, usually comes from outside forces such as anxious parents, college administrators, and college faculty. Teacher-training institutions actually resist reform; in fact, the academic qualifications of teachers are comparatively low when compared with other college-educated and professional groups. Extensive studies done with national samples by the Educational Testing Service and others show that students who major in education score lower on comprehensive tests of verbal and mathematical competence than do majors in almost every other field (Chauncy, 1952).

Figure 19.8 Teachers, especially those in large cities, have organized into unions and gone on strike over the issues of poor pay and crowded classrooms.

The traditional low pay and low prestige of school teachers no doubt adds to the recruitment of the less academically able. Ironically, the pattern of recruitment of the academically less able is reinforced by the tremendous growth of higher education; academically able men and women interested in teaching tend to be drawn not to high schools but to expanding colleges and junior colleges across the nation in hopes of higher prestige and higher pay.

The introduction of televised teaching, although hailed as impersonal by many educators, is one means of overcoming the low academic quality of teachers. The televised teachers are more likely to be subject-matter specialists, with aims closer to college teachers of the same subjects. The televised teacher is not concerned with the interpersonal problems between teacher and student but only with the subject to be taught.

The quality of education will continue to be a persistent concern in American life because the United States and other industrial societies make formal education certificates the primary means of gaining desired occupational statuses. The demands made for higher-quality schools will continue to transform the nature of education—and the solutions to the perceived problems in education will no doubt create new problems that will have to be solved.

THE FUTURE OF AMERICAN EDUCATION

The precise future of education in the United States is difficult to predict. However, there is no reason to doubt that educational institutions at the precollege and college levels will continue to expand and grow. The increase in educational requirements for jobs at all levels has increased the population's demand for education. In addition, the explicit goal of American education has always been to maximize economic and cultural opportunity. In so far as this goal is achieved, the society becomes more fluid, barriers to social mobility are reduced, and people at the lower end of the social hierarchy share more fully in the material and cultural goods of society. On the other hand, there is a counterbalancing purpose of education, which is to pass on the advantages of parents to their children.

Any predictions about the nature and direction of education will have to take into account the pervasive influence of social stratification within society. Debates concerning the quality of education or access to educational institutions clearly reflect attempts by various groups to control the future life chances of the child, whatever his family's status. As long as certification by formal educational institutions is the major vehicle of role allocation within the entire social structure, there is little doubt that schools will continue to be the center of heated political conflict.

It seems reasonably certain that educational institutions will change (and in fact are changing) what they teach and when they teach it. Technological change has become so rapid that it is no longer feasible to give a person early in life all the education he is going to need. Education is already a life-time activity for people in many professions. We can no longer accurately predict what people are going to need to know twenty years from now when they have finished school. Increasingly, schools must therefore teach people *how* to learn, rather than simply what to learn. Many futurists such as Peter F. Drucker (1969) expect that the traditional pattern of getting a college education between eighteen and twenty-one may be replaced by a pattern of frequent returns to school. If life-long education seems im-

probable to you, it would be well to recall that our present goal of nearly universal higher education would have seemed absurd only twenty years ago.

SUGGESTED READINGS

Coleman, James S. "Class Integration—A Fundamental Break With the Past," *Saturday Review,* 55 (May 27, 1972), 58–59.

Collins, Randall. "Functional and Conflict Theories of Educational Stratification," *American Sociological Review,* 36 (December, 1971), 1002–1019.

Silberman, Charles. *Crisis in the Classroom.* New York: Random House, 1970.

Trow, Martin. "The Democratization of Higher Education in America," *European Journal of Sociology,* 3 (1962), 231–263.

Chapter 20 Religion and Society

THE STUDY OF RELIGION by the social sciences enjoyed a Golden Age from the latter part of the nineteenth century until the first part of the twentieth century. All of the prominent early figures of social science, including Karl Marx, Emile Durkheim, Max Weber, Sigmund Freud, and William James, paid considerable attention to religious institutions and religious behavior. But around the end of World War I, the study of religion went into eclipse. One reason for this decline was that the battle between religion and science, so bitter during the disputes over Darwin's theory of evolution, had died down. Religion no longer threatened science. Furthermore, as James H. Leuba's studies showed, most American scientists and social scientists no longer accepted religious beliefs (1916). Social scientists therefore assumed that religion was on the wane. Why study what would soon be unimportant? The sociology of religion languished, and many introductory textbooks no longer included chapters on religion.

Then, following World War II, religion began to attract new interest. Religious institutions in America began to experience a sudden increase in membership and the mass media began to speak of a religious revival. Furthermore, sociologists working on such diverse problems as voting and the birth rate found it necessary to consider the sizable and stubborn role played by religion in explaining these phenomena. Slowly the sociology of religion regained importance, for sociologists must deal with the world as it is, not as they expect it to be. Since 1960 two journals wholly devoted to the topic have been founded, and chapters on religion are back in the textbooks: Religious institutions have remained a fundamental feature of modern society.

One of the first tasks faced by sociologists when they reopened the study of religion was to figure out what they meant by the term religion. This was a problem that had vexed the founding fathers and had been left unsettled. In Chapter 18 it is pointed out that the family has many forms in different societies. If anything, religious institutions are even more varied, and an adequate definition must encompass all of these variations. Consequently, the first task of this chapter is to

define religion. We will then examine a number of theories about religion: why do religious institutions persist in society and why are individuals religious? Next we will examine how religious institutions operate. Finally, the present state of religion in America will be discussed and speculations about future trends will be made.

WHAT IS RELIGION?

One of the most influential early sociologists, Emile Durkheim (1858–1917), a Frenchman, provided the first important step to a workable definition of religion. In his book *The Elementary Forms of Religious Life* (1915) Durkheim began by arguing that all known religions are based on the assumption that everything—from thoughts, words, actions, and objects, to places and animals—can be separated into two opposed classes: the *sacred* and the *profane*. According to Durkheim, sacred things are "set apart and forbidden," whereas profane objects are simply ordinary. He also argued that sacredness resides not in the object itself, but in the mind of the beholder. An object may be considered sacred in one society, profane in another society.

Working from his distinction between the sacred and the profane, Durkheim proposed the following definition of religion:

A religion is a unified system of beliefs and practices relative to sacred things . . . beliefs and practices which unite into a single moral community called a Church, all those who adhere to them (1915).

The question is, of course, what things will be defined as sacred and why. We shall consider Durkheim's answers in the next section where we consider theories of religion.

Modern sociologists have changed Durkheim's definition somewhat. Typically, they define religion as *an institutionalized system of symbols, beliefs, values and practices focused on questions of ultimate meaning* (Glock and Stark, 1965). The word "institutionalized" indicates that religion is a relatively permanent property of groups. But the key phrase is "questions of ultimate meaning," which means questions about the nature and

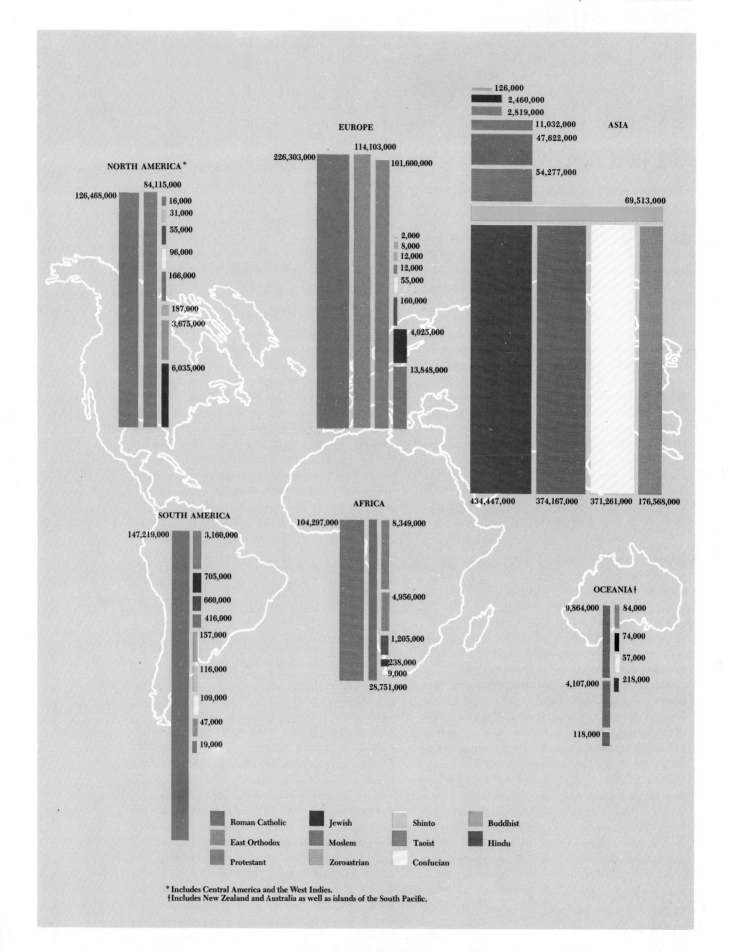

ASIA
126,000
2,460,000
2,819,000
11,032,000
47,622,000
54,277,000
69,513,000
434,447,000   374,167,000   371,261,000   176,568,000

EUROPE
226,303,000   114,103,000   101,600,000
2,000
8,000
12,000
12,000
55,000
160,000
4,025,000
13,848,000

NORTH AMERICA °
126,468,000   84,115,000
16,000
31,000
55,000
96,000
166,000
187,000
3,675,000
6,035,000

SOUTH AMERICA
147,219,000   3,160,000
705,000
660,000
416,000
157,000
116,000
109,000
47,000
19,000

AFRICA
104,297,000   8,349,000
4,956,000
1,205,000
238,000
9,000
28,751,000

OCEANIA†
9,864,000   84,000
74,000
57,000
218,000
4,107,000
118,000

Roman Catholic   Jewish   Shinto   Buddhist

East Orthodox   Moslem   Taoist   Hindu

Protestant   Zoroastrian   Confucian

° Includes Central America and the West Indies.
†Includes New Zealand and Australia as well as islands of the South Pacific.

Figure 20.1   The estimated religious population of
the world. The coexistence of different religions
within countries contributes to cultural diversity, but
conflicts among various religions have at times
led to civil and international wars.
(Adapted from 1968 Brittannica Book of the Year.)

meaning of reality. Questions of ultimate meaning
are questions about the purpose, origin, and fate
of the world: why do we exist, what can we expect,
and very important, what happens when we die?
Sociologists suggest that things will be regarded
as sacred if they are believed to provide or symbolize *solutions* to such ultimate questions.

Value Orientations

As we shall see in the next section, sociologists
have found it worthwhile to suggest that religious
institutions are a necessary component of societies, that without religious institutions a society
could not endure. But this is obviously false if we
define religion in terms of belief in the existence
of a supernatural world—God, heaven, spirits, a
Creator. Some societies, such as the Soviet Union,
officially reject the supernatural. You will notice
that the definition given by modern sociologists
does not say that some set of beliefs has to be
supernatural in order to be called a religion. Marxism, science, and a variety of doctrines without a
supernatural element deal with questions of ultimate meaning and therefore would be classified
as religions under the definition provided by modern sociologists. This saves the claim that societies
must have religious institutions, but it causes a
great deal of confusion.

Many sociologists therefore use the term *value
orientation* instead of religion when treating
the similarities of Catholicism and Communism
(Kluckhohn, 1962). They then distinguish between *religious* and *humanistic* value orientations. Value orientations that contain a supernatural component are identified as religious, those
without such a component are identified as humanistic (Glock and Stark, 1965). Both are alternative kinds of answers to the same ultimate questions. It is obvious, however, that religious value
orientations are by far the most common variety.
It is mainly through religion that humans have
told and continue to tell themselves who they are,
why they exist, and how they ought to behave.

Individual Religiousness

Thus far we have discussed religion as a group
property. But, as you will see, it is also useful to

define individual religiousness. Sociologists ask
not only why societies have religious institutions
but why individuals are religious. The most often
used conception of individual religious commitment was first proposed by Charles Y. Glock in the
late 1950s and was refined in subsequent work
(Stark and Glock, 1968). Glock proposed that all
religious institutions make certain demands on
their members. The extent to which one meets
these demands indicates the extent of one's religiousness. Obviously, different religions make different demands. But Glock argued that all of these
variations fit within five general kinds of demands
and that all religious institutions make all five
kinds of demands on their members. Glock called
these the dimensions of religious commitment.

First, all religions require members to hold
certain *beliefs*. Second, all religions ask their
members to participate in certain *rituals*. In addition, all religions expect members to have a certain amount of *knowledge* about the history and
traditions of their faith. Obviously this knowledge
is linked with belief, but the two are not identical.
For example, one can know the Ten Commandments but not believe in them—or one can believe in the Ten Commandments but be ignorant
of the tradition that God gave these commandments to Moses on Mount Sinai. A fourth demand
of religions is that their members will experience
certain kinds of religious *feelings*. These feelings
can vary from such ecstatic experiences as feeling
seized by the Holy Ghost to quiet feelings of awe
and devotion. Finally, all religions expect certain
behavioral *consequences* of faith. True believers,
for examples, will keep the commandments, will
not eat pork, will grow beards, or will abstain from
alcohol. Studies based on these five dimensions of
religious commitment have found that although
each varies somewhat independently of the others, all are necessary to assess individual religiousness adequately (Faulkner and De Jong, 1966;
Stark and Glock, 1968).

THEORIES OF RELIGION

As we have pointed out, the questions of why societies have religious institutions and why individuals are religious are logically independent.

Figure 20.2   Emile Durkheim (1858–1917) was one of the most influential founders of modern sociology. A Frenchman and a socialist, he set out to demonstrate that social factors cannot be reduced to psychology or physiology—that there are social forces, such as norms, outside the individual that shape individual behavior. His first major book was *The Division of Labor* (1893) (see Chapters 9 and 22). He is best remembered today for his major contributions to scientific sociology. *Suicide* (1897) was the first major, quantitative study of a social problem and stands today as model for empirical research. Furthermore, in analyzing data on suicide rates Durkheim found considerable empirical support for his views that social facts influence individual behavior. His *Elementary Forms of Religious Life* (1912) was long regarded as a classic, but lately its data and major premises have been called into question.

The answer to one may not be the answer to the other. Persons may be individually religious and their religiousness may benefit the group as a whole, but the religious motives of individuals may be entirely unrelated to the group consequences of their religiousness. We shall first examine theories that explain why societies have religious institutions and will then examine theories that explain why individuals are religious.

Theories of Religious Institutions

Three major theorists concerned with why societies have religion all started from the functionalist premise that religion contributes to the operation of societies as systems. All three men—Emile Durkheim, Karl Marx, and Max Weber—agreed that religion can serve as a primary source of social unification: religion serves as a moral cement that holds societies together. But beyond this initial agreement, Durkheim, Marx, and Weber disagreed strongly on the social functions of religious institutions in societies.

Emile Durkheim   Emile Durkheim argued that religious *belief systems* make the values of society sacred. Religious *rituals* reinforce identification with and commitment to these values. And through its unique system of eternal *rewards* and *punishments* religion helps to insure conformity to social norms—deviance is not only unlawful but sinful. Durkheim argued that one consequence of religion is a cohesive society and that, in turn, group cohesion becomes the source of religious sentiments.

To shape his theory of religion, Durkheim studied anthropological accounts of primitive societies. He observed that these small tribal groups were extremely cohesive—there was high agreement on norms and values and very close relations among group members. These groups also seemed to give their highest expression of group solidarity during religious ceremonies and celebrations. From these observations, Durkheim drew his famous and controversial conclusion: *religion is the worship of society*. Society, according to Durkheim, gives the sensation of perpetuity—it is actually society that is eternal. Furthermore, groups (societies) impose pressures on the individual to conform even if rational calculation might challenge the basis of conformity. Certainly later studies, such as the Asch experiment, support Durkheim on this point (see Chapter 8).

Because societies impose moral pressure upon their members, Durkheim explained, it is natural that such a force should inspire sentiments of awe, reverence, and sacredness. It is intrinsic to the very nature of societies, he wrote, that "outside of us there exists something greater than us, something with which we enter into communication." This "something" is, of course, society itself. Durkheim came to the conclusion that religion is "a system of ideas with which individuals represent to themselves the society of which they are members" (Durkheim, 1915). Not only is religion a social phenomenon, but society is a religious phenomenon (Parsons, 1937). Humans worship their society and thus are bound together in a system of sacred norms and values. Thus is society held together.

Durkheim's position has been very influential in the work of modern functionalists. In particular, Talcott Parsons (1937, 1951) has strongly supported the idea of religion as a source of social integration and cohesion.

Karl Marx   Marx agreed with Durkheim in many respects. He, too, regarded religion as a reflection of society, particularly of the economic relations of a society. But Marx disliked what he saw. He concluded that social arrangements under which most persons are exploited are made sacred through religion. The religious ideas of a society are the religious ideas of the ruling classes of the society. As such, they are a conservative force that justifies the power of the ruling classes. Religion serves as an "opium of the people" that fosters "false consciousness." As long as workers believe that kings have the Divine Right to rule over them or that worldly success reflects the will of God and the virtuousness of the wealthy, they will remain victims of exploitation. Thus, in the Marxist view, priests and clergymen are agents of the ruling class and, as such, enemies of the people.

But both Durkheim and Marx overemphasized the conservative and socially unifying character of religion. Durkheim ignored the fact that even in the very simple societies he studied, the principal religious unit was not the tribe but the clans within the tribe, each with its own special totems and worship. Worship of sacred objects, therefore, had little bearing on integrating the tribe as a whole and in fact even permitted the possibility of religious friction between clans within the same society (Demerath and Hammond, 1969). This possibility of friction becomes even greater in complex modern societies—within each exist a variety of competing faiths. Knowing that civil wars have been fought on religious grounds, can we say that religion inevitably serves to bind societies together, to perpetuate existing social arrangements, and thus to impede conflicts or social change? Here Marx took issue with Durkheim.

Both Durkheim and Marx regarded religion as a reflection of society. But Marx argued that religious ideas are completely determined by economic interests. And unlike Durkheim, Marx recognized that religion can serve as a disruptive force in societies. Marx argued that most earlier revolutionary movements had occurred under the banner of religion—that new religious ideologies arose in order to integrate and justify the rise of a new class to power. Thus Marx and Engels, and later Karl Kautsky (1953), argued that Christianity was essentially an early instance of a proletarian movement.

Max Weber Weber agreed with much of Marx's social analysis. He was therefore not so intent upon refuting Marx as upon correcting and expanding the Marxist point of view. He rejected the Marxist premise that religious ideas are totally determined by, and are the mere reflections of, economic interests of social classes.

In his classic essay, *The Protestant Ethic and the Spirit of Capitalism* (1930), first published in 1905, Weber argued that values—both religious and nonreligious—are not only reflections of economic relations, but can play an *independent* role in governing economic relations. At least sometimes, societies shape their institutions to some

extent to fit their moral commitments or values, instead of shaping their values to justify their institutions. Thus Weber argued that the rise of Protestantism preceded and was necessary for the development of capitalism. The traditional religious values of Catholicism deterred the development of rational and disciplined economic activity. Protestantism stressed the importance of work as an end in itself and regarded worldly success as evidence of God's favor. Eventually this led to seeing hard work and worldly success not merely as signs of salvation but as means for earning salvation. This theological position, according to Weber, gave rise to the spirit of capitalism—religion motivated economic zeal and the pursuit of wealth that undergirded capitalism. Protestant values encouraged both the pursuit of money and personal frugality—profits were not to be spent on luxuries but plowed back into the firm to earn more money. In this way capitalism was encouraged.

There have been many objections raised against Weber's analysis. Unfortunately, his work has been represented primarily by his short essay on the Protestant Ethic because his more highly developed work on the subject—*The Sociology of Religion*—went untranslated until 1963. In the latter work, Weber took a more Marxist position and built a more general theory. Nevertheless, when all the criticisms are taken into account (even Weber's own criticisms in his later work), his general claim that values can influence social structure survives (Demerath and Hammond, 1969). Weber never argued that values alone determine social structure; he accepted the importance of social structure in determining values. He merely claimed that the two interact, each shaping the other. As we shall see later, one of Weber's most important applications of this position was in church-sect theory. This body of theory captures the dynamic of religious change and conflict within societies, the question that both Weber and Marx recognized but that Durkheim glossed over.

Modern View Today most sociologists accept the idea that religious institutions are present in society because they serve some important purpose

Figure 20.3 The church can be a force for change in society, or it can be a conservative institution. At times, it is both: the Berrigan brothers, Roman Catholic priests (*left*), have been radical activists in America, whereas the late Cardinal Spellman (*right*) was staunchly on the side of official government policy and traditional patriotic values.

and that an analysis of the social functions of religion reveals why religious institutions persist. They agree that religion serves to integrate societies, to legitimate existing social arrangements, to provide a sacred sense to the norms and values of societies, and to provide humans with a shared set of solutions to questions of ultimate meaning. They recognize that several religions may exist within the same society and that such differences in beliefs may lead to conflict. When such conflict occurs, the functions of religion must be examined separately for each of the competing religious groups; it is probable that religion is fulfilling the previously noted functions within each group, even if not for society as a whole. Indeed, the conflict between groups is at least partly due to the fact that the groups are not integrated into one society through their religious institutions. Furthermore, you will recall from our earlier discussion that religion is only one kind of value orientation that can fulfill these functions. The institutions based on Communism seem fully as effective as religion in fulfilling these functions.

But not all sociologists today uncritically accept the notion that religion is a primary source of social integration. They observe the extensive religious pluralism of societies such as the United States and wonder whether religion is providing the integrating values. Some suggest that it is not religion but secular values such as faith in democracy, in the rule of law, and in political and cultural traditions that integrate American society. Robert Bellah (1968) has called these elements a "civil religion." Others have challenged the whole notion that societies need consensus on major values in order to hold together. It may be precisely because religious values are no longer so important and thus no longer a source of divisiveness that modern industrial nations have found ways to accommodate competing faiths, conflicting interests, and cultural diversity.

One important piece of evidence against Durkheim and the extreme functionalist position involves the assertion that religion helps integrate society because its system of eternal rewards and punishments strengthens adherence to social norms. A large-scale study of American teen-agers found that those who strongly believed that God punishes sins were no less likely to commit delinquent acts than were teen-agers who did not believe in divine judgment (Hirschi and Stark, 1969). Just how vital religion is for social integration therefore remains in doubt.

Theories of Individual Religiousness

Speculations about why people are religious have, from the writing of the Apostle Paul down to the present, struck a common theme. Religion offers us comfort against the frustrations of life, gives purpose to our existence, and guides our behavior. But some people are more religious than are others. What accounts for this difference? Two mirror-image answers have predominated. Some argue that people who most need the comforts of faith—those who suffer the greatest frustration and whose lives seem most meaningless—will be the most religious. Others have argued that religion reflects the highest ideals of a society and will therefore appeal most to those whose social advantages encourage commitment to the society (Glock, Ringer, and Babbie, 1967).

Sociologists today consider both of these positions inadequate. N. J. Demerath III (1965) has argued that religious institutions are multifaceted and can strongly appeal to both the advantaged and the disadvantaged. Working from Glock's dimensions of individual religious commitment, Demerath suggests that the poor will be more religious in those dimensions that serve to comfort earthly frustrations and that the rich will be more religious on those dimensions that confirm their high social status. Chapter 14 reports research by Rodney Stark that confirms Demerath's views. The lower classes are more religious when it comes to belief and prayer. The middle and upper classes are more religious when it comes to church membership, church attendance, and religious knowledge.

In work presently being completed, Stark and Glock expand this position. First, they distinguish three elements in religion. Some aspects of religious commitment in and of themselves are *rewarding*. For example, participation in religious organizations offers rewards similar to those provided by any kind of social club. Second, some aspects of religious commitment can serve as *compensations* for rewards one is denied through lack of power, prestige, or property. Thus, religious belief can offer hope for justice in the world to come and can suggest the impermanence of earthly rewards; ritual activities such as prayer can offer the means for seeking comforts from the sorrows of life. Finally, Stark and Glock discern two kinds of compensations: those that compensate for rewards that less powerful persons are denied and those that compensate for rewards everyone is denied. For example, rich or poor, all humans die. The promise of life beyond death thus compensates all persons, not just the poor.

Stark and Glock have constructed a general theory of religious commitment that predicts that various people will be to greater or lesser degrees involved in the rewarding aspects of religion, the compensatory aspect for rewards that some are denied, and the compensations for rewards that all are denied. They conclude that *powerful* groups in society will seek to control, promote, and demonstrate commitment in religious institutions in order to (1) obtain the rewards available through religious institutions; (2) seek compensa-

tions for deprivations for which no direct reward exists (death, for example); and (3) encourage *others* to accept compensations instead of taking actions to enlarge their share of those rewards that do exist. Similarly, they conclude that the *powerless* will manifest commitment to religion in terms of both kinds of compensations but will tend to be excluded from those aspects of religion (church membership, church organizations, leadership) that are directly rewarding.

In examining the relationship between religiousness and four sources of power—wealth, status, physical advantages, and mental advantages—Stark and Glock have found support for their theory. For example, they point out that although a variety of studies show that the more intelligent a person is the less likely he is to hold traditional religious beliefs, other data show that the more intelligent a person is the more likely he is to belong to a church and participate in religious organizations. Stark and Glock themselves warn that sociological understanding of religious commitment is at a very early stage. Further studies will undoubtedly reveal many inconsistencies and force many revisions in theories of individual religious commitment.

THE NATURE OF RELIGIOUS INSTITUTIONS

Religious institutions differ greatly from society to society, over time, and even from one religion to another within the same society. One major variation is in the degree to which religions are formally organized. Some religions are very informally organized; others are huge bureaucratic organizations. Furthermore, religions differ in the extent to which they are fused with or separated from other social institutions. In ancient Egypt, for example, religious and political institutions were virtually identical. The state was ruled by the Pharaoh, who was himself considered divine and who, through his person, linked the gods in heaven with humans on earth. In a sense, the gods owned and ruled the country. In contrast, the United States Constitution specifically separates church and state. Although it is obvious that political and religious institutions in the United States

Figure 20.4   Religious symbols (*from top to bottom*): the Hindu cosmic diagram Shri-Yantra; the Chinese Confucian and Taoist Yang and Yin joined in a circle symbolizing the Great Ultimate and representing the two basic, interacting, harmonious forces of the cosmos; the Christian Tau Cross combined with the Anchor; the Christian Cross; the Jewish Mogen David, the Shield or Star of David; the Buddhist Dharmachakra, or Wheel of the (Universal) Law, with spokes representing the Eightfold Path to enlightenment—right speech, right action, right livelihood, right effort, right mindfulness, and right concentration; the Islamic sacred formula representing belief in one God; the Hindu sacred word OM or AUM, meaning "aye" or "amen," which represents the sound for the whole of consciousness-existence and at the same time its willing affirmation.

mutually influence one another, it is equally obvious that they are separate institutions.

In this section we will examine three aspects of religious organizations: the nature of religious leadership and religious roles; the development of rituals, beliefs and symbols; and finally, the tensions inherent in religious institutions that result in the dynamic process of sect formation and the transformation of sects into churches.

Religious Leadership

Even in hunting and gathering societies, the key roles of religious leadership appear. Particular persons take charge of religious activities, usually on a parttime basis. With the advent of simple horticultural societies, full-time religious roles appear, and some minimum organization of religion develops. Specialized religious roles possess a more than ordinary degree of authority because those who occupy such roles claim to have a special relationship with the ultimate. A number of such religious roles can be identified.

The religious founder is a person who presents to his followers, by preaching, teaching, and example, a special call to the religious life. He communicates to others elements of his own unique and profound religious experience and thereby intentionally or unintentionally provides the basis for establishing a new religious community. Jesus, Gautama Buddha, and Muhammad are examples of religious founders.

The prophet, on the other hand, speaks within an established religious tradition; the prophet may in turn deepen and expand the tradition or demand that its injunctions be followed to the letter. The prophets of the Old Testament are obvious examples. Max Weber (1952) distinguished two types of prophets. *Exemplary* prophets, such as Gandhi and Martin Luther King, Jr., communicate their messages through personal example. *Ethical* prophets, like most in the Old Testament, criticize the present state of affairs and exhort believers to penitence and rededication to their faith.

The *priest* owes his authority to the power of his office—anyone in the role of priest is deemed to have priestly powers, whether or not he is personally virtuous. This is in contrast with prophets who base their authority on their own personal *charismatic* qualities (see Chapter 13). The priest is the official and authorized celebrant of the rituals and is often an official and authorized teacher who counsels the ordinary believer. Although most Protestant denominations prefer the title of minister to that of priest, ministers occupy the priestly role, as sociologists define it.

The prophetic and priestly roles are often regarded as opposites (as we shall see in the discussion of churches and sects). The prophet usually decries the imperfections of current religious institutions, and the priest, as an "organization man," usually defends these institutions.

Rituals, Beliefs, and Symbols

The development of religions ordinarily proceeds along three main dimensions: the establishment of rituals, the systematization of beliefs, and the development of symbols.

Rituals involve a complex of words, gestures, and acts in which some experience or event of primary importance to the religion is represented and symbolically reenacted. For example, the Catholic Mass, with its ritual of Holy Communion, reenacts the Last Supper of Christ. Participants in a ritual do not spontaneously express their personal feelings as much as they participate in and share with others the feelings, attitudes, and relationships they have been taught to associate with the ritual.

Durkheim argued that rituals function to reinforce commitment to religious values and to increase solidarity among adherents. But rituals also serve private personal needs. Rituals can provide comfort in the face of uncertainty or anguish. Consider how the ritual of the funeral service can fulfill both group and individual needs. Through gathering and participating in the service, the group regains the solidarity that the loss of a member has threatened. And by means of the service, each individual is comforted for the loss of a loved one and against the fear of his own death.

Beliefs give meaning to rituals and, in turn, are reinforced by being represented in rituals. Obviously, the Mass is meaningless without beliefs concerning God, redemption through Christ, and the authority of the priesthood. Over time, religious beliefs tend to become more and more rationalized, codified, and elaborated. The longer a religious tradition is served by priestly specialists, the more beliefs tend to be transformed into theological systems. Once developed, such systems are less fluid than are a set of beliefs; therefore, religions that develop theologies tend to be more institutionally stable. As we shall see shortly, this stability is often gained at the price of rigidity.

Religious symbols begin as representations of beliefs and rituals and, like all symbols, soon take on religious meanings of their own; they become sacred in their own right. The cross is not simply a reminder of the Crucifixion of Jesus or of salvation through faith but is itself an object of awe and reverence. The same is true of religious statues, which sometimes come to be worshiped not as representations of divinity but as divine.

The development of rituals, beliefs, symbols, and religious roles contains potential dysfunctions. Powerful religious roles raise the problem of self-interest over community interest. Combined with highly developed rituals and a codified theology, power in religious institutions tends toward rigidity, legalistic interpretations, resistance to change, and temptation to coerce adherence to the faith. Furthermore, the representation of the religious experience to the worshipers is necessarily symbolic, as in rituals and religious icons. However, the continual use of symbols tends to stereotype and routinize them and thus to slowly empty them of their ability to represent the religious experience. The development and success of a religious movement may therefore carry with it the seeds of its own decline. It may begin to oppress the faithful at the same time that it loses its ability to satisfy their religious needs. This brings us to the question of the rise and fall of religious institutions.

Church and Sect

Max Weber gave the original impetus to what has come to be called *church-sect* theory. He noted that two types of religious institutions characterized Christianity. On the one hand were highly institutionalized religious organizations that were dominated by the priestly role and that were relatively at ease with their surrounding culture. These he called *churches*. The other types of organizations were less organized, dominated by the prophetic role, and defined in opposition to the surrounding culture. These he called *sects* (Weber, 1946). However, it was actually Weber's contemporary, the German historian Ernst Troeltsch, who first made extensive use of the concepts of church and sect.

Troeltsch (1949) defined the church as an organization that members are born into and that tries to encompass the whole population of a society. The church conducts public worship, mediates divine grace through such formal means as sacraments administered by a priestly hierarchy, and has a highly codified theology and system of formal rituals.

By contrast, the sect separates itself from society in general—its members may even be quite hostile toward outsiders and toward society's institutions. Moreover, the sect emphasizes voluntary or converted membership instead of membership by birth and sees itself as a society of the saved.

Sects and Religions Change For Troeltsch, however, the concepts of church and sect were merely useful for organizing historical data. It remained for a theologian, H. Richard Niebuhr (1929), to use these concepts to formulate a theory of *religious* change. Niebuhr suggested that the sect is inherently unstable. It is founded by people whose religious needs are currently not met by the churches of their society. These disenchanted people break away and start a new faith in order to give revitalized expression to their religious concerns. As such, sects appeal to the socially disadvantaged and disinherited. They begin as a society of committed converts embattled against the world. But this posture does not last. Sometimes they are crushed as heresies. Sometimes they merely die out as members get old. But frequently they begin to come more and more to terms with their surrounding society and *eventually become churches*. In fact, sometimes they completely replace the previous churches.

Figure 20.5   Niebuhr's theory of religious change.
Churches and sects are not static religious bodies but
undergo continual change. Through the generations,
sects tend to crystallize into churches, and dissatisfied
members of churches often split off to form sects.
In order to chart the life of a sect, begin at the top of
the diagram and work downward.

One mechanism that promotes the change from sect to church is the arrival of the second generation, which means that the sect no longer has exclusively converted members. Soon it begins to have members who did not join out of conviction or firm dissatisfaction with society. Another factor is that over time many sect members improve their economic position. As they cease to be a uniformly dispossessed group and as the wealthier members play a prominent internal role in sect affairs, the group becomes less hostile to worldly affairs. When they begin to require their clergymen to undergo formal training for the ministry, sects are moving well down the road to becoming churches. At this point, the process repeats itself. The sect-becoming-a-church begins to lose those qualities that originally attract alienated and dispossessed members. Many members still are alienated and dispossessed. Thus conflict ensues, and frequently some members split off to found a new sect. Niebuhr isolated an endless cycle of schism, birth, development, schism, and rebirth (see Figure 20.1). Most Protestant denominations began as sects within the Christian community. Indeed, Christianity itself began as a sect within the Jewish community.

Church-Sect Theory and Politics   Church-sect theory offers powerful insights into the formation and transformation of religious groups. But it also offers insights into social and political movements in general (see Chapter 28). Such movements frequently begin with very radical positions which reject the institutions of their society. And frequently, if they grow and endure, they begin to move toward increasingly moderate positions. It is worth remembering that the Republican Party of Abraham Lincoln's day was considered a dangerously radical party by many Americans and only came to power because the majority of voters were divided between two moderate candidates.

There is, however, an even closer link between radical politics and church-sect theory. Niebuhr pointed out that no important sect movements have occurred among the Western European working classes since the rise of Methodism. He suggested that since the start of the nine-

teenth century, working-class dissatisfactions have been channeled mainly into radical politics instead of religion. This trend was also noticed by early socialists. In fact, Leon Trotsky was so aware of the similarity of revolutionary Marxism and sectarianism that in the late 1890s he successfully recruited the first working-class members of the South Russian Workers Union from among adherents to religious sects (Lipset, 1960).

Recent research shows that there is a connection between religion and radical politics in a number of Western nations, including the United States (Glock and Stark, 1965). Persons tend to be either politically radical *or* religious, not both. Similarly, Gary Marx (1967) found in a nationwide study of black Americans that there was a strong negative relationship between religiousness and militancy. The more religious a black person was, the less militant he was about securing justice for black people.

In light of the discussion presented earlier in this chapter, which classified radical politics and religion as alternative value orientations fulfilling the same functions, these findings should come as no surprise. We do not expect people to adhere to two religious faiths. To expect someone to be both a Communist and a Catholic is similarly inconsistent (although humans are a blithly inconsistent species and many people nevertheless do hold to such a dual commitment).

TRENDS IN AMERICAN RELIGION

Niebuhr pointed out that sect formation on any large scale had ceased in Western Europe by the start of the nineteenth century. But in America, sects continued to emerge in considerable numbers. Such bodies as the Nazarenes, the Mormons, the Seventh-Day Adventists, Christian Scientists, and Jehovah's Witnesses are among the most important native American religious movements. As a consequence, there are more than 250 separate, organized religious denominations in the United States (Landis, 1963). Seymour Martin Lipset (1960) suggests that continuing sect formation in America is related to the failure of radical politics

SECT TO CHURCH

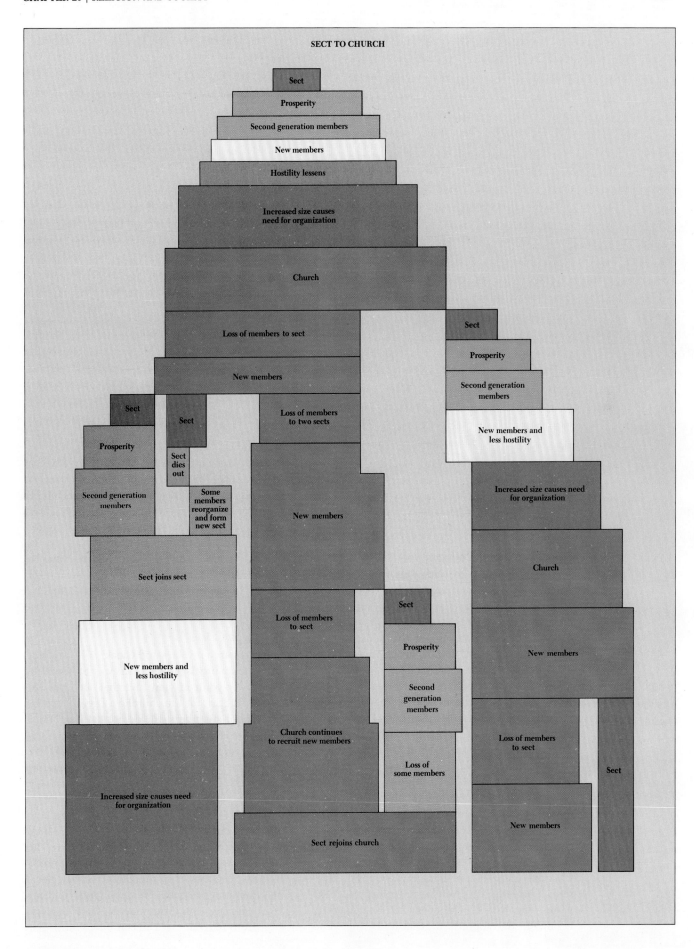

Figure 20.6   The style of presentation of religious doctrine, as well as doctrine itself, often varies to accord with the society. The "drive-in" church may fit well with the habits of modern suburban America.

to develop to any significant extent. Whatever the case, the United States is truly a nation of religious diversity.

Denominational Differences

Over the past fifteen years a number of major religious groups have merged or have discussed merger. These mergers and talks of mergers led many to write about the demise of denominationalism in America—to suggest that old doctrinal differences, at least within Protestantism, had been settled. In fact, some sociologists attempted sophisticated explanations of why denominationalism had broken down and a "common-core Protestantism" had emerged (Lee, 1960). As it turned out, they were trying to explain something that had not happened. When Glock and Stark (1965) conducted a large-scale survey of religious beliefs, they found that, if anything, denominational differences were greater than ever. Some of their findings appear in Table 20.1.

In Table 20.1 you can see that Protestant denominations differ greatly in the proportion of members who accept the traditional tenets of Christian faith. In denominations such as the Missouri Lutherans, the Southern Baptists, and the various small sects, the overwhelming majority believe in the virgin birth, that Jesus walked on

water, that Jesus will come again, that there is a Devil, and that Biblical miracles are real. In denominations such as the Congregationalists, Methodists, and Episcopalians, the overwhelming majority reject these beliefs. Indeed, fewer than half of the Congregationalists and only 60 percent of the Methodists express unqualified belief in God. Old differences among the Protestant denominations were based on controversies over adult or infant Baptism and over the style of ritual appropriate for worship services. Such differences seem trivial compared with the disagreement on basic articles of faith that these data reveal. A subsequent study of American Protestant clergymen by Jeffrey K. Hadden (1967) revealed virtually identical patterns to the ones found among laymen.

It seems reasonable to suppose that seventy-five years ago the majority of Congregationalists, Methodists, and Episcopalians, like the Southern Baptists today, believed in these doctrines. If so, then Glock and Stark's data indicate that the religious outlook of many American Protestants has changed considerably. If such change continues, traditional Christianity may become a minority point of view in America in the near future.

Religious Crises

Later research by Stark and Glock (1968) suggests that Christianity is indeed on its way to becoming a minority point of view and that such changes portend a crisis for the churches. Their data show that church members who do not hold traditional religious views are relatively apathetic about religion in other ways. They are much less likely to contribute funds to support their church and they are much less likely to attend worship services regularly. (However, less religious persons are considerably more inclined to give time and money to charitable organizations than are more religious persons.)

There are other signs of a growing crisis in religious institutions in the United States. Recall that the rapid rise in church attendance following World War II caused the mass media to speak of a religious revival. The rise continued during the

Table 20.1 Denomination and Professed Religious Belief

Denomination	Belief in Existence of God [a]	Belief in Virgin Birth [b]	Belief in Jesus' Walking on Water [c]	Belief in Jesus' Future Return [d]	Belief in Miracles [e]	Belief in Existence of Devil [f]
Congregational	41%	21%	19%	13%	28%	6%
Methodist	60	34	26	21	37	13
Episcopalian	63	39	30	24	41	17
Disciples of Christ	76	62	62	36	62	18
Presbyterian	75	57	51	43	58	31
American Lutheran	73	66	58	54	69	49
American Baptist	78	69	62	57	62	49
Missouri Lutheran	81	92	83	75	89	77
Southern Baptist	99	99	99	94	92	92
Sects	96	96	94	89	92	90
Total Protestant	71%	51%	50%	44%	57%	38%
Roman Catholic	81%	81%	71%	47%	74%	66%

a. Percentage of people in each denomination agreeing with the statement "I know God really exists and I have no doubts about it."

b. Percentage of people responding "Completely true" to the statement "Jesus was born of a virgin."

c. Percentage of people responding "Completely true" to the statement "Jesus walked on water."

d. Percentage of people responding "Definitely" to the question "Do you believe Jesus will actually return to earth some day?"

e. Percentage of people agreeing with the statement "Miracles actually happened just as the Bible says they did."

f. Percentage of people responding "Completely true" to the statement "The Devil actually exists."

Source: Rodney Stark and Charles Y. Glock, *American Piety: The Nature of Religious Commitment* (Berkeley: University of California Press, 1968).

1950s until it reached a high point in 1957. That year the Gallup poll reported that 51 percent of Americans claimed to attend church weekly. But since then attendance has been steadily declining. In 1971 only 40 percent claimed to be weekly attenders. It is now believed that part of the post-war revival stemmed from the baby-boom that began immediately after the war (see Chapter 23). It is well known that family church attendance rises when there are younger children in the home and declines when the children are grown (Glock, Ringer, and Babbie, 1967). But this is hardly the whole story—the Gallup findings indicate that the decline in church attendance has been steepest among young people, not among the middle-aged; between 1958 and 1966 the proportion of weekly church attenders among young adults dropped 11 percentage points. If young people persist in less church attendance as they get older, the downward trend in attendance is certain to continue.

In addition, Americans now generally believe that religion is losing influence in contemporary life. Gallup reported in 1957—the year of the high point in church attendance—that only 14 percent of the nation's Christians thought religion was losing influence; 69 percent thought it was increasing. Ten years later this picture had virtually reversed: 57 percent thought religion was losing influence, and only 23 percent thought it was gaining influence. If we take these findings as a measure of individual attitudes about religion, they mark a massive loss of confidence in religion.

A further source of religious crisis has been the developing conflict between clergy and church congregations over the role of the churches in issues concerning social justice. In his book *The Gathering Storm in the Churches* (1969), Jeffrey K. Hadden reported on a series of studies of the involvement of the clergy in the civil-rights movement and the reactions of church members to such clergy activism. He noted that his study of clergymen's religious beliefs produced nearly identical results with Glock and Stark's findings for members. However, he found that these results did not mean that theologically liberal clergymen in denominations such as the Congregationalists, Methodists, or Episcopalians tended to serve congregations who shared their liberal views. For the fact is that in the liberal denominations the most active members—the ones who fill the pews and with whom the minister has most contact—tend to be that minority of members who hold conservative religious views; the liberal-minded majority tends to be less active. These facts indicate an obvious source of conflict within the theologically liberal denominations.

Second, Hadden's national study revealed that if the religious beliefs of church members did resemble those of the clergy, their views on civil rights did not. Regardless of their theological outlook, church members were less supportive of the civil-rights movement than were clergymen.

Furthermore, the majority of church members strongly disapproved of the involvement of the clergy in the civil-rights movement. Nevertheless, the clergy tended to favor activism on behalf of civil rights. During the early 1960s the prominence of clergymen in the civil-rights movement, and then in the peace movement, led to many proclamations about an emerging "New Breed" of clergymen.

The major changes in the Catholic Church following the Vatican II Council further encouraged such hopes for a vigorous new clergy and revitalized religious institutions. Hadden predicted, however, that the young, liberal, activist clergymen were on a collision course with their congre-

gations. Church members strongly preferred their clergymen to restrict themselves to traditional pastoral activities—visiting the sick, leading young people's groups, and preaching salvation.

In many ways Hadden's predictions have been supported by subsequent events. Most denominations have reported financial difficulty over the past few years and blame much of it on members' resentment of an activist clergy. A later study of the Protestant clergy by Stark and others (1971) found that the majority of clergymen were conforming to the expectations of their congregations and were not speaking out on social issues. During the year from the spring of 1967 to the spring of 1968—a year in which Detroit and many other American cities burned during ghetto riots and that ended with the assassination of Martin Luther King in Memphis—more than half of the Protestant clergymen in the state of California *did not* devote even a section of one of their sermons to "racial problems." Furthermore, as Hadden anticipated, conflict within the churches had caused a tremendous disillusionment in the young "New Breed" of clergymen.

Table 20.2 shows that only 14 percent of the most theologically liberal clergymen said they definitely would choose to enter the ministry if they had to make the choice over again. In contrast, 75 percent of the theologically conservative clergy said they definitely would choose to enter

Table 20.2   Degree of Doctrinal Orthodoxy and Attitude Toward Vocation

Doctrinal Orthodoxy [a] (Doctrine-Index Rating)	Reconsideration of Vocation [b]				
	Definitely Would Reenter	*Probably Would*	*Not Sure*	*Probably Would Not*	*Definitely Would Not*
0 (Most liberal)	14%	39%	21%	22%	4%
1	22	40	19	18	1
2	45	32	15	6	2
3	54	31	13	2	0
4 (Most conservative)	75	18	4	3	0
Average	56	27	11	5	1

a. Degree of liberalism-conservatism with respect to traditional doctrinal beliefs as measured by the Doctrine Index, a questionnaire based on strong adherence to the five traditional doctrines: existence of a personal God, the divinity of Jesus, the existence of life beyond death, the existence of the Devil, and the necessity to salvation of a belief in Jesus: A rating of 0 represents acceptance of none of these beliefs, and a rating of 4 represents acceptance of 4 *or all 5* of them.

b. Answer to "Looking back on things—if you had it to do over—how certain are you that you would enter the ministry?"

Source: Adapted from Rodney Stark, Bruce O. Foster, Charles Y. Glock, and Harold Quinley, *Wayward Shepherds: Prejudice and the Protestant Clergy* (New York: Harper & Row, 1971).

the clergy. Clergymen who seem to regret their choice to become clergymen obviously have very low morale. These findings confirm speculation in the mass media that the "New Breed" clergy have become prone to leave the ministry.

Will Religion Persist?

In light of all these findings, what can we conclude about the future of religion in America? Many individuals, including theologians, suspect that the religious doctrine established in horticultural and agrarian societies cannot serve or survive in advanced industrial societies. In his influential book *The Sacred Canopy* (1967), Peter Berger traces the change in Christianity from a faith that bound believers into a social and moral community to a faith that in contemporary times has become "privitized"—a faith that each individual must construct for himself because no dominating religious institution exists to do it for him. Berger argues that in modern society people live in a world of many religions as well as in a world with many nonreligious "reality defining agencies," none of which is dominant. Thus he argues that "one cannot really talk about religion anymore [because] religion no longer refers to the cosmos or to history but to individual *Existence* or psychology." The theologian Harvey Cox advanced similar arguments in his best-seller *The Secular City* (1966). Cox defined the modern age as the age of "no religion at all."

Many sociologists agree with these gloomy predictions about the future of Christianity. However, it does not follow from any of the trends we have discussed that we are about to become a "godless" society. As we have already noted, all of the evidence and the theoretical speculation of social scientists point to the conclusion that religion has always been an important component of all human societies. How then do we confront the contradicting claims of social scientists? On the one hand, they argue that religion has always been present in human societies; on the other, they present empirical and theoretical evidence

that points to the demise of Christianity in the Western world. Several responses are possible. First, it may be that the theoretical arguments about the universal presence of religion in societies are wrong. Second, it may be that sociologists who predict the demise of Christianity are wrong. Third, sociologists may be right on both accounts but wrong in their assumption that religion is necessary for the integration of societies. People in postindustrial societies may be moving into an age in which religion is no longer necessary—or one in which religion will be replaced by some "functional equivalent." Fourth, sociologists may be right on both accounts, and the final demise of religion may spell the end of human beings. Certainly there is plenty of evidence for our ability to extinguish ourselves. Perhaps the death of religion will spell the death of all hope for people to find a common core of shared values by which they can agree to live. This is a frightening proposition that most of us would not want to accept.

There is yet a fifth possibility that deserves attention. Possibly, we are about to experience an era when people create a new faith that is more capable than that of the Old and New Testaments of managing the affairs of a complex world. As Harvey Wheeler (1971) argues, as cultural forms change, so must people's gods; otherwise people are doomed to cultural stagnation—". . . a death-of-God era is also a god-building era. . . . " We can only wait to see whether this era will create a new faith.

SUGGESTED READINGS

Glock, Charles Y., and Rodney Stark. *Religion and Society in Tension.* Chicago: Rand McNally, 1965.

Durkheim, Emile. *The Elementary Forms of Religious Life.* Joseph Ward Swain (tr.). Glencoe, Ill.: Free Press, 1954; first published in English, 1915.

Niebuhr, H. Richard. *The Social Sources of Denominationalism.* New York: Holt, 1929.

Weber, Max. *The Protestant Ethic and the Spirit of Capitalism.* New York: Scribner, 1930.

Chapter 21 Politics

IN AMERICAN SOCIETY, the word "politics" has come to have a tarnished meaning in popular usage. Politics brings forth an image of shifty-eyed men deciding issues in smoke-filled rooms. It tends to suggest the primacy of compromise and self-interest over principle, of might over right, of unreason over reason. This attests to the feeling that politics as an activity is inevitably corrupting and debasing and that, in fact, it is possible to have societies without such political behavior.

This popular view of politics is not useful, however, in gaining an understanding of how political processes actually work. When social investigators speak of *politics*, they are referring to the process by which decisions about the allocation of wealth, power, and other scarce resources to competing social groups are *made* and *legitimated*.

POLITICS AS AN ACTIVITY

Making political decisions is often a complex process, as well as one that involves a great deal of secretiveness. Political decisions involve giving some advantage to one group and denying this same advantage to another group that also wants it—one group's gain means another group's loss. Therefore, such decisions entail making informed guesses about the effects they might have on the social system as a whole or at least on its political institutions and its repositories of power. In this sense, every major political decision implies a potential risk to those in power. Groups whose demands are not met might cease to follow the directives of those in power. This situation may be described as the loss of legitimate authority, or *legitimacy*.

In order to minimize the possibility that their power to compel or command obedience will be lost, rulers attempt to justify, or *legitimate*, their decisions and policies as well as they can. The particular form the process of legitimation takes depends heavily on how complex the society is, on its type of culture, and on the historical era. Later on in this chapter the form legitimation has taken in modern industrial states, where it falls to the political theoreticians and intellectuals allied to the ruling class, is examined.

The Political Arena

As long as social institutions are involved in the making of decisions about the allocation of wealth and power, politics will exist in one form or another. Political activity, the struggle for power and resources, has taken many *forms* because it occurs in societies of many different types. It takes place in many different *arenas* as well. Political sociology is largely concerned with the allocation of power and resources in arenas or settings as small as the *community* and as large as the *state* or the *international system*.

It certainly also makes sense to speak of politics in very different settings. The psychological and political theorist Wilhelm Reich (1970) speaks of a political economy of the *family unit*. C. P. Snow's entertaining novels about British academia (see, for example, *The Masters*) portray the politics of the major British universities. Kate Millett (1970) and many other women have begun to document the politics of male-female relations in Western society. Following the lead of Max Weber, we might study the politics of various government *bureaucracies*. Any institution or organization—whatever its function or stated purpose—may be considered a political arena and thus be analyzed in political terms.

The present chapter aims to give you some idea of the political in society, of what political structures, institutions, and processes are. Some of the universals of all known political systems are pointed out, and the institutions that characterize modern industrial states such as ours—parties, political machines, pluralistic politics, particular voting patterns, and so on—are explored. A basic issue that concerns political sociologists is how order is normally maintained in society—how the consent of the governed is obtained. In suggesting where the answers to this question of political stability might lie, the chapter briefly traces the historical development of preindustrial and industrial societies to give some idea of how different economic, social, and political arrangements and circumstances affect political stability.

Rather than dealing exhaustively with political institutions in each era, the chapter focuses on a different historical situation in order to illuminate each of these concerns: political structures in society, political parties, community politics, the locus of power in advanced industrial society, and the social bases of national politics.

Approaches to Investigating Politics

Social investigations that focus on the political usually organize data in one or more of the following ways. The data may be drawn from a single political unit at a given period in time. This system is then analyzed in terms of what the political institutions and processes are, who holds the power and controls the wealth, how authority is legitimated, which groups in the society lend their support to the rulers or decision makers and which do not, and so on. In another type of political analysis, the comparative approach, data are drawn from several different political systems. These systems are compared to see how they agree and how they differ. The comparative approach can involve a look at data drawn from groups or societies chosen for certain *similarities* (advanced industrialization, say, or the presence of many minority groups, or some other characteristic), from societies of *different types* (communist and capitalist, for example), or from societies of different levels of *social complexity* (hunting and gathering and horticultural societies or preindustrial and industrial societies, for instance). In a third approach, the changing political configurations that occur in one or more societies as they move through different *historical* eras are examined. This type of political analysis concentrates on change and development.

Political sociologists frequently focus on politics at the national level. But the great majority of people *experience* politics most immediately at the local level. In their neighborhoods and their cities, seemingly trivial controversies over garbage collection, traffic lights, and (especially in cities) "crime in the streets" may arouse people's emotions and enlist their actions to a higher degree than do questions of war and peace. In general, the more obvious the connections are between political decisions and one's life situations, the more likely one is to become involved in

political processes. The more personal knowledge people have of their leaders, the more likely they are to become involved in political movements with these leaders. Both these conditions are most likely to be found in local-level politics. But community politics in the United States takes place in the context of a large industrialized society with a powerful national government. Accordingly, it differs from community politics in other societies in both the range and types of decisions it makes and in the way it makes them. Thus, to understand the politics you experience in everyday life, it is necessary to understand important features of the political functioning of societies in general.

THE MAINTENANCE OF SOCIAL ORDER

Most of the investigation of and theorizing about political phenomena has concerned politics at the level of national government, or the *state*. Every state has at least two classes of individuals, the *rulers* and the *ruled*. The problem of social order may be posed in its political form as follows: What accounts for situations in which the ruled accept the authority of their rulers? The corollary question is that of social change: Under what circumstances do the ruled refuse to accept the authority of their rulers? Sociologists differ in how they try to answer these two questions.

The Functionalist Perspective

Functionalists, and their followers among the behavioral political scientists, have tended to emphasize the role of *values* in the integration of political units, or *polities*. The classical statement of this position comes from the work of the pioneering French sociologist Emile Durkheim, whose *conscience collective* is, roughly, a set of shared values that operates to integrate a society, no matter how simple or complex. According to this view, in fairly simple societies the members actually agree *ideologically*, largely because of shared religious beliefs. In complex societies there is no need to claim the existence of shared material interests or specific values in the society at large. In complex societies, those having a high degree of division of labor and therefore many

Figure 21.1 The conscience collective (Durkheim's name for the set of shared values that serves to integrate a society) in simple, preindustrial societies is often based on people's ideological consensus on social goals. In contrast, people in complex, industrial societies tend to be tied together by their agreement on the types of means used to accomplish diverse ends. During a transitional period between a preindustrial and industrial society, both shared social goals and a common commitment to social procedures, such as "the democratic process," make up a society's conscience collective. Pictured here are villagers in the eastern highlands of Papua, New Guinea, loading ballot boxes into a helicopter; they are voting in 1972 elections for the territory's House of Assembly. The conscience collective of these villagers is in a transitional phase in which both procedural and ideological values are shared.

different social roles, the conscience collective (unifying cultural values) takes the form of commitments to *procedures*. That is, the members of society are committed to certain means rather than goals, or, as it is often expressed, to "rules of the game." They do not share common political goals, but they all believe in the ground rules by which political decisions are arrived at, and this shared belief operates to maintain social order. In the United States, for example, members of the John Birch Society and political leftists or members of manufacturing interest groups and consumer groups may all share a belief in "democratic processes," although each group wants to win the game, which means, as was pointed out earlier, that their opponents lose.

The Conflict Perspective

Two other important theoretical perspectives on the maintenance of political order stem from the views of Karl Marx and Max Weber. Both the Marxian and Weberian political perspectives play down the role of a prior or abiding social agreement on values. Instead, Marx and Weber, each in his own way, emphasize the role of conflict, or *struggle*. For them, the form that authority takes in society as a whole is the outcome of struggle between competing politically organized groups. In this view the dominance of particular groups ultimately rests on their *control* over specific economic and political resources. Control of these key resources leads to political power. The control of resources makes it likely (although not necessary) that the authority of the controlling group will be legitimated. Weber did not propose a single solution to the problem of explaining how a particular group becomes the ruling one. Marx tended toward the view that the group controlling the society's means of economic production would, in the long run, assume political dominance as part and parcel of this control. Marx believed that in most situations such control rests on direct ownership of the means of production, but, as Eric Hobsbawm has pointed out, Marx's discussion of "Asiatic despotism" shows that he did not consider this to be always so (Marx, 1966).

The crux of the argument between functionalist and conflict approaches is this: Functionalists tend to view polities as being usually integrated. Therefore, they pay a great deal of attention to political socialization, the process by which members of society learn and internalize the political values, attitudes, and beliefs deemed appropriate by their society. Crises of legitimacy are seen as highly unusual, and politics is seen as benign in that all groups have a stake in maintaining order by following the rules of the game. For those holding the conflict approach, legitimacy is much more of a problem. Many Marxists deny that legitimacy plays any part in the creating of political stability; they contend that coercion of the ruled by the rulers does the job. In their view, the polity tends to divide into unalterably opposed groups, on either class or status-group lines.

Political structures differ greatly in societies of different degrees of complexity and of different historical eras. These structural differences result from the fact that economic organization, social organization, and political organization are closely tied. A sensible way to approach the study of *political structures* is to trace their development historically in terms of general world-historical trends and to note differences between the political structures of societies that have different kinds of economic orders.

POLITICAL STRUCTURES

In the beginning there was no state. Recall from Chapter 12 that in hunting and gathering societies no social roles are reserved specifically for political as against familial, economic, or religious responsibilities. Formal political structures do not occur until there regularly is a surplus of production beyond the subsistence level. A regular surplus in production can come about only when relatively sophisticated technology is used to satisfy social needs. The development of *agriculture* was the first giant step toward the realization of an economic surplus. Preagricultural societies depended on the hunting of seasonal game and the

gathering of seasonal plants in order to survive and were frequently forced to follow a nomadic way of life. Learning to plant and somewhat control the growing conditions led to greater yields —and to a settled life. Agricultural societies have had many different types of political structures. These vary from the relatively simple political structures of horticultural societies to the enormously complex empires of agrarian societies.

Preindustrial Societies

Agricultural societies, no matter how different they are in other ways, all tend to be quite *decentralized* politically in comparison to industrial societies. Guenther Roth (1968) notes that *personal rule* is common in agricultural societies. A classic example of such rule is provided by Marc Bloch in *Feudal Society* (1964), which gives a description of the medieval European ceremony of *homage:*

Imagine two men face to face; one wishing to serve, the other willing or anxious to be served. The former puts his hands together and places them, thus joined, between the hands of the other man—a plain symbol of submission, the significance of which was sometimes further emphasized by a kneeling posture. At the same time, the person proffering his hands utters a few words—a very short declaration—by which he acknowledges himself to be the "man" of the person facing him. Then chief and subordinate kiss each other on the mouth, symbolizing accord and friendship. Such were the gestures—very simple ones, eminently fitted to make an impression on minds so sensitive to visible things—which served to cement one of the strongest social bonds known in the feudal era.

Homage linked the vassal, or subordinate, to the lord, or superordinate, who occupied different levels of the social structure. One man's lord might be vassal to a higher lord, and so on up the status ladder. The highest lord in such a society was the king.

The example of ancient China, however, serves to illustrate that not all preindustrial societies had such a high degree of personal rule. Ancient Chinese society, as Weber (1958*b*) pointed out, had developed a remarkably efficient system of bureaucratic rule by the educated *literati:* A

Figure 21.2 The Flemish artist Pol de Limburg and his two brothers Hermann and Jan depicted in a series of twelve miniatures (one for each month of the year) a visual calendar of seasonal life in a feudal society. The paintings were bound into a book of "hours" (indicating times for prayer), *Les Très Riches Heures du Duc de Berry* (1413–1416), for the brother of the king of France. The painting below, for the month of July, illustrates that the personal rulership of a feudal lord is a tangible reality in peoples' lives—the lord's elegant castle in the background is a constant reminder of this fact. His vassals do the work of an agricultural society; in the summer season they harvest grain and shear the sheep.

person achieved high political office by excelling on special examinations. In theory, at least, this system made social mobility possible for talented individuals of all social classes.

Political administration based on personal rulership is somewhat unreliable. The unreliability occurs partly because few rulers have the personal magnetism, or *charisma*, to bind the loyalty of their allies. There is also difficulty when a patrimonial ruler dies. A crisis often arises over who will become the next leader because frequently there is no single, obvious choice. Political stability often suffers. Once in power the new ruler faces the hard job of spurring coalitions among potential supporters, so as to solidify his rule.

Most preindustrial societies have inevitably had *weak* central governments. Often the central ruler could not obtain enough resources to allow a clear domination over potential rivals. The most important of these resources has been money. Once a ruler gained wealth he could easily convert it into military power by hiring *mercenaries* to fight for his cause. V. G. Kiernan (1965) has traced the extensive use of such mercenaries in Western Europe until the eighteenth century. There were certain limits, however, to the ruler's ability to tax his subjects. First, until the development of a *monetary economy*, all taxes were paid directly in goods and were therefore difficult for the ruler to collect. Kings would travel across their territories in order literally to consume their taxes. Second, after the development of the monetary economy, taxation methods were highly inefficient. In addition, tax collectors kept large parts of their take. The establishment of separate offices, such as the Exchequer in England, concerned with finances marked the first significant differentiation of government structures—the differentiation of the ruler (political decision maker) from the revenue official.

Growth of Centralized Political Power

The central regime's stay in power depended on the resources it could command to reward its internal allies and punish its enemies. Going to war was one obvious way to enrich the ruler's coffers: territorial expansion would bring in new revenues. War also gave rulers the chance to reward the faithful by granting them new lands. In the years 1660 to 1815 the maritime states of Western Europe, such as Spain and France, were becoming centralized politically under absolutist rulers. Absolutist kings created large armies that could be used to put down threats to their authority. They also were very concerned with strengthening their states' economic bases. Internal trade was encouraged, as well as the attempt to gain precious metals from international trade. Most decisively, these states promoted economic power by any and all means (such as war, slavery, piracy, and colonialism).

The intrusiveness of the state in promoting economic growth continued into—and beyond— the period in which theories of economic *laissez faire,* or unhindered competition in the marketplace, prevailed. The standard view of the *laissez-faire* period of economic growth (which began in the early nineteenth century and continued well until about the period of the antitrust acts, at the close of the nineteenth century) is that the government played little or no part in controlling or aiding the course of economic development. *In Growth and Welfare in the American Past* (1966), Douglass C. North documents a contrary view. He notes that "a large number of studies have shown conclusively that government intervened significantly in the American economy in the nineteenth century." He goes on to show that both the federal government and those of the states invested in, subsidized, and in other ways heavily supported a wide variety of economic activities, including public works, private corporations, and the building of canals and railroads.

In American society today, it has frequently been asserted that if military spending (which makes up half of all government expenditures) were to cease or to be cut significantly, the economy would probably be thrown into severe depression, and serious political instability would result. Whether or not this prediction is correct, it is certainly clear that state intervention in the economy for the sake of promoting economic growth has great political significance. One reason for this is because such intervention is often on behalf of specific classes, status groups, or parties. The nature of the state, be it capitalist or socialist, is therefore a most important factor in determining the course of a society's future development.

We have briefly traced the development of political centralization from the relatively decentralized political structures of agricultural socie-

ties and their consequently weak central governments to the rise of states with the strong, centralized governments characteristic of industrial societies. A comparison of some of the characteristics of patrimonial regimes (inherited personal rulership) with those characteristics of modern industrial states might be helpful.

Whereas most patrimonial regimes were decentralized and unstable, most modern industrial states are extremely centralized in terms of authority as well as extremely stable politically. The administration of such states tends to approach Weber's description of modern bureaucracy (see Chapter 9). Modern bureaucracy is highly specialized in contrast to the relatively undifferentiated patrimonial bureaucracy. A high degree of specialization carries with it clear-cut areas of command and responsibility. Whereas patrimonial rule was personal, modern bureaucratic authority is impersonal: Power rests in the office (theoretically, at least) rather than in the individual occupying it. The patrimonial system recruits office holders on ascriptive criteria, the modern bureaucracy on the basis of ability and technical knowledge. In modern bureaucracy, unlike in patrimonial rule, there is a differentiation of private and official income. For Weber (1958a), bureaucracy ultimately implied a system of control on the basis of *technical knowledge;* hence he called it "rational."

INDUSTRIALIZATION AND POLITICAL STABILITY

One of the central questions in political sociology is: Why do the ruled accept the domination of their rulers? Political regimes tend to achieve a high degree of legitimacy among the ruled (and thus to be relatively stable) when they are regarded by their citizens as able to deliver what they promise. In modern societies since the era of absolute rulership, the job of legitimating rule has fallen to intellectuals allied to the ruling circles, as was noted earlier. They have constructed sophisticated social theories to justify the existence of the state. The points they raise in arguing the necessity of the state can be regarded as constitut-

Figure 21.3   The political views of Thomas Hobbes (1588–1679). In the left cartoon, a war of all against all results from each individual's pursuing his own self-interest. Hobbes assumed that people are, by nature, self-seeking and hedonistic. Hobbes' solution to the "war" is for the populace to make a "contract" to establish peace. He believed that only one man with total authority could prohibit individuals from breaking the contract. The populace—original makers of the contract—would then become subjects under a ruler they had agreed to obey. (*Right*) In Hobbes' view the monarch's right to decide all moral questions is absolute. And because his power is legitimated by social contact, his good is—theoretically, at least—also the people's good.

ing the promises the regime is willing to make to its citizens in exchange for their allegiance. Thomas Hobbes (1588–1670) serves as a justly famous example of such an apologist.

In his classic *Leviathan* Hobbes argued brilliantly from common-sense notions of social psychology that human nature is individualistic. It was very popular for eighteenth-century intellectuals, of whom Hobbes was one, to speculate about government by imagining what people did in the "natural state," a (mythical) primal period in human history when people were people but had not yet formed themselves into governments and states such as existed in later times. People in the natural state, Hobbes wrote, do not form themselves into societies but constantly war against each other for scarce resources. Continual warfare is the result as well as the cost of individual freedom. But Hobbes saw this cost as too severe: it prevents the development of civilization, which provides the possibility that individu-

als and groups can live in peace and security. Free people can never agree with one another long enough to engage in trade; so no material progress that benefits humankind as a whole could occur. Hobbes saw a simple way out of this bleak situation: the renunciation of individual freedom and the voluntary ceding of all political power to a king. For Hobbes, the renunciation of freedom leads to many demonstrable benefits—peace, prosperity, and culture.

We can regard these benefits as the covert promises offered to the polity that we referred to earlier. To the extent that the citizens see the promises as being fulfilled, they may regard the regime as effective. This gives it a good chance of achieving legitimacy and political stability.

The Promise of Democracy and Freedom

After many political struggles (such as the French Revolution) states have come to promise not only peace, prosperity, and progress but individual

Figure 21.4   Do the candidates from different
political parties really represent significantly different
viewpoints? In the United States, the differences
between major candidates, and their political parties,
may be less important than their similarities.

freedom as well. This particular package of promises is in fact the claim of most industrialized societies and universally goes under the name *democracy*. The Soviet Union, for example, and other communist countries claim democracy, as do capitalist societies. Thus, democracy may be the form of government toward which industrial society tends and under which it achieves its greatest stability. But before we can decide whether this statement is true, we ought to be clear about what a democracy is, for certainly modern industrial states differ greatly in the degree of individual freedom they allow. The definition of democracy usually includes two important elements. First, a democratic state provides processes such as elections in which particular people can be replaced by others or retained as leaders (rather than rulers) at relatively frequent intervals. Second, the theory of democracy claims that if such leaders are chosen properly they in fact will be representative of the large majority of the population. Unpopular or ineffective leaders can be replaced through orderly procedures guaranteed *by the state itself*. The ruled need never resort to violence because the regime is regarded as being, in a fundamental sense, self-correcting.

Problems of Formally Democratic States

In practice, the definition of democracy, like Hobbes' vision of the English monarchy, may be a theoretical statement more than a factual description. Many observers insist that the Soviet Union, for example, is not a democratic regime, despite the occurrence of periodic and regular elections in the Soviet Union. A major complaint is that Soviet elections are a sham—mere formal exercises of democracy—because all candidates come from one political party, the Communist

Figure 21.5 Seymour Martin Lipset received his doctorate from Columbia University in 1949. He has been a prolific and influential writer on a wide range of topics. He has written several important volumes on stratification with Reinhard Bendix (see Chapter 13) and has recently written extensively on student protest movements. His major work has been in political sociology. He is coauthor of *Union Democracy* (1956) and author of *Agrarian Socialism* (1950), *Political Man* (1959), *The First New Nation* (1963), and *The Politics of Unreason* (1970, written with Earl Raab). After a decade as a professor at Berkeley, Lipset moved to Harvard, where he is now a professor in the Department of Social Relations.

Party. In the American system, it is argued, there are many *competing* political parties—or, more realistically speaking, two such parties, the Democratic and the Republican. In the Soviet Union all candidates for political office are Communists; in the United States the major candidates can be either Democrats or Republicans.

How do we decide whether this argument is valid? The key *empirical* question, of course, concerns how to measure the characteristic "competing," because this characteristic is what the argument hinges on. It is not inconceivable that two members of the same American political party might represent polar alternatives on a wide range of issues—such as George Wallace and George McGovern in the Democratic Party or Jacob Javits and John Tower among the Republicans. Quite different positions are represented within the Soviet Communist Party between their "hawks" and "doves." It has frequently been noted that both the American Democratic and Republican parties are *capitalistic parties*, committed, among other things, to the preservation of private ownership of the means of economic production. In this sense they may not really meet the requirement of offering the voters a real choice, if that is construed to mean a choice between *types* of social systems.

Another difficulty with the notion of democracy is that the assumption that elected officials are representative of the people who have elected them may not be warranted. In *Political Parties* (1949), originally published in 1914, the German sociologist Robert Michels specifically attacked this vital link in the theory of democracy. In his view, all large-scale formal democratic organizations tend to degenerate into oligarchical structures; that is, delegated *leaders* become subtly transformed into *rulers*, who dictate public policy rather than respond to the electorate's wishes.

Other limits of a democracy that embodies majority rule have been known for some time. Alexis de Tocqueville (1805–1859) commented in the early nineteenth century about the tendency toward a "tyranny of the majority" emerging from democratic structures, and his warning has never seemed more pertinent than it does today. Minority status groups, particularly ethnic groups, exist in every formally democratic society. Such groups have a collective identity that differs in some respects from that of the rest of the society. The result is that such groups have somewhat divergent interests from the rest of society. Their interests, therefore, will not be entirely served by the functioning of regular democratic procedures. In particular, these minorities will always be defeated in elections if the opposition is united, because they can never muster enough votes. William Gamson (1968*b*) has noted that in politics this situation leads to what he has aptly described as *stable unrepresentation*. Stokely Carmichael and Charles V. Hamilton (1967) have used the term *institutional racism* to denote similar problems in spheres other than the political one.

Democracy as the Political Form of Industrialized Countries

These considerations imply that as an objective term the word "democracy" is singularly difficult to use in a precise and fully meaningful fashion. It is clearly difficult to try to measure the extent to which various "formally democratic" societies are democratic in practice; nonetheless, all industrial societies today claim to be democratic in some sense. In many less developed societies no such claims are made. Seymour Martin Lipset (1960) has noted, as have numerous other observers, that there is a positive association between the degree of industrialization of a society and the trappings—the formal procedures, if not the facts—of formal democracy it contains. There has never been a satisfactory account of the significance of this association, but the following explanation may be offered as a broad outline.

Industrial societies are typically *wealthier* and provide more *educational opportunity* than the less developed countries, and both these attributes probably have great significance for political stability. The greater wealth of industrial societies is also distributed in such a way that *more than half their populations are considered to be above the level of poverty* (see Chapter 12). Said

Figure 21.6   The caucus type of political organization is prominent in preindustrial societies. America's "founding fathers" are shown here being chosen from among the members of the social and political elite. Such political caucuses do not exist in the United States today, but members of Congress, although elected by popular vote, are still largely drawn from the upper class and the upper-middle professional class, and especially from the profession of law.

another way, these societies tend to have a large middle class. This is a new phenomenon in history. In earlier times only a *minority* of the population could be regarded as well-off. The existence of this substantial middle class probably serves to give a majority of the polity the idea that they themselves *have a stake in the existing political system.* This idea is reinforced by the possibility of upward mobility, which is much greater in industrial society than in many Third World societies. Social mobility tends to be tied to the expansion of educational opportunities, and that, again, is characteristic of the industrial setting. Industrial societies can afford democratic governments and yet maintain political stability, as long as their economic growth proceeds in a predictable fashion. That is, such societies need not fear that they sign their own death warrant by allowing people many personal liberties, because the citizens, who feel they have a stake in the existing system, would have to be foolish to want to seriously tamper with the political order. Therefore, despite periods of great dissatisfaction among minority groups in such societies, political revolutions are usually considered highly unlikely by political theorists: At any given time, the vast majority of the citizens feel themselves to be deriving enough benefit from the system not to want to risk radical change.

The less developed countries, on the other hand, are continually faced with the reality that

any opposition party could in theory enlist vast support from a largely dissatisfied populace. And the gap between rich and poor nations seems to be widening, which probably means that democracy remains only a distant hope for the poorer societies.

Although industrial societies enjoy relatively stable political regimes, the members, as was noted earlier, agree not so much on their political goals as much as on the means by which those goals are rightly to be achieved. The members of these societies tend to ally themselves with different long-term political institutions that have formed for the purposes of gaining political power and thus controlling, to some degree, the allocation of wealth and resources. Such institutions, the political parties, may be formed around a variety of different concerns. It is to an investigation of these parties that we now turn.

POLITICAL PARTIES: THEIR STRUCTURE AND EVOLUTION

Political parties have existed, in one form or another, for centuries. Whigs and Tories, to give an example, were clearly distinctive political groups in England as long ago as the late seventeenth century. But the vast changes in social structure that accompanied industrialization transformed the nature and organization of political parties.

Most preindustrial parties were associations of *notables* that organized into what Maurice Duverger (1954) has termed *caucuses.* The caucus was, by nature, a limited and exclusive group. In most preindustrial societies having representative legislative bodies, such caucuses were loosely constructed on territorial bases. One party might be composed of the king and his court and allies among commercial groups. Another might be dominated by groups of nobles jealously trying to keep the central authority from imposing its rule on their outlying territories.

The caucus type of party never sought to recruit new members from the community at large. Membership was increased, much as in a social club, through formal nomination. The party made no attempt to broaden its base of political support because its power ultimately depended on the *reputation* of its members. Members were chosen on the basis of their individual qualities and personal influence. They were not chosen as delegates, or representatives of a given group. By and large, party strife in the preindustrial era was tame. This was so largely because most participants in the political process were of elite status in the society as a whole. Few commoners had political rights.

Industrialization in Western Europe and North America brought with it decisive consequences for party structure. In the so-called *ancien regime* the political arena was traditionally dominated, of course, by the nobility, also known as the landed aristocracy. This domination became increasingly oppressive to the people who were involved in the development of industry, the bourgeoisie. In particular, the growing manufacturing interests were held back by laws that had their origin in the preindustrial period. Such legislation included provisions guaranteeing that people who could not find enough work in the countryside to keep them alive would be given subsistence. As long as such essentially feudal welfare laws existed, agricultural laborers who were pushed off their lands could choose to remain in the countryside rather than face migration to the overcrowded and disease-ridden cities.

As long as migration from the countryside to the city was thus limited, *wages* in new factory industries could not be kept as low as they might be otherwise. Additionally, there were often struggles between urban and rural interests with regard to protective tariffs: Free trade, by bringing goods to the largest possible markets and forcing down the price of staple foods for the new industrial proletariat, or working class, would greatly benefit the urban manufacturers. Consequently, representative industrialists urgently pressed for it. Farmers, on the other hand, suffered when imports depressed the price of farm commodities and thus sought protective tariffs.

Such economic issues were not the only basis for the disenchantment of the bourgeoisie with the prevailing government. Access to status-confirming institutions—universities, the Court, legislative bodies, high bureaucratic office in church and military institutions—in the *ancien regime* tended to be reserved for the sons of the aristocracy. The wealthy industrialists and their allies deeply resented the fact that their *economic* preeminence could not buy them *social* honor and *political* power. The values they espoused in their social theories, such as utilitarianism, and in their literature favored equality, not privilege.

In their struggle for political and social advantage the bourgeoisie enlisted the aid of the newly created *proletariat*, or working class. Especially at issue was the right of all men to vote. Traditionally, only men who owned land (real property) could vote, but society could not be considered democratic until men without property could participate in the political process. (The rights of women were undreamed of—the issue was not fairness but the new classes' struggle for power.) Propagandists and spokesmen of the bourgeoisie—the ideologists of democracy—were opposed by such conservatives as Edmund Burke (1729–1797), who warned of the dangers of extending the right to vote. The conservatives' argument was a simple one. To open legitimate political participation to the masses—who had no stake in the social system, being in the main impoverished—would be to invite the prospect of revolution. (Remember that it was stated earlier that poor countries face the prospect of revolutions waged by the dissatisfied, poor majorities of their populations.) History has proved the conservatives wrong, but why they were is still debated.

There was a great deal of political struggle over the suffrage issue, some of it from within the political system and some of it outside, such as the mass movements and uprisings that carried the threats of violence or force. Eventually, the right of universal male suffrage was won by the second half of the last century. Thomas H. Marshall (1964) has traced the course of this struggle. Once all men could vote, political parties had to seek support among the working-class masses because they constituted the great majority of *citizens*, or people entitled to participate in political decision making. This, as might be imagined, imposed grave strains on the caucus type of party organization. Exclusive, aristocratic parties of notables could not hope to attain power in the industrial setting. In consequence, *mass parties* were born. They are called mass parties because their basis of power is in the masses of people rather than in any specific elite—or so it seems. The nature of such modern parties is not entirely clear, as the following discussion shows.

Mass parties tend to be highly centralized, and they attempt to enroll many members to increase their chance of winning elections. They do this by proposing political decisions that appeal to the largest number of voters. In Western Europe, but not in the United States, mass parties were founded on a trade-union base.

The major goal of a modern political party is to *gain power*. In reaching for this goal, political principles are frequently compromised. Party members in general, the *rank and file*, have little influence in party affairs. Although this situation is bewailed by men like Joseph Schumpeter (1883–1950), it is indeed the essence of political democracy. Schumpeter writes: "A party is not, as classical doctrine (or Edmund Burke) would have us believe, a group of men who intend to promote public welfare 'upon some principle on which they are all agreed.'" Schumpeter notes that political principles or planks may be characteristic of the parties that espouse them much as certain brands of goods may be characteristic of the department stores that sell them. "But the department store cannot be defined in terms of its brands and party cannot be defined in terms of its principles." Rather, the party is defined by the fact that its members are united in the struggle for political power, and different parties may well adopt almost identical programs. Schumpeter continues: "Party and machine politicians are simply the response to the fact that the electoral mass is incapable of action other than a stampede, and they constitute an attempt to regulate political competition exactly similar to the corresponding tactics of a trade association. The psychotechnics of party management and party ad-

vertising, slogans, and marching tunes, are not accessories. They are the essence of politics. So is the political boss" (Schumpeter, 1962).

The political boss operates on the level of community politics but often serves as a bridge to the national parties, which essentially come into existence once every four years, when a president must be elected. The boss controls votes in the community—but that is the subject of the next section, which treats local politics.

COMMUNITY POLITICAL SYSTEMS

The community level is where people experience politics most immediately. Community political institutions reveal the processes that involve different types of people in politics in general. Our look at community politics concentrates on the development of local-level urban political structures in an advanced industrial state—the United States—in the past century, with a glance at its origins in the late eighteenth century. The two types of political configurations focused on are the politics of pluralism and the political machine.

In eighteenth-century and early nineteenth-century American communities, wealthy landowners, merchants, and ambitious industrialists took on the "burden" of community governance to enhance their family status and, at times, for financial profit. In New England and Virginia, town meetings and local legislatures also brought middle-class farmers and bureaucrats into local politics. Landless tenants and factory hands, however, did not participate much in the political life of their communities. Towns and cities with large numbers of such residents were governed largely by men from the oldest and wealthiest families. In some communities, control over local political and economic institutions by a monied local "aristocracy" persisted well into the twentieth century. This type of *pyramidal power structure*, in which economic and political power is held by a small group of wealthy families, was perhaps best documented by Helen Lynd and Robert Lynd in *Middletown* (1929), the report of their studies of the small industrial city of Muncie, Indiana.

When the Lynds lived and worked in "Middletown," between 1924 and 1935, the city was dominated by one wealthy and powerful family, which the authors referred to as the *X* family. Members of the *X* family were industrialists and professionals who owned and operated an important local industry. Their hold over the processes of decision making and over the life chances of Middletown residents was so strong that the Lynds, in *Middletown in Transition* (1937), report one of their informants, an average Middletown resident, as saying:

If I'm out of work I go to the *X* plant; if I need money I go to the *X* bank, and if they don't like me I don't get it; my children go to *X* college; when I get sick I go to the *X* hospital, and my wife goes downtown to buy clothes at the *X* department store; if my dog strays away he is put in the *X* pound; I buy *X* milk; I drink *X* beer; I vote for *X* political parties. . . .

This pattern of family dominance in a community is a form of bossism by the economic elite. Here politicians, both party workers and elected officials, owe their primary allegiance not to the party organization but to the small number of ruling families at the top of the pyramid.

In the nineteenth and early twentieth centuries, many towns and cities developed more complex political structures. During this period, national corporations grew rapidly, and control over locally owned industries often passed into the hands of boards of directors in distant cities. Often such changes in the structure of the economy acted to weaken the power of local business elites. At the same time, American communities were receiving large influxes of foreign immigrants whose needs and numbers would make local leadership seem a thankless task for the traditional local elite.

The number of foreign immigrants in American cities in the late nineteenth and early twentieth centuries created a situation in which it was possible for a new type of politician to emerge. By capturing the loyalty and the votes of the immigrants and their children, a politician could act as an independent broker between competing elite families. Given the requisite neighborhood organization, and the organization of coalitions of var-

ious ethnic leaders, a politician with little family status or money could potentially control the course of community elections over a decade or more. In the face of such organized opposition from people they tended to disdain, the traditional business elite in American communities often withdrew from public politics. This important change in the pattern of American community politics is evident in Robert Dahl's study (1961) of the history and sociology of city politics in New Haven, Connecticut.

Pluralism

In his study of New Haven politics in the past and present, Dahl shows that the ruling families of the town had lost control of its politics by the end of the nineteenth century. As the immigrant population of the town swelled between 1840 and 1870, the ruling families could no longer translate their wealth directly into political power. Men whom Dahl refers to as *ex-plebes*—sons of immigrants—developed political followings in their ethnic groups, used this base of support to build popularity in the community at large, and gained control of the vote. In this new political system, Dahl explains, "Popularity had been split off from both wealth and social standing. Popularity meant votes; votes meant office; office meant influence. Thus the ex-plebes completed the transition from the old patterns of oligarchy based upon cumulative inequalities to new patterns of leadership based upon dispersed inequalities."

New Haven's current politics is often held up as an example of *pluralistic power structure*. Popular politicians emerged there who could act as brokers between competing political parties. If the Irish align themselves solidly behind the Democratic party, the Italians, the second largest ethnic group in the city, will support Republican candidates. The competing parties, in addition to lining up the support of different ethnic groups, also attracted different factions of the town's upper-class activists. Dahl thus demonstrates that power in New Haven is not centralized in the hands of a small elite. Instead, various issues move different segments of the town's population to varying degrees. A politician who wants to accomplish any project in the city must gain the support of broadly based coalitions of citizens from different ethnic groups and different classes.

The Political Machine

An alternative to the development of pluralist community politics in America has been the evolution of the *political machine*. Many of America's greatest cities, including New York, Chicago, Boston, and San Francisco, have been machine towns at one time or another. The machine is a dying political structure in America, but some cities—particularly Mayor Daley's Chicago—still maintain it. In general, the urban machine places a virtual monopoly on political power in the hands of people from working-class backgrounds (Cornwell, 1968; Dahl, 1961). A machine *boss*, such as Chicago's Mayor Daley, is the dominant political figure in the community. The machine probably got its name from the fact that its parts are so well organized and its operations so smooth and continuous. Votes of a faithful majority are "delivered" for candidates chosen by the machine boss and his ward captains. The boss and his captains wield control over an organization of ethnic and neighborhood leaders, who themselves organize precinct organizers. In return for their votes and their work, the party faithful receive "friendship" ranging from mere attention to *patronage* in the form of jobs or services.

The machine boss acts as an entrepreneur who exchanges political power for a share in the control over the economic wealth of the community. This he again trades for more control over votes and thus more power. In response to the criticism that the machine boss espouses no political ideology, there is the saying "The machine boss has seven principles, two fishes and five loaves." Loaves, fishes, chickens, and jobs, all these and more can be used before election day in exchange for votes and political power. On the other hand, the determining feature of the machine's existence is that the population *needs* its services. The more affluent the community becomes, the less attractive become the loaves and fishes that the machine has to offer. The more educated its popu-

lation, the less demand there is for patronage jobs in city hall. Competing institutions in the areas of public welfare and civil service have also damaged the machine's power by eliminating the need among many people for its services.

After World War II many urban machines—in Boston, New York, Pittsburgh, and other major cities—were experiencing what Edwin O'Connor (1956) called "the last hurrah" in his book of that title. Institutions of the welfare state had stripped this political structure of its usefulness; the growth of metropolitan areas beyond city limits made local-level politics seem increasingly irrelevant in comparison to politics at the national level. But the question of how to organize political institutions in local communities remains an extremely interesting one. With the decline of political machines and the giving up of political control on the part of economic elites, there often exists a vacuum of political power and influence at the local level that increases the potential for manipulation of the population from the national level.

Accordingly, it would be wise to go on to a discussion of just who is in a position of power in modern industrial America and other advanced industrial societies—who determines in which direction most major political decisions will go? Who is making the decisions? No matter how much the current American resurgence of interest in regaining a measure of local control succeeds in revitalizing community governments, the fact is that in societies such as ours the power to make the most far-reaching and deeply affecting decisions lies on the national level.

POWER IN ADVANCED INDUSTRIAL SOCIETY

One of the most perplexing questions about advanced industrial society is where political power is located. The attention of investigators has focused primarily on American society, but looking at other political systems as well, as Ralph Miliband (1969) has done, may be fruitful. Many observers feel that power rests with politicians and political structures. In contrast, some observ-

Figure 21.7 Mayor Richard Daley (*far right*)
and Mrs. Nixon at a Columbus Day parade in 1972.
Daley is the boss of the Chicago political machine,
one of the few urban machines that still exist in
contemporary politics in the United States.

Figure 21.8 The political machine trades favors
and patronage—shares in the control over the economic wealth of the community—for votes and power.
But the proverbial piece of cheese, whether prom-
ised by a machine boss or by campaigning political-
party leaders, often turns out to be smaller than
expected (see Figure 21.4).

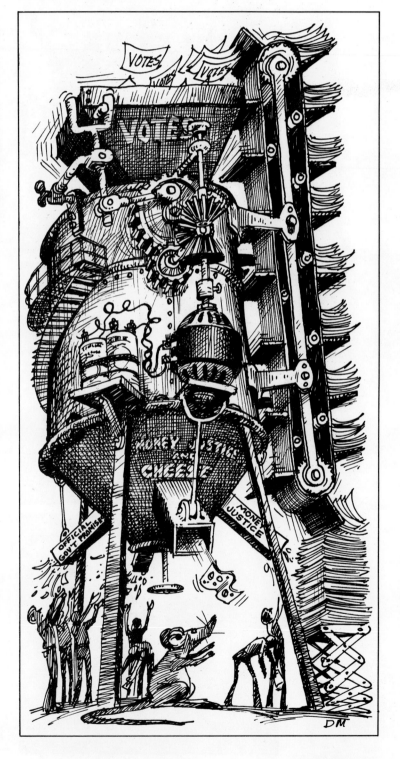

ers hold that there is a *power elite,* a group that
derives its strength from its control of large institutions in the *social* structure.

Perhaps the most engaging representative of
the former view is Joseph Schumpeter. Schumpeter (1962) sees the political boss as the leading
example of the independence of the politically
powerful in society at large. The boss, according
to Schumpeter, is an entrepreneur, someone who
wheels and deals, but in votes, not in money. His
power derives directly from this ability, not from
any social status he occupies. He has a unique
power in a legislative society because he can
promise different groups the ability to deliver
votes on a given issue. The number of separate
interest groups in our society is staggeringly great.
Each of these groups seeks certain advantages—
tax breaks, favorable regulation, protective tariffs,
labor settlements, or licenses—to increase its own
resources. The political leader serves to create
some harmony of interest among these competing
groups, offering support to some, hindering others, and, at other times, effecting compromise
among them. For a system this complex to persist
it is necessary for certain individuals to work in
the gaps between institutions, interest groups,
and the public. This is the functional role of the
politician. Because such men are indispensable to
the proper maintenance of the political system,
they have great political power. Furthermore,
this power is *autonomous*—independent of any

Figure 21.9   C. Wright Mills investigated the extent to which military chiefs, political leaders, and corporation executives are drawn from the same social class and make up a power elite. Barry Goldwater, for example, pictured here, is a well-known political and military leader, as well as a successful businessman.

one group in the polity—because the political leader is free to back first one interest and then another. The politician is thus similar to a *catalyst* in enabling competitive forces to decide between alternative policies.

Schumpeter's view is at the heart of the *pluralist* position on power. The key to this position is that power is never *monopolized* by any particular group but always moves from one group to others over time. There is an additional proviso that membership in potential interest groups is, for practical purposes, open and that such membership cuts across lines of classes and status groups. If the cleavages between interest groups do not cut across class and status groups but instead coincide with them, then some interest groups will be powerless to prevent a monopoly on power by their competitor.

This view of the autonomous power of politicians—and of the functional importance of politics in capitalist society—has been forcefully challenged by C. Wright Mills and his followers. In his influential book *The Power Elite* (1956), Mills spelled out his conception that power in American society rests largely in the hands of a *power elite*. This elite is principally composed of individuals who run corporate, military, and governmental (especially the executive branch) institutions. This group, which may number no more than five hundred men, is seen to be relatively cohesive and in basic agreement on most important national issues. They come from similar social backgrounds and belong to the same clubs; they have all attended prestigious colleges and professional schools. They also share the view that government and large corporations can fruitfully exist in symbiosis. This symbiotic relationship is most closely approximated in the so-called "military-industrial complex," the group composed of people who run either the military, large industry (which has enormously profitable defense contracts), or both, which President Eisenhower warned against in his final speech before leaving office. Seymour Melman (1971) has written a number of books documenting the interdependence of military and industry in contemporary America.

Figure 21.10   C. Wright Mills (1916–1962) was a severe critic of the American political and academic establishment. He produced an amazing number of books and articles during a relatively short career. Among his most important books are *White Collar* (1951), *The Power Elite* (1956), and *The Sociological* *Imagination* (1959). He also was an early and important Weber scholar and with H. H. Gerth selected and translated a collection of Weber's essays in 1946. Mills received his doctorate from the University of Wisconsin. At the time of his death he was an associate professor of sociology at Columbia University.

Whereas the pluralists conceive power to be up for grabs among several competing groups, to Mills and his followers the major sources of power are *monopolized* by a group maintaining control of the dominant institutions in the society. Politicians, in this view, occupy only what Mills called "the middle levels of power." There they compete with one another to see who controls what piece of the resource pie. But it is at the high levels of power that policy is made—the decisions about national security, the size of the budget, the nature of foreign policy, and the direction of future social investments. These decisions tend to be made without the consent of Congress and sometimes, as in the Tonkin Gulf resolution or the Bay of Pigs invasion, by deception of the public as well as their legislators.

There is no question that certain individuals, because of their institutional position or control over vast portions of the economy, have great power. The debate between pluralists and the various proponents of the power-elite thesis has tended to focus on how much these powerful individuals, and their institutions, stick together when it comes to making policy. This debate remains unresolved—partly because of insufficient research and partly because of the difficulties of doing research on powerful elites that have much to conceal from the general public.

Having looked at the question of where power is located in advanced industrial society, let us now turn to this question: On what basis does such power rest in society as a whole?

THE SOCIAL BASES OF NATIONAL POLITICS

There seem to be three types of social bases for politics in any society: Classes (positions in the occupational structure), status groups (ethnic, religious, or regional groups), and parties (coalitions voluntarily established on the basis of shared political interest). In the long run, political parties tend to rest on either a class or a status-group basis. The more a given society is modernized, or industrialized, the more it is expected that splits between classes will characterize its politics.

The tool most often used by social scientists in studying the bases of parties in society is the *voting study:* who votes for whom and why. In 1963 Robert Alford reported on a survey of voting patterns for four Anglo-American societies: the United States, Great Britain, Canada, and Australia. Alford noted that support for national political parties seemed to be most clearly divided along class lines in those countries that had moved furthest away from political identities founded on regional or religious loyalties and toward national political identities. For example, politics are more class based in Great Britain than in Canada; Canada has more pronounced regional and religious divisions than has Great Britain.

However, no society has yet approached totally class-based politics. In France and Italy, for example, the Communist Party is very largely supported by industrial workers, whereas the various more moderate parties tend to be supported by the middle classes and professionals. But there are still plenty of workers who support conservative parties and many middle-class and professional persons who vote left. Furthermore, there are also ethnic and religious parties in both societies that claim another basis of support among voters. These parties practice what has been termed *status-group politics.*

In the United States the major political parties do not divide neatly along class or status-group lines. Even so, it is possible to say that the Democratic Party is generally supported by the working class, whereas Republican support tends to occur in the middle and upper-middle classes and in rural areas. Of course, there are exceptions to these generalizations. For one thing, class lines and rural-urban differences do not fully coincide with the divisions among such status groups as racial, religious, and ethnic minorities and majorities. In American society today status-group politics frequently counts for more than class politics. Table 21.1 shows the proportion of persons preferring the Democratic Party in the 1960 election—the year John F. Kennedy defeated Richard M. Nixon for the presidency. The table shows that a majority (60 percent) of the polled Americans in blue-collar occupations preferred the Demo-

Table 21.1   Percentage Preferring Democrats in 1960, by Occupational Type and Religion°

Occupational Type	Religion		
	Catholic	*Protestant*	*Total*
Blue Collar	79%	51%	60%
White Collar	73	32	46%
Total	76%	40%	

° Different bases were used in computing the percentages for occupation and for religion. Jews were included in the occupational sample.

Source: Adapted from Robert R. Alford, *Party and Society: The Anglo-American Democracies* (Chicago: Rand McNally, 1963), p. 243.

crats, and the majority of white-collar workers did not (only 46 percent said Democrat). These data support the claim that class influences political preference in the United States. But looking further at the table you will notice that class played a much weaker role in political preference than did religion. Regardless of their class, Catholics overwhelmingly preferred the Democrats. But only a bare majority (51 percent) of Protestant blue-collar workers preferred the Democrats; two-thirds of Protestant white-collar workers did not. Similarly, blacks and Jews have overwhelmingly been supporters of the Democratic Party regardless of their social class. Until recently Southerners too voted as a status group. But lately Southerners have been turning to two-party voting along class lines (Campbell *et al.,* 1960).

Thus, among certain religious, ethnic, or regional groups, status-group voting appears to be the *norm.* This tendency can be further demonstrated by Sidney G. Tarrow's comparison (1967) of the social base of the most class-oriented political party—the Communist Party—in two regions of Italy, the north and south. In the north, the party's members live mostly in medium and large cities, whereas in the south they live in the countryside. The northern party is predominantly working class; the southern, peasant. In the south, disproportionate numbers of the upper class support the Communist Party, especially intellectuals and students. The character of party organization is radically different in the two settings: centralized in the north, loose in the south. In conclusion,

it might be said that there are *two* Communist parties in Italy and that the social base of Italian Communism is correspondingly muddled. In large part, this situation results from the fact that Italy has two different socioeconomic structures in the two regions. In fact, as Michael Hechter (1971) has shown, these differing structures can be seen as resulting from an internal colonial pattern of development. The north of Italy is industrialized, whereas the south bears many similarities to less developed countries. In consequence, southern Italian politics tends to focus on prospects for regional development and this emphasis gives it a status-group character.

THE FUTURE OF POLITICAL STRUGGLE

Political order, as we have seen, ultimately rests on the agreement of the rank-and-file members of society to abide by the decisions of their rulers or leaders. Such agreement is either voluntary, because of shared values, or is the course dictated by prudence in the face of the superior force commanded by the politically powerful. Yet, as we have also seen, the structures and processes of a state's politics do not always operate to the benefit of many or even most of its members. For example, in the discussion of problems of formally democratic societies, we noted that situations of stable unrepresentation and institutional racism often occur: Some status groups—racial minorities in the United States, or the Catholics in Northern Ireland—are always the "have nots" in the society. The twin questions of *repression* and *exploitation* of such groups have hardly been touched on here (except to be noted in passing, with reference to the desire of the new industrial classes to exploit the emigrants from the farms to the cities). Disaffection on the part of organized groups in society is always likely to be met with violence if other measures do not suffice.

The persistence of political struggle, much of it violent, in the technologically sophisticated West in the 1960s and 1970s is a fact, though to many an unpleasant one. There has been much recent discussion of a *postindustrial society* governed largely by scientific consensus, or the agreement of the experts. The postindustrial society is theorized to be less politicized than older societal forms. This is so because politics, concerned as it is with competition on the basis of power, will ostensibly give way to rational planning, conducted by many individuals with expert knowledge about diverse aspects of social management. But the continuation of status-group politics within highly technological societies would seem to belie these expectations. As long as social groups are divided by systematic differences of wealth, power, and prestige, violent politics may be anticipated, both within and between nations.

SUGGESTED READINGS

Campbell, Angus, *et al. The American Voter.* New York: Wiley, 1960.

Dahl, Robert. *Who Governs?* New Haven, Conn.: Yale University Press, 1961.

Lipset, Seymour Martin. *Political Man.* Garden City, New York: Doubleday, 1960.

Mills, C. Wright. *The Power Elite.* New York: Oxford University Press, 1956.

Chapter 22 Economics and the World of Work

ALL INDIVIDUALS AND ALL SOCIETIES must find ways to make a living. The two key elements in this process are *production* and *exchange*. Commodities such as food, machines, and weapons are produced, and together with labor they are exchanged between individuals and groups. In industrial societies this whole process is facilitated by the use of money and credit; in most simple societies goods and services are bartered directly back and forth.

Roles, groups, and organizations that are primarily concerned with production and exchange constitute the economic institutions of society. The present chapter will give little attention to exchange. That seems better left for economics courses. Instead, this chapter will concentrate on production, specifically on that part of production that constitutes work. We shall consider the nature of work, why people work, the organization of work, the role of unions, and the relationships between work and inequality.

THE NATURE OF WORK

No society can exist without work activities. People must work to produce and prepare food, provide shelter and clothing, defend against enemies, treat illness, and develop language, religion, and the arts. Even activities as basic as these require specialized skills. In nonliterate societies, for example, hunters, house builders, and medicine men have distinct skills. Social scientists call the differentiation of skills *the division of labor*. In contemporary industrial societies there are thousands of clearly distinguishable skills and functions, each of which is organized into an occupation. Skills are so differentiated in the United States that 21,741 separate ones were identified in 1965 (U.S. Department of Labor, 1965).

The actual and potential workers in the population of an industrial society constitute its *labor force*. The labor force includes not only those who are gainfully employed but also those who want to work but are temporarily or involuntarily unemployed. It excludes those who are underage, unemployable, or not seeking work. Every society also has some members who, because of advanced age or severe physical or mental handicaps, must be supported by the labor force. It should be noted that societies differ in the ways they define who is included in the labor force. For example, part-time laborers who do not want more work may or may not be considered part of the labor force—and the same is true of newsboys and others under sixteen who work part-time before or after school hours.

In the United States in 1970, 61 percent of the total national population of persons sixteen years old or over were considered to be in the labor force—81 percent of the males and 43 percent of the females (U.S. Department of Labor, 1971). These percentages may change because many people who have traditionally been excluded from the labor force census owing to physical handicaps or family responsibilities—for example, mothers of young children—are increasingly expressing desires to participate.

Work activities are of interest to sociologists not only because they usually take up at least one-half of workers' waking hours but also because they constitute a vital part of society.

Work in the Past: Preindustrial Societies

To understand the social ramifications of work in modern society, we should review what work was like in preindustrial societies. Glimpses of early patterns can be constructed from studies of isolated societies that have not yet been much affected by industrial civilization.

The division of labor in primitive societies is sex-based; men and women have different jobs regardless of the overall characteristics of the society. In her classical study of the peaceful, mountain-dwelling Arapesh of New Guinea, Margaret Mead found:

Cooking everyday food, bringing firewood and water, weeding and carrying—these are women's work; cooking ceremonial food, carrying pigs and heavy logs, house building, sewing thatch, clearing and fencing, carving, hunting, and growing yams—these are the work of both men and women. If the wife's task is the more urgent—if there are no greens for the evening meal, or a haunch of meat must be carried to a neighbour in the next village—the husband stays at home and takes care of the baby.

In a very different kind of society among the fierce, cannibalistic Mundugumor, Mead found:

What work the men do can easily be done alone. They make yam gardens, and they cut down sago-palms for sago-working and to rot upon the ground so that the edible sago-grub will flourish in the rotting trunk. The women do everything else. . . . Upon this basis of women's work, the men can be as active or as lazy, as quarrelsome or as peaceful, as they like. And the rhythm of the men's life is in fact an alternation between periods of supreme individualism, in which each man stays at home with his wives and engages in a little desultory labour, even an occasional hunting excursion with his bow and arrows, and the periods when there is some big enterprise on foot. The competitiveness and hostility of one Mundugumor for another are very slightly expressed in economic terms. They quarrel principally over women (Mead, 1935).

In civilizations, or societies characterized by city life, the division of labor became more complex. The population of Egypt in the time of the Pharaohs (about 2,500 to 1,000 B.C.) was divided into the nobility, the priesthood, the army, the bureaucracy (scribes), and the peasants. The peasant class included not only farmers but skilled and semiskilled artisans: draftsmen, quarriers, masons, carpenters, bricklayers, sculptors, painters, chariot makers, armorers, leather workers, boat builders, physicians, and morticians. At the bottom of the social hierarchy were the increasing numbers of slaves captured during foreign conquests, who had to do the most menial tasks of manual labor (Casson, 1965). Ironically, the system of slavery in ancient Greece freed philosophers and scholars from menial toil, thus allowing the flowering of noble ideals and political concepts of democracy.

A similar division of labor persisted in Western civilization up through the feudal period, but feudalism added a new dimension of institutional commitment between the landed aristocracy and the serfs who supported them: The oaths of fidelity bound a servant to his lord and made the lord paternalistically responsible for the welfare of the servant. However, through the same period the growth of commerce and money exchange contributed to the development of trade centers in cities—and the commerce led to the break-up of the feudal loyalties between employer and employee; ultimately, it laid the basis for industrialization (Gibbs, 1953).

From Preindustrial to Modern Society

One of the founders of modern sociology, Emile Durkheim (1858–1917), described the transition from precommercial and preindustrial to modern society as a change from a social system based upon what he called *mechanical solidarity* to one based upon *organic solidarity*. Mechanical solidarity characterizes total societies that are held together by common values and a moral consensus, which he termed the "collective conscience." Organic solidarity, which characterizes industrial societies, is based less upon shared moral norms than upon recognition of an individual's interdependence with many other individuals and groups in the society (Durkheim, 1966; Hall, 1969). The assembly line inside a modern factory epitomizes Durkheim's concept of organic solidarity. From the moment the first part or subassembly appears at the beginning of the line until the finished product moves off the end, what each worker does depends on what the worker before him up the line has done. The only values that these workers need to share with each other are certain work-related expectations necessary to complete the transaction.

Another important forerunner of modern sociological thinking, Karl Marx (1818–1883), argued that the factory system represented the final degradation in the continuing plight of the working classes throughout history. Marx theorized that workers had always been alienated from control over the means of production because these means (property and tools) had been owned by a few, who appropriated the benefits (profits) for their own use. In factories, workers were finally separated even from the few benefits they had previously derived from the paternal concern of their landlord employers. Men became appendages of machines and enslaved by the methods of mass production.

At the same time, Marx reasoned that factories provided an opportunity for improvement in this paradoxical situation because factories brought together large numbers of previously isolated groups of workers under one roof, so that they had an opportunity to recognize their mutual plight—that is, to develop a class consciousness—and to prepare for the revolution that Marx saw as necessary to stop industrial exploitation; in fact, he was convinced the revolution was inevitable under these circumstances (Marx, 1936). Marx did not foresee the extent to which changing managerial ideologies would blunt this revolutionary potential and channel it into different directions in industrializing nations such as Great Britain and the United States. (Some different views on revolutionary potential are discussed in Chapter 29.)

In a notable study, Reinhard Bendix (1956) showed that in different countries and at different stages in the process of industrialization, industrial management developed ideologies to justify their activities and their authority. Originally in England, the first nation to industrialize on a large scale, factory management devoted attention to justifying industrialization against more traditional agricultural and commercial pursuits and adopted what Bendix called an "entrepreneurial ideology." Later in England, the United States, and other Western societies, the emphasis turned to "managerial ideology" to justify managers' claims to need considerable freedom for themselves and obedience from workers. Entrepreneurial ideology was directed against the old preindustrial order; managerial ideology sought to buttress the new industrial one.

Frederick W. Taylor (1967) and the school of scientific management in the early decades of the twentieth century tried to establish a scientific basis for job specification and for assigning individuals to job positions. The later studies of Elton Mayo and his colleagues, in what became known as the human-relations school of industrial research in the 1930s and 1940s, pointed to the dangers of overspecialization and to the startling fact (startling to researchers not previously edu-

cated in the social sciences) that informal groups of workers tend to develop in every factory situation. These informal groups behave in ways that may either support or undermine overall production goals of their employers, depending upon the degree of correspondence between work-group norms and management goals (Mayo, 1933). The findings and methods of both the scientific-management and the human-relations schools of industrial research have been used extensively by modern industrial management to try to increase cohesion and productivity in organized work situations of all types.

WORK MOTIVATION AND REWARDS

Sociologists, psychologists, and economists not only study work activities in industrial societies but wonder why men and women work at all. What motivates their toil? What satisfactions and rewards do they get from it?

These questions do not have the same significance when one asks them with reference to simple, primitive forms of society. In societies such as those examined by Margaret Mead and other cultural anthropologists, a person works so that he and his family can survive, and there is no viable alternative to work. To ask the question why persons work in such situations is to ask why they want to go on living.

The question about work motivation takes on a different meaning in more complex, modern societies. Remember that these are societies characterized by a much more complex division of labor. Many different kinds of jobs and different kinds of work situations exist, and the individual has at least some degree of choice in his occupation. What work he will do is not predetermined for him from the time of his birth; occupational opportunities become available to him within a system of *achieved* rather than *ascribed* status (both types of status are discussed in Chapter 12). Why do men and women aspire to or choose one kind of work rather than another?

Workers in modern industrial societies, unlike preindustrial workers, have to learn new work *disciplines.* Especially in parts of the world where industrialization, bureaucratization, and modern-

Figure 22.1   What motivates people to work?
Sources of work motivation may be extrinsic
or intrinsic. Extrinsic rewards, such as money and
prestige, may serve as an important source of
motivation for the commercial artist (*top*). Intrinsic
rewards—the satisfaction gained from the activity
itself—may be more important to the Navajo
sand painter (*bottom*).

ization have been occurring only within the past generation, people cannot learn work disciplines from their families or communities; in fact, there is often conflict between agrarian community standards or ways of life and the requirements of the modern factory, store, or office. Even within comparatively modernized nations such as the United States, the cultural patterns of native people—the American Indians—still persist in marked contrast to the work requirements of the urban industrial system. For example, the concept of working strictly according to a time schedule or punching a time clock is quite foreign to people who have been accustomed to regulating their lives by such natural measures of time as seasons of the year, daily cycles of the sun, and monthly cycles of the moon. People whose roots are deep in an agrarian mode of living probably would not understand the highly sophisticated concerns of New York City dwellers who a few years ago reportedly petitioned the management of the city subway system to schedule a new train at two-and-one-half minutes after the hour because they were dissatisfied with existing trains that ran on the hour and five minutes after!

The concept of working for a boss who is neither a kinsman nor a personal acquaintance can also strike persons with a preindustrial, agrarian background as very strange and perhaps incomprehensible. Similarly strange is the idea that a person devotes only part of himself to his work and that the obligations between employer and employee are strictly limited. Yet these are important characteristics of modern bureaucratic work organization, which we shall discuss in a later section of the chapter. Working by the clock and impersonality in the supervisory relationship are, in fact, two characteristics of work that need to be offset by special incentives that motivate people to submit to industrial discipline.

Theories of Work Motivation

So we return to the fundamental question: what incentives does the modern industrial system provide for work activities? One answer comes from classic economic theory. From Adam Smith (1723–1790) on, economists in the classical tradi-

Figure 22.2   The Protestant Ethic, depicted in Grant Wood's painting *American Gothic* (1930), stresses hard work in the service of God as the basis of life.

tion have argued that money is the main motivation for work. In this school of thought, the modern person has been viewed as an economic being who rationally calculates ways to maximize his individual financial gain, whether he works at a station on an assembly line or invests his capital in a corporation.

This view of human nature has been rejected, or at least significantly modified, in the theories of many sociologists and psychologists. People do not always act in what might objectively be called their own best interests and do not always behave in ways that would maximize their financial gain. Individuals have often been known to take somewhat lower-paying but more satisfying jobs. Furthermore, the studies of Elton Mayo and many others have provided convincing evidence that *group* influences are often more powerful determinants of behavior at work than are considerations of private gain (Mayo, 1933; Roethlisberger and Dickson, 1939).

One of Max Weber's important contributions to sociological theory is his analysis of the relationship between religious ideology and economic behavior, especially the motivation to work. Weber demonstrated how changes in the religious sphere of human activity can cause changes in work motivation. More specifically, Weber argued that capitalism, the primary mode of economic behavior in Western civilization, arose not out of general greed for economic gain but out of the ability to *restrain* this greed through ideologies, or values, of hard work and saving. Before capitalistic enterprise really took hold in the Western nations, the Protestant Reformation had occurred. The Reformation took several forms, but one major form, Calvinism, laid particular stress on the idea that salvation (although predestined by God) is demonstrated by worldly success achieved by the strict disciplines of hard work and conscientious saving—called the Protestant Ethic or the Puritan Ethic.

Weber argued that the Protestant Ethic provided the ideological basis for Western capitalism; other factors, he said, also contributed to its development: for example, the separation of industry from household activities; the development of ra-

tional bookkeeping methods; the separation of corporate and communal property; and the development of a rational legal system of government. Weber (1930) proved the importance of the Protestant Ethic by showing that those who became Calvinists and formed the new middle class in Western societies, or who at least felt strongly influenced by the Protestant Ethic, were most likely to engage in commercial and industrial activities. Among the middle classes in the United States and countries of Western Europe, religious justifications for work have long since become persistent everyday attitudes: those who are physically able should work, and idleness is reprehensible.

More recently, several social psychologists have developed theories about work motivation that have gained widespread attention. One of these is Abraham Maslow's "hierarchy of needs." He maintained that people's motives fall into five categories: (1) simple needs for survival, safety, and security; (2) social and affiliative needs; (3) ego-satisfaction and self-esteem needs; (4) needs for autonomy and independence; and (5) self-actualization needs for the maximum development of an individual's creative potential. Maslow claimed that human beings have to satisfy lower levels of need before they can become concerned with higher levels. The challenge to modern industrial society is to create work opportunities that provide human satisfactions at the highest level of self-actualization (Maslow, 1954). In a somewhat similar theory, Frederick Herzberg distinguished between "hygienic factors," the rudiments of job satisfaction, and "motivators," the factors associated with a sense of positive job satisfaction, accomplishment, and personal competence (Herzberg, Mauser, and Snyderman, 1959).

Douglas McGregor became known for his distinction between "Theory-X" and "Theory-Y" conceptions of worker motivation. Theory X says that because people are inherently irrational, lazy, and uncommitted to management's goals, management must use outside incentives to instill enough discipline and self-control in workers to get them to perform satisfactorily. Theory Y says that people are naturally active and that they try to do good work; they take pride in their work as they do in other activities, do not necessarily have goals contradictory to management's, and are capable of and interested in joint participation in managerial concerns. McGregor argues that many failures in managing enterprises can be attributed to management's Theory-X approach to worker motivation (McGregor, 1960).

Occupational Differences

The theories of work motivation outlined in the preceding section attempt to define what motivates workers in general. Some social scientists have done studies of specific kinds of workers and work activities to see what in particular motivates them. In observing production workers, for example, William F. Whyte (1955) found:

1. Among production workers, the proportion primarily motivated by money to engage in individual behavior contrary to work group norms is very low; perhaps as few as 10 percent will respond to an individual incentive scheme and ignore group pressures to restrict output.
2. When an incentive scheme works, whether it is an individual or a group incentive, it often works for reasons other than making more money. In fact, (a) workers may perceive the meeting of production goals to be a sort of game; they work hard because the game is fun; (b) workers may work to meet higher quotas in order to maintain good relations with their supervisor or to minimize the pressure for production from him; and (c) workers may produce at a brisk pace because it is often less boring or fatiguing than an erratic or slow pace.
3. "Rate busters," who produce above the group norms, differ in their background and personality from "restrictors," who work at the level of group norms. The rate busters are more individualistic, come from homes in which economic individualism is highly prized (such as a farm family), and do not seem to have strong social needs. Restrictors come from urban working-class homes, value cooperation and getting along with others, and have stronger social needs as evidenced by a higher rate of joining outside social groups.

Other studies have found (1) that managers appear to be motivated by different incentives from those that ordinarily motivate production workers and (2) that managers themselves differ in their motivations. For example, a review of the literature by Victor H. Vroom (1964a; 1964b) reports that sales and personnel managers are more likely to indicate strong social or affiliative needs but that production managers tend to have strong interests in working with mechanical things. Higher-level managers are more likely to express needs for personal growth, self-actualization, and autonomy than are lower levels of management.

Saul W. Gellerman (1963) has shown that even workers who appear to be primarily motivated by money attach different meanings to economic rewards. For some, money represents security and love; for others, power. For some, money is a measure of achievement in society, and for still others, it is merely the means to the end of comfortable and sumptuous living.

No one explanation covers all work situations; men and women work for varied reasons. People socialized in the Protestant Ethic probably feel compelled to work and gain intrinsic satisfaction from doing a "good job." Others see work quite consciously as a means to an end that is important to them. The motivations for work among most

Figure 22.3   This man installs right-front windows
in automobiles eight hours a day. Such dull,
repetitive work, not uncommon in industrial societies,
has resulted in alienation and anomie among the
industrial proletariat. People who must do this type
of work rely solely on extrinsic rewards; there
is no intrinsic satisfaction in the job itself.

people, however, represent a mixture of intrinsic
and extrinsic elements.

Factors in Job Satisfaction and Dissatisfaction

Marxian theory postulates that in capitalist society
factory technology, increasing division of labor,
and nonownership of property result in widespread *alienation* of industrial workers from control over their work, from meaningful social relationships with each other, and even from their
own self-respect. Durkheim suggested a similar
concept of *anomie* to describe the detachment
felt by many individuals in relation to work and
other institutions in modern society.

Blue Collar   Although assembly-line workers—
who have been most deprived of autonomy and
freedom of action in modern factories—do experience considerable job dissatisfaction and alienation, the large majority of industrial workers
have not expressed dissatisfaction. Robert
Blauner reported that in a 1964 nationwide Roper

survey of American workers, 61 percent of the
automobile workers felt their jobs were monotonous all or most of the time, but only 38 percent
of the unskilled men in the entire sample felt their
jobs were dull. Automobile workers were more
likely than other factory workers to feel that their
jobs make them work too fast, that the jobs are too
simple for their best abilities, and that they do not
lead to any higher positions within their company.
Blauner found that craft technologies in the construction industry and a variety of service industries permit more freedom and individual discretion to the worker than manufacturing industries
do, and because both these industries are gaining
more workers than manufacturing is, craftsmen
represent an increasing proportion of satisfied
workers. Job satisfaction is also wide-spread
among workers in continuous-process technology
industries, such as oil refineries and highly automated, computer-controlled plants (Blauner,
1964). Workers are most likely to be dissatisfied
in industries where technology is changing from
individual craftsmanship to automation and

Figure 22.4   A master craftsman passing
skills on to an apprentice. Once learned, the basic skills
gained can be applied in producing various
types of products. For example, a carpenter can learn
to make carts, build cabinets, or frame houses without
major retraining. The carpenter's skills open to him a
broad range of activities that stand in marked
contrast to the specialized functions performed by
most factory workers.

where human labor is becoming excessively frac-
tionated and viewed simply as an appendage to
machinery.

White Collar   C. Wright Mills in his classic study
of white-collar employees (1953) found that overall job satisfaction is much higher in white-collar
than in blue-collar or hourly-wage categories and
that the extent of job satisfaction is actually correlated with the way one's occupation is ranked
by level of skill and prestige; the prestige rankings
of some specific occupations in the United States
are given in Chapter 12. Mills found that 86 percent of professional employees, 74 percent of
managers, 56 percent of skilled workers, 48 percent of semiskilled workers, and 42 percent of
commercial employees were satisfied with their
work situations.

A number of studies have shown that physical
scientists rank high on scales of occupational prestige; also, except for those employed in universities, they are likely to view themselves as having
different goals from those of their employers. A
nationwide survey of scientists by Howard
Vollmer found 66 percent of the total sample indicating that they were satisfied or very satisfied
in their work situations. The percentage satisfied
was 71 in universities but only 57 for scientists
employed in industrial companies. This difference
in satisfaction may be explained by figures showing that 94 percent of those in universities reported that they had a large degree of freedom
to select their work activities, but only 65 percent
of those in industrial companies did so (Vollmer,
1965). Flexibility, freedom of action, and individual discretion on the job, then, are correlates
of job satisfaction for people at both ends of the
occupational skill spectrum.

THE ORGANIZATION OF WORK

We have discussed the division of labor and individual responses to job situations in industrial
societies, but what about the jobs themselves?
How does work become organized? The division
of labor constitutes one major dimension of the
organization of work. In modern complex socie-

ties work is divided into a host of occupational
groupings. Within the same work establishment,
persons doing the same kind of work are likely to
be classified into distinct *jobs* or job *positions*. In
many cases, the qualifications for recruiting workers and the work to be performed by occupants
of these positions are formally written up in job
descriptions. Typically, these descriptions indicate not only what the individual is expected to
do but also the supervisor to whom he reports.
The other major dimension of work organization
is the *hierarchy of authority*, which tells who su-
pervises whom, so that the work activities of a
number of individuals can be coordinated toward
an overall purpose. Chapter 9 discusses the hierarchy of authority as a vertical dimension of organization and the division of labor as a horizontal one.

Sociologists usually characterize these aspects
of work organization in terms of *roles*—the rights,
obligations, and patterns of behavior that are expected of occupants of different positions in society. Roles have functions, and these functions
differ in different kinds of work. For example, the
roles of those at different levels of supervisory

responsibility differ in authority. Roles are discussed at length in Chapter 7.

Preunion Systems and Work Relations

Before unions became a part of workers' lives in modern industrial societies, people organized work activities and relationships much differently. In most early societies workers and employers had close ties based on mutual obligations. These relationships began to break down with the growth of industry, and workers had to find new ways to organize work activities and relationships.

Associations The division of labor into separate crafts and occupations in the early civilizations of the Middle East and the Mediterranean resulted in *craft associations,* where novices could learn special skills and perform work under the direction of journeymen and master craftsmen. Apprenticeship on the job became the common method for transmitting and controlling work skills among the working class.

For many centuries only a minority of the entire population was included in skilled occupational groups, which performed specialized services for the nobility (from whom some of the workers learned the mysteries of religion and the arts of war as well as secular skills). The vast majority of people were relatively unskilled agrarian peasants kept in serfdom or slavery.

Guilds In the late Middle Ages economic difficulties beset feudal agriculture, and population expansion created a surplus of peasant labor, part of which drifted into new commercial pursuits in expanding urban centers of trade. Peasants with rural experience in carpentry, stone cutting, smithing, weaving, or leather working might expect full-time work in town. The demand was even greater for weavers, armorers, potters, silversmiths, and other skilled craftsmen of goods that the nobility and the military required. Craftsmen in these and other trades formed *merchant guilds* that purchased their own materials, rented their own shops, and sold their own products.

Under the merchant-guild system, master craftsmen employed journeymen and appren-

Figure 22.5 Institutions are interrelated and mutually influence each other. Workers who belong to a union (an economic institution) develop, to some degree, a working-class consciousness. Politicians and parties (part of the political institution) try to secure the support of workers at election time by addressing themselves to the political and economic needs most important to workers.

tices. This was an intimate, close-working relationship, where the employer and employee were likely to know each other well for a long period of time—perhaps even for a lifetime—and to develop mutual feelings of obligation.

The Breakdown of Relations During the period starting with migration to the Americas in the sixteenth century through the beginnings of the industrial revolution in the eighteenth century, the close working relationships between employer and employee began to change. Observers of these changes were concerned with what would replace the paternalistic merchant-guild system. The Frenchman Alexis de Tocqueville (1805–1859) was one of these observers. "Between the workman and the master," he wrote in the 1830s, "there are frequent relations but no real associations." He noted that political democratization in North America was associated with the growth of industry and that industry in turn also caused the development of a labor force freed from the interpersonal obligations that had characterized the preindustrial order. Tocqueville feared that a "new aristocracy" would arise in industry that would seek to exercise power in an unrestrained way; yet he also saw the possibility that new norms and expectations would develop to govern the relationship between employers and employees in industrial enterprises. "The rule is different," he wrote, "but there is a rule" (Tocqueville, 1954).

As we have noted, Marx had predicted that the alienation of workers, accelerated by industrialization and the factory system, would inevitably lead to revolution—the complete overthrow of the capitalistic system. However, the general response of workers in Western European countries and America was to organize themselves to deal with management in new ways through a process that became known as *collective bargaining*. Unionization became a major alternative to revolution in the West. The capitalistic system was not overthrown in many countries, but union organization certainly contributed to the modification of this system in significant ways.

Unions

Until the 1930s, unionization in the United States mainly followed craft lines. For example, machinists, electricians, carpenters, teamsters, and operating engineers formed unions. Craft unions are still the predominant form of union organization in industries such as construction, which depend heavily upon skilled or semiskilled labor. These craft unions later organized themselves into the American Federation of Labor (AFL), to increase their collective power to bargain effectively with management and government at the national level. Although there was some industry-wide organization of skilled, semiskilled, and unskilled workers before the 1930s—for example, of mine workers and longshoremen—it was not until this decade that unions such as the automobile workers and the steelworkers really organized. During the 1930s, the New Deal policies of President Franklin D. Roosevelt gave the collective-bargaining process government support and recognition. It not only became legally permissible for the majority of workers at any plant site to organize themselves into a union, but federal law *required*

employers to bargain with duly constituted unions on the setting of wages, working conditions, and other matters of interest to workers. Industry-wide unions organized themselves at the national level into the Congress of Industrial Organizations (CIO), and the CIO was later merged into a superorganization now known as the AFL-CIO.

In contrast to the situation in a number of European countries, the union movement in the United States has focused primarily on improving conditions directly associated with jobs—wages, hours of work, safety at the work site, and the like—rather than on making broad social or economic changes in the capitalistic system (Perlman and Taft, 1935). Workers' direct contact with the union is usually through a shop steward or representative of the union "local," which, in turn, is typically affiliated with a national union organized along craft or industry lines (often called the "international" union because it has Canadian or possibly Latin American affiliates). Union members have the right to vote on the programs and policies of their union local, but in fact few members participate actively in local affairs, especially in recent years; many younger workers seem to feel that because most of the great battles for job rights have already been won, it is no longer necessary to lay one's body on the line for the sake of the union.

Professions

An industrializing society also becomes a professionalizing society. Like unionization, professionalization strongly affects occupational groups, but not necessarily in the same ways (Vollmer and Mills, 1966; Hughes, 1958). Here are some characteristics of professionalized occupations: (1) having work activity based upon a systematic body of theory; (2) developing group authority that client groups will recognize; (3) gaining community approval and sanction for this authority through certification or licensing; (4) developing a code of ethics to regulate professional relations; and (5) establishing a professional culture sustained by professional associations (Greenwood, 1957).

Some unionized occupational groups can be said to become more professionalized as they take on these characteristics, and some relatively more professionalized occupational groups may become unionized, such as engineers and scientists in some parts of the aerospace industry. However, the two processes are conceptually and sociologically different: unionism in American society has mostly had a job-specific economic orientation; professionalization, on the other hand, implies a deeper commitment to an occupational group over a lifelong career.

Bureaucracies

Whereas professionalization affects *occupational groups* to a greater or lesser degree, bureaucratization affects the *organizations* that employ workers in modern societies. Max Weber characterized the process of bureaucratization as including at least these three elements: (1) the classification of authority relations between job positions (what Weber called "offices") in a systematic hierarchy; (2) the prescription of rights and duties for job positions; and (3) the formal regulation of the recruitment, promotion, and separation of personnel (Weber, 1947; Gerth and Mills, 1946). Organization charts illustrate Weber's first characteristic: when an organization is too large to be managed solely by face-to-face relations, management draws up organization charts that unambiguously set out the hierarchy of authority. The use of formal job descriptions (Weber's second characteristic) is not universal in modern organizations, but the principle that "the man should be selected to fill the requirements of a particular job" is accepted in most work situations. Under certain circumstances, some organizations, however, give highly professionalized personnel considerable latitude to tailor their jobs to their own particular interests.

In a series of studies, Philip Selznick and Howard Vollmer saw how Weber's third major characteristic of bureaucratization has shown up in present-day work organizations. They noted that employees develop concepts about rights that restrict management from arbitrarily firing, disciplining, or otherwise countering expectations about the modern employment relationship. The combination of these pressures—brought to bear by unionization—and the corporate needs for coordination and control of work activities have led to institutionalized restrictions on managerial authority. Evidence from a variety of industries indicates that these restrictions apply to such matters as:

1. *The scope of managerial control:* Most managers and workers in all situations agree that management authority is limited only to matters strictly relevant to job performance.
2. *The establishment of just cause for removal:* The large majority of workers and increasing numbers of managers believe that the burden of proof should rest upon management to establish "just cause" for a worker to be removed from any job position.
3. *Due process in employee discipline:* The large majority of workers and increasing numbers of managers are recognizing that employees should not be disciplined for unsatisfactory performance or for alleged misconduct unless they have been given adequate warning, unless proof of intent is established for wrongdoing, and unless adequate procedures for hearing and grievance review are available.
4. *Consistency in rule enforcement:* Managers and employees alike are recognizing that management cannot seek to enforce any rules or regulations that are not consistently applied (Vollmer, 1960; Selznick, 1969).

It is clear that the role relationship between employers and employees is becoming institutionalized and that new expectations are being defined in new ways.

INEQUALITIES AT WORK

Not all people have equal access to all kinds of work positions in modern industrial society. Some groups of people in the general population who have always had less power in the total society also have less opportunity to enter more desirable job positions. Employers also have used job prerequisites to exclude certain individuals from jobs.

Categoric Exclusion

Categoric exclusion has been based on sex, age, race, religion, national origin, social origin, and physical appearance. Probably the most commonly used of these criteria has been sex. Until the late 1960s, most jobs were classified and advertised by sex, and women were excluded from applying for jobs in the male categories. Jobs classified as suitable for females were most often ones suitable for traditional female roles: teacher, nurse, secretary. Especially in Western societies, working for money has been considered a typically male obligation, and most females have been unpaid homemakers. In the United States this situation has changed significantly since World War II. Chapter 28 sets out these changes in detail. In other societies the change has been even more dramatic. For example, the medical and dental professions have been considered as suitable only for males (some medical schools had quotas on the number of females they would admit). Consequently, only a tiny percentage of American medical and dental practitioners are women. In Finland, however, approximately 75 percent of all dentists are women, and in the Soviet Union some 85 percent of physicians are now women.

Race, religion, and national origin are still categories that serve to limit job opportunities in the United States. In communist societies, coming from a bourgeois background or being an active churchgoer may effectively exclude one from holding a wide range of highly rewarded occupations, regardless of personal ability.

In recent years, increasing numbers of older persons have been protesting their exclusion from the labor force. When a worker reaches sixty-five years of age, he is forced into retirement in most American work situations. Some employers encourage even earlier retirement; early retirement is a built-in expectation in certain commercial, athletic, military, and entertainment occupations. Yet numerous studies have shown that many if not most workers are still physically and mentally able to continue work, at least on a reduced time basis, after age sixty-five (Hanson, 1972).

Opponents of age discrimination have advocated medical screening to make physiological age rather than chronological age a basis for retirement. Peter Drucker has pointed out that American employers might learn something from Japanese employers, who require employees to retire at age fifty-five but continue to employ them on a part-time basis so that the flexibility of the workforce is increased and the individual is assured that he is still needed at work from time to time (Drucker, 1972).

Rarely do such criteria of categoric exclusion remain rigid over long periods of time. As the bases of categoric exclusion from particular kinds of jobs change, so do the opportunities of the previously excluded groups. This change in opportunities is one of the major sources of social mobility within a society and of social change in general. (Mobility is discussed further in Chapter 13; social change, in Chapter 26.)

Disadvantaged groups who want equality of opportunity are demanding shifts in or abolition of the criteria of exclusion. Job discrimination against individuals of both sexes and of different racial, ethnic, or age backgrounds appears to be decreasing in the United States, and employers have been required by the federal government to institute "affirmative action programs" in employment practices. These programs are intended to correct previous inequities through formal training programs, reorientation of existing employees, and other positive actions. Physical and mental handicaps that were previously the bases for excluding individuals from many jobs are also being reexamined.

All these developments represent further progress toward universalistic, achievement-oriented criteria of employment, rather than ascriptive criteria. Chapter 12 further discusses achievement and ascription as bases for perpetuating inequality. In the future we may expect men and women to be hired and placed on jobs more and more in terms of what they can do, or be trained to do, rather than in terms of what groups they belong to in the outside society.

Job Prerequisites

Among the most common prerequisites for admission to various kinds of work in modern societies are certain levels of formal education, specialized training, or equivalent experience. In an increasing number of occupations, though by no means in all, the amount and type of formal education

Figure 22.6 Categoric exclusion has been part of the official hiring practices of most firms. Age and gender criteria have been prominently featured in job advertisements, whereas racial criteria have not but have been at least as important historically. Such hiring and advertising practices help maintain institutional racism, sexism, and age discrimination. Recent federal legislation has been directed toward eliminating them. Consequently, jobs that were traditionally sex-typed, for example, such as telephone operator and television-camera operator, are now being opened up to both sexes.

is considered more important than "equivalent experience."

Often educational prerequisites are *not* necessary. In times of national emergency—for example, during World War II—desperate shortages of skilled workers and professionals made it necessary to recruit many people who had insufficient educational preparation. Because increasing emphasis is being placed on formal education qualifications in the United States, the educational system (discussed at length in Chapter 19) is becoming the most important single channel of social mobility for those born at the lower-status levels of the society. Education is also the basis for mobility of the occupation itself: as occupational groups require more formal education of individuals, the occupation becomes more professionalized and is more likely to acquire a higher status in the world of work.

By insisting on highly specialized or idiosyncratic characteristics as requirements for holding certain kinds of jobs, employers can use job prerequisites to discriminate against people they want to exclude. The definition of the right kind of person for a particular job may, in effect, exclude all applicants except those who come from favored racial, ethnic, religious, or social-class backgrounds. Such criteria have been applied not only to employment opportunities but also to membership in "exclusive" schools and clubs.

WORK IN THE FUTURE

It is useful to view human societies as social systems. The various parts of these social systems are interrelated, and change in one part is likely to have consequences in others. In the twentieth century, work in societies around the world has been significantly affected by legal, technological, institutional, and economic changes that are likely to affect what people do in their work and the values they attach to it.

Legislation: Past and Future

The general desire for job security has prompted much work-related legislation and government action. People want to make institutional relationships predictable so that they can plan for the

Before the company hires her... you should make sure she's not pregnant.

Figure 22.7   During the industrial revolution, factory conditions were so horrible that the factories were called "sweat shops." People who worked in them were considered little more than toiling beasts by the factory bosses. Even children worked as many as fourteen hours per day at hazardous jobs for low pay. Such conditions prompted workers to organize in order to gain a modicum of security, a standard of safety on the job, and a shorter working day.

future. As we have seen, the industrial revolution upset the predictability of work relations that had endured for centuries. Labor became free; individuals could sign on to work wherever they pleased. However, at the same time that the oppressive bonds of obligation in systems of slavery and serfdom had been broken in Western industrial nations, the obligations of employers to the welfare of their employees were also shattered. Employers could dismiss employees at any time for lack of work, and in a free labor market it was up to the individual employee to find work elsewhere. This meant that employees often had to uproot their families and travel to other communities or areas to find new work—and this still occurs, as may be witnessed by recent migrations of workers that have been caused by layoffs in American defense-related industries.

Workers in modern society look to unionization as one answer to their insecurity and powerlessness in the face of massive labor displacement. Seeking assistance through legislation and government programs has been another. In response to the dislocations of the Great Depression, the federal government in 1935 launched a comprehensive program to assure income for the unemployed, aged, blind, and disabled and provided aid to dependent children and a retirement fund through the Social Security Act, which had been strongly supported by the AFL and other labor organizations. Since then, state legislation has been expanded to provide unemployment insurance in many areas. Nevertheless, union groups have continued to press for a guaranteed annual wage that would provide a more stable and predictable income for members of the labor force.

Federal legislation related to education and retraining, such as the Manpower Training and Development Act and more recent legislation in 1972 to support college tuition payments through federal grants, has provided additional support for greater security in employment. However, security still has not been provided to the degree desired by many groups. Workers from minority groups that have been greatly restricted in employment opportunities are likely to be hardest hit in massive layoffs. They are the "last to be hired, first to be fired," because layoffs, according to the rules in most formally organized work situations, are supposed to occur in the order of reversed seniority. Workers who are employed in demand-sensitive industries, such as those that produce luxuries that are subject to widespread variations in civilian consumption and demand, are also likely to be especially insecure in their prospects for future employment.

We can therefore expect the pressure for legislative and governmental assistance for life-time employment security to continue in American society, as it has in other Western societies. Opponents of governmental action are likely to continue to condemn ideas of a "welfare state," saying perhaps that it would be tantamount to replacing the capitalistic system with socialism. Proponents are likely to use counter-slogans such as "workfare" to describe the intent of new legislative programs to guarantee work opportunities for all, as opposed to welfare plans that provide financial support for the unemployed. The safest prediction is that the United States will be in-

Figure 22.8 One of the effects of automation is that operating personnel (*top*) are increasingly replaced by maintenance personnel (*bottom*). Maintenance work, especially on complex machines, may require long periods of special training and experience. It is not possible for operating personnel simply to shift over to maintenance as their jobs become automated. This situation has led to a condition of technological unemployment—people being replaced by machines.

volved in a continuing compromise between capitalistic and socialistic forms of social and economic structure in the future.

Automation

The replacement of human control of machines with automatically controlled machinery (aided by computers) in continuous production processes has been the most dramatic technological change affecting work situations in recent decades. Computerized operations have also replaced human skills in many office situations.

Studies by James Bright and others have shown that the affects of automation on labor requirements and the conditions of work are difficult to pin down (Bright, 1958; Mann and Hoffmann, 1960; Friedman, 1955). The most widespread generalization is that automation considerably reduces the demand for *operating* personnel in factories and offices. At the same time, the introduction of highly sophisticated machinery increases the demand for *maintenance* personnel; the consequences of one machine breaking down can be economically devastating to an employer if an entire production line has to be shut down until the machine is repaired. It is naive to assume that the total labor displacement caused by automation would be very slight because operating personnel could simply transfer into maintenance work. The answer is not so simple: the kind of maintenance work required for computers and highly sophisticated production machinery requires high-level skills based upon considerable formal training. Most production workers do not have such skills and training; they are semiskilled at best, having learned certain machine-operating skills by on-the-job training.

Automation is therefore likely to cause what is known as *technological unemployment.* Individuals must be retrained for new kinds of work at the cost of considerable time and financial expense. Who will provide the financial support for such retraining? Many have argued that it is unfair for individual workers to have to entirely pay for the retraining necessitated by technological changes outside of their control. Others have pointed out that it is often economically unfeasi-

ble for employers to bear the burden of technological retraining expenses themselves. If one
believes that the problem of technological unemployment is a problem of the total society, the
most feasible solutions appear to be cost-sharing
schemes, including individual employee participation and employer support for federal government sponsored retraining programs.

Leisure

Many sociologists have been interested in the relationship between work and leisure, as well as
that between work and retirement in modern society. Robert Dubin (1963) found in a notable
study that leisure rather than work constituted
the "central life interest" for the large majority of
factory workers. Louis Orzack found that work is
the central life interest of more professionalized
groups, which coincides with previous remarks in
this chapter on the orientation of professionals
(Orzack, 1963). Studies by Eugene A. Friedmann
and Robert J. Havighurst (1954), and more recently by Robert Atchley (1972), show that upper
white-collar and more highly professionalized employees are more reluctant to leave their work for
retirement; however, they are more likely to adjust to leisure activities when retired because they
are more likely than manual workers to have developed skills that are readily transferable to leisure activities.

Predicting the reaction of workers to shorten-
ing the normal work week to less than forty hours
and to experimenting with new kinds of retirement policies is therefore a complex matter. The
extent to which individuals favor these changes is
likely to vary depending upon the kind of work
they do and their particular work situation.

Attitudes About Careers and Education

Widespread technological unemployment and
the tendency for certain occupations to "peak
out" early, implying early retirement as the expected norm, have very significant consequences
for working careers and for educational institutions. For centuries, people thought that an individual would learn his trade or profession when
he was young and would spend the rest of his
working life practicing what he learned in his
youth, but this idea is rapidly becoming passé. As
technology changes more and more rapidly in
many fields, what an individual originally learned
about his work rapidly becomes out-of-date. It has
been estimated, for example, that the "half life"
of an engineering education is only from five to
ten years; that is to say, half of what an engineering student learns will be out of date within ten
years (the half-life time has been estimated at five
years for electronics engineers and at ten for those
in civil engineering).

The consequence of these trends is that educating oneself for a given job is being viewed
more and more as a lifelong pursuit rather than
a one-time affair. Lifelong learning is becoming
necessary for all individuals in the more technical
fields of work simply to keep up-to-date with their
fields, as well as to prepare for possible career
changes. As a result, educational institutions will
have to respond to the increasing demand for
adult education courses.

Multiple careers also are gaining attention
among sociologists interested in work behavior.
As more individuals recognize that they are likely
to have more than one kind of career during their
lives, their views on the meaning of work, as well
as on the relationship between education and
work, are likely to change in ways that are not
completely foreseeable at present.

Finally, as economic security—assured income
and assured employment for those who want it—
becomes widespread in modern society, profound
changes in the preferred type of work will probably occur, at least among a notable minority of the
population—the youth. As the need to work for
money simply to keep from starving essentially
disappears, groups of young people across the college campuses of the nation are seeking alternative careers and life styles. These youths reject the
Protestant Ethic that work is a justifiable end in
itself. They also are likely to reject the belief that
it is desirable to compete and acquire goods and
property for separate nuclear families. They believe instead that they are in the vanguard of new
forms of work and new patterns of living that emphasize the value of communal enterprise and

deemphasize monetary gain. Their answer to the increasing leisure-oriented culture of middle- and upper-class persons is to propose new forms of communal living in urban or rural environments and to engage in "alternative occupations" in areas of human service—for example, in voluntary day-care centers, clinics, and welfare work—or in areas of community support such as raising food and maintaining dwellings in a communal environment.

Most sociologists would agree that it is too early yet to determine the degree to which these new experiments in communal living and associated work occupations will be satisfactory and enduring or will replace more traditional occupations and work institutions in a larger society. It is likely that these innovations will not completely replace the socioeconomic structure of the larger society, but they may influence its character and goals in significant ways in the future. Even as the

craft guilds in ancient Egypt, the monasteries in the Middle Ages, and the merchant guilds at the beginning of the Renaissance nurtured skills and values that in later eras found fuller expression, the youth communes of today may be harbingers of new activities in the world of work in the coming postindustrial era.

SUGGESTED READINGS

Bendix, Reinhard. *Work and Authority in Industry.* New York: Wiley, 1956.

Hughes, Everett C. *Men and Their Work.* Glencoe, Illinois: Free Press, 1958.

Vollmer, Howard M., and Donald L. Mills. *Professionalism.* Englewood Cliffs, New Jersey: Prentice-Hall, 1966.

Weber, Max. *The Protestant Ethic and the Spirit of Capitalism.* Talcott Parsons (tr.). New York: Scribner, 1930.

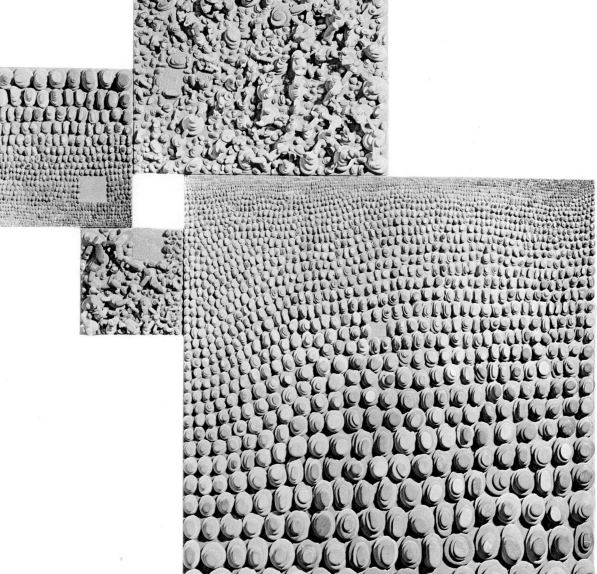

Progressions by Mary Bauermeister (1963); The Museum of Modern Art Collection.

Before introducing this unit, it seems useful to review how we got here. Unit III was concerned with the individual; it examined biological and social sources of humanness. Unit IV expanded our scope to the social environment; it examined roles, groups, and organizations. Unit V introduced a vertical dimension into this social environment. We saw that all groups are stratified internally and that societies are composed of groups holding higher and lower positions. Unit VI marked a greater expansion of scope. We saw that stratified sets of roles, groups, and organizations are clustered around certain social functions. These clusters are institutions—for example, the family, education, religion, politics, and work. A cluster of institutions makes up a society. Having worked our way from the newborn human infant to society, we now take up special aspects of societies. ¶ Societies are made up of populations. They also exist in a physical location. The characteristics of populations and physical locations impose major problems and limits for all societies. For example, populations may grow rapidly, or they may decline rapidly. They may be made up primarily of young people or of older people. Such variations have profound effects on societies. Furthermore, populations may be scattered sparsely across the countryside, or they may be compressed densely in cities. The spatial distribution of societies also profoundly influences the way they operate. ¶ Study of the characteristics of human populations is called *demography*. It comes from the Greek word *demos*, which means the people. Demography is the science of vital statistics: births, deaths, migration, and the like; Chapter 23 provides an introduction to demography. The study of human locations and the relationships between society and its physical setting is called *human ecology*. Chapter 24 concentrates on urbanization and the ecology of the city. Chapter 25 examines human ecology worldwide.

UNIT VII
DEMOGRAPHY
AND ECOLOGY

Chapter 23 The Population Problem

THE POPULATIONS OF MANY NATIONS in Asia, Latin America, and Africa are expanding very rapidly. The rates of growth in some nations are in excess of any known to human history. Some of these nations are crowded and some are not, but all must adjust to rapid growth. In this chapter we will examine Venezuela's population growth in detail. Venezuela is not heavily populated, but its numbers are rapidly increasing, and its growth is causing serious social and economic difficulties for Venezuela. We will inquire into the causes of this growth and ask how long it will continue.

For comparison, we will examine the demographic history of England. England's experience is typical of that of many Western European nations, just as Venezuela's experience is similar to that of many developing nations. England and other Western European nations were experiencing rather rapid rates of population growth a century ago, but the rate of growth in these nations has slowed since then. Our interest is in determining whether the presently developing nations will follow a path similar to England's and reduce their growth rates before the pressure of population brings disaster. Finally, we will consider the demographic future of the United States: What problems do we encounter when we make efforts to halt our population growth?

VENEZUELA'S DEMOGRAPHIC HISTORY

The demographic history of Venezuela is typical of that of many Third-World countries. Before the mid-1940s the population of Venezuela grew slowly, more slowly in fact than did the populations of the United States and many European nations. At this point growth picked up and became extremely rapid through the 1960s and 1970s. The annual rate of growth in Venezuela was estimated at 3.7 percent in 1970. At this growth rate, a population will double in nineteen years (see Figure 23.1). In this same year, the growth rate of the American population was only 0.8 percent.

The sudden, recent increase in numbers for Venezuela is displayed in Figure 23.2. The orange line traces the actual size of the population from 1890 to 1970, with a projection to 1980.

It is unlikely that this projection will miss the actual figure by very much. The graph indicates that the population of Venezuela will have increased nearly tenfold: from 1.6 million in 1890 to 15.0 million in 1980. In the first sixty years 2.9 million people were added to the population, but in the thirty-year span from 1950 to 1980, 10.5 million more will have been added—over three times as many in just half the time.

The brown line in Figure 23.2 shows the numbers by which Venezuela's population *would have* increased if the pre-1945 rates had continued to govern population growth. The gap between the two lines is more than a mathematical statement: the diverging lines show divergent ways of life—the one known in Venezuela today and another, probably richer, way that Venezuelan people might have realized.

The Problems of City Growth

The rural population grows in Venezuela, but the farms and plantations will not support the excess. Young Venezuelan men and women therefore abandon the countryside for the city, searching for a better livelihood. Many come to Caracas, headquarters for a multimillion-dollar petroleum industry that has made Venezuela the world's second largest oil producer. Migrants stream to this opulent capital city, where they find nearly the highest cost of living on earth and a poor labor market to receive them.

The Labor Market Rural migration causes the urban population of Venezuela to grow at the spectacular rate of 6.0 percent per year while the rural rate of population growth remains stationary; the growth rate across the entire nation is 3.7 percent. The urban labor market can scarcely employ the expanding supply of local labor and is simply unable to absorb the migrants. The city of Caracas is bordered by sprawling shantytowns inhabited by these displaced individuals. Most are only intermittently employed, and when they do work their wages are low and their employment is insecure (Hauser, 1961; Beyer, 1967). The average income is high in Venezuela, relative to most developing nations, but it is most unevenly dis-

Figure 23.1   Doubling time is the number of years
in which the size of a population will be doubled. The actual
number of years depends, of course, on the
annual growth rate of the population.

Figure 23.2   Venezuela's population growth charted from 1890,
with a projection to 1980. The orange line traces actual population
increase; the brown line traces population growth that would
have occurred if the pre-1945 growth rate had continued. The gap
between the lines shows the great difference between Venezuelans'
real standard of living and a better one they might have had if the
growth rate had not increased so drastically.

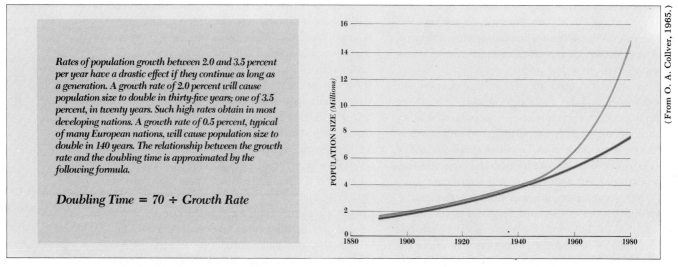

*Rates of population growth between 2.0 and 3.5 percent
per year have a drastic effect if they continue as long as
a generation. A growth rate of 2.0 percent will cause
population size to double in thirty-five years; one of 3.5
percent, in twenty years. Such high rates obtain in most
developing nations. A growth rate of 0.5 percent, typical
of many European nations, will cause population size to
double in 140 years. The relationship between the growth
rate and the doubling time is approximated by the
following formula.*

Doubling Time = 70 ÷ Growth Rate

(From O. A. Collver, 1965.)

tributed. It is estimated that 45 percent of the
entire population earns less than $150 per year.
The short end of the stick falls to the countryside
population and to the urban migrants.

Economic Growth   Rapid population growth not
only generates labor-market imbalances but also
impedes reform of these conditions. The value of
goods and services produced in Venezuela increased 4.5 percent per year in the early 1960s,
just short of the 5.0 percent rate experienced by
the United States in the same period. These goods
and services represent money that might be used
to develop industries and increase the demand for
labor. Unfortunately, however, rapid population
growth competes with economic development.

Although the economic growth rate was 4.5
percent in the aggregate, per-capita growth was
only 1.0 percent per year. The value of goods and
services per person in Venezuela increased rather
slowly because the number of individuals over
whom the gain would be divided was increasing
almost as rapidly as production. On the other
hand, the United States, which experienced a
much lower rate of population increase in this
period, realized a 3.5 percent per capita annual
rate of economic growth from its gross 5.0 percent
rate (Nortman, 1971).

Among the cruelest of ironies for developing
nations is the fact that rapid population growth

counteracts economic growth. In Venezuela,
problems attendant on population growth can
only be solved by industrial development, but
population growth is the very condition that frus-
trates development.

Expansion of the labor supply is an important
and problematic consequence of high population
growth rates. Also of significance is the fact that
high birth rates generate youthful age structures.
In 1968, 46 percent of Venezuela's population
were under age fifteen; 51 percent were of working age. Children cannot be put to productive use
in cities and towns as they could be in a traditional
rural economy. In urban situations, children are
simply an added burden for underemployed and
poorly paid adults.

Urbanization and Change

Substantial changes in the organization of society
typically attend high levels of population growth.
One particularly significant change that has accompanied population growth in modern times is
urbanization, or the transformation of rural, traditionally agricultural societies into nations of cities. In 1940, only 11 percent of Venezuela's population lived in cities; by 1950, 22 percent of the
population was urban; and today over one-half of
Venezuela's citizens are city dwellers.

Venezuela and many other nations in Latin
America and Africa are rapidly approaching

Figure 23.3 (*Top left*) Trends in birth and
death rates in Venezuela from 1890 to 1970. (*Top
right*) Urban slum conditions prevail in Venezuelan
cities; large numbers of people migrate from the countryside, hoping to find work in Caracas and other urban
centers. Large urban slums are characteristic of all
developing countries in Asia, Africa, and Latin America.
(*Bottom right*) Urban-renewal programs and housing
projects in Venezuela attempt to alleviate slum conditions.

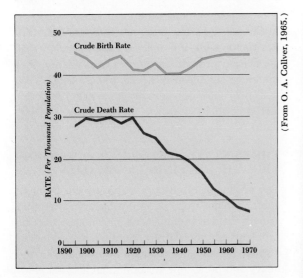

(From O. A. Collver, 1965.)

European and American levels of urban concentration. We pointed out earlier that the migration
of young adults from rural areas is a major factor
in urban expansion. The existence of such large
numbers of migrants derives from the high rates
of population increase. In the next section we will
consider some of the causes of overall population
growth in Venezuela. Three facts should be reviewed at this point:

1. Venezuela grows at 3.7 percent a year.
2. The cities grow at 6.0 percent per year.
3. The rural population remains stationary.

All of Venezuela's population growth is therefore urban growth.

These rates and proportions outline a process
of rapid change in social life. The rural sector is
characterized by strong extended family ties, pervasive religious traditions, relatively simple economic arrangements, and an impermeable social-
class system. For years, the tenant or small farmer
was concerned only with local and family affairs,
and his knowledge of events beyond the local setting was severely circumscribed. Urbanization
changes this arrangement and makes life very different: Extended family ties and permanent social
relations are replaced by looser social bonds; the
opportunities and frustrations of a complex labor
market replace simpler rural pursuits; national
policies become everyman's concern; the influ-

Figure 23.4   World-wide crude birth and death
rates, from 1970 to 1975, as projected in 1963 by the
United Nations.
(Adapted from United Nations, 1966.)

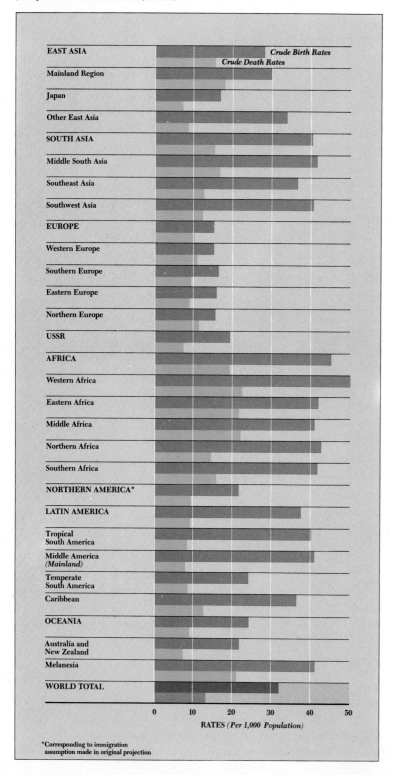

ence of religion and traditional values weakens.
In Chapter 24 we will say more about urban life.
For the present, it is sufficient to remember that
population growth accelerates urbanization and
therefore significantly affects social change. We
shall now look into several factors that have affected population growth in Venezuela.

THE CENTRAL FACTOR IN POPULATION GROWTH: DECLINING MORTALITY

The origins of rapid population growth point to
another major irony of recent history: The rapid
growth that has brought such enormous economic
problems and social dislocations is a by-product of
a great benefit to humankind—a decline in the
heavy and persistent loss of human life that characterizes preindustrial societies. The levels of
mortality that governed population in Venezuela
and other Third-World nations prior to World
War II were very high. In 1941, 181 out of every
1000 infants died before reaching their first birthdays; an additional 77 died before five years of
age. By 1961, only 56 infants died before age one,
and all but 25 of the survivors lived to their fifth
birthday.

Venezuelan mortality in 1940 was heaviest for
children, but the risk of death exceeded 1960 levels for all age categories. Out of every 1000 persons, 20 died in 1940; today less than 10 per 1000
die each year. The number of persons per 1000
who die in a year is called the *crude death rate*.
The value of the crude death rate in Venezuela
is plotted as the brown line in Figure 23.3 for the
period from 1890 to 1970. The graph indicates
that the high level of mortality was stationary until 1920, at which point it began to decline. After
1940 the rate of decline accelerated.

This decline generated the rapid population
increase that Venezuela has experienced in recent years. To appreciate why this is so, examine
the other line in Figure 23.3. The orange line
traces the *crude birth rate*, or the number of
births per 1000 persons in a year. This rate does
not change very much over the years; its value
remains between 40 and 45 throughout the entire
period.

The gap between the birth and death rates indicates the rate at which the population increases in a year. In 1920, there were roughly 42 births and 29 deaths per 1000 persons. Thirteen more persons were added through birth than were lost through death per 1000 population. *Natural increase*—the number of births exceeding deaths—was, then, 13 per 1000 or 1.3 percent. In 1940, the birth rate per 1000 was 40 and the death rate 20; natural increase, accordingly, rose to 2.0 percent. And in 1965, the birth rate per 1000 was estimated to be 44, the death rate to be 7, and natural increase to be 3.7 percent. Rates of increase have gone up in Venezuela because mortality has declined.

It is not incorrect to say that high birth rates cause the present rapid expansion of many human populations; the birth rates in the developing countries are high, and Venezuela's current value of 44 per 1000 is typical. If the birth rates were lower, the growth rate would, of course, be lower. The birth rate, however, has always been high in developing countries. The *change* responsible for rapid population growth is the recent *decline in mortality* (Arriaga, 1968; Collver, 1965).

Death rates in Latin America, Asia, and Africa were traditionally high, but have now fallen. Populations are expanding because young people who twenty years ago would have perished in infancy are now surviving to bear children themselves. We have reviewed the role of migration in Venezuela's urban growth, but that role is secondary to the role that the recent decline in death rates has played in Venezuela's rapid growth.

Why did the vital rates follow the paths they did? To find out why, we shall examine the reasons for the decline in mortality.

The Role of Environment and Disease

High mortality rates governed Venezuela's population until recent years because Venezuelans had to endure (1) an unhealthy environment, (2) inadequate medical facilities and personnel, and (3) inferior diets. Improvements in these conditions over the past few decades—most significantly in the quality of the environment—are re-

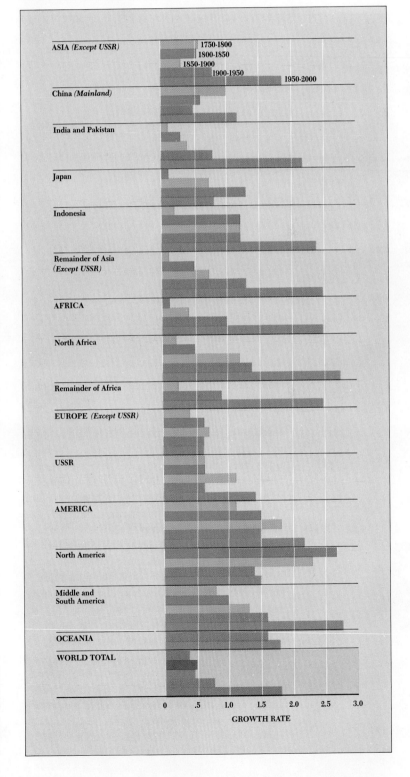

Figure 23.5   World-wide population growth rates. From 1750 to 1900 the world's population rose 0.5 percent per year, a rate that doubled the population during that century and a half. Between 1900 and 1950 the rate rose to 0.8 percent per year, and the doubling time decreased to eighty-eight years. It is estimated that the rate of increase over the second half of the twentieth century will be an average of 1.8 percent. At that rate, the world's population will double in thirty-nine years. (From J. D. Durand, 1967.)

Figure 23.6 Widespread communicable diseases account for most deaths in underdeveloped countries such as Guyana (formerly British Guiana). In contrast, the major causes of death in industrialized nations are associated with stress. (*Below*) Death rates for the five major causes of death in Guyana from 1911 to 1960. (From J. R. Mandle, 1970.)

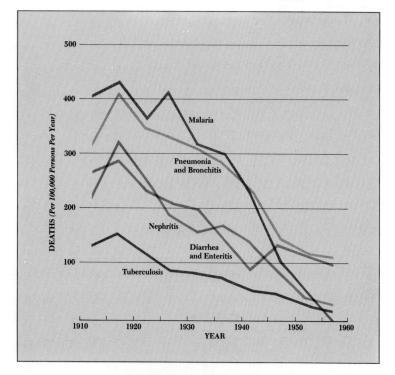

these five causes accounted for only one-fourth of the deaths. Such diseases as nephritis, pneumonia, and bronchitis, for example, are indirectly related to environmental conditions. These infectious diseases often accompany a disease that is actually one of the environmental group. In fact, the incidence of infectious diseases increases as the environmental diseases become prevalent, especially in unhealthy bodies that have little resistance to infection. A population in poor health supports infectious diseases. The decline of these diseases contributed strongly to lower death rates.

Operating on the Environment

As Figure 23.6 indicates, malaria was the most serious cause of death in British Guiana until the early 1940s. At this point it began to decline sharply, and by the late 1950s it had virtually disappeared as a cause of death. The related infectious disease nephritis also declined sharply over this period. Getting rid of malaria was a central factor in the fall in the death rates not only in British Guiana but also in numerous other countries in Asia, Africa, and Latin America (Davis, 1956). The key to the eradication of malaria is the elimination of the mosquito that carries the disease. The elimination of malaria was accomplished not by using hospitals and doctors or treating the population but by operating on the environment in which the population lived.

Two general methods were used: One was the tedious draining and filling of the swamps and stagnant waters in which the mosquito develops. These procedures were initiated in British Guiana in the 1920s and contributed to the decline of the disease from that time until the end of World War II. In the postwar period, DDT became available, and its use is responsible for the subsequent rapid disappearance of the disease. The dangers of DDT are current concerns of everyone, but it is necessary to realize that for people who must choose between high infant-mortality rates and the possible dangers of DDT, the choice will be to spray with DDT.

The high death rates from diarrhea and enteritis in British Guiana and many other nations of

sponsible for the sharp decline in the Venezuelan death rate.

Environmental conditions that made the death rate high in Venezuela included swamps and marshes that supported the malaria-bearing mosquito, impure water supplies that gave people diarrhea and stomach disorders, and unsanitary living conditions that promoted tuberculosis and other diseases. Even when these conditions are not fatal, they weaken people, reduce their resistance to infections, and generally increase their risk of death. Although historical cause-of-death statistics are not available for Venezuela, a useful series extending from 1911 is available for nearby British Guiana (now known as Guyana, having achieved independence in 1966), and these statistics provide a rough picture of what probably occurred in Venezuela (Mandle, 1970).

Figure 23.6 shows the average rates of mortality from the five major causes of death in British Guiana from 1911 to 1960. These five causes accounted for about one-half of the deaths in that country from 1911 to 1935, but in the late 1950s,

Figure 23.7   Changes in the crude death rates of
six developing nations from 1940 to 1965. The death
rates of these countries are typical of most countries in
Africa, Asia, and Latin America.

CRUDE DEATH RATES						
	TAIWAN	CEYLON	GUATEMALA	CHILE	MAURITIUS*	ALGERIA*
1940–1944	18.3	19.7	27.8	19.8	20.7	21.1
1965	7.5	7.5	15.4	10.7	8.6	10.0

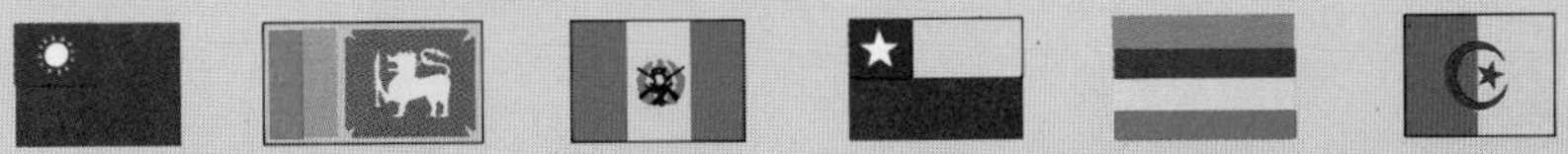

Rates are for the years 1946–1950.

Latin America, Asia, and Africa are a result of
water supplies severely polluted with human
waste. The more careful disposal of waste and the
gradual improvement of water supplies have contributed to a fifty-percent decline in the death
rates from diarrhea and enteritis. The general improvements in sanitation also had the effect of
lowering the death rates from tuberculosis and
other diseases. By 1960, mortality had fallen to
one-third the level of 1920.

The major diseases in British Guiana were essentially controlled by environmental intervention. It should be noted, however, that infant mortality was strongly reduced through educational
programs directed at mothers (Mandle, 1970).
Similarly, the targets in developing areas of the
world in the postwar period were everywhere the
water supplies and the minds of young mothers.
In most regions the mosquito, too, was a target.
As Figure 23.7 demonstrates, the effects on the
mortality rates were spectacular.

THE POPULATION EXPLOSION

The decline in the death rates brought in its wake
a population explosion. If the population explosion is to be contained and the recent gains in
mortality are to be sustained, the high levels of
fertility, or birth rates, in developing countries
must be reduced.

High Fertility

The birth rate in Venezuela is about 44 per 1000.

This level of fertility has been maintained in
Venezuela for many years, and there is no statistical indication that it is changing. Similar high levels of fertility hold throughout the developing
Third World.

Two factors account for these high fertility
rates: First, most women in developing nations
marry or have sexual intercourse throughout
nearly all the years in which they are biologically
capable of bearing children. In Venezuela, a
woman who lives to age fifty will, on the average,
have given birth to about six children; this average includes women who are sterile and women
who never married (Collver, 1965; Arriaga, 1968;
and Nortman, 1971). Western European populations never experienced the very high growth
rates that now govern the populations of the developing nations because they never showed patterns of youthful and nearly universal sexual associations. Second, there is little effective effort
made by people in developing nations to control
the fertility of these sexual unions; contraception
is not widely used, and abortion and sterilization
are appealed to only by a fraction of the population. Michael Bamberger and Margaret Earle's
investigation (1971) of 200 women of childbearing
age in Caracas found that only 19 were using contraception. It turned out that only 13.4 percent of
women exposed to the risk of childbearing were
doing anything to modify the risk. The 19 women
who were using contraception had had, on the
average, 6.6 previous pregnancies. The use of contraception, then, if it ever begins, begins after

Figure 23.8   One way for a society to approach the
population problem is to calculate its optimal
population level and, through rational family planning,
to maintain the population at that level. India, with
the most urgent population problem of any country, has
successfully introduced a number of family-planning
services, which have resulted in some decline in
the birth rate. A person from the Indian family-planning
service hangs a poster that says, "Happiness is a
two-child home."

Figure 23.9   Thomas Malthus (1766–1834), an Englishman, is regarded as the father of modern population studies. In his "Essay on the Principle of Population" (1798), he argued that humans naturally stand in danger of a population explosion. He contended that whereas human populations grow geometrically, or exponentially (2, 4, 8, 16, . . .), resources, such as food, at best increase only in an arithmetic ratio (2, 4, 6, 8, . . .). Thus, populations will outstrip the food supply, and mass starvation will result. Malthus also argued that certain factors work to keep such a population explosion from happening. He identified *preventive* checks that lowered fertility—deferred marriage and celibacy. But he gave major weight to *positive* checks—starvation, disease, war, and vice.

family size is large; it does not prevent the formation of large families.

The pattern of large-family preferences and of very limited and belated contraceptive use is the rule in Latin America, Asia, and Africa. Surveys regarding fertility attitudes and behavior have been conducted in many nations in these regions. The results of these studies indicate that the ideal of a large family is strongly entrenched in non-Western, non-European cultures and that most women have little awareness of contraception and are even skeptical that they can control their fertility (Nortman, 1971).

Attitudes About Women, the Family, and Contraception

The values and traditions of developing nations underlie the high fertility of their populations. In many areas early and universal sexual unions are viewed as natural and appropriate and are expected of all members of society. These societies offer women no means of support except through the family. A woman's alternatives are either to burden parents and siblings (who view the support of unmarried adult females as an imposition) or to marry. The latter course is almost invariably chosen, if, indeed, it can be considered a choice.

The large-family ideal derives from the long experience of high rates of infant and child mortality. To be assured that one son would survive to continue the family line, to take over the father's land or trade, and to care for parents in their old age, parents had to have two or three sons. Because only about one-half of the infants born are male, rather heavy fertility was required to achieve these objectives. Although the abrupt decline in mortality levels in the developing regions has made it possible to achieve these objectives with smaller families, the time-honored ideal of a large family persists.

The traditional agricultural economies of developing nations are also frequently supportive of the large-family ideal. Because children are able to perform useful, productive agricultural work, they contribute to the household income from an early age. However, as the children grow into adulthood, problems arise. If more than one son should survive, the family plot must be divided, or some of the sons must seek employment elsewhere. With levels of mortality low, as they are today, surplus population results from high fertility levels in developing nations.

The consequences of high fertility are evidently not yet understood by many people in the developing countries. Couples persist in bearing many children despite the fact that this behavior no longer involves social or economic gain. In fact, high fertility is even exhibited by couples who report a preference for small families. Several factors account for this persistence of high fertility. First, contraceptives are not readily available in some areas of Latin America, Asia, and Africa. Second, even when contraceptives are available, it is frequently the case that many people are unaware of their availability. Finally, even when contraception is available and its availability is known, there is all too often a pervasive pessimism regarding its effectiveness. People view the claims of contraception, like those of magic, with suspicion. Traditional societies never had effective means of controlling natural events of any sort, and the belief that such control is beyond human capacity is rather strong (Stycos, 1968).

ENGLAND AND THE MALTHUSIAN THEORY OF POPULATION

No certain prediction can be made of the future path of Venezuela's population except that present levels of growth will not continue indefinitely. If existing rates of increase were to persist for two centuries, Venezuela would contain more persons than presently inhabit the earth! The question, then, is not whether present growth will continue but how growth will be stopped or slowed.

There are two theories of population that lead to different predictions. One, *Malthusian theory,* developed by British political economist Thomas Robert Malthus (1766–1834), predicts that the growth rates will fall as a result of rising mortality. The other, *demographic transition theory,* outlined by Kingsley Davis in 1945, predicts that growth rates will fall as a result of a decline in

Figure 23.10   According to Malthusian theory, population increases geometrically (2, 4, 8, 16, . . .), but food resources increase arithmetically (2, 4, 6, 8, . . .).

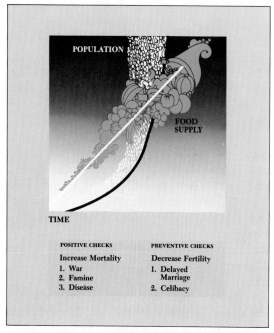

POPULATION

FOOD SUPPLY

TIME

POSITIVE CHECKS	PREVENTIVE CHECKS
Increase Mortality	Decrease Fertility
1. War	1. Delayed Marriage
2. Famine	2. Celibacy
3. Disease	

fertility. Both theories involve fairly encompassing explanations of population change. But despite their wide sweep, both theories are strongly conditioned by the historical experience of the Western European populations. We shall see that Malthusian theory fits much of the experience of preindustrial Europe and that transition theory fits the demographic history of industrializing Europe. In a later section, we will ask whether either of these formulations applies to the developing nations.

One basic principle of Malthusian theory is that as per capita income rises, population will increase, and when per capita income falls to low levels, population growth will go into decline (Malthus, 1960). Mortality is the factor mediating the relationship between per capita income—or the well-being of a society's members—and population size. For example, rising incomes or stable but comfortable incomes assure a sufficient supply of food and other necessities. When the population is healthy, the level of mortality will, accordingly, be low. Low or falling incomes, on the other hand, imply declining levels of nutrition and inadequate clothing and shelter. As a result of these conditions, the health of the population de-

clines, and mortality rises. Fertility generally remains constant throughout (however, in a later section we will see that fertility is a factor to be reckoned with even in preindustrial England).

Population growth, according to Malthus, is governed entirely by mortality, which is, in turn, governed by changes in income. Per capita income, however, is itself affected by population growth. In particular, as population size increases, the goods society produces must be divided among a larger number of persons; each person then has less, and the per capita amount falls (as happened in Venezuela). High or rising incomes—because they lower mortality and increase population numbers—actually lead to future falling incomes. One might argue that production may also increase as population grows and that therefore goods per capita need not decline with an increase in numbers. This point leads to a second principle of Malthusian theory: Increases in production or income will not, over a long period of time, keep pace with increases in population; ultimately, per capita income will fall.

Preindustrial England
Certain features of the demographic history of medieval and early modern European history conform to the Malthusian model. The experience of famine and disease in preindustrial England provides us with a good example of how mortality governs population growth in preindustrial societies. We shall now see how rising standards of living in the countryside lowered mortality and increased population in England.

The Farming Population: Famine
England, around 1100, was rather thinly settled, with a population estimated at 2,500,000. Much of the territory was marsh and forest, and only a fraction of the arable land was under cultivation. Despite primitive agricultural methods, yields from this fertile land were good, and crop failures were few. If poor care and prolonged use lowered the fertility of the soil, new land could always be cleared and planted. The available evidence indicates that food production was adequate at this time (Pollard and Crossley, 1969).

Figure 23.11   In the mid-fourteenth century, Londoners fled to the countryside to escape the bubonic plague. Dogs were believed to carry the plague, and thousands of them were killed on sight, but no one paid attention to the rats, which were really responsible for the epidemic. Unsanitary conditions and dense concentration of people in cities predispose to such epidemics.

Population increased in England after 1100. The main reason for this increase was low mortality supported by favorable standards of living. The growth in population numbers increased the demand for food. An expanding labor force moved in to cultivate new territories. Land was cleared of forest; swamps and marshes were drained; and agricultural production grew. But by the middle of the twelfth century, good land had become scarce. Increased population made necessary the use of marginal land, and good land became so overworked that its fertility began to fall. Production per capita declined accordingly.

The tenant farmers, who comprised most of England's population, were squeezed by lower crop yields and increasing high rents, which they typically paid directly to landlords in agricultural products. Less food was left for the farmers to consume. Standards of living and the health of much of the population fell (Pollard and Crossley, 1969). The situation became disastrous in the years 1315 and 1316. Heavy rains in those years damaged the crops and resulted in exceptionally poor harvests. The marginal land, much of it poorly drained, was particularly unproductive. Famine resulted, and death rates rose. Local and periodic crop failures bred famine and checked any increase in population size.

Concentration of Population: Disease

Despite the deterioration of agriculture, life in Britain had in some ways improved. Towns of modest size had developed over the previous few centuries. These towns supplied services to the countryside. Tradesmen such as blacksmiths and shoemakers provided tools and other goods for the farming community. The administration of law was carried out formally by appointed officials. Agricultural products could be sold or exchanged in the marketplace. In sum, the organization of social and economic life had become at once more efficient and complex. Such developments are necessary before industrial and economic growth can begin, but the concentration of population may lead to disaster—as it did in fourteenth-century English towns. Population concentration in these towns unfortunately prepared the conditions for the 1348 epidemic of the bubonic plague.

The bubonic plague is spread by a flea *(P. pestus)* that lives on a particular type of rat *(R. rattus)*. When the disease is epidemic in the rats, it will become a serious threat to any nearby creatures. The typical form of the disease is spread from rat to man by way of the flea.

Two conditions must be present if the disease is to become epidemic among men: The population of *R. rattus* must be dense, and the human population must live close to the rats. Towns of at least modest size are also a requirement not only because the rat requires human shelter to survive in European climates but also because a dense population of infected rats can only occur when many rat-infested buildings or houses are close to one another. Ill-lit dwellings with thatched roofs and eaves provided an ideal habitat for *R. rattus,* and the careless storage of grain assured it an adequate diet. People were ignorant of the health hazard and made no serious attempt to exterminate or control the rodent. That the epidemic of bubonic plague wreaked such havoc on the human population of the English towns in the years 1348 through 1350 implies that rat infestation was extreme indeed.

When the disease was introduced to England in 1348, it spread rapidly and widely, destroying perhaps one-fourth of the population (Deaux, 1969; Shrewsbury, 1970). The plague spread to England from Europe, probably carried by rat-infested ships, and reduced the population drastically in the short space of two years. England never again faced a visitation so fierce, but lesser epidemics occurred during the next centuries.

Only in the last century were England and other European nations able to assure better health for their urban populations. Until very recently, frequent outbreaks of typhus, smallpox, and cholera and a steady high rate of intestinal infections resulted in substantially higher death rates in urban areas than in the countryside. Premodern conditions assured that crowding would increase mortality.

Changes in Population in Premodern England

England's population numbered about 4,000,000 in 1315, but over two centuries passed before it exceeded this value. During these two centuries the *Malthusian checks* of famine and disease periodically cut back any strong short-term growth. Around 1540, the population of England again began to increase, growing to 6,000,000 by 1640. It may be that improved housing, more effective agricultural methods, and a run of good harvests reduced the level of mortality and permitted the surge of growth. Also, it is possible that the periodic epidemics were less frequent and less severe in this century. Such explanations are consistent with Malthusian theory, which holds that the key to population growth is a relaxation of mortality,

which is, itself, at least partly a result of improved living conditions.

On the other hand, there is some evidence that fertility was high during this period because there were changes in marriage patterns. Records for Colyton, a town near London, indicate that women were marrying young during this century of growth and were bearing large numbers of children (Wrigley, 1969). Fertility also may have played a role in the population growth that occurred after 1100. It is likely that the marriage age at that time was also low. Because land was cheap, young people could marry and rear children without waiting for inheritance.

Population growth ceased around 1640, and numbers remained stationary for the next century. Just as Malthusian theory predicts, agricultural production did not keep pace with population increase. Grain prices rose dramatically, indicating food was scarce, and the level of living declined for much of the population. The bubonic plague and other epidemics visited the crowded cities and towns. Rising population numbers strained resources; the available goods per person declined; and the level of mortality rose. However, there is also evidence that fertility was lower from 1650 to 1750 than it had been in the last century. Women in Colyton, for example, married later and bore fewer children in this period than they had in the previous era (Wrigley, 1969).

The Relative Importance of Mortality and Fertility

It is reasonable to conclude from this demographic view of the history of England that a somewhat modified Malthusian model applies to preindustrial populations. Increases in income—which follow the opening of new land, improved agricultural methods, and commercial development—have the effect of lowering mortality and thereby increasing population. Improvements in housing and sanitation have the same result. The growth, however, soon outstrips the gains in income, and crowding wipes out the gains in health that housing and sanitation improvements have brought about. The level of mortality rises again,

Figure 23.12.   According to the theory of demographic transition, there are three population patterns that correspond to the three stages in a society's transition to mature industrialization. In the *preindustrial pattern*, a high death rate is offset by an equally high birth rate, and population is relatively stable. In the *industrializing pattern*, mortality and fertility rates decline, but the mortality rate declines first and to a greater degree than the fertility rate. The result is rapid population growth. In the *postindustrial pattern*, a low death rate is balanced by a low birth rate, and the population is in a state of equilibrium.

checking and sometimes rolling back the gain in population numbers.

However, it is also true that changes in fertility are responses to changes in income. Apparently, fewer persons marry and marriage occurs later in life when incomes and living conditions are unfavorable (Wrigley, 1969). As a consequence, fewer children are born. Evidently, the high cost of living and the scarcity of land make it difficult for young men to marry and to take on the responsibility of supporting a family. Low birth rates reduce some of the excess population and therefore modify the impact of mortality.

Changes in fertility show that people make social responses to overpopulation. These responses indicate that human populations, even in preindustrial contexts, are not entirely governed by mortality and the ruthless biology of famine and disease. However, it is clear that mortality plays an important role in determining population size and change in preindustrial societies.

DEMOGRAPHIC TRANSITION THEORY

As we shall see when we review the history of modern England, the economic growth that attended industrial development was sufficiently rapid to assure stable or rising incomes despite declining mortality and increasing population numbers. *Demographic transition theory* exempts the case of industrial growth from the Malthusian cycle of rising income⟶falling mortality⟶rising population⟶falling income⟶and rising mortality. The theory specifies declining fertility as a consequence of industrialization.

The fact that industrialism concentrates population in urban areas has much to do with declining fertility. Children increase household expenses but do not contribute to the support of the family, as they do in agricultural contexts. Although children cost more in industrial societies than they do in agrarian societies, the numbers of children increase because industrial growth has caused a decline in mortality; that is, fewer children are lost in infancy and early childhood. Industrialization increases family size at a time

Figure 23.13   During the industrial revolution in England, newly appointed civil-service administrators concerned with public health had to contend with unsanitary conditions and practices. The woman at the window is emptying a chamberpot into a public street.

when reduction of family size is preferred. Fertility is the factor that comes into play: Ultimately, the pressure is relieved by the parents, who control their fertility, as did middle-class couples in nineteenth-century England, in order to avert the burden of large families (Banks and Banks, 1964).

Modern England

In 1750 the population of England again began to increase. Growth continued to 1930 at a pace more rapid than England had known in any earlier period. When growth ceased, the population

of England had increased to 40,000,000. The major factor behind this protracted growth was a decline in mortality. However, the ultimate cessation of growth in the 1930s was entirely due to a decline in fertility. Mortality had nothing to do with the discontinuation of this surge of growth. In fact, death rates were declining when growth ceased. It is significant that the decline in fertility did not occur in response to falling incomes, as in the preindustrial era. The fall in birth rates occurred in the years 1870 to 1930—a time when incomes and living conditions were improving. Thus the predictions of Malthusian theory are flatly contradicted by the history of modern England (Wrigley, 1969).

England in the eighteenth century underwent a major social and economic transformation. The production of clothing, tools, and other commodities was transferred from crude home and village manufacture to urban mass production assisted by machinery. A series of technological breakthroughs sharply increased the efficiency of manufacturing and led to a dramatic rise in English industrial output. The increased availability of, and income from, the factory-produced goods in England improved the lot of the British people. Some of the wealth was invested in new machinery and in experimentation with new technological possibilities.

Science and engineering were spurred, and the result was still greater increases in industrial production. Some of the improvements spilled over into the areas of medicine and sanitation, lowering mortality at some points and preventing its rise at other points. Finally, there was a major revolution in agriculture that led to large increases in the amount and quality of food produced. The income realized from industry also made possible the purchase of food abroad.

The rise in per capita income did generate an increase in population, but population growth, in contrast to earlier periods, did not dilute the gains in income or lower standards of living. The Malthusian principle that population ultimately outstrips resources did not apply during the period of industrial growth.

Industrialism

As we have seen, the broad outline of modern English demographic history follows the path implied by transition theory. Industrial development expanded in the years 1750 to 1930, and death rates declined from 25 to 30 per 1000 at the beginning of the period to 12 to 14 per 1000 at its close. Population and living standards increased. Around 1870 the birth rate went into decline, falling from 35 per 1000 to 14 per 1000 in the space of two generations. In the 1930s, the population stopped increasing (Finn, 1970).

The decline in mortality was effected by advances in technology and medical knowledge and by the organized application of this knowledge. The decline was assisted by improvements in the production and distribution of food, which provided more and more people with diets to keep them healthy. It is to be noted, however, that technical innovations account only for part of the improvement. Only the organization of medicine, science, and public health made it possible to apply knowledge effectively across the population.

Both the technological and organizational developments are closely related to the process of industrialization. The rise of large-scale industry concentrated populations in cities, which required fairly detailed political and civil-service administrations (Deane and Cole, 1969). These administrations ultimately took responsibility for public health. They made use of experts, studied health problems, and generated considerable useful information. The government took responsibility for sanitation, the water supply, the disposal of waste, and the enforcement of quarantines. Such extensive and rational organization could never have developed in the semifeudal society of premodern England.

The rise of industry bred a respect for scientific learning and experimentation. Invention had contributed in obvious ways to the improvements in the production of manufactures, and persons engaged in science and experimental study were accorded increasing social respect. Professionals in the fields of science and medicine exchanged information, examined previous ideas about disease

and human health, tested preventive and therapeutic methods, and replaced folk remedies with effective procedures. Experimentation was also applied to agriculture. Scientists found more effective fertilizers that produced better grain, and they established sorting and breeding methods to develop better animals.

Industrialism is directly responsible for the improvements in transportation. The industrial and commercial centers needed raw materials and food from the countryside and therefore had to have access to the hinterland to carry on production. Just as important, finished goods had to be delivered to consumers. Out of these demands arose an elaborate and fairly rapid system of roads, canals, and, finally, railways. A substantial merchant fleet for international trade was also built.

In summary, the major factors that improved health—medical technology, organized public health, scientific agriculture, and an elaborate transportation system—all resulted from the process of industrialism, which is discussed in greater detail in Chapter 12. These developments could not have occurred in a medieval agrarian society.

Decline in Birth and Death Rates

The decline in mortality began early in the industrial revolution and proceeded relatively slowly over the period. The progress was uneven, with the death rates leveling in the middle of the era before continuing to fall (Mitchell and Deane, 1971). However, by the close of the period the level of mortality was far below the levels experienced in the mid-eighteenth century or, for that matter, in any other period of English history. The birth rate did not begin to decline until after 1870, and it fell over a sixty-year span, without interruption, to modern low levels. Fertility in the 1930s had, like mortality, reached an unprecedented low level. The growth induced by falling mortality after 1760 was halted by declining fertility in the 1930s. The reasons for the decline in the death rates have already been indicated. The causes of this decline in fertility must now be explored.

The fall in birth rates in England and elsewhere in Europe in the nineteenth century did not occur as a consequence of shifts in the marriage age or in the number of people marrying. The immediate cause of the decline was the effective intervention by married couples in the process of fertility. Contraception and, to a lesser extent, abortion were employed to control family size. This fact is interesting, for it marks the first time that these methods figured in the fertility of the English population.

To say that birth control caused the decline in fertility is to give a less-than-adequate account of the sharp fall in birth rates. We must ask instead why so many couples resorted to birth control in the late nineteenth century. This fundamental question has to do with social behavior, and it is not easily answered.

Prior to 1870 people shunned birth control even though knowledge of procedures had existed for centuries. The use of birth control was almost universally condemned as immoral. Prostitutes practiced contraception, but respectable married couples did not. The sale and advertisement of contraceptives was illegal in most nations, and there was little support for the repeal of such legislation. Churches, as one might expect, condemned the practice of birth control, but the clergy took a minor interest in the matter because the "evil" was not widespread.

The Middle Class

In the 1870s and 1880s the practice of contraception was adopted by the urban middle classes. This group, which valued so highly their manners and ethical postures, which was so enthusiastically committed to rigid Victorian morality, was the first class in English society to take up the practice of contraception (Banks and Banks, 1964).

It is not surprising, however, that the diffusion of contraceptive practices began with the middle classes. They were especially well-informed and literate and were therefore more likely to be aware of the advantages of contraception. In addition, the middle classes were strongly oriented to economic rationality; they wanted to lead planned, not accidental, lives. The middle classes

were the innovative group in late nineteenth-century English society. They were, for example, responsible for the industrial and administrative adaptions that revolutionized not only the economy but all of British life.

The adaptive and innovative character of the Victorian middle classes may explain why they, rather than some other segments of the population, initiated the practice of family planning, but it does not entirely explain why the practice was taken up in the late nineteenth century rather than some earlier time. The question is a very important one because it bears on the future course of fertility in the developing nations.

EUROPE AND THE DEVELOPING NATIONS

If we could isolate the conditions that caused the European populations to adopt family planning, we would have a basis for determining whether similar developments are imminent in the high-fertility areas of Latin America, Asia, and Africa. Unfortunately, it is not yet possible to give a reliable and detailed explanation for the spread of family planning in Europe in the late nineteenth century.

Certain events, however, did take place in nineteenth-century Europe that created a climate for birth control. Increases in household size, housing problems, and the cost of rearing children generated pressures for lower fertility. At the same time, religious values were weakening, and traditional moral pressures against the use of birth control therefore lost some of their force.

Falling death rates in the nineteenth century increased the chances that an infant would survive to maturity. Families therefore grew larger although fertility remained fairly steady. Women bearing the same number of children as their parents had borne found themselves with larger families. Having more children obviously means having to spend more for food, clothing, and other necessities. These pressures occurred at a time when the populations of Britain and other Western European nations were concentrating in cities and towns. Housing in the cities was scarce, and large families meant crowded quarters. Thus, declining mortality and urbanization conspired to increase the expense and discomfort of high fertility, and people responded by having fewer children in their families.

The costs of childbearing increased as the strength of traditional norms and values waned. Because the Church no longer held a central position in social life, its ancient strictures against birth control were no longer morally binding. Pressures favoring the adoption of family planning practices were thus stronger than pressures against it in the late nineteenth century.

We have seen that contraception was first used by the urban middle classes. After the 1880s the practice spread rapidly. In less than two generations the working classes and people in rural areas of Europe and Britain had adopted it. By 1930, resistance to the practice was limited to the least educated segment of the population and to some Catholics. Virtually the entire population became interested in family planning.

Demographic transition theory says that declining fertility will result from long-term economic improvements combined with declining mortality. It is clear that the decline in fertility in modern Europe *did follow* a period of economic growth and gains over mortality, but it is not entirely certain that either declining mortality or economic growth *caused* the decline in fertility.

Certain other European nations, notably France, had rather different experiences. Fertility in France began declining in 1800, well before the advent of large-scale industrial growth in that country. Mortality and fertility fell at the same time in France; so lower death rates did not precede the fall in birth rates. In other words, the logic of demographic transition theory cannot be proven to hold for all Western European countries. Its predicted sequence of events occurred in most Western European nations but not in all.

Transition theory, then, is not always consistent with modern European history, but Malthusian theory is almost always inconsistent with the history of modern England and modern Western Europe. Increasing birth rates in modern England did not lead to increasing death rates. The birth rate did not remain high and invariant but fell.

Improved levels of living brought a lower, not a higher, rate of population growth.

Even so, Europe itself is not free from modern examples of Malthusianism. Ireland is a case in point. From 1750 to 1845, improved agricultural methods and products as well as changes in the laws and customs governing the use of land made it possible for a larger proportion of the Irish to farm a plot of land capable of supporting a family. More married and married younger, and the population expanded. The added population was accommodated by subdividing the land holdings; the smaller farms could support a family because of the increased use of potatoes as a crop. However, Ireland was not growing industrially. In 1845, the potato crop failed. The island could not feed its expanded population, and about one-sixth of the population died and another one-sixth fled to other countries. Ireland, like preindustrial Europe, could not adapt to short-term reverses.

The inconsistencies we have noted do not prove that the developing nations, like most European ones, will lower their birth rates and escape Malthusian predictions. One has to be cautious when considering whether a theory based on a particular set of historical conditions may apply to nations whose historical conditions differ. It is obvious that Latin America, Asia, and Africa are not in all ways similar to modern industrial Europe, and it is not reasonable to predict they will have the same destiny. For instance, the developing nations have higher birth rates and higher rates of population growth than Europe ever had. The pressures of growth in these nations are therefore more severe, and the required adjustments in fertility are far greater than were those in industrializing Europe. Although these Third-World nations are called developing nations, not all of them are advancing economically. And, of those that are developing, many are not achieving economic gains sufficient to improve the lot of their expanding numbers of people.

THE DEMOGRAPHIC FUTURE OF THE UNITED STATES

Many Americans have become worried about the rapid growth of our population. There are 204

Figure 23.14   The birth rate in the United States has
steadily declined since 1900, except for the period
from 1940 to 1955, when there was a sharp reversal in
the trend. The period of rapid increase was called
the postwar "baby boom."
(Adapted from R. A. Easterlin, 1968.)

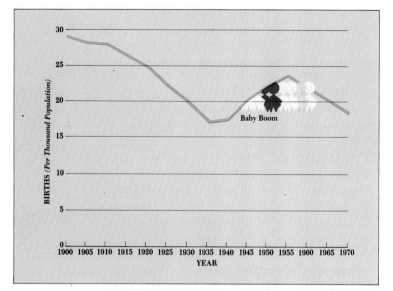

million of us now, and at the present rate of
growth there will be 300 million of us in about
thirty-five years. Our cities, parks, freeways, and
beaches are already overcrowded. We face shortages of natural resources. Many social scientists
are now concerned. To conclude this chapter we
examine some critical questions about the demographic future of the United States. Prediction
must rest on solid understanding of the past, so
this section is particularly aimed at dispelling
some common misconceptions about what has
caused our birth rate to rise and fall. It also examines the difficulties in halting population growth
and suggests some unpleasant consequences of
stopping growth abruptly.

Recent Fertility Patterns

Fertility in the United States declined sharply in
the early part of this century. The crude birth rate
was 27 per 1000 persons in 1900. By 1933 it had
dropped to 18. The annual rate of population increase was less than 1 percent during the 1930s.
At that time it was believed that fertility would
continue to fall (Peterson, 1969).

But that is not what happened. Just before
World War II the birth rate began to rise again.
The rise was interrupted by the war, but after the
war the rate streaked up again, and the period
from the late 1940s through about 1960 is now

described as the *baby boom.* Then, almost equally
suddenly, the birth rate began to drop again. By
1970 the birth rate had fallen to 17 per 1000.

According to demographic transition theory,
fertility should be low once industrialization has
occurred. The United States and Western Europe
have been highly industrialized since the turn of
the century. During this period they have had low
fertility only some of the time—and nearly all
these nations have had a baby boom. Why? And
will such booms occur again?

The Baby Boom

These questions are urgent because population
growth in the United States depends almost entirely on the birth rate—the death rate is virtually
stationary at 9 deaths per 1000 persons each year.
If the 1970 birth rate were to continue, our population would double in eighty-eight years. But if
the baby-boom pattern is cyclical and thus happens again—fifteen years of high fertility followed
by fifteen years of low fertility—the population for
the United States would double on the average
every forty-seven years.

It is popular to explain the low fertility of the
1930s on economic grounds. This was the time of
the Great Depression, and it seems plausible that
fertility was low because people could not afford
to have children. Similarly, the high birth rate
after World War II is often explained by saying
that prosperity made large families possible again.
But the facts do not fit this interpretation. The
birth rate did hit a historic low during the Depression, but it already had been falling sharply
throughout the prosperous decade of the 1920s.
Although fertility was high in the prosperous
1950s, it declined rapidly in the no-less-prosper-
ous early 1960s. Fertility today is at Depression
levels, but our current economic problems are
hardly comparable to the conditions of the 1930s.
In fact, there have been many economic crises
during the past two centuries, but the response of
the birth rate to them has generally been slight.
Economics does not explain the baby boom.

Two other popular notions about American
population growth are equally at variance with
the facts. Many believe that the decline in the

birth rate since the early 1960s has been a consequence of improved contraception—the pill and the intrauterine device (IUD). But fertility had already declined substantially before these items came into widespread use. Furthermore, fertility was as low in the 1930s as it is now, and neither device was available then. It is also thought that the recent decline in the birth rate has been a response to public concern over population growth. But it was not until the late 1960s that much publicity was given to the environmental dangers of population growth; by then fertility was already low.

The fact is that we do not really know why the baby boom occurred, and we do not know if one will occur again. But we do know that at the current birth rate the population will reach 300 million by the year 2008, and if the birth rate does suddenly soar again, we will reach that number much sooner. In fact, many people believe that even our present rate of population growth is unacceptable. There is growing support for the idea of *zero population growth*—stabilization of our population at some acceptable size.

Zero Population Growth

Several ways of stabilizing population size seem possible. We will look at two of them and at some possible consequences of their use, consequences that may surprise you.

Two Parents, Two Children   One method of attaining a zero growth rate is to reduce the average size of American families to two children. With just two children for each set of parents, growth should eventually cease. In fact, population size should, in time, begin to decline because some prospective parents will not survive to have children. Although the method seems reasonable, it would not work immediately. Even if couples were suddenly to decide, be persuaded, or be constrained to reduce their fertility to two children per family, growth would continue for many years. Figure 23.15 shows that, given an average of two children per couple and no migration, the population would grow to 250 million by the year 2000 and to 275 million in 2020, at which time

Figure 23.15   Because people born during the postwar baby boom are now reaching child-bearing age, the population in the United States is likely to continue growing through 2020, even if most couples decide to have only two children.
(From D. J. Bogue, 1969.)

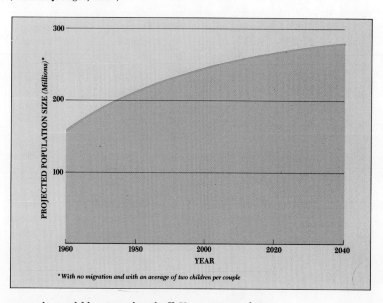

growth would begin to level off. You can see, then, that zero population growth through families with two children would not become effective for about fifty years.

The reason for the continuing growth is that the population presently contains many young people but relatively few older persons. The babies born during the baby boom discussed earlier are now coming into childbearing age, and even if their childbearing is restrained, considerable numbers will be added to the population. To state the matter coldly, there are simply not enough older Americans to produce a number of deaths sufficient to balance the births—nor will there be enough until the baby-boom children reach retirement age. That will occur around the years 2010 to 2025.

If the birth rate remains at two children per couple, ultimately the American population will stop growing. But not until the secondary effects of the baby boom have added to it tens of millions of new members.

Adjustment of the Birth Rate   There is another method of halting the growth of population, which, if it could be enforced, would certainly be effective. If the birth rate were adjusted each year to equal the death rate, natural increase would, by definition, be zero. If there were no migration,

Figure 23.16   The age structure of a population in a given society may have profound effects on its social and economic conditions. (For example, the effects on the United States labor market of the baby-boom children when they reached working age were considerable.) The graphs below show the age structure for American females in selected years, given that population growth was zero from 1965 on. (From T. Frejka, 1968.)

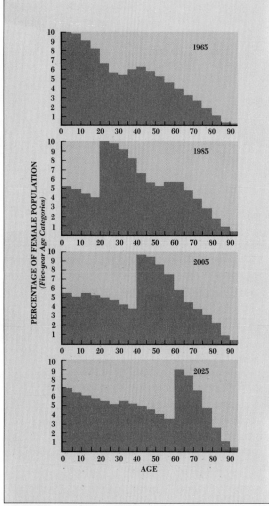

growth was zero for many years, another drastic adjustment would be required when the baby-boom crop started to be heavily cut by mortality, around 2030 to 2045—if one did not want a sharp decline in population. To replace them, it would be necessary to raise the birth rate substantially. The maintenance of constant numbers would require just under 3.0 children per couple in this period. It is difficult to imagine the tactics by which such sharp reversals in childbearing behavior could be induced.

Changes in America's Age Structure   Even if a policy ensuring zero population growth were operational, the consequences of its implementation raise doubts about its acceptability. Tomas Frejka (1968) computed the age structure of the American population that would result if zero population growth were suddenly to happen. Figure 23.16 shows the age structure for several future years, given that growth stopped in 1965. In 1985, there would be a remarkably small number of children and adolescents in the population because of the steep drop in the birth rate twenty years earlier. There would be only half as many from birth to age nineteen as there had been in 1965. Educators would be put out of work. Industries that make products for young adults and children would face a crisis.

Also, the number of persons of working age would increase sharply in the years 1965 to 1985 as baby-boom children entered adulthood. This sharp increase in the number of persons available for work would be likely to create employment problems no matter what course fertility followed in later years.

After a few decades, these particular problems would disappear but would be replaced by other dislocations. Between the years 2005 and 2030, those born during the baby boom would be passing through the postretirement ages. The task of supporting and caring for them would fall to the relatively small group of prime-age adults born after 1965. Resources would have to be poured into the training of medical and social-service personnel and into the construction of facilities to meet the needs of an aging population. The man-

overall population growth would also be zero, and population numbers would remain constant. This method introduces very serious problems, however. In order to achieve zero population growth today, the birth rate would have to fall to 9 per 1000 per year, and for another twenty years couples would have to content themselves with an average 1.2 children per family! The baby-boom children, who were raised in families averaging 3.0 to 3.5 children, would be required to make considerable sacrifices to assure that the fertility of their parents was not reflected in the number of children in the third generation.

Given that this adjustment in the birth rate could somehow be effected and that population

power requirements and the expense would seriously burden the small labor force. And not long after the personnel had been trained and facilities built up, these services would be unneeded because the baby-boom crop of people would finally have died.

A Dilemma

The curtailment of population growth in the United States raises a dilemma. If growth were made to cease by adjusting birth rate to death rate, the cost would be serious social and economic dislocations, and these would persist for two generations. A less drastic approach—maintaining average family size at two children—would not generate such dislocations and would ultimately bring growth to zero but would entail a substantial increase in population numbers before growth ended.

No solution to our population problems is going to be easily accomplished. But the worst possible course would be to find no solution at all.

SUGGESTED READINGS

Davis, Kingsley. "The Amazing Decline of Mortality in Underdeveloped Areas," *American Economic Review*, 46 (May, 1956), 305–318.

Malthus, Thomas, Julian Huxley and Frederick Osborn. *Three Essays on Population*. New York: (Mentor) New American Library, 1960.

Peterson, William. *Population*. 2nd ed. New York: Macmillan, 1969.

Wrigley, E. A. *Population and History*. New York: McGraw-Hill, 1969.

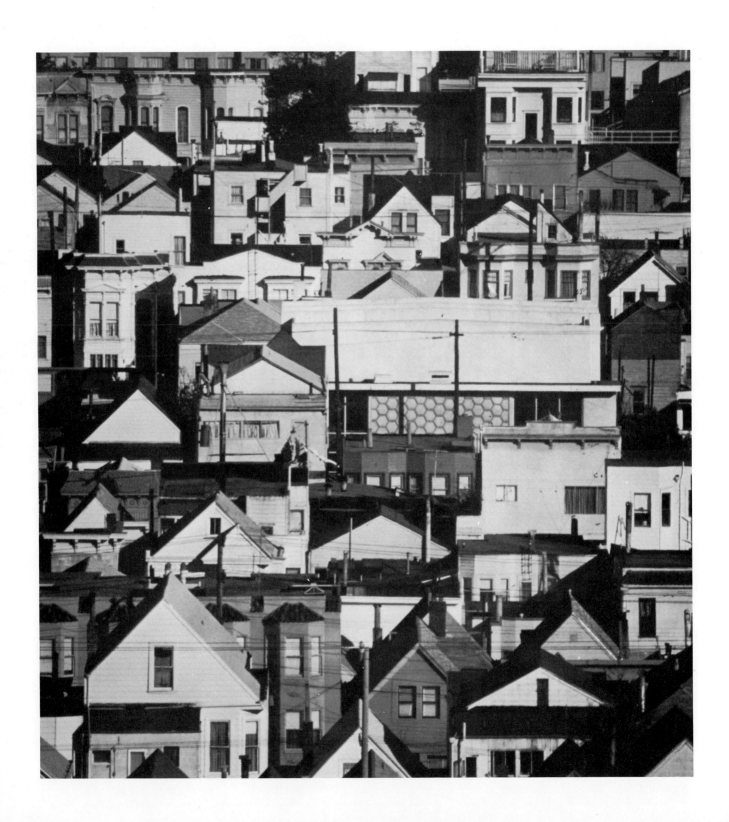

Chapter 24 The Urban Community

CITIES AND CIVILIZATION ARE INSEPARABLE. All that is meant by the word "civilized" began to develop only with the rise of cities 6,000 years ago in the river valleys of ancient Mesopotamia. Art, literature, philosophy, music, architecture, science, fashion, and higher education flourished in cities where the concentration of population and the variety of interactions were great enough to support such specialized areas of human culture. And the lure of cities has been all but irresistible to most men from that time to this.

Not even the undeniable drawbacks of city life have been able to separate civilization and cities. Urban dwellers have always regretted the overcrowding and traffic congestion—in ancient Rome it was carts, not cars. They have always had to endure filth and pollution. At the height of their glory, the ancient Athenians and Romans persisted in dumping their garbage in the streets outside their doors. And the frenzy and unpredictability of life were as typical of Constantinople as they are of Manhattan. But the opportunities to develop and the stimulation afforded by civilization and city life have always been too precious to forego.

Despite all the warnings sounded over the past two centuries against the moral and physical dangers of city life, since 1790 more and more Americans have made their way into the city. In that year 5.1 percent of Americans lived in areas defined as urban; today an estimated 52.7 percent live in such areas, with fully 69.9 percent of the latter in large metropolitan areas composed of a central city and its suburban rings. Most Americans who still live in small towns, in hamlets, and on farms now lead a way of life permeated, even dominated, by the values and artifacts of urban culture. Except for deliberate vacation excursions into the countryside, most people, from birth to death, remain citizens of an urban world.

On an evolutionary scale the city dweller is a very recent variety of the human species. If one thinks of the history of our species as a trip of 1,000 miles, only after 950 of them did we begin to see any farms, and only during the last 10 did cities appear. Yet, during the last 2.5 miles the number of cities has begun to increase rapidly, and within the past mile entirely urbanized societies have suddenly appeared.

WORLD URBANIZATION

A hundred years ago no society was predominantly urban. At the beginning of this century only Great Britain could be regarded as a highly urbanized society. Now all industrial nations are highly urbanized, and the rate of urbanization continues to accelerate even in nonindustrial and developing societies. The distribution of population by size of locality and the world-wide growth of urban population are shown in Figure 24.1. Should the pattern of accelerating urbanization continue, by the next century more than half the world's people will live in cities of over 100,000 and yet another sizable percentage will reside in smaller urban communities.

This increasing urbanization of the human species creates problems and possibilities for which past experience provides few guidelines. For a century and a half, the shift of population from countryside to cities in the now highly urbanized societies occurred step by step with industrialization and a gradually rising per capita income. This correlation between urbanization, industrialization, and standard of living is often, if not always, found in the developing nations.

Developing Nations

In many developing societies, migration from the farms and rural villages into the cities is increasing far more rapidly than is industrialization. Moreover, the high mortality rates of the nineteenth-century industrial city, which made room for more rural migrants, are now a thing of the past. The correlated urbanization and industrialization of the nineteenth and early twentieth centuries solved the problem of rural overpopulation by providing jobs for the surplus population in the cities while simultaneously increasing food production for the population.

However, many of the developing nations do not follow this pattern; instead, their rural population increases while agricultural production lags.

Figure 24.1   Graph of the change in urban population
throughout the world from 1920 to 1960. Industrialization, which brings with it a high concentration
of people in urban areas, is responsible for the steady
overall increase since 1920.
(From United Nations, 1968.)

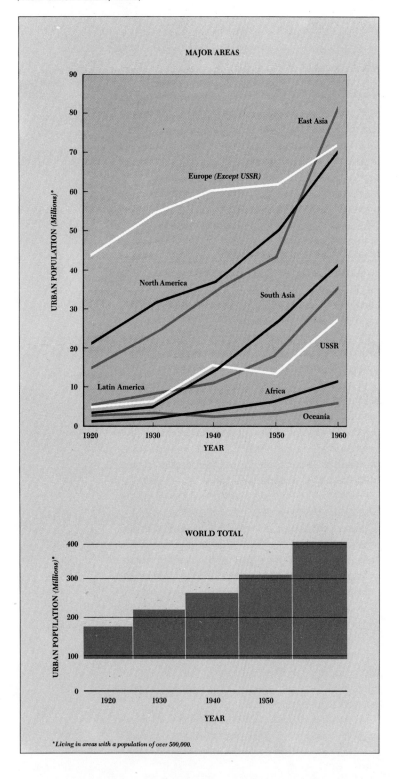

Their cities grow ever more crowded as a result
of migration from the overpopulated countryside
and of natural increase permitted by a falling mortality rate, while industrialization proceeds too
slowly to absorb the surplus of people. Chapter 23
discusses problems attendant on rapid urbanization in Venezuela. Most of Asia, Africa, and Latin
America are thus not simply repeating the demographic history of Western Europe and the United
States but are forging a new pattern.

More than 250 urban areas throughout the
world today have a population of half a million or
more, and the total number of such areas and the
size of each continue to increase. Almost half of
these are in the less industrialized nations and, for
the most part, antedate the great industrial city-
building era in the West. Only a few of them exhibit the ecological patterns of Western industrial
cities. They display rather the typical pattern of
the preindustrial city.

In urban areas of many developing nations, the
areas of poverty, generally "squatters" settlements, are usually on the city's periphery, although smaller slum areas frequently are found
adjacent to or directly in the old center. Ethnically distinct groups usually occupy separate areas
or "quarters"; many unassimilated rural migrants
and peasants try to establish villagelike enclaves
within the city and to maintain strong ties with
their home villages. The wealthy live in the most
desirable sites, most often near the center but also
in recently built, nearby suburbs.

Industry usually comes late in developing nations and is generally located in peripheral, dis-
continuous zones along railroads and major road-
ways. Although there are proportionately fewer
cars in cities in developing nations, the narrow,
poorly paved streets cannot effectively accommodate present motor traffic, and mass transit is
inadequate in such cities.

The Imbalance of Urban Growth

This pattern of urbanization in developing nations
is evident in the rapid growth of cities in sub-
Saharan Africa during the last decade. In many of
the African nations, a single city, often the political and economic capital of the country, attracts

Figure 24.2   Urbanization in countries in sub-Saharan Africa has followed the pattern of increasingly high concentrations of people in one primary city within each country. This pattern is typical of many developing nations; urban populations are a necessary condition for modernization.
(Adapted from W. A. Hance, 1970.)

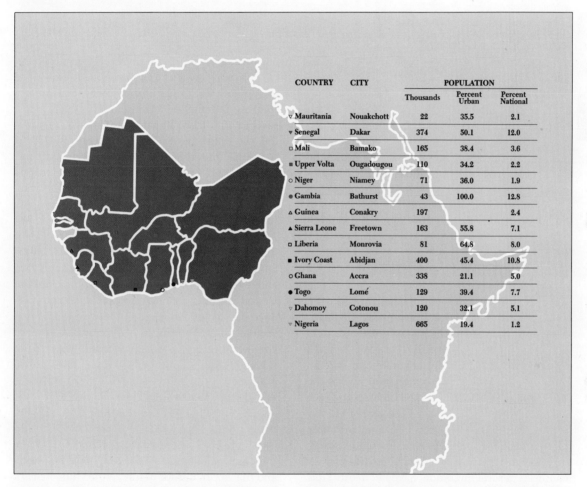

| COUNTRY | CITY | POPULATION | | |
		Thousands	Percent Urban	Percent National
▽ Mauritania	Nouakchott	22	35.5	2.1
▼ Senegal	Dakar	374	50.1	12.0
▯ Mali	Bamako	165	38.4	3.6
▪ Upper Volta	Ougadougou	110	34.2	2.2
○ Niger	Niamey	71	36.0	1.9
● Gambia	Bathurst	43	100.0	12.8
△ Guinea	Conakry	197		2.4
▲ Sierra Leone	Freetown	163	55.8	7.1
▯ Liberia	Monrovia	81	64.8	8.0
▪ Ivory Coast	Abidjan	400	45.4	10.8
○ Ghana	Accra	338	21.1	5.0
● Togo	Lomé	129	39.4	7.7
▽ Dahomey	Cotonou	120	32.1	5.1
▽ Nigeria	Lagos	665	19.4	1.2

much of the nation's investment capital and skilled population. As Figure 24.2 demonstrates, cities such as Abidjan, Dakar, Freetown, Bathurst, and Monrovia account for over 40 percent of the urban populations of their respective nations. (A notable exception to this pattern is Lagos, Nigeria, whose population—in excess of 700,000—accounts for less than 20 percent of the urban population of the country.)

The general pattern of urban growth in African nations has caused certain imbalances: When growth takes place primarily in one city, it prevents a more even distribution of regional economic and social development. Concentration of political and economic elites in one city may result in increased conflict between urban and rural sectors of the population, which may, in turn, impede the development of the nation's political institutions and contribute to the instability of African governments.

However, one should not exaggerate the negative aspects of urban growth in Africa and other rapidly urbanizing areas of the world. For example, it is not always clear that such primary-city growth leads to political instability. Countries such as Senegal and the Ivory Coast have had some of the most stable political institutions in Africa since their independence in the early 1960s. The growth of great cities in the African nations also may be a prelude to the overall urbanization and economic development of those countries in the future.

In the 1970s the populations of some of the cities listed in Figure 24.2 will surpass one million.

Figure 24.3.1   Robert E. Park (1864–1944) (*top left*) was one of the key figures in the "Chicago School" of sociology during the 1920s. After working as a newspaper reporter he went to Germany, and he received his doctorate from Heidelberg in 1904. From 1905 to 1914 he served as secretary and companion to Booker T. Washington. From then until his retirement in 1933 he was a professor of sociology at the University of Chicago, where he played a major role in stimulating extensive urban research. He coauthored with Ernest W. Burgess *Introduction to the Science of Sociology* (1921) and *The City* (1925).

Cities such as Abidjan, Dakar, and Lagos are already taking their place among the *world cities,* cities which reach far beyond national borders to attract people and trade. Although they are difficult to measure, the positive economic and social contributions of such primary cities are no doubt significant. Some scholars point out that growth of primary cities such as Paris and London was of central importance in the development of France and Great Britain. How one weighs the economic and social gains against the imbalances is a controversial issue that students of modernization argue about—the theoretical grounds for differences of opinion on several issues are discussed at length in Chapter 29.

URBANIZATION IN INDUSTRIAL SOCIETIES

In the highly urbanized industrial societies the movement of people from farm to rural hamlet, to city, and to metropolis has almost reached its limits. Indeed, there already is evident a small movement of nonagricultural families far enough into the countryside to take them out of what the census defines as the metropolitan area and into what is now called exurbia. At the same time, urban centers continue to grow in size and absolute numbers. What will life be like when all vestiges of rural values, hitherto brought to the city by centuries of rural migration, have been lost? How will continuing increases in productivity be used by a fully urbanized society, and what kind of culture will it create?

The Urban Region

Whatever the differences in spatial structure, social organization, and cultural patterns, a development that characterizes urbanization in all industrialized societies is the emergence of the *urban region*. For a relatively brief period—hardly more than a century—industrial cities had well-defined boundaries and exerted little influence on the older town form of urban life. The functions of these cities were primarily commercial and governmental. Today political boundaries no longer correspond to economic or social realities. Residential, commercial, and industrial areas flow

Figure 24.3.2   Ernest W. Burgess (1886–1966) (*bottom left*) was born in Canada and completed his doctorate at the University of Chicago in 1913. He returned to teach at Chicago in 1919 and remained there until his retirement in 1957. He collaborated with Park in writing an introductory sociology text (1921) and *The City* (1925) and in directing the urban research characteristic of the "Chicago School." He also did considerable research on the family and, with Harvey J. Locke, was the author of *The Family* (1945).

across such artificial boundaries, and newspapers, the telephone, radio, and television have effectively extended the influence of the metropolis outward to encompass farms and townships lying well beyond the official suburbs. The merchandising operations of the metropolis now constitute a single system that penetrates into the farthermost reaches of exurbia. Rapid transit and expressways link the entire hinterland to the central city.

In the United States these sprawling, complex metropolitan areas have developed around one central-city nucleus, which serves as a dominating economic and cultural focus for the entire region. In Europe such areas have been created by *conurbation,* a process in which two or more adjacent industrial and commercial cities, such as may be found along a riverway or rail line, expand toward and eventually merge into each other. In the United States this same process has begun to produce the *megalopolis,* a multimetropolitan region such as that emerging on the eastern seaboard between Boston and Washington. By the end of this century, most of the people in highly industrialized societies will live in urban regions that are metropolitan, if not megalopolitan.

Metropolitan Dominance

The influence of the major metropolitan areas of the United States reaches throughout the nation and the world. Earlier in this century Robert Park showed that the metropolitan daily press was read far beyond the limits of the city (Park and Burgess, 1925). Within a fifty-mile radius of Chicago, the majority of newspaper subscribers read the Chicago papers, either exclusively or in addition to the local weekly papers. If anything, the phenomenon of metropolitan dominance has increased in the years since Park conducted his research. The map of transcontinental rail lines shows that all roads pass through Chicago, making that city the shipping and mercantile capital of the interior of the nation.

Today town officials regularly trek to Washington, D.C., to request funds for crucial local development projects. The electronic media have contributed to the cultural dominance of the New York and Los Angeles metropolitan regions. Mil-

Figure 24.4 As metropolitan areas have begun to expand and to merge with each other, a new type of urban entity has emerged—the megalopolis. The megalopolis is a region of two or more cities, once separated by countryside, now joined by continuous strips of urban and suburban settlement. Megalopolitan areas are emerging on the northeastern seaboard from Boston to Washington, D.C., and, to a less advanced degree, along the shores of the Great Lakes, in Texas, in California, and in parts of Europe.
(From J. Gottman, 1961.)

(*Bottom right*) Columbia, located in the Washington-Baltimore corridor. In contrast to most cities and suburbs, Columbia is a city planned for its residents. The master plan calls for this new town to consist of ten villages, each one divided into five neighborhoods. Each town, village, and neighborhood has its own center. A bus route, which is closed to automobiles, connects eight village centers with the town center; the other two villages are for residents who wish to use cars. There is open space between villages and between the town center and the villages, and industry is separated from residential areas. Schools, stores, offices, recreational and religious facilities, cultural and entertainment activities, and industrial firms are located in appropriate and convenient areas throughout the city.

POPULATION DENSITY PER SQUARE MILE

- 1-50
- 50-150
- 150-500
- 500-1000
- 1000 AND OVER

MEGALOPOLIS

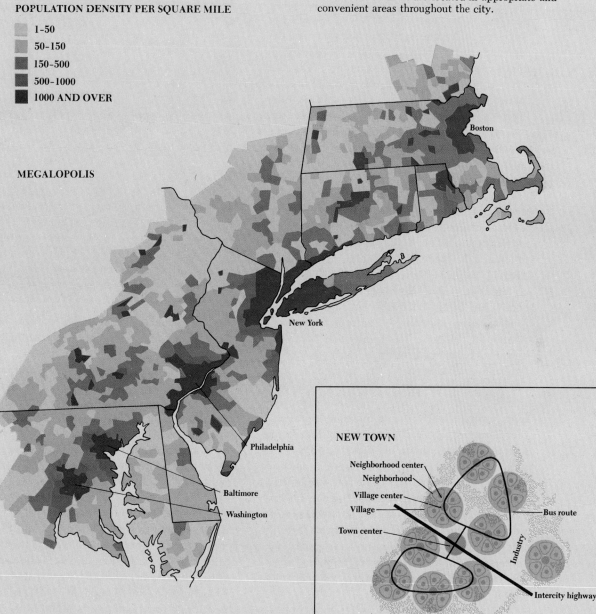

Boston

New York

Philadelphia

Baltimore

Washington

NEW TOWN

Neighborhood center
Neighborhood
Village center
Village
Town center
Bus route
Industry
Intercity highway

lions of television viewers in rural communities far from the coastal metropolitan cultural centers nightly view shows that are created and staffed by people who live and work in New York and Los Angeles. On the one hand, the central cities, the suburbs, and the rural towns and villages are all interconnected and interdependent. On the other hand, although all areas of social life are influenced by these centers, the dominant influence is not found in any one metropolitan center.

Perhaps nowhere is the far-reaching influence of metropolitan centers more evident than in the small agricultural towns and villages of the United States and Canada. For example, as metropolitan centers have grown, the milk-producing regions that supply them have had to become increasingly mechanized and dependent on a complex network of markets and transport lines whose function is directed by metropolitan organizations. Arthur J. Vidich and Joseph Bensman (1960) made an intensive study of Springdale, a dairy-farming community dominated by the vast New York metropolitan area. They wanted to study the foundations of social life in a community that "lacks the power to control the institutions that regulate and determine its existence." In Springdale, they found that townspeople and farmers alike believe that the cities are evil and corrupt and that problems in rural life are created by influences of city life. However, the authors also found that this negative image of urban life went "hand in hand with respect for the power, the wealth, and the legitimacy of acceptance of urban values." In spite of negative attitudes about urban institutions, the farmers, businessmen, and local professionals—all the major social strata of the village—spent much of their time competing for success in institutions whose operation and rules are established by the markets and cultural facilities of New York City.

Shifts in the price of milk and changes in governmental policies about road building or price supports are all decisions made largely by urbanites, but they may have immediate and profound effects on small towns like Springdale. In light of his political and economic dependence on urban institutions, the small-town resident's insistence

Figure 24.5   As middle-class people attempt to escape the problems of city life by moving to outlying areas, these areas become suburbs of the city. The suburbanization of the regions around America's cities has intensified greatly since World War II and in many cases has involved the creation of series after series of haphazardly joined, poorly planned housing tracts that deteriorate rapidly.

on values of self-sufficiency and individual effort seems anachronistic, and his negative images of the city appear defensive and unrealistic.

The effects of metropolitan dominance in rural areas are not always obvious. As indicated in the Springdale study, these influences operate just beneath the surface of the seemingly pastoral, small-town society. In the central cities, however —in the luxury high-rise districts, in the inner-city slums, and in the congested arterials—the effects of metropolitan growth are painfully clear.

Slums and Suburban Communities

Since the 1920s and especially since 1950, the outlying portions of metropolitan areas in the United States have been growing much faster than the central cities, some of which have remained stable or have even declined in population. Disparity in growth rates has been most marked in the larger and older urban areas, whose inner cores are likely to be plagued by poverty and physical deterioration. Moreover, the larger and older cities are more likely to be surrounded by suburbs or suburban centers in which employment, shopping, and recreational opportunities have been increasing. This pattern further diminishes people's involvement in and concern for the central city. Finally, the older and larger the metropolitan community, the more likely the outer area's population will have a higher socioeconomic status than that of the central city and the more likely—except in Southern metropolises—the proportion of blacks in the center will be rapidly increasing.

Increasing differentiation within a metropolitan area can lead to social disorganization if means are not found to integrate the parts into a truly functional community. Suburbs are viable only if most of their residents go to the central city to work; even when suburbs develop into self-sufficient satellite cities with their own industry and offices, these communities must be economically integrated with the total metropolitan area. The failure to bring blacks and other minority-group communities into the economic and political life of the city has produced much of the increasing alienation, frustration, and violent behavior of disadvantaged minorities in the United States. Most white suburbs are voluntary ghettos based on their residents' homogeneous social, cultural, and economic characteristics. They often incorporate their areas into suburban towns, thereby reinforcing natural, or ecological, boundaries with political ones. Black ghettos, on the other hand, are involuntary communities that lack political power; their residents have been excluded from the opportunity structure of the metropolis.

In an earlier era, foreign-born immigrants inhabited most of the involuntary ghettos in the United States. Today ghettos are more likely to be populated by Indians, blacks, and Appalachian whites, a trend that is documented in Chapter 25. The ghetto is typically in the "inner city," often near industrial areas where the only available housing in general is substandard.

Unemployment in the inner city is undoubtedly the major cause of the grinding poverty that marks the lives of ghetto residents. Unemployment rates for urban blacks have remained above the 6 percent level since 1954, even in periods of sustained economic growth. Black unemployment is always at least twice as serious as it is for

urban whites, and in times of recession it may immediately jump to three or four times higher.

Still more damning are rates of *underemployment* in the inner city. Underemployed people are those who work part time while looking for full-time jobs or who work full time but earn below 3,000 dollars a year. In the late 1960s, the underemployed and unemployed accounted for almost 33 percent of the labor force in ten major inner-city ghetto communities (Kerner Commission, Report of the National Advisory Commission on Civil Disorders, 1968). This figure was nine times higher than that of the general urban population. Inside the cities, the better jobs quite simply belong to those who have been given educational and other advantages that the average ghetto resident does not command.

The Ghetto Jungle After surveying the major inner-city slum areas in the late 1960s, the Kerner Commission accepted the view that some inner-city slum areas are human jungles (Kerner Commission, 1968). A section of their report headed "The Jungle" states

The culture of poverty that results from unemployment and family disorganization generates a system of ruthless, exploitative relationships within the ghetto. Prostitution, dope addiction, casual sexual affairs, and crime create an environmental jungle characterized by personal insecurity and tension.

Thus addiction to heroin and other lethal narcotics is heavily concentrated in low-income neighborhoods, particularly in New York City. The commission also reported that blacks represented just over 50 percent of addicts known to the United States Bureau of Narcotics at the end of 1966. Of the 59,720 known addicts, "over 52 percent . . . lived in New York State, mostly in Harlem and other Negro neighborhoods. These figures undoubtedly underestimate the actual number of persons using narcotics regularly —especially those under 21." In concluding this section of the report, the investigators note that the social pathology of inner-city slums is affecting a generation of children as well as adults. In the cities they surveyed, 1.2 million nonwhite chil-

Chapter 24.6   The oppressive physical
conditions of ghetto life have contributed greatly to
the widespread social alienation felt by ghetto
residents. Black consciousness, stressing shared experiences, both of common oppression and of a
common culture, is an attempt on the part of black
people to develop the identity and pride
necessary to overcome the problems of ghetto life.
Urban-renewal projects, while providing improved
living conditions, threaten black identity and
recreate conditions of alienation.

dren under 16 live in families that rely on one
woman for support. In the large majority of these
cases the children are growing up in poverty.

The Ghetto Culture   The view of the inner-city
slum as a jungle supporting conditions that make
poor children "better candidates for crime and
civil disorder than for jobs providing an entry into
American society" (Kerner Commission, 1968)
should be tempered with another point of view.
Racism, exploitation, and neglect have caused
inner-city ghettos to exist, but many writers have
pointed to the cultural processes that nevertheless

form cohesive neighborhoods out of the chaos of
slum conditions.

Slum neighborhoods produce cultural patterns
that sustain people and allow them to survive under the most extreme circumstances. Ghetto culture is not merely a "culture of poverty" that sets
ground rules for coping with drugs, poverty, and
welfare. The culture of slum neighborhoods is
created in the peer groups that meet in street
corners, beauty parlors, and neighborhood taverns (Liebow, 1967). In these groups people can
prove themselves worthy of reputation and dignity, and they can learn who may be trusted and

who is to be avoided. Slum neighborhoods develop their own forms of expression, such as the Italian concept of *omertà*, or code of silence, and the black tradition of the blues (Keil, 1966).

Out of the misery of slum life have come some of the most genuinely creative contributions to the culture of the larger society. For example, discussing his early years in Harlem, Langston Hughes writes,

When I came back to New York in 1925 the Negro renaissance was in full swing. . . . I spent as much time as I could in Harlem, and this I have done ever since. I was in love with Harlem long before I got there, and I still am in love with it. Everybody seemed to make me welcome. The sheer dark size of Harlem intrigued me. And the fact that at that time poets and writers like James Weldon Johnson and Jessie Faust lived there, and Bert Williams, Duke Ellington, Ethel Waters, and Walter White, too, fascinated me. Had I been a rich man, I would have bought a house in Harlem and built musical steps up to the front door, and installed chimes that at the press of a button played Ellington tunes (Hughes, 1964).

One of the severest of inner-city problems is the deleterious effect that urban-renewal programs have on such culture-producing neighborhoods.

Urban Renewal and the Neighborhood

Although humanitarian goals often motivate urban renewal, the construction of large public-housing projects frequently makes it more difficult for inner-city residents to establish local cultures and areas of trust and safety in their neighborhoods. In an excellent study of morality and trust in a slum community, Gerald D. Suttles (1968) found that residents of a large public-housing project were placed at a serious disadvantage in their relationships with residents of surrounding slum neighborhoods. As Suttles concluded,

The most important consequence of project living may be the way it restricts most opportunities to achieve a stake in the prospects of the local community and to develop the kind of leadership and social differentiation that is so critical in forming a stable moral community. In the Jane Addams Projects the Negroes can never alter the buildings to their own use, and all that keeps them there are

a few friends and an income too small to rent better housing. If they become more affluent, they leave. . . . The result is an overwhelming homogeneity in which differences of income, education, political influence, and occupation are so lacking as to fail to designate potential leaders and spokesmen.

Jane Jacobs (1961), in her perceptive study of housing in New York City, reaches similar conclusions about the problems of urban-renewal housing projects. Jacobs finds that in destroying old urban neighborhoods and replacing them with new but sterile housing projects, planners may destroy all the mechanisms that allow people to take responsibility for one another in the city; rather than heal the ills of the inner city, large project developments often intensify them.

This is not to say that we should not reconstruct decaying urban neighborhoods but that we should pay more attention to building the possibilities in those renewed areas for the continuation or rebirth of neighborhood cultures. The issue relates not only to physical safety in inner-city places but to the personalities of the people who live and grow up in the city.

Urban Life and Personality

It is impossible for people to become uprooted from neighborhoods and communities they have known for their entire lives without suffering potentially serious personality disorders. For the immigrant generation to American and Canadian cities, the experience of coming to a new culture and creating new communities always left indelible marks on their personalities. Similarly, when a neighborhood is torn down to make room for an expressway or for new urban-renewal housing, the displaced people may suffer acute mental stress. In his paper "Grieving For a Lost Home," Marc Fried describes the effects of the destruction of an inner-city neighborhood in Boston (Fried, 1963). Here the sense of loss experienced by the relocatees was "indistinguishable from an acute grief reaction" and often required intensive psychological care.

What are the relationships between community and personality formation, and how does urban life affect the individual? The German sociologist Georg Simmel (1858–1918) asserted that modern urban life is both overstimulating and impersonal. Most urban people seek privacy and relate to others not as whole persons but only in their functionally specific roles. Relationships are therefore secondary rather than primary. Above all, people tend to measure everything by the standard of money. At the same time, Simmel recognized the limitless potentialities of urban life and its culture-creating role (Simmel, 1950).

Louis Wirth (1938) agreed with Simmel's pessimistic assessment of the very fragmenting and alienating effects of urban life, but he did not recognize as clearly its positive side. For Wirth, urban people's extreme indifference and blasé outlook were devices they used to insulate themselves from the personal claims and demands of others. Such insulation leads people to believe that they can live their own lives as they wish.

Pessimistic pictures of urban life such as Wirth's are excessively one-sided. For example, the family—the basic primary group—remains a significant part of urban social organization in developing nations (United Nations, 1957). Industrial cities do not necessarily disrupt kinship, friendship, and neighborhood groups but clearly cause them to be organized on new bases (Breese, 1966). The friendship group, for example, may now be physically dispersed throughout the urban area. The neighborhood may be more a psychological than an ecological reality. Modern means of communication and transportation, especially the combination of telephone and automobile, have made possible this new organization of primary groups.

The urban way of life can thus be thought of on at least three levels. Of central importance to the urbanite are his family, his kin, his friends, and, in some cases, his neighbors. This is the level of *primary group interaction.* Next is the level of *secondary group interaction,* in which job and job-related contacts are usually of the greatest importance. Finally, much interchange takes place anonymously rather than intimately—as *interaction between roles* rather than between persons in their entirety. It is on the basis of this latter type

of interaction that natives and foreigners, rich and poor, can be treated alike; that the stranger can be responded to at all; and that the blasé outlook so vividly characterized by Wirth does indeed show itself.

Most urban dwellers, especially those with children, presently seem to desire to live in an area with others like them, an area protected from activities considered evil, dangerous, or disruptive. Security in the pursuit of one's preferred life style is valued equally in an affluent white suburb, a black inner-city neighborhood, or a commune. To the extent that life styles vary with income, education, ethnic background, and religion, the processes of voluntary ecological segregation in the modern metropolis produce social areas with differing or even unique dominant values and behavior patterns among their residents; ecological segregation is discussed in Chapter 25. However, incessant population mobility has rendered some areas almost perpetually transitional; others remain too diffuse or heterogeneous to develop and sustain a life style any more distinctive than "mainstream middle-class American."

CITY PLANNING AND ORGANIZATION

City planning is as old as cities. One of the first known planners was Hippodamus, the Greek architect who planned the Piraeus, the port of Athens, in the fifth century B.C. For almost nine-tenths of urban history, however, most city planning has been minimal, with limited objectives prescribed by the elite: defending the city; maintaining a governmental, religious, or commercial center; beautifying and servicing the elite's residential areas; routing traffic; or providing necessary facilities and amenities, whether baths or tombs, stadiums or churches.

The much-praised original "planning" of Washington, D.C., at the end of the eighteenth century hardly went beyond the conception stage. It is instructive to compare that city's present physical and social disarray and its ugly slums with the orderly and well-managed growth of Stockholm, Sweden, which has had a planning office for more than three centuries. In Stockholm, planning has emphasized the provision of housing and other facilities, the integration of central-city and suburban growth, and the coordination of transportation with economic and residential development—all with an awareness of how probable demographic and economic trends are likely to affect the particular area's future growth (Sidenbladh, 1965).

Where planning is concerned, the United States lags behind other industrialized societies. A strong antiplanning ideology is partly responsible for Americans' aversion to political and social planning. Perhaps Americans associate planning with socialist ideas. It is likely that their aversion is partly a result of the tradition of local autonomy.

American planners have just begun to concern themselves with broader problems than those of land use, tax bases, and traffic flow, and they remain uncertain whether they should attempt to plan institutional change and the reform of the entire social system. Even in societies where planning is far more advanced than in the United States, planners do not grasp all the ways in which urban society is changing. They do not see the necessity of making planning part of the very process of urban evolution and do not accept the need for changes in the fundamental conceptions of planning itself.

Political Issues

Case studies of urban planning in the United States have generally emphasized the conflict of interests in municipal politics. Professional planners produce imagined allocations of space, and those with authority alter the plans in response to pressures from local centers of political and economic power. These "feasible plans" are presented publicly, sometimes evoking dramatic but ineffective protests by such relatively powerless groups as residents of the area and social scientists; so the essentially unmodified plans are formally adopted.

In the larger cities, those who shape decisions usually are most effective when dealing with matters directly related to the interests of their constituencies, and no one group exerts decisive power in all areas of action. Controversial issues

Figure 24.7 City planning is an important issue today. Alleviation of the crowding, environmental pollution, and urban decay that plague American cities calls for long-range, comprehensive plans. But such plans and their execution seem to require increasing centralization of power as administrative and enforcement agencies are brought together under a single jurisdiction.

are usually compromised through the "brokerage politics" practiced in city halls and county courthouses. Until recently, planning decisions were left largely to government bodies, commissions, and professional staffs, whose members were usually made up of more affluent people. But blacks and the organized poor in a number of cities, trapped in their decaying cores and subject to well-planned disruption by expressway and renewal projects, have begun to resist this established coalition of political, professional, and "aesthetic" interests. For the next decade or two, many planning projects will reflect this conflict over who should and can decide the future of a given neighborhood.

Increased participation by previously excluded groups has been further stimulated and facilitated by the federal government, by powerful labor unions, and by foundations. Municipal political leaders and local elites have resisted the steady decline in the autonomy of their cities, but further erosion of their power is likely because national business and financial corporations are becoming more involved in urban renewal and because departments of urban and local affairs are growing at the state level. Planning and plan implementation thus provide one major arena in which established local power structures try to defend control over the fate of "their" cities.

The imperatives of the Federal Community Action Agency and Model Cities Program have forced independent domains of decision making in the urban political structure to integrate and centralize. Departments of traffic, welfare, zoning, law enforcement, education, industrial development, and public housing traditionally have had their own separate bodies of decision makers and independent staffs of professional personnel; there has been little coordination and collaboration among the various groups. The politics of planning in the years ahead will reflect some people's efforts to preserve this long-established autonomy against both local and higher-level pressures for greater integration of functions and broader community participation.

Professional planners have rarely been prepared to deal with the social and institutional dimensions of urban problems or with the politics of planning and plan implementation. New kinds of professionals are claiming a place in the planning process, but "advocacy planning" is also emerging as one means of allowing groups that used to be excluded from the planning process to challenge the programs formulated by the entrenched establishment. Thus, the role of the expert in the urban power structure is finally being challenged.

The division between "inner" and "outer" cities in the metropolis and the fragmentation of the outer area into a multitude of municipalities and districts make effective planning almost impossible. If this situation cannot be reversed through local political action, it will eventually have to be dealt with by state or federal government.

Community Organization

Life in urban communities has always been organized through a combination of formal government relationships and informal relationships built on traditional values and customs. Primary-group communities are organized according to kinship patterns and face-to-face relationships; large, differentiated urban communities—with their written records, laws, and formal government structures—are more consciously organized types of community structures.

The emergence of commercial and industrial cities and, later, of the urbanized society has increased the role of contractual relationships and formal organizational structures in the life of the urban citizen. This increase may, at first, mean a further extension of the elite's power to manage and govern, but eventually, through the spread of literacy and the enlargement of legal rights, more urbanites may be able to participate in the processes by which urban life is organized.

Community Participation Power and participation in decision making reinforce each other in the modern metropolis. Most organizations and associations of citizens, however, have little influence in determining community policies. In spite of the direct involvement of labor-union officials and leaders of ethnic and racial groups in some community decisions, the great majority of powerful people in the community are still those with high education, income, and occupational status. Not only the poor and the black minorities but also the young, the aged, women, and rural migrants are not well represented and lack access to economic and political power (Bloomberg, 1966).

Except for the limited choice offered in general elections, participation in relevant organizations and associations is the only way for people with less power, property, and prestige to make effective demands. The vicious circle of nonparticipation in planning programs has to be broken; so far, deprivation has meant nonparticipation, and nonparticipation means further deprivation.

Community Action Programs It stands to reason that when elites establish reform programs for disadvantaged people in the community, such programs are often less likely to meet their needs than are programs created and controlled by the disadvantaged themselves. There is little evidence to support the idea that the poor are intrinsically unable to deal effectively with the problems of urban society that beset them. But how do they begin their self-help projects without access to the resources controlled by the urban elite and the middle classes and without the skills that those in power have acquired through education and experience? Recent action programs controlled and substantially staffed by poor people and black people indicate that their motivation and organizational capabilities are far greater than the stereotypes suggest.

Occasionally settlement houses have become centers for ethnic community organization and local politicking. Union-based political action has enabled residents of working-class districts to establish influence in city hall and to have a spokesman on the school board and on various appointed commissions. More militant organizing both for community self-help projects and in order to influence crucial political decisions have been a byproduct of the civil-rights and black-power movements and have been promoted by such advocates of community organization as the late Saul Alinsky and his Industrial Areas Foundation.

All of these efforts have met with substantial, though seldom unanimous, opposition from the local establishment. The community-action phase of the Antipoverty Program became the focal point of local opposition to the whole program, even though its emphasis was on providing career opportunities for the poor and on giving them an active voice in programs launched by conventional public and private agencies—not on enhancing their political power or helping them create their own agencies for community change.

Race, Poverty, and Urban Policy

Problems of race and poverty intersect. The question of who will control action programs and urban policy has been at least as divisive as the issue over the causes and cure of racism and deprivation. Those who shape policy for urban areas find it difficult to focus attention and resources on problems such as mental health, education, and environmental pollution when they are so preoccupied by poverty, racism, and disparities in power that have created conflict and violence.

Almost all new attempts to deal with these issues in the past several decades have come from outside the local community: from the Federal Government and state governments; from the national and regional offices of business and financial corporations and labor unions; from regional and national conferences of professional groups or committees created by them; and from university personnel financed by foundations and federal agencies. Those in control of the local government have, in the main, resisted innovations and sought to control whatever resources—especially money—the agents of reform might offer. The policy and power struggles in American cities today are episodes in the continuing nationalization of the social order. We have seen the tremendous impact of industrialization, mass communication, and the rise of the metropolis on the social order. Industrialization exerts pressures toward greater equality and upward mobility, and urbanization presses to change the tradition of local autonomy.

Pressures have mounted for change in the organization and distribution of local power. Black communities and organized poverty groups have begun to push for smaller units of government with limited functions within the inner city—such as multi-neighborhood districts, decentralized school districts, and neighborhood corporations—but segments of the upper class, especially those still living in the inner city, have sought to increase the scope and power of county government or to establish new forms of metropolitan government. The drive for greater metropolitan control may make political authority more congruent with the functional distribution of people and problems in the metropolitan area, but it will prevent passing control over the inner city into the hands of the lower and lower-middle classes who form an ever increasing proportion of its population. How these underlying issues of power distribution and government reorganization are resolved will greatly affect the future of American cities and American society.

SUGGESTED READINGS

Gist, Noel P., and Sylvia F. Fava. *Urban Society.* 5th ed. New York: Crowell, 1964.

Jacobs, Jane. *The Death and Life of Great American Cities.* New York: Random House, 1961.

Liebow, Elliot. *Tally's Corner: A Study of Negro Streetcorner Men.* Boston: Little, Brown, 1967.

Suttles, Gerald D. *The Social Order of the Slum.* Chicago: University of Chicago Press, 1968.

Chapter 25 Human Ecology

WE PLAY OUT OUR LIVES in space as well as in time, and the places we inhabit become rich with social meanings. Locality itself is a proper element of social structure and plays an important part in shaping the content of human relationships. Think of how many struggles are waged over the boundaries of neighborhoods and nations or of how proud neighborhoods in cities become modern ruins after one or two generations have passed through them. The overcrowding and decay in large cities are, to be sure, major objects of the current concern over environmental problems. The study of human ecology, which has focused on such problems for several decades, is basic to their future solution.

SOCIETY AND ECOLOGY

The term *ecology* was introduced in biology and was first applied to the study of plants. Only later was it applied to the study of zoology and later still—in fact, not until the 1920s—to the study of human communities. In recent years, ecology has come to mean the study of the relationship between people and their natural environment, and the term has become very popular in discussions of pollution, which focus attention on the way people use and misuse their natural environment.

Early enthusiasts, however, viewed ecology in enormously broad terms, describing it as the study of *all* relations of *all* organisms to the totality of their environments. Ecology became a usable concept only after it was restricted to the study of (1) the patterns in which organisms or activities distribute themselves in space with reference to other organisms and activities and (2) the way organisms adapt to and change the physical aspects of their environment. Precursors of modern ecological thought are found in French sociology of the late nineteenth century, especially in the work of Emile Durkheim and his students. Durkheim emphasized *social morphology,* or the environmental basis of social organization. He was particularly concerned with population size and density as determinants of the division of labor in society. This concern in French sociology was most fully developed in the famous Chicago-school ecological studies early in this century.

Social ecology, as developed by Robert E. Park, Ernest W. Burgess, and their colleagues at the University of Chicago after World War I, stressed relationships among men, their organic and inorganic environments, and their ongoing social activities. The ecological approach emphasized that nothing by itself has fixed meaning and that meaning instead is always a matter of the relationship of objects and activities to one other. Not only does environment significantly modify people's behavior but people's behavior always results in the reshaping of their environments.

Ecological studies begin with the explicit assumption that the interactions between organisms and their environments are patterned and recurrent rather than undesigned and random. Ecological studies also assume that the number and kinds of patterns vary with the number and complexity of the variables involved. Human ecological patterns exhibit the greatest complexity and variability. The uniquely human factor of rationality—and, by implication, irrationality—and the human being's ability to consciously modify his behavior and environment make the study of human ecology more complex than that of plant and animal ecology.

The cultural and social superstructures that human beings build on the basis of their needs and out of their environment are sometimes extremely detrimental to the welfare of the species. The scourges of unplanned urbanism and pollution suggest that man may have at last developed a way of destroying the very environment that supports him. It must not be assumed that the mere existence of a particular ecological pattern warrants the conclusion that the pattern is based on sound reasoning and judgment or that it should be allowed to continue.

Even though all social ecologists consider the accumulated culture to be an essential factor in ecological analysis, some do not believe the scope of that influence is very large. Yet every cultural item and social institution influences the spatial distribution of people and their artifacts, which in

Figure 25.1 An important assumption underlying industrialization is that people can conquer nature. In the short range, rapid industrialization brings great material prosperity. But the search for raw materials for industry brings with it the use of such techniques as strip mining (shown here) and clear cutting of timber and such accidents as oil spillage that in the longer range may be ecologically devastating.

turn affects culture and institutions in a continuing process of interaction. It is the interactive character of ecological patterns that makes futile any attempt to discover regularities in, for example, land-use patterns that do not take into account the sentiments and attitudes attached to the land in question. Land-use patterns are never the result of purely rational calculations. Only when all the influences on land use are identical—a rare occurrence—can one expect to discover identical ecological relationships.

THE ECOLOGY OF SIMPLER SOCIETIES

Simpler societies generally adapt to their physical environments without significantly modifying them. In fact, the basic criterion used for identifying a primitive culture is the absence of any significant modification of the biological or geophysical environment of that culture. People in primitive societies must move to new territory each time their food supply becomes depleted. In such cultures a limited technology appears to be the critical determinant of ecological patterning.

The Tikopia Islanders: Population Control

The Tikopia islanders provide an important example of simpler cultures. Earlier in this century, Raymond Firth, a pioneer of British social anthropology, went to the Solomon Islands to study the people of Tikopia.

When Firth lived among the islanders, they maintained a culture that was intimately linked to the natural food sources of their tropical islands. The yearly cycle of biological reproduction on the island and the natural supply of fish and edible plants established limits on the number of people that the island could support. Some means of maintaining a stable population was essential to the culture's continued existence in the natural environment of the islands. The Tikopia chose to practice infanticide—"proportioned to the food," as the islanders explained it to Firth. The islanders claimed that they practiced infanticide unwillingly, but they continued to do so because of the islands' limited resources; "only after at least one child of each sex has been born is the act carried out. The infant is buried without ceremony, since it has barely lived and has not become a full fledged member of society" (Firth, 1963).

Although the Tikopia culture is severely constrained by environmental conditions, the Tikopia recognize that they exist at the top of a food chain that can support only a finite population. This insight has become part of their moral code.

Nomadic Communities and Feudal Societies

Communities of herding nomads, such as the ancient Arabs or medieval Tartars, are somewhat more complex in their ecological relationships than are the Tikopia islanders. Regardless of locale, the nomads adapt to their environment and move to new locations when their animals have exhausted the foraging potential in a given area. Nomads modify their environment to some degree by domesticating animals, but their communities lack physical stability because of the constant necessity to move on. Cultures that develop an agricultural technology that does not rapidly exhaust the land do not need to continue moving to new territories, or at least need to move less often; the Iroquois tribes, for example, moved only every ten or twelve years.

In cultures relying upon plow agriculture, the fertility of the land has been the principal determinant of ecological patterns, but the influence of political and military factors also has been strong.

Figure 25.2 Preindustrial societies are far more at the mercy of environmental vicissitudes than industrial societies are. Although nomads do modify their environment to some extent by domesticating animals, they face the constant necessity of adapting to their environment: they must move to new locations when their animals have exhausted the foraging potential of an area. These Amharic nomads of Ethiopia are proud of their nomadic heritage and prefer their mobility to physical stability and accumulation of wealth.

A case in point is the agricultural-political-military culture of the Western medieval period, which largely persisted into the early modern era. In one of the most authoritative studies of feudal society, Marc Bloch (1964) writes:

The disorders of the early Middle Ages had in many cases induced men to draw nearer to each other, but these aggregations in which people lived cheek by jowl were separated by empty spaces. The arable land from which the village derived its sustenance was necessarily much larger in proportion to the number of inhabitants than it is today. For agriculture was a great devourer of space. In the tilled fields, incompletely ploughed and almost always inadequately manured, the ears of corn grew neither very heavy nor very dense. The most advanced systems of crop rotation known to the age required that every year half or a third of the cultivated soil should lie fallow.

Beyond the cultivated lands around the feudal villages stretched wastelands of scrub forest and dunes. They were "immense wildernesses, seldom uninhabited by man, though whoever dwelt there as charcoal-burner, shepherd, hermit or outlaw did so only at the cost of a long separation from his fellow men" (Bloch, 1964).

The size and shape of European feudal villages and the human relationships that characterized the medieval period were highly dependent upon the evolution of feudal political institutions. But the rise of medieval kingdoms and the growth of trading settlements depended, in turn, on the repopulation of Europe in the period from 1050 to 1250. Bloch's study demonstrates that one immediate effect of this repopulation was the closer association of human groups.

Between the different settlements, except in some particularly neglected regions, the vast empty spaces thenceforth disappeared. Such distances as still separated the settlements became, in any case, easier to traverse. For powers now arose or were consolidated—their rise being favoured by current demographic trends—whose enlarged horizons brought them new responsibilities. Such were the urban middle classes, which owed everything to trade. Such also were the kings and princes; they too were interested in the prosperity of commerce because they derived large sums of money from it in the form of duties and tolls; moreover they were aware—much more so than in the past—of the vital importance to them of the free transmission of orders and the free movement of armies (Bloch, 1964).

American Homesteads

Political institutions also have affected the distribution of people in the modern era. The Homestead Act of 1862, for example, offered a quarter section, or 160 acres, of land in the then Western territory to anyone who would live on it and farm it for five years. The land rush and settlement that followed therefore populated and civilized the American West but destroyed the Indians by taking away the open range required by nomadic populations and by using armed conflict to seize the range land.

In the period of American homesteading, the farmer's community was restricted to his immediate geographical neighborhood. Transportation was slow and limited to horse and wagon, except for those few communities served by early railroads. As technology revolutionized American agriculture in the early twentieth century, the

Figure 25.3   From 1900 to 1950 there was a steady migration from rural to urban areas in the United States. Since 1950 a new trend, suburbanization, has developed as people move out of the city centers and into the surrounding communities. (Adapted from D. Bogue, 1955.)

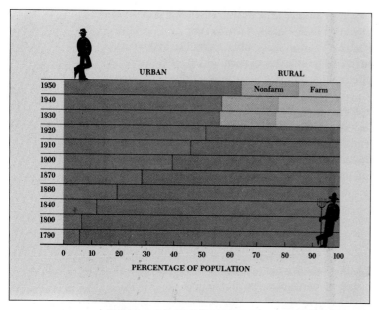

a highly diverse population over a limited territory and those that regularize relationships based on interdependence. Two general ecological patterns of urban communities have been identified from the numerous studies of urban ecology: the *preindustrial*, or pedestrian, city and the *industrial*, or mechanized, city.

In perhaps the most complete study on the subject, Gideon Sjoberg (1955) examines the ecology and social structure of preindustrial cities throughout the world and over history. He finds that in the preindustrial city the center of the settlement is the favored residence of the elite. The economically disadvantaged residents of the city fan out toward the periphery, and the very poorest and the outcasts live beyond the walls or in the "suburbs," which literally translated means "under the walls."

Except in the most favored center of the city, "most streets are mere passageways for people and for animals used in transport. Buildings are low and crowded together. The congested conditions, combined with limited scientific knowledge, have fostered serious sanitation problems."

According to Sjoberg, more significant than the generally poor living conditions in preindustrial cities is

the rigid social segregation which typically has led to the formation of "quarters" or "wards." In Fez, Morocco, and Aleppo, Syria . . . these were sealed off from each other by walls, whose gates were locked at night. The quarters reflect the sharp local social divisions. Thus ethnic groups live in special sections. And the occupational groupings, some being at the same time ethnic in character, typically reside apart from one another. Often a special street or sector of the city is occupied almost exclusively by members of a particular trade; cities in such divergent cultures as medieval Europe and modern Afghanistan contain streets with names like "street of the goldsmiths."

Despite rigid segregation, the evidence suggests no real specialization of land use such as is functionally necessary in industrial-urban communities. In medieval Europe and in other areas, city dwellings often serve as workshops, and religious structures are used as schools or marketing centers.

Finally, the "business district" does not hold the position of dominance that it enjoys in the

160-acre farm became an increasingly uneconomical unit of production. Competition for larger land holdings drove thousands of farm families from the land in the period from 1900 to 1950. As Figure 25.3 demonstrates, the rural people who were displaced from the land swelled the populations of cities and towns.

Even though the ecological basis of American society changed during these decades, the influence of earlier ecological relationships has persisted in American social institutions. American politics has kept the values of self-sufficiency and individual achievement and the idea that abundance and success are available to any who will simply work for them. How long these values will persist, now that the ecological relationships that nurtured them have largely disappeared, is a question that remains open.

ECOLOGY OF PREINDUSTRIAL CITIES

Unlike the people of simpler societies, the urbanite lives in a predominantly man-made environment. In the city, interdependence rather than self-sufficiency is the dominant mode of life, and people have claim upon each other on the basis of mere propinquity. The most important ecological processes in cities are those that order

Figure 25.4   An early print depicting the fortress town of Arles, France. Preindustrial cities such as Arles were characterized by compact organization and well-defined physical and social boundaries. In these cities the elite lived at the center of town, the artisans and workers around them, and the poor at or beyond the city walls. In modern industrial cities the middle and upper classes are moving away from the city center, and the poor are crowded into the downtown areas.

industrial-urban community. Thus, in the Middle East the principal mosque, or in medieval Europe the cathedral, is usually the focal point of community life. The center of Peiping is the Forbidden City (Sjoberg, 1955).

Examples of this kind of ecological pattern are not, however, limited to ancient cities or cities of the new nations. With some modifications, this pattern was characteristic of American cities before the early decades of the present century when modern technology, particularly rapid mass transit and the automobile, began reshaping the ecology of our cities. For example, what is now the Boston metropolitan area was, in 1850, a tightly packed central city and a group of peripheral, equally compact independent towns. Careful study of the period led Sam B. Warner (1962) to conclude:

Throughout the tiny metropolitan region of 1850, streets of the well-to-do lay hard by workers' barracks and tenements of the poor; many artisans kept shop and home in the same building or suite; and factories, wharves, and offices were but a few blocks from middle-class homes. Buildings in both [Boston and peripheral towns] were eminently suited to a city short of land, a city which depended on people walking for its means of transportation, a city which depended upon face-to-face relationships as its means of communication.

Evidence abounds that this general pattern was common to both large and small cities in the pedestrian era prior to the development of manufacturing techniques and mechanized transportation. Within walking distance of the central business district of nearly every large city of the United States and Canada, one can even today see the skeletons of splendid residences that have been converted to commercial use or to multiple dwellings for lower-income occupants.

ECOLOGY OF INDUSTRIAL CITIES

There are many differences between preindustrial and industrial cities. Walled cities are anachronisms in the modern era. The center of the city is no longer always the safest and wealthiest part. Most significant of all, the means of transportation, after plodding along at a pedestrian pace for millennia, have been rapidly accelerated.

There are several other factors that have gone into shaping the ecological patterns of today. For example, the people of contemporary industrial cities have insisted on retaining their ethnic, class, and religious prejudices. Also, the newer modes of transportation, coupled with persisting economic differentiation, have enabled the more affluent city dwellers to move outside of the city proper or well above its sidewalks.

As previously mentioned, systematic work in social ecology began only after World War I, with the work of Robert E. Park and Ernest W. Burgess and the so-called Chicago school of sociologists, who together created the discipline of urban sociology in the United States. Burgess' *concentric-circle* scheme of urban growth, set forth in the mid-1920s, has undoubtedly been the most influential model in the study of social ecology. It was followed in the late 1930s by the *sector* model of Homer Hoyt, and in the mid-1940s by the *multiple-nuclei* model developed by Chauncy Harris and Edward Ullman.

Concentric-Circle Model

Burgess conceived of a city composed of what he and Robert Park called *natural areas*—areas of homogeneous population and land use that are

Figure 25.5 Three theories of urban ecology: Ernest W. Burgess's concentric-zone model (*top left*), which was applied to Chicago in the 1920s; Homer Hoyt's sector model (*top right*), which modified Burgess's model and accounted for changes brought about by the automobile; and the multiple-nuclei model of Chauncy Harris and Edward L. Ullman (*bottom*), which attempted to account for new patterns resulting from differentiated activities in modern industrial cities. Each model represents an attempt to describe land-use patterns in large cities during different periods of urban growth in the United States.

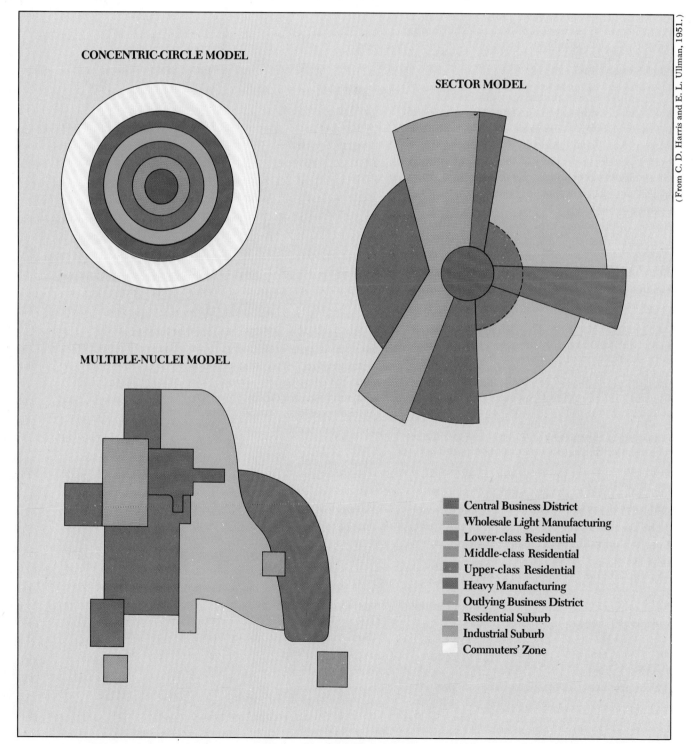

(From C. D. Harris and E. L. Ullman, 1951.)

CONCENTRIC-CIRCLE MODEL

SECTOR MODEL

MULTIPLE-NUCLEI MODEL

Central Business District
Wholesale Light Manufacturing
Lower-class Residential
Middle-class Residential
Upper-class Residential
Heavy Manufacturing
Outlying Business District
Residential Suburb
Industrial Suburb
Commuters' Zone

not the result of deliberate planning. Figure 25.5 displays the concentric-circle model. Zone I, the central business district, is the zone of highest land values, an area dominated by large commercial and financial enterprises. Zone II, usually called the zone of transition, arises in the course of the city's growth as a result of the expansion of Zone I. Zone II also illustrates the ecological processes of *competition, invasion,* and *succession.* In the Chicago that Burgess and his colleagues studied in the 1920s, Zone II was perceptibly moving: At its inner edge, where it joined the central business district, succession was complete: new commercial buildings had either replaced or overshadowed the older residential tenements; on its outer edge, where it abutted Zone III, the process of invasion was incomplete. Here rickety tenements and light industry competed for available space; invasions of new migrants began here, always threatening to drive out the older settlers; and no sooner was one pattern of land use established than another invasion would begin. Land speculation was usual in this area, and the current uses of land for rooming houses or slums were seen as temporary, pending the time when the property could be sold at high prices for commercial or industrial use. In this zone, again toward its inner edge, are the pawnshops, the burlesque houses, and the skid-row area, with its variety of cheap bars and flophouses.

Zone III in this model is characterized as an area of workingmen's homes, usually two-family dwellings but sometimes four- and five-story walkups. Dwellings were usually packed close together and were typically overcrowded, but the area had the great advantage of being near the working place of its inhabitants. Residents of this area were themselves often in transition from the life of the slums to that of Zone IV, where better houses on larger lots and more desirable apartments for the middle class were to be found. In this area, neighborhood shopping centers and the "bright light" areas provided appealing amenities and diversions. Beyond this zone was the area of commuters in which the wealthier families lived in still larger houses on still more spacious lots.

No matter how rigidly the concentric-circle scheme has sometimes been applied by Burgess' successors, it was conceived as a dynamic model of a growing city, in which the tendency was for "each inner zone to extend its area by the invasion of the next outer zone" (Burgess, 1925).

Sector Model

Homer Hoyt's sector theory, which he developed as an explicit modification of Burgess' model, conceives of the spatial distribution of population and activities in a city as a group of pie-shaped wedges or sectors that tend to run radially from the center of the city and thus cut across a concentric land-use pattern (see Figure 25.5). Although Hoyt acknowledged the applicability of Burgess's model to the previous development of cities, his observation of the changes introduced by the automobile led him to conclude that the pattern sketched by Burgess was no longer adequate, descriptively or conceptually (Hoyt, 1939).

Unique topography, such as the existence of a river or hills, shaped the pattern of industrial land use so that it rarely conformed to the theoretical shape of a circle. Because most workingmen lived near their places of employment, the absence of any fixed pattern of industrial land use precluded the development of any similarly fixed pattern of workingmen's residential areas. Hoyt's research was concerned primarily with middle- or upper-class residential areas, and he concluded that high-rent districts tend to progress toward and ultimately occupy high ground; to spread along waterways not used for industrial purposes; to move toward open land on the edges of the city; to follow the same general direction as new office buildings, banks, and stores; to develop along the lines of fastest transportation; and, once started, to continue in the same direction over a long period of time, influenced but slightly by real-estate promoters and their activities. However, he saw the distribution of higher-income commuter areas as often remaining more or less in keeping with the concentric circle model, which was developed as an ideal type rather than as a description of the growth pattern of any particular city.

Since the 1920s, in accordance with the pattern postulated by Burgess, the richest people have tended to move further out into the suburbs, but the upper-middle and lower-middle classes have occupied identifiable bands at distances from the center of the city that are in proportion to their income. The centrifugal distribution of these groups is illustrated by the fact that in 1890 the new housing construction for the middle and the upper classes lay between two-and-a-half and three-and-a-half and between three-and-a-half and ten miles, respectively, from the center of the city; but by 1900, new construction for these two classes had moved to bands that were three-and-a-half to six, and five to fifteen miles, respectively, from the city center. The rapidly increasing use of the automobile after World War I intensified this movement, filling the areas between railway and street-car lines with roads and, at times, replacing the older transportation forms. Los Angeles, which has experienced its greatest growth during the age of the automobile, exemplifies the ecological patterns of a city built for motorists.

Modern shopping centers, in sharp contrast to the commercial districts of the central city, are accessible only by car and are consequently forced into the relatively open areas on the city's periphery in order to provide the needed parking space. These shopping centers in turn attract home builders and home buyers and therefore contribute to the urban sprawl within which the majority of Americans now live.

Multiple-Nuclei Model

Chauncey Harris and Edward L. Ullman (1951), although acknowledging the insights of both Burgess' and Hoyt's models of urban ecology, suggested that a modern industrial city is characterized by a number of spatially separate nuclei around which differentiated activities grow.

Four factors affect the rise of these differentiated districts, which are shown in Figure 25.5. First, certain activities require special facilities. Most retail districts are located at the point of maximum accessibility to intracity transportation, but manufacturing districts require large blocks of land together with adequate water or rail con-

nections. Second, similar activities congregate because they profit from proximity. For example, retail establishments cluster together because they all benefit from the increased customer traffic made possible by such clustering, and financial and office districts benefit from the ease of intercommunication made possible by physical proximity. Third, certain dissimilar districts are inherently antagonistic to each other, such as a factory area close to a high-rent residential district. Finally, certain people whose activities might benefit from a particular location may be unable to afford the rent for the most advantageous sites.

It is true that certain districts—wholesale and light manufacturing areas, heavy industrial areas, residential districts, retail shopping centers, and areas of cultural and educational activity—can be observed in all large cities, as Harris and Ullman's model suggests; however, the multiple-nuclei model is less a theory than a post-factum description and attempt at explanation. Its value in predicting patterns of urban growth has proved to be virtually nil.

All of the foregoing models suffer from the underlying assumption that land-use patterns are rational and that they represent attempts to maximize economic return. The profit motive, however, is not always the most important force in urban dynamics. For more comprehensive theories of urban growth, one must turn again to the influence of cultural attachments, the role of local political institutions, and the life cycle of urban populations. Clearly this area of ecology is open to competing theories, but it is equally clear that no simple theory will ever account for the overwhelming complexity of even one city's human ecology. It is for this reason that contemporary ecologists often limit their analysis to discrete subunits, such as local communities in cities.

Natural Areas

One of the most compelling concepts in urban ecology is that of the *natural area*, which was discussed earlier in the chapter. Park and Burgess (1925) say that a natural area "comes into existence without design, and performs a function, though the function, as in the case of the slum,

Figure 25.7 (*Bottom*) Invasion and succession take place as one group moves into and comes to dominate a city neighborhood formerly occupied by another. Two contrasting patterns have occurred in large industrial cities in the United States. In one pattern, immigrant groups have moved into industrial city centers to replace other immigrant groups who have moved out as their members became upwardly mobile. In some city

areas, however, such as New York's Greenwich Village, poor artists and others have moved into areas formerly occupied by the immigrant poor to form bohemian communities. The chart below indicates the parentage of the white residents of Greenwich Village, compared with those of Manhattan and New York City as a whole, in 1910, 1920, and 1930. (Adapted from C. Ware, 1935.)

may be contrary to anybody's desire. It is a natural area because it has a natural history." Here Park and Burgess were thinking about the great diversity of communities to be found in large cities; these natural-area communities include the bohemian quarters of artists and writers, the segregated ghetto communities, and the fancy districts of the rich and powerful. One of the important features of such natural areas is that they develop their own cultural systems; in Park's view each "has its own standards, its own conception of what is proper, decent, and worthy of respect."

Bohemian Communities The bohemian community is an example of a natural area that has exerted profound influence over the development of American culture during this century.

The Haight-Ashbury district of San Francisco nurtured ideas and life styles that have influenced the thinking of a generation of Americans. But the Haight-Ashbury district was born with the counterculture of the late 1960s. As a community, it could not withstand the commercialization of its culture, and by the early 1970s it was no longer the ecological base of the life style it nurtured.

Other bohemian communities, often those that adjoin great urban universities, have sustained avant-garde movements for centuries. The Latin Quarter in Paris is an example of an urban district that has supported revolutions in morality and politics ever since the Middle Ages. The strikes and riots that helped depose the French government in 1968 were only the most recent of revolutionary movements that the district has fostered. In other periods, such as that between the World Wars, the Latin Quarter was a base for such artists as Braque, Picasso, James Joyce, and Richard Wright, who made their revolutions in the arts rather than in politics.

New York's Greenwich Village is another example of a bohemian community within the city. In her study of this community in 1920 and 1930, Caroline Ware describes how the ecology of that section of Manhattan Island made it possible for a bohemian community to flourish there (Ware, 1935). Originally a zone of first settlement for Irish and Italian immigrants, Greenwich Village

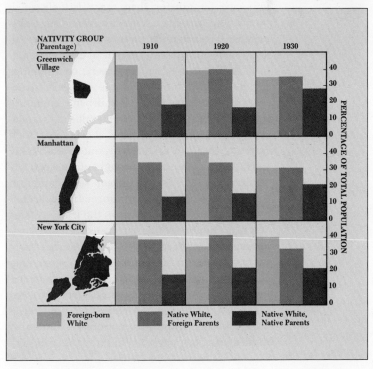

in 1920 began to lose its ethnic population as the American-born children of the immigrants moved to other sections of the city (see Figure 25.7). Their leaving made it possible for artists and intellectuals with limited incomes to move into the newly vacated tenements of the Village. Ware (1935) notes that once this new population group had become somewhat established in the community, "the Village acted as a magnet which drew to it a wide variety of people with one quality in common, their repudiation of the social standards of the communities in which they had been reared." The importance of Greenwich Village in the vast New York metropolitan area cannot be exaggerated. Since the 1920s this relatively small community has served as the cultural base and training ground for the most restless and creative youths in each generation.

Segregated Communities Studies of communities within the metropolis often elaborate the theme that settlements within the city develop their own cultures. These cultures may have influence beyond the borders of the urban place itself, influence far greater than the relatively small populations of such communities would suggest is possible. The bohemian culture of Greenwich Village is only one example of such an urban community. Segregated ethnic and racial communities also develop their own cultures and social structures. Although the segregated urban community may be a denial of the American ethic of assimilation, ecological studies have shown that such "ghetto" communities are a frequent and highly persistent phenomenon throughout the world.

Ecological studies of urban segregation in America most often rely on information collected by the Census Bureau. Cities in the United States and Canada are divided into *census tracts*, small geographical units for which the appropriate census bureau lists basic information on population composition, labor-force characteristics, and housing conditions. The average census tract has about four thousand residents. Census-tract boundaries are established with the intention of maintaining them over a long period of time, so that compari-

sons may be made from census to census. There are now 180 census areas in the United States. Thus census-tract data are available for most cities with populations of fifty thousand or more and the areas surrounding those cities. The census tract is an extremely powerful tool because it allows ecologists to measure changes in the population composition of very small urban areas. Such information can be used to study the dynamics of urban settlement as well as a host of urban problems ranging from juvenile delinquency to the segregation of ethnic and racial minorities.

Ecologists such as Otis D. Duncan, Stanley Lieberson, and Karl and Alma Taeuber have used census-tract data to study patterns of residential segregation in American cities. Their studies compare patterns of segregation across a wide range of cities, and they also measure changes in ethnic and racial segregation over time. Such comparisons are made possible through the use of the *segregation index*—a statistical measure of urban segregation that is calculated from census-tract data. For example, a Negro-white segregation index of zero for a given city means that the residential distribution of Negroes and whites is even throughout that city; conversely, if each city block contains only whites or only Negroes, the value of the segregation index for that city is 100.

The figures listed in Figure 25.9 show the indexes of Negro-white residential segregation in a selection of cities in the United States (Taeuber and Taeuber, 1965). Taking Chicago as an example, the figure shows that in 1960 that city had a segregation index of 92.6. This means that 92.6 percent of Chicago's black population would have to redistribute itself throughout the city in order to achieve complete racial integration, or a zero segregation index. The figure also shows that Chicago's racial segregation declined by almost three percentage points from 1940 to 1950 but that segregation in that city increased between 1950 and 1960. Negro-white segregation indexes calculated by the Taeubers show that American cities are highly segregated indeed and that the patterns of change seen for Chicago were common in many other major cities during the same

Figure 25.8   Residential segregation in twenty
American cities. Southern cities have been no more
racially segregated than Northern cities; the idea of
a segregated South as opposed to an integrated North
is not borne out by the facts. But since 1940 the
South has become more segregated while the North
has become increasingly integrated.
(Adapted from K. Taeuber and A. Taeuber, 1965.)

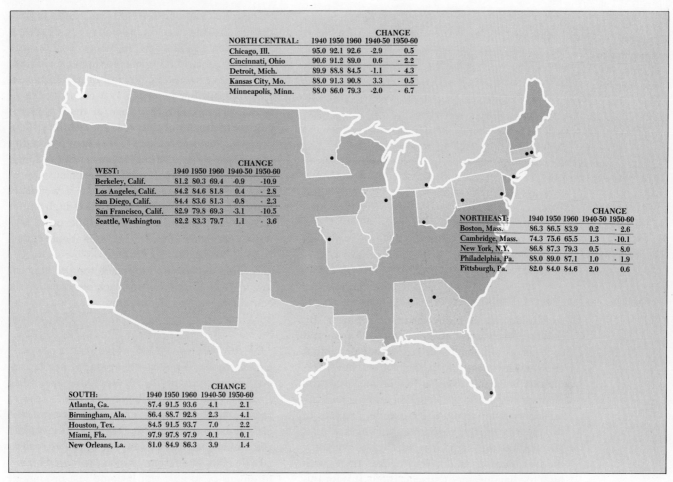

NORTH CENTRAL:	1940	1950	1960	CHANGE 1940-50	1950-60
Chicago, Ill.	95.0	92.1	92.6	-2.9	0.5
Cincinnati, Ohio	90.6	91.2	89.0	0.6	- 2.2
Detroit, Mich.	89.9	88.8	84.5	-1.1	- 4.3
Kansas City, Mo.	88.0	91.3	90.8	3.3	- 0.5
Minneapolis, Minn.	88.0	86.0	79.3	-2.0	- 6.7

WEST:	1940	1950	1960	CHANGE 1940-50	1950-60
Berkeley, Calif.	81.2	80.3	69.4	-0.9	-10.9
Los Angeles, Calif.	84.2	84.6	81.8	0.4	- 2.8
San Diego, Calif.	84.4	83.6	81.3	-0.8	- 2.3
San Francisco, Calif.	82.9	79.8	69.3	-3.1	-10.5
Seattle, Washington	82.2	83.3	79.7	1.1	- 3.6

NORTHEAST:	1940	1950	1960	CHANGE 1940-50	1950-60
Boston, Mass.	86.3	86.5	83.9	0.2	- 2.6
Cambridge, Mass.	74.3	75.6	65.5	1.3	-10.1
New York, N.Y.	86.8	87.3	79.3	0.5	- 8.0
Philadelphia, Pa.	88.0	89.0	87.1	1.0	- 1.9
Pittsburgh, Pa.	82.0	84.0	84.6	2.0	0.6

SOUTH:	1940	1950	1960	CHANGE 1940-50	1950-60
Atlanta, Ga.	87.4	91.5	93.6	4.1	2.1
Birmingham, Ala.	86.4	88.7	92.8	2.3	4.1
Houston, Tex.	84.5	91.5	93.7	7.0	2.2
Miami, Fla.	97.9	97.8	97.9	-0.1	0.1
New Orleans, La.	81.0	84.9	86.3	3.9	1.4

period. The 1970 census will include more data
on contemporary trends, but the analysis has not
been completed as of this writing.

Indexes of segregation also can be used to compare changes in segregation patterns among various groups in a given city. When the Taeubers
(1965) compared the segregation of whites,
Negroes, and other races for San Francisco during
the period of 1940 to 1960, they found that "the
other races were dispersing residentially, becoming less segregated from whites, and, in the process, more segregated from Negroes." This trend
was even more marked in the case of persons with
Spanish surnames, as research indicated. In general, the Taeubers' research confirmed an earlier
ecological study by Stanley Lieberson (1963),
which had found that "in terms of sheer magni-
tude, the Negroes are far more highly segregated
than are the immigrant groups."

Of course, most adult Americans know from
their own experience that they live in a racially
segregated society. The importance of these ecological studies is that they provide information on
how much segregation there is, where it occurs,
and which changes are actually taking place in
urban residential segregation.

Ecological Correlations

The separation of urban areas into distinctive
natural areas, zones, and subcommunities has provided sociologists with data that have often been
helpful in developing insights, hypotheses, and

Figure 25.9   Changes in segregation indexes for whites, blacks, and other races in San Francisco, from 1940 to 1960. In 1940, there were 603,000 whites, 5,000 blacks, 18,000 Chinese, 5,000 Japanese, and 3,000 Filipinos in San Francisco. The number of whites remained fairly constant over the twenty-year period, but by 1960 the number of blacks had increased to 74,000, and the numbers of Chinese, Japanese, and Filipinos had increased to 36,000, 9,000, and 12,000, respectively. The decline in residential segregation between whites and nonwhites has occurred mainly between whites and races other than black. And segregation of any minority group from blacks is almost always greater than that group's segregation from other minority groups.

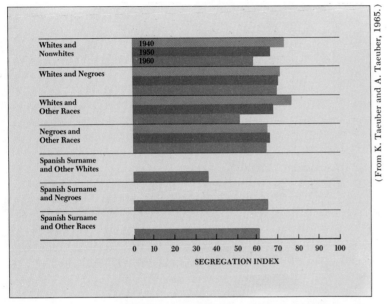

(From K. Taeuber and A. Taeuber, 1965.)

lation to suicide. Because the suicide rates for any population are quite low, a small group can make a great deal of difference in rates.

These remarks also point to the fallacy of *ecological determinism*. Ecological determinism entails interpreting behavior as a consequence of spatial properties rather than of the social and cultural character of the area. For example, some urban ecological areas have been found to retain high crime rates over half a decade, even though a succession of ethnic, racial, and religious groups have moved into and out of them. It would be fallacious to consider the continued high crime rates as evidence of the peculiar properties of that ecological space. Rather, the rates should be attributed to the districts' qualities as low-rent areas and zones of transition in which the problems of low income, migration, and lack of education all contribute to high crime rates.

THE SHAPE OF THE FUTURE

Unless there are radical changes in American social values and attitudes, it can be expected that spatial segregation in urban areas on the basis of race, ethnic origin, religious affiliation, and social-class status will change slowly, if at all, over the remaining years of this century. If poverty can in fact be eliminated, segregated areas based on differentials of wealth will become less prominent without ever disappearing entirely. The fear that the elimination of such segregated ecological areas will lead to cities that are dull, uninteresting, flat, and culturally homogeneous is probably baseless. Although "consciousness of kind" will still be reflected in and through ecologically distinct areas, more objective criteria, such as vocational and avocational interests, age, and personal compatibility, may replace the older irrational criteria as the formative bases for such areas.

If social attitudes change, involuntary ghettos may be eliminated. New modes of mass transportation may provide the urban dweller of the future with a flexibility and a convenience unknown today and may significantly shape the land-use patterns of tomorrow. The ability to predict fu-

conclusions about many forms of behavior. By finding correlations between ecological areas and such forms of behavior as crime, suicide, voting choices, and race riots, sociologists have frequently been able to draw conclusions about the characteristics of populations in an area and the behavior under study. For example, analyses of urban crime rates have often discovered that crime rates are high in census tracts with low median incomes and low in census tracts with high median incomes (Hirschi, 1969). It is for this reason that there is said to be a high correlation between low income and high crime rates.

Although this method generally has been useful, it carries with it a danger. The measure of a population is one of central tendency, but the behavior under study might largely be due to contrasting or marginal elements in the population. For example, the association of high suicide rates with areas of newly arrived immigrants may mask the contribution of select and nonimmigrant groups to the high suicide rates. Also, areas of recent immigration are likely to be ones of low rent and of diminished social and legal controls over nonimmigrants. As a result, these areas may attract the elderly poor, the unattached, and other persons more prone than the general popu-

ture ecological patterns rests, however, upon the ability to control the direction of social change in urban areas and in the society at large. Governmental action will also help to determine the shape of tomorrow's urban community. Whether that action will be directed toward making the presently overcrowded and unpleasant inner cities more livable, toward the development of new dispersed communities on the model of the English New Towns, or toward some other, as yet unforeseen alternative are questions that must be answered soon if we are to be able to plan the land uses of the future. American society can no longer afford unplanned urban development.

SUGGESTED READINGS

Bloch, Marc. *Feudal Society.* L. A. Manyon (tr.). Chicago: University of Chicago Press, 1964, VI.

Firth, Raymond. *We, The Tikopia: A Sociological Study of Kinship in Primitive Polynesia.* 2nd ed. London: Allen & Unwin, 1961.

Lieberson, Stanley. *Ethnic Patterns in American Cities.* New York: Free Press, 1963.

Taeuber, Karl, and Alma Taeuber. *Negroes in Cities.* Chicago: Aldine, 1965.

Turner, Ralph (ed.). *Robert E. Park on Social Control and Collective Behavior.* Chicago: University of Chicago Press, 1967.

Ware, Caroline. *Greenwich Village 1920–1930.* New York: Harper, 1935.

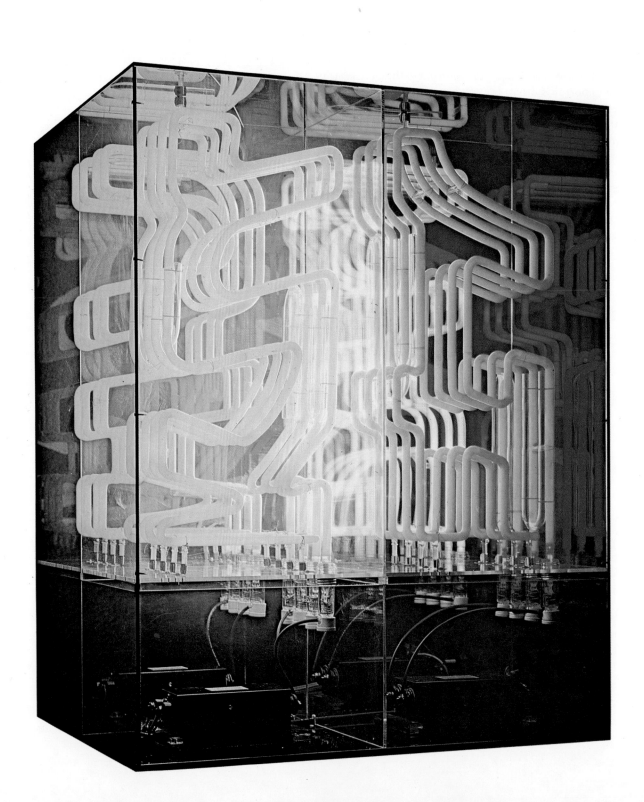

Previous units examined the constituent parts of societies. Throughout these discussions it was obvious that societies are not static. Instead, they are constantly undergoing changes. Sometimes these changes are extremely slow, and the passing generations can hardly detect them. Sometimes changes occur rapidly, even abruptly. ¶ To conclude this introduction to sociology, we now take up the question of social change. In so doing, we must also take up the question of social stability.. How are societies held together? To what extent do the forces that hold societies together facilitate or resist change? Why do societies change? How do they change? Chapter 26 discusses these questions. ¶ Clearly, a major threat to social stability and a major source of social change are sudden, relatively spontaneous outbursts of joint activity on the part of a significant number of persons—such incidents include panics, crazes, riots, protest movements, rebellions, and revolutions. Sociologists analyze these phenomena as instances of collective behavior. Chapter 27 discusses the characteristics, forms, and sources of collective behavior. ¶ The most enduring and socially significant forms of collective behavior are social movements. These movements are characterized by relatively organized group activity, and their goal is to change some basic aspect or aspects of society: the civil-rights movement, the

UNIT VIII STABILITY AND CHANGE

peace movement, and the John Birch Society are examples of contemporary American social movements. The first half of Chapter 28 outlines what sociologists know about social movements; the second half offers a thorough analysis of the contemporary Women's Liberation Movement. ¶ The major form of social change throughout the world is modernization. The problems faced by developing nations, their prospects for becoming modernized, and the tensions between developed and developing nations are discussed in Chapter 29.

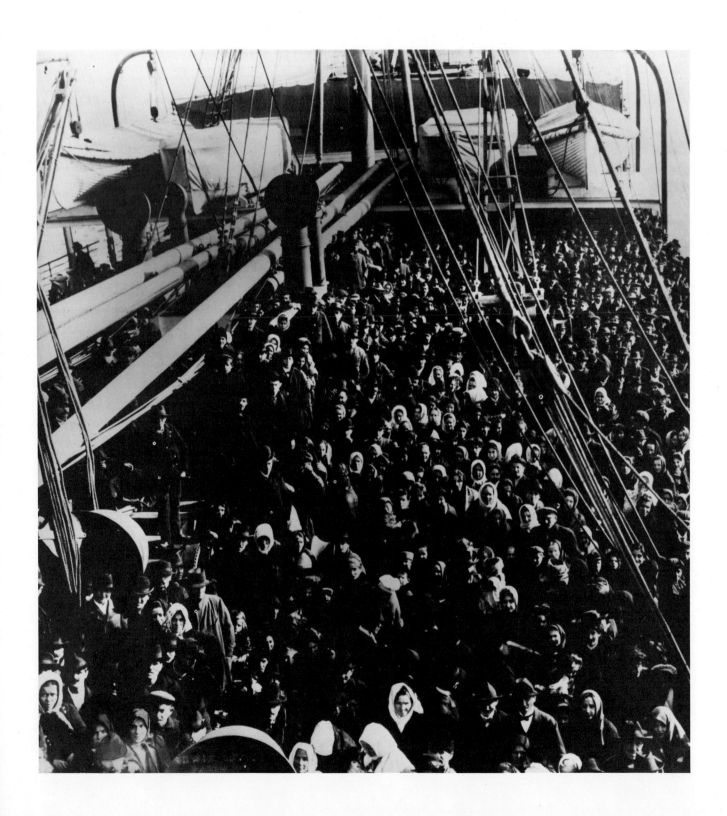

Chapter 26 Social Integration and Social Change

THIS CHAPTER ELABORATES and amends the old cliché that everything changes but remains the same. To ask how societies maintain their continuity is also to ask how they fail to do so. To ask how they hold together is also to ask how they fall apart. To ask how societies resist change is also to ask how they change. The first half of the chapter is devoted to analyzing how societies maintain their social integration in the face of internal and external pressures. The second half of the chapter takes up how and why societies change.

THE STUDY OF SOCIAL INTEGRATION

The word "society" was defined earlier as a high-level abstraction symbolizing countless millions of patterned, normatively oriented interactions among individuals (often playing highly specialized roles) and groups. How are all these discrete interactions organized and coordinated to give a social structure coherent form or integration? Or, why is it that some societies fail to attain a reasonable degree of integration and are thus plagued by chronic and often widespread instability and conflict?

Integration can be explored at any level of a society, from that of the society as a whole down through the set of roles occupied by a given individual. We require two points of reference to adequately assess the integration of any system, whether that system is a group, an institution, or the whole society. We must ask both how well a particular system's own constituent parts are adapted to one another (*internal integration*) and how well that particular system is accommodated to other similar systems or to the larger social system (*external integration*). These two viewpoints are necessary because a high degree of one type of integration may be and often is accompanied by a low degree of the other. For example, a religious sect or denomination may be tightly integrated internally and at the same time very poorly integrated with the external society—as were the Mormons in America during the nineteenth century. Similarly, although a group may serve important integrating functions for its own members, conflicts between it and competing groups may be malintegrative for the whole society (Coser, 1956).

Society is a *system* of action (see the functionalist account of systems in Chapter 4) and not a random collection of unrelated behaviors; therefore, social change, social integration, and social malintegration are both causes and effects of each other. A change in one part of the system, for example, may enhance integration in that part but cause malintegration in another part or at another level. Such malintegration may generate pressures for further change, which may, in turn, have both integrative and malintegrative consequences. It is important to understand that integration is a continuing *process*, not a state.

Social systems at the same level—whether they are all cultures, total societies, institutions, collectivities, roles, or personalities—do not necessarily have the same degree of internal or external integration. Our primary concern in this chapter will be with integration on the institutional or normative level of the society because the lack of integration among institutions is a leading cause of change within a social system. An examination of institutions will typically reveal different degrees of integration, which means that strains and pressures for change are unequally distributed throughout the social structure and concentrated at certain stress points. Also, because there is probably no *essential* difference between the internal processes that engender change and those that maintain stability in a social system, a discussion of the way institutions are integrated—or malintegrated—both internally and externally is critical both to an understanding of social change and to an understanding of social stability.

One might object to discussion on the institutional level by saying that it is far too abstract. One might assert—with some justification—that abstract cultural and institutional norms tell us little about the actual integration of a system, which is inevitably mediated through the personalities of individuals. Individuals are, after all, the irreducible units of any social structure. However, it is precisely because norms and roles do influence

Figure 26.1   According to functionalist theory, the
normal state of a social system is equilibrium, in
which social institutions are well integrated. If changes
(either internally or externally caused) occur, a
disequilibrium results. The system then achieves a
reintegration at a different level and regains
equilibrium. The social processes of integration,
malintegration, and reintegration can be likened to a
chemical process. For example, the inorganic substance
ammonium cyanate is in a state of equilibrium until
heat, in the form of a flame, is applied. The flame acts
as a catalyst that brings about the malintegration of
this substance. The end result of the process set into
motion by the application of heat is a molecular
reintegration into another form—urea, an organic
substance found in all living things.

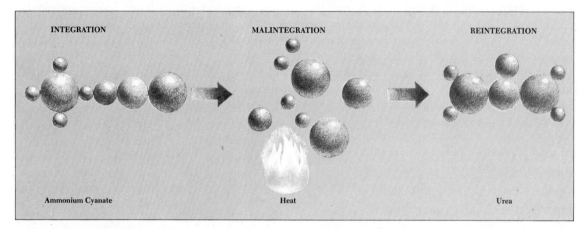

INTEGRATION   MALINTEGRATION   REINTEGRATION

Ammonium Cyanate   Heat   Urea

behavior—in some cases strongly—that social integration can sensibly be discussed at the abstract level of social structure. Sociologists do not lose sight of the fact that social action is always human action, affected by the needs, goals, and predispositions of individuals, and if relatively little is said about personality factors here, it is because sociologists' primary interest lies in the larger social system. As the next chapter makes clear, changes in the consciousness of individuals and groups may be important sources of social change and always underlie such changes. In the words of W. I. Thomas, "If men define situations as real they are real in their consequences." This chapter's discussion of integration and change, however, deals primarily with the larger social system.

SOURCES OF INTEGRATION

If we lived in the best of all possible societies, we would not find inconsistencies among the normative demands made upon us and would therefore accept them all. But no such perfectly integrated society has ever existed. Especially in complex societies, there are inconsistencies at every level of the social structure—among the varying injunctions of values and norms and the diverse demands of collectivities and roles. In addition, there has never been a society in which all individuals or even all major groups accepted the existing social order as completely legitimate.

However, some societies are more highly inte-

grated than others and are therefore more stable than others, at least temporarily. Any society that remains a going concern over a reasonable length of time must, by definition, have attained at least a minimal integration, or it would, also by definition, have collapsed. Sociologists have identified a variety of factors that promote the dynamic integration of a social system. The factors discussed in what follows constitute most of the major sources of societal integration.

Belief in Legitimacy

Always internalized in the personalities of individuals is the belief that the system is "good," that it is "my" or "our" system, that its existence is morally justified, and that its commands and decisions "ought" to be loyally obeyed, even when they run counter to the short-run interests of particular individuals or groups. People have different bases for believing in the legitimacy of a system (Weber, 1947). Whatever the basis of belief, it signifies a moral consensus regarding the "right" of a government to rule and to make binding decisions for and on behalf of the entire political community. Legitimacy may be accorded in varying degrees to the political community as a whole (the nation), to the community's political institutions, or to the political regime of the moment (the current administration). William A. Gamson (1968b) calls the according of such legitimacy "trust." In democratic societies, a higher degree of legitimacy is typically given to

Figure 26.2 An important mainstay of social integration is the belief held by the members of a social institution in its legitimacy. For example, the Pope (*top*) is the final source of authority for the Catholic Church and is accorded a high degree of legitimacy by members of this church. However, the legitimacy of a religious institution can also be challenged by its members, as the newspaper article (*below*) reports. The "feminist theses" demand a recognition of the roles women play and an end to sexist practices in Christian churches.

Clerics' Wives to Nail 'Feminist Theses' to Door

PASADENA, Calif., Oct. 25 (UPI) — Just as Martin Luther nailed his historic 95 theses to a church door in Germany, so a group of militant women plan to nail or tape a list of "feminist theses" to church doors this Sunday.

A group of four women, all ministers' wives, nailed the theses yesterday to the entrance of the Southern California headquarters of the United Church of Christ.

Among other things, they challenge the tradition of referring to God as "Him" and the restrictions in most denominations against women being ordained ministers. The United Church of Christ does ordain women.

Human beings were created in the image of God — male and female — and so "it is heresy to refer to God exclusively in the male gender," argued one of the theses.

The theses are the work of the Women's Task Force of the United Church of Christ, but they are addressed to all Christian churches.

They plan to nail or tape the theses to the doors of a dozen United Church of Christ churches in Southern California this Sunday, which is celebrated as Reformation Sunday. They are going to mail copies to other churches and church-connected women's groups across the country.

The 15-member force of women was created by the church's regional convention last year. The theses complained that churches "exploit women through volunteerism," treat women as "chattels" in traditional marriage services and that "without women in its official ministry, a church's leadership is stagnant at nearly every level."

the political community, political institutions, and ideology than to the regime currently in power. Elections, from this point of view, become devices by which an administration's legitimacy is periodically tested; if it is deemed insufficiently legitimate or trustworthy, it will be replaced by another one.

Legitimacy, then, is not permanently accorded. Quite the contrary. Legitimacy is a highly volatile "commodity" that must constantly be renewed by the system (Nieburg, 1969).

A system's continued existence and vitality depend on the ability of its institutions and leaders to produce "outputs"—decisions and policies—that satisfy the needs and interests expressed by all the system's important social groups and to indicate to those groups that the system will respond with reasonable justice and speed to their legitimate demands (Easton, 1965). Such "outputs" are what the system exchanges for the diffuse loyalty and support, or legitimacy, that it demands from its members (Parsons, 1959).

Maintenance of a high degree of legitimacy is probably the single most effective and economical means of social integration because it almost automatically assures a high level of obedience to the decisions of authorities and it largely eliminates the need for the use of force. Yet the maintenance of high legitimacy depends, in the long run, on the performance of the system—its ability to fulfill the expectations and demands of its constituent groups. Poor or biased performance can erode a system's legitimacy, both in the minds of those groups whose demands are consistently ignored or slighted in the social bargaining process and in the view of those who take seriously such ideals of the system as equality and justice. Declining legitimacy, in turn, provides one of the strongest normative justifications for the use of violence by dissidents who demand structural change and reintegration (Gurr, 1970).

Success in Attaining Goals

A society needs the ability both to attain collective goals—including the goals of self-maintenance, national power, a favorable balance of payments, and cultural glory—and to provide the opportuni-

ties and resources for the attainment by individuals and groups of their goals. In both cases the goals must be weighed against the costs. To achieve a goal at exorbitant cost may seriously deplete the system's resources; a system with depleted resources undermines its own capacity to maintain itself and therefore jeopardizes its legitimacy. Whether a cost is deemed exorbitant will, of course, depend on the nature of the goal, the way it is presented to members of the society, and the degree of popular allegiance it commands; for example, a war that can be presented as "defensive" is likely to command greater support and elicit greater sacrifice than one presented as overtly "aggressive." Within the limits of reasonable cost, successful attainment of collective goals will almost surely enhance the system's legitimacy and the allegiance given it, as will its "adaptive capacity" to permit groups in the system to attain their pluralistic goals (Williams, 1970). In the words of Leon Trotsky (1934), "... even in the court of the severest critic, success is the highest praise."

Adherence to Cultural Values and Symbols

A regime often invokes adherence to abstract values and symbols in order to stifle opposition and dissent—to justify itself and its actions in a period when satisfaction with its performance and its perceived legitimacy is declining. At such a time, authorities may make attempts to restore stability and legitimacy by appealing to *cultural* values and symbols. Historically, appeals to religious values and symbols have most commonly been used to legitimize institutional arrangements and the actions of authorities—the divine right of kings, for example. Since the French Revolution, however, secular symbols, such as the nation or "the people," and ideologies, such as democracy, fascism, or communism, have increasingly been invoked for the same purposes. Recently, a number of students of religion and symbolism, including W. Lloyd Warner (1959), Will Herberg (1960), and Robert Bellah (1968), have pointed to the rise of a "civil religion" in the United States, which tends to justify the existing institutional structure and to resist changes in it by appealing to a presuma-

Figure 26.3   The legal system tends to favor the rich over the poor. Courtrooms are crowded with the disadvantaged, who are more likely than the wealthy to be arrested and booked and to go to court and be convicted (*left*). But although the system of justice in practice favors certain groups over others, the laws of the land are committed to upholding certain constitutional rights, such as the right of assembly (*right*).

bly monolithic and agreed upon "American way of life."

Appeals to overarching cultural values or to ideologies—sacred or secular—can have a unifying effect, however, only if there exists wide-spread agreement among the members of a society on the meaning and the legitimacy of the symbols and beliefs. Where this is not the case, where the loyalties of the populace are divided among two or more antithetical or competing systems of ultimate values, such appeals are actually likely to stimulate overt conflict, even to the point of violence. The religious wars between Catholics and Protestants that rent Europe during the sixteenth and seventeenth centuries are vivid examples of what happens when competing systems of ultimate values are appealed to. The struggle between the same religious groups in Northern Ireland (Ulster) is a recent example. The struggle in Ireland is particularly complicated because antithetical political symbols as well as religious ones are involved: Many, perhaps most, of the Catholics identify with "Ireland," and most of the Protestants give allegiance to "England." The situation in Ulster brings to life an abstract point made earlier: what may be integrative at one level or

for one collectivity in a social structure may be malintegrative or grossly disruptive at another level or for other groups.

In addition to values and symbols, goals may be used to rally society's members. Appealing to ultimate goals is a variant of justifying the means by the end, whether that end be "victory," "peace," "the Great Society," "equality," "*la gloire,*" or "perfect communism." Such appeals may be effective in the short run but cannot be used repeatedly in the face of lost credibility from consistently poor system performance, like that of Soviet agriculture since 1928 or American promises of victory in Vietnam.

Adherence to the Normative Order

In advanced industrial societies the social structure is integrated in part through the society's official normative order, which consists of the legal system and those agencies responsible for creating, modifying, interpreting, and enforcing law. Informal traditional devices are rarely able to deal adequately with the disputes and conflicts that proliferate in complex, rapidly evolving social systems. In such systems, formal law has become the primary, but not the only, means for

Figure 26.4   In the spring of 1942, during World
War II, 110,000 Japanese-Americans, under Executive
Order 9066, were "relocated" into concentration
camps like the Manzanar Relocation Camp (*top*).
The relocation (*bottom*) was ostensibly carried out
to protect the "internal security" of the United States
but is today regarded by many as a result of
wartime hysteria and racism.

reconciling the demands of competing groups and
distributing finite resources in response to a multitude of demands.

Law, however, is always the product of political processes. It is the outcome of direct or representative bargaining among a variety of social
groups or interests, which command varying resources and influence in the formal political
realm. For this reason, law is never impartial and
always unstable. Because the interests in the
political bargaining process are never evenly
matched, law always favors some group or groups
at others' expense (Nieburg, 1969; Easton, 1965).

Law represents a crystallization of the relationships among the effective social forces at a
particular moment in time, even though those relationships are in reality forever shifting. Social
change thus always runs ahead of its expression in
law—sometimes so far ahead as to threaten the
stability of the society. This is another way of saying that formal law is a conservative force, not
because of any inertia inherent in law itself, but
because existing law is always defended by those
groups whose interests it favors, groups that may
retain for a long time influence or power to block
changes that will hurt their interests.

If law is to be an effective means of social integration, it must match its demand for adherence
with responsiveness to shifts in the balance of social power. It must have mechanisms for including new groups in the political bargaining process.
Groups that have been weak or excluded must
believe that, as they gain in strength and organization, the official legal and political orders will be
responsive to their legitimate interests and demands. Where the normative order is unresponsive or where there is dogmatic insistence on adherence to "law and order," there is likely to be
disruption and even violent protest. In the late
1960s American blacks and university students,
for example, resorted to violence aimed at making
the normative order more responsive to their interests.

It is interesting to note that in the Soviet Union
and the United States, both advanced industrial
countries, "law and order" is an important public
issue. The protection of property and property

rights—in the United States "private property" and in the Soviet Union "the people's property" —is basic to their respective legal systems.

All societies, whether they call themselves democratic, authoritarian, or totalitarian, possess some recognized means to effectively change the system without recourse to violence. To what extent and how rapidly these mechanisms will be mobilized in response to nonviolent petitions and demands are questions that can only be answered through specific historical analysis. What does seem certain is that the legal system can be a powerful means of integration when it is readily and rapidly responsive to changes in the relative strengths of competing social interests, when it recognizes legitimate demands of minority groups, and when its operation is perceived as generally fair and just by all important interests in the society.

When the formal legal system (as well as other structures) remains unresponsive to important changes in the social balance of power or to considerations of social justice, a society can expect alienation among the excluded or disadvantaged groups. If such disaffection is intense, it can lead to a withdrawal of legitimacy or trust from the larger social system.

Quarantine or Insulation

Quarantine, as the label implies, is an attempt to neutralize malintegrative forces in the society by controlling the contact or communication among units of the larger society. Quarantine may be enforced literally by relocating or isolating population groups, as was done to 110,000 Americans of Japanese ancestry on the West Coast early in 1942 and to the Volga Germans in the Soviet Union somewhat earlier; it may also be enforced informally, as it is in many American urban ghettos. It may be carried out more subtly by refusing to publicize information about the grievances, the activities, or even the very existence of alienated social groups. An example of such a "conspiracy of silence" is the treatment, prior to the early 1960s, of what Michael Harrington has called "the invisible poor" in America (1962). As political leaders and theorists have always known intui-

tively, control of information is a critical element in the maintenance of social control and social integration.

If the grievances of a disaffected group are deeply felt and touch issues fundamental to its existence and integrity as a group, quarantine attempts are likely to provoke defensive violence, which may then be used by the authorities as an excuse for outright repression or even extermination, as was the case with the American Indians.

Quarantine is unlikely to be effective if alienation from the system is widespread, and it is always a costly strategy because it diverts the system's resources and at the same time deprives the society of potential resources in the lost allegiance, energy, and talents of alienated groups.

Invocation of Threats

A threat to a society's existence, whether from another society or from groups inside the society, has often been used to heighten integration (Coser, 1956). Since World War II, both the United States and the Soviet Union have used each other's system as a threat. The function served for the Soviet regime by the evil spirit of "capitalist imperialism" is no different, sociologically speaking, from the functions served for American authorities by the specter of "communist infiltration." Each calls the other evil to justify its own internal and foreign policies.

Whether such threats are "real" is irrelevant. What is important is that powerful groups in the society believe they are and act accordingly. Reference to the threat can be used to rally support for the policies of the regime and to stifle dissent by identifying dissenters with the enemy. This technique was used repeatedly by J. Edgar Hoover and the FBI, who ascribed every significant movement of dissent in the United States after the end of World War II to the work of Communist Party members or *agents provocateurs* (Stark, 1972b).

Where genuine internal threats to the social order exist, they usually if not always are rooted in the demands of previously excluded or exploited groups for a greater share of social "goods," such as property, power, and prestige

—and opportunities to get them. Both the "black-power" movement and its complement of "white backlash" are vivid examples of reactions to perceived threats on the part of significant groups within American society.

Too great emphasis by authorities on the danger of internal threats to social order runs the serious risk of polarizing the society into hostile segments, making social integration by any means short of force difficult if not virtually impossible.

Invoking either external or internal threats as a means of increasing integration commits a society to the staggering costs of maintaining a huge military establishment, numerous paramilitary police, and intelligence and counterintelligence forces. Invoking threats also increases faith in the efficacy of force as a means of solving all problems within and between nations. In fact, the emphasis on threats—the threat of a breakdown of "law and order," for example—is often a way of avoiding or denying the need for radical structural change.

Force

Realist political theorists, including Kautilya in the fourth century (*The Artha Sāstra*) and Machiavelli in the sixteenth (*The Prince*), have always emphasized the importance of force and violence in maintaining a system of government. Liberal democratic political theorists, on the other hand, beginning with John Locke and Thomas Hobbes in the seventeenth century, have emphasized the role of consensus (the "social contract") in creating and maintaining social order and have tended to underrate the efficacy of force as a means of social integration (Pareto, 1935).

Over the short run, which may be a generation or longer, overt force or the threat of its use can be extremely effective, especially if it is occasionally and ruthlessly unleashed as violence (Parsons, 1964). Howard Polsky, in his study of delinquent boys, noted that "violence is a direct, uncomplicated, pervasive and economical form of social control" (1962). Force is even more costly than quarantine because it necessitates the maintenance of large armies and police forces. Systems that are established by force inevitably attempt to win legitimacy not only through their actions and

policies but through an ideology, or what Gaetano Mosca (1939) called a "political formula." In the long run, force as a means of social integration is probably unstable and ineffective not only because it costs a great deal but because its continued use convinces dissenters—whose numbers must be very great to require force in the first place—that only through counterforce and violence can they change the system. When no satisfactory alternatives exist, force logically and inexorably breeds counterforce, and violence breeds counterviolence.

Vested Interests

The factor of vested interests is related to several factors we have already discussed (legitimacy, for example). A society retains stability because certain groups and individuals who derive advantages from the status quo will defend the system against fundamental changes. In effect, vested-interest groups identify their personal advantages and their destinies with the continued existence of the system. The opposition to change expressed by such groups is often little more than a rationalization for maintaining intact a social structure and a distribution of power, property, and prestige that favors them over rising groups. When such vested interests are both numerous and powerful, their opposition to structural change will likely be strong and supported by a coherent ideology. Such groups are almost certain to support "their" regime should it decide—sometimes at their own urging—to resort to policies of quarantine or policies of force.

Vested interests that have become intense and rigid in their outlook may, by their rigidity, precipitate a revolutionary situation, as has often happened in the course of history, to wit, the Russian and French revolutions.

Social Inertia or Apathy

Half a century ago, in *Human Nature and Conduct*, John Dewey, following the lead of William James, wrote that "man is a creature of habit, not of reason nor yet of impulse." Dewey was probably closer to the truth than most ordinary people or even most social scientists care to admit. People all too easily become accustomed or resigned to social arrangements that seem intolerable to outsiders; they are often reluctant to exchange an unpalatable present for an indeterminate future. Such inertia or traditionalism—fundamentally a characteristic of individual personalities and only through them of social structure—is probably most pronounced in agrarian and other preindustrial societies, but its force in even the most highly industrialized systems cannot be discounted.

From another point of view, such inertia may be characterized as apathy, or a basic satisfaction with the way the system works. Pervasive apathy can hold back the political mobilization needed for radical or rapid social change (Berelson *et al.*, 1954). Overcoming this inertia seems to require some drastic shock or trauma to the existing social order and its members, like the shock that has historically come through defeat in war, contact with a stronger and more technologically advanced civilization, economic collapse, or the diffusion of new ideas, often religious in character (see Chapter 20). Continued poor performance by a society will not break through social inertia if nothing else exists to compare its performance with or if such performance has come to be accepted by members of the society as "in the nature of things." Under these conditions, maintaining the system's typical performance may be enough to win a high degree of legitimacy and thus of stability.

THE STUDY OF SOCIAL CHANGE

We have examined some features of societies that permit them to persist by overcoming internal conflicts and pressures that threaten to disrupt them. To some extent the sources of social integration are conservative; they tend to keep the society as it is. As such, they can be seen as those features of society that resist changes in the society's organization and operation. But that is only a partial picture. Integration and change, as we noted earlier, are not opposites.

The need for social integration can be a cause of social change, and change can serve to inte-

grate societies. For example, roles may be redefined in ways that reduce conflict between them. Institutions may be changed to reduce the grievances of some group or class. Norms may be changed to accommodate technological advances.

To conclude this chapter we take up social change. What is it? What are its sources? What models do sociologists use to describe social change? And what are the major features of change in contemporary society?

Social change is a relative concept. It does not denote a total and radical discontinuity between the structure of a society at two different points in time. Some characteristics of the social structure must remain the same for the structure to be considered the same entity—there must be some continuity. In studying social change in a particular culture or society, the sociologist is interested in defining precisely how the social structure has changed, in identifying why it has changed in those particular ways, and, if possible, in discerning what the final outcome of the changes may be.

Three distinctions are useful in the study of social change. The first distinction views social change as either *manifest* or *latent* (see Chapter 4). In any society, but especially in modern industrial societies, some social changes will be recognized by most of the society's members (manifest), and others will go largely or wholly unremarked (latent). Most people, for example, recognize the social changes that the mass media, especially television, have brought about. Another example of a manifest social change is the attainment, following World War II, of political independence by many colonial areas.

The sociologist, however, is often interested in those processes of change that are not apparent to most members of the society itself. Much of what sociologists contribute to the understanding of social change and of social systems generally comes from studying latent processes and making them manifest.

The second distinction is between *absolute* and *relative* change. In analyzing a social structure, the sociologist is interested not only in how various elements themselves change over time but also in how they change relative to other ele-

Figure 26.5   The median income of families headed by blacks or people of other races rose approximately 400 percent between 1947 and 1970. This absolute change in income is considerable, but the position of such families compared to that of families headed by whites has remained disadvantaged, as is shown by the continuing disparity between their median incomes. This distinction between absolute and relative changes is a central consideration in any evaluation of social change.
(From U.S. Bureau of the Census, 1971.)

MEDIAN INCOME OF FAMILIES
(By Race Of Head)

YEAR	White	Negro and Other Races	YEAR	White	Negro and Other Races
1947	$3,157	$1,614	1959	$5,643	$2,917
1948	3,310	1,768	1960	5,835	3,233
1949	3,232	1,650	1961	5,981	3,191
1950	3,445	1,869	1962	6,237	3,330
1951	3,859	2,032	1963	6,548	3,465
1952	4,114	2,338	1964	6,858	3,839
1953	4,392	2,461	1965	7,251	3,994
1954	4,339	2,410	1966	7,792	4,674
1955	4,605	2,549	1967	8,274	5,141
1956	4,993	2,628	1968	8,937	5,590
1957	5,116	2,764	1969	9,794	6,191
1958	5,300	2,711	1970	10,236	6,516

ments. In an absolute sense, black Americans have made great gains in average income and education during the past twenty years. However, these gains have not greatly decreased their disadvantaged position relative to whites. It is important to keep the distinction between absolute and relative changes constantly in mind because people's perception of social change is affected by whether they focus on absolute or relative dimensions.

A third dichotomy is between change that is *continuous* and change that is *abrupt*. Sociologists have often concerned themselves with the former, a good example of which is the industrial revolution, a label for a long series of changes in the technology and the organization of work, in the relationship between employers and workers, in the development of new market relationships, and in the increasing division and specialization of the work process itself. Such changes occurred over a long period of time—some of them are not complete even today—and their impact has been more or less continuous, expressed in long and often involved consequences. It is almost impossible to give an exact date to the industrial revolution. Growth in population and the process of structural differentiation are other examples of significant continuous changes.

By contrast, those abrupt political and social changes associated with revolutions can be exactly dated, even though their consequences may be as long in unfolding as those of less dramatic and more protracted processes. Often historians and sociologists attempt to discover the long-term changes that may have culminated in an abrupt event; at the same time, they realize that a sudden event, such as a military defeat or a natural disaster, may significantly change the structure and the direction of an entire society.

GENERAL SOURCES OF CHANGE

In discussing the sources of social change, it has been customary to distinguish between internal changes that arise from the workings of the given system itself and external changes that arise from forces impinging on the social system from one or another of its various environments. A purely mechanistic view of social life might suggest that once in operation, a society will continue unchanged, except as external forces compel such change. In point of fact, such a model is entirely inadequate. Because societies are only imperfectly integrated, they generate in the course of their own operation strains, dissatisfactions, and pressures, out of which changes develop regardless of the external forces acting on the society.

Internal Sources

Internally generated changes typically occur over fairly long periods of time and are usually continuous rather than abrupt. An example of this process can be seen in the political consequences of immigration. The arrival of millions of Europeans in the United States between the late 1880s and the outbreak of World War I meant that beginning shortly after the end of that war, both the foreign born and their children would become a major political force, especially in the large urban areas where most had settled. Some observers foresaw this development around the turn of the century, but it did not become obvious to the country at large until the presidential election of 1928. Today one can see the same process at work as more and more blacks move from the rural South into the large Northern and Western metropolitan centers, thus increasing their effective political influence, an increase further magnified by the flight of many middle-class whites into the suburbs.

One way of conceptualizing the sources of internal change is to see change in terms of action and reaction. The idea of this dialectical relationship has entered the mainstream of sociological thought through the work of Karl Marx, which is discussed at greater length in Chapters 4 and 15. The process, however, is by no means confined to class conflict; its general application suggests that elements of a social system, such as institutions, often generate conflicts in the course of their own operation that may produce new social realities. For example, Marx predicted that as economic concentration proceeded under capitalism, factory units and their work forces would become increasingly larger. He predicted that this change would facilitate the organization of the workers —of the very group that would eventually overthrow capitalism. Thus, the process of economic concentration would set in motion countervailing forces that would lead to an outcome quite different from that intended by those who initiated the process. The dialectical process can easily be observed in the American racial situation.

Another emphasis in the study of internal sources of structural change focuses on interdependence of all the elements of a social system. Because all elements of a social system are interrelated, change in any one part will produce strain and consequent pressures for change in many other parts. For example, the building of elaborate highway systems in and around major metropolitan areas—itself a response to the invention and mass production of the automobile—has, since the 1920s, greatly facilitated the process of suburbanization. As Chapter 24 points out, one result of suburbanization has been to remove large segments of the middle and upper socioeconomic groups from the central city, where their social and administrative skills are desperately needed. The building of highways can thus be seen as a cause of the urban crisis; however, it can

also be seen as a consequence of the acceptance of a technological innovation. As the discussion of manifest and latent functions in Chapter 4 makes clear, sometimes a change in one part of the society makes manifest a previously latent structure of interrelationships. It is the concern with such interrelationships that is a hallmark of the sociological analysis of change.

External Sources

External factors may be at least as important as internal ones in the genesis of social change. Some external sources of change are cultural diffusion, war, and natural events.

Cultural Diffusion Historically, cultural diffusion—the borrowing of the ideas, technologies, material artifacts, or behavior patterns of one culture by another—has been one of the major sources of change. Logically, the greater the contact one society has with others, the greater will be its exposure to and adoption of foreign cultural items. But diffusion never occurs wholesale or at random. It depends upon the needs of the receiving society, the tightness of its own integration, the way in which new cultural items are presented to it, and the way these items "fit" with strongly held values and habit patterns across the culture. The short hair styles of American women during the 1920s, for example, never took hold among the Indian women of Northwest California because in that culture short hair signified a widow in mourning for her dead husband. The Japanese, who venerate age, are unlikely to establish nursing homes and retirement communities on the American pattern. Thus, existing cultural meanings prevent the adoption of foreign cultural items that might otherwise be welcomed.

Sometimes diffusion is reciprocal, but often it moves from the politically more powerful cultures to the less powerful ones. The impact of American culture on Japan has been much greater than the reverse impact, although borrowing has proceeded in both directions. The Japanese language, for example, has taken over many American terms, especially in the areas of science and tech-

Figure 26.6   The diffusion of cultural artifacts has steadily increased, and the products of advanced industrial nations can be found in remote areas of the world. The effects of such diffusion on the cultural life of other peoples are often profound.

merce, tourism, conscious borrowing, and gradual spread through intermediaries have all, in various cultures and at various times, been important.

War   War has also been a major source of social change both because it usually necessitates internal changes in the structure of the participant societies and because it increases intercultural contact. When war results in conquest, the conquered nation may experience fundamental changes in its social structure. The American occupation of Japan following World War II, for example, produced substantial changes in Japanese political institutions and in some sectors of its economy. Some of these changes might not have occurred at all, and some would have taken a far longer time had Japan not been decisively defeated in war and occupied by a foreign power. On the other hand, war may so weaken a society as to pave the way for internal upheaval. The Russian experience in World War I, which helped open the way to the Bolshevik revolution, is an example of such a situation.

Natural Events   Finally, natural events such as climatic shifts, earthquakes, plagues, floods, famines, and other similar disasters may deeply affect the course of a society's life and its social structure. Karl A. Wittfogel (1957) has suggested that the social and political structures of a number of ancient empires were determined by the necessity to control floods and manage the society's water resources. Wittfogel's thesis remains controversial, however, and many commentators have rejected it. Precisely because natural disasters are unpredictable, they usually are not incorporated into systematic theories of social change.

EXPLANATIONS OF SOCIAL CHANGE

Speculation on the pattern and direction of social change can be found in the works of the very earliest philosophers in both the Occident and the Orient. From such philosophical speculation and from the more recent work of sociologists, a number of models of social change have emerged.

nology. Linguistic borrowing from Japanese into English is virtually nonexistent. The culture of a mother country has typically exercised decisive influence over that of her colonies, especially where the colonies have lacked strong, well-integrated cultural traditions of their own. The actual mechanisms of cultural diffusion are varied; migration, colonization, warfare and conquest, com-

Models

The oldest model, which finds expression in the works of the ancient Indian and Greek philosophers as well as in many modern works, is the model of the *cycle*. In its pure form the cyclical model assumes that a particular course of events is endlessly repeated, either exactly or approximately. The idea is succinctly embodied in a refrain from the Book of Ecclesiastes: "There is nothing new under the sun."

A second view, one that dominated the social thought of the nineteenth century, was the *evolutionary* model. In its nineteenth-century version, this view assumed that all societies passed through an invariant sequence of stages on their way to some final stage, which was usually identified (by Western European thinkers) with the contemporary societies of Western Europe. Although this unilinear model of social evolution has today been abandoned, the evolutionary idea itself remains in more sophisticated forms. It has reappeared in various theories of the stages of a society's economic development, especially that advanced by W. W. Rostow (1960). Rostow's theory posits five stages through which a traditional society moves on its way to a modern industrial economy: traditional society, the pre-take-off period, the take-off, the drive to maturity, and the age of high mass consumption. Chapter 29 discusses the stages at greater length.

Models incorporating an evolutionary viewpoint sometimes view the developmental stages as aspects of "progress," that is, as representing movement toward a "better" or "higher" stage or as advance toward some end point, such as a high standard of living for the society's members, political democracy, or national power and greatness. But, obviously, there is no guarantee that changes will be for the better. For example, it is perfectly possible that technical progress can result in political repression or even the destruction of life on earth.

Another highly influential model of social change, derived from Marx's work, is the *conflict* model. In its Marxist version, this model sees class conflict as the basic—indeed, the only—form through which significant social and political changes occur. Because any ruling group or class develops vested interests in continuing its own domination, only through violent class struggle can society move to a new form of social structure dominated by a different group or, in Marx's vision, ultimately by no group at all.

Each of these models of social change is related to one or another political orientation or ideology. A cyclical model of change implies both inevitability and a kind of fatalism that discourages or negates purposive social planning and action. The evolutionary conception was historically linked to nineteenth-century liberal democracy and the idea of progress, with its ultimate optimism that all social problems could be solved and the "good society" attained. At the same time, because evolution was deemed inevitable, active intervention in social processes was discouraged. The conflict model, precisely because it sees violence and conflict as the only way to effect change, supports an activist and often totalitarian political interpretation while retaining as much or even more optimism than the evolutionary view. Although few sociologists today adhere rigidly to any one of these models, the basic models form the background of most discussions of social change.

Long-term Changes and Types of Societies

The nature of long-term changes tells much about the basic character of modern industrial societies and suggests the problems that confront traditional societies on their path toward modernization. Transitions in Western societies have usually been conceptualized as the movements from one ideal type of social structure to another. (To view long-term trends this way is to select an evolutionary model of social change.) The change is always from intimate community to organizational complex. The ideal types envisioned by Ferdinand Tönnies (*Gemeinschaft* and *Gesellschaft*) are discussed in Chapter 8. Emile Durkheim's distinction between mechanical and organic solidarity is treated in Chapter 22. Tönnie's ideas were not new when he published them in 1887. Already in 1861, the British scholar Sir Henry Maine, in his book *Ancient Law*, had suggested that as societies evolved from the primitive to the modern, the force that held them together changed from "status," or traditional kinship-based bonds, to "contract," or bonds based upon explicit, mutually advantageous agreements.

This way of thinking in terms of polarities of ideal types of societies has been so influential that it reappears again and again in the social and sociological thought of the late nineteenth and twentieth centuries. It is encountered, for example, in Herbert Spencer's (1820–1903) dichotomy of the "simple homogeneity" and "complex heterogeneity" or "military" and "industrial" societies (1967); in Max Weber's more sophisticated distinction between traditional and rational-legal political orders (1947); and even in anthropologist Robert Redfield's "folk society" and "urban society" (1947). Redfield's typology, derived from his actual anthropological field experience, conceives of the folk society as a small, isolated, relatively self-sufficient social system characterized by a rudimentary division of labor. The urban society is, as always, the polar opposite: large, densely populated, in constant contact with other societies, and characterized by a complex, highly specialized division of labor. Redfield's model points to urbanization as a critical aspect of the process through which relationships among men change from those based on family and kinship to those based on impersonal contract.

All modern industrial societies, including the United States, continue to display some elements of status, traditionalism, or mechanical solidarity, but these elements are less important than those of contract, rationalization, and organic solidarity. The contrast between the ideal types is exemplified in the difference between the family or local neighborhood and the bureaucratically organized industrial corporation.

CONTEMPORARY CHANGE: PATTERNS AND VARIABLES

Most of the theories and models of social change that we have discussed are efforts to explain the historical experience of Western civilization since the Renaissance. Today rapid social change is a world-wide phenomenon, and one may well question whether theories derived solely from the Western experience are relevant either to non-Western societies or to Western societies in which social change is now the result of deliberation and planning. The question is discussed in other chapters in terms of such major processes now underway in the developing areas of the world as population growth, urbanization, and modernization (see Chapters 23, 24, and 29).

In this chapter the question will be explored in terms of the processes of modernization, Westernization, and especially industrialization. These three terms are often mistakenly used as synonyms for certain structural processes at work in many developing nations, but each implies different approaches and different outcomes for nations following the road that leads from traditionalism to modernity.

Modernization and Westernization

In studying modernization, one of the most useful concepts is *structural differentiation* (Smelser, 1963; Parsons, 1961). One way of defining modernization is by the degree to which various functions in a society become differentiated and come to be served by increasingly specialized institutions. Chapter 29 discusses the differentiation in modernizing societies of many functions that are separately treated in various chapters throughout the book; it discusses the way modernization affects work, the family, roles, the political order, stratification criteria, and other variables.

Modernization and Westernization—although often equated—are not necessarily the same processes. What distinguishes the two is precisely the forms that modernization may take. For example, in Western countries, large-scale social institutions such as trade unions may take on notably different patterns from the ones in non-Western nations. Yet in both areas the unions may be considered as one of the indexes of modernization. Differences between Japan and Western countries with respect to unions are a case in point.

Another distinction between modernization and Westernization may be made by examining the differences in the quality of life in societies that have predominant urban centers. Although Japan, like most Western societies, may be characterized as urban, life in Japanese cities tends to have the closed character of the village (Dore, 1958; Vogel, 1963). This quality may be regarded as an aspect of Japanese social structure that is still premodern, or it may be regarded as fully modern but non-Western. Similar distinctions between modernization and Westernization may be made by looking at the character of other institutions and structures in Western and non-Western societies that are indexes of modernization—for example, education, the mass media, and the applications of science and technology.

Industrialization

The term *industrialization* is more descriptive and emotionally more neutral than either modernization or Westernization. Industrialization, however, may be thought of as the single most critical aspect and source of modernization because it is central to the overall processes of specialization and differentiation. Although industrialization is based on technology and is itself principally an economic process, it is intimately related to political, legal, and other institutional processes. For example, industrialization creates a sharp separation between management and labor. As societies become increasingly industrialized, the functions of each of these groups become more and more differentiated.

Industrialism, at least in the world's experience so far, does not come to the preindustrial society in one fell swoop. However, once the process gets underway, it continues to advance, no matter what the cultural or national setting in which it is taking place. One can say that a society has become industrialized (in a statistical sense) when at least half its working population is engaged in production and service sectors of nonagricultural occupations. Although only a handful of all the nations of the world have achieved ma-

Figure 26.7   Modernization for many Third World countries has meant Westernization, as the Western dress of these Indian men suggests.

ture industrialization, it has become a national objective throughout the world.

Industrialization may well prove to be a process compatible with traditional agrarian, religious, and other cultural values, even though in the West it has, in fact, undermined these older values. India may well be a test case of the ability of large-scale industrialization to coexist with older agrarian traditions, although it has already become obvious in India that many of those traditions are under serious strain. Most students of modernization believe that the industrialization process itself will, sooner or later, force the abandonment of traditional structures and relationships. This belief that industrialism as such molds social structure and social action has given rise to the *convergence hypothesis.*

The convergence hypothesis states that as industrialization proceeds, the pattern of social structure will increasingly resemble the pattern of advanced industrial societies—regardless of the unique characteristics of the society in its preindustrial period—for industrialism carries its own special set of values and institutions (Kerr *et al.,* 1964). Industrialization rests upon the foundations of science and technology. And both science and its technological application demand a level of rationalization and intellectual sophistication far beyond any known in the preindustrial age.

The convergence hypothesis implies that technology, politics, economics, sociology, and psychology in the industrializing society take on a configuration that supports the continued spread of industrialization throughout the society and increases its complexity. For example, the hypothesis would lead us to expect relationships in industrial work to eventually take on the same characteristics, regardless of the setting and regardless of the pace and structure of industrialization along the way. Wherever industrialization takes place, the end results expected are (1) work specialization, for which scientific training and education are all important; (2) occupational professionalism; (3) complete flexibility and mobility of the labor force in its allocation to industrial processes; (4) a reward or compensation system geared to rational economic contributions; (5) increasing economic bargaining, on a collective basis, on the part of occupational or professional groups; (6) an all-pervasive ethic of the value of science and scientific innovation; (7) a diffusion of political power throughout the society; and (8) the release of the individual from personal or nonrational controls over his behavior both at work and outside work (see Chapter 22).

One way to characterize this evolution is to see it as the transformation of a society based on status relationships to one based on contract, or of particularistic to universalistic relationships. In terms of the classical theories of social change, what is suggested is the shift from *Gemeinschaft* to *Gesellschaft* (Tönnies, 1957) or, in Durkheim's terms, a shift from a society based upon mechanical solidarity to one based upon organic solidarity.

Technology, Invention, and Culture

The development of technology is not, in and of itself, a social change. According to the distinctions made in Chapter 3, technological innovation is a product of the cultural, not the social, system. Once embodied in social organization, however, technology has an immediate impact on social structure.

Some sociologists, especially William F. Ogburn (1922), have pointed to technological innovation as the most powerful single cause of social change since the industrial revolution. Ogburn made one of the only systematic attempts to measure the effects of technological innovation on social change. He believed that changes in culture rather than changes in the physical environment or in human biology explain most social change. Chief among these cultural factors are accumulation, adjustment, diffusion, and especially invention. He defined *invention* as either the combination of existing cultural elements, material or nonmaterial, into new wholes, or the modification of an existing element to form a new one. In his analysis, Ogburn did not confine the concept of invention to the mechanical and technical realms but included "social inventions," such as political forms, religious beliefs and rituals, or an alphabet. The existing stock of cultural elements (the cultural base) is importantly related to the rate of change: when the base is small, inventions tend to be few; when it is large, they tend to be many.

During the 1920s and 1930s, Ogburn and others studied the general social effects of technological innovation and concluded that the more advanced the level of technology, the faster the rate of social change (Ogburn and Gilfillan, 1938; Rosen and Rosen, 1931). When Ogburn investigated the effects of technological innovation on

Figure 26.8 Technology tends to develop more
rapidly than the social structure necessary to deal
with it. The proliferation of modern weaponry, the
technology of war, threatens the existence of life
on earth because social means capable of adequately
regulating or preventing the use of such weapons
do not yet exist.

institutions, especially those that developed in response to new technology, he found that the rate
of institutional change was always slower than
that of technological change; to describe this discrepancy, he coined the term *cultural lag*. Thus,
because technological change typically occurs
more rapidly than society can assimilate its im-

plications into its institutional structure, it places
the social system under strain, and, as we have
already seen, strain is one of the primary causes
of social change.

The accelerating pace of such change can perhaps best be illustrated by the following "time
map"—it scales down events in time as a map

scales down distances. Assume that civilized man's history extends back not ten thousand years but only fifty years. After living in a cave for about thirty-nine years and obtaining his food by hunting and fishing, man left the cave and began to build "houses" and to live in open-air settlements. About three years ago he succeeded in domesticating certain food plants and animals. About two years ago most of the great founded religions—Judaism, Christianity, Buddhism, Mohammedanism, and Confucianism—appeared; about fifteen months ago the printing press was developed; ten days ago electricity was discovered; yesterday morning the airplane was invented, last night radio, this morning television, and, since you began to read this paragraph, atomic energy. This model serves to illustrate the ever increasing rate of change that Ogburn's work suggested.

The effects of technology are felt both by the society as a whole and, differentially, by groups and individuals within it. The benefits and costs are always relative. In the space of two decades, for example, the automobile threw thousands of carriage makers and harness makers out of work, but in the end it created millions of new jobs. The relative benefits, however, do not deny the reality of technological unemployment or the hardship it works on those whose jobs and skills are suddenly rendered obsolete. There has always been opposition to technological innovation or at least to its social utilization—from the early nineteenth-century Luddite riots in the British textile industry to the current opposition of organized labor to widespread automation.

Technological change uproots otherwise stable populations and directly affects life styles and routines. The family, for example, alters with technological changes that open new employment to women, increase available leisure time, deny jobs to middle-aged or older workers and open them to youth, and radically alter the hours spent at work and in the home. The stratification system also may be radically changed by technological developments. With the substitution of machines for skills, status and prestige rankings

change. The machine repairman may now replace the skilled craftsman who formerly produced a finished product for the trade; the accelerated mechanization and automation of office work increasingly deflates the claims of white-collar workers to superior status. Technological development may increase or decrease the relative homogeneity of the working class, depending upon whether the development tends to equalize or differentiate jobs (Schneider, 1969).

Technology alone or even in combination with a base of natural resources does not guarantee that a society will successfully modernize. Cultural factors significantly influence the direction that any society will take. One problem for developing societies is how to institutionalize technological innovation in a traditional cultural and social structure. Often, policies or particular decisions that are rational in economic or technical terms are rejected because they conflict with deeply held values and sentiments. Some investigators have suggested that innovations are usually made by persons marginal to their society, persons who feel excluded or alienated from the existing social structure and who therefore reject many of the traditional values and norms. Successful modernization may therefore depend in part upon the appearance of socially marginal personalities, who, given appropriate opportunities, can initiate the technological and structural shifts that such modernization inevitably involves (Hoselitz, 1964). However, all such generalizations regarding the importance of marginality for innovation are by no means universal. Another view maintains that socialization patterns produce persons who have a powerful drive to achieve status through innovation and therefore may be termed "innovative personalities" (Hagen, 1962). In the West, after the spirit of capitalism had become institutionalized, economic innovation became a valued form of activity, and entrepreneurs carried high prestige.

In the developing world today, technological and economic innovation is usually encouraged and, at times, even introduced by the government with the support of at least some section of the traditional elite. To the extent that comparison with standards of living in the more advanced societies leads to a revolution of rising expectations in the less advanced ones (see Chapter 14), there will be a degree of dissatisfaction with the status quo and a relative readiness to accept innovation. From this perspective, the process of modernization becomes less a technological, economic, or even political problem and more a social-psychological problem.

This chapter has largely neglected social-psychological aspects of change; its primary orientation has been toward institutions. Still, members of a society not only react to change but, by means of collective behavior, can themselves constitute a major source of social change. Under the press of either internal strains or external threats, some members of society respond collectively, and the responses may range from crazes to riots to revolutionary movements. The following chapter assesses the nature, causes, and effects of collective behavior.

SUGGESTED READINGS

Allen, Francis R. *Socio-cultural Dynamics: An Introduction to Social Change.* New York: Macmillan, 1971.

Applebaum, Richard P. *Theories of Social Change.* Chicago: Markham, 1970.

Hagen, Everett E. *On the Theory of Social Change.* Homewood, Ill.: Dorsey Press, 1962.

Ogburn, William F. *Social Change.* New York: Viking, 1950.

Chapter 27 Collective Behavior

WHENEVER GREAT NUMBERS of people engage in similar behavior it is socially and historically significant. Thousands of slaves were made to work together in the construction of the Egyptian pyramids; millions of soldiers were arrayed against one another in World War II; some 80 million Americans go to the polls every fourth year to elect a president. But the motivations, goals, and limitations of such mass enterprises as these are known to their initiators and participants. This is not true of all collective behavior.

In fact, the most awe-inspiring and often most socially disruptive mass actions are spontaneous and unplanned, transient and unpredictable. Often during times of social stress and transformation spontaneous bursts of collective activity occur that energize and sweep in their path thousands or even millions of people without, at the beginning, the benefit of conscious planning or central direction.

Such spontaneous outbursts of collective action may center harmlessly on trivial objects, symbolic actions, or such vague goals as hair and clothing styles, musical forms, or modes of consciousness; they may be irrationally destructive, as were the witch hunts of the sixteenth and seventeenth centuries; or they may change the course of political and social history, as did the early Crusades in medieval Europe.

THE STUDY OF COLLECTIVE BEHAVIOR

Collective behavior refers to those similar actions of a multiplicity of individuals that are spontaneous and transitory and therefore in contrast to the routine, predictable interactions of everyday life. Thus defined, collective behavior encompasses a wide variety of phenomena, including fashions, fads, riots, revolutions, religious sects, and social movements of all sorts. The term also has been used to describe the ebb and flow of public opinion and the effects of propaganda, rumor, and mass communications. Collective behavior is therefore a comprehensive category that includes much more than the social movements described in the next chapter of this book. Although all social movements are examples of collective behavior, not all collective behavior exhibits the organization characteristic of social movements.

The Criteria

Historically, the most common criteria used to define collective behavior were psychological. Gustave Le Bon (1895) and Sigmund Freud (1921) both viewed crowd phenomena as examples of the effects of a type of primitive mentality that grips the participants. More recently, Roger Brown (1954), a social psychologist, has identified collective behavior in terms of how frequently collective attention is polarized and how permanently participants identify with a particular group. Other investigators have identified collective action as a function of a distinctive kind of communication or interaction, for example, "imitation" or "social contagion." Herbert Blumer (1951) uses these criteria to distinguish some types of collective behavior from other types. Neil J. Smelser (1962) views collective behavior as the attempt of people to reconstitute their social environment under conditions of uncertainty and strain. In episodes of collective behavior people try to structure their environment on the basis of what Smelser calls a *generalized belief*, a belief that will plausibly explain their situation and justify their collective behavior. Not all sociologists agree on the most salient identifying characteristics of collective behavior, but most would concur that such behavior shows spontaneity, transitoriness, and lack of institutionalization.

Three Questions

Approaching an analysis of an episode of collective behavior, the sociologist asks three broad questions: What are the causes of the collective behavior? What are the mechanisms and processes by which collective actions unfold? What are the consequences of such behavior?

Causes With respect to causes, the sociologist must first consider the social environment of the individuals involved and the kinds of strains, deprivations, and frustrations, such as unemployment

Figure 27.1   Chart of the different approaches
to the study of collective behavior discussed in the text.

	PSYCHOLOGICAL	SOCIAL
THEORIST(S)	Le Bon Freud and others	Marx and others
MAJOR VARIABLES OR MECHANISMS	Contagion Imitation Suggestion or Social facilitation Identification and psychological regression (Freud)	Economic deprivation Social disorganization Value conflict
TYPE OF COLLECTIVE BEHAVIOR	Crowd behavior	Class action
FOCUS OF INTEREST	The individual	Objective social conditions
PREDISPOSING FACTORS	Suggestibility of crowd	Social conditions: oppression of proletariat by bourgeoisie
PRECIPITATING FACTORS	Manipulation by leader	Aggravating incident
RESOLUTION	Dissipation of crowd	Revolution or further oppression
EXAMPLE	Lynch mob	The Paris revolt of 1968

and political repression, that are likely to predispose them to act. The sociologist would assess the absolute level of strain in terms of the expectations and standards of individuals, the opportunities for involvement in collective behavior, as well as the obstacles to involvement. If an individual, for example, is involved with family responsibilities and belongs to many different social groups, he may be less likely to engage in spontaneous collective behavior than an individual who is less firmly rooted in the social structure and has few family or group obligations.

Mechanisms and Processes   A sociologist's investigation of the mechanisms and processes of col-

lective behavior involves the way in which a large number of discrete, unorganized people arrive at shared definitions of situations through the spread of rumor, the creation of generalized beliefs, and the growth of ideologies. The impact of leaders (their qualities and actions) can be decisive for the growth of an incipient movement. What are the consequences, for example, when leaders with different characteristics and appeals begin to appear—for example, the mobilizer, the propagandist, the ideologist, the bureaucrat? Do these different types of leaders tend to come into conflict with one another, or are modes of cooperation worked out among them? What are the consequences of success or failure to a movement itself

INTERACTIONIST	NATURAL-HISTORY	VALUE-ADDED	
Park and Burgess Blumer Turner and Killian Lang and Lang	Dawson and Gettys Brinton	Smelser	
Restlessness Feedback Milling Collective excitement Social contagion	1. Preliminary stage 2. Popular stage 3. Stage of formal organization 4. Institutionalization	1. Structural conduciveness 2. Structural strain 3. Generalized belief 4. Precipitating factors 5. Mobilization for action 6. Social control	
Rumor Redefinition of social reality	Social movement	Craze, mass hysteria Undirected	Social movement, riot Directed
The process of the development of collective behavior	Stages of social movements or acts of collective behavior	Process or stages of collective behavior	Conditions, Processes, Resolution
Unstructured situation	Social unrest	Boredom	Social conditions
Milling crowd	Collective excitement	An incident	The last-straw type of incident
Redefinition of social reality	Institutionalization or dissolution	Rumor dispelled, participants discredited	Riot control Improved conditions or revolution
Reaction to bombing of Pearl Harbor	United States civil-rights movement	Mad gasser	1967 urban riots

as well as to the larger society? Does a successful movement become strengthened or undermined by success? Under what conditions does failure either demoralize or reinvigorate a movement? Much collective behavior, of course, never becomes crystallized into the organizational forms that many social movements take on. Therefore, the long-range influences of much collective behavior are inordinately difficult to assess.

Consequences In considering the consequences of collective behavior, the older school of scholars viewed such behavior as mainly disruptive and destructive to social order. Recently, however, attempts have been made to inquire empirically into the actual social consequences of collective behavior. Many investigators now see such behavior as an important mechanism in social change. In the wake of many spontaneous collective actions more formal organizations—such as pressure groups, clubs, voluntary associations, and networks of friendship—may grow. In addition, episodes of collective behavior frequently are responsible for the creation of laws or the appearance of new customs and new values.

ANALYSIS OF COLLECTIVE BEHAVIOR

So far, it appears that collective behavior is a catchall label that refers to many, often tenuously related, aspects of human behavior. Some of these

Figure 27.2   According to Gustave Le Bon, when people congregate in a crowd, a new mentality is created. By using this crowd mind, leaders can manipulate people into mob action. Le Bon held that the processes of imitation, suggestion, and social contagion "take over" normal rational thought as people are caught up in such action.

aspects have to do with individual participants: their motives, their attitudes, and the meanings they assign to their behavior. Other aspects are concerned with a behavioral episode itself: its genesis, its characteristics, its development, and its results. Still others concern the kinds of social organization and the collectivities that may arise in the course or as the result of a collective episode: division of roles among participants, patterns of leadership, and types of organizational structure. Some of these aspects may even be cultural in nature, involving the kinds of meaning systems that may develop out of the matrix of collective action.

The multifaceted character of the concept *collective behavior* becomes apparent when viewing the history of attempts to analyze it. A particular theorist will focus on one facet and attempt to develop, on the basis of that facet, a coherent theory. Another theorist will fasten onto another facet and fashion a theory solely around it. What has been less explored in the history of thought about collective behavior is how the diverse facets of such behavior can be interrelated.

Collective behavior poses special difficulties of analysis for the sociologist, in part because episodes of collective action typically excite strong emotional reactions that distort objective analysis. Observers are too ready to praise or blame, to

defend or denounce actions or ideologies and therefore unable dispassionately to investigate the development of the behavior. Moreover, incidents of collective behavior, because they often occur in a surprising and sudden fashion, cannot be controlled experimentally. There exist ethical obstacles to experimentation—for example, an experimenter may not create a real panic simply in order to observe it. Further, it is often difficult to observe episodes of collective behavior directly, because the time and place of dramatic or otherwise unusual actions cannot be predicted. Bystanders, journalists, and others who do observe such episodes often neither notice nor report those characteristics that would most interest social scientists. Finally, it is virtually impossible to sample collective behavior. The analyst of collective behavior often must settle for a scattering of possibly inaccurate, sometimes overdramatized accounts of collective actions.

The Psychological Approach

Prior to 1920 the chief approaches to the analysis of collective behavior were the psychological and the social. The psychological approach was divided into two branches, one of which relied on a single explanatory mechanism—either "contagion," "imitation," "suggestion," or "social facilitation"—to account for the occurrence of collective actions. The work of Gustave Le Bon (1895), for example, was based on the assumption that the gathering of people into a crowd creates a new mentality that is particularly receptive to suggestion and psychic contagion. From this mentality develops behavior that is irrational, impulsive, dangerous, and susceptible to easy manipulation by leaders.

The second psychological tradition proceeds from Freudian psychoanalysis. Freud (1921) accepted Le Bon's characterization of a crowd, but he emphasized psychological regression as the basis for the emergence of these characteristics. The key mechanism for Freud was *identification* (for a definition of this mechanism see Chapter 6). Like young children, the members of a crowd identify with a leader and, through him, with one another, thus creating a potential for mass action. Freud also viewed the crowd as emotional, impatient, impulsive, irrational, and thirsting for direction. He maintained that the mentality of the crowd corresponds to a state of regression—a primitive mental level. Both of these psychological approaches primarily attribute the main features of crowd behavior to an internal psychic mechanism that operates within the individuals making up the crowd.

The Social Approach

The social approach to the explanation of collective behavior is typified in Karl Marx's theory of revolution, even though Marx is not usually thought of as a theorist of collective behavior. As Chapter 14 points out, Marx regarded political revolutions as resulting primarily from a convergence of economic and social forces at a given stage in the evolution of a society. In particular, he predicted that the proletarian revolution, which would overthrow capitalism, would be caused by the aggravation of inherent social and economic contradictions within capitalist society, particularly the exploitation of the working class by the capitalists. Accordingly, the revolutionaries' psychology was unimportant to Marx because, like revolution itself, it too is a product of inexorable laws of social development. Although not all sociologists who have emphasized the social approach have been Marxists, this approach has usually involved the identification of those conditions that give rise to episodes of collective behavior—such conditions as economic deprivation, social disorganization, and value conflict.

Both the psychological and the social traditions remain alive in contemporary sociology, but a number of others have arisen since the 1920s. These newer approaches cannot simply be described as psychological or social because each of them involves some combination of orientations.

The Interactionist Approach

The first of these approaches, called the *interactionist approach*, is associated with Robert E. Park and Ernest Burgess (who were at the University

Figure 27.3 The social approach to the study of collective behavior, which focuses on the underlying conditions that give rise to collective action, is useful in studying revolutionary situations. Here, students and workers are shown building a barricade of wooden planks and parts of metal tree guards near the Place de la Bastille during their strike in Paris in 1968.

of Chicago during the 1920s) and has been developed by Herbert Blumer, Ralph Turner, and Lewis Killian (1957), and by Kurt Lang and Gladys Lang (1961). Though there are several variants of the interactionist tradition, the central concern is the means by which individuals communicate with one another during periods when their life situation is unstructured. The emphasis is on how new meanings and new social structures are created. For Blumer, the central characteristic of elementary collective behavior is a restlessness, communicated through a circular or "feedback" process from one individual to another, whereby the response of one person reproduces and transmits the stimulation he has received from another person.

Various other mechanisms characterize this state of unrest—aimless milling about, collective excitement, and social contagion. Interactionists also have studied such phenomena as the spread of rumor, the collective redefinition of social structure in a crisis, and patterns of mobilization, manipulation, and control by leaders. This approach is characterized by a concentration on the *process* by which collective behavior develops rather than by a search for underlying causes or conditions. In addition, the interactionist tradition views incidents of collective behavior as involving groups of individuals collectively arriving at new

Figure 27.4   The interactionist approach to collective behavior is concerned with the type of communication that takes place among participants in an unstructured situation. New meanings and new social structures may arise as a result of the "feedback" process, in which individuals keep reproducing stimulation they receive from each other. For example, the university students' interaction in a discussion group (*top*) may result in new formulation of their grievances. (*Bottom*) Their collective decision is then to confront a member of the university administration. The students' collective behavior may generate new meanings and new structures for student participation in their academic community.

meanings. It shies away from the view that these individuals are being coerced in any automatic way by larger social or psychological forces.

The Natural-History Approach

The second approach that has appeared during the last few decades is the *natural-history approach* to collective behavior, associated with the sociologists Carl A. Dawson and Warner E. Gettys and with the historian Crane Brinton. In its simplest form, this approach involves the assertion that there exist certain empirical uniformities of sequence in the unfolding of collective behaviors. A classic model of the stages of a social movement has been developed by Dawson and Gettys (1929): Beginning with a "preliminary stage of social unrest," the social movement passes through a "popular stage of collective excitement" to a "stage of formal organization" and finally reaches, if successful in its aims, a terminal point of "institutionalization." The culmination of the sequence introduces some new institutional form—a sect, a law, a new kind of family structure, or a political reform. Brinton (1938) has developed a comparable model for the sequence of stages that occur in the development of a revolutionary movement.

The Value-Added Approach

The third modern approach, formulated by Neil J. Smelser (1962) has been termed the *value-added approach*. This approach maintains that there are many determinants or necessary conditions—some social, some psychological, and some cultural—that must be present for any kind of collective action to occur. The value-added approach insists, however, that these determinants must combine in a definite pattern. As they combine, theoretically possible outcomes are gradually eliminated, and the actual outcome becomes increasingly determined. Smelser identifies the following determinants in order of increasing specificity.

First, *structural conduciveness* refers to the kinds of structural elements present in a society and the implications these elements have for the occurrence of various types of collective behavior. For example, the existence of a stock market, in contrast to other types of exchange mechanisms, provides a setting that makes possible the occurrence of financial speculation, of economic "booms" and "busts."

Second, *structural strain* refers to some deprivation, conflict, ambiguity, or discrepancy in the social environment that disposes members of the society to make collective attempts to relieve the strain. In order to be a determinant of an incident of collective behavior, however, strain must combine with the condition of conduciveness; the two sets of variables act together to increase the probability of a particular kind of collective behavior.

The third variable identified by Smelser is the growth and spread of a *generalized belief*. In order that the social situation may be diagnosed and people may undertake action in a purposive way, some system of meaning must be created. A generalized belief identifies the source of strain, attributes certain characteristics to that source, and specifies certain responses to the strain as possible and appropriate. It functions much like an ideology, and, in fact, the study of generalized beliefs necessarily merges with the study of rumors, ideologies, and systems of religious belief.

A further condition, that of *precipitating factors*, refers to dramatic, often fortuitous events that occur in the context of the other variables and that may trigger the outbreak of collective action.

Next, the participants must be *mobilized for action*. Given the existence of the previous conditions, collective behavior still must await the mobilization of potential actors. At this stage the behavior of leaders is often decisive.

Finally, the operation of mechanisms of *social control* refers to those counterdeterminants that prevent, interrupt, deflect, inhibit, or suppress the accumulating force of all the other determinants. Social control refers to the ways in which the surrounding society reacts to an actual or impending episode of collective behavior. The agencies involved include the police, the courts, the press, legislative and community leaders, and or-

ganized public opinion. Whether attempts at social control succeed in preventing or suppressing the behavior in question depends partly on the degree to which those who act as the agents of control represent in their actions the sentiments of the larger community and partly on their willingness and ability to use force to maintain the existing social order.

RENAISSANCE OF INTEREST

Since World War II, the study of collective behavior has undergone a renaissance. In addition to those already mentioned, numerous studies from a variety of perspectives have appeared during the last two decades. One of the best historical studies is George Rudé's *The Crowd in the French Revolution* (1959). Rudé delved into the archives of the French Revolution, the records of arrests, and the history of crowd formation. By a careful analysis of the occupation, sex, and social status of participants, Rudé was able to demonstrate why people became involved in the various riots during the Revolution. In particular, he was able to relate the incidence of and participation in riots to changes in the price of bread—and the classes of people it affected—during the years from 1789 to 1794. Unlike most previous studies of crowd behavior, Rudé's research is marked by careful attention to historical detail.

Another example of an excellent case study, this one by an anthropologist, is James Slotkin's *The Peyote Religion* (1956), in which he traces the origin and fate of drug cults among American Indian tribes in the late nineteenth century. Slotkin shows how war, defeat, and repression by the colonial authorities drove the Indians into an increasing passivity. Their collective orientation became more and more resigned, passive, and dominated by fantasies of world regeneration. This collective orientation culminated in the development of religious cults dominated by the use of hallucinatory drugs, specifically the peyote cactus.

A second feature of the renaissance of interest in collective behavior is that contemporary investigators are at last making a systematic attempt to bring empirical data to bear on hypotheses

Figure 27.5   Renewed interest in the study of collective behavior was signaled by such work as George Rudé's study of the French Revolution, illustrated by the drawing below. Another important study that served to reawaken interest in collective behavior was James Slotkin's research on native American peyote cults. It is interesting to note that the collective behavior studied by Rudé was directed toward changing the world, whereas that studied by Slotkin was inner-directed.

and as the number of black policeman per each thousand blacks in the population declines.

Although these findings are tentative and require further research before they can be asserted as valid generalizations, Lieberson and Silverman's investigation is a far cry from the speculative work of earlier writers who, from their armchairs and without reference to the facts, blamed such groups as the riffraff, the troublemakers, or the agents of a repressive regime for the outbreak of riots.

A third feature of the new interest in collective behavior stems from current disturbances. Investigators are devoting increasing attention to such events as campus revolts, peace demonstrations, civil-rights protests, and racial militancy. Two major national commissions, the National Advisory Commission on Civil Disorders, usually referred to as the Kerner Commission, and the National Advisory Commission on the Causes and Prevention of Violence, have contributed to the interest in generating both better data and better explanations regarding current collective movements.

emerging from theories of collective behavior. Stanley Lieberson and Arnold R. Silverman (1965) gathered seventy-two descriptions of what they classified as black-white race riots that occurred in the years between 1913 and 1963. They analyzed these in terms of their immediate precipitating incidents, as well as in terms of various underlying conditions. They discovered that a sizable proportion of precipitating incidents appeared to have involved interracial violations of social norms—particularly fights, bodily injuries, and killings.

To examine the underlying conditions that contribute to race riots, the authors used a systematic paired-comparison analysis. Each city that had experienced a riot was compared with a city as similar as possible in size and geographic region that had not experienced such a riot in the ten years preceding or following the riot date. In this way, the authors could discover, approximately at least, those features of riot-prone cities that set them apart from cities that had not experienced riots. They found that the probability of rioting increases as blacks attain more occupations traditionally held by whites, as the percentage of white store owners in black areas increases,

VARIETIES OF COLLECTIVE BEHAVIOR

A major feature of Smelser's value-added model of collective behavior is that it identifies the underlying similarities between very shortlived outbursts of collective behavior, such as a craze, and more elaborate varieties, such as riots or social movements. He argues that as people develop more elaborate definitions of what it is that is bothering them—generalized beliefs about what is wrong and who is to blame—the form their collective behavior will take becomes more complex. Thus, persons experiencing certain stressful circumstances (strains) who lack any clear understanding of what is wrong will be prone to crazes or outbursts of mass hysteria, but they are unlikely to riot and are certainly unable to organize a social movement. In contrast, Smelser argues that riots, for example, are a directed form of social action—people riot against someone (or some institution) whom they blame for causing a disturbing state of affairs. Clearly, revolutionary social movements have a highly developed theory of whom they are in opposition to and why.

In crazes and mass hysterias people are responding with little comprehension of what is bothering them or what needs to be done to remove the source of their troubles. It is precisely this lack of what Marx called *consciousness of objective conditions* that makes mass hysterias and crazes "irrational." We judge rationality in terms of the degree to which action is guided by comprehension of its motives and is directed toward achieving clearly defined goals. When people "know what they are doing" we may strongly disapprove of what they are doing, but we do not regard them as "nutty." But when people seem unaware of the real reasons behind their behavior we often call their behavior irrational. We do this because such action typically is irrelevant to the real strains bothering people—it is not directed toward removing the source of the problem.

In order to make these distinctions clearer, and to provide some understanding of the dynamics of collective behavior, the remainder of this chapter is devoted to two studies of collective behavior. The first is an account of an outburst of mass hysteria. The second is excerpted from the investigation of ghetto riots conducted by the Kerner Commission.

The "Phantom Anesthetist" of Mattoon

During World War II, on the first night of September, 1944, a woman in Mattoon, Illinois, reported to local police that someone had opened her bedroom window and sprayed her with a noxiously sweet-smelling gas that partially paralyzed her legs for about half an hour and made her ill. The local paper reported the story on page one under the headline: "ANESTHETIC PROWLER ON LOOSE." The following day three more women reported being gassed in a similar manner. From then on, the number of the attacks rapidly grew. By September 10th, seventeen attacks had occurred, and that night, despite massive patrolling by local and state police and armed citizens, seven attacks were reported. But after one more attack the next night, the incidents ceased. The "mad gasser" was never caught. Indeed, after the press had sensationalized the story for more than a

week, press accounts turned suddenly skeptical. Headlines such as "STATE HUNTS GAS MADMAN" were replaced by long interviews with social scientists on the dynamics of mass hysteria. Soon authorities were convinced there never had been a phantom anesthetist loose in Mattoon.

Donald M. Johnson, a social scientist at the University of Illinois, went to Mattoon and conducted a systematic study of the incident. He interviewed the gasser's victims, police, and local officials. He carefully assembled data on all police calls during the period. He assessed the newspaper coverage. From these materials he wrote a classic account of collective hysteria (1945).

Johnson's first task was to establish that what occurred really was hysteria, not the work of an incredibly clever gasser, who, police claimed, would have needed to be able to turn invisible in order to carry out numerous attacks despite massive police-citizen patrols. Johnson based his case against a real gasser on a number of arguments. First, the gasser merely gassed. He took nothing. He did not utilize the semi-paralyzed state of his female victims for sexual assaults. And no dogs barked at his presence. But more definitive is the fact that gas experts throughout the country said no gas existed with the characteristics necessary to confirm the stories of the victims. In fact, experts said no gas with such properties *could* be developed. The gas would have to be extremely stable and potent to act virtually instantly on victims from a considerable distance—yet it had to disperse harmlessly and instantly because it usually did not affect others in the same room with the victim.

With the possibility of a real gasser disposed of, Johnson set about an analysis of how mass hysteria had been generated. Figure 27.6 shows the patterns of phone calls to the police for the relevant period. Notice that the prowler calls rose in the same pattern as did gasser calls (total police calls also rose in the same pattern). Interestingly enough, shortly after the gasser calls ceased so did prowler calls. This is extremely abnormal. One might expect prowler calls to return to their usual level, but not to disappear. Johnson argued that this demonstrates the effects of counter-suggesta-

Figure 27.6   In his research on mass hysteria
Johnson noted the patterns of prowler and gasser calls
made to the police in Mattoon, Illinois.
(From D. M. Johnson, 1945.)

Figure 27.7   Headlines from a Mattoon newspaper
show how the press sensationalized the mad-gasser
incident. This sensationalism may have contributed to
the mass hysteria in Mattoon, Illinois, in
September, 1944.

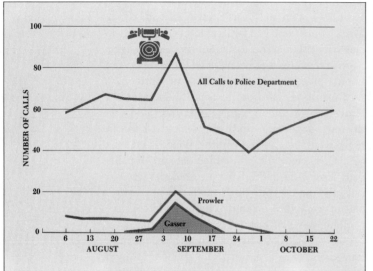

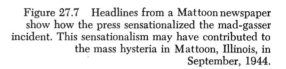

bility that had set in after the newspapers began to ridicule the gasser incident as hysteria. People were unwilling, for awhile, to report even routine prowler activity. Note too that police calls in general, although not disappearing, fell below normal levels following the end of the gasser incident, and then rose back toward normal levels. Apparently, people became generally reluctant to call the police, lest they be thought hysterical.

Through interviews, Johnson found that the victims did not know one another and that knowledge of the gasser had not spread through personal interaction but mainly through the press. The first incident became a page-one sensation, and the number of incidents steadily rose as press coverage grew more and more sensational and lengthy. Incidents subsided in response to a change in press coverage from "mad gasser hits again" to "mass gasser is imaginary." He thus concluded that the press was the stimulus for the mass hysteria.

But not just anyone or everyone in Mattoon had become a victim. Who had reacted to the stimulus of the press by joining in the mass hysteria? Johnson's data on victims revealed that they were indeed subject to considerable strain—something was bothering them. First, he discovered that not a single gasser "attack" had oc-

curred in either of Mattoon's two high-income areas. Indeed, not a single person in Mattoon who had been to college, for however brief a period, was a victim. In fact, three-fourths of the victims had not gone beyond grade school. And although 60 percent of the homes in Mattoon had telephones at that time, only a third of the victims had phones. Clearly, then, those caught up in the mass hysteria were the poor and uneducated.

There were other striking characteristics of the victims as well. Of the twenty-nine victims interviewed, twenty-seven were women; the two men who were victims had been gassed with their wives (and the wives had noticed the attack first). In part, this could have been the result of the initial definition of the situation—a male prowler with a strange paralytic gas had attacked a woman. Such an incident has clear sexual overtones and would seem to exclude men from the victim category.

Yet there probably is more to the fact that, for all practical purposes, only women were caught up in the mass hysteria. For one thing, Johnson reported a number of laboratory studies on suggestibility and clinical studies of hysteria that show that women are usually much more prone to such responses. Second, we have now come to understand that women have long suffered under considerable strain because of their disadvantaged position in society. But, as is taken up in detail in the next chapter, there was no women's movement in the 1940s at the time of the Mattoon incident. Women had problems, but they had not collectively become aware of their shared problems; they had not defined the source of their dissatisfactions as social and sex-based rather than individual.

Does reference to sex-role deprivations and dissatisfactions make any sense in this context? In retrospect, it seems so. Johnson found that all but one of the women "attacked" by the gasser were married. Furthermore, they were not elderly. Instead, they were disproportionately between the ages of twenty and twenty-nine. The gasser thus typically "struck" young mothers (with little education and little income) whose husbands were either blue-collar workers or away in the army. It is precisely these women who are most oppressed by the traditional wife and mother role. They have a house full of young children. They lack labor-saving conveniences and cannot afford baby-sitters. They have poor communication with their husbands (recall Chapter 14). Lacking education, they have fewer resources for coping with their problems and fewer leisure pursuits to relieve their tedium. Being young, they are still close to their girlhood dreams and hopes. But these young housewives of Mattoon had no theory of what was wrong or who was to blame. Smelser's model of collective behavior would pick them as prime targets for the "Phantom Anesthetist of Mattoon." And they were.

GHETTO RIOTS: THE KERNER COMMISSION FINDINGS

During the summer of 1967 riots erupted in the black ghettos of many major American cities. Eighty-three persons died during these riots, stores were burned and looted, and many people feared that racial tensions were leading America into an era of urban guerrilla warfare. The emergency prompted President Lyndon Johnson to appoint a commission to investigate the circum-

stances surrounding the riots. The commission was officially named the National Advisory Commission on Civil Disorders (1968), but it came to be known as the Kerner Commission after its chairman, Otto G. Kerner. In its report the commission said bluntly that white racism was the principal cause of the disorders. The excerpts from the commission report, which conclude this chapter, describe the circumstances that led to riots and offer a profile of the typical rioter.

You will recall that Smelser takes the position that the difference between a riot and mass hysteria, such as the case of the gasser of Mattoon, is one of consciousness of collective grievances. The women of Mattoon did not understand what was bothering them. But, as you will see, black Americans did know what was bothering them: years of injustice and suffering for which white America is to blame. The following paragraphs are excerpts from Chapter Two of the Kerner Commission's report, which was published in 1968.

THE RIOT PROCESS

The Commission has found no "typical" disorder in 1967 in terms of intensity of violence and extensiveness of damage. To determine whether, as is sometimes suggested, there was a typical "riot process," we examined 24 disorders which occurred during 1967 in 20 cities and three university settings. We have concentrated on four aspects of that process:

The accumulating reservoir of grievances in the Negro community;
"Precipitating" incidents and their relationship to the reservoir of grievances;
The development of violence after its initial outbreak;
The control effort, including official force, negotiation, and persuasion.

We found a common social process operating in all 24 disorders in certain critical respects. These events developed similarly, over a period of time and out of an accumulation of grievances and increasing tension in the Negro community. Almost invariably, they exploded in ways related

Figure 27.8 According to the Kerner Commission, two aspects of the riot process are an accumulation of grievances in the ghetto community and "precipitating" incidents (and their relationship to the reservoir of grievances). Ghetto inhabitants can be pushed by the facts of their everyday lives—abominable living conditions and oppressive environments (*right and top left*), discriminatory treatment by the police and others, unemployment, and a frustrated sense of their inability to change these conditions—to a point where an arrest in their neighborhood (*bottom right*) will provoke them to riot.

to the local community and its particular problems and conflicts. But once violence erupted, there began a complex interaction of many elements—rioters, official control forces, counterrioters—in which the differences between various disorders were more pronounced than the similarities.

The Reservoir of Grievances in the Negro Community

Our examination of the background of the surveyed disorders revealed a typical pattern of deeply held grievances which were widely shared by many members of the Negro community. The specific content of the expressed grievances varied somewhat from city to city. But in general, grievances among Negroes in all the cities related to prejudice, discrimination, severely disadvantaged living conditions, and a general sense of frustration about their inability to change those conditions.

Specific events or incidents exemplified and reinforced the shared sense of grievance. News of such incidents spread quickly throughout the community and added to the reservoir. Grievances about police practices, unemployment and underemployment, housing, and other objective conditions in the ghetto were aggravated in the minds of many Negroes by the inaction of municipal authorities.

Out of this reservoir of grievance and frustration, the riot process began in the cities which we surveyed.

Precipitating Incidents

In virtually every case a single "triggering" or "precipitating" incident can be identified as having immediately preceded—within a few hours and in generally the same location—the outbreak of disorder. But this incident was usually a relatively minor, even trivial one, by itself substantially disproportionate to the scale of violence that followed. Often it was an incident of a type which had occurred frequently in the same community in the past without provoking violence.

We found that violence was generated by an increasingly disturbed social atmosphere, in which typically not one, but a series of incidents occurred over a period of weeks or months prior to the outbreak of disorder. Most cities had three or more such incidents; Houston had 10 over a 5-month period. These earlier or prior incidents were linked in the minds of many Negroes to the preexisting reservoir of underlying grievances. With each such incident, frustration and tension grew until at some point a final incident, often similar to the incidents preceding it, occurred and was followed almost immediately by violence.

As we see it, the prior incidents and the reservoir of underlying grievances contributed to a cumulative process of mounting tension that spilled over into violence when the final incident occurred. In this sense the entire chain—the grievances, the series of prior tension-heightening incidents, and the final incident—was the "precipitant" of disorder.

This chain describes the central trend in the disorders we surveyed and not necessarily all aspects of the riots or of all rioters. For example, incidents have not always increased tension; and tension has not always resulted in violence. We conclude only that both processes did occur in the disorders we examined.

Similarly, we do not suggest that all rioters shared the conditions or the grievances of their Negro neighbors: some may deliberately have exploited the chaos created out of the frustration of others; some may have been drawn into the melee merely because they identified with, or wished to emulate, others. Some who shared the adverse conditions and grievances did not riot.

We found that the majority of the rioters did share the adverse conditions and grievances, although they did not necessarily articulate in their own minds the connection between that background and their actions.

Newark and Detroit presented typical sequences of prior incidents, a buildup of tensions, a final incident, and the outbreak of violence:

NEWARK

Prior Incidents

1965: A Newark policeman shot and killed an 18-year-old Negro boy. After the policeman had stated that he had fallen and his gun had discharged accidentally, he later claimed that the youth had assaulted another officer and was shot as he fled. At a hearing it was decided that the patrolman had not used excessive force. The patrolman remained on duty, and his occasional assignment to Negro areas was a continuing source of irritation in the Negro community.

April 1967: Approximately 15 Negroes were arrested while picketing a grocery store which they claimed sold bad meat and used unfair credit practices.

Late May, early June: Negro leaders had for several months voiced strong opposition to a proposed medical-dental center to be built on 150 acres of land in the predominantly Negro central ward. The dispute centered mainly around the lack of relocation provisions for those who would be displaced by the medical center. The issue became extremely volatile in late May when public "blight hearings" were held regarding the land to be condemned. The hearings became a public forum in which many residents spoke against the proposed center. The city did not change its plan.

Late May, June: The mayor recommended appointment of a white city councilman who had no more than a high school education to the position of secretary to the board of education. Reportedly, there was widespread support from both whites and Negroes for a Negro candidate who held a master's degree and was considered more qualified. The mayor did not change his recommendation. Ultimately, the original secretary retained his position and neither candidate was appointed.

July 8: Several Newark policemen, allegedly including the patrolman involved in the 1965 killing, entered East Orange to assist the East Orange police during an altercation with a group of Negro men.

Final Incident

July 12, approximately 9:30 P.M.: A Negro cab driver was injured during or after a traffic arrest in the heart of the central ward. Word spread quickly, and a crowd gathered in front of the Fourth Precinct stationhouse across the street from a large public housing project.

Initial Violence

Same day, approximately 11:30 P.M.: The crowd continued to grow until it reached 300 to 500 people. One or two Molotov cocktails were thrown at the stationhouse. Shortly after midnight the police dispersed the crowd, and window-breaking and looting began a few minutes later. By about 1 A.M., the peak level of violence for the first night was reached.

DETROIT

Prior Incidents

August 1966: A crowd formed during a routine arrest of several Negro youths in the Kercheval section of the city. Tensions were high for several hours, but no serious violence occurred.

June 1967: A Negro prostitute was shot to death on her front steps. Rumors in the Negro community attributed the killing to a vice-squad officer. A police investigation later unearthed leads to a disgruntled pimp. No arrests were made.

June 26: A young Negro man on a picnic was shot to death while reportedly trying to protect his pregnant wife from assault by seven youths. The wife witnessed the slaying and miscarried shortly thereafter. Of the white youths, only one was charged. The others were released.

Final Incident

July 23, approximately 3:45 A.M.: Police raided a "blind pig," a type of night club in the Negro area which served drinks after hours. Eighty persons were in the club—more than the police had anticipated—attending a party for several servicemen, two of whom had recently returned from Vietnam. A crowd of about 200 persons gathered as the police escorted the patrons into the police wagons.

Initial Violence

Approximately 5:00 A.M.: As the last police cars drove away from the "blind pig," the crowd began to throw rocks. By 8:00 A.M., looting had become widespread. Violence continued to increase throughout the day, and by evening reached a peak level for the first day.

In the 24 disorders surveyed, the events identified as tension-heightening incidents, whether prior or final, involved issues which generally paralleled the grievances we found in these cities. The incidents identified were of the following types:

Police Actions Some 40 percent of the prior incidents involved allegedly abusive or discriminatory police actions. Most of the police incidents began routinely and involved a response to, at most, a few persons rather than a large group.

A typical incident occurred in Bridgeton, N.J., 5 days before the disturbance when two police officers went to the home of a young Negro man to investigate a nonsupport complaint. A fight ensued when the officers attempted to take the man to the police station, and the Negro was critically injured and partially paralyzed. A Negro minister representing the injured man's family asked for suspension of the two officers involved pending investigation. This procedure had been followed

Figure 27.9 In a riot situation, after an initial outbreak of violence, such as the breaking of store windows, looting (*top*) usually follows. Fires (*middle*) seem to break out later in the riot process (during the middle cycles of riots that last several days), although it remains unclear whether fires are set only after looting occurs or before as well. Such crimes are often regarded as a way of protesting against the structure and organization of society. At times, official forces used in the riot-control effort have included the National Guard. (*Bottom*) A ghetto inhabitant who refused to move at orders of a National Guardsman is seized by a policeman.

previously when three policemen were accused of collusion in the robbery of a white-owned store. The Negro's request was not granted.

Police actions were also identified as the final incident preceding 12 of the 24 disturbances. Again, in all but two cases, the police action which became the final incident began routinely.

The final incident in Grand Rapids occurred when police attempted to apprehend a Negro driving an allegedly stolen car. A crowd of 30 to 40 Negro spectators gathered. The suspect had one arm in a cast, and some of the younger Negroes in the crowd intervened because they thought the police were handling him too roughly.

. . .

THE DEVELOPMENT OF VIOLENCE

Once the series of precipitating incidents culminated in violence, the riot process did not follow a uniform pattern in the 24 disorders surveyed. However, some similarities emerge.

The final incident before the outbreak of disorder, and the initial violence itself, generally occurred at a time and place in which it was normal for many people to be on the streets. In most of the 24 disorders, groups generally estimated at 50 or more persons were on the street at the time and place of the first outbreak.

In all 24 disturbances, including the three university-related disorders, the initial disturb-

ance area consisted of streets with relatively high concentrations of pedestrian and automobile traffic at the time. In all but two cases—Detroit and Milwaukee—violence started between 7 P.M. and 12:30 P.M., when the largest numbers of pedestrians could be expected. Ten of the 24 disorders erupted on Friday night, Saturday, or Sunday.

In most instances, the temperature during the day on which violence first erupted was quite high. This contributed to the size of the crowds on the street, particularly in areas of congested housing.

Major violence occurred in all 24 disorders during the evening and night hours, between 6 P.M. and 6 A.M., and in most cases between 9 P.M. and 3 A.M. In only a few disorders, including Detroit and Newark, did substantial violence occur or continue during the daytime. Generally, the night-day cycles continued in daily succession through the early period of the disorder.

At the beginning of disorder, violence generally flared almost immediately after the final precipitating incident. It then escalated quickly to its peak level, in the case of 1-night disorders, and to the first night peak in the case of continuing disorders. In Detroit and Newark, the first outbreaks began within two hours and reached severe, although not the highest, levels within 3 hours.

In almost all of the subsequent night-day cycles, the change from relative order to a state of disorder by a number of people typically occurred extremely rapidly—within 1 or 2 hours at the most.

Nineteen of the surveyed disorders lasted more than 1 night. In 10 of these, violence peaked on the first night, and the level of activity on subsequent nights was the same or less. In the other nine disorders, however, the peak was reached on a subsequent night.

Disorder generally began with less serious violence against property, such as rock and bottle-throwing and window-breaking. These were usually the materials and the targets closest to hand at the place of the initial outbreak.

Once store windows were broken, looting usually followed. Whether fires were set only after looting occurred is unclear. Reported instances of fire-bombing and Molotov cocktails in the 24 disorders appeared to occur as frequently during one cycle of violence as during another in disorders which continued through more than one cycle. However, fires seemed to break out more frequently during the middle cycles of riots lasting several days. Gunfire and sniping were also reported more frequently during the middle cycles.

. . .

THE RIOT PARTICIPANT

It is sometimes assumed that the rioters were criminal types, overactive social deviants, or riffraff—recent migrants, members of an uneducated underclass, alienated from responsible Negroes, and without broad social or political concerns. It is often implied that there was no effort within the Negro community to attempt to reduce the violence.

We have obtained data on participation from four different sources:

Eyewitness accounts from more than 1,200 interviews in our staff reconnaissance survey of 20 cities;
Interview surveys based on probability samples of riot area residents in the two major riot cities—Detroit and Newark—designed to elicit anonymous self-identification of participants as rioters, counterrioters or noninvolved;
Arrest records from 22 cities; and
A special study of arrestees in Detroit.

Only partial information is available on the total numbers of participants. In the Detroit survey, approximately 11 percent of the sampled residents over the age of 15 in the two disturbance areas admittedly participated in rioting; another 20 to 25 percent admitted to having been bystanders but claimed that they had not participated; approximately 16 percent claimed they had engaged in counterriot activity; and the largest proportion (48 to 53 percent) claimed they were at home or elsewhere and did not participate. However, a large proportion of the Negro community apparently believed that more was gained than lost through rioting, according to the Newark and Detroit surveys.

Greater precision is possible in describing the characteristics of those who participated. We have combined the data from the four sources to construct a profile of the typical rioter and to compare him with the counterrioter and the noninvolved.

. . .

The typical rioter in the summer of 1967 was a Negro, unmarried male between the ages of 15 and 24. He was in many ways very different from the stereotype. He was not a migrant. He was born in the state and was a lifelong resident of the city in which the riot took place. Economically his position was about the same as his Negro neighbors who did not actively participate in the riot.

Although he had not, usually, graduated from high school, he was somewhat better educated than the average inner-city Negro, having at least attended high school for a time.

Nevertheless, he was more likely to be working in a menial or low status job as an unskilled laborer. If he was employed, he was not working full time and his employment was frequently interrupted by periods of unemployment.

He feels strongly that he deserves a better job and that he is barred from achieving it, not be-cause of lack of training, ability, or ambition, but because of discrimination by employers.

He rejects the white bigot's stereotype of the Negro as ignorant and shiftless. He takes great pride in his race and believes that in some respects Negroes are superior to whites. He is extremely hostile to whites, but his hostility is more apt to be a product of social and economic class than of race; he is almost equally hostile toward middle class Negroes.

He is substantially better informed about politics than Negroes who were not involved in the riots. He is more likely to be actively engaged in civil rights efforts, but is extremely distrustful of the political system and of political leaders.

SUGGESTED READINGS

Blumer, Herbert. "Collective Behavior," in Alfred M. Lee (ed.), *New Outline of the Principles of Sociology.* New York: Barnes & Noble, 1951.

Brown, Roger W. "Mass Phenomena," in Gardner Lindsey (ed.), *Handbook of Social Psychology.* Reading, Mass.: Addison-Wesley, 1954, II, 833–876.

Lang, Kurt, and Gladys E. Lang. *Collective Dynamics.* New York: Crowell, 1961.

Smelser, Neil J. *Theory of Collective Behavior.* New York: Free Press, 1962.

Chapter 28 Social Movements

MANY KINDS OF COLLECTIVE BEHAVIOR, as Chapter 27 points out, are short-lived and without lasting social effects. Fads come and go. Crazes pass. Riots do not go on indefinitely. But not all collective behavior is transitory. Often people respond to their grievances and dissatisfactions by uniting in an organized, long-term effort to change their society (or to resist changes). Such organized activities directed toward change or resisting change are *social movements* (Turner and Killian, 1957).

Sociologists have searched for the common features of such diverse phenomena as the rise of Christianity, the Russian Revolution, the Women's Christian Temperance Union, the civil rights movement, and the John Birch Society. Their search has uncovered many characteristic features of all such movements. This chapter reviews the sociological understanding of social movements. A particular contemporary social movement—the Women's Liberation Movement —is then analyzed in order to give concreteness to the earlier discussion.

THE NATURE OF SOCIAL MOVEMENTS

A number of elements of social movements can be distinguished. First, social movements develop in response to some sources of *discontent*. Contented people do not organize to change the world. Second, all social movements have some set of *goals*—and to implement these goals, *a program* for change. The ideas that justify this program and its goals constitute the *ideology* of the movement.

Furthermore, social movements are made up of people acting together as groups and often through formal organizations. As such they must deal with organizational problems (recall Chapters 8 and 9). Thus, social movements develop sets of roles and norms governing member behavior, face problems of maintaining legitimate leadership, and must recruit and properly socialize new members. Social movements are subject to having one set of goals transformed into another, internal factionalism, bureaucratization, stratification, and other contingencies faced by all human organizations in all societies.

Sources of Discontent

Every member of every society in the course of his or her life experiences frustration, fear, disappointment, and anger. But it is only when *large numbers of persons share common dissatisfactions and feel that something can be done about them* that a social movement is likely to develop.

As is pointed out in Chapter 26, widespread dissatisfaction is likely to be produced by strains that may occur in various aspects of society. Such strains may first become apparent within a society's *situational facilities*—the resources available for the satisfaction of human needs. Strain may also develop among social institutions—the way roles are organized in one institutional setting may be incompatible with the way roles in other institutions are organized. For example, educational roles may encourage women to seek careers while family roles encourage them to stay at home. Or strains may develop in social norms, especially when the norms appear to hinder, rather than to promote, human needs and aspirations. The norms of racial segregation are an obvious example.

There may even be strain at the level of values when the most basic tenets by which people have been accustomed to live no longer seem appropriate to the realities of their lives. In the United States the meaning of national loyalty, for example, has been brought into question as the government has embroiled the nation in various foreign military ventures not clearly related to the nation's security or to its traditional stance in foreign affairs. Strain within the system of values or norms may also result from a society's different population groups' adhering to different and conflicting values and norms—strains may be produced by the immigration of peoples with diverse cultural heritages, the isolation of groups through physical or social segregation, and the uniqueness of the social or cultural environment in which each successive generation grows to maturity. (See Chapter 16.)

Role of Communications The communication system within a society can affect the fate of social

Figure 28.1 People who share common discontents may be easily manipulated by a strong leader, especially if the leader forcefully presents a plan of action and if channels of communication among people are blocked.

discontent. If channels of communication become closed or clogged by too much "noise," people may come to feel that "nobody listens to their troubles," that their "messages" do not get through. Their confidence in the usual mechanisms by which grievances are redressed is thus reduced. On the other hand, free access to channels of communication can increase discontent as scattered individuals learn that there are others who share their feelings.

There are those in the United States today who hold the mass media primarily responsible for the rapid proliferation of both racial and student demonstrations since the mid-1960s. Even if this charge exaggerates the power of the media, it is nevertheless true that radio and television communication can give coherence to a movement whose members are widely dispersed physically and who may never all come together at any one time or place. To avoid such eventualities, totalitarian regimes attempt to control all channels of communication and to restrict individual freedom of expression in order to isolate and neutralize dissident members of the society. And, of course, even in the United States, not all groups have equal access to the media.

Weakening of Existing Political Order Another condition leading to the rise of social movements is the inability of an established government to maintain order and to alleviate persistent social

problems (Hertzler, 1940). As people begin to lose confidence in the existing political order, they become susceptible to the appeal of movements that promise to restore order or improve conditions. They may be willing to accept a "strong man" who promises simple, drastic solutions to complex problems, even at the price of their liberty. Would-be dictators, such as Adolf Hitler during the early 1930s, have sometimes employed terrorist tactics against the population or selected groups within it in order to spread fear and undermine confidence in the existing regime, thus feeding demands for order through the institution of a new government.

Relative Deprivation Most students of social movements agree that hardship and frustration, no matter how widespread, do not of themselves give rise to organized social movements. Belief in the real possibility of better conditions also must exist. In fact, the development of a generalized conviction that something both *must* be done and *can* be done is a necessary element in the development of a coherent social movement.

As is considered at length in Chapter 14, it is not the most disadvantaged groups in a population that are most likely to launch a social movement or foment a revolution but those who are somewhat better off, yet still dissatisfied. The concept of *relative deprivation* attempts to explain such a phenomenon by claiming that people become discontented not because of the absolute severity of their situation but because they compare their actual condition with what they believe it could and should be. For example, members of the National Farmers Organization (NFO), a movement of militant farmers in the Midwest, are, on the whole, economically better off than the typical nonmember farmer in the same region. The NFO members have, on the average, more formal education, more military service, and more labor-union experience than nonmembers. As a result, their aspirations are higher than those of poorer farmers with more restricted experiences (Morrison and Steeves, 1967).

Closely related to the concept of relative deprivation is that of the *revolution of rising expecta-*

tions, which proposes that the experience of somewhat improved conditions leads to the expectation of, and thus the demand for, still further improvement. When improvement fails to materialize or comes too slowly, major disturbances and even revolution may ensue (Geschwender, 1968). Historically, this idea gains credence from the experience of several major social revolutions. The Puritan Revolution in England (1640–1648) and the French Revolution (1789–1794) were both spearheaded by middle-class groups whose economic condition had improved conspicuously during the preceding two generations. However, these groups had also been effectively excluded from participation in political power and social honor. The Russian Revolutions of 1917 were led by the relatively well-off urban industrial workers and by intellectuals drawn either from the middle classes or, in the case of Lenin, from the minor nobility.

The folk adage "The more they have, the more they want" should not, however, be allowed to divert attention from another pattern of change that has been called the *J-Curve* of rising and declining satisfactions. As is discussed in Chapter 14, sometimes a period of both rising satisfactions and rising expectations is followed by a period of an absolute, rather than a relative, decline in rewards. James Davies (1969) has argued that the black insurrections of the 1960s resulted not merely from blacks' aspirations rising faster than progress toward equality was being made, but they also stemmed from a sudden increase in white violence against blacks that constituted an absolute decline in blacks' position in society.

Goals of Social Movements

Classifying movements in terms of their goals or orientations is not as easy as it might appear at first glance. Such common classifications as "right" and "left," "reform" and "radical," or "revolutionary," "moderate," and "extremist," often reflect misleading simplifications of complex situations of thought and action. One way of classifying social movements is by how they relate to the existing social order: a *progressive* movement proposes

new goals and supposedly better, or at least more effective, ways of doing things; a *reactionary* movement advocates the restoration of a real or imagined preexisting (and presumably superior) state of affairs; and a *conservative* movement works for the preservation of existing features of the society. The last two types usually constitute a *countermovement,* opposing some other movement that advocates change.

Social movements also can be classified as *expressive* and *institutional,* although a movement often changes from one of these types to the other (Lang and Lang, 1961). Expressive movements concentrate on reforming their participants, often as preparation for an inevitable change in society, such as the coming of a Messiah. The early Christian or the contemporary Jehovah's Witnesses serve as examples. Institutional movements, such as organized pressure groups or third-party movements, on the other hand, work to change the existing institutions of society. Sometimes these two types are differentiated respectively as primarily *religious* or *political* in their thrust.

Ideology: The Development of Collective Meaning

A social movement develops a culture—a body of shared understandings, meanings, and behavior. A primary shared understanding in a movement's development is a sense of discontent with the status quo. Herbert Blumer (1951) has analyzed the role of the agitator in the process of crystalizing discontent. The agitator calls people's attention to sources of discontent that they may sense only vaguely and makes them aware that others share their dissatisfaction, thus setting the stage for leaders to advance a program and recruit a following.

An ideology serves to justify the proposed action program and, when necessary, acts as a force for changing or redirecting this program. Mao Tse-tung (1971), an important Marxist ideologist of the twentieth century, believes that the ideology, or theory, of a social movement should be in constant interplay—a give-and-take relationship—with the practice of a social movement.

Figure 28.2   If a social movement appears to threaten a society's values, it will encounter repression and will be forced to use more severe, often illegal, tactics in order to gain its ends. In the early stages of the black movement, for example, peaceful marches and sit-ins were met by a countermovement of "white backlash." As a result, the black movement became radicalized through the militancy of such organizations as the Student Nonviolent Coordinating Committee (SNCC) and the Black Panther Party.

Ideally, thought and action should proceed and feed back into each other in order to effect the goals of the movement—to bring about social change.

Intellectuals play a prominent role in the creation and elaboration of ideology; their theories are reflected in terms, slogans, and labels that constitute the vocabulary of the movement. An interpretation of history that asserts that the movement's goals are in harmony with the traditions of the society, with divine or natural law, or with the movement of world history is usually a part of the ideology. In addition, there may be two visions of the future: the utopia that will result from the success of the movement, and the chaos that will prevail if it fails.

Finally, a movement's ideology often will invert the prevailing evaluation of social groups—the idea that "the last shall be first"—and will then cast social heroes and villains accordingly. To Marxists, capitalists and bourgeoisie are the villains, whereas to the bourgeoisie, radicals and communists are the epitome of evil.

Radical or Reform

The most common distinction between movements of reform and radical movements is based on the comprehensiveness of their goals. Reform movements usually advocate changes in some part of the social order, changes that are compatible with the basic values and institutions of the society. Radical movements, however, characteristically aim at comprehensive changes in all social institutions—political, economic, religious, and educational—and the substitution of new values and social relationships for the old. Reform movements typically try to achieve their goals through legitimate, peaceful means. Frequently, but not always, radical groups resort to force to overcome the opposition of vested interests. When radical groups use a considerable amount of force they are considered revolutionary movements.

This classification raises problems, however, because it depends in large part on the subjectivity of the classifier's judgment. What *are* the basic values of a given society? Even the most violent radical movements often proclaim that

their goals, not the establishment's, reflect the true, original values of the society. In effect, it is the public definition of a social movement, not its intrinsic character, that makes it radical or revolutionary. If a movement is publicly defined as threatening to the society's basic values, it will almost certainly encounter severe repression and will be forced more and more toward the use of illegal tactics.

Separatist or secessionist movements go beyond the goal of changing the social order and seek to withdraw from it entirely. Typically, a movement develops such a goal after its members despair of effecting change within the existing social structure. The numerous utopian communities in the United States during the nineteenth century are examples of separatist movements, as are such separatist religious groups as the Mormons and the Hutterites.

The Organization of Social Movements

A social movement always develops some internal organization and typical patterns of behavior among its members. The membership quickly divides into leaders and followers, but the influence of the leaders may not initially be recognized as formal authority. Membership often is not formalized either, partly because the size of the following often fluctuates rapidly and cannot be precisely defined or controlled, and partly because the very need for such formalization is often denied by the movement's ideology. Members vary in degree of devotion to the movement and its goals and often disagree among themselves as to who the real leaders are.

Leaders

A social movement often is identified with the name of a single, symbolic leader (for example, Christ or Muhammad, Lenin or Ho Chi Minh), but its nucleus is almost invariably a group whose members occupy differentiated roles and serve varying leadership functions. The creative or the *charismatic* leader who (because of his or her extraordinary personal qualities) is identified by both members and outsiders as the founding figure, is only one type of leader, albeit the most

memorable. Less conspicuous but equally important is the *administrative* leader who is concerned with the prosaic details of organization, finances, and other practical matters (for example, Saint Paul or Stalin). A third type of leader, the intellectual or *ideologist*, enlarges the ideology of the movement beyond the level of basic ideas and appealing slogans to a theory that justifies the movement, its means, and its goals. Often a charismatic leader also functions as an ideological leader. For example, the writings of Mao Tsetung, a charismatic leader, have been of primary ideological importance to the Chinese revolutionary movement.

Just as the membership of a social movement may often be ill-defined and fluctuating, the leadership may often be unstable and shifting. Various groups may vie for power, and, following the death of the founder, individual charismatic successors often compete for recognition. Many movements have foundered because of divisive internal struggles for leadership. The more loosely organized the movement is, the greater is the danger of schism or even total disintegration at this critical point.

A major problem in understanding social movements, on the part of both social scientists and laymen, has been in overestimating the role of leaders in charting the goals of the movement. You will recall from Chapter 8 that leaders of groups frequently are very limited in the degree to which they can exert authority. Recent studies of the peace movement, prepared for the President's Commission on the Causes and Consequences of Violence, indicate that the mobilization of large demonstrations was outside the power of movement leaders (Skolnick, 1969). Mass support was generated by events in Vietnam and Washington, not by leaders' calls to action. Others report the same process in regard to student protest—mass support came not in response to the actions of leaders but in response to actions by administrators, politicians, or the police (McEvoy and Miller, 1969).

The leadership of a strong social movement is often the nerve center of a loosely organized, vaguely defined body of members who support

Figure 28.3   Some social movements rely for their following on highly intense mass appeal. Such movements are typified by the rallies of Reverend Billy Graham, shown here speaking to a large crowd. People who join such movements tend to identify strongly with the movement at first but then gradually lose interest. Those who join social movements such as the Divine Precepts movement discussed in Chapter 2 that tend to rely on *personal* recruitment are likely to remain active longer, although their initial excitement may not be as great.

the movement with varying intensity. Such leadership must be attuned to the heterogeneous, contradictory, and often inarticulate grievances of this following and must try to formulate these grievances into specific complaints symbolized by appealing slogans and easily understood demands for action. To the extent that leaders accurately sense and satisfactorily formulate the mood of a movement's membership, followers feel that the ideas of the leaders are really their own. The result of a leader's accurate articulation of grievances and goals may be an increased cohesion among the existing members and an often dramatic entrance of new members.

Followers

Not all members are equally devoted to the cause. Some become *converts*, fully committed to the doctrines enunciated by the leaders, but a larger number are merely *adherents*, those who accept only part of the doctrine and whose loyalty and obedience vary with time and situation (Pettee, 1938). The devotion of others is little more than nominal, stemming more from the influence of reference groups with which they identify than from genuine conviction or conversion to a new way of thinking. And some members must be

counted primarily as *adventurers* or *opportunists* who participate in the movement in an attempt to advance their private goals (Hoffer, 1951). One of the greatest challenges to leadership is that of welding the members of a movement into a unified, disciplined collectivity able to act with determination and sustained effectiveness. Often this challenge goes unmet, and the movement gradually disintegrates.

Other movements, especially those of an illegal, conspiratorial character, are typically small, tightly organized, strictly disciplined, and highly restrictive of admission although they may seek and attract the support of a substantial number of sympathizers or "fellow travelers." The Bolshevik party in Russia between 1903 and 1917, as organized by V. I. Lenin, is probably the most successful case in recent history of such a small, dedicated, tightly knit movement.

Recruitment

One of the most important questions in the study of social movements is: Who joins and why? You will recall from Chapter 2 that this question was a major focus of John Lofland's study of the Divine Precepts group. Many hypotheses have been advanced to explain "participation proneness" among particular sectors of the society. None is fully satisfactory.

One popular explanation is that the type of person most likely to join a social movement is a misfit, an alienated individual, socially or psychologically maladjusted before he becomes a member, who seeks in the movement a "home" or a solution to his personal problem. A popular version of this old argument was advanced in the 1950s by Eric Hoffer, a longshoreman turned social philosopher, in his book *The True Believer* (1951). Hoffer argues that the fanatical members of all movements, "the true believers," share feelings of frustration, disaffection from society, and rejection by it. They become converts out of their own psychological needs rather than because of the doctrines of the movement or any deep desire for social reconstruction. Although such factors seem to play a role in individual cases, Hoffer's thesis seems oversimple and unconvincing as a comprehensive explanation.

Specific psychological traits that have been mentioned as predisposing people to membership include an authoritarian personality, unresolved childhood conflicts, and general rebellion against authority. In contrast, some social scientists look for attitudes, such as *alienation*, that reflect the current experience and the life style of joiners (Zeitlin, 1966). There are several reasons why individuals associate themselves with a given social movement; these reasons may be as various as the personality needs and social situations of the joiners. It is also probable that quite different motives separate those who join a reform movement from those who ally themselves with revolutionary groups. But any generalizations in this area would, at the moment, be premature and presumptuous.

Because people usually belong to other groups and have some status in society before joining a movement, the social characteristics of members have been the subject of some research. Adherents of specific movements tend to be drawn from particular socioeconomic levels. The current student left, for example, is largely made up of people with upper-middle-class backgrounds (Westby and Braungart, 1966).

Some researchers have examined the influence of *status inconsistencies,* such as when an individual is relatively wealthy yet a member of a minority group, on the tendency to join various types of movements (Rush, 1967; Broom, 1959; Geschwender, 1968). Thus, Gary Marx (1967) found that middle-class blacks were considerably more militant and more active in militant organizations than were working-class blacks. In a comprehensive series of studies, age, education, religion, political preference, and participation in community life were examined as sources of predisposition to join a social movement. The authors of the study concluded that people's background characteristics and their consequent attitudes are more important in determining whether people will join a movement (and in determining the movement's course) than are the leaders' activities (Morrison and Steeves, 1967).

Recruitment also greatly depends on the process of human interaction—people usually join movements only if they are recruited personally. At the end of his study on recruitment into the Divine Precepts movement, John Lofland reflected on the possible competitive advantages the Divine Precepts might have had in contrast to other movements in securing a particular convert. He concluded that they did not have ideological advantages over a great many other social movements. Instead, their advantage lay in being the particular social movement that established interactional bonds with a given convert at the appropriate moment. Converts did not choose the Divine Precepts after careful consideration of the doctrines of several competing groups. They chose the Divine Precepts because the Divine Precepts chose them. (See Chapter 2.)

Development of Norms

Any movement must have some degree of internal organization so that norms may develop. Obedience to these norms will symbolize the loyalty of members, strengthen their identification with the movement, and set them apart —sometimes radically and visibly—from nonmembers. Actual conformity to these norms varies as widely as the intensity of each member's commitment to the movement's goals.

Prescribed positions on specific issues are defined, and expression of these views becomes a mark of loyalty to the group. The norms may even suggest modes of dress (for example, the brown shirts of the early Nazis or the Mao peasant costume), styles of address (such as "Comrade" as a salutation among Communist Party members), and forms of recreation that are deemed appropriate for members. A special language may develop, including terms and phrases that encapsulate the movement's attitude on certain issues or toward certain groups. Joining the movement may, for the individual, have the significance of a "rite of passage" that dramatizes and signifies separation from his previous life and his reintegration into a new order of existence. At the extreme, almost every aspect of life is regulated by the

Figure 28.4   Social movements are often directed toward the realistic satisfaction of human needs. Farm workers in California, faced with oppressive circumstances, such as incomes below the subsistence level, frequent layoffs, and substandard housing, organized a social movement. The program included the organization of the United Farm Workers union as a bargaining group and, to support their demands, nation-wide boycotts of grapes and lettuce picked by nonunion workers.

movement, as was the case with Divine Precepts converts. Each convert was expected to enter communal life, give all his money to the movement, and devote all his time to the movement goals—to make the movement his whole concern.

The values and norms of a movement are communicated to members and are sustained in a variety of ways. The dissemination of printed propaganda and the speeches of leaders are two of the most important today. Equally important is the informal communication that takes place among members at meetings. Rallies are also important in creating a sense of solidarity. Such rallies are, in effect, rituals of integration for the group. Even music—the songs of the movement—sustain values, and a sense of fellowship is enhanced by such physical signs as buttons, medallions, banners, and auto-bumper stickers.

The Myth

To outsiders and critics, the program of a social movement often appears impractical and visionary, and its members may seem like utopians willing to disrupt the social order in the quest for an unattainable dream. Yet a social movement must offer a utopian vision of a better world if it is to inspire its members to make the sacrifices demanded of them. Georges Sorel, a nineteenth-century French writer, called this utopian vision "the myth" and argued that it was important not because it could ever be realized but because it could move people to action in the present (Sorel,

1950). Martin Luther King, Jr.'s, famous speech from the steps of the Lincoln Memorial, in which he proclaimed, "I have a dream," (1963) signaled the birth of such a myth. Millennial myths, such as the belief in the imminence of Christ's second coming, have led people to change their entire mode of living—as did the Divine Precepts, who believed Christ had already returned in Korea. To urge that social movements limit their vision only to what is practical is to ask them to forgo the possibility of mobilizing the deepest sources of human commitment and the noblest actions of which people are capable.

THE FATE OF SOCIAL MOVEMENTS

Social movements have been classified on the basis of their goals, their tactics, and their public definition, but any particular movement inevitably undergoes changes during the course of its existence. Thus, it becomes necessary to know what forces contribute to these changes in order to accurately characterize a movement throughout its career.

Changes in the *composition* and *size of membership* are two of the most important factors that can alter the character of a social movement. New types of followers, attracted by some part of the program but not all of it, may contribute to change in the movement's goals. The addition of a large number of new adherents may make organization and control of the membership more difficult, at least for a time; may lead to greater vagueness and abstraction of goals; and may make increase in numbers and wealth, rather than actual changes in the social order, the measure of the movement's success. (Recall the discussion of the transformation of sects into churches in Chapter 20.) What once were means can become ends.

On the other hand, the failure to attract a substantial following may influence the movement to rely increasingly on conspiratorial tactics designed to gain its ends in the absence of popular support. In other cases, such failure may presage the movement's rapid or gradual dissolution, as actual and potential members gravitate to more attractive groups or retreat into apathy.

The nature of the opposition to a movement also influences its career. Some religious revival movements have had little effect on the social order partly because they encountered so little opposition. Publicly defined from the beginning as respectable, they have elicited verbal support, but little action, from large numbers of adherents. A movement that encounters strong opposition may, as already noted, become radicalized. Frustrated in their attempts to effect change by legal means, its leaders may embark on illegal activities. Criticisms of a movement's values may also lead to fanatical, self-righteous defense and an intemperate denunciation of all critics. Finally, under external pressure, a movement may split over personalities or questions of tactics into competing wings that fight each other as well as their opposition. Such dissension was the fate of the Social Democratic party in Tsarist Russia, which, in 1903, split into the bitterly hostile Bolshevik and Menshevik factions, largely over questions of political tactics.

A social movement may fail as as a result of repression and the destruction of its organization or the removal of its leader, by death or otherwise. The rapid demise of Marcus Garvey's "back-to-Africa" movement in the 1920s, for example, can be ascribed to Garvey's conviction and imprisonment on charges of mail fraud. Furthermore, a movement may lapse into insignificance after a brief moment in the sun, as did "technocracy" in the 1930s, a movement that urged control of society by technical experts.

As a movement may fail, so may it succeed in a variety of ways. The greater single success is the actual attainment of power in the political arena through a successful revolution. Such occurrences are rare but are usually decisive when they do take place, as in Russia in 1917 or China in 1949. The accomplishment of secession by a separatist movement constitutes success in its own terms.

Sometimes movements achieve many of their goals without ever attaining power. Their programs are accepted by the larger society or by existing power groups, put into practice, and their personnel co-opted into the existing, now somewhat modified, institutional structure. The labor movement in the United States achieved such a success with the passage of the National Labor Relations Act in 1934, which institutionalized collective bargaining and the rights of labor unions. Sometimes major parties may be forced to incorporate into their own platforms some of the goals and programs advocated by third parties (parties built around one or a few issues). This was the ultimate fate of American Populism of the 1890s, the Townsend movement of the mid-1930s that demanded old-age insurance, and even much of Norman Thomas' socialism of the 1920s and 1930s, whose platform was virtually completely taken over by the Democratic and eventually even the Republican parties. Probably as many social movements have withered because of this kind of "success" as have declined as a result of either repression or natural attrition.

Even when a social movement may seem to have failed, it may have lasting covert effects. The utopian religious movements of the fifteenth and sixteenth centuries in Europe, such as Anabaptism, failed to usher in a new, divinely decreed and just social order, but these movements did lead to more active participation of the masses in politics and religious life. Marcus Garvey saw his black-separatist movement collapse, but some of his ideas lived on and were revived long after his death by the black-power movement.

The worldly success of a movement does not, however, mean that its program as envisioned in its myth, will become reality. Access to power, in whatever degree, imposes new requirements on the leaders of a movement. Successful revolutionary movements promising freedom and justice may be followed by a reign of terror in which dissent from the victorious new regime is ruthlessly and violently suppressed. The program of a successful movement may have to be modified in response to the often intractable difficulties encountered in making it a reality; and the myth proves to have been only an illusion, more a means of attaining power than a guide to using it. Yet people will continue to dream their dreams and strive to realize utopias on earth through collective action, despite the experiences and failures of their forebears.

Figure 28.5

Figure 28.6   Isabella (Sojourner Truth) was born in 1797 and died in 1883. For thirty years she was a slave on a Dutch estate in New York and was finally freed by the 1827 New York State emancipation laws. Her owner demanded that she continue to serve a year longer, but she fled with her infant daughter. She took the name Sojourner, and later Truth. She was deeply religious and an ardent abolitionist. She also eloquently fought for women's rights. During the Civil War she became the first female "freedom rider," striving to enforce the desegregation of public trans-portation. In 1864 she went to visit Lincoln at the White House and then remained in Washington, D.C., to work among the newly freed blacks whose children were being kidnapped and taken to Maryland, still a slave state. She organized posses to stop the slavers and convinced mothers to swear out warrants. Later she worked to influence legislation to gain the freedmen land in the West so they could support themselves. Her work made her a legend in her own time and a great figure in the history of black America.

WOMEN'S LIBERATION: CASE STUDY OF A SOCIAL MOVEMENT

Now that we have reviewed many general characteristics of social movements, let us turn to an analysis of a particular, contemporary movement—the women's movement. As you read about the development of this movement, try to determine how the features of social movements outlined in the previous discussion pertain to this specific case study.

A BRIEF HISTORY

There was a vigorous feminist movement in both the United States and Great Britain in the late nineteenth and early twentieth centuries. It began, in the United States, at least, with women who either were active abolitionists, such as Elizabeth Cady Stanton (1815–1902), Lucretia Mott (1793–1880), and Lucy Stone (1818–1893), or were inspired by the abolition (antislavery) movement. The discrimination, both legal and social, that they experienced as women working in the abolition movement awakened them to the need for a women's movement. For example, in 1840, the women members of the American delegation to the World Anti-Slavery Conference in London had been refused seats—an occurrence that serves to remind us that social issues can be very narrowly defined. Such treatment led them to establish (at a conference held at Seneca Falls, New York, in 1848) a movement for the emancipation of women.

The issue of women's rights was not, of course, a new one, having been an important question in the Western middle class for quite a while. For example, at the beginning of the nineteenth century Mary Wollstonecraft wrote an eloquent essay on the subject of women's rights and their position in society. Abigail Adams wrote a letter to her husband, President John Adams, warning him that if women's rights was not a high-priority issue, women would make it one. According to sociologist Carol Andreas (1971), many women's clubs and educational-meetings groups sprang up among discontented women, chiefly the wives of

Dat man ober dar say dat women needs to be helped into carriages, and lifted ober ditches, and to have de best place every whar. Nobody eber help me into carriages, or ober mud puddles, or gives me any best place, . . . and ar'n't I a woman? Look at me! Look at my arm! . . . I have plowed, and planted, and gathered into barns, and no man could head me—and ar'n't I a woman? I could work as much and eat as much as a man (when I could get it), and bear de lash as well—and ar'n't I a woman? I have borne thirteen chilern and seen 'em mos' all sold off into slavery, and when I cried out with a mother's grief, none but Jesus heard—and ar'n't I a woman? . . . Den dat little man in black dar, he say women can't have as much rights as man, cause Christ w'ant a woman. Whar did your Christ come from? . . . From God and a woman. Man had nothing to do with him. SOJOURNER TRUTH

Olive Gilbert, *Narrative of Sojourner Truth*, William Loren Katz, general ed. (New York: Arno Press, 1968).

Midwestern businessmen in the 1830s. In some experimental communes of the 1830s and 1840s, equality of the sexes was often attempted in all spheres—socially, in work, intellectually, and sexually. During the Civil War, of course, women were important participants in the labor force, doing jobs in support of the war effort and the jobs left vacant by men.

After the war, the "woman question" was widely debated. Many adherents of the women's movement expected that when the right to vote was granted to blacks it would be extended to women as well. Their dismay at the lack of support even from their fellow abolitionists caused some of the spokeswomen to oppose passage of the Fourteenth Amendment to the Constitution, which enfranchised black men.

In the early years of the movement, agitation and propaganda to awaken attention to the injustices women suffered were primary tasks. At first the feminists faced tenacious opposition and much ridicule. Amelia Bloomer and others who tried to do away with the restrictive, steel-ribbed and whalebone corsets simply earned abuse and the lasting derogatory term "bloomers" for their more reasonable clothing. But as the ranks of the feminists steadily grew, their tactics became bolder. They held mass rallies and marches, en-

Figure 28.7 Women earn less than men for the same type of work (*top*). The pay gap is wider for jobs held predominantly by women (*bottom*) than in male-dominated jobs—which are, by definition, of higher status.
(Adapted from U.S. Department of Labor.)

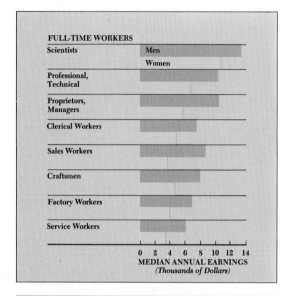

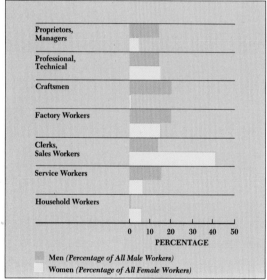

ance by no means guaranteed the entrance of women from lower social classes, or even of able women from the upper classes.

Feminists turned their attention to a great number of issues, including reforms in education, dress, industrial working conditions, religion, marriage, and divorce laws. By the turn of the twentieth century, they also concerned themselves with peace, prohibition of liquor, and economic legislation.

By the time the women's movement entered its second generation, toward the end of the nineteenth century, many of its leaders were educated and professional women, whereas formerly many had been housewives and poor women. Many of these new leaders had orthodox views on subjects other than suffrage. Questions of a "new morality," such as that championed by flamboyant Victoria Woodhull (1838–1927), and of a radical rethinking of the family, such as that put forth by Elizabeth Stanton (who identified domestic slavery as the source of women's oppression), now tended to fade. The country had in the meantime been transformed from an agrarian society to an industrial one, and the change brought great concern with the evils and ills of city life. Great waves of immigrants reached America, to suffer in the filth of the cities. Many women, such as Jane Addams (1860–1935), who might have concentrated their attention on feminist issues were drawn into social work and efforts at social reform.

The basis of the struggle for the vote changed in the teens of the new century from one with a strongly radical feminist emphasis to one with an emphasis on the service that "feminine virtues" could provide for government. In the words of Waltraud Ireland (1970), "Women's emancipation had essentially been reduced to the right to vote." During World War I much of the political rhetoric in America centered on "making the world safe for democracy," and, as is usual in war, women also took on many new roles—yet they still were not entitled to a share in that democracy. Late in 1919, after lobbying, demonstrations, and picket lines that resulted in the jailing of militant women, and with the reluctant support of President Wilson, the vote was granted women by pas-

gaged in civil disobedience, went to jail, and steadily gained support.

In the second half of the nineteenth century, when there was widespread concern about education, many women's colleges were founded. Despite much social opposition, even graduate education and training in professions like medicine and law were opened—although only to *exceptional* women. Most of these women were from comfortable social backgrounds, and their accept-

Figure 28.8   Since 1964, when Alice S. Rossi (*opposite*) published "Equality Between the Sexes: An Immodest Proposal" in the respected journal *Daedalus*, Ms. Rossi has brought her professional sociological skills to bear upon the tasks of understanding the place of women in American society and supporting large-scale meaningful change. Rossi's papers have been published in such diverse sources as *Science, American Sociological Review, The Humanist, Dissent,* and *Redbook*. She has noted that her work represents her as a woman, a

feminist, and a professional sociologist. She was a founding member of the National Organization for Women (NOW), and she has served on many national councils and task forces related to women, family law, and family life. Alice Rossi is presently a professor of sociology at Goucher College in Baltimore.

Figure 28.9   Portrait of a revolution: Mothers in the labor force, from 1940 to 1967.
(Adapted from Women's Bureau, 1969.)

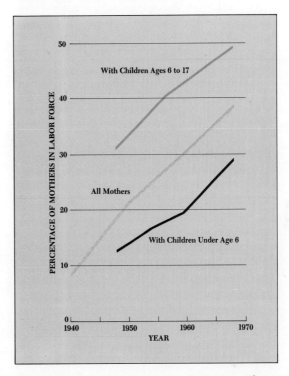

sage of the Nineteenth Amendment. But American women failed to win broader social reforms.

Shortly thereafter, feminism disappeared as a mass-based social movement. But suddenly in the mid-1960s the feminist movement was reborn.

Some commentators dated the rebirth of the women's movement from the publication in 1963 of Betty Friedan's book *The Feminine Mystique,* which eloquently and powerfully stated the grievances of contemporary middle-class women. Certainly this book was of great importance. But books do not create social movements. Indeed, all during the period beginning in 1920, when the women's movement lay dormant, important and eloquent books and articles stating the case for women continued to appear: Suzanne La Follette's *Concerning Women* in 1926, Gunnar Myrdal's "A Parallel to the Negro Problem" in 1944, Ruth Hershberger's *Adam's Rib* in 1948, Edith M. Stern's "Women Are Household Slaves" in 1949, Helen Hacker's "Women as a Minority Group" in 1951, and Simone de Beauvoir's *Second Sex,* in 1953, were among the best. But none of these writings started a social movement. Thus, Friedan's book seems to have appeared at a time when conditions were ripe for a movement to occur. What were these conditions?

SOURCES OF DISCONTENT

Earlier in this chapter the sources of strain that give rise to social movements are described as discrepancies between actual social conditions and the needs and aspirations of individuals. Furthermore, as the gap between the two widens, social movements are especially likely to result. In 1964, Alice S. Rossi, who has since become a major sociological investigator of sex inequalities, pointed out that women had not simply been standing still in terms of equality since the 1920s—they had actually been losing ground. In the same year Jessie Bernard, another prominent sociologist, published data showing that the proportion of women in the learned professions had actually *decreased* since the end of the nineteenth century. Since these early studies, considerable data have been gathered showing that the position of large numbers of American women rela-

tive to that of men has been declining. Three major factors must be considered: (1) changes in women's participation in the labor force; (2) changes in the duties of the wife-mother role; and (3) changes in educational achievement accompanied by a widening pay and status gaps between men and women.

Women in the Labor Force

Since 1940 there has been a considerable increase in the proportion of women who do full-time or part-time work outside the home. The largest and most significant increases have been in the proportions of working wives and mothers. In 1940, 12.5 percent of white wives held jobs; in 1966, more than 34 percent were working. The proportion of working nonwhite wives almost doubled in the same period: 27.3 percent of them worked in 1940, whereas 47.6 percent held jobs in 1966 (Ridley, 1969).

Changes were even more marked for mothers (see Figure 28.9). In 1940, only 8.6 percent of mothers were members of the labor force, but by 1967, 38.2 percent of mothers worked (Bernard,

Figure 28.10 Jessie Bernard has been researching and writing about marriage, the family, and women for thirty years. By her own admission, however it was not until her consciousness was raised by the women's liberation movement in the late 1960s that she began to question the underlying assumptions of the research she had accepted, contributed to, and taught. Dr. Bernard is presently putting together a volume in which she examines the major paradigms of the social and behavioral sciences for deficiencies that result from male biases in these sciences. Her books include *American Family Behavior* (1942, reissued, 1973), *Academic Women* (1964), *The Sex Game* (1968), *Women and the Public Image, An Essay on Policy and Protest* (1971), *The Future of Marriage* (1972), and the *Future of Motherhood* (1973). Jessie Bernard is presently Research Scholar Honoris Causa at Pennsylvania State University, where she had previously taught, from 1947 to 1964.

1971*a*). Whereas some of this increase is accounted for by women entering the labor force after their children were grown, there were also substantial changes among women with children still at home. Among women with children between the ages of six and seventeen, the proportion who worked rose from 31 percent in 1947 to 49 percent in 1967. Mothers with children under the age of six more than doubled their participation in the labor force in the same period—their numbers increased from 13 percent working in 1947 to 29 percent working in 1967 (Bernard, 1971*a*).

The increased participation in the labor force by wives and mothers created a number of strains. First, although increasing numbers of mothers with young children were working, child care was expensive and hard to find. Second, although many husbands of working women undoubtedly helped out with some domestic chores, such work was not defined as part of the role of husband and father, and thus most working women were also "homemakers." Third, disapproval of married women who worked continued to run relatively high—48 percent of the population disapproved in 1936, and 46 percent disapproved in 1960, despite the great changes during this period in the proportions of wives who did work (Oppenheimer, 1969). These pressures on working wives and mothers came to be felt by more and more women as more and more of them took jobs outside the home.

Perhaps the majority of women who entered the labor force did so out of economic necessity. For example, 79.2 percent of American families below the poverty line are families that have a woman as head of the household (United States Bureau of the Census, 1968). Obviously such women do not have the choice of being supported by a man. And, to some extent, as we shall see shortly, the poverty of such families stems from the low wages paid women and the low-paying jobs open to them. But in addition to families without a male wage earner are families in which both the husband's and the wife's incomes are required to maintain a modestly comfortable life style. Such women must choose between working or having their families do without many things they want and need.

During World War II, women again reentered the work force in large numbers, with the active encouragement of spokesmen and propagandists from government and other social institutions, such as churches and schools. "Rosie the Riveter" became a popular symbol of women's capacity to fill traditionally male work roles. Child care was made available, usually at places of work. After the war, official voices (echoed by the media) pressured women to relinquish their jobs to returning veterans and to resume their former roles, so that the men could find an America "just the way we left it." Child-care facilities closed down as the women left the factories.

Through the 1950s and 1960s cultural spokesmen decreed that the maintenance of the American home was a woman's highest calling and greatest fulfillment. Opinion leaders such as Dr. Benjamin Spock reinforced the newly developing idea that children could not be healthy or intelligent without full-time attention from their mothers. The definition of woman's role, for the first time in history, was posed almost solely in terms of service rather than productivity. There was concurrent emphasis on the definition of marriage as an institution with an emotional base—romantic love between husband and wife was the cement. Women who did not marry were increasingly derogated as loveless, desexualized, and "castrating" freaks. The question was posed: "Career or family?" with tacit agreement that one could not have both. But, as the Advisory Commission on the Status of Women (1969) has stated, fully ninety percent of women will work at some point in their lives—many, if not most, out of necessity. Cultural mythology and reality obviously are discrepant.

Changes in the Role of Wife and Mother

Since the early 1930s American women have tended to complete their families while they are quite young; the mean age of the American mother at the birth of her last child has been stable at about twenty-six or twenty-seven. Consequently, by the time the average mother is in her middle thirties, she no longer faces the demanding and time-consuming care of small children. Instead she faces the opportunity and perhaps the need to find something else to do with the time she once spent on infant care. In addition, the average life span has increased, so that most women have about forty-five years of life ahead of them by the time their youngest child begins school.

Labor-saving appliances, services, and products have reduced the time consumed by housekeeping duties. For example, before automatic washers and dryers became widely available after World War II, and before the development of synthetic fabrics and permanently pressed clothing, wives often spent one full day washing clothes and another full day ironing them. Nevertheless, the Chase Manhattan Bank asserts that women at home still put in over ninety-nine hours of housework a week (Mitchell, n.d.). But more and more women have come to recognize that the amount of work that *has* to be put in to maintain a reasonable home is far less. The wife's role has historically included much more than simple child care. The reduction of this role to housecleaner and nurse, plus the possibility of having more leisure time, led to growing unhappiness among many women, especially those isolated in "bedroom" suburbs. The pressures on mothers to elaborate these reduced roles to an absurd degree only intensified their oppressiveness in many women's eyes. The frustration and sense of uselessness such women experienced is poignantly described in Friedan's *Feminine Mystique*. The reduced requirements of women's family roles also led to women's increasing reentry into the labor force. And there they found that the nature of their jobs and pay magnified their frustration and discontent.

Education and Pay

The proportions of Americans completing high school and attending college have increased dramatically over the past few decades, as Chapter 18 points out. These increases occurred among both men and women, but men are still considerably more likely than women to obtain higher edu-

Figure 28.11 Women, even with college degrees, are often hired in supportive capacities, such as secretary and typist. Their work is usually menial, requiring little creativity or imagination other than in the ingenuity exercised in "keeping the boss happy," and the pay is usually quite low.

cation. In 1956, 37.7 percent of women high-school graduates went on to college (Bernard, 1964), whereas 54 percent of them did so in 1967 (Harris, 1970). The corresponding percentages for men were 65.6 and 71.

But it is not so much the lag in achieving college educations that has produced discontent among women as it is the fact that such achievement is so much less rewarded for women than for men. It is pointed out in Chapter 13 that educational achievement has much less effect on social mobility for blacks than it does for whites. The same difference occurs between the sexes. Several years ago the median income of women with bachelor's degrees was approximately equal to that earned by men with eighth-grade educations! Indeed, as Joreen (1970) shows, the median income of women with college degrees is only 51 percent of that of men with degrees. This is partly accounted for by the positions women achieve in the labor force. Bernard (1971*b*) concludes that most of the increase in working women who had been to college was absorbed by *clerical* occupations. These are low-paying, low-prestige, and dead-end occupations: typist, file clerk, receptionist. In 1968 more than 48 percent of employed women with from one to three years of college education were in clerical occupations.

It is true that women with degrees are generally employed in professional and technical occupations. However, they are heavily concentrated in the lowest-paying and lowest-status occupations in this group. Women dominate such occupations as nurse, teacher, social worker, and medical and dental technician, but they are rare in the ranks of doctors, lawyers, and college professors. For example, Rossi (1969) pointed out that although women in 1969 made up 30 percent of doctoral candidates in sociology and 31 percent of sociology graduate students who were teaching undergraduates, they made up only 14 percent of full-time assistant professors, 9 percent of full-time associate professors, 4 percent of full-time professors, 1 percent of "chairmen" of graduate sociology departments, and 0 percent of the forty-four full professors at the five elite departments (Berkeley, Chicago, Columbia, Harvard, and Michigan).

By the mid-1960s, then, there had developed a large and growing number of women whose status in terms of educational achievement was far higher than it was in terms of their income and occupational prestige. They were overqualified for the jobs they held. This is a clear example of status inconsistency as that concept is developed in Chapters 12 and 14. Women who had come, during the process of achieving college degrees, to see themselves as intelligent and socially valuable were assigned boring tasks, were denied authority, and were frequently expected to be office servants—to make the coffee, tidy up the office, run personal errands for the boss, and massage his ego. Worse yet, they often had to accept significantly lower pay than men, and sometimes lower job titles, for identical jobs. The proportion of women attending college continued to increase, and, therefore, so did the number of women caught in inconsistent statuses.

Furthermore, since World War II the position of women relative to men has been getting *worse*. In 1940 working women were slightly more likely than working men to hold jobs in the two highest-status occupational categories—"professional-technical" and "managers and officials." But as Dean D. Knudsen (1969) points out, by 1969

working men were almost twice as likely as working women to hold these high-paying and high-status jobs (27.2 percent versus 16.4 percent). Thus, the general rise in high-status positions and the decline in unskilled ones that has characterized the American economy over past decades has benefited only men.

Moreover, the gap between the incomes of men and women *increased* by a stunning amount between 1945 and 1966. In 1945 the median income for women was $910 less than the median income for men (see Figure 28.8). In 1966 the gap had widened to $3,668. For all their increases in schooling, and for all of their greater participation in the labor force, women were falling further behind men in the prestige of the jobs they held and in the salaries they earned. Recall the discussion of Davies' J-Curve theory of revolutions. Davies predicts that radical social movements are likely to occur when the gap between expectations and actual rewards increases. Women's expectations were rapidly rising because of their gains in education, but the actualities of their relative rewards in the labor force were declining. Under these conditions, Davies' model would predict the occurrence of a social movement aimed at the redress of grievances. That is what, in fact, happened.

BUILDING A WOMEN'S MOVEMENT

Grievances do not automatically translate themselves into a social movement. Instead, in response to grievances people must develop a common awareness of their problems and unite in a *collective* effort to deal with these problems. Several factors played a major role in bringing many women together with a shared awareness of the need for change.

One was probably the rise of the black civil-rights movement, which provided a model for many other disadvantaged groups. It sensitized many Americans to the mechanisms of discrimination and by example demonstrated how unified protest could provoke change. A second factor was disillusionment with the Civil Rights Act of 1964. The only feature of the act that included women was the section on equality in employment. It was quickly demonstrated that these provisions would not be enforced on behalf of women. A third factor was that increasing entry into the labor force brought women out of the isolation of their homes and into contact with one another in offices and factories. Recall from Chapter 14 that Marx predicted that industrialization would lead to revolution because the isolated peasantry would be gathered into factories where they could develop a common consciousness of their circumstances. Although the revolution did not occur where Marx expected it to, a vigorous labor movement did, which suggests that Marx was at least on the right track. The case of women moving into work situations seems somewhat similar. Increased opportunities for interaction helped women build a shared definition of their situation. At this point books and articles on the oppression of women no longer went unheeded. Instead, such materials provided the basis for developing an ideology.

New formal and informal organizations appeared that were devoted to the cause of women's rights. One of the first formal organizations to appear was the National Organization for Women (NOW), founded in 1966. Differences among groups within the contemporary women's movement are often not clear-cut, but it seems fair to consider NOW a moderate, reformist group.

Another major orientation within the women's movement is represented by a more radical perspective. Young women of the New Left working in civil-rights and antiwar groups experienced discrimination that was similar to that experienced by women abolitionists over 100 years before. By 1967 these women had formed independent groups in New York, Chicago, Boston, and many other locations throughout the United States, using the name "Women's Liberation Movement" (Salper, 1972; Ware, 1970). Since then the name has been generally applied to the women's movement and consequently to groups not associated with left-wing politics.

Some groups that began on the left have ceased their affiliation with any traditional political perspective on the status of women, noting

Figure 28.12 *Current Population Reports* published in 1963 and 1967 by the United States Bureau of the Census indicates that the gap between women's and men's median annual incomes has increased steadily from 1945 to 1966. This trend points to one of the severe, concrete grievances that helped trigger the women's movement for social change.
(Adapted from U.S. Bureau of the Census, 1963 and 1967.)

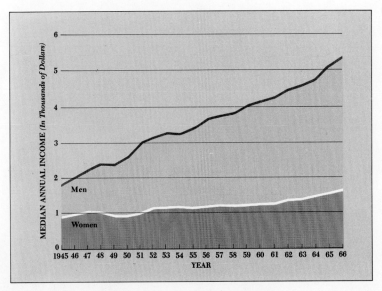

that social revolution has not *necessarily* meant the liberation of women. Yet such groups (who sometimes call themselves Radical Feminists) remain radical in the sense that they believe solutions to social inequalities will require massive reorganization of society, rather than reform. However, other groups that consider themselves part of the Women's Liberation Movement do remain associated with left-wing politics in that they analyze their position in a society divided along class and racial lines, as well as by sex. These groups (who sometimes refer to themselves as socialist feminists) feel that solutions to social oppression and exploitation require the total restructuring of social institutions. And these groups do incorporate many aspects of leftist politics in their assumptions of how social change shall be effected (McAfee and Wood, 1972).

THE IDEOLOGY AND PROGRAMS OF FEMINISM

The ideology of feminism is open-ended and undergoing continual revision. Yet there are some consistent features that can be pointed out. For the purpose of our discussion we will speak of the two main ideological forces in feminism as the "moderate" and the "radical." Ideological differences between them, as noted earlier, often are

Figure 28.13   Language reflects culture. Men's
attitude toward women is reflected in the language
they use to refer to women. Women have been
called chicks, foxes, pigs, pussies, and dogs. They have
also been called broads, skirts, birds, and numerous
other things. These terms may seem rather innocuous
in themselves, but the concepts they represent—
and the inferior status they imply—help shape women's
self-images. These self-images, in turn, help shape
the kinds of subordinate behavior that contribute to
women's inferior status and to their oppression.

not clear-cut; in some areas, they are differences in degree; in other areas, they reflect differing goals and programs. Such differences are discussed in more detail later in the chapter. But whatever their differences, it must be noted that moderates and radicals often work together and that many groups do contain both moderate and radical women.

Many feminists identify the historical failure of the women's movement as one that resulted from lack of a unified social, political, and economic analysis of women's situation in society and also from people's identification of "the woman question" with the vote. Today's feminists, in the process of learning a lesson from history, give more emphasis to the analysis of society and to the question of how to reorganize the society to bring about social equality.

At its first national conference in 1967, NOW adopted a set of demands that virtually all feminist groups support: an end to discrimination by gender in employment; paid maternity leave; publicly supported child care; equal opportunity in education and job training; repeal of all abortion laws; and unrestricted access to contraceptive information and devices (NOW, 1970). It was in response to efforts by the National Women's Political Caucus (NWPC), NOW, and other women's groups, that the Democratic Party adopted reformed rules giving women a major role for the first time in the convention of 1972. Reformist groups such as NOW and NWPC have made many other efforts to get their programs into law at both the state and national level.

The more moderate feminists have concentrated on legislative reform programs. They tend to feel that solutions to women's problems lie in the provision of equal opportunities for and equal treatment of the two sexes. They hope that social attitudes—women's feelings about themselves and the behavior expected of them, as well as men's feelings about women and expectations of them—will change under the pressure of agitation, law, and education. The more radical feminists, especially many of those with working-class backgrounds, doubt whether legislative reform would sufficiently alter existing social, political,

and economic institutions so that the lot of all women (and, indeed, of men and children) would improve. Social change, they point out, cannot simply be legislated. However, all feminists recognize that legislative reform is necessary.

The Feminist Viewpoint

What do feminists in general currently believe? The basic feminist viewpoint today is that neither women nor men are given the opportunity to define themselves or to develop their potentialities because of restrictive role definitions. Feminists point out that psychologists have found that on psychological scales there are greater differences among people of the same sex than there are between the norms for males and females, despite cultural training—shouldn't people be allowed to develop their individuality? Feminists hold that people cannot know whether any real, biologically determined differences relevant to modern life and work exist between men and women until constrictive cultural distinctions are eradicated. Women are kept socially subordinate not only by their own internalized role training, values, and beliefs but by unfair practices and discrimination both deliberate and unintended.

This basic social inequality—discrimination on the basis of gender—is termed *sexism*. Sexism is, simply put, the tendency to see "sex" (gender) as a factor of great importance in the organization of all aspects of society. As with racism, its counterpart, the dominant group sees its own orientation as the only right one. Just as racism in Western society results in white supremacy, sexism results in male supremacy. So, as Jessie Bernard (1971b) has pointed out, sexism amounts to the unconscious, unexamined, and unchallenged belief that the world as men see it is the only world, that the way of dealing with life that men have created is the only way to deal with it, and that what men think about women is the only way to think about women.

But sexism is not just a point of view restricted to men; women hold it as well. Women frequently are harsh judges of other women whose behavior deviates from role-prescribed behavior, and, of course, it is mostly mothers who socialize their

Figure 28.14   A social movement may contain both moderate and radical factions. In the women's movement of the late nineteenth and early twentieth centuries, the moderate faction focused on the attempt to get the vote for women and looked to existing institutions to accomplish its goals. The more radical faction was aimed at a wider goal: a complete end to the oppression of women. Women working toward such a goal were forced to bypass existing male-dominated institutions and their legitimately validated authority structure and thus often left themselves open to criminal prosecution.

daughters into traditional feminine roles. Sexism permeates our culture. We use the words "man" and "mankind," "he," "him" and "his," to refer to all human beings (a practice that has been avoided in this textbook—to the extent that English usage permits—except in direct quotations from other sources). Adult women are frequently called "girls"; this practice is analogous to calling an adult black man "boy." Perhaps more importantly, advertising, adult and children's literature, and most social institutions have actively promoted a view of women as narcissistic, silly, weak, headachy, emotionally unstable, and generally competent only to judge the whiteness of the wash. The honorifics "Miss" and "Mrs." categorize women according to their marital status, but men are referred to as "Mr." whether they are married or not. (Many women now prefer to use "Ms."—a title that does not depend on marital status.)

Feminists have given considerable attention to how the emphasis on female attractiveness—the pressure to be seen as attractive by men—is both produced by and supportive of male dominance. In addition, those who don't spend much of their time altering their natural appearances are, like the Bloomer girls, condemned; they earn the epithets "slob," "dog," "unfeminine," "dyke," and so forth.

The pressures to be attractive to men divide women by making them rivals and also make them dependent upon men: it is men who decide which women are attractive. Feminists identify this tendency to judge other women by their appearances as treating women as *sex objects*. Consequently, they oppose such cultural forces as *Playboy*, which operate to maintain the preoccupation with a woman's body as a commodity, and the me-too attempts of such sexual-liberation-oriented magazines as *Cosmopolitan* to foster the same preoccupation with men's bodies. They also deplore the "counterculture's" picture of women, such as that celebrated in the lyrics of many rock songs, and the role of nurturing "Earth Mother" that women, especially in communes, are expected to play.

The essence of the traditional female role is widely held to be *service* to the emotional and physical needs of others—preeminently those of children and husbands, and often elderly parents as well. Indeed, the wishes and feelings of others must take priority over women's own; this contributes to the inherent inferiority of the traditional female sex role in terms of power and decision-making force.

To the extent that women are sensitive to others' emotional needs, men can receive fulfillment of their demands upon women *without having to ask*. This has several important consequences. For one thing, men may exercise power over women without appearing to do so. Thus, both marriage partners and even outside observers may believe that unequal situations are situations of equality. The frequency of automatic service that men receive gives them the impression that women *ought* to please them, and it encourages anger and disdain toward women who do not. Such male expectations and reactions are central to sexist ideologies.

The use of physical violence and force is seen as symptomatic of the syndrome of sexism that results in the subjugation of women. Rape, wife beating, and other examples of the male use of force demonstrate that men do use force to dominate women (as they too often do to dominate other men). The fear of force makes women dependent on men to protect them from other men. Physical dominance by males results not simply

Figure 28.15   Women, observing the third annual Women's Rights Day (September 25, 1972), demonstrate outside the American stock exchange in New York to protest the lack of women brokers on the floor. Some radical women's groups believe that such demonstrations for equal rights are characteristically addressed to the concerns of middle-class women. Radical women point to a split between the concerns of working-class and middle-class, mostly professional women as a failing of the women's movement. As

evidence of such a split they point to the Equal Rights Amendment, which, at the time of this writing, is awaiting ratification by the states and which is enthusiastically backed by a broad spectrum of middle-class women's groups—most prominently, the National Organization for Women (NOW). The amendment is opposed by many working-women's groups because it *removes* protective legislation that applies to women—rather than extending such legislation to men (Jordan, 1970).

from size and strength differences but also from role training. The activist approach to this issue has included the establishment of rape clinics by women's groups to help victims, who are often ill-treated by police and doctors. This approach has also included the training of women in techniques of physical self-defense on the twofold rationale that well-prepared women will be better able to defend themselves and that, more importantly, women have been socialized into the passive, victim's role and consequently have hardly any sense of what they are capable of physically.

Much feminist analysis has grown out of women sharing their concrete personal experiences in small groups. Many women meet regularly in these small groups, called *consciousness-raising groups*, to exchange and discuss their experiences and feelings so that they may come to realize that the difficulties women experience are common to them as a group and not the product of emotional weakness (as has often been implied). Through this sharing, women have achieved fuller understanding of how sexism operates in society.

Radical Analysis

Many of the efforts of the feminists, particularly the more radical ones, are aimed at helping women gain a sense of their untapped capabilities, both physical and psychological, and a sense of potency as individuals. They recognize the need for individual women to struggle against their own personal histories, which include socialization into the subordinate, relatively passive women's role; to regain or achieve a sense of *personal* dignity; to accept the worth of their own needs and desires rather than allowing everyone else's to take priority; and to strive for some kind of meaningful activity and achievement that will bring self-respect. Radical feminists emphasize the need to achieve wider change. They are united in their condemnation of the individualist bias that often weakens social movements. Thus, they emphasize *collective* effort, as women working together with other women, and also with men, to overcome distinctions between people on

the basis of irrelevant social categories. The consciousness-raising group, therefore, is meant to raise women's consciousness not only of their individual plights but also of the plights of other women and, more broadly, of everyone whose human powers are diminished by society because of the role definitions foisted on them by virtue of their age, gender, social class, race and so on.

Radical groups generally agree that people should participate as much as possible in making decisions that affect their own lives. As one aspect of their attempt to put this belief into practice they often try numerous ways to facilitate women's active participation in the movement, and many of them deny that the movement has fixed leaders. They acknowledge certain spokeswomen but repudiate the attempt by mass media to identify certain women, such as Gloria Steinem or Germaine Greer, as leaders.

Radical feminists think that to define the problem primarily in terms of changing laws will definitely doom the movement to failure in achieving the substantial changes needed to overcome the problems faced by women. As stated earlier, they believe that to concentrate on legislation is to travel down the same road to failure that brought an end to the earlier women's movement. Instead, they feel that radical changes in the organization of society's institutions are vital.

Figure 28.16 "Oh, she's average—smokes sometimes, drinks punch, frequently kissed—Oh, yes—common knowledge—one of the effects of war, you know." So goes the description of a woman in F. Scott Fitzgerald's *This Side of Paradise* (New York: Charles Scribner's Sons, 1920). Cultural changes in postwar America, including the achievement of the right to vote, led to the false idea that women had been "liberated"—that is, had achieved full social equality.

Figure 28.17 Mary Harris "Mother" Jones (1830–1930) was fifty years old when she left a career of teaching and dressmaking to become a full-time union organizer. She vehemently pointed out that women's failure to challenge role definitions on every level plays into the hands of the powerful in a male-supremacist society. She said "No matter what your fight . . . don't be ladylike. God Almighty made women and the Rockefeller gang of thieves made ladies."

They argue that the solutions to women's problems proposed by many moderate feminists are inapplicable to working-class women: get a job or go back to school and hire a maid to do your housework and perhaps care for the kids. This, radical feminists note, merely shifts the derogating, low-status jobs to women who are often too poor to have much choice about how they earn their living. Thus, there is actually a danger that middle-class women's liberation will be achieved at the expense of lower-class women—and men.

The more moderate organizations have often accepted such criticism and attempted to alter their proposals to mitigate possible ill effects. But on the whole they do not share the more radical women's belief that the system has always divided the poor from the middle class (to the detriment of the poor).

Furthermore, such class analysis is mainly restricted to those radical feminists who have retained a commitment to the political left. The majority of radical feminists see sexism as a more fundamental split in society than class division. Thus, they do not concern themselves with political reform as much as with total cultural reform. In the words of Ellen Willis (1970):

The radical [political] movement has been dominated by men. Its theory, priorities, and strategies reflect male interests. . . . An anti-capitalist, anti-imperialist analysis is insufficient for our purposes. Women's oppression antedated capitalism . . . and has outlasted it in socialist countries. . . . We must provide a place for women to be friends, exchange personal griefs and give their sisters more support—in short, develop group consciousness. . . . It is not only possible but imperative for women to build a specifically feminist radical consciousness.

They therefore organize on many fronts—political, personal, social, and cultural: collective-living experiments; alternative institutions, such as day care and gynecological clinics that provide care and also teach women to perform simple examinations themselves; educational groups; and consciousness-raising groups.

Generally speaking, moderate feminists find the analysis of the radicals implausible and utopian. They doubt that radical feminists understand practical politics. They see little to be gained by implacable opposition to compromise. Unlike radical feminists, they doubt sex-based inequalities are inextricably tied to most other social ills. Many believe not only that radical feminists call for unnecessarily radical changes but that in so doing they do damage to the movement by alienating potential supporters and allies who oppose the radical remaking of society as a whole.

THE FUTURE OF THE MOVEMENT

The women's movement was reborn innocently, without a sense of its past. Women in the "dormant" period between 1920 and the late 1960s

Figure 28.18   *The Illegal Operation* by Edward Kienholz shows the apparatus of illegal abortion. Kienholz created the protest art piece in 1962, ten years before the Supreme Court upheld women's rights to legal abortion.

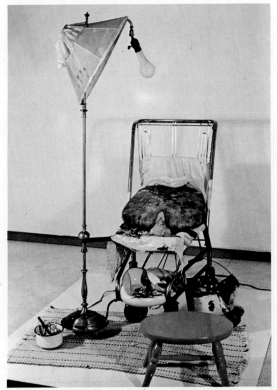

considered themselves to have achieved social equality. Everyone could laugh at those silly old suffragettes who took themselves so seriously! Women could congratulate themselves on being "liberated": they could buy and use cigarettes, display themselves as sexual objects for the pleasure of men, make themselves available sexually as never before—none of which challenged male domination in any sphere. Even *Playboy* took the opportunity to congratulate the new "girl" on her—primarily sexual—liberation and to contrast her with the old fuddy-duddies of the past (Holmes, 1968).

Women soon discovered, however, that the "liberated" woman (or girl) was not the same as women's liberation and that women would simply have to stop letting other people define them, tell them what they were and what they should be, should do, and should want. Women are gradually discovering the past history of their movement. Putting all the manifestations and causes of sexism

and other discrimination together into an anaylsis of how discrimination affects *all* of a society and its participants—old, middle-aged and young, female *and* male—and then attacking these causes and manifestations will, they hope, lead to a radical readjustment of the whole system.

As has been pointed out, the contemporary women's movement is still fluid; its ideology is open-ended, and its proposed solutions are under continual revision. But the present central issues are likely to remain central to the development of the movement.

The simple fact that women are not a minority group (indeed, they are the majority) makes it likely that they will achieve many changes. Major alterations in childhood socialization, the family, and the economy may well take place. But it is not yet possible to say just what these changes will be. Obviously, the claims of some radical feminists that the liberation of women will establish a utopian age of peace and total equality among people are unlikely to prove accurate. But it does seem probable that society will be greatly changed.

SUGGESTED READINGS

General References

Turner, Ralph H., and Lewis M. Killian. *Collective Behavior.* Englewood Cliffs, N.J.: Prentice-Hall, 1959.

Toch, Hans. *The Social Psychology of Social Movements.* Indianapolis: Bobbs-Merrill, 1965.

The Women's Movement

Bernard, Jessie. *Women and the Public Interest: An Essay in Policy and Protest.* Chicago: Aldine-Atherton, 1971.

Cade, Toni (ed.). *Black Woman.* New York: (Signet Books) New American Library, 1970.

Firestone, Shulamith. *The Dialectics of Sex.* New York: William Morrow, 1970.

Gornick, Vivian, and Barbara K. Moran (eds.). *Women in Sexist Society: Studies in Power and Powerlessness.* New York: Basic Books, 1971.

Morgan, Robin (ed.). *Sisterhood Is Powerful.* New York: Random House, 1970.

Chapter 29 Modernization

SOME PEOPLE AND GROUPS enjoy a life with a high degree of comfort while others have difficulty scraping by; within any society there is an unequal distribution of power, property, and prestige. Similarly, the world is divided into rich nations and poor nations. *Modernization* is the word denoting the process by which agrarian societies become wealthy industrial nations—and by which the poor Third-World nations of Asia, Africa, and South America hope to do likewise.

Modernization involves every aspect of national life—social, economic, and political. It brings with it changes in the laws of a nation, in the organization of work, and in the beliefs of individuals. It is reflected in community organization, mass communication, health services, and in transportation. The term modernization describes an ideology as well as a process. The ideology of modernization invokes the goal of a greatly improved life in the future and urges people to change their behavior in order to bring this future about. As an ideology of the future, modernization everywhere has similar goals: national independence, economic well-being, and social equality. As a process, modernization requires different methods in different places to achieve these goals.

This final chapter treats modernization both as a dependent and as an independent variable so that you can observe the way modernization is affected by and in turn affects other variables discussed throughout the book. The particular course that modernization follows within any individual society varies with both internal needs and external forces. But no matter what the particular forces shaping it are, once modernization is under way, it always brings about major changes in a society's role systems, organizations, and institutions, as well as in its criteria and systems of stratification (see Chapter 12).

MEASURES OF MODERNIZATION

Because the process of modernization involves change in social, political, and economic institutions, it is quite difficult to assess the rate at which it is proceeding or the course it is taking simply on the basis of a single set of characteristics.

Economic Development

Gross national product (GNP) per capita is the most widely used indicator of national modernization because it has the advantage of summarizing great quantities of information in a single number. The GNP per capita is the total monetary value of all final goods and services produced in a nation in one year divided by the number of people in that nation. However, it has serious drawbacks, aside from the obvious one that, because it concerns only economic information, it does not permit evaluation of social or political modernization: (1) It does not indicate whether a nation is modernizing, for it describes the present state of a nation, not how it is changing. (2) By summarizing so many pieces of information, it obscures the distinct roles played by the various parts of a nation's economy. (3) It fails to take into account the unequal distribution of wealth, which especially characterizes predominantly agrarian societies (see Chapter 12). GNP per capita as an assessment of modernization should be supplemented by other indexes. Among the other most frequently measured variables are population growth, level of urbanization, quality of educational and medical services, diffusion of consumer goods, labor organization, political stability, and political participation.

Per-capita national income, or average income, is another commonly used measure of economic modernization. Looking at Table 29.1, which gives the per-capita income of various countries, you can see that there is disparity among developing nations themselves, between developing nations and advanced ones, and between nations that have different types of economies—*planned economies* (the socialist countries) and *market economies* (the capitalist ones). Developed socialist countries, having planned economies—for example, the Soviet Union, East Germany, and the other Eastern European socialist countries—have lower per-capita incomes than do the developed capitalist countries, those having market economies. The developed capitalist countries are the United States, Japan, Israel, and the countries of the British Commonwealth and Western Europe. Except for Israel, these countries experienced the benefits of the industrial revolution of the nineteenth century and went from agrarian to industrialized nations. Before the end of World War II, most of these countries had established empires throughout the world—networks of colonies that served as sources of cheap labor and raw materials and as markets for manufactured goods.

Most of the underdeveloped countries of Africa, Asia, and Latin America stood in official colonial status with respect to the advanced capitalist countries until the end of World War II. These underdeveloped countries, which are located in clusters on three continents, are known collectively as the Third World. They rely almost exclusively on agriculture and the mining of raw materials. As Table 29.1 shows, these predominantly agrarian countries are extremely poor. Although there are differences in per-capita national income among the countries of the Third World—the Latin American countries, for example, have an average per-capita income that is two and a half times that of the Asian countries and twice that of the African countries—the Third World taken as a whole is extremely disadvantaged compared with the developed nations.

Taking the unequal distribution of wealth in Third World countries into account, the differences between per-capita income of the agrarian Third World countries and the advanced socialist and capitalist countries are even more glaring. For example, the per-capita income in Brazil is $130, but this figure does not take into account the uneven distribution of income throughout the population. A few high-level officials or plantation owners make thousands or even hundreds of thousands of dollars a year while the average peasant nearly starves. In the industrialized countries the incomes are more evenly distributed, and per-capita income gives a better picture of the economic well-being of a population.

Measures of industrialization are important supplements to per-capita income in assessing modernization in developing countries. A country has to industrialize in order to modernize. Many people must give up farming and take up factory work before substantial economic growth can take place. The two best measures of industrialization in a given country are its per-capita consumption of energy and its per-capita consumption of industrial steel. Columns two and three of Table 29.1 give these figures for our groups of countries. It is clear that most of the countries of Asia, Africa, and Latin America are extremely far behind in industrialization. In order to develop economically, these countries will have to undergo drastic and rapid industrialization.

Social Development

It is important to measure social as well as economic development to know whether and how a country is modernizing. Measures of social development, as we shall see, are important indicators of modernization. Countries express different values in their social development according to what they choose to spend their money on. Thus, some developing nations stress heavy industry, such as steel mills, and others emphasize education.

Table 29.2 gives several indexes of social development. If we compare the advanced socialist countries with the advanced capitalist countries, we can see that the two types are about equally developed socially. However, although these two groups of countries have approximately the same number of doctors, teachers, registered pupils, books, and radio receivers, certain differences reflect differences in values. The socialist countries are slightly ahead in medicine and education, and the advanced capitalist countries are slightly ahead in consumer goods (measured by the number of inhabitants per radio receiver).

The glaring differences occur when the advanced socialist and capitalist countries are compared with the underdeveloped, nonindustrialized Third World. The level of social development in Third World countries of Asia, Africa, and Latin America lags far behind that of the industrially developed countries. Dividing the population by the number of doctors, we find that a doctor in Nigeria must serve the medical needs of 34,000 people, whereas a doctor in the United States serves only 690 people. Similarly, for each of the

Table 29.1   Indexes of Economic Development *a*

Country	Per Capita National Income *d*	Per Capita Consumption, 1964	
		Energy of Coal	Industrial Steel
United States	(1964) $2700	8772 kg*e*	615 kg
United Kingdom	(1964) 1365	5079	438
West Germany	(1964) 1415	4230	579
France	(1964) 1370	2933	356
Italy	(1964) 760	1659	221
Sweden	(1964) 2025	4320	623
Average b	1605	4500	470
Soviet Union	(1964) 890	3430	355
East Germany	(1964) 1205	5569	424
Czechoslovakia	(1964) 1685	5789	498
Hungary	(1964) 1445	2824	224
Bulgaria	(1964) 650	2410	124
Cuba	(1964) 575	931	29
Average b	1075	3490	275
Pakistan	(1963) 80	86	11
India	(1963) 80	161	16
Malaysia	(1963) 235	373	43
Thailand	(1963) 95	106	13
Iraq	(1963) 210	666	28
Average b	140	280	22
United Arab Republic *c*	(1961) 130	321	24
Morocco	(1964) 170	149	16
Zambia	(1964) 195	431	22
Nigeria	(1962) 90	38	6
Ghana	(1964) 250	120	11
Average b	165	210	16
Peru	(1964) 235	602	24
Argentina	(1964) 685	1242	93
Brazil	(1960) 130	364	43
Chile	(1964) 445	1078	74
Colombia	(1963) 230	494	31
Average b	345	755	53

a. Data have been drawn from the United Nations Statistical Yearbook (1965), various tables.
b. All averages are simple averages.
c. Egypt and Syria until mid-1961, when Syria withdrew.
d. All figures are in dollars and were calculated from the data and conversion rates supplied by the United Nations Statistical Year-book. For the socialist countries (excluding Cuba), the net material product at market prices was used and the conversions were made at the "base price."
e. Or equivalent.
Source: Pierre Jalée, *The Third World in World Economy* (New York: Monthly Review Press, 1969).

Table 29.2   Indexes of Social Development *a*

Country	Number of inhabitants per				
	Doctor 1960–1963	Teacher 1963–1964	Registered pupil 1963–1964	Number of book titles produced 1964	Radio receiver 1962–1964
United States	690	88	3.7	6,753	1.00
United Kingdom	840	135	5.8	2,077	3.39
West Germany	670	158	6.1	2,226	3.21
France	870	112	4.5	3,585	3.23
Italy	610	103	5.9	5,682	4.91
Sweden	960	93	5.4	1,161	2.60
Average	775	115	5.2	3,580	3.05
Soviet Union	510	118	4.4	2,910	3.15
East Germany	*c*	113	4.7	2,862	2.78
Czechoslovakia	570	95	4.4	1,648	3.80
Hungary	650	110	5.1	2,108	4.05
Bulgaria	620	93	4.2	2,367	4.16
Cuba	1,200	141	4.7	14,120	*c*
Average	710	112	4.6	4,336	3.59
Without Cuba	587			2,380	
Pakistan	7,000	383	11.3	65,000	183
India	5,800	*c*	8.3	35,920	110
Malaysia	10,500	144	5.3	18,280	20
Thailand	7,600	193	6.1	7,245	*c*
Iraq	4,800	164	6.2	24,170	10
Average	7,140	121	7.4	30,120	81
United Arab Republic *b*	2,500	215	7.0	10,870	13
Morocco	9,700	375 *d*	11.0 *d*	*c*	20
Zambia	8,900	*c*	9.5	*c*	300
Nigeria	34,000	509	17.4	213,700	94
Ghana	12,000	208	6.1	34,080	13.5
Average	13,420	327	10.2	86,220	88
Peru	2,200	149	4.9	11,900	5.5
Argentina	670	89	5.4	6,635	3.6
Brazil	2,700	170	7.0	14,910	10.5
Chile	1,800	*c*	4.9	5,380	5.4
Colombia	2,000	181	6.7	*c*	5.5
Average	1,875	147	5.8	9,760	6.1

a. Data drawn from the United Nations Statistical Yearbook (1965), various tables.

b. Egypt and Syria until mid-1961, when Syria withdrew.

c. Unknown.

d. State education only.

Source: Pierre Jalée, *The Third World in World Economy* (New York: Monthly Review Press, 1969).

other indicators of social development, the Third World is appallingly far behind.

PATTERNS OF MODERNIZATION

Earlier, it was noted that diverse conditions in developing nations call for diverse methods and patterns of change. However, poor societies have much in common despite their diversity, and we may point to some common features of the changes they have experienced.

Recent history has shown that the paths nations may follow in modernizing are numerous. Social scientists, in evaluating these alternative patterns, must try to assess the effects of broad national changes such as agrarian reform, capital accumulation, industrialization, and urbanization, along with changes in the behaviors and normative orientations of individuals. Important, also, is a comparison of the experience of the nations that had taken great modernizing strides before the breakup of the colonial world with those that are modernizing now.

One pattern that no modernizing nation has so far been able to avoid is bureaucratization. Because modernization means the transformation of entire societies, it requires rational planning, skillful coordination, and organizational structures that will sustain it over time. Bureaucracy, which is discussed in Chapter 9, has been the preeminent organizational form for accomplishing these ends in modernizing nations.

In all nations, government has played a major role in stimulating and directing modernization. The United States and the Soviet Union have long, contrasting histories of modernization, but both nations have relied on formal bureaucratic organizations. Bureaucratic organization is as important to private enterprise in the United States as it is to government-owned enterprises in the Soviet Union.

Modernizing nations similarly require the rational organization of resources. Achieving rationality in such nations is no simple task, for traditional approaches to the recruitment and supervision of employees are hard to change.

When achievement supplants ascription as the basis for assigning status (see Chapter 12), personal loyalties and routines must be deemphasized, and behavior must be oriented toward accomplishing the task at hand. Modernization requires the development of organizations that effectively blend formal and informal obligations.

SOURCES OF MODERNIZATION

For nations that are now in the beginning stages of the process of modernization, the most obvious source of change is contact with nations that have advanced further in the process. The two most common and enduring patterns that such contact has taken are *colonialism,* which is, in essence, political control, and *imperialism,* which is, in essence, economic control.

Colonialism

For more than four hundred years colonialism linked the preindustrial areas of Latin America, Asia, and Africa to more modern nations in Europe. Spain, Portugal, England, France, Holland, Italy, and Germany all sought riches, raw materials, markets, power, and religious converts through the formation of colonies. When the goals of adventure and the simple extraction of riches became supplanted by the more complex ones of creating markets, obtaining raw materials, and becoming politically powerful, each European nation had to create organizations within its colonies that in effect laid the foundations for the formation of the new nations that the colonies ultimately became.

For example, in order to exploit the resources of their colonies, European nations had to pacify the territory and then control it, so that their enterprises could continue and expand. Control required the establishment of a transportation and communications system and the introduction of money into the national economy. The expansion of agriculture, mining, services, and the small amount of industry that was introduced was facilitated by the creation of rudimentary educational systems. Western religion and life styles were also introduced where it suited the colonizers' ideological or practical ends. Such changes most affected the relatively small class of indigenous people who had fairly direct contact with the colonizers, either because they worked in the colonial administration or because they owned businesses that largely depended on colonial contact. This group became the new middle class.

As the ideology of modernization gained momentum in the colonial world, discrepancies between the colonizers and the colonized became politically important. A newly developed nationalist consciousness led to the demand for an end to social, economic, and political subjugation; the colonial administration became the target of attack. The once-artificial geographical boundaries set up by the nations that had carved out the colonies took on new meaning as they came to define nations that sought independence from their European colonial masters.

Imperialism

Because the colonial powers needed the raw materials and markets provided by their colonies and the colonies needed the goods, capital, and political support of the colonial power, a degree of mutual dependence between the two countries developed. This dependence endured after the former colonies had gained independent national status. Patterns of world power shifted, adding the United States, the Soviet Union, and Japan to the list of economically dominant powers. Strong economic and political ties were maintained through formal organizational channels, such as the Commonwealth of Nations and SEATO, or through the more informal means of "economic aid" and "foreign investment."

The fact that developed nations are to some degree dependent on developing ones does not mean that any particular developing one can exercise power over a developed one. In fact, although the benefits of aid to developing nations cannot be denied, the balance of power lies securely with the developed nations. Differential economic power has come to replace direct political control. To some extent, developing nations

Figure 29.1 The Sheraton-San Cristobal in Santiago, Chile, pictured here, was owned by the International Telephone and Telegraph Corporation (ITT), a large corporation based in the United States. Such private corporations based in advanced industrial nations frequently invest in the hotel industries of developing nations and realize large profits. Since his election in 1970, however, Chilean President Salvador Allende has authorized the confiscation of property owned by several American companies, among them ITT properties.

vie with one another to gain preferred status with a developed nation.

In the United States, a quota system guarantees the purchase of stated amounts of agricultural goods from dependent nations at prices above the world market level, and both Britain and France have similar arrangements with former members of their colonial empires. The Soviet Union also has such arrangements with developing nations although they were not former colonies—such as the sugar-trade agreements it maintains with Cuba. Such trade agreements guarantee developed nations a steady supply of raw materials and serve to continue the economic dependence of developing nations. The developed nation, for example, can lower its quota determining how much of the developing nation's main export product it will accept, and this ability can serve as a powerful threat in international relations. On the other hand, such trade arrangements do offer developing nations a secure market at advantageous prices, thus providing them additional capital to use in modernization. Unfortunately, a secure market arrangement with a developed nation often leads a developing nation to remain a one-crop or one-commodity economy. Thus it remains dependent, and its modernization is in many respects thwarted. Such nations have neither the necessity nor even the flexibility to redeploy manpower and capital into diversification. Furthermore, they constantly risk economic disas-

Figure 29.2 Charismatic leaders are important sources of direction during the early stages of social and economic revolutions. But an appropriate form of social organization must be developed in order to bring desired changes about. Cuban revolutionary society is based on the socialist model.

ter should the one crop fail or technological change (such as the invention of synthetic rubber) make the single commodity less valuable.

Aside from preferential trade agreements, direct economic aid, in the forms of loans, technical assistance, and some outright grants, is extended by the more modern nations to the developing ones, both directly and through the offices of international organizations. Such aid has been especially directed at the development of new sources of electrical power and the construction of improved transportation and communication networks in the developing countries.

It has been estimated that in 1965 the advanced industrial nations gave or loaned the Third World countries over $10 billion in aid, nearly $4 billion of which was in outright gifts such as surplus agricultural products (Jalée, 1969). The remainder was in the form of either long-term loans or private investment of foreign companies in the Third World countries. This aid is naturally quite welcome, but it constitutes only a small proportion of the capital flow between more and less modern nations.

With respect to technical assistance, in 1965 the advanced nations sent 35,800 trained technical personnel to assist in the economic modernization of the Third World countries (Lambe, 1967). These technical advisers engaged in agricultural research, attempting to find ways to increase crop yields, helped design roads, bridges, and other

transportation facilities, and helped build factories and research facilities. Assistance in such social-modernization projects as raising literacy is considered later in this chapter.

Foreign investment, the entrance of business firms based in more developed nations into former colonial areas, can be a boon to modernization because it provides additional sources of capital and establishes relatively modern organizations where they are sorely needed. However, the fact that profits are returned to the home country is a focus of agitation for anti-imperialistic nationalism. All too often, the modern firm extracts favorable economic concessions, such as low tax rates, cheap labor, and market monopolies, from the modernizing society as the price of locating their business enterprise there.

POLITICAL MODERNIZATION

The transfer of the people's allegiance from the colonial power to the national state is a decisive event in the political modernization of new states. The new nation can command profound loyalty; it can mobilize large-scale human effort for social, economic, or military ends; it can give masses of individuals a common identity and infuse them with a common consciousness.

As the formation of new nations redirects allegiance, it restructures kinship, social class, and community ties. The social organization needed to sustain and direct newly aroused national enthusiasm also needs to be developed. Loyalty and spirit can be maintained in the short run by a charismatic leader with great personal attraction or by the redirection of frustrations to external causes through propaganda or warfare (see Chapter 26). However, a nation must develop the ability to fulfill the promise that sparks initial enthusiasm. Otherwise, potential for change can be directed against national rulers and lead to internal conflicts that halt the process of development.

The ability of the political process to deal with nationalism and with feelings of frustration is crucial in determining the forms of political participation that are possible in a given nation. National elites, both military and civilian, value national cohesion and political stability.

National elites are the men in the middle. In one sense they are the masters of the status quo, so it is not always in their interest to overhaul the society they dominate. However, if they do not respond to changing national demands, they may find themselves suddenly displaced. In situations with such changing demands, therefore, they must promote some form of modernization in order to retain their status. They usually do not suffer if they can help guide the process of modernization. Their position of power and their experience with the workings of society usually enable them to anticipate the direction of change and benefit from it. In the Mexican Revolution, even after the countryside had been ravaged and far-reaching land reform had been instituted, a relatively unchanging elite group managed to control much of the agricultural production.

The nature of a nation's elites is important in determining whether a dictatorship will be established and political freedom curtailed. If a nation's elite is monolithic—if landholders, industrialists, politicians, and churchmen act as one—its ability to do what it pleases is greatly enhanced.

The priority that elites put on modernization is also important in determining the rate at which it will advance and the course it will take. In some nations, such as Haiti and Syria, dictatorships seem to have been imposed simply to maintain the power of specific groups. Peru, Cuba, Thailand, and Pakistan assert that their dictatorships are necessary to maintain stability and will be replaced when constructive change is more firmly institutionalized.

In a world where newly developing nations must compete with more modern counterparts, political stability is an important condition for rapid purposive growth. A stable pattern of political participation fits best the ideology of modernization; closely held political power serves this ideology better than does an unstable democracy. Sacrifices on the part of the people are often necessary, especially in consumer goods, and people frequently are not willing to vote for sacrifices even if they would be better off in the long run. Developing nations frequently are subject to one-party or even dictatorial rule. Interestingly

enough, Seymour Martin Lipset (1967) points out that America—the first "new nation" to emerge from a colonial past—experienced an initial period of one-party rule. The Founding Fathers were a "power elite," and in most states only property owners could vote. As nation building progressed, the country became more democratic, and presumably this trend toward greater democracy is a possibility for nations that are now undergoing modernization.

THEORIES OF MODERNIZATION

Theories of modernization and development offer interpretations—often polemical ones—of the patterns we have just discussed. We will distinguish two types of theories of modernization: *diffusionist* theories and *nationalist* theories. Diffusionist theories stress the fact that the current modern industrial nations, especially the capitalist ones, have already undergone modernization and can aid the underdeveloped countries in their modernization efforts in two major ways. First, because the advanced nations have already modernized, they can serve as demonstration models for the underdeveloped countries of the Third World; they can show Third World countries of Asia, Africa, and Latin America that modernization is possible. Second, the industrialized countries can assist the underdeveloped countries more directly by supplying economic and technical assistance and by helping to diffuse the kinds of values and social structures necessary for modernization throughout the Third World. According to these theories, the route to modernization for the underdeveloped countries lies in following the one laid out by the advanced industrial nations and accepting their assistance.

Stemming from the Marxist viewpoint, nationalist theories about the route to modernization maintain that the history of relations between the advanced capitalist countries and the Third World is not a history of demonstration and assistance but one of imperialism and exploitation. Nationalist theorists contend that the advanced nations have helped the underdeveloped countries only in those areas that benefit the rich countries. For example, rich nations develop the raw materials of poor nations for their own, not the under-developed nation's, benefit. The modern industrial countries get richer as the predominantly agrarian, underdeveloped countries get poorer. Nationalist theorists maintain that continued close ties with the advanced capitalist countries will lead only to continued underdevelopment of the Third World and to a worsening of their conditions. The road to development, according to nationalist theory, is for Third World countries to dissolve bonds that tie them to the advanced capitalist nations and to seek independently their own forms of modernization. Because each of the countries of the Third World has a unique history and unique problems, modernization should be an individual national concern.

Diffusionist Theories

In this discussion of diffusionist theories, we will focus on the one developed by W. W. Rostow (1960), which may be called the stages-of-growth theory. In order to isolate the process that nations must go through in order to modernize, Rostow studied the countries that modernized during the industrial revolution of the nineteenth and early twentieth centuries. He found that as the methods of science and technology were increasingly applied, nations went through a series of five developmental stages: (1) traditional society, (2) preconditions for take-off, (3) take-off, (4) increasing maturity, and (5) high mass consumption.

Traditional societies, those in the first stage, are predominantly agrarian; science and technology are not developed to a very high degree, and productivity, even in agriculture, is low. Societies begin to modernize at the second stage of growth, *preconditions for take-off,* which is a period of transition. During this second stage, countries begin to apply science and develop technology in order to increase productivity in agriculture; they also begin mining the raw materials necessary for industrialization and start to develop manufacturing industries. Modernization is impeded, however, by what remains of the traditional society, which exists side by side with the emerging industrial society. During this transitional stage, it is as if there were two societies

Figure 29.3 Two cultures may exist simultaneously within the same developing country. According to diffusionist theorists, especially dualists, modern Western-style cultures emerge out of traditional environments and eventually displace the traditional cultures.

in one. But the traditional society is seen by modernizing groups as holding back the process of modernization, and a new social structure and set of values that aid modernization are developed and replace those of the old.

It is not until *take-off,* the third stage in the modernization process, that a country achieves sustained growth. The society develops all economic bases, agricultural and industrial alike, through the application of science and technology. Values of progress fully displace values of tradition.

A society that has experienced a take-off into sustained growth is free to explore new paths to modernization. During the fourth stage of modernization, that of *increasing maturity,* the fruits of the new productivity are applied to the continued development of the society. The members of a society in the process of attaining maturity can experiment and can explore new possibilities for the uses of modern industry, technology, and science and at the same time further develop the technology and science necessary for the continued rapid growth of industry. The economy enables the society to move into new enterprises beyond the industries that powered the take-off.

The final stage, according to Rostow's theory of modernization, is the stage of *high mass consumption.* Following the initial excitement and exploration of the drive to maturity, the question arises: how is the new wealth to be used? At this stage the demand for consumer goods rises. Items that were available only to a few during the drive to maturity become increasingly available to the middle and working classes. The development of mass education and the rise in social-welfare services are also characteristic of societies that have reached the stage of high mass consumption.

Recall that Rostow developed his theory by reviewing the development of countries that began to modernize during the industrial revolution of the nineteenth and early twentieth centuries. If we apply his theory to the underdeveloped countries today, we see that none of the Third World countries has reached the fourth or fifth stages of growth; it is questionable whether they have even experienced take-off into sustained growth. From Rostow's point of view, during each of these stages—especially at the preconditions stage and the take-off stage—the advanced industrial countries can greatly assist the Third World to modernize socially and economically.

As we noted earlier, during the preconditions stage, two societies seem to exist within the same country. There is a traditional society with an agriculturally based economy, a low level of productivity, and a traditional social structure. But within the same country an industrial society is emerging with an increasingly modern, predominantly urban social structure. The theory of *dualism* has been developed within the diffusionist framework by such social scientists as Benjamin Higgins (1956) to explain this observation.

According to this theory, even though the traditional society in Third World countries exists side by side with the growing industrial society, the two societies function independently. The traditional society is domestically based and therefore oriented toward the needs of its own population. The industrializing society, on the other hand, is oriented outward because it needs economic and technical assistance from the more developed countries. Countries that have already become modern nations can provide markets for its new goods and at the same time provide the scientific and technological knowledge necessary for increased industrialization.

Figure 29.4 Third World countries, such as Cuba and Chile, are turning toward nationalism in the attempt to solve their social and economic problems. From the nationalist viewpoint, foreign economic or political domination is generally unacceptable; therefore, foreign interests in countries adopting such a viewpoint are usually asked or forced to leave.

According to diffusionist theories, developed countries can assist Third World countries in the preconditions stage in their social as well as their economic modernization. In order for take-off to occur, a country must not only advance economically but also develop a social structure that supports modernization. The traditional society must be destroyed while the new social structure is fostered. A predominantly rural society does not favor modernization; so people must move from the countryside into cities. As nations in the take-off stage develop modern forms of social organization and institutions, modern industrial nations can give assistance; technical and educational experts help developing countries in building the social structure and the economy needed to break the bonds of tradition (Sufrin, 1966). Economic and technological assistance is discussed earlier in this chapter.

One of the primary impediments to social modernization is illiteracy. Helping an underdeveloped nation educate its population may be seen as a form of social aid. A modern industrial country needs a population that can read and write and that can perform specific functions within an increasingly complex division of labor. In the United States, the most highly developed country in the world, only 2 percent of the population are illiterate, but in Nigeria, 88 percent of the population are. In literacy, as in per-capita income, the Latin American nations are slightly ahead, but the figure for Peru—39.4 percent illiteracy in 1961—for example, shows that illiteracy is still very high compared with the advanced nations. To help raise the level of literacy and education, the developed countries in 1965 sent 56,000 teachers to serve as educational advisers to the Third World countries.

The proponents of the diffusionist theories of modernization hope that the economic and social aid given by the advanced countries will help the developing nations achieve sustained growth and thus become equal partners in a modern world.

Nationalist Theories

There are a growing number of social scientists (Jalée, 1969; Frank, 1969; Magdoff, 1969; O'Connor, 1970) in the Marxist tradition who see the relationships between the advanced capitalist countries and the Third World countries as a system of imperialism. Since shortly after Columbus' voyage to America, well before the industrial revolution, the advanced capitalist countries of Western Europe, particularly England, have had a virtual stranglehold on Asia, Africa, and Latin America. During the industrial revolution and until World War II these underdeveloped countries were brought under political control (colonialism) and economic control (imperialism) and served as sources of cheap labor and raw materials and as markets for a growing capitalist system.

According to Marxist scholars, the European powers made these continents into dependent subjects. The underdeveloped countries were not allowed to develop into competitive countries on the world stage but were kept in the position of supplying the advanced countries with the materials, notably iron ore and petroleum, necessary for the further industrialization and modernization of the advanced capitalist countries (O'Connor, 1970). Marxist critics of diffusionist theories maintain that the relationships among countries must be examined from a world-wide perspective. The diffusionists contend that the advanced countries of Europe and North America industrialized while the rest of the world remained stagnant; nationalist theorists argue that

the advanced industrial nations industrialized at the expense of the underdeveloped Third World.

Diffusionists would argue that once the advanced countries did industrialize—whether at the expense of the rest of the world or not—they turned around and began to assist the countries of the Third World. Diffusionists can point to the political independence given to former colonial possessions of the European powers since the end of World War II.

Social scientists who argue that imperialism, not assistance, is the major characteristic of the relations between the advanced capitalist countries and the Third World countries maintain that even though official colonialism has ended, imperialist economic control is still a fact (Jalée, 1968). In discussing the economic control exercised by advanced nations, André Gunder Frank (1969) points out that the United States between 1950 and 1965 invested $23.9 billion in other countries, and during that same period the inflow into the United States in the form of profits was $37 billion. Of the $23.9 billion it invested, $14.9 billion went to Europe and Canada, while only $11.4 billion flowed into the United States from these areas. The situation with respect to the other countries, mostly underdeveloped, to which the investment went is quite different: The United States invested $9 billion in underdeveloped countries but received a net inflow of $16.6 billion from them. This is hardly an example of aid from the developed countries to the underdeveloped ones; if anything, the Third World countries are assisting the advanced industrialized countries to develop further.

Social Change or Revolution

Chapter 14 asked the question, "Why haven't revolutions occurred in the advanced capitalist countries as Marx predicted?" Within any capitalist society, according to the Marxist perspective, there are two antagonistic classes: the *bourgeoisie,* the owners of the means of production, and the *proletariat,* those who must sell their labor power to the owners of the means of production. These two classes are locked in an unceasing conflict. During Marx's lifetime, the conflict was intense,

Figure 29.5 Traditional societies relying on simple technological means, such as the agricultural techniques shown here, cannot hope to meet the needs of the expanding populations in Third World countries. Some form of industrialization seems necessary to reach higher levels of productivity.

and it looked as though the proletariat might overthrow the bourgeoisie, especially in England, and establish a socialist state. Chapter 14 explains that the development of unions and collective bargaining, which Marx had not foreseen, reduced social inequalities and class conflict and therefore reduced the likelihood of revolution.

The views of nationalist theorists, however, suggest that Marx's predictions may still hold true. Consider the class-conflict model on an international scale. The international capitalist class (bourgeoisie) has interests in maximizing its profits. Underdeveloped countries (on analogy with the proletariat) are good sources of raw materials and cheap labor, and the rate of profit is consistently higher than in the advanced countries. Consider too that as the class conflicts in Europe became intense during the industrial revolution, the capitalists were able to stave off revolutions by transferring their greatest exploitation from their own workers to those in underdeveloped nations.

In a sense, then, the people of the Third World have become the new international proletariat while the working classes in the advanced capitalist countries have received a share in the increased productivity of the world capitalist system.

If this analysis is accurate, the revolutions Marx predicted—or at least the socialism he foresaw—are more likely to occur in Third World countries than in the advanced capitalist countries. The working classes in the advanced countries are too comfortable at present to have revolutionary potential, but the situation in the Third World is far different. The people of these countries are falling further and further behind in economic and social modernization. In 1948, Mao Tse-tung ended a long period of upheaval in China by coming to power and turning China toward socialism and modernization; about ten years later, in 1959, Cuba experienced a socialist revolution; and about ten years after that, Chile became the first Latin American country to elect a Marxist president, Salvador Allende. These and other nations in Asia, Africa, and Latin America are beginning to turn toward nationalism and socialism as a solution to their problems. The social scientists who advocate the nationalist road to modernization predict that the countries of the Third World will make greater efforts to modernize without the intervention of advanced nations.

THE EFFECTS OF MODERNIZATION ON SOCIAL LIFE

The period during which modernization takes place, regardless of the path taken, is a period of rapid social change. This provides an opportunity for social scientists to study the dynamics of social change; changes in variables discussed in earlier chapters of the book occur within a short period. Viewing the process of modernization as an independent variable, we can now examine some of the ways in which modernization affects the various aspect of social life.

Whether the underdeveloped countries travel the capitalist road to modernization or choose instead to travel the socialist road (both are nationalistic), there are certain processes that all modernizing nations undergo, as noted earlier. These processes lead to changes in institutions, organizations, groups, roles, and, as we saw in Unit V, systems of stratification.

Whether socialist or capitalist, any modernizing country must industrialize; that is, the focus of economic activity must shift from agriculture to industry and manufacturing. Tilling of the soil in agrarian societies is accomplished with relatively simple technology; horse-drawn plows and human physical labor are all that is necessary. But the products of a modern nation—cars, radios, televisions, and the like—require a much more sophisticated technology and consequently a much more complex division of labor. How does a social structure that supports increasing industrialization emerge?

Institutions and Organizations

In modernizing nations the several institutions discussed in Unit VI undergo changes in the direction of increased specialization. For example, modernization affects the world of work (discussed in Chapter 22). A person in an agrarian society may be expected to perform, at one time or another, most of the tasks associated with farming. Within a modern factory, however, the production of a single manufactured product may require the performance of hundreds or even thousands of separate tasks. A man or woman can perform only a very small, specialized portion of the total work necessary to produce such a product. In the production of an automobile, for example, there are hundreds of different steps, from tightening bolts to inspecting the finished product. The typical manufacturing pattern has been to have an assembly line in which each of these separate tasks is performed by a different person who is specifically trained for the job.

Specialization in the world of work requires specialization of education (see Chapter 19). In agrarian societies there is little need for formal education. If a person is likely to spend his or her life working in the fields as a peasant, there is no real need to learn to read or write. The education that one attains is general knowledge acquired in the family or from other community members

and directed toward maintaining a traditional social structure. In modernizing nations, however, education must be directed toward the needs of an industrializing nation. General education becomes increasingly technical, and work training becomes more and more specialized. Higher education, too, must be geared to the needs of an increasingly complex technology; industrial nations require engineers and technicians who can "build bridges" from tradition to modernization (Lipset, 1967).

The family also undergoes basic changes during modernization (see Chapter 18). In traditional societies, children are an economic asset, and families tend to be large and organized on an extended-family basis in which parents, children, and other relatives live in one household and share the responsibilities of daily life. The more people there are to work the fields, the higher agricultural productivity will be. With modernization, however, comes a shift in emphasis from the extended-family system to the nuclear family. Children are no longer an economic asset. They cannot come into the factory and help their parents with their jobs; rather, they are dependent on their parents for support. Family size decreases in modernizing nations, and families become increasingly separate units of parents and children. Some remnants of the extended-family system, however, still remain even in modern industrial nations, especially in culturally homogeneous neighborhoods in large cities (Gans, 1965).

Many social scientists have pointed to the increasing alienation experienced by the individual in modern industrial societies (Marcuse, 1964). As the division of labor becomes more and more complex and as individuals perform increasingly specialized tasks, people lose their sense of control over the entire process of production. Various other factors associated with modernization—including the stress on individual achievement over group welfare, the need to move to pursue job opportunities, and the competitive ethic fostered at the expense of the cooperative one by these changing social requirements—help turn individuals into isolated units.

Families also become isolated units, and the

Figure 29.6 "Habitat," a community housing structure designed for the Montreal exposition "Expo 67" by Israeli architect Moshe Safdie, embodies the idea that in modern societies dwellings should use living space economically, leaving outside space uncluttered and open.

high degree of physical mobility increases this trend. A breakdown of the patriarchal extended-family structure, in which the older adults have authority and command respect, is hastened in industrial societies partly because the older people's values differ from those of the young: Their societies have undergone such rapid shifts that basic personal orientations have shifted between one generation and the next. The old tend to be repositories of tradition, whereas the young value change. Since the beginning of this century in socialist countries—and more recently in capitalist countries—a new family system has been developing in response to this growing alienation. Some people in capitalist countries are turning to a communal way of life in which tasks are shared equally among members of the unit and children are raised collectively—patriarchal authority structure is replaced by the collectivity. (Chapter 18 discusses possible further changes the family in Western society may undergo.) In China the communal system, including collective farms, is an integral part of the social and economic system of the society.

As the institutions of a society become increasingly specialized and complex in order to meet the needs of the increasingly complex division of labor in industrialization, organizational forms must be developed that integrate these diversities (see Chapter 9). As noted earlier, the main organizational trend in modernizing nations is bureaucratization. Emphasis in industrial nations is placed on efficiency and rationality because so many specific functions have to be integrated and organized. Traditional societies are loosely organized; people have a great deal of leeway in defining their activities, and they are chosen for jobs on the basis of friendship and family ties. In modern industrial societies the situation is quite different. People are chosen for jobs mostly on the basis of whether they can do the job well (Unit V), and the organizations themselves are organized rationally so that the specific functions to be performed are performed efficiently. Tasks are well-specified, and training and education are geared toward the efficient performance of those tasks.

Roles and Mass Society

Modernization results in individuals occupying increasing numbers of roles, thus dividing their lives into smaller segments. Furthermore, the extent to which an individual's roles are segregated—performed in widely separated places and before different audiences—increases with modernization. For example, a person in a traditional society may act out the roles of shopkeeper, friend, and parent within the immediate vicinity of his or her combination shop and living quarters. Today a person may play several distinct roles within a large office building (art director, friend), while his or her domestic roles are performed forty miles away in a suburb. Those who interact with the person at work may never see him or her in the domestic roles. Furthermore, many roles in modern societies involve impersonal interaction with strangers. For example, we rarely know persons who wait on us in stores. All this is relatively new. In agrarian societies people rarely interact with strangers and are rarely called upon to behave impersonally.

The development of many highly segregated roles and impersonal patterns of interaction has alarmed a number of sociologists (Kornhauser,

1959; Selznick, 1960). They believe that something important has gone out of human relations as a result of the transformation of society from the close-knit intimacy of the small town and the stable urban neighborhood to the impersonality of modern metropolitan life. They use the term "mass society" to indicate the lack of close bonds among people in modern societies. But whether the changes in human relations have been good or bad, they seem likely to be permanent or at least long-range. Role segregation and impersonality so far have been inherent in large, complex, industrialized societies. As developing nations become modernized, it is quite likely that fewer and fewer of their citizens will remain in close-knit villages. If this represents an evil of modernization, it is one few nations can overcome.

SUGGESTED READINGS

Frank, André Gunder. *Capitalism and Underdevelopment in Latin America*. New York: Monthly Review Press, 1969.

Heilbroner, Robert. *The Great Assent*. New York: Harper & Row, 1963.

Jalée, Pierre. *The Third World in World Economy*. New York. Monthly Review Press, 1969.

Mead, Margaret. *Cultural Patterns and Technical Change, UNESCO*. New York: Mentor, 1955.

Contributing Consultants

Ronald L. Akers holds a Ph.D. from the University of Kentucky. He has taught at several universities, including Kent State University, the University of Alberta, San Diego State College (now California State University at San Diego), and the University of Washington; he is now professor of criminology and deviant behavior at Florida State University. He has written numerous articles and research papers, and a book (in press) pertaining to his various areas of interest: criminology, juvenile delinquency, deviant behavior, law and society, and the sociology of occupations and professions. Professor Akers is responsible for the Deviance and Conformity chapter.

Helen Chiros Arbini earned a B.A. in sociology at the University of the Pacific and an M.A. at the University of California at Davis; she is currently completing her Ph.D. in sociology at Davis. Her major interests are the sociology of work, education, and the family. She is now doing a study of the American high school as a "custodial" institution in American society. Ms. Arbini is presently teaching in the sociology department of the California State University at San Diego. She contributed to the Education chapter.

Richard Dewey, professor of sociology and former chairman of the department at the University of New Hampshire, took his Ph.D. at the University of Wisconsin. He has taught in many parts of the United States and has been involved in urban-planning projects in Chicago and Milwaukee. His numerous articles and books range in content from social psychology to urban problems to the forerunners of modern sociological thought. His current efforts include research and teaching in the field of rural-urban sociology and social psychology; his newly cultivated interest is in developing visual aids—movies and colored slides—for use in college and university classrooms. Professor Dewey contributed to the Human Ecology chapter.

Bruce K. Eckland, professor of sociology at the University of North Carolina, received his Ph.D. from the University of Illinois in 1964. His numerous articles focus on the relations between sociology and genetics and on studies of social mobility and education. He currently is a member of the editorial boards of *Social Forces, American Journal of Sociology, Sociology of Education, Behavior Genetics,* and *Social Biology.* Professor Eckland is responsible for the following chapter: The Biological Basis of Society.

Glenn A. Goodwin is an assistant professor of sociology at Pitzer College. He received his Ph.D. from Tulane University and, before going to Pitzer, taught at Wayne State University. In addition to writing on the sociology of the absurd and the development of the sociology of sociology as a viable theoretical framework, Goodwin is interested in the history and development of sociological theory, with an emphasis upon examining problems of epistemology inherent in the science of sociology. He has taught the introductory course for over seven years and still finds it one of the most challenging courses to teach in the entire sociology curriculum. Professor Goodwin is responsible for the Basic Concepts chapter.

Richard Greenbaum has received degrees from the University of Chicago, New York University, and Harvard University in such diverse fields as English, sociology, Russian regional studies, political science, history, and television and film production. He has taught at Harvard University, New York University, and Hunter College. He is currently affiliated with John Jay College of Criminal Justice of the City University of New York. For two years he was a research associate at the Harvard Medical School. His chief avocations are creative writing and film making. He contributed to the following chapter: Social Integration and Social Change.

Jeffrey K. Hadden is a professor of sociology and urban studies at the University of Virginia in Charlottesville. He received his Ph.D. in sociology from the University of Wisconsin in 1963. He has been a research consultant for the Educational Testing Service, the National Council of Churches, and the Lutheran Church in America, among other organizations. Hadden's research has embraced a wide range of interests. He has published books and articles on urban politics, religion, riots, the family, and nuclear war. He is the author of *The Gathering Storm in the Churches* and coauthor of *Marriage and the Family* and *Metropolis in Crisis: Social and Political Perspectives.* Professor Hadden contributed to the following chapters: Family and Kinship, Education, and Religion and Society.

Michael Hechter, assistant professor of sociology at the University of Washington, did his undergraduate and graduate studies at Columbia University. He is primarily concerned with processes of social change and is presently investigating national development in the British Isles and France. A forthcoming book, *Internal Colonialism: The Celtic Fringe in British National Development,* will report on some preliminary findings of this research. Professor Hechter is responsible for the Politics chapter.

Bernard Karsh, who studied engineering and economics before receiving an M.A. and the Ph.D. in sociology from the University of Chicago, is a professor of sociology at the University of Illinois in the department of sociology and in the Institute of Labor and Industrial Relations. He has written or participated in the writing of *Diary of a Strike, The Worker Views His Union,* and *Labor and the New Deal* and has published about forty articles in academic journals during the past fifteen years. His current research interests are in the area of social change, particularly in the impact of technology on social change, and his forthcoming book deals with the structure of industrial relations in contemporary Japan. Professor Karsh contributed to the following chapter: Social Integration and Social Change.

Lewis M. Killian, a native of Georgia, holds the Ph.D. in sociology from the University of Chicago. In 1969 he joined the faculty of the University of Massachusetts as professor of sociology, after having taught at Florida State University, the University of Oklahoma, the University of Connecticut, and the University of California at Los Angeles. His interests in race relations and social movements are reflected in three books: *Collective Behavior* (with Ralph H. Turner); *Racial Crisis in America* (with Charles M. Grigg); and, most recently, *The Impossible Revolution?,* a study of the development of the black-power movement. Professor Killian contributed to the first portion of the Social Movements chapter.

William Kornblum, assistant professor of sociology at the University of Washington, Seattle, received his Ph.D. from the University of Chicago. He is an urban sociologist interested in ethnicity, community structure, and local political processes. He has conducted research in Abidjan, Paris, Ljubljana, New York, Chicago, and Seattle on such subjects as urban gypsies, socialist democracy in Yugoslav communities, and working-class ethnicity in the United States. His most recent work will appear in *Steel and Ethnicity: The Social Dimensions of a Working Class Community.* Professor Kornblum contributed to the following chapters: The Urban Community, and Human Ecology.

James C. McCann received his Ph.D. from Brown University in 1972. He is an assistant professor of sociology at the University of Washington at Seattle. His major research area is the sociology of mortality. He is the author of several articles that have appeared in scholarly journals. Professor McCann is responsible for the following chapter: The Population Problem.

Marianne Rice is currently working toward the Ph.D. degree. She received a B.A. from Stanford in 1966 and an M.A. from the University of Washington in 1971. Her main areas of research interest are social psychology and the sociology of sex roles. Ms. Rice contributed to the study of women's liberation in the Social Movements chapter.

Peter I. Rose holds a Ph.D. from Cornell and is chairman of the department of sociology and anthropology at Smith College and a member of the graduate faculty of the University of Massachusetts. He has also been a visiting professor at Wesleyan, Colorado, Clark, Amherst, and Yale and a Fulbright Lecturer at the University of Leicester (England) and Flinders University (Australia). His books include *They and We, The Study of Society, The Subject Is Race, The Ghetto and Beyond, Americans from Africa, Nation of Nations,* and *Seeing Ourselves.* Professor Rose is responsible for the Race and Ethnicity chapter.

John Finley Scott is an associate professor of sociology at the University of California at Davis. He received his B.A. in philosophy from Reed College and the Ph.D. in sociology from the University of California at Berkeley. He is the author of *Internalization of Norms* and of numerous papers on sociological theory and on education and the family. Professor Scott is responsible for the Theoretical Perspectives chapter.

W. Richard Scott, professor of sociology and chairman of the department of sociology at Stanford University, took his Ph.D. at the University of Chicago. He has served on the editorial boards of the *Pacific Sociological Review, Administrative Science Quarterly, American Journal of Sociology,* and *American Sociological Review.* His wide range of interest is reflected in his publications, which include *Formal Organizations: A Comparative Approach* (with Peter M. Blau), *Metropolis and Region* (with Otis Dudley Duncan and others), *Medical Care* (with Edmund H. Volkart), and *Social Processes and Social Structures.* His most recent research deals with evaluations and authority in formal organizations. Professor Scott is responsible for the Formal Organizations chapter.

Neil J. Smelser, associate director of the Institute of International Studies and professor of sociology at the University of California at Berkeley, received his Ph.D. in sociology from Harvard University in 1958. After completing his undergraduate education at Harvard, he was a Rhodes Scholar at Magdalen College, Oxford. In recent years he has served as consultant to the President's Advisory Commission on the Causes and Prevention of Violence. His publications include *The Sociology of Economic Life, Theory of Collective Behavior,* and *Essays in Sociological Explanation.* Professor Smelser is responsible for the Collective Behavior chapter.

Mark Solomon, Ph.D. candidate at the University of Oregon, received his B.A. and M.A. from San Diego State University (now California State University at San Diego). His interests are social movements, especially the women's movement, and world revolution. Solomon contributed to the following chapters: Social Roles and Interaction, and Modernization.

Rodney Stark received his Ph.D. in sociology from the University of California at Berkeley in 1971. Since then he has been professor of sociology at the University of Washington. He is the author of six books. Five of them, coauthored with Charles Y. Glock, have dealt with religious behavior. His most recent book, *Police Riots,* was published in 1972. He has also written a number of articles, some of which have appeared in *Harpers, Trans-action,* and *Psychology Today.* Stark contributed to many chapters in this book, including the Theoretical Perspectives chapter, and served as general adviser. He is particularly responsible for the following chapters: What Is Sociology and How Is It Possible?, Doing Sociology, Stratification, Social Mobility, Consequences of Inequality, and Is Inequality Necessary?

Jeffrey W. Stone took his B.A. in 1967 from the University of California at Irvine, received his M.A. in 1969 from the University of Illinois, and is now a Ph.D. candidate at the University of California at San Diego. He has been an instructor at UCSD and is currently teaching at Pomona College. His interests include the sociology of science (his thesis area), sociological theory, organizations, and the sociology of knowledge. Professor Stone contributed to The Nature and Variety of Groups chapter and is responsible for the Adult Socialization and Resocialization chapter.

Martin Trow is a professor of sociology in the Graduate School of Public Policy at the University of California at Berkeley. He has also taught at Hofstra College, Columbia's School of General Studies, and Bennington College. He has held an appointment at Berkeley since 1957. His main research interests are in the sociology of politics and education. Between 1968 and 1971 he was director of the National Surveys of Higher Education for the Carnegie Commission on Higher Education and has been a member of the advisory committee to the Commission. Professor Trow is also a member of the National Academy of Education. He is coauthor of *Union Democracy* and, most recently with A. H. Halsey, of *The British Academics.* Professor Trow contributed to the Education chapter.

Pierre L. van den Berghe, professor at the University of Washington since 1965, has also taught at the Sorbonne, Wesleyan University, and the State University of New York at Buffalo and was a Visiting Rockefeller Professor for two years at the University of East Africa, Kenya, and the University of Ibadan, Nigeria. He received his Ph.D. from Harvard University. His fields of professional interest are ethnic and race relations, social stratification, social theory, social change, comparative sociology, political sociology, and sociolinguistics, with the geographical specialization of Sub-Saharan Africa and Mesoamerica. Van den Berghe has a fluent knowledge of four languages and a reading knowledge of four others. He has written nine books and numerous articles on his varied interests. Professor van den Berghe is responsible for the following chapter: Sex and Age: The Tyranny of Older Men.

Howard M. Vollmer received a B.A. in psychology and an M.A. in sociology from Stanford University and a Ph.D. in sociology from the University of California at Berkeley. He was associated for over twelve years with the Stanford Research Institute, where he conducted research and consulted with numerous government agencies, private corporations, and scientific and educational institutions on problems of organization and management. Currently, he is chairman of the department of sociology at American University in Washington, D.C. He is coeditor of *Professionalization* and is the author of *Employee Rights and the Employment Relationship* and numerous articles on work, occupations, and related institutions. Professor Vollmer is responsible for the following chapter: Economics and the World of Work.

Rita Weisbrod received a B.A. in 1955 and an M.A. in 1959 in sociology from the University of Minnesota and has engaged in research studies at UCLA, the Bell Telephone Laboratories at Murray Hill, New Jersey, and Cornell University. She received her Ph.D. in 1972 from Cornell in social psychology. Her current research includes studies on children's understanding of norms and the development of social competence. She is responsible for the following chapter: The Cultural Basis of Society: Childhood Socialization.

References

A

Adorno, Theodor W., Else Frenkel-Brunswik, Daniel J. Levinson, and R. Nevitt Sanford. *The Authoritarian Personality.* New York: Harper, 1950. [2]

Advisory Commission on the Status of Women. *California Women: Report of the Advisory Commission on the Status of Women.* Sacramento, Calif.: State of California Documents Section, 1969. [28]

Akers, Ronald L. "Socio-Economic Status and Delinquent Behavior: A Retest," *Journal of Research in Crime and Delinquency,* 1 (January, 1964), 38–46. [11]
———. *Deviant Behavior: A Social Learning Approach.* Belmont, Calif.: Wadsworth, 1973. [4, 11]

Akers, Ronald L., Robert L. Burgess, and Weldon Johnson. "Opiate Use, Addiction, and Relapse," *Social Problems,* 15 (Spring, 1968), 459–569. [11]

Albert, Ethel. "The Roles of Women: A Question of Values," in S. M. Farber and R. H. L. Wilson (eds.), *The Potential of Woman.* New York: McGraw-Hill, 1963, 105–115. [18]

Alford, Robert. *Party and Society: The Anglo-American Democracies.* Chicago: Rand McNally, 1963. [21]

Andreas, Carol. *Sex and Caste in America.* Englewood Cliffs, N.J.: Prentice-Hall, 1971. [28]

Argyris, Chris. *Personality and Organization.* New York: Harper, 1958. [9]

Arriaga, Eduardo E. *New Life Tables for Latin American Populations.* Institute of International Studies. Berkeley: University of California Press, 1968. [23]

Asch, Solomon. "Effects of Group Pressure Upon the Modification and Distortion of Judgements," in Guy Swanson, Theodore M. Newcomb, and Eugene L. Hartley (eds.), *Readings in Social Psychology.* New York: Holt, 1952, 2–11. [8]

Asimov, Isaac. Introduction to Chapter 24, "The Individual and His Groups," in *Psychology Today: An Introduction.* 2nd ed. Del Mar, Calif.: CRM Books, 1972, 471. [8]

Atchley, Robert C. "Retirement and Leisure Participation: Continuity or Crisis," *Industrial Gerontology,* 1, no. 12 (Winter, 1972), 100–101. [22]

B

Bain, Read. "The Self-and-Other Words of a Child," *American Journal of Sociology,* 41 (May, 1936), 767–775. [7]

Bales, Robert F. "The Equilibrium Problem in Small Groups," in Talcott Parsons, Robert F. Bales, and Edward A. Shils, *Working Papers in the Theory of Action.* Glencoe, Ill.: Free Press, 1953, 111–161. [8]

Bales, Robert F., and Edgar F. Borgatta. "Size of Group as a Factor in the Interaction Profile," in A. Paul Hare, Edgar F. Borgatta, and Robert F. Bales (eds.), *Small Groups: Studies in Social Interaction.* New York: Knopf, 1955, 396–413. [8]

Bales, Robert F., Fred L. Strodtbeck, Theodore M. Mills, and Mary E. Roseborough. "Channels of Communication in Small Groups," *American Sociological Review,* 16 (August, 1951), 461–468. [8]

Baltzell, E. Digby. *The Protestant Establishment: Aristocracy and Caste in America.* New York: Random House, 1964. [13]

Bamburger, Michael, and Margaret Earle. "Factors Affecting Family Planning in a Low Income Caracas Neighborhood," *Studies in Family Planning,* 2 (1971), 175–178. [23]

Bandura, Albert. *Principles of Behavioral Modification.* New York: Holt, Rinehart and Winston, 1969. [6]

Bandura, Albert, and Richard H. Walters. *Social Learning and Personality Development.* New York: Holt, Rinehart and Winston, 1963. [6]

Banks, J. A., and Olive Banks. *Feminism and Family Planning in Victorian England.* New York: Schocken, 1964. [23]

Barber, Bernard. *Social Stratification; A Comparative Analysis of Structure and Process.* New York: Harcourt, Brace, 1957. [13]

Barker, Ernest. *The Development of Public Services in Western Europe 1660–1930.* New York: Oxford University Press, 1944. [9]

Beauvoir, Simone de. *The Second Sex.* H. M. Parshley (ed. and tr.). New York: Knopf, 1953. [28]

Becker, Howard P. *Through Values to Social Interpretation.* Durham, N.C.: Duke University Press, 1950. [8]

Becker, Howard S. *The Outsiders.* New York: Free Press, 1963. [10, 11]
———. (ed.). *The Other Side.* New York: Free Press, 1964. [11]

Becker, Howard S., Blanche Geer, Everett Hughes, and Anselm L. Strauss. *Boys in White: Student Culture in Medical School.* Chicago: University of Chicago Press, 1961. [10]

Bedau, Hugo A. (ed.). *The Death Penalty in America: An Anthology.* Chicago: Aldine, 1964. [11]

Bell, Norman W., and Ezra F. Vogel (eds.). *A Modern Introduction to the Family.* Rev. ed. New York: Free Press, 1968. [18]

Bellah, Robert N. "Civil Religion in America," in William G. McLoughlin and Robert N. Bellah (eds.), *Religion in America.* Boston: Beacon Press, 1968, 3–23. [14, 20, 26]

Ben-David, Joseph. "The Growth of the Professions and the Class System," *Current Sociology,* 12, no. 3 (1963–64), 256–277. [19]

Bendix, Reinhard. "Bureaucracy and the Problem of Power," in Robert K. Merton *et al.* (eds.), *Reader in Bureaucracy.* Glencoe, Ill.: Free Press, 1952, 114–134. [9]
———. *Work and Authority in Industry.* New York: Wiley, 1956. [9, 22]

Bendix, Reinhard, and Seymour Martin Lipset (eds.). *Class, Status and Power.* Glencoe, Ill.: Free Press, 1953. 2nd ed., New York, 1966. [12]

Benedict, Ruth. *Patterns of Culture.* New York: (Mentor) New American Library, 1959. [5]

Berelson, Bernard, and Gary A. Steiner. *Human Behavior: An Inventory of Scientific Findings.* New York: Harcourt, Brace & World, 1964. [3, 8, 10]

Berelson, Bernard, Paul Lazarsfeld, and William N. McPhee. *Voting: A Study of Opinion Formation in a Presidential Campaign.* Chicago: University of Chicago Press, 1954. [26]

Berger, Peter L. *The Sacred Canopy: Elements of a Sociological Theory of Religion.* Garden City, N.Y.: Doubleday, 1967. [20]

Berger, Peter L., and Brigitte Berger. "The Blueing of America," *New Republic,* 164 (April 3, 1971), 20–23. [13]

Bernard, Jessie. *Academic Women.* Cleveland: World Publishing, 1964. [28]
———. "Changing Family Lifestyles: One Role, Two Roles, Shared Roles," *Issues in Industrial Society,* 2 (1971a), 21–28. [28]
———. *Women and the Public Interest: An Essay on Policy and Protest.* Chicago: Aldine-Atherton, 1971b. [28]

Berscheid, Ellen, Karen Dion, Elaine Walster, and G. William Walster. "Physical Attractiveness and Dating Choice: A Test of the Matching Hypothesis," *Journal of Experimental Social Psychology,* 7 (March, 1971), 173–189. [2]

Beyer, Glenn H. *The Urban Explosion in Latin America.* Ithaca, N.Y.: Cornell University Press, 1967. [23]

Bird, Caroline, and Sara Welles Briller. *Born Female: The High Cost of Keeping*

Women Down. New York: David McKay, 1968. [28]

Blalock, Hubert M. "The Identification Problem and Theory Building: The Case of Status Inconsistency," *American Sociological Review,* 31 (February, 1966), 52–61. [12]

Blau, Peter M. *Dynamics of Bureaucracy; A Study of Interpersonal Relations in Two Government Agencies.* Chicago: University of Chicago Press, 1955. [9]

————. *Bureaucracy in Modern Society.* New York: Random House, 1956. [9]

————. *Exchange and Power in Social Life.* New York: Wiley, 1964. [9]

Blau, Peter M., and Otis Dudley Duncan. *The American Occupational Structure.* New York: Wiley, 1967. [13, 14]

Blau, Peter M., and W. Richard Scott. *Formal Organizations.* San Francisco: Chandler, 1962. [9]

Blauner, Robert. *Alienation and Freedom.* Chicago: University of Chicago Press, 1964. [9, 22]

Bloch, Marc. *Feudal Society.* L. A. Manyon (tr.). Chicago: University of Chicago Press, 1964. [21, 25]

Bloomberg, Warner, Jr. "Community Organization," in Howard S. Becker (ed.), *Social Problems: A Modern Approach.* New York: Wiley, 1966, 359–425. [24]

Blum, Richard. "Mind-Altering Drugs and Dangerous Behavior: Narcotics," in *President's Commission on Law Enforcement and the Administration of Justice, Task Force Report: Narcotics and Drug Abuse.* Washington, D.C.: U.S. Government Printing Office, 1967, 40–63. [11]

Blumer, Herbert. "Collective Behavior," in Alfred M. Lee (ed.), *New Outline of the Principles of Sociology.* New York: Barnes & Noble, 1951, 167–222. [27, 28]

————. "Society as Symbolic Interaction," in Arnold Rose (ed.), *Human Behavior and Symbolic Processes: An Interactionist Approach.* Boston: Houghton Mifflin, 1962, 179–192. [4]

Breese, Gerald. *Urbanization in Newly Developing Countries.* Englewood Cliffs, N.J.: Prentice-Hall, 1966. [24]

Bright, James. *Automation and Management.* Cambridge, Mass.: Harvard University Press, 1958. [22]

Brim, Orville G., Jr. "Socialization Through the Life Cycle," in Orville G. Brim, Jr., and Stanton Wheeler, *Socialization After Childhood.* New York: Wiley, 1966, 1–49. [10]

Brim, Orville G., Jr., and Stanton Wheeler. *Socialization After Childhood.* New York: Wiley, 1966. [10]

Brinton, Crane. *An Anatomy of Revolution.* Rev. ed. New York: (Vintage) Random House, 1957; first printing, 1938. [27]

Bronfenbrenner, Urie. "Socialization and Social Class Through Time and Space," in Eleanor E. Maccoby, Theodore M. Newcomb, and Eugene L. Hartley (eds.), *Readings in Social Psychology.* 3rd ed. New York: Holt, Rinehart and Winston, 1958, 400–425. [6]

Broom, Leonard. "Social Differentiation and Stratification," in Robert K. Merton, Leonard Broom, and Leonard S. Cottrell

(eds.), *Sociology Today.* New York: Basic Books, 1959, 429–441. [28]

Brown, Roger W. "Mass Phenomena," in Gardner Lindzey (ed.), *Handbook of Social Psychology.* Reading, Mass.: Addison-Wesley, 1954, II, 833–876. [27]

Brown, Roger, and Ursula Bellugi. "Three Processes in the Child's Acquisition of Syntax," *Harvard Educational Review,* 34 (1964), 133–151. [6]

Bullock, Henry A. "Significance of the Racial Factor in the Length of Prison Sentences," *Journal of Criminal Law, Criminology, and Police Science,* 52 (November-December, 1961), 411–417. [11]

Burgess, Ernest W. "The Growth of the City: An Introduction to a Research Project," in Robert E. Park, Ernest W. Burgess, and Roderick D. McKenzie, *The City.* Chicago: University of Chicago Press, 1925, 47–62. [25]

Burgess, Robert L., and Robert L. Akers. "A Differential Association-Reinforcement Theory of Criminal Behavior," *Social Problems,* 14 (Fall, 1966), 128–147. [11]

C

Cahalan, Don. *Problem Drinkers.* San Francisco: Jossey-Bass, 1970. [11]

Campbell, Angus, Philip Converse, Warren Miller, and Donald Stokes. *The American Voter.* New York: Wiley, 1960. [14, 21]

Caplovitz, David, and Candace Rogers. *Swastika 1960: The Epidemic of Anti-Semitic Vandalism in America.* New York: Anti-Defamation League of B'nai B'rith, 1960. [2]

Carmichael, Stokely, and Charles V. Hamilton. *Black Power: The Politics of Liberation in America.* New York: Random House, 1967. [16, 21]

Carter, H. D. "Twin Similarities in Occupational Interests," *Journal of Educational Psychology,* 23 (1932), 641–655. [5]

Cartter, Allan M. *An Assessment of Quality in Graduate Education.* Washington, D.C.: American Council on Education, 1966. [14]

Casson, Lionel. *Ancient Egypt.* New York: Time-Life Books, 1965. [22]

Chambliss, William J., and Richard Nagasawa. "On the Validity of Official Statistics—A Comparative Study of White, Black, and Japanese High-School Boys," *Journal of Research in Crime and Delinquency,* 6 (January, 1969), 71–77. [11]

Chambliss, William J., and Robert B. Seidman. *Law, Order, and Power.* Reading, Mass.: Addison-Wesley, 1971. [11]

Chauncy, Henry. "The Use of the Selective Service Qualification Test on the Deferment of College Students," *Science,* 116 (July, 1952), 75–85. [19]

Chein, Isidor, and others, with the collaboration of Daniel M. Wilner. *The Road to H: Narcotics, Delinquency, and Social Policy.* New York: Basic Books, 1964. [11]

Childe, V. Gordon. *Man Makes Himself.* New York: (Mentor) New American Library, 1951. [5]

Chinoy, Ely. *Automobile Workers and the American Dream.* Garden City, N.Y.: Doubleday, 1955. [9]

————. *Sociological Perspective.* 2nd ed. New York: Random House, 1968. [3]

Chiricos, Theodore G., and Gordon P. Waldo. "Punishment and Crime: An Examination of Some Empirical Evidence," *Social Problems,* 18 (Fall, 1970), 200–217. [11]

Chomsky, Noam. *Aspects of the Theory of Syntax.* Cambridge, Mass.: MIT Press, 1965. [5]

Clark, Burton R. *The Open Door College.* New York: McGraw-Hill, 1960. [19]

————. *Educating the Expert Society.* San Francisco: Chandler, 1962. [19]

Clausen, John A. "Family Structure, Socialization and Personality," in Martin L. Hoffman and Lois W. Hoffman (eds.), *Review of Child Development Research.* New York: Russell Sage Foundation, 1966, II, 1–53. [6]

Clinard, Marshall B. *Sociology of Deviant Behavior.* New York: Holt, Rinehart and Winston, 1968. [11]

Clough, Shepard Bancroft, and Charles Woolsey Cole. *Economic History of Europe.* Boston: D. C. Heath, 1941. [12]

Cloward, Richard, and Lloyd Ohlin. *Delinquency and Opportunity.* Glencoe, Ill.: Free Press, 1961. [11]

Cohen, Albert K. *Delinquent Boys.* Glencoe, Ill.: Free Press, 1955. [11]

Cohn, Norman. *The Pursuit of the Millennium.* New York: Harper & Row, 1961. [4]

Cohn, Werner. "The Politics of American Jews," in Marshall Sklare (ed.), *The Jews: Social Patterns of an American Group.* Glencoe, Ill.: Free Press, 1958. [13]

Coleman, James S. *Equality of Educational Opportunity.* Department of Health, Education, and Welfare. Washington, D.C.: U.S. Government Printing Office, 1966. [13, 19]

————. "Class Integration—A Fundamental Break With the Past," *Saturday Review,* 55 (May 27, 1972), 58–59. [19]

Collins, Randall. "Functional and Conflict Theories of Educational Stratification," *American Sociological Review,* 36 (December, 1971), 1002–1019. [19]

Collver, O. Andrew. *Birth Rates in Latin America: New Estimates of Historical Trends and Fluctuations.* Institute of International Studies. Berkeley: University of California Press, 1965. [23]

Commission on Obscenity and Pornography. *The Report of the Commission on Obscenity and Pornography.* New York: Bantam, 1970. [11]

Cooley, Charles Horton. *Social Organization.* New York: Scribner, 1909. [8]

————. *Human Nature and the Social Order.* New York: Scribner, 1922. [6, 7]

Cornwell, Elmer E., Jr. "Bosses, Machines, and Ethnic Groups," in Lawrence E. Fuchs (ed.), *American Ethnic Politics.* New York: Harper & Row, 1968, 194–216. [21]

Corwin, Ronald G. "Role Conception and Career Aspiration: A Study of Identity in Nursing," *Sociological Quarterly,* 2 (April, 1961), 69–86. [7]

Coser, Lewis. *The Functions of Social Conflict.* Glencoe, Ill.: Free Press, 1956. [3, 26]

Cox, Harvey. *The Secular City.* Rev. ed. New York: Macmillan, 1966. [20]

Cremin, Lawrence. *The Transformation of the School: Progressivism in American Education 1876–1957.* New York: (Vintage) Random House, 1964. [19]

Cressey, Donald R. (ed.). *The Prison.* New York: Holt, Rinehart and Winston, 1961.[11]

D

Dahl, Robert. *Who Governs? Democracy and Power in an American City.* New Haven, Conn.: Yale University Press, 1961. [21]

Dalton, Melville. *Men Who Manage; Fusions of Feeling and Theory in Administration.* New York: Wiley, 1959. [9]

D'Andrade, Roy G. "Sex Differences and Cultural Institutions," in Eleanor E. Maccoby (ed.), *The Development of Sex Differences.* Stanford, Calif.: Stanford University Press, 1966. [17]

Davies, James C. "The J-Curve of Rising and Declining Satisfactions as a Cause of Some Great Revolutions and a Contained Rebellion," in Hugh Davis Graham and Ted Robert Gurr (eds.), *Violence in America: Historical and Comparative Perspectives.* New York: Bantam, 1969, 690–730. [14, 28]

Davis, Kingsley. "Extreme Social Isolation of a Child," *American Journal of Sociology,* 45 (January, 1940a), 554–564. [6]

———. "The Sociology of Parent-Youth Conflict," *American Sociological Review,* 5 (August, 1940b), 523–535. [10]

———. "A Conceptual Analysis of Stratification," *American Sociological Review,* 7 (June, 1942), 309–321. [15]

———. "The World Demographic Transition," *Annals of the American Academy of Political and Social Sciences,* 237 (January, 1945), 1–11. [23]

———. "Final Note on a Case of Extreme Isolation," *American Journal of Sociology,* 50 (March, 1947), 432–437. [6]

———. *Human Society.* New York: Macmillan, 1949. [4, 6, 8, 15]

———. "Reply to Tumin," *American Sociological Review,* 18 (August, 1953), 394–397. [15]

———. "The Origin and Growth of Urbanization in the World," *American Journal of Sociology,* 60 (March, 1955), 429–437. [12]

———. "The Amazing Decline of Mortality in Underdeveloped Areas," *American Economic Review,* 46 (May, 1956), 305–318. [23]

———. "Sexual Behavior," in Robert K. Merton and Robert A. Nisbet (eds.), *Contemporary Social Problems.* 2nd ed. New York: Harcourt, Brace & World, 1966. [11]

Davis, Kingsley, and Wilbert Moore. "Some Principles of Stratification," *American Sociological Review,* 10 (April, 1945), 242–249. [15]

Dawson, Carl A., and W. E. Gettys. *An Introduction to Sociology.* New York: Ronald Press, 1929. [27]

Deane, Phyllis, and W. A. Cole. *British Economic Growth: 1688–1959.* Cambridge, Mass.: Cambridge University Press, 1969. [23]

Deaux, George. *The Black Death: 1347.* New York: Weybright and Talley, 1969. [23]

Deck, Leland. "Short Workers of the World, Unite!" *Psychology Today,* 5 (August, 1971), 102. [13]

Demerath, N. J. III. *Social Class in American Protestantism.* Chicago: Rand McNally, 1965. [20]

Demerath, N. J. III, and Phillip E. Hammond. *Religion in Social Context.* New York: Random House, 1969. [20]

Dennis, Wayne. "Causes of Retardation Among Institutional Children: Iran," *Journal of Genetic Psychology,* 96 (1960), 47–59. [6]

———. "Infant Development Under Conditions of Restricted Practice and of Minimal Social Stimulation: A Preliminary Report," *Journal of Genetic Psychology,* 53 (1938), 149–158. [6]

Deutsch, Martin P. "The Disadvantaged Child and the Learning Process," in A. Harry Passow (ed.), *Education in Depressed Areas.* New York: Columbia University Press, 1963, 163–179. [19]

Dimond, Stuart J. *The Social Behavior of Animals.* New York: Harper & Row, 1970. [5]

Dion, Karen. "Physical Attractiveness and Evaluations of Children's Transgressions," *Journal of Personality and Social Psychology* (1972). [2]

Dion, Karen, Ellen Berscheid, and Elaine Walster. "What Is Beautiful Is Good," *Journal of Personality and Social Psychology,* in press. [2]

Divorce Statistics Analysis, United States, 1963. U.S. Department of Health, Education, and Welfare; Public Health Service Publication, No. 1000, Series 21, No. 13. Washington, D.C.: U.S. Government Printing Office, 1964. [18]

Dore, Ronald P. *City Life in Japan: A Study of a Tokyo Ward.* Berkeley: University of California Press, 1958. [26]

Drucker, Peter F. *The Age of Discontinuity; Guidelines to Our Changing Society.* New York: Harper & Row, 1969. [12, 19]

———. "What We Can Learn From Japanese Management," *Industrial Gerontology,* 1, no. 12 (Winter, 1972), 89–91. [22]

Dubin, Robert. *The World of Work; Industrial Society and Human Relations.* Englewood Cliffs, N.J.: Prentice-Hall, 1958. [9]

———. "Industrial Workers' World: A Study of the 'Central Life Interests' of Industrial Workers," in Erwin O. Smigel (ed.), *Work and Leisure.* New Haven, Conn.: College and University Press, 1963, 53–72. [22]

Duncan, Beverly. "Dropouts and the Unemployed," *Journal of Political Economy,* 73 (April, 1964), 121–134. [19]

Dunham, H. Warren. *Community and Schizophrenia: An Epidemiological Analysis.* Detroit, Mich.: Wayne State University Press, 1965. [11]

Durkheim, Emile. *The Elementary Forms of the Religious Life.* Joseph W. Swain (tr.). Glencoe, Ill.: Free Press, 1954; first published in English, 1915. [20]

———. *Suicide: A Study in Sociology.* John A. Spaulding and George Simpson (trs.). Glencoe, Ill.: Free Press, 1951. [5, 11]

———. *The Division of Labor in Society.* George Simpson (tr.). New York: Free Press, 1966. [22]

Duverger, Maurice. *Political Parties, Their Organization and Activity in the Modern State.* Barbara and Robert North (trs.). New York: Wiley, 1954. [21]

E

Easton, David. *A Systems Analysis of Political Life.* New York: Wiley, 1965. [26]

Eberhard, Wolfram. "Social Mobility and Stratification in China," in Reinhard Bendix and Seymour Martin Lipset (eds.), *Class, Status and Power.* 2nd ed. New York: Free Press, 1966, 171–182. [13]

Eckland, Bruce K. "Genetics and Sociology: A Reconsideration," *American Sociological Review,* 32 (April, 1967), 173–194. [5, 13]

Eisenstadt, S. N. *From Generation to Generation: Age-Groups and Social Structure.* Glencoe, Ill.: Free Press, 1956. [19]

———. "Bureaucracy, Bureaucratization, and De-Bureaucratization," *Administrative Science Quarterly,* 4 (December, 1959), 302–320. [9]

———. *The Political Systems of Empires.* New York: Free Press, 1963. [9]

Elder, Glen H., Jr. "Appearance and Education in Marriage Mobility," *American Sociological Review,* 34 (August, 1969), 519–533. [5]

Elder, Glen H., Jr., and Charles E. Bowerman. "Family Structure and Child Rearing Patterns: The Effect of Family Size and Sex Composition," *American Sociological Review,* 28 (December, 1963), 891–905. [6]

Ellul, Jacques. *The Technological Society.* John Wilkinson (tr.). 1st American ed. New York: Knopf, 1964. [9]

Empey, LaMar T., and Steven G. Lubeck. *The Silverlake Experiment.* Chicago: Aldine, 1971. [11]

Engels, Friedrich. *Origin of the Family, Private Property, and the State.* 4th ed. New York: International Publishers, 1964; first printing, 1882. [17, 18]

Ennis, Phillip H. "Crime, Victims, and the Police," *Trans-action,* 4 (June, 1967), 36–44. [11]

Epstein, Cynthia Fuchs. *Woman's Place: Options and Limits in Professional Careers.* Berkeley: University of California Press, 1971. [28]

Erikson, Kai T. *Wayward Puritans.* New York: Wiley, 1966. [11]

Erlanger, Howard S. "The Anatomy of Violence: An Empirical Examination of Sociological Theories of Interpersonal Aggression." (Unpublished Ph.D. dissertation, University of California, Berkeley, Sept. 1971). [14]

Etzioni, Amitai. *A Comparative Analysis*

of Complex Organizations. New York: Free Press, 1962. [9]

Evans-Pritchard, Edward E. *The Nuer.* New York: Oxford University Press, 1940. [18]

Eysenck, H. J., and D. B. Prell. "The Inheritance of Neuroticism: An Experimental Study," *Journal of Mental Science,* 97 (1951), 441–465. [5]

F

Fadiman, Clifton. "Is There an Upper-Class American Language?" *Holiday,* (October, 1956), 8–10. [14]

Faris, Robert E. L. *Social Disorganization.* Rev. ed. New York: Ronald Press, 1955, [11]

Faris, Robert E. L., and H. Warren Dunham. *Mental Disorders in Urban Areas.* Chicago: University of Chicago Press, 1939. [11]

Faulkner, Joseph E., and Gordon F. DeJong. "Religiosity in 5-D: An Empirical Analysis," *Social Forces,* 45 (December, 1966), 246–254. [20]

Faunce, William A. *Problems of an Industrial Society.* New York: McGraw-Hill, 1968. [9]

Federal Bureau of Investigation. *Crime in the United States, Uniform Crime Reports—1969.* Washington, D.C.: U.S. Government Printing Office, 1970. [11]

——. *Crime in the United States, Uniform Crime Reports—1970.* Washington, D.C.: U.S. Government Printing Office, 1971. [11]

Feldman, Saul. "The Presentation of Shortness in Everyday Life: Height and Heightism in American Society: Toward a Sociology of Stature." Paper presented at the American Sociological Association Convention, Denver, 1971. [13]

Ferdinand, Theodore N., and Elmer G. Luchterhand. "Inner-City Youth, the Police, the Juvenile Courts, and Justice," *Social Problems,* 17 (Spring, 1971), 510–527. [11]

Ferster, C. B., and B. F. Skinner. *Schedules of Reinforcement.* New York: Appleton-Century-Crofts, 1957. [6]

Festinger, Leon, Stanley Schachter, and Kurt Back. *Social Pressures in Informal Groups.* New York: Harper & Row, 1950. [8]

Festinger, Leon, and John Thibaut. "Interpersonal Communication in Small Groups," *Journal of Abnormal and Social Psychology,* 46 (January, 1951), 92–99. [8]

Finn, M. W. *British Population Growth: 1700 to 1850.* Glasgow, Scotland: University Press, 1970. [23]

Firestone, Shulamith. *The Dialectics of Sex: The Case for Feminist Revolution.* New York: William Morrow, 1970. [28]

Firth, Raymond. *We, The Tikopia: A Sociological Study of Kinship in Primitive Polynesia.* 2nd ed. London: Allen & Unwin, 1963. [25]

——. *Human Types.* New York: Rockefeller University Press, 1968. [5]

Flexner, Eleanor. *Century of Struggle: The Woman's Rights Movement in the*

United States. Cambridge, Mass.: Harvard University Press, 1959. [28]

Forbes, Gordon, R. Kent Tevault, and Harry F. Gromoll. "Political Stamping Grounds," *Psychology Today,* 4 (April, 1971), 74. [1]

Frank, André Gunder. *Latin America: Underdevelopment or Revolution.* New York: Monthly Review Press, 1969. [29]

Freud, Sigmund. *Group Psychology and the Analysis of the Ego.* James Strachey (tr.). New York: Bantam, 1960; first published in 1921. [27]

Fried, Marc. "Grieving for a Lost Home," in Leonard Duhl (ed.) with the assistance of John Powell, *Urban Condition: People and Policy in the Metropolis.* New York: Basic Books, 1963, 151–171. [24]

Friedan, Betty. *The Feminine Mystique.* New York: Norton, 1963. [28]

Friedman, Georges. *Industrial Society: The Emergence of the Human Problems of Automation.* Glencoe, Ill.: Free Press, 1955. [22]

Friedmann, Eugene A., and Robert J. Havighurst. *The Meaning of Work and Retirement.* Chicago: University of Chicago Press, 1954, 183–194. [22]

G

Galbraith, John Kenneth. *The New Industrial State.* Boston: Houghton-Mifflin, 1967. [12]

Gamson, William A. *Power and Discontent.* Homewood, Ill.: Dorsey, 1968*a*. [26]

——. "Stable Unrepresentation in American Society," *American Behavioral Scientist,* 12 (November, 1968*b*), 15–21. [21]

Gans, Herbert J. *The Urban Villagers.* New York: Free Press, 1965. [29]

Geiger, H. Kent. "The Fate of the Family in Soviet Russia: 1917–1944," in Norman W. Bell and Ezra E. Vogel (eds.), *A Modern Introduction to the Family.* Rev. ed. New York: Free Press, 1968, 48–67. [18]

Gellerman, Saul W. *Motivation and Productivity.* New York: American Management Association, 1963. [22]

Gerth, H. H., and C. Wright Mills. (eds. and trs.). *From Max Weber: Essays in Sociology.* New York: Oxford University Press, 1946. [9, 22]

Geschwender, James A. "Explorations in the Theory of Social Movements and Revolutions," *Social Forces,* 47 (December, 1968), 127–135. [28]

Gesell, Arnold, and Frances L. Ilg, in collaboration with Louise B. Ames and Janet Learned. *Infant and Child in the Culture of Today; the Guidance of Development in Home and Nursery School.* New York: Harper, 1943. [6]

Gibb, Cecil A. "Leadership," in Gardner Lindzey (ed.), *Handbook of Social Psychology.* Reading, Mass.: Addison-Wesley, 1954, II, 877–920. [8]

Gibbs, Jack P., and Walter T. Martin. *Status Integration and Suicide.* Eugene, Ore.: University of Oregon Press, 1964. [11]

Gibbs, Marion. *Feudal Order, A Study of*

the Origins and Development of English Feudal Society. New York: Schuman, 1953. [22]

Gist, Noel P., and Sylvia F. Fava. *Urban Society.* 5th ed. New York: Crowell, 1964. [24]

Claser, Daniel. *The Effectiveness of a Prison and Parole System.* Indianapolis, Ind.: Bobbs-Merrill, 1964. [11]

Glasscote, Raymond, James N. Sussex, et al. *The Treatment of Drug Abuse.* Washington, D.C.: Government Information Service of APA and NAMH, 1972. [11]

Glazer, Nathan. "A New Look at the Melting Pot," *The Public Interest,* 16 (Summer, 1969), 180–187. [16]

Glazer, Nathan, and Daniel Patrick Moynihan. *Beyond the Melting Pot: The Negroes, Puerto Ricans, Jews, Italians, and Irish of New York City.* Rev. ed. Cambridge, Mass.: MIT and Harvard University Press, 1971. [16]

Glock, Charles Y., Benjamin B. Ringer, and Earl R. Babbie. *To Comfort and to Challenge: A Dilemma of the Contemporary Church.* Berkeley: University of California Press, 1967. [20]

Glock, Charles Y., and Rodney Stark. *Religion and Society in Tension.* Chicago: Rand McNally, 1965. [14, 20]

——. *Christian Beliefs and Anti-Semitism.* New York: Harper & Row, 1966. [2]

Goffman, Erving. *Asylums: Essays on the Social Situation of Mental Patients and Other Inmates.* Chicago: Aldine, 1961. [9, 10, 11]

——. *Encounters: Two Studies in the Sociology of Interaction.* Indianapolis, Ind.: Bobbs-Merrill, 1961. [7]

——. *Stigma.* Englewood Cliffs, N.J.: Prentice-Hall, 1963. [11]

Goldschmidt, Walter. *Man's Way: A Preface to the Understanding of Human Society.* New York: Holt, 1959. [12]

Goode, Erich. *The Marijuana Smokers.* New York: Basic Books, 1970. [11]

Goode, William J. "Community Within a Community, the Professions," *American Sociological Review,* 22 (April, 1957), 194–200. [9]

——. "Marital Satisfaction and Instability: A Cross-Cultural Analysis of Divorce Rates," *International Social Science Journal,* 14 (1962), 507–526. [14, 18]

——. *World Revolution and Family Patterns.* New York: Free Press, 1963. [17, 18]

Gordon, Milton. *Assimilation in American Life.* New York: Oxford University Press, 1964. [16]

Gordon, Robert A., and James E. Howell. *Higher Education in Business.* New York: Columbia University Press, 1959. [19]

Goslin, David A. (ed.). *Handbook of Socialization Theory and Research.* Chicago: Rand McNally, 1969. [6]

Gottesman, I. I. "Heritability of Personality: A Demonstration," *Psychological Monographs,* 77, no. 9 (1963). [5]

Gottschalk, Louis. *The Era of the French Revolution.* Boston: Houghton-Mifflin, 1929. [12]

Gough, E. Kathleen. "The Nayars and the Definition of Marriage," *Journal of the Royal Anthropological Institute,* 89, Part 1 (1959), 23–34. [18]

———. "The Origin of the Family," *Journal of Marriage and the Family,* 33 (November, 1971), 760–770. [17]

Gouldner, Alvin W. *Patterns of Industrial Bureaucracy.* Glencoe, Ill.: Free Press, 1954. [9]

———. "Cosmopolitans and Locals: Towards an Analysis of Latent Social Roles," *Administrative Science Quarterly,* 2 (December, 1957), 281–292. [8]

———. "Organizational Analysis," in Robert K. Merton, Leonard Broom, and Leonard S. Cottrell, Jr. (eds.), *Sociology Today.* New York: Basic Books, 1959, 400–410. [9]

Graham, Hugh Davis, and Ted Robert Gurr. *History of Violence in America: Historical and Comparative Perspectives.* New York: Praeger, 1969. [8]

Greenstein, Fred I. "New Light on Changing American Values: A Forgotten Body of Survey Data," *Social Forces,* 42 (May, 1964), 441–450. [8]

Greenwood, Ernest. "Attributes of a Profession," *Social Work,* 2 (July, 1957), 44–55. [22]

Gross, Neal, Ward S. Mason, and Alexander W. McEachern. *Explorations in Role Analysis: Studies of the School Superintendency Role.* New York: Wiley, 1958. [7]

Gunther, Mavis. "Infant Behavior at the Breast," in B. M. Foss (ed.), *Determinants of Infant Behavior.* London: Methuen, 1961, I. [6]

Gurr, Ted Robert. *Why Men Rebel.* Princeton, N.J.: Princeton University Press, 1970. [26]

H

Hacker, Helen Mayer. "Women as a Minority Group," *Social Forces,* 30 (October, 1951), 60–69. [28]

Hadden, Jeffrey K. *The Gathering Storm in the Churches.* Garden City, N.Y: Doubleday, 1969. [20]

———. "A Protestant Paradox—Divided They Merge," *Trans-action,* 4 (July-August, 1967), 63–69. [20]

Hagen, Everett E. *On the Theory of Social Change.* Homewood, Ill.: Dorsey Press, 1962. [26]

Hall, Richard H. "Some Organizational Considerations in the Professional-Organization Relationship," *Administrative Science Quarterly,* 12 (December, 1967), 461–478. [9]

———. *Occupations and the Social Structure.* Englewood Cliffs, N.J.: Prentice-Hall, 1969. [22]

Hanson, Pamela Marsters. "Age and Physical Capacity to Work," *Industrial Gerontology,* 1, no. 12 (Winter, 1972), 20–41. [22]

Hare, A. Paul, Edgar F. Borgatta, and Robert F. Bales (eds.). *Small Groups: Studies in Social Interaction.* 3rd ed. New York: Knopf, 1962. [6]

Harlow, Harry F., and Margaret K. Harlow. "Social Deprivation in Monkeys," *Scientific American,* 207 (November, 1962), 137–147. [6]

———. "The Affectional Systems," in Allan Schrier, Harry Harlow, and Fred Stollnitz (eds.), *Behavior of Nonhuman Primates: Modern Research Trends.* New York: Academic Press, 1965, II, 287–333. [6]

Harrington, Michael. *The Other America.* Baltimore, Md.: Penguin, 1962. [26]

Harris, Ann Sutherland. "The Second Sex in Academe," *American Association of University Professors Bulletin,* 56 (September, 1970), 283–295. [28]

Harris, Chauncy, and Edward L. Ullman. "The Nature of Cities," in Paul K. Hatt and Albert J. Reiss, Jr. (eds.), *Reader in Urban Sociology.* Glencoe, Ill.: Free Press, 1951, 222–232. [25]

Harris, Marvin. "Race," *International Encyclopedia of the Social Sciences.* New York: Macmillan, 1968, XIII, 263–267. [16]

Hauser, Philip M. (ed.). *Urbanization in Latin America.* New York: Columbia University Press, 1961. [23]

Hazelrigg, Lawrence (ed.). *Prison Within Society.* Garden City, N.Y.: (Anchor) Doubleday, 1969. [11]

Hechter, Michael. "Towards a Theory of Ethnic Change," *Politics and Society,* 2 (Fall, 1971), 21–45. [21]

Herberg, Will. *Protestant, Catholic, Jew.* Rev. ed. Garden City, N.Y.: (Anchor) Doubleday, 1960. [26]

"The Heroin Plague," *Newsweek,* 78 (July 5, 1971), 27–32. [11]

Herrnstein, Richard. "I.Q.," *Atlantic,* 228 (September, 1971), 43–64. [5]

Hershberger, Ruth. *Adam's Rib.* New York: Pellegrini & Cudahy, 1948. [28]

Hertzler, J. O. "Crisis and Dictatorships," *American Sociological Review,* 5 (April, 1940), 157–169. [28]

Herzberg, Frederick, Bernard Mauser, and Barbara B. Snyderman. *The Motivation to Work.* New York: Wiley, 1959. [22]

Higgins, Benjamin. "The 'Dualistic Theory' of Underdeveloped Areas," *Economic Development and Cultural Change,* 4 (January, 1956), 99–115. [29]

Hintze, Otto. "Die Entstehung der modernen Staatminsterien," *Historische Zeitschrift,* 100 (1908), 53–111. [9]

Hirschi, Travis. *Causes of Delinquency.* Berkeley: University of California Press, 1969. [11, 13, 14, 25]

Hirschi, Travis, and Rodney Stark. "Hellfire and Delinquency," *Social Problems,* 17 (Fall, 1969), 202–213. [20]

Hoetink, Harry. *The Two Variants on Caribbean Race Relations: A Contribution to the Sociology of Segmented Societies.* New York: Oxford University Press, 1967. [16]

Hoffer, Eric. *The True Believer.* New York: (Mentor) New American Library, 1951. [28]

Hoffman, Martin L., and Herbert D. Saltzstein. "Parent Discipline and the Child's Moral Development," *Journal of Personality and Social Psychology,* 5 (January, 1967), 45–57. [6]

Hollingshead, August B., and Frederick C. Redlich. *Social Class and Mental Illness.* New York: Wiley, 1958. [11]

Holmberg, Allan. *Nomads of the Long Bow: The Siriono of Eastern Bolivia.* Smithsonian Institution, Institute of Social Anthropology, Publication No. 10. Washington, D.C.: U.S. Government Printing Office, 1950. [12]

Holmes, John Clellon. "The New Girl," *Playboy,* 15 (January, 1968), 179–186, 214–216. [28]

Homans, George C. *Social Behavior: Its Elementary Forms.* New York: Harcourt, Brace & World, 1961. [4, 8, 9]

———. "Bringing Men Back In," *American Sociology Review,* 29 (December, 1964), 809–818. [4]

———. *The Nature of Social Sciences.* New York: Harcourt, Brace & World, 1967. [1, 4]

Hook, Sidney. *The Hero in History: A Study in Limitation and Possibility.* Boston: Beacon Press, 1943. [15]

Hoselitz, Bert. "A Sociological Approach to Economic Development," in David E. Novack and Robert Lekachman (eds.), *Development and Society.* New York: St. Martin's Press, 1964, 150–163. [26]

Hoyt, Homer. *The Structure and Growth of Residential Neighborhoods in American Cities.* Washington, D.C.: U.S. Government Printing Office, 1939. [25]

Hughes, Everett C. *Men and Their Work.* Glencoe, Ill.: Free Press, 1958. [22]

Hughes, Langston. "My Early Days in Harlem," in John Hendrik Clarke (ed.), *Harlem: A Community in Transition.* New York: Citadel, 1964, 62–64. [24]

Humphreys, Laud. "Tearoom Trade: Impersonal Sex in Public Places," *Transaction,* 7 (January, 1970) 10–14 +. [11]

Hyman, Martin D. "Determining the Effects of Status Inconsistency," *Public Opinion Quarterly,* 30 (Spring, 1966), 120–129. [12]

I

Inhelder, Bärbel, and Jean Piaget. *The Growth of Logical Thinking From Childhood to Adolescence.* New York: Basic Books, 1958. [6]

Ireland, Waltraud. "The Rise and Fall of the Suffrage Movement," *Leviathan,* 2, no. 1 (May, 1970), 4–7, 44–46. [28]

Irwin, John. *Felon.* Englewood Cliffs, N.J.: Prentice-Hall, 1970. [11]

J

Jacob, Herbert. *German Administration Since Bismarck: Central Authority Versus Local Autonomy.* New Haven, Conn.: Yale University Press, 1963. [9]

Jacobs, Jane. *The Death and Life of Great American Cities.* New York: Random House, 1961. [24]

Jalée, Pierre. *The Pillage of the Third World.* Mary Klopper (tr.). New York: Monthly Review Press, 1968. [29]

———. *The Third World in World Economy.* Mary Klopper (tr.). New York: Monthly Review Press, 1969. [29]

Jensen, Arthur R. "How Much Can We Boost I.Q. and Scholastic Achievement?"

Harvard Educational Review, 39 (Winter, Summer, 1969), 1–123, 449–483. [5, 13]

Johnson, Donald M. "The 'Phantom Anesthetist' of Mattoon: A Field Study of Mass Hysteria," *Journal of Abnormal and Social Psychology*, 40 (April, 1945), 175–186. [27]

Jordan, Joan. "Comment: Working Women and the Equal Rights Amendment," *Trans-action*, 8 (November-December, 1970), 16–22. [28]

Joreen. "The 51 Percent Minority Group: A Statistical Essay," in Robin Morgan (ed.), *Sisterhood Is Powerful*. New York: Random House, 1970, 37–46. [28]

K

Kadushin, Charles. "Social Class and the Experience of Ill Health," *Sociological Inquiry*, 34 (Winter, 1964), 67–80. [14]

Kagan, Jerome. "On Cultural Deprivation." Paper presented at Russell Sage and Rockefeller Conference, New York, 1967. [6]

Kaij, Lennart. *Alcoholism in Twins*. Stockholm: Almquist and Wiksell, 1960. [5]

Kallman, Franz J. *Heredity in Health and Mental Disorder*. New York: Norton, 1953. [5]

Kaplan, John. *Marijuana; The New Prohibition*. New York: Pocket Books, 1971. [11]

Kassebaum, Gene, David Wood, and Daniel Wilner. *Prison Treatment and Parole Survival*. New York: Wiley, 1971. [11]

Kautsky, Karl. *Foundations of Christianity*. Henry F. Mins (tr.). New York: Russell and Russell, 1953. [20]

Keil, Charles. *Urban Blues*. Chicago: University of Chicago Press, 1966. [24]

Keller, Suzanne, and Marisa Zavalloni. "Ambition and Social Class: A Respecification," *Social Forces*, 43 (October, 1964), 58–70. [13]

Kelley, Harold H., and John W. Thibaut. "Experimental Studies of Group Problem Solving and Process," in Gardner Lindzey (ed.), *Handbook of Social Psychology*. Reading, Mass.: Addison-Wesley, 1954, II, 735–785. [8]

Kerr, Clark, *et al. Industrialism and Industrial Man: The Problems of Labor and Management in Economic Growth*. New York: Oxford University Press, 1964. [26]

Kiernan, V. G. "Foreign Mercenaries and Absolute Monarchy," in Trevor Aston (ed.), *Crisis in Europe, 1560–1660*. New York: Basic Books, 1965, 117–140. [21]

Killian, Lewis A. *White Southerners*. New York: Random House, 1970. [16]

Kitsuse, John I., and Aaron V. Cicourel. "A Note on the Use of Official Statistics," *Social Problems*, 11 (Fall, 1963), 131–139. [11]

Klopfer, Peter H., and Jack P. Hailman. *An Introduction to Animal Behavior*. Englewood Cliffs, N.J.: Prentice-Hall, 1967. [5]

Kluckhohn, Clyde. *Mirror for Man*. New York: McGraw-Hill, 1949. [4]

———. "Values and Value-Orientations in the Theory of Action: An Exploration in Definition and Classification," in Talcott Parsons and Edward Shils (eds.), *Toward a General Theory of Action*. New York: Harper & Row, 1962, 388–433. [20]

Knudsen, Dean D. "The Declining Status of Women: Popular Myths and the Failure of Functionalist Thought," *Social Forces*, 48 (December, 1969), 183–193.[28]

Kohn, Melvin. *Class and Conformity*. Homewood, Ill.: Dorsey Press, 1969. [6]

Komarovsky, Mirra. *Blue-Collar Marriage*. New York: Random House, 1964. [14]

Kornhauser, William. *The Politics of Mass Society*. New York: Free Press, 1959. [29]

Kuhn, Manford, and Thomas S. McPartland. "An Empirical Investigation of Self-Attitudes," *American Sociological Review*, 19 (February, 1954), 68–76. [7]

Kummer, Hans. *Primate Societies*. Chicago: Aldine-Atherton, 1971. [5, 17]

L

LaBarre, Weston. *The Human Animal*. Chicago: University of Chicago Press, 1955. [5]

Labovitz, Sanford. "Variation in Suicide Rates," in Jack P. Gibbs (ed.), *Suicide*. New York: Harper & Row, 1968, 57–73. [11]

LaFollette, Suzanne. *Concerning Women*. New York: Albert and Charles Boni, 1926. [28]

Lambe, James. *Rich World/Poor World*. London: Arrow, 1967. [29]

Landis, Benson Y. (ed.). *Yearbook of American Churches for 1963*. New York: National Council of Churches of Christ in the U.S.A., 1963. [20]

Landtman, Gunnar. *The Kiwai Papuans of British New Guinea*. New York: Macmillan, 1927. [12]

Lang, Kurt, and Gladys E. Lang. *Collective Dynamics*. New York: Crowell, 1961. [27, 28]

Lassiter, Roy L. *The Association of Income and Educational Achievement*. Gainesville: University of Florida Press, 1966. [13]

Le Bon, Gustave. *The Crowd: A Study of the Popular Mind*. New York: Viking, 1960; first printing, 1895. [27]

Lee, Robert. *The Social Sources of Church Unity*. Nashville, Tenn.: Abingdon Press, 1960. [20]

Lemert, Edwin M. *Human Deviance, Social Problems, and Social Control*. 2nd ed. Englewood Cliffs, N.J.: Prentice-Hall, 1972. [11]

Lenneberg, Eric. "On Explaining Language," *Science*, 164 (May 9, 1969), 635–643. [6]

Lenski, Gerhard. "Status Crystallization: A Non-Vertical Dimension of Social Status," *American Sociological Review*, 19 (August, 1954), 405–413. [12]

———. "Social Participation and Status Crystallization," *American Sociological Review*, 21 (August, 1956), 458–464. [12]

———. *Power and Privilege: The Theory of Social Stratification*. New York: McGraw-Hill, 1966. [12, 13, 15]

Lerman, Paul. "Evaluative Studies of Institutions for Delinquents," in Paul Lerman (ed.), *Delinquency and Social Policy*. New York: Praeger, 1970, 317–328. [11]

Lerner, I. Michael. *Heredity, Evolution and Society*. San Francisco: W. H. Freeman, 1968. [5]

Leuba, James H. *The Belief in God and Immortality*. Boston: Sherman French, 1916. [20]

Lévi-Strauss, Claude. *The Elementary Structure of Kinship*. Boston: Beacon Press, 1968. [17]

Lieberson, Stanley. *Ethnic Patterns in American Cities*. New York: Free Press 1963. [25]

Lieberson, Stanley, and Arnold R. Silverman. "The Precipitants and Underlying Conditions of Race Riots," *American Sociological Review*, 30 (December, 1965), 887–898. [27]

Liebow, Elliot. *Tally's Corner: A Study of Negro Streetcorner Men*. Boston: Little, Brown, 1967. [10, 24]

Lipset, Seymour Martin. *Agrarian Socialism; the Cooperative Commonwealth Federation in Saskatchewan, a Study in Political Sociology*. Berkeley: University of California Press, 1950. [9]

———. *Political Man*. Garden City, N.Y.: Doubleday, 1960. [14, 20, 21]

———. "University Student Politics," in Seymour M. Lipset and Sheldon S. Wolin (eds.), *The Berkeley Student Revolt*. Garden City, N.Y.: (Anchor) Doubleday, 1965, 1–9. [10]

Lipset, Seymour Martin, and Reinhard Bendix. *Social Mobility in Industrial Society*. Berkeley: University of California Press, 1958. [13, 14, 19]

Lipset, Seymour Martin, and Aldo Solari. *Elites in Latin America*. New York: Oxford University Press, 1967. [29]

Litwak, Eugene. "Models of Bureaucracy Which Permit Conflict," *American Journal of Sociology*, 67 (September, 1961), 177–184. [9]

Lofland, John. *Doomsday Cult*. Englewood Cliffs, N.J.: Prentice-Hall, 1966. [2]

———. *Deviance and Identity*. Englewood Cliffs, N.J.: Prentice-Hall, 1969. [2, 11]

———. *Analyzing Social Settings*. Belmont, Calif.: Wadsworth, 1971. [2]

Lofland, John, and Rodney Stark. "On Becoming a World Saver: A Theory of Conversion to a Deviant Perspective," *American Sociological Review*, 30 (December, 1965), 862–875. [2]

Lorenz, Konrad. *Evolution and Modification of Behavior*. Chicago: University of Chicago Press, 1965. [5]

———. *On Aggression*. New York: Harcourt, Brace & World, 1966. [5, 6]

Luckey, Eleanore B., and G. D. Nass. "A Comparison of Sexual Attitudes and Behavior in an International Sample," *Journal of Marriage and the Family*, 31 (May, 1969), 364–379. [18]

Luckman, Thomas, and Peter L. Berger. "Social Mobility and Personal Identity," *European Journal of Sociology (Archives européennes de sociologie)*, 5 (1964), 331–344. [13]

Lynd, Robert S., and Helen M. Lynd. *Middletown, A Study in American Culture*. New York: Harcourt, Brace, 1929. [21]

———. *Middletown in Transition; A Study*

in Cultural Conflicts. New York: Harcourt, Brace, 1937. [21]

M

McAfee, Kathy, and Myrna Wood. "Bread and Roses," in Roberta Salper (ed.), *Female Liberation: History and Current Politics.* New York: Knopf, 1972. [28]

McCandless, Boyd R. *Children: Behavior and Development.* 2nd ed. New York: Holt, Rinehart and Winston, 1967. [6]

McClelland, David. *The Achieving Society.* Princeton, N.J.: Van Nostrand, 1961. [13]

Maccoby, Eleanor E. (ed.). *The Development of Sex Differences.* Stanford, Calif.: Stanford University Press, 1966. [17]

McEvoy, James, and Abraham Miller. *Black Power and Student Rebellion: Conflict on the American Campus.* Belmont, Calif.: Wadsworth, 1969. [28]

McGregor, Douglas. *The Human Side of Enterprise.* New York: McGraw-Hill, 1960. [22]

MacIver, Robert M. *The Web of Government.* New York: Macmillan, 1947. [9]

McKee, John P., and Alex C. Sherriffs. "Men's and Women's Beliefs, Ideals, and Self-Concepts," *American Journal of Sociology,* 64 (January, 1959), 356–363. [7]

McLuhan, Marshall. *Understanding Media: The Extensions of Man.* New York: McGraw-Hill, 1965. [10]

McNemar, Q. "Twin Resemblances in Motor Skills, and the Effect of Practice Thereon," *Journal of Genetic Psychology,* 42 (1933), 70–99. [5]

Maehr, Martin L., Josef Mensing, and Samuel Nafzger. "Concept of Self and the Reaction of Others," *Sociometry,* 25 (December, 1962), 353–357. [7]

Magdoff, Harry. *The Age of Imperialism.* New York: Monthly Review Press, 1969. [29]

Maine, Sir Henry J. Sumner. *Ancient Law: Its Connection With the Early History of Society, and Its Relation to Modern Ideas.* New York: Dutton, 1965; first printing, 1861. [26]

Malinowski, Bronislaw. *Magic, Science and Religion.* Glencoe, Ill.: Free Press, 1948. [4]

Malthus, Thomas. *On Population.* Gertrude Himmelfarb (ed.). New York: Modern Library, 1960. [23]

Mandle, Jay R. "The Decline in Mortality in British Guiana, 1911–1960," *Demography,* 7 (August, 1970), 301–315. [12]

Manis, Jerome G., and Bernard N. Meltzer (eds.). *Symbolic Interaction: A Reader in Social Psychology.* Boston: Allyn and Bacon, 1967. [7]

Mann, Floyd, and Richard Hoffman. *Automation and the Worker: A Study of Social Change in Power Plants.* New York: Holt, Rinehart and Winston, 1960. [22]

Mannheim, Karl. *Man and Society in an Age of Reconstruction.* New York: Harcourt, 1950. [9]

Mao Tse-tung. *Selected Readings From the Works of Mao Tse-tung.* Peking, People's Republic of China: Foreign Language Press, 1971. [28]

March, James G., and Herbert A. Simon. *Organizations.* New York: Wiley, 1958. [9]

Marcuse, Herbert. *One Dimensional Man: Studies in the Ideology of Advanced Industrial Society.* Boston: Beacon Press, 1964. [29]

Maris, Ronald W. *Social Forces in Urban Suicide.* Homewood, Ill.: Dorsey Press, 1969. [11]

Marlowe, David, and Kenneth J. Gergen. "Personality and Social Interaction," in Gardner Lindzey and Elliot Aronson (eds.), *Handbook of Social Psychology.* Rev. ed. Reading, Mass.: Addison-Wesley, 1968, III, 590–665. [8]

Marshall, Thomas H. *Class, Citizenship and Social Development.* Garden City, N.Y.: Doubleday, 1964. [21]

Marx, Gary T. *Protest and Prejudice.* New York: Harper & Row, 1967. [14, 20, 28]

Marx, Karl. *Capital.* Max Eastman (ed.). New York: Modern Library, 1936. [22]

———. *The Communist Manifesto.* Chicago: Regnery, 1960; originally published in 1848. [4]

———. *Pre-capitalist Economic Formations.* Eric Hobsbawm (ed.), Jack Cohen (tr.). 1st U.S. ed. New York: International Publishers, 1965. [21]

Maslow, Abraham. *Motivation and Personality.* New York: Harper, 1954. [22]

Mayo, Elton. *Human Problems of an Industrial Civilization.* New York: Macmillan, 1933. [22]

Mazur, Allan, and Leon S. Robertson. *Biology and Social Behavior.* New York: Free Press, 1972. [5]

Mead, George Herbert. *Mind, Self and Society.* Chicago: University of Chicago Press, 1934. [7]

———. *On Social Psychology; Selected Papers.* Anselm Strauss (ed.). Rev. ed. Chicago: University of Chicago Press, 1964. [6]

Mead, Margaret. *Sex and Temperament in Three Primitive Societies.* New York: Morrow, 1935. [17, 22]

Melman, Seymour. *Pentagon Capitalism: The Management of the New Imperialism.* New York: McGraw-Hill, 1971. [21]

Merei, Ferenc. "Group Leadership and Institutionalization," in Eleanor E. Maccoby, Theodore M. Newcomb, and Eugene L. Hartley (eds.), *Readings in Social Psychology.* 3rd ed. New York: Holt, Rinehart and Winston, 1958, 522–532. [8]

Merrill, Francis E. "Stendahl and the Self: A Study in the Sociology of Literature," *American Journal of Sociology,* 66 (March, 1961), 446–453. [7]

Merton, Robert K. "Social Structure and Anomie," *American Sociological Review,* 3 (October, 1938), 672–682. [11]

———. "Discrimination and the American Creed," in Robert M. MacIver (ed.), *Discrimination and National Welfare.* New York: Harper, 1949. [16]

———. *Social Theory and Social Structure.* Rev. ed. Glencoe, Ill.: Free Press, 1957. [1, 4, 9]

Michels, Robert. *Political Parties.* Eden Paul and Cedar Paul (trs.). Glencoe, Ill.: Free Press, 1949. [9, 21]

Milgram, Stanley. "Nationality and Conformity," *Scientific American,* 205 (December, 1961), 45–51. [8]

Miliband, Ralph. *The State in Capitalist Society: An Analysis of the Western System of Power.* New York: Basic Books, 1969. [21]

Miller, Neal, and John Dollard. *Social Learning and Imitation.* New Haven, Conn.: Yale University Press, 1941. [4]

Miller, S. M., and Frank Reissman. "The Working-Class Subculture," in Arthur B. Shostak and William Gomberg (eds.), *Blue-Collar World: Studies of American Workers.* Englewood Cliffs, N.J.: Prentice-Hall, 1964. [13]

Miller, Walter B. "Lower Class Culture as a Generating Milieu of Gang Delinquency," *Journal of Social Issues,* 14, no. 3 (1958), 5–19. [11]

Millett, Kate. *Sexual Politics.* Garden City, N.Y.: Doubleday, 1970. [21]

Mills, C. Wright. *White Collar.* New York: Oxford University Press, 1953. [22]

———. *The Power Elite.* New York: Oxford University Press, 1956. [14, 21]

Milner, Murray. *The Myth of Equality.* San Francisco: Jossey-Bass, 1972. [19]

Minturn, Leigh, and William W. Lambert. *Mothers of Six Cultures.* New York: Wiley, 1964. [6]

Mischel, Walter. "Father Absence and Delay of Gratification: Cross-Cultural Comparisons," *Journal of Abnormal and Social Psychology,* 63 (July, 1961), 116–124. [6]

Mitchell, B. R., and Phyllis Deane. *Abstract of British Historical Statistics.* New York: Cambridge University Press, 1971. [23]

Mitchell, Juliet. *Women: The Longest Revolution.* Boston: New England Free Press, n.d. [28]

Morgan, Elaine. *The Descent of Woman.* New York: Stein and Day, 1972. [5, 8]

Morley, Sylvanus G. *The Ancient Maya.* Stanford, Calif.: Stanford University Press, 1946. [12]

Morrison, Denton E., and Allan D. Steeves. "Deprivation, Discontent, and Social Movement Participation: Evidence on a Contemporary Farmers' Movement, the NFO," *Rural Sociology,* 32 (December, 1967), 414–434. [28]

Morse, Nancy Carter, and R. S. Weiss. "Function and Meaning of Work and the Job," *American Sociological Review,* 20 (April, 1955), 191–198. [9]

Mosca, Gaetano. *The Ruling Class.* Hannah D. Kahn (tr.). New York: McGraw-Hill, 1939. [15, 26]

Murdock, George P. *Our Primitive Contemporaries.* New York: Macmillan, 1934. [12]

———. *Social Structure.* New York: Macmillan, 1949. [5, 17, 18]

———. "World Ethnographic Sample." *American Anthropologist,* 59 (August, 1957), 664–687. [18]

Mussen, Paul H., and Luther Distler. "Masculinity, Identification and Father-Son Relationships," *Journal of Abnormal and Social Psychology,* 59 (November, 1959), 350–356. [6]

Mussen, Paul H., and Eldred Rutherford. "Parent-Child Relations and Parental Personality in Relation to Young Children's Sex-Role Preferences," *Child Development*, 34 (1963), 589–608. [6]

Myrdal, Gunnar. *An American Dilemma: The Negro Problem and Modern Democracy.* New York: Harper, 1944. [16]

————. "A Parallel to the Negro Problem," (Appendix 5) in *An American Dilemma: The Negro Problem and Modern Democracy.* New York: Harper, 1944, 1073–1078. [28]

N

National Advisory Commission on Civil Disorders. (Kerner Commission). *Report of the National Advisory Commission on Civil Disorders.* New York: Bantam, 1968. [11, 24, 27]

National Commission on Marijuana and Drug Abuse. *Marijuana: A Signal of Misunderstanding.* New York: New American Library, 1972. [11]

Newman, Donald J. "Pleading Guilty for Consideration: A Study of Bargain Justice," *Journal of Criminal Law, Criminology, and Police Science*, 46 (March-April, 1956), 780–790. [11]

Newman, H. H., F. N. Freeman, and K. J. Holzinger. *Twins: A Study of Heredity and Environment.* Chicago: University of Chicago Press, 1937. [5]

Niebuhr, H. Richard. *The Social Sources of Denominationalism.* New York: Holt, 1929. [20]

Nieburg, Harold L. *Political Violence: The Behavioral Process.* New York: St. Martin's Press, 1969. [26]

North, Douglass C. *Growth and Welfare in the American Past: A New Economic History.* Englewood Cliffs, N.J.: Prentice-Hall, 1966. [21]

Nortman, Dorothy. "Population and Family Planning Programs: A Factbook," *Reports on Population and Family Planning*, No. 2. New York: The Population Council, 1971. [23]

NOW. *Bill of Rights* (adopted at the First National Conference of the National Organization for Women, Washington, D.C., 1967), in Robin Morgan (ed.), *Sisterhood Is Powerful.* New York: Random House, 1970, 512–514. [28]

————. *Revolution: From the Doll's House to the White House.* Report of the Fifth Annual Conference of the National Organization for Women, Los Angeles, California, 1971. (Available from NOW National Office, 1957 E. 73rd Street, Chicago, Illinois 60649.) [28]

Nye, F. Ivan. "Child Adjustment in Broken and in Unhappy Broken Homes," *Marriage and Family Living*, 19 (1957), 365–371. [18]

Nye, F. Ivan, James F. Short, Jr., and Virgil J. Olson. "Socio-Economic Status and Delinquent Behavior," *American Journal of Sociology*, 63 (January, 1958), 381–389. [11]

O

O'Connor, Edwin. *The Last Hurrah.* Boston: Little, Brown, 1956. [21]

O'Connor, James. "The Meaning of Economic Imperialism," in Robert I. Rhodes

(ed.), *Imperialism and Underdevelopment: A Reader.* New York: Monthly Review Press, 1970, 101–150. [29]

O'Donnell, John A., and John C. Ball (eds.). *Narcotic Addiction.* New York: Harper & Row, 1966. [11]

O'Neill, William L. *Everyone Was Brave: The Rise and Fall of Feminism in America.* Chicago: Quadrangle, 1969. [28]

Office of Juvenile Delinquency and Youth Development. *Juvenile Court Statistics.* Washington, D.C.: U.S. Government Printing Office, 1970. [11]

Ogburn, William F. *Social Change.* New York: Viking, 1950; first printing, 1922. [26]

Ogburn, William F., and S. C. Gilfillan. *Recent Social Trends.* New York: McGraw-Hill, 1938. [26]

Ogburn, William F., and Meyer F. Nimkoff. *Sociology.* 4th ed. Boston: Houghton Mifflin, 1964. [3]

Oppenheimer, Valerie Kincade. *The Female Labor Force in the United States: Demographic and Economic Factors Governing Its Growth and Changing Composition.* (Population Monograph Series No. 5.) Institute of International Studies. Berkeley: University of California Press, 1969. [28]

Orzack, Louis H. "Work as a 'Central Life Interest' of Professionals," in Erwin O. Smigel (ed.), *Work and Leisure.* New Haven, Conn.: College and University Press, 1963, 73–84. [22]

Osborne, Richard H. (ed.). *The Biological and Social Meaning of Race.* San Francisco: W. H. Freeman, 1971. [5]

Ossowski, Stanislaw. *Class Structure in the Social Consciousness.* Sheila Patterson (tr.). New York: Free Press, 1963. [15]

P

Palmer, Francis H. "Inferences to the Socialization of the Child from Animal Studies," in David Goslin (ed.), *The Handbook of Socialization Theory and Research.* Chicago: Rand McNally, 1969. [6]

Pareto, Vilfredo. *The Mind and Society: A Treatise on General Sociology.* Arthur Livingston (tr.). New York: Harcourt, Brace, 1935, I–IV. [13, 26]

Park, Robert E., and Ernest W. Burgess. *Introduction to the Science of Sociology.* Chicago: University of Chicago Press, 1924. [27]

Park, Robert E., Ernest W. Burgess, and Roderick D. McKenzie. *The City.* Chicago: University of Chicago Press, 1925. [24, 25]

Parsons, Talcott. *The Structure of Social Action.* New York: McGraw-Hill, 1937. [20]

————. "Introduction," in Max Weber, *The Theory of Social and Economic Organization.* A. M. Henderson and Talcott Parsons (trs.). Glencoe, Ill.: Free Press, 1947, 1–86. [9]

————. *The Social System.* Glencoe, Ill.: Free Press, 1951. [9, 20]

————. "Family Structure and the Socialization of the Child," in Talcott Parsons and Robert F. Bales (eds.), *Family, Socialization and Interaction Process.* Glen-

coe, Ill.: Free Press, 1955, 35–131. [6]

————. "'Voting' and the Equilibrium of the American Political System," in Eugene Burdick and Arthur J. Brodbeck (eds.), *American Voting Behavior.* Glencoe, Ill.: Free Press, 1959, 80–120. [26]

————. *Structure and Process in Modern Society.* Glencoe, Ill.: Free Press, 1960. [9]

————. "Some Considerations on the Theory of Social Change," *Rural Sociology*, 26 (September, 1961), 219–235. [26]

————. "Some Reflections on the Place of Force in Social Process," in Harry Eckstein (ed.), *Internal War.* New York: Free Press, 1964, 33–70. [26]

Perlman, I. Richard. "Antisocial Behavior of the Minor in the United States," *Federal Probation*, 29 (December, 1964), 23–30. [11]

Perlman, Selig. *A History of Trade Unionism in the United States.* New York: Macmillan, 1923. [14]

Perlman, Selig, and Philip Taft. *History of Labor in the United States.* New York: Macmillan, 1935. [22]

Perrow, Charles B. "Analysis of Goals in Complex Organizations," *American Sociological Review*, 26 (December, 1961), 854–866. [9]

————. "A Framework for the Comparative Analysis of Organizations," *American Sociological Review*, 23 (April, 1967), 194–208. [9]

Pettee, George S. *The Process of Revolution.* New York: Harper, 1938. [28]

Piaget, Jean. "Developmental Psychology: A Theory of Development," in *The Encyclopedia of the Social Sciences.* New York: Macmillan, 1968, IV, 140–147. [6]

————. *The Language and Thought of the Child.* 3rd ed. New York: Humanities Press, 1962. [6]

Ping-ti, Ho. *The Ladder of Success in Imperial China. Aspects of Social Mobility, 1368–1911.* New York: Columbia University Press, 1962. [13]

Pinkney, Alphonso. *Black Americans.* Englewood Cliffs, N.J.: Prentice-Hall, 1969. [16]

Platt, Anthony. *The Child Savers.* Chicago: University of Chicago Press, 1969. [11]

Plunkett, M. "School and Early Work Experience of Youth," *Occupational Outlook Quarterly*, 4 (1960), 22–27. [19]

Pollard, Sydney, and David W. Crossley. *The Wealth of England 1085–1966.* New York: Schocken, 1969. [23]

Polsky, Howard W. *Cottage Six.* New York: Russell Sage Foundation, 1962. [26]

Porter, John. "The Future of Upward Mobility," *American Sociological Review*, 33 (February, 1968), 5–19. [13]

President's Commission on Law Enforcement and Administration of Justice. *Task Force Report: The Courts.* Washington, D.C.: U.S. Government Printing Office, 1967. [11]

Putney, Snell. *The Conquest of Society.* Belmont, Calif.: (Focus Books) Wadsworth, 1972. [10, 12]

Q

Quinney, Richard. *The Social Reality of Crime.* Boston: Little, Brown, 1970. [11]

R

Radcliffe-Brown, Alfred Reginald. *The Andaman Islanders*. Glencoe, Ill.: Free Press, 1948. [12]

Reay, Marie. *The Kuma*. Melbourne, Australia: Melbourne University Press, 1959. [12]

Reckless, Walter C. *The Crime Problem*. 4th ed. New York: Appleton-Century-Crofts, 1967. [11]

Reckless, Walter C., Simon Dinitz, and Ellen Murray. "Self Concept as an Insulator Against Delinquency," *American Sociological Review*, 21 (December, 1956), 744–746. [7, 11]

Redfield, Robert. "The Folk Society," *American Journal of Sociology*, 52 (January, 1947), 293–308. [26]

Reich, Wilhelm. *The Mass Psychology of Fascism*. Vincent R. Carfagno (tr.). New York: (Noonday) Farrar, Strauss & Giroux, 1970. [21]

Reiss, Albert J., Jr. "Police Brutality—Answers to Key Questions," *Trans-action*, 5 (July, 1968), 10–19. [1, 11]

Ridley, Jeanne Clare. "The Changing Position of American Women: Education, Labor Force Participation, and Fertility," in *Fogarty International Center Proceedings, No. 3—The Family in Transition*. Washington, D.C.: U.S. Government Printing Office, 1969. [28]

Rieken, Henry W., and George C. Homans. "Psychological Aspects of Social Structure," in Gardner Lindzey (ed.), *Handbook of Social Psychology*. Reading, Mass.: Addison-Wesley, 1954, II, 786–832. [8]

Riesman, David, in collaboration with Reuel Denney and Nathan Glaser. *The Lonely Crowd*. New Haven, Conn.: Yale University Press, 1961. [8]

Rivers, Caryl. "Genetic Engineering Portends a Grave New World," *Saturday Review*, 55 (April 8, 1972), 23–27. [17]

Roethlisberger, Fritz J., and William J. Dickson. *Management and the Worker*. Cambridge, Mass.: Harvard University Press, 1939. [9, 22]

Rose, Peter I. "Red, White, Blue—and Black," *Massachusetts Review*, 6 (Autumn, 1965), 851–858. [16]

———. *The Subject Is Race: Traditional Ideologies and the Teaching of Race Relations*. New York: Oxford University Press, 1968. [16]

———. *They and We: Racial and Ethnic Relations in the United States*. Rev. ed. New York: Random House, 1973. [16]

Rosen, Bernard C., and Roy D'Andrade. "The Psychosocial Origins of Achievement Motivation," *Sociometry*, 22 (September, 1959), 185–218. [6]

Rosen, S. McKee, and Laura Rosen. *Technology and Society*. New York: Macmillan, 1941. [26]

Rosenberg, Hans. *Bureaucracy, Aristocracy and Autocracy: The Prussian Experience, 1660–1815*. Cambridge, Mass.: Harvard University Press, 1958. [21]

Rosengren, William R. "The Self in the Emotionally Disturbed," *American Journal of Sociology*, 66 (March, 1961), 454–462. [7]

Rossi, Alice. "Sex Equality: The Beginning of Ideology," in Betty Roszak and Theodore Roszak (eds.), *Masculine/Feminine: Readings in Sexual Mythology and the Liberation of Women*. New York: Harper & Row, 1969, 173–186. [28]

Rostow, W. W. *The Stages of Economic Growth: A Non-Communist Manifesto*. New York: Cambridge University Press, 1960. [26, 29]

Roth, Guenther. "Personal Rulership, Patrimonialism, and Empire-Building in the New States," *World Politics*, 20 (January, 1968), 194–206. [21]

Roy, Donald. "Efficiency and 'the Fix': Informal Intergroup Relations in a Piecework Machine Shop," *American Journal of Sociology*, 60 (November, 1954), 255–266. [9]

Rudé, George. *The Crowd in the French Revolution*. Oxford: Clarendon Press, 1959. [27]

Rush, David. "Perinatal Mortality, Race, Social Status, and Hospital of Birth: The Association with Birth Weight," *Proceedings of Birth Defects Symposium, III*. Albany, N.Y.: New York State Department of Health, Birth Defects Institute, 1972. [13]

Rush, Gary B. "Status Consistency and Right Wing Extremism," *American Sociological Review*, 32 (February, 1967), 86–92. [28]

Russell, J. C. "Late and Ancient Medieval Population," *Transactions of the American Philosophical Society*, 48, Part 3 (June, 1958). [12]

S

Salapatek, Philip, and William Kessen. "Visual Scanning of Triangles by the Human Newborn," *Journal of Experimental Child Psychology*, 3 (1966), 155–167. [6]

Salper, Roberta. "The Development of the American Women's Liberation Movement, 1967–1971," in Roberta Salper (ed.), *Female Liberation: History and Current Politics*. New York: Knopf, 1972. [28]

Sarbin, Theodore R. "Role Enactment," in Bruce J. Biddle and Edwin J. Thomas (eds.), *Role Theory: Concepts and Research*. New York: Wiley, 1966, 195–200. [7]

Schein, Edgar H. "The Chinese Indoctrination Program for Prisoners of War: A Study of Attempted Brainwashing," *Psychiatry*, 19 (May, 1956), 149–172. [10]

Schermerhorn, Richard A. *Comparative Ethnic Relations: A Framework for Theory and Research*. New York: Random House, 1970. [16]

Schneider, Eugene V. *Industry and Society*. New York: McGraw-Hill, 1969. [26]

Schumpeter, Joseph A. *Capitalism, Socialism, and Democracy*. New York: Harper & Row, 1962. [21]

Schur, Edwin M. *Crimes Without Victims*. Englewood Cliffs, N.J.: Prentice-Hall, 1965. [11]

Scott, John Finley. "A Comment on 'Do American Women Marry Up,'" *American Sociological Review*, 34 (October, 1969), 725–727. [13]

———. *Internalization of Norms: A Sociological Theory of Moral Commitment*. Englewood Cliffs, N.J.: Prentice-Hall, 1971. [4, 10]

———. "Stratification and the Family: Status Ascription and Stratum Mobility," in Gerald W. Thielbar and Saul D. Feldman (eds.), *Issues in Social Inequality*. Boston: Little, Brown, 1972, 580–597. [13, 17]

Scott, John Paul. *Animal Behavior*. Garden City, N.Y.: Doubleday, 1963. [5]

Scott, W. Richard. *Social Structures and Social Processes*. New York: Holt, Rinehart and Winston, 1970. [9]

Scott, W. Richard, Stanford M. Dornbusch, Bruce C. Bushing, and James D. Laing. "Organizational Evaluation and Authority," *Administrative Science Quarterly*, 12 (June, 1967), 93–117. [9]

Sears, Robert, Eleanor Maccoby, and Harry Levin, in collaboration with Edgar Lowell, Pauline Sears, and John W. M. Whiting. *Patterns of Child Rearing*. Evanston, Ill.: Row, Peterson, 1957. [6]

Sellin, Thorsten. *Culture, Conflict, and Crime*. New York: Social Science Research Council, 1938. [11]

Selznick, Gertrude, and Stephen Steinberg. *The Tenacity of Prejudice*. New York: Harper & Row, 1969. [2, 14]

Selznick, Philip. *TVA and the Grass Roots*. Berkeley: University of California Press, 1949. [9]

———. *The Organizational Weapon*. Glencoe, Ill.: Free Press, 1960. [29]

———. *Law, Society, and Industrial Justice*. New York: Russell Sage Foundation, 1969. [22]

Sewell, William H. "Inequality of Opportunity for Higher Education," *American Sociological Review*, 36 (October, 1971), 793–809. [19]

Sherif, Muzafer, and Carolyn W. Sherif. *Groups in Harmony and Tension; an Integration of Studies on Intergroup Relations*. New York: Harper, 1953. [8]

Sherwood, John J. "Self Identity and Referent Other," *Sociometry*, 28 (March, 1965), 66–81. [7]

Shibutani, Tamotsu. "Reference Groups as Perspectives," *American Journal of Sociology*, 60 (May, 1955), 562–569. [8]

Shibutani, Tamotsu, and Kian M. Kwan. *Ethic Stratification: A Comparative Approach*. New York: Macmillan, 1965. [3, 16]

Shrewsbury, J. F. D. *A History of the Bubonic Plague in the British Isles*. Cambridge, Mass.: Cambridge University Press, 1970. [23]

Sidenbladh, Goran. "Stockholm: A Planned City," *Scientific American*, 213 (September, 1965), 106–118. [24]

Silberman, Charles. *Crisis in the Classroom*. New York: Random House, 1970. [19]

Sills, David L. *The Volunteers*. Glencoe, Ill.: Free Press, 1957. [9]

Simmel, Georg. *Sociology*. Kurt H. Wolff (tr.). Glencoe, Ill.: Free Press, 1950. [24]

Simmons, J. L., with the assistance of Hazel Chambers. "Public Stereotypes of

Deviants," *Social Problems,* 13 (Fall, 1965), 223–232. [11]

Simon, Herbert A. *Administrative Behavior.* 2nd ed. New York: Macmillan, 1957. [9]

Sinclair, Andrew. *The Emancipation of the American Woman.* New York: Harper & Row, 1965. [28]

Sjoberg, Gideon. "The Preindustrial City," *American Journal of Sociology,* 60 (March, 1955), 438–445. [25]

———. *The Preindustrial City, Past and Present.* Glencoe, Ill.: Free Press, 1960. [12]

Skinner, B. F. *Beyond Freedom and Dignity.* New York: Knopf, 1971. [4, 6]

Skodak, Marie, and Harold M. Skeels. "A Final Follow-Up Study of One Hundred Adopted Children," *Journal of Genetic Psychology,* 75 (1949), 85–125. [5]

Skolnick, Jerome. *Politics of Protest.* New York: Simon and Schuster, 1969. [28]

Slater, Eliot. "Genetic Investigations in Twins," *Journal of Mental Science,* 99 (1953), 44–52. [5]

Slater, Philip E. "Role Differentiation in Small Groups," in A. Paul Hare, Edgar F. Borgatta, and Robert F. Bales (eds.), *Small Groups: Studies in Social Interaction.* New York: Knopf, 1955, 498–515. [8]

Slotkin, James S. *The Peyote Religion: A Study in Indian-White Relations.* Glencoe, Ill.: Free Press, 1956. [27]

Smelser, Neil J. *Theory of Collective Behavior.* New York: Free Press, 1962. [27]

———. "Mechanisms of Change and Adjustment to Change," in Bert Hoselitz and Wilbert Moore (eds.), *Industrialization and Society.* New York: Humanities Press, 1963, 32–54. [26]

Snow, C. P. *The Masters.* Garden City, N.Y.: Doubleday, 1959. [21]

Snyder, Charles R. "Inebriety, Alcoholism, and Anomie," in Marshall B. Clinard (ed.), *Anomie and Deviant Behavior.* New York: Free Press, 1964, 189–212. [11]

Solari, Aldo. "Secondary Education and the Development of Elites," in Seymour M. Lipset and Aldo Solari (eds.), *Elites in Latin America.* New York: Oxford University Press, 1967, 457–483. [19]

Sorel, Georges. *Reflections on Violence.* T. E. Hulme and J. Roth (trs.). Glencoe, Ill.: Free Press, 1950. [28]

Spencer, Herbert. *Evolution of Society.* Robert L. Carneiro (ed.). Chicago: University of Chicago Press, 1967. [26]

Spiro, Melford E. "Is the Family Universal?—The Israeli Case," in Norman W. Bell and Ezra F. Vogel (eds.), *A Modern Introduction to the Family.* Rev. ed. New York: Free Press, 1968, 68–79. [18]

Srole, Lee, Thomas S. Langer, Stanley T. Michael, Marvin K. Opler, and Thomas A. C. Rennie. *Mental Health in the Metropolis.* New York: McGraw-Hill, 1962. [11, 14]

Stark, Rodney. "Class, Radicalism and Religious Involvement," *American Sociological Review,* 29 (October, 1964), 698–706. [14]

———. "The Economics of Piety: Religious Commitment and Social Class," in Ger-

ald W. Thielbar and Saul D. Feldman (eds.), *Issues in Social Inequality.* Boston: Little, Brown, 1972a, 483–503. [14]

———. *Police Riots.* Belmont, Calif.: (Focus Books) Wadsworth, 1972b. [10, 11, 26]

Stark, Rodney, and Charles Y. Glock. *American Piety: The Nature of Religious Commitment.* Berkeley: University of California Press, 1968. [8, 14, 20]

Stark, Rodney, and James McEvoy III. "Middle-Class Violence," *Psychology Today,* 4 (November, 1970), 52–54, 110–112. [14]

Stark, Rodney, Bruce D. Foster, Charles Y. Glock, and Harold E. Quinley. *Wayward Shepherds: Prejudice and the Protestant Clergy.* New York: Harper & Row, 1971. [2, 20]

Starr, Roger. "Power and Powerlessness in a Regional City," *The Public Interest,* 16 (Summer, 1969), 3–24. [16]

Stearns, Marion S. *Report on Preschool Programs: The Effectiveness of Preschool Programs on Disadvantaged Children and Their Families.* Department of Health, Education and Welfare. Washington, D.C.: U.S. Government Printing Office, 1971. [19]

Stephens, William N. *The Family in Cross-Cultural Perspective.* New York: Holt, Rinehart and Winston, 1963. [17]

Stern, Edith M. "Women Are Household Slaves," *American Mercury,* 68 (1949), 71–76. [28]

Stevenson, Harold, Jerome Kagan, and Charles Spiker (eds.). *Child Psychology.* Chicago: National Society for the Study of Education, distributed by the University of Chicago Press, 1963. [6]

Steward, Julian, and Louis Faron. *Native Peoples of South America.* New York: McGraw-Hill, 1959. [12]

Stinchcombe, Arthur L. *Constructing Social Theory.* New York: Harcourt Brace Jovanovich, 1968. [4]

Stouffer, Samuel A. *Communism, Conformity, and Civil Liberties.* Garden City, N.Y.: Doubleday, 1955. [8, 14]

Stouffer, Samuel A., Edward A. Suchman, Leland C. DeVinney, Shirley A. Star, and Robin M. Williams, Jr. *The American Soldier: Adjustment During Army Life.* Princeton, N.J.: Princeton University Press, 1949, I. [14]

Strauss, George. "Some Notes on Power Equalization," in Harold Leavitt (ed.), *The Social Science of Organizations: Four Perspectives.* Englewood Cliffs, N.J.: Prentice-Hall, 1963, 39–84. [9]

Stycos, J. Myrone. *Human Fertility in Latin America: Sociological Perspectives.* Ithaca, N.Y.: Cornell University Press, 1968. [23]

Sufrin, Sidney C. *Technical Assistance—Theory and Guidelines.* Syracuse, N.Y.: Syracuse University Press, 1966. [29]

Sumner, William Graham. *Folkways: A Study of the Sociological Importance of Usages, Manners, Customs, Mores, and Morals.* New York: Dover, 1959. [3, 11, 16]

Sutherland, Edwin H. *Principles of Criminology.* 4th ed. Chicago: J. B. Lippincott, 1947. [11]

Sutherland, Edwin H., and Donald R. Cressey. *Criminology.* 8th ed. Philadelphia: J. B. Lippincott, 1970. [11]

Suttles, Gerald D. *The Social Order of the Slum.* Chicago: University of Chicago Press, 1968, 119–131. [24]

Sutton-Smith, Brian, and B. G. Rosenberg. *The Sibling.* New York: Holt, Rinehart and Winston, 1970. [6]

Sykes, Gresham M. *The Society of Captives.* Princeton, N.J.: Princeton University Press, 1958. [10]

T

Taeuber, Karl E., and Alma F. Taeuber. *Negroes in Cities.* Chicago: Aldine, 1965. [25]

Tarrow, Sidney G. "Political Dualism and Italian Communism," *American Political Science Review,* 61 (March, 1967), 39–53. [21]

Taylor, Frederick W. *The Principles of Scientific Management.* New York: Norton, 1967. [22]

Teeters, Negley, and David Matza. "The Extent of Delinquency in the United States," *Journal of Negro Education,* 28 (Summer, 1959), 200–213. [11]

Terry, Robert M. "Discrimination in the Handling of Juvenile Offenders by Social Control Agencies," *Journal of Research in Crime and Delinquency,* 4 (July, 1967), 218–230. [11]

Thiessan, Delbert D. *Gene Organization and Behavior.* New York: Random House, 1972. [5]

Thompson, James D., and Frederick L. Bates. "Technology, Organization, and Administration," *Administrative Science Quarterly,* 2 (December, 1957), 325–343. [9]

Tittle, Charles. "Crime Rates and Legal Sanctions," *Social Problems,* 16 (Spring, 1969), 409–423. [11]

Tocqueville, Alexis de. *Democracy in America.* Phillips Bradley (ed. and tr.). New York: (Vintage) Random House, 1954, II. [22]

Toffler, Alvin. *Future Shock.* New York: Random House, 1970. [10]

Tönnies, Ferdinand. *Community and Society—Gemeinschaft and Gesellschaft.* Charles F. Loomis (ed. and tr.). East Lansing, Mich.: Michigan State University Press, 1957. [8, 26]

Tout, Thomas Frederick. *The English Civil Service in the Fourteenth Century.* Manchester, England: University Press, 1916. [9]

Townsend, Robert. *Up the Organization.* New York: Knopf, 1970. [8]

Troeltsch, Ernst. *Social Teachings of the Christian Churches.* New York: Macmillan, 1949, I, 331–343. [20]

Trotsky, Leon. *The History of the Russian Revolution.* Max Eastman (tr.). London: Gollancz, 1934. [26]

Trow, Martin. "The Second Transformation of American Secondary Education," *International Journal of Comparative Sociology,* 2 (September, 1961), 146–166. [19]

———. "The Democratization of Higher Education in America," *European Jour-*

nal of Sociology (Archives européennes de sociologie), 3 (1962) 231–263. [19]

———. "Two Problems in American Public Education," in Howard S. Becker (ed.), Social Problems: A Modern Approach. New York: Wiley, 1966, 76–116. [19]

Tumin, Melvin M. "Some Principles of Stratification: A Critical Analysis," American Sociological Review, 18 (August, 1953), 387–393. [15]

Turner, Ralph H., and Lewis M. Killian. Collective Behavior. Englewood Cliffs, N.J.: Prentice-Hall, 1957. [27, 28]

Tyler, Edward Brunett. The Origins of Culture. New York: Harper & Row, 1958, I. [3]

U

Udy, Stanley H., Jr. "Administrative Rationality, Social Setting, and Organizational Development," American Journal of Sociology, 68 (November, 1962), 299–308. [9]

Ullman, Albert D. "Sociocultural Background of Alcoholism," Annals of the American Academy of Social and Political Sciences, 315 (January, 1958), 48–54. [11]

United Nations. Report on the World Social Situation: 1957. New York: United Nations, 1957. [24]

U.S. Bureau of the Census. "Family Income Advances; Poverty Reduced in 1967. (Preliminary Data from March, 1968 Sample Survey.)," Current Population Reports; Consumer Income, Series P-60, No. 55. Department of Commerce. Washington, D.C.: U.S. Government Printing Office, 1968. [28]

U.S. Department of Labor. Dictionary of Occupational Titles. 3rd ed. Washington, D.C.: U.S. Government Printing Office, 1965. [22]

U.S. Department of Labor. Handbook of Labor Statistics. Washington, D.C.: U.S. Government Printing Office, 1971. [22]

V

van den Berghe, Pierre L. "Dialectic and Functionalism: Toward a Theoretical Synthesis," American Sociological Review, 28 (October, 1963), 695–705. [4]

———. Race and Racism: A Comparative Perspective. New York: Wiley, 1967. [16]

van Lawick-Goodall, Jane. "Mother-Offspring Relationships in Free-ranging Chimpanzees," in Desmond Morris (ed.), Primate Ethology. Garden City, N.Y.: Doubleday, 1969, 287–346. [5]

Veblen, Thorstein. Higher Learning in America; A Memorandum on the Conduct of Universities by Business Men. New York: A. M. Kelley, 1918. [9]

Videbeck, Richard. "Self-Conception and the Reactions of Others," Sociometry, 23 (December, 1960), 351–359. [7]

Vidich, Arthur J., and Joseph Bensman. Small Town in Mass Society. Garden City, N.Y.: Doubleday, 1960. [24]

Vogel, Ezra F. Japan's New Middle Class: The Salary Man and His Family in a Tokyo Suburb. Berkeley: University of California Press, 1963. [26]

Vold, George B. Theoretical Criminology. New York: Oxford University Press, 1958. [11]

Vollmer, Howard M. Employee Rights and the Employment Relationship. Berkeley: University of California Press, 1960. [22]

———. Work Activities and Attitudes of Scientists and Research Managers: Data from a National Survey. Menlo Park, Calif.: Stanford Research Institute, 1965. [22]

Vollmer, Howard M., and Donald L. Mills. Professionalization. Englewood Cliffs, N.J.: Prentice-Hall, 1966. [22]

von Hagen, Victor W. The Ancient Sun Kingdom of the Americas: Aztec, Maya, Inca. Cleveland: World Publications, 1961. [12]

Voss, Harwin L. "Socio-Economic Status and Reported Delinquent Behavior," Social Problems, 13 (Winter, 1966), 314–324. [11]

Voss, Harwin L., and David M. Peterson (eds.). Ecology, Crime, and Delinquency. New York: Appleton-Century-Crofts, 1971. [11]

Vroom, Victor H. Motivation in Management. New York: American Foundation for Management Research, 1964a. [22]

———. Work and Motivation. New York: Wiley, 1964b. [22]

W

Waldo, Gordon P., and Theodore G. Chiricos. "Perceived Penal Sanction and Self-Reported Criminality: A Neglected Approach to Deterrence Research," Social Problems, 19 (Spring, 1972), 522–540. [11]

Walker, Daniel. Rights in Conflict. New York: New American Library, 1968. [11]

Waller, Jerome H. "Achievement and Social Mobility: Relationships Among IQ Score, Education, and Occupation in Two Generations," Social Biology, 18 (September, 1971), 252–259. [5]

Walster, Elaine, Vera Aronson, Darcy Abrahams, and Leon Rottman. "Importance of Physical Attractiveness in Dating Behavior," Journal of Personality and Social Psychology, 4 (1966), 508–516. [2]

Ware, Caroline. Greenwich Village 1920–1930. New York: Harper, 1935. [25]

Ware, Cellestine. Woman Power: The Movement for Women's Liberation. New York: Tower, 1970. [28]

Warner, Sam B. Streetcar Suburbs. Cambridge, Mass.: Harvard University Press and MIT Press, 1962. [25]

Warner, W. Lloyd. The Living and the Dead: A Study of the Symbolic Life of Americans. New Haven, Conn.: Yale University Press, 1959. [26]

Washburn, S. L., and I. DeVore. "Social Behavior of Baboons and Early Man," Viking Fund Publications in Anthropology, 31 (1961), 91–105. [17]

Watson, Ernest H., and George H. Lowery. Growth and Development of Children. 5th ed. Chicago: Year Book Medical Publishers, 1967. [13]

Watson, Goodwin. Action for Unity. New York: Harper, 1947. [16]

Webb, Eugene J., et al. Unobtrusive Measures; Nonactive Research in the Social Sciences. Chicago: Rand McNally, 1966. [1]

Weber, Max. The Protestant Ethic and the Spirit of Capitalism. Talcott Parsons (tr.). Glencoe, Ill.: Scribner, 1930. [20, 22]

———. "The Social Psychology of the World's Religions," in H. H. Gerth and C. Wright Mills (eds. and trs.), From Max Weber: Essays in Sociology. New York: Oxford University Press, 1946, 267–301. [20]

———. The Theory of Social and Economic Organization. A. M. Henderson and Talcott Parsons (trs.). Glencoe, Ill.: Free Press, 1947. [9, 22, 26]

———. Ancient Judaism. Hans H. Gerth and Don Martindale (trs.). Glencoe, Ill.: Free Press, 1952. [20]

———. "Bureaucracy," in H. H. Gerth and C. Wright Mills (eds. and trs.), From Max Weber: Essays in Sociology. New York: Oxford University Press, 1958a, 196–244. [21]

———. "The Chinese Literati," in H. H. Gerth and C. Wright Mills (eds. and trs.), From Max Weber: Essays in Sociology. New York: Oxford University Press, 1958b, 416–444. [21]

———. The Sociology of Religion. Ephraim Fischoff (tr.). Boston: Beacon Press, 1963. [20]

———. Basic Concepts in Sociology. H. P. Secher (tr.). 3rd ed. New York: Citadel, 1964. [3]

Weinberg, S. K. (ed.). The Sociology of Mental Disorders. Chicago: Aldine, 1967. [11]

Weiss, Carin. "The Development of Professional Role Commitments Among Graduate Students." (Unpublished M.A. Thesis, University of Washington, 1972.) [10]

Westby, David L., and R. G. Braungart. "Class and Politics in the Family Backgrounds of Student Political Activists," American Sociological Review, 31 (October, 1966), 690–692. [28]

Westley, William A. "Violence and the Police," American Journal of Sociology, 59 (July, 1953), 34–41. [11]

Wheeler, Harvey. "The Phenomenon of God," Center Magazine, 4 (March-April, 1971), 7–12. [20]

Wheeler, Stanton. "The Structure of Formally Organized Socialization Settings," in Orville G. Brim, Jr., and Stanton Wheeler, Socialization After Childhood. New York: Wiley, 1966, 51–116. [10]

White, Ralph K., and Ronald O. Lippitt. Autocracy and Democracy. New York: Harper & Row, 1960. [8]

Whiting, John W. M. "Sorcery, Sin and the Superego: A Cross-Cultural Study of Some Mechanisms of Social Control," in Marshall R. Jones (ed.), Nebraska Symposium on Motivation. Lincoln, Neb.: University of Nebraska Press, 1959, 174–197. [6]

Whyte, William F. Street Corner Society.

Chicago: University of Chicago Press, 1943. [11]

———. *Money and Motivation*. New York: Harper & Row, 1955. [22]

Whyte, William H., Jr. *The Organization Man*. New York: Simon and Schuster, 1956. [10]

Wickler, Wolfgang. *The Sexual Code: The Social Behavior of Animals and Men*. Garden City, N.Y.: Doubleday, 1972. [5]

Wilensky, Harold L., and Charles N. Lebeaux. *Industrial Society and Social Welfare*. New York: Russell Sage Foundation, 1958. [9]

Williams, Robin. *American Society: A Sociological Interpretation*. 3rd ed. New York: Knopf, 1970. [26]

Williams, Thomas Rhys. *Introduction to Socialization: Human Culture Transmitted*. St. Louis, Mo.: C. V. Mosby, 1972. [5]

Willis, Ellen. "Women and the Left," in Shulamith Firestone and Anne Koedt (eds.), *Notes From the Second Year: Women's Liberation*. 1970, 55–58.

(Available from Radical Feminism, P.O. Box AA, Old Chelsea Station, New York, N.Y. 10011.) [29]

Wilson, James Q. *The Amateur Democrats*. Chicago: University of Chicago Press, 1962. [9]

Wirth, Louis. "Urbanism as a Way of Life," *American Journal of Sociology*, 44 (July, 1938), 1–24. [24]

Wittfogel, Karl A. *Oriental Despotism: A Comparative Study of Total Power*. New Haven, Conn.: Yale University Press, 1957. [26]

Wohl, Richard R. "The Rags to Riches Story: An Episode of Secular Idealism," in Reinhard Bendix and Seymour Martin Lipset (eds.), *Class, Status and Power*. Glencoe, Ill.: Free Press, 1953, 388–395. [13]

Wrigley, E. A. *Population and History*. New York: McGraw-Hill, 1969. [23]

Wrong, Dennis H. "Trends in Class Fertility in Western Nations," *Canadian Journal of Economics and Political Science*, 24 (May, 1958), 216–229. [14]

Y

Yinger, J. Milton. "Contraculture and Subculture," *American Sociological Review*, 25 (October, 1960), 625–635. [3]

Young, Kimball, and Raymond W. Mack. *Sociology and Social Life*. 3rd ed. New York: American Book, 1965. [3]

Z

Zeitlin, Maurice. "Alienation and Revolution," *Social Forces*, 45 (December, 1966), 224–236. [28]

Zetkin, Klara. *Reminiscences of Lenin; Dealing with Lenin's Views on the Position of Women and Other Questions*. London: Modern Books, 1929. [18]

Zigler, Edward, and Irwin L. Child. "Socialization," in Gardner Lindzey and Elliot Aronson (eds.), *The Handbook of Social Psychology*. Reading, Mass.: Addison-Wesley, 1969, III, 450–589. [6]

Glossary

A

absolute change. The amount of change in relation to points in time. See also *relative change.*

accommodation. A reciprocal process by which conflicting groups mutually adjust their discordant attitudes and behaviors, so as to establish a relationship of relative equilibrium. See also *assimilation.*

acculturation. The process by which members of one culture assimilate the traits of another.

achieved status. Social position based on the actions of an individual or group—position based on what you do, not who you are. See also *ascribed status.*

adherents. Those who join a social movement and accept its doctrine.

adolescence. An age grade, usually set as between the onset of puberty and the reaching of "maturity," containing that part of the population no longer children but not quite adults.

age grading. The process through which age categories become institutionalized and rights and obligations distributed differentially to each category.

age set. A social group in which all members are judged to be of equivalent age; a group of age peers. In many societies, a group of persons who undergo initiation rites at the same time.

agrarian society. A farm-based society having little or no industrialization.

alienation. A feeling of estrangement from and hostility toward society.

anarchy. The denial of any and all political authority.

anomie. A term used by Emile Durkheim to indicate a social condition characterized by the absence or breakdown of norms that govern group and individual behavior. Sometimes used to indicate an individual's feelings of normlessness.

anthropomorphism. The imputing of human characteristics to a being or thing not human, such as deity, animal, plant, or material object.

anticipatory socialization. The process by which an individual learns the major values and some of the behavior patterns of members of a significant reference group as preliminary to possible membership in the group.

ascribed status. Social position based on birth and determined by such factors as family, caste, race, sex, age, religion, or ethnicity. See also *achieved status.*

ascription, ascriptive. See *ascribed status.*

assimilation. The process through which one group, either voluntarily or under compulsion, adopts the styles of life, attitudes, and behaviors of a politically or culturally dominant group, leading eventually to the former's disappearance as an independent, identifiable unit. See also *accommodation.*

assortative mating. The tendency of either similar or dissimilar phenotypes to mate together.

attitude. An individual's evaluation (positive or negative) of some aspect of the world around him and a predisposition to act on the basis of this evaluation. Thus, a person with negative attitudes toward blacks is predisposed to act in discriminatory ways toward blacks.

authoritarian personality. A personality type characterized by intolerance, rigidity, and extreme reliance on authority.

authority. Formal and legitimate uses of power.

B

behavior modification. A therapeutic technique based on the principles of learning theory that seeks to directly alter undesirable behavior rather than to change behavior through changing the personality.

behaviorism. That group of social-science theories that stress study of overt behavior and discount the utility of studying private states of mind such as an individual's feelings, inner thoughts, or states of consciousness.

bourgeoisie. A term used by Karl Marx to denote the class that owned the means of production in capitalist societies. More generally used to denote the middle class. See also *proletariat.*

bride price. In most societies, a payment made by a man to the family of his bride, so that the marriage becomes a form of exchange of goods for a bride.

bureaucracy. A trained and specialized permanent administrative staff responsible for devising, overseeing, and coordinating the activities of other participants in an organization.

bureaucratization. The development over time of the specialized administrative apparatus of bureaucracy in an organization or a society.

C

capitalism. An economic institution that is characterized by private ownership and control of economic capital and production and that is guided by the economic principle of achieving maximum profits through exchange.

career. The sequence of social positions that the individual enters and leaves over his life cycle.

caste. A group whose status is based mainly on ascriptive criteria.

caste system. A type of social organization composed of ranked, mutually exclusive units between which virtually no social mobility is permitted.

categoric exclusion criteria. The characteristics of a class of citizens that are used to define the class as inappropriate candidates for particular kinds of work. These characteristics include sex, race, social origins, and physical status.

census. A periodic enumeration of a total population and some of the population's characteristics, such as age, sex, or occupation.

charisma. An extraordinary (sometimes mystical and supernatural) personal quality attributed to some leaders that causes others to accept their authority; frequently seen as the basis of trust and devotion given religious founders and prophets but also attributed to some political leaders.

church. According to Ernst Troeltsch, an organization characterized by de facto membership by birth; administration of formal means of grace, such as sacraments; administration of public worship; a priestly hierarchy; a development of dogma; inclusiveness of all social groups; and an orientation to convert everyone. See also *sect.*

class. According to Max Weber, a number of people who have a specific causal component of their life opportunities in common as a result of a common position in the labor market. See also *social class.*

class consciousness. According to Karl Marx, the awareness of the proletariat of its common market position and exploitation.

cognitive development. The development of the abilities to perceive, imagine, reason, and judge.

collective behavior. Those similar actions of a multiplicity of individuals that are spontaneous and transitory and therefore in contrast to the routine structured interactions of everyday life.

collectivity. A general term referring to a number of individuals, whether aggregated or dispersed, organized or unorganized, as a recognizable unit without specifying characteristics or type.

colonialism. The extension by a national political power of its control to other national areas and peoples.

communication. In its broadest sense, all procedures by which one person may, through the mediation of symbols, affect or influence another.

communism. In its most basic sense, the political-economic system characterized by common ownership of the means of production.

concentric–circle model. Ernest W. Burgess' concept of urban ecology. He described the city as being composed of five concentric circles, the innermost being the business district (Zone I), surrounded successively by a mixture of residences and businesses (Zone II), workingmen's homes (Zone III), better homes and shopping centers (Zone IV), and commuters' and wealthier homes (Zone V). See also *multiple–nuclei model; sector model.*

concept. A name or category used by scientists to identify some phenomenon.

conditioning. Denotes the learning process by which some stimulus becomes linked with some behavior in such a way that the stimulus will cause the behavior to occur; for example, as when the sight of a dog invariably produces crying in a particular child.

conflict theory. Theory that views society as a collection of antagonistic groups, institutions, and classes, each contending for dominance. See also *functionalism.*

conformity. Adherence to society's normative requirements and performance patterns.

conjugal family. See *nuclear family.*

consanguinity. Descent from a common ancestor.

conservatism. The ideology that sees government as an instrument for the maintenance of order and as a tool for integrating the various parts of the society into a harmonious whole. See also *liberalism; radicalism.*

conservative movement. A social movement that works for the preservation of existing features of the society. See also *progressive movement; reactionary movement.*

conspicuous consumption. Thorstein Veblen's term for ostentatiously wasteful use of expensive articles as a means of demonstrating one's social standing.

control. A statistical process of holding constant all factors other than the independent variable in order to see if a relationship between independent and dependent variables holds when all else is equal. In experiments, controls are accomplished through randomization of subjects; in nonexperimental analysis, by statistical manipulation of the data.

conurbation. The process by which several nearby cities expand toward and eventually merge into one another.

corporation. A body chartered by the state and consisting of a formal agreement or contract among people joined in a common purpose to hold property, contract, sue, and be sued.

countermovement. A social movement that exists solely to oppose some other movement.

"crimes without victims." Legally prohibited actions that involve no injured, unwilling, or complaining victim; for example, drug addiction, alcoholism, and prostitution.

crowd. An unstructured collectivity that reacts to a common focus of attention and engages in spontaneous interaction.

crude death rate. The ratio of the number of deaths in a year to the total population, usually expressed per 1,000 members of the population.

cultural diffusion. The spread or dispersion of artifacts, beliefs or patterns of behavior from one culture to another.

cultural lag. The difference between the rate of change of a given kind of technology and of the institutions that arise in response to that technology.

cultural values. A set of ideas about which goals should be desirable or preferable within and for a culture by members of that culture. See also *instrumental values; terminal values.*

culture. The set of artifacts, interaction patterns, beliefs, symbols, values, norms, and customs distinguishing one social group from another.

custom. A norm or pattern of thought or behavior that is supported by tradition. Violation of customs is not strongly sanctioned.

D

data. Systematic observations against which scientists test theories. Frequently implies observations that have been quantified (put in numerical form).

demographic transition theory. The theory that sees population change as related to the process of industrialization and its concomitant social changes. Under this theory, populations go through three stages: a preindustrial stage, in which both the birth rate and mortality rate are high; an early industrialization stage, in which the birth rate is high and mortality declines; and a mature industrialization stage, in which both the birth rate and the mortality rate are low.

demography. The study of population.

denominations. Sects that have accommodated to the society.

dependent variable. The phenomenon that one is trying to explain. The phenomenon that is caused by the independent variable(s).

deviant behavior. Any behavior that does not conform to commonly accepted standards and is adversely perceived.

deviant role. A situation in which a person is regularly engaged in deviance, organizes his life around deviance, and is viewed by himself and others as deviant.

diffusion. See *cultural diffusion.*

discrimination. A pattern of behavior that deprives the members of a social category of legal rights and social opportunities, not because of their behavior or beliefs but solely because of their membership in that category.

division of labor. The division of a social group into parts differentiated on the basis of their functional contribution.

division of labor, horizontal dimension of. Functional specialization of tasks within organizations.

division of labor, vertical dimension of. A hierarchical organization structure in which those at the top have the greatest authority within the organization.

dominant groups. Social groups that have the power to control the life chances of persons in subordinate groups.

E

ecology. The study of the patterned ways in which organisms distribute themselves in space with reference to other organisms and to inorganic aspects of the territorially limited environment.

economic exchange. According to Max Weber, any voluntary agreement involving the offer of any present, continuing, or future utility in exchange for any utilities offered in return.

egalitarian society. A society based on the principle that all men are entitled to equal treatment and rights in the society. See also *hierarchical society.*

empirical investigation. The method of acquiring primary knowledge by direct sensory observation, experimentation, and the testing of hypotheses.

endogamous marriage. Marriage within the same social class or ethnic, tribal, racial, religious, or national group. See also *exogamous marriage.*

endogenous change. Change that emerges from sources within the society. See also *exogenous change.*

esteem. The honor an individual receives from his colleagues of the same status for his skill on the job. See also *prestige.*

ethclass. According to Milton Gordon, a subsociety created by the intersection of the vertical stratification of ethnicity with the horizontal stratification of social class.

ethical prophet. A prophet who exhorts men to repentance and change. See also *exemplary prophet.*

ethnic group. A group consisting of people who conceive of themselves and are regarded by others as belonging together by virtue of a common ancestry, real or fictitious, and a common cultural background. See also *social race.*

ethnic identity. The derivation of one's identity primarily from one's ethnic origins or ethnic group membership.

ethnic stratification. A system in which some relatively fixed or ascribed group membership (for example, race, religion, or nationality) is used as an important criterion for distributing social positions, with their concomitant rewards.

ethnocentrism. The belief that one's ethnic group is superior to all others.

ethology. The study of animal behavior.

evolutionary change. The model of social change based on the idea that societies are shifting from one form to another with some direction, often toward some specific end point. See also *revolutionary change.*

exemplary prophet. A prophet whose chief mode of communication is the example of his own life. See also *ethical prophet.*

exogamous marriage. Marriage to a person outside of the group. See also *endogamous marriage.*

exogenous change. Change that emerges from sources external to the society in which the change occurs. See also *endogenous change.*

experiment. Research permitting deliberate manipulation of the independent variable and control of all extraneous variables.

expressive leadership. That aspect of leadership that serves to create harmony and affection among group members.

expressive movement. A social movement that provides a means for expressing the feelings of its participants. See also *institutional movement.*

extended family. A family of several generations of kin living in the same household or in proximity.

F

families of orientation. The families in which the husband and wife of a nuclear family were raised.

folkways. Norms of behavior about which there is little moral concern, such as the conventions of etiquette. See also *law; mores.*

free enterprise. The economic system under which the task of meeting consumer demands is left to private business. Government is restricted to protecting the rights of individuals.

functionalism. In sociology, the view of society as an interdependent set of institutions, each providing a vital need for the maintenance of the social system. See also *conflict theory.*

G

Gemeinschaft. According to Ferdinand Tönnies, a type of community in which there is a high degree of social cohesion based on value and normative consensus and a high degree of commitment to the community. Social bonds are natural rather than voluntary. See also *Gesellschaft.*

genes. The basic units of heredity, transmitted in the chromosomes.

genetics. The study of the transmission of hereditary characteristics.

genotype. The characteristics of an organism that are inherited and that can be transmitted to offspring. See also *phenotype.*

gerontocracy. Rule by the eldest members of a social group.

Gesellschaft. According to Ferdinand Tönnies, a type of society in which social bonds are deliberately created on the basis of mutual interests and exchange. See also *Gemeinschaft.*

ghetto. Ecological unit in which suppressed minorities, such as blacks in America, are forced to live through legal, social, or economic constraints. Originally the term referred to the separate sections of European cities in which Jews were forced to live.

goal specificity. The extent to which goals are explicit and clearly defined, providing criteria for choosing among alternative courses of action.

gross national product (GNP). The measure of the total monetary value of all final goods and services produced in a country during one year.

group. A set of individuals who are bound by a set of social relations that differentiate these individuals from others. See also *dominant groups; ethnic group; primary groups; reference groups; secondary groups; subordinate groups.*

H

heritability. The extent to which a behavioral trait is determined by heredity.

horticultural society. A society whose economy is based on gardening or primitive farming and the domestication of animals.

hunting and gathering society. A society whose economy is based on the killing of wild animals and the gathering of wild food.

hypothesis. A statement, usually derived from a theory, that predicts an empirical relationship between two or more variables.

I

identification. In children, associating one's self with certain significant adults whom one tries to emulate.

identity. Those aspects of an individual's social placement, roles, and self-conceptions that constitute answers to the question, "Who am I?"

ideology. A general interpretation of reality in terms of a combination of values or preferences and objective descriptions of events.

immanent change. The idea that once set in motion, actions may tend to create and generate new actions.

imperialism. The practice of extending the controlled sphere of a nation by military, political, economic, or legal means.

imputing a role to others. See *role taking.*

incest taboo. The prohibition against sexual relationships between primary relatives (such as between parent and child or between siblings).

independent variable. A phenomenon that is judged to be the cause of another phenomenon. The independent variable causes changes in the dependent variable.

inner city. The most central and oldest part of a large city.

instinct. An inherited (unlearned) pattern of behavior.

institutions. Relatively permanent patterns of specialized roles; groups and procedures through which major social functions are performed.

instrumental leadership. That aspect of leadership that is directed toward the pursuit of group goals. Sometimes called task leadership. See also *expressive leadership.*

integration. The mutual accommodation of parts of a society to each other, producing a situation of minimal conflict. See also *domination; mediation.*

intergenerational mobility. The upward or downward occupational movement of an individual in comparison with the occupational status of his father or son. See also *intragenerational mobility; vertical mobility.*

internalization. The incorporation of social norms into the self or the personality, so that violations of norms will produce a sense of guilt.

intragenerational mobility. The upward or downward occupational movement of an individual over his lifetime. See also *intergenerational mobility; vertical mobility.*

L

labeling theory. The point of view that deviance lies not in the actions of the "deviant" but depends upon the evaluation put upon a particular action and actor by society.

latent change. Social change that is not apparent to most members of the society in which it is occurring. See also *manifest change.*

latent function. Unintended, and often unnoticed, consequences of some social arrangement(s). A latent function of intermarriage among the royal houses of Europe was to greatly increase the incidence of genetic defects among royalty. See also *manifest function.*

law. A set of codified and written norms of behavior enforced by specialized personnel. See also *folkways; mores.*

leader, intellectual. A leader who enlarges the ideology of a movement and formulates a theory that justifies the movement, its means, and its goals.

leader, symbolic. A charismatic leader who, because of his extraordinary personal qualities, is identified by both members and outsiders as representing a particular movement.

learning. The acquisition of knowledge, behaviors, and certain skills.

liberalism. The ideology that supports change within gradual and orderly limits and sees government as a neutral instrument responding to the many and various demands placed upon it. See also *conservatism; radicalism.*

life style. A person's life style includes the kinds of goods and services he consumes, the way in which they are consumed, and the way in which his time is spent.

looking-glass self. The symbolic-interactionist proposition that the self develops out of interaction with others and thus is a product of how others see one. The looking-glass self is the way an individual sees himself in the eyes of others.

M

macro theory. A theory dealing with large-scale social relations, such as the influence of one institution upon another. See also *micro theory.*

malintegration. The failure of a social system to run effectively and smoothly; instability. See also *societal integration.*

Malthusian theory. The idea, originated by Thomas Robert Malthus, that human populations increase geometrically (2, 4, 8, 16, 32 . . .) and are dependent ultimately on the means of subsistence, which increase arithmetically (2, 4, 6, 8, 10 . . .).

manifest change. Social change that is obvious to the members of a society in which it is occurring. See also *latent change.*

manifest function. The recognized and intended consequences of particular social arrangements. See also *latent function*.

market system. The economic system in which production, distribution, income, interest, and wages are determined by exchange.

martyr. A person who becomes a source of inspiration, internal integration, and loyalty to a social movement because of his death or imprisonment.

mass communication. Rapid and frequent communication of information to significantly large portions of the society.

mass media. Centralized media of mass communication, including the press, radio, television, and motion pictures.

mass organizations. Organizations in which members are related to one another through common attachment to the central leadership rather than through primary ties such as kinship or ethnicity.

mass society. Society characterized by large-scale industrialization and bureaucratization, as well as by other impersonal, specialized, and uniform organizations and activities. It is organized to deal with people in large numbers rather than individuals.

matrilineal system. The system of determining descent through the female line. See also *patrilineal system*.

matrilocal residence. The sharing of residence, by the nuclear family, with the bride's parents. See also *neolocal residence; patrilocal residence*.

mean. The average of a set of values computed by adding the values of all items in the set and then dividing by the number of items in the set. The average height of a group is the total height of all members divided by the total number of members.

mechanical solidarity. Emile Durkheim's term for the binding together of human groups by their similarities. See also *organic solidarity*.

megalopolis. A metropolitan region consisting of several large cities and suburbs that adjoin one another, such as is found in New York, in London, and in Tokyo.

metropolitan areas. Sprawling, complex, multicentered regions developed around one central city, such as Chicago, Louisville, and Kansas City.

micro theory. A theory dealing with small-scale, observable social phenomena, such as the influence of intensive interaction between persons upon how well they come to like one another. See also *macro theory*.

mobility. The movement of people in a population, as from place to place, from job to job, or from one social position to another.

model. A representation that serves as a copy of a process, an object, or an event.

modernization. The process by which agrarian societies are transformed into industrial or modern societies. It involves not only technological changes but also changes in political, social, and economic arrangements.

monogamy. Marriage involving only one husband and one wife.

monopoly. A situation in which a market or segment of a market is controlled by a single organization.

mores. Norms of behavior invested with great moral importance. They involve matters of health, sex, religion, property, and other activities that are deemed vital. See also *folkways; law*.

multiple–nuclei model. Chauncy Harris and Edward Ullman's theory of urban ecology, a modification of the theories of Ernest W. Burgess and Homer Hoyt. Their theory suggests that the rise of separate nuclei and differentiated districts reflects a combination of four factors: (1) certain activities require special facilities; (2) certain like activities group together because they profit from cohesion; (3) certain unlike districts are detrimental to each other; and (4) certain activities are unable to afford the high rents of most desirable sites. See also *concentric–circle model; sector model*.

myth. The expression of religious thought in dramatic and symbolic form through a narrative.

N

nation-state. A political organization consisting of a relatively homogeneous group of people sharing a sense of common nationality and living within the boundaries of a sovereign state.

nationalism. A sense of allegiance to one's own nation over all others.

natural areas. Geographical areas within a community, inhabited by persons of the same subculture. See also *social areas*.

natural selection. Any environmental force that promotes reproduction of certain members of the population who carry certain genes.

negative reference groups. Reference groups whose standards and values are actually rejected by the individual, so that they serve as antimodels, as in the phenomenon of adolescent rebellion against adult values. See also *positive reference groups*.

neolocal residence. The separation of the household of the nuclear family from that of the extended family. See also *matrilocal residence; patrilocal residence*.

nonverbal communication. Communication by means other than spoken language.

normative group structure. The formal and informal rules governing what is expected of people in situations, what is required of them, and what is forbidden to them.

norms. Prescriptions for correct behavior, ordinarily couched in moral terms.

nuclear family. A married couple and their children. Also known as the conjugal family.

O

objective class. A person's position in the stratification system that is based on publicly observable criteria such as income, education and prestige and that is independent of what the person may think his class position to be. See also *subjective class*.

operant behavior. Behavior that affects the social or physical environment in ways that in turn affect the future occurrence of the behavior. See *reinforcers*.

organic solidarity. Emile Durkheim's term for the binding together of human groups through their functional differences in the cooperative division of labor. See also *mechanical solidarity*.

organizations, rational-system view of. The view that an organization is an instrument, a rationally conceived means to the realization of goals. See also *rationality*.

organizations, social-system view of. The view that few organizations pursue specific goals but rather have multiple, complex, diffuse, and often conflicting purposes.

P

particularistic criteria. Criteria that distinguish between people by their membership in a particular and unique group rather than by relation to a task. See also *universalistic criteria*.

patrilineal system. The system of determining descent through the male line. See also *matrilineal system*.

patrilocal residence. The sharing of residence, by the nuclear family, with the groom's parents. See also *matrilocal residence; neolocal residence*.

peer. A comember of a given social category, such as age or social class.

phenotype. The observable characteristics of an organism; a product of both heredity and environment. See also *genotype*.

phonemes. The smallest sound units of speech.

pluralism. The social condition in which a variety of ethnic groups and subcultures maintain autonomy and develop their cultural traditions within a single complex society.

polyandry. A marriage pattern in which women have two or more husbands.

polygamy. Marriage involving multiple spouses. A generic term that includes the forms known as polygyny and polyandry.

polygenic trait. A trait that is controlled by more than one gene pair.

polygyny. A marriage pattern in which men have two or more wives.

position. The location of a person within a set of persistent interactional relationships with others.

positive checks. Factors that increase mortality in a population—famine, disease, wars. See also *preventive checks*.

positive reference groups. Reference groups with which the individual shares an initial value consensus, so that he adapts and models his attitudes and behaviors in accordance with the groups' standards as he perceives them. See also *negative reference groups*.

power. The ability to secure one's way or to achieve one's ends even against opposition. See also *authority; role-specific power*.

preindustrial city. A community that has not reached a high-level technology, so that transportation is primarily by foot, communication is primarily by word of mouth, and agriculture and handicrafts monopolize labor.

presentation of self. The way a person

communicates his identification of his own role.

prestige. The differential honor a status receives, as compared with other statuses. See also *esteem.*

preventive checks. Factors that lower fertility in a population—moral restraint, late marriage, chastity, birth control. See also *positive checks.*

primary groups. Small, face-to-face groups with a degree of permanence, such as the family, children's play groups, peer and friendship groups, and the "old-fashioned" community. See also *reference groups; secondary groups.*

primogeniture. The system under which the first-born child or eldest son receives all inheritance and succeeds to the parents' role.

private property. Property that is exclusively controlled, used, and disposed of by private individuals or groups of individuals. See also *public property; semipublic property.*

profane, the. According to Emile Durkheim, all ordinary, routine experience. See also *the sacred.*

progressive movement. A social movement that proposes new goals or new and supposedly more effective ways of doing things. See also *conservative movement; reactionary movement.*

proletariat. The class of people in a society that does not own or control the process of producing goods. See also *bourgeoisie.*

property. The exclusive right to possess, enjoy, and dispose of a good or service. See also *private property; public property; role-reward property; role-use property; semipublic property.*

property right. A legal right to make contracts, to conduct a business, to labor, or to use, enjoy, and dispose of property.

prophet. A charismatic figure within a religious tradition who claims a special relation to the beyond. See also *ethical prophet; exemplary prophet; religious founder.*

puberty rite. A ceremony or ritual that serves to ease the transition from childhood to adulthood.

public property. Property that is owned and operated by a government for use of the public, such as the post office and public parks. See also *private property; semipublic property.*

R

race. An aggregate of persons who share a set of genetically transmitted physical characteristics.

racism. Invidious judgments of, and discriminatory behavior toward, others based on racial differences.

radicalism. The ideology that rejects most of the premises upon which the institutions of the existing society are based and sees the government as an instrument of domination over the people. See also *conservatism; liberalism.*

rationality. Functionally, the extent to which a series of actions is organized in such a manner that the actions lead to a previously defined goal.

reactionary movement. A social movement that advocates the restoration of a real or imagined preexisting and presumably superior state of affairs. See also *conservative movement; progressive movement.*

recidivism. The commission of a criminal offense by someone previously convicted of a crime.

reference groups. Groups to which the individual refers for comparative self-judgments. He evaluates himself relative to the values and standards of his reference groups and his behavior is oriented toward them. See also *negative reference groups; positive reference groups; primary groups.*

reform movement. A social movement that advocates changes in some part of the social order without disrupting the basic values and institutions of the society. See also *revolutionary movement.*

reinforcers. Stimuli that cause increases in the rate at which a behavior occurs. Positive reinforcers are stimuli whose occurrence increases the frequency of a response; negative reinforcers are stimuli whose removal increases the frequency of a response.

relative change. How things change in relation to each other. See also *absolute change.*

relative deprivation. The idea that people become discontented not because of the absolute severity of their situation but because they compare their actual condition with what they believe it could and should be.

religious founder. A charismatic figure who presents to his fellows by preaching, teaching, and example a special call to the religious life, thereby providing the basis for a new religious community based on his own unique and profound religious experience and insights. See also *prophet.*

replication. The repetition of a scientific study upon new data.

revolution of rising expectations. The idea that the experiencing of somewhat improved conditions leads people to expect, and thus to demand, still further improvement.

revolutionary change. The model of social change based on the idea that societies tend to develop modes of resistance to change and vested interests in the maintenance of a given form of society and that only through overt conflict can society move to new and valuable forms of social structure. See also *evolutionary change.*

revolutionary movement. A social movement that advocates comprehensive changes in all social institutions and the substitution of new values and social relationships for the old. See also *reform movement.*

rite of passage. A ceremony or ritual that serves to ease the transition of individuals from one status to another.

ritual. Prescribed, repetitive religious action.

role. A set of expectations or evaluative standards applied to an individual or to a position. See also *social roles.*

role acquisition. The learning of specific behaviors appropriate to a social role.

role conflict. Competition or conflict among the expectations involved in a person's various social roles.

role distance. A separation of the individual and the self afforded a person by his role.

role relationship. Expectations between any pair of positions.

role-reward property. The property an individual receives as a reward for playing his role, such as the salary and other job benefits a worker gets for doing his job. See also *role-use property.*

role set. The set of role relationships connected with a given position.

role-specific power. The capacity to achieve certain stated ends that accrue to one in his role, such as the teacher's power to assign homework or the father's power to discipline his child. See also *power.*

role taking. The capacity to imagine how the other person will play his role. For example, the patient expects doctorlike activity from his physician.

role-use property. The property an individual receives in order to play a role, such as the materials a worker uses in order to get his job done. See also *role-reward property.*

S

sacred. Phenomena that are believed to be related to the supernatural in an important way and are consequently highly valued; holy.

sacred, the. According to Emile Durkheim, the individual's internalized experiencing of the norms of society, arousing an attitude of intense respect and a sense of obligation. See also *the profane.*

sacred society. A society characterized by primary group relations and guided by tradition and belief in the mystical and supernatural. See also *secular society.*

secondary groups. Groups in which relations are impersonal, as opposed to the personal relations of primary groups. The distinguishing feature of secondary relations is that interaction tends to be stereotyped, involving only specialized segments of the individual, as, for example, in the relation between clerk and customer or between coworkers who know little of each other's lives outside of the work place. See also *primary groups.*

sect. According to Ernst Troeltsch, a voluntary society composed of strict and definite behaviors, in which members are bound to each other by the fact that all have experienced a spiritual rebirth; it is withdrawn from the general society and it may even be militantly opposed to it. See also *church.*

sector model. Homer Hoyt's modification of Ernest W. Burgess' theory of urban ecology. The sector scheme conceives of the city's ecological pattern as consisting of pie-shaped sectors that tend to run axially or radially and thus to break up any concentricity of land-use patterns. See also *concentric-circle model; multiple-nuclei model.*

secular society. A society characterized by change, science, innovation, and a lack of sacred, traditional values. See also *sacred society*.

self-conception. The way in which an individual sees himself.

semipublic property. Property that is privately owned and operated but to which the public is given guaranteed access by a government, as in such utilities as a telephone company or a transportation system. See also *private property; public property*.

sensorimotor development. The development of behaviors that require coordination between the senses and motor abilities, as in walking or eating.

separatist movements. Social movements that go beyond the goal of changing the social order and seek to withdraw from it entirely.

serf. A member of a caste required to perform agricultural labor. Typically, serfs are legally bound to the land and thus are sold along with the land.

sex role. A social role that entails different behavioral expectations based on the person's sex.

sexism. Prejudice and discrimination against persons wholly on the basis of their sex. Normally implies prejudice and discrimination against females.

sibling. A brother or sister.

situational facilities. The resources available in a society for the satisfaction of human needs.

social areas. Divisions of a population based on social rank, urbanization, and segregation, unbound by a geographical frame of reference or by degrees of interaction. A social area contains persons having the same level and way of life and the same ethnic background. See also *natural areas*.

social categories. Aggregates of people who share some characteristic, such as ethnic heritage, income, or age.

social change. Change in the structure of a society, primarily but not exclusively in its institutional structure.

social class. A social stratum or category differentiated from other strata on the basis of such economic considerations as wealth, occupation, and property ownership.

social control. Any social arrangement that acts to enforce conformity to norms and thus to curtail deviance.

social interaction. The mutual adjustment of individual lines of action; the mutual or reciprocal influencing of the behavior of all persons involved.

social mobility. An individual's movement from one occupation to another or from one social position to another. See also *intergenerational mobility; intragenerational mobility; vertical mobility*.

social movement. An organized aggregate of people who have joined together to bring about certain alterations in the social order.

social race. Pierre van den Berghe's term for a group that is socially defined on the basis of physical criteria. See also *ethnic group*.

social roles. Differentiated expectations associated with positions, particularly with regard to the division of labor among a set of positions.

social self. The idea that the self is formed and shaped through primary group interaction, so that the individual can view himself from the standpoint of those around him and can also take the role of the other and empathize with him.

social stratification. Levels of society delineated on the basis of power, property, and prestige.

social system. Any group of two or more individuals interacting with each other with regard to a common focus.

socialism. The political-economic system characterized by government ownership and administration of the means of production and distribution of the products.

socialization. The process through which persons learn the culture and social roles of their society and come to perform the roles expected of them. See also *anticipatory socialization; norms; values*.

societal integration. The way in which the various parts and subunits of a social system fit together so that the system runs relatively smoothly and efficiently with a minimum of friction.

socioeconomic status. A general estimate of position within the system of social stratification. Often measured by combining education, income, and occupational prestige. Frequently abbreviated as SES.

specialization. The repeated performance of a single activity, or complex of activities, that results in the production of the same good or service.

statistical significance. The mathematical probability that a given research result was not produced by chance.

status. Place of an individual within a structure of positions in relation to other such positions.

status-group politics. Politics based on a submerged racial, religious, or ethnic-group membership rather than on economic considerations.

stereotyping. The categorization of people on the basis of general beliefs and feelings rather than on the basis of accurate information or firsthand experience.

structural differentiation. The differentiation of special institutions out of more amorphous and homogeneous collectivities. The process by which societies become more complex.

structural strain. The existence of incompatible or conflicting demands on parts of a social system and ultimately on the individuals within it.

subculture. A group within a culture that either does not hold all the beliefs of the larger culture or gives them a very different emphasis.

subjective class. The social class to which an individual thinks he belongs. See also *objective class*.

subordinate groups. Social groups that lack effective power and are therefore controlled by dominant groups.

symbol. Any idea, object, or event that stands for or represents something else.

symbolic interaction. A general theoretical perspective in sociology that places emphasis on three elements of social phenomena: communication processes, interaction patterns, and the subjective meanings of social phenomena to the participants involved. The individual assesses the meanings of these phenomena and conducts himself in terms of such meanings.

T

taboo. A strongly proscriptive norm, usually infused with supernatural prohibitions.

tautology. A statement that is always true by virtue of the definitions of its terms and the logical relations among them.

technology. The application of theoretical knowledge to the solution of practical problems; the means for making available to people the products of their civilization.

Third World. A political term referring to the developing nations of Asia, Africa, and Latin America. Sometimes applied to coalitions of nonwhite minority members. The term designates those who are not members of either the developed capitalist or communist "worlds" of nations.

total institution. An institution within which all of an individual's activities take place. Membership may be voluntary (convents, communes) or involuntary (prisons, mental hospitals).

totalitarianism. Social organization characterized by a centralized power having absolute or near absolute control. Usually all sectors of the society are utilized to achieve ends determined by those in control.

traditionalism. The notion that it is correct for people to accept their condition in this world as it exists.

U

universalistic criteria. Criteria applied uniformly to the group of persons or objects being studied. See also *particularistic criteria*.

urban region. An area containing many cities of different sizes with merging boundaries.

urbanization. The process of changing from a rural to an urban mode of living. This process includes industrialization, population increases, and complex division of labor.

V

values. General standards about what is desirable, how things should be, the ultimate goals to be pursued. Democracy is a value in American society, as are justice and economic well-being.

vertical mobility. The upward or downward occupational movement of an individual. See also *intergenerational mobility; intragenerational mobility*.

vital statistics. The births, deaths, and marriages in a population, used to measure such factors as the relative force of fertility and mortality in a society.

Name Index

Subject Index

Credits and Acknowledgments

Unit I
Sociology: A Study and an Activity

2—*Study: Falling Man* by Ernest Trova (1965), from the collection of the Walker Art Center, Minneapolis.

Chapter 1 What Is Sociology and How Is It Possible?

4—George Gardner; 7—(top left) John Oldenkamp/IBOL, (top right) The Summer Institute of Linguistics, (bottom left) courtesy of the Office of Economic Opportunity, (bottom right) Lawrence Frank/Rapho Guillumette; 9—Alan Mercer; 10—Dick Corten.

Chapter 2 Doing Sociology

12—Ken Heyman; 15—based on John Lofland, *Doomsday Cult*, Prentice-Hall, 1966; 17—Victor Friedman; 18—photo by Dick Corten; 19—Michael Lowy; 20—courtesy of Karen Dion; 21—(left) Michael Alexander, (center) Jason Laure/Rapho Guillumette, (right) John Dawson; 24—(left) Leon Bolognese, (right) courtesy of Charles Glock; 25—UPI Compix 26—Doug Armstrong, adapted from Rodney Stark, B. D. Foster, C. Y. Glock, and H. E. Quinley, *Wayward Shepherds: Prejudice and the Protestant Clergy*, Harper & Row, 1971, p. 81; 28—from C. Y. Glock and Rodney Stark, *Christian Beliefs and Anti-Semitism*, Harper and Row, 1966. 29—Doug Armstrong, after Rodney Stark, 1972.

Unit II
The Principles of Sociology

34—*The Letter* by David Smith, courtesy of Munson-Williams-Proctor Institute, Utica, New York.

Chapter 3 Basic Concepts

36—George Gardner; 39—(top) Karl Nicholason, (bottom) courtesy of NASA; 40—(top) Welden Anderson/Photophile, (bottom) UPI Compix; 41—courtesy of the American Sociological Association; 43—Karl Nicholason; 44—Jacques Jangoux; 46-49—UPI Compix; 50—Marty Gunsaullus.

Chapter 4 Theoretical Perspectives

54—Joe Molnar; 57—John Dawson; 60—Doug Armstrong; 63—Steve McCarroll; 64—Joseph Toussaint; 65 and 67—courtesy of the American Sociological Association; 72—The Granger Collection.

Unit III
The Interplay of Heredity and Environment

74—*Rotating Sphere with Interior Sphere* by Arnold Pomodoro, courtesy of the Fine Arts Gallery of San Diego, gift of Mr. and Mrs. Philip L. Gildred.

Chapter 5 The Biological Basis of Society

76—Alan Mercer; 78—from John C. Lilly, *The Mind of the Dolphin*, © 1967 by John Cunningham Lilly, Doubleday & Co., used with permission of the publisher; 79—Tom Lewis, adapted from John Napier, "The Antiquity of Human Walking," © 1967 by Scientific American, Inc., all rights reserved; 80—(top left) John Olden-kamp/IBOL, (top right) Irven DeVore, (bottom) John Dawson; 81—Tom Lewis, adapted from W. C. Allee, *The Social Life of Animals*, W. W. Norton, 1938; 82—R. A. and B. T. Gardner; 83—The Granger Collection; 84—courtesy of World Medical News; 85—Robert Isaacs; 87—(top) Doug Armstrong, adapted from L. B. Arey, *Developmental Anatomy* (6th ed.), W. B. Saunders Co., 1954.

Chapter 6 The Cultural Basis of Society: Childhood Socialization

90—courtesy of the Girl Scouts of America; 92—courtesy of Harry H. Harlow, Wisconsin Regional Primate Center; 93—Michael Alexander; 94—Ted Polumbaum for *Psychology Today;* 95—Marv Rubin; 96—courtesy of David Hicks; 97—Eric Schaal for *Psychology Today;* 98—Steve Wells/IBOL; 101—The Granger Collection; 104—Ken Heyman; 106 and 110—Bill MacDonald/IBOL.

Unit IV
Primary Components of Social Organization

112—sculpture by Max Finkelstein from private collection.

Chapter 7 Social Roles and Interaction

114—George Gardner; 117—(left) courtesy of the American Sociological Association, (right) The Granger Collection; 118—John Oldenkamp/IBOL; 119—Karl Nicholason; 122—Patti Peck; 125—(top left) Ray Ellis/Rapho Guillumette, (top right) Rogier Gregoire, (bottom) Alfred Eisenstaedt for *Life* Magazine, © Time, Inc.

Chapter 8 The Nature and Variety of Groups

128—Nancy Chase Black; 130—(left) Charles Gatewood, (center) Harry Crosby, (right) Steve McCarroll/IBOL; 133—(left) courtesy of Japan National Tourist Organization, (right) Fred Lombardi; 135—adapted from Leon Festinger et al., *Social Pressures in Informal Groups*, Stanford University Press, 1963, pp. 36 and 38; 137—courtesy of Solomon Asch; 138—William Vandivert; 141—adapted from M. Roff and S. B. Sells, "Relations Between Intelligence and Sociometric Status in Groups Differing in Sex and Socioeconomic Background," *Psychological Reports* (1965), 16:515.

Chapter 9 Formal Organizations

144—Ron Thal; 147—Dick Raphael for *Sports Illustrated*, © 1972 Time, Inc.; 149—courtesy of Peter Blau; 150—used by permission of United Press International; 152—Howard Saunders; 153—The Granger Collection; 157—Karl Nicholason; 158—Wide World Photos.

Chapter 10 Adult Socialization and Resocialization

160—Arthur Sirdofsky; 162—Reginald Von Muchow; 163—Paul Slick; 165—(left) Ken Heyman, (right) Charles Gatewood; 166—UPI Compix; 170—Terry Lamb; 171—Burk Uzzle/Magnum Photos.

Chapter 11 Deviance and Conformity

174—Alan Mercer; 176—(top) John Oldenkamp/IBOL, (bottom) Kim Nelson; 178—(left) adapted from Federal Bureau of Investigation, *Crime in the United States, Uniform Crime Reports, 1970,* Government Printing Office, 1971, (right) adapted from Office of Juvenile Delinquency and Youth Development, *Juvenile Court Statistics*, Government Printing Office, 1970; 182—UPI Compix; 184—courtesy of the American Sociological Association; 186—Jack Brembeck: Director of Advertising and Public Relations, KABC-TV, Richter & Mracky-Bates, Inc.: Advertising Agency for KABC-TV, Stanley Davis: Art Director, Richter & Mracky-Bates, Inc., Carol Corbett: Copywriter, Richter & Mracky-Bates, Inc., Robert M. Klosterman: Account Supervisor, Richter & Mracky-Bates, Inc.; 188—Patti Peck, after Ronald Akers, 1972; 189—(top) UPI Compix, (bottom) Julian Wasser for *Time* Magazine, © 1972 Time, Inc.

Unit V
Structures and Processes of Inequality

192—*Moon-Homage* by Louise Nevelson, courtesy of the Pace Gallery, New York;

Chapter 12 Stratification

194—Charles Gatewood; 196—Marv Rubin; 197—(top) adapted from Evelyn M. Kitagawa, "Social and Economic Differentials in Mortality in the United States, 1960," *International Population Conference, London, 1969*, Vol. II, pp. 980–985, The International Union for the Scientific Study of Population, 1971, (bottom) adapted from Norman Bradburn and David Caplovitz, *Reports on Happiness*, Aldine, 1965, p. 9; 199—Karl Nicholason; 200—from Robert W. Hodge, Paul M. Seigel, and Peter H. Rossi, "Occupational Prestige in the United States, 1925–1963," *American Journal of Sociology* (1964), 70:286–302, © 1964 by the University of Chicago, used with permission; 202—Tom Lewis; 203—adapted from Rodney Stark, 1972; 204—University of North Carolina Photo Lab; 207—(left) Photographic Library of Australia, (right) William Davenport; 208–209—Cynthia Bassett and Nat Antler; 211—Karl Nicholason.

Chapter 13 Social Mobility

216—Mark Haven; 218—adapted from H. F. Cline, *Mexico*, Oxford University Press, 1963, p. 124; 219—(left) The Library of Congress, (top right) UPI Compix, (bottom right) courtesy of VISTA; 220—Tom Lewis; 221—courtesy of the American Sociological Association; 222—(top) adapted from Seymour Lipset and Richard Bendix, *Social Mobility in Industrial Society*, University of California Press, 1958, 224—adapted from U.S. Bureau of the Census, *Current Population Reports: Consumer Income*, Series P-60, No. 80, "Income in 1970 of Families and Persons in the United States," Government Printing Office, 1971, p. 105; 226—courtesy of the Office of Economic Opportunity; 227—(left) courtesy of the Department of Housing and Urban Development, (top right) Ken Heyman, (bottom right) Jill Krementz; 229—Marv Rubin.

Chapter 14 Consequences of Inequality

232—Joe Molnar; 236—Warner Brothers; 237—(top) Michael Alexander, (bottom) reproduced by permission of World Publishing Company from *Still Hungry in America*, text by Robert Coles, photographs by Al Clayton. Photographs © 1969 by Al Clayton, text © 1969 by Robert Coles; 238—(top left) Jill Krementz, (bottom left) courtesy of VISTA, (right) The New York Times; 239—(top) courtesy of the Office of Economic Opportunity, (center) Burk Uzzle/Magnum Photos, (bottom) Charles Harbutt/Magnum Photos; 241—art by Darrel Millsap/Millsap and Kinyon; 244—courtesy of Volkswagen of America; 245—Alan Mercer; 246—from James C. Davies in Hugh Graham and Ted Gurr (eds.), *History of Violence in America: Historical and Comparative Perspectives* (Report to the National Commission on the Causes and Prevention of Violence), Bantam, 1969.

Chapter 15 Is Inequality Necessary?
248—courtesy of the Office of Economic Opportunity; 250—Terry Lamb; 252—courtesy of the American Sociological Association; 254—Marc Riboud/Magnum Photos; 255—(top) René Burri/Magnum Photos, (bottom) Hugh Wilkerson; 257—Culver Pictures, Inc.

Chapter 16 Race and Ethnicity
260—Paolo Koch/Rapho Guillumette; 262—(top) Alan Mercer, (bottom) Jason Lauré/Rapho Guillumette; 263—(left) George Holton/Photo Researchers, (top right) Carl Frank/Photo Researchers, (bottom right) Wide World Photos; 264—The Granger Collection; 265—(top left, top right, and center right) Yvonne Freund, (bottom left) Dan McCoy/Black Star, (bottom right) Marion Bernstein; 270—Doug Armstrong.

**Chapter 17 Sex and Age:
The Tyranny of Older Men**
272—Charles Gatewood; 276—(top left and bottom right) courtesy of the United Nations, (top right) courtesy of ACTION, (bottom left) courtesy of the Office of Economic Opportunity; 278—Burk Uzzle/Magnum Photos; 280—Joyce Fitzgerald; 282—The Art Works, after Dr. Victor A. McKusick; 283—UPI Compix; 285—Phillip V. Tobias, Department of Anatomy, University of the Witwatersrand, Johannesburg; 288—(top left) courtesy of United Air Lines, (top right) from the Bureau of Business Practice, Waterford, Connecticut, (bottom) courtesy of The Institute of High Fidelity, Inc.

**Unit VI
Social Institutions**
290—*CUBI XXVII* by David Smith (1965), courtesy of the Solomon R. Guggenheim Museum Collection, New York.

Chapter 18 Family and Kinship
292—Wayne McLoughlin; 295—Alan Mercer; 297—Tom Lewis; 298—Doug Armstrong; 300—Marv Rubin; 303—Gerald Berreman; 305—courtesy of William Goode; 306—Doug Armstrong, adapted from U.S. Department of Health, Education, and Welfare, National Center for Health Statistics.

Chapter 19 Education
308—George Gardner; 310—courtesy of Title Insurance and Trust Co., San Diego, California; 311—Doug Armstrong; 312—Terry Lamb; 316—photo by Richard W. Linfield; 318—UPI Compix; 320—Jane Bown; 322—Michael Alexander; 324—Dick Corten.

Chapter 20 Religion and Society
326—Don Peterson; 328—Doug Armstrong, adapted from *1968 Britannica Book of the Year*, Encyclopaedia Britannica, Inc., 1968; 330—New York Public Library Picture Collection; 332—UPI Compix; 334—John Dawson; 337—Doug Armstrong; 338—Kim Nelson.

Chapter 21 Politics
342—Larry Leach; 345—UPI Compix; 347—Photographie Giraudon; 349—Karl Nichola-

son; 350—Darrel Millsap/Millsap and Kinyon; 351—Lida Moser; 352—courtesy of Wadsworth Atheneum, Hartford, Connecticut; 357—(left) UPI Compix, (right) Darrel Millsap/Millsap and Kinyon; 358—(top and center) Wide World Photos, (bottom) UPI Compix; 359—Ben Martin for *Time* Magazine, © 1956 Time, Inc.

Chapter 22 Economics and the World of Work
362—George Hall; 366—(top) Alan Mercer, (bottom) George Pressler/Photophile; 367—courtesy of the Art Institute of Chicago; 369—Michael Mauney for *Life* Magazine, © 1972 Time, Inc.; 370—Culver Pictures, Inc.; 371—Henry Leland/Nancy Palmer Agency; 376—The Bettmann Archive, Inc.; 377—Leon Bolognese.

**Unit VII
Demography and Ecology**
380—*Progressions* by Mary Baurmeister (1963), stones and sand on plywood, 51¼" × 47⅜" × 4¾", collection The Museum of Modern Art, New York, Matthew T. Mellon Foundation Fund.

Chapter 23 The Population Problem
382—Don Peterson; 384 and 385 (left)—Doug Armstrong, adapted from O. Andrew Collver, *Birth Rates in Latin America: New Estimates of Historical Trends and Fluctuations*, Institute of International Studies, University of California Press, 1965; 185—(right) Ken Heyman; 186—Doug Armstrong, adapted from United Nations, *World Population Prospects as Assessed in 1963*, Population Studies, No. 41, United Nations, 1966, pp. 34–35; 387—Doug Armstrong, adapted from John D. Durand, "The Modern Expansion of World Population," *Proceedings of the American Philosophical Society*, (1967), Vol. 3, No. 3; 388—Felicia Fry, adapted from Jay R. Mandle, "The Decline of Mortality in British Guiana, 1911–1960," *Demography* (1970), 7:301–315; 389—Alice Harmon and Doug Armstrong, after James McCann, 1972; 390—Raghubir Singh/Nancy Palmer Agency; 391—The Granger Collection; 392—Tom Lewis; 393—The Granger Collection; 395—Howard Saunders; 396—The Granger Collection; 400—Doug Armstrong, adapted from Richard A. Easterlin, "The American Baby Boom in Historical Perspective," *Population, Labor Force, and Long Swings in Economic Growth*, National Bureau of Economic Research, 1964; 401—Felicia Fry, adapted from Donald J. Bogue, *Principles of Demography*, Wiley, 1969, p. 130; 402—Doug Armstrong, adapted from Thomas Frejka, "Reflections on the Demographic Conditions Required to Establish a U.S. Stationary Population Growth," *Population Studies*, (1968), 22:385.

Chapter 24 The Urban Community
404—George Hall; 406—Doug Armstrong, adapted from United Nations, *Urbanization: Development Policies and Planning*, International Social Development Review No. 1, United Nations, 1968, p. 13; 407—Doug Armstrong, adapted from William Hance, *Population, Migration, and Urbanization in Africa*, Columbia University Press, 1970, p. 232; 408—courtesy of the American Sociological Association; 409—Tom Lewis and Doug Armstrong, adapted from Jean Gottman, *Megalopolis: The Urbanized Northeastern Seaboard of the United States*, Twentieth Century Fund, 1961; 410—George Hall; 412—(top left) courtesy of the Office of Economic Opportunity, (top right) Joe Molnar, (bottom left) Tibor Hirsch, (bottom right) courtesy of the Department of Housing and Urban Development; 415—George Hall.

Chapter 25 Human Ecology
418 and 420—George Hall; 421—Otto Lang/Photophile; 422—Tom Lewis and Doug Armstrong, adapted from Donald Bogue, "Urbanism in the United States, 1950," *American Journal of Sociology* (1955), p. 473; 423—The Bettmann Archive, Inc.; 424—Doug Armstrong, adapted from

Chauncy D. Harris, and Edward L. Ullman, "The Nature of Cities," in Paul K. Hatt and Albert J. Reiss, Jr. (eds.), *Cities in Society*, © 1951, 1957 by The Free Press, reprinted by permission of The Macmillan Co.; 427—(top) Alan Mercer, (bottom) Doug Armstrong, adapted from Caroline Ware, *Greenwich Village, 1920–1930*, Harper & Row, 1935, p. 464; 429 and 430—Doug Armstrong, adapted from Karl Taeuber and Alma Taeuber, *Negroes in Cities*, Aldine, 1965, pp. 39–41.

**Unit VIII
Stability and Change**
432—*Fragment for the Gates to Times Square II*, by Chryssa (1966), courtesy of the Whitney Museum, New York.

Chapter 26 Social Integration and Social Change
434—The Granger Collection; 436—John Dawson; 437—(top) Henri Cartier-Bresson/Magnum Photos, (bottom) used by permission of United Press International; 439—(left) Bob Van Doren, (right) Jason Laure/Rapho Guillumette; 440—Dorothea Lange/National Archives; 444—U.S. Bureau of the Census, 1971; 446—UPI Compix; 449—Toronto Star Syndicate; 451—Darrel Millsap/Millsap and Kinyon.

Chapter 27 Collective Behavior
454—George Gardner; 458—The Granger Collection; 459—Wide World Photos; 460—Michael Alexander; 462—The Bettmann Archive, Inc.; 464—(left) Felicia Fry, adapted from Donald M. Johnson, "The 'Phantom Anethetist' of Mattoon: A Field Study of Mass Hysteria," *Journal of Abnormal and Social Psychology* (1945), 40:175–186, (right) courtesy of the Illinois State Historical Society Library; 466—(top left and right) Charles Gatewood, (bottom left) John Oldenkamp/IBOL; 469—(top) Jason Lauré, (center and bottom) UPI Compix.

Chapter 28 Social Movements
472—Paolo Koch/Rapho Guillumette; 474—UPI Compix; 476—Norris McNamara/Nancy Palmer Agency; 478—UPI Compix; 480—Jason Lauré; 482—George Gardner; 484—(right) Doug Armstrong, adapted from U.S. Department of Labor, National Science Foundation, data for 1968, (right) Stan Wayman for *Psychology Today*; 485—adapted from Women's Bureau, *Handbook of Women Workers*, Bulletin 294, 1969, pp. 24, 26, and 41; 486—Claude Bernard; 487—George Gardner; 489—data from U.S. Bureau of the Census, "Income in 1966 of Families and Persons in the United States," *Current Population Reports*, Series P-60, No. 53, U.S. Government Printing Office, 1967, and "Income of Families and Persons in the United States: 1961," *Current Population Reports*, Series P-60, No. 53, 1963; 490—Karl Nicholason; 492—The Bettmann Archive; 493—Wide World Photos; 494—(left) The Granger Collection, (right) The Bettmann Archive, Inc.; 495—*The Illegal Operation* by Edward Kienholtz, from the collection of Mr. and Mrs. Monte Factor.

Chapter 29 Modernization
496—Peter Anderson; 502—UPI Compix; 503—Lee Lockwood/Black Star; 505—Elliott Erwitt/Magnum Photos; 506—Peace Corps Photo; 508—Dr. Conrad C. and Toini Jaffe; 510—Bill Strode/Black Star.

Cover design—Tom Lewis

Cover photograph—John Oldenkamp/IBOL

Society Today, Second Edition, Book Team

Roger G. Emblen, *Publisher*

Barbara Rose, *Publishing Coordinator*

Cynthia Farden, *Editor*

Susan Orlofsky, *Associate Editor*

Martha Rosler, *Consulting Editor*

Janet Lanphier, *Editorial Assistant*

Patricia Campbell, *Research Assistant*

Leon Bolognese, *Designer*

Nat Antler, Cynthia Bassett, *Associate Designers*

Alice Harmon, Bonnie Weber, *Art Assistants*

Nancy Hutchison Sjöberg, *Rights and Permissions Supervisor*

Phyllis Barton, *Production Supervisor*

Sandie Marcus, *Production Assistant*

John Ochse, *Sales Manager*

Howard Smith, *Social Sciences Marketing Manager*

Pat Boyce, Mary Moon,

Cheryl Riehl, Lindy Cooper Wisdom, *Sales Coordinators*

CRM Books

Richard Holme, *President and Publisher*

John H. Painter, Jr., *Publisher, Life and Physical Sciences*

Roger G. Emblen, *Publisher, Social Sciences*

Tom Suzuki, *Director of Design*

Charles Jackson, *Managing Editor*

Henry Ratz, *Director of Production*

Officers of Communications Research Machines, Inc.

Charles C. Tillinghast III, *President*

Richard Holme, *Vice-President*

James B. Horton, *Vice-President*

Paul N. Lazarus III, *Vice-President*

Wayne E. Sheppard, *Vice-President*